Fundamental Algebra and Trigonometry

MERVIN L. KEEDY PURDUE UNIVERSITY

MARVIN L. BITTINGER INDIANA UNIVERSITY –
PURDUE UNIVERSITY AT INDIANAPOLIS

ADDISON-WESLEY PUBLISHING COMPANY

Reading, Massachusetts
Menlo Park, California
London
Amsterdam
Don Mills, Ontario
Sydney

Fourth printing, May 1979

Portions of this text originally appeared in *Algebra and Trigonometry: A Functions Approach* by Mervin L. Keedy and Marvin L. Bittinger, copyright © 1974 by Addison-Wesley Publishing Company, Inc.

ISBN 0-201-03767-X
BCDEFGHIJK-VB-89876543210

Preface

This text is based on *Algebra and Trigonometry: A Functions Approach* (Addison-Wesley, 1974) but there has been a major revision. Among the changes that have been made are the following.

1. *Calculators.* This book recognizes the fact that calculators are readily available today. In many exercise sets there are optional sections, marked ▦ . These exercises are designed to be worked with a calculator. For most of them, the simplest of calculators will suffice. Square-root capability would be helpful on occasion, but ordinary arithmetic capability is all that is actually required.

2. *Challenging problems.* In many exercise sets, exercises that require something of the student beyond the abilities stated in the objectives have been included. These are marked ▶. Some of them are difficult and highly challenging, but many are not.

3. *The metric system.* Many of the exercises and examples now use metric units.

4. *Triangles.* Since some instructors prefer to approach trigonometry initially through the use of triangles, rather than circular functions, we have arranged material so that this is possible (see p. 204).

5. *Polar coordinates.* An introduction to polar coordinates has been included.

6. *Rational functions.* A fairly comprehensive lesson on rational functions and their graphs has been added.

7. *Linear systems.* The material on solving systems of linear equations has been completely rewritten. The objective is to make the solving of these systems strictly algorithmic. This was done because of the great success many instructors have found in using this approach, and because of the fact that the world is now full of calculators and computers.

8. *Study supplement.* In the margins of *Algebra and Trigonometry: A Functions Approach* there are developmental exercises and objectives for each lesson. That material has not been included in this book, but has been placed in a separate booklet, called a *Study Supplement.* The text is keyed to that supplement. When a symbol such as **[5–7]** occurs in the text the student is to turn to the supplement and work the

exercises indicated. The use of the Study Supplement is optional, but highly recommended, because the use of the developmental exercises has proved so effective.

9. *Smoothing and correcting.* Much of the textual material has been rewritten or polished, to make the reading easier and more understandable. Errors, where noted, have of course been corrected, and passages that were found to be misleading have been rewritten in an effort to make them clearer.

Among the salient features of the text that have been retained are the following.

1. *Functions and transformations.* After an honest and straightforward review of elementary algebraic skills in Chapter 1 and a treatment of equations in Chapter 2, the concepts of relation, function, and transformation are introduced in Chapter 3. The concept of function is then emphasized throughout the remainder of the text. The ideas of transformations make this chapter unique and they set up the study of later material. Instructors report that students need a little extra push through Chapter 3, but that the payoffs are great. In Chapter 4, for example, transformations are used to

simplify the concepts related to quadratic functions and they provide a new approach to solving inequalities with absolute value, a traditionally difficult topic. In Chapter 7, the first chapter on trigonometry, the transformation ideas make the development of certain trigonometric identities very simple. Instructors tell us of cases in which students are afraid that they may not be understanding the material because they grasp the ideas so readily.

2. *Exercises.* Great care has been given to constructing the exercises, which number over 4500. They are based on the behavioral objectives, except for those mentioned earlier, and they are graded. The first ones in an exercise set are usually easy and they become progressively more difficult. For the most part, the exercises occur in matching pairs; that is, any odd-numbered exercise is very much like the one that immediately follows it.

3. *Flexibility.* There are many ways in which to use this book and its *Study Supplement.* The instructor who wishes to use it in a traditional way should simply ignore the supplement. The instructor who wishes to

use the lecture method primarily, but also wants to introduce some student-centered activity into the class, can easily do so by interrupting the lecture and having students work the exercises in the supplement at appropriate times. On the other hand, the book, with the supplement, is well suited for use in audio-tutorial or other systems of individualized instruction, or in any approach that is essentially a self-study program. When the supplement is used, the book can be used with minimal instructor guidance, thus making it particularly effective for use in large classes.

4. *Supplementary materials.* In addition to the *Study Supplement* the following materials are available.

- An Answer Booklet containing the answers to even-numbered exercises.
- A Diagnostic Test which will assist in placing students in any of the developmental and precalculus texts by the authors, including this text.
- A Test Booklet, originally prepared for *Algebra and Trigonometry: A Functions Approach*, which contains five alternate forms of each chapter test and the final examination, with answers spaced for easy grading.

The authors wish to thank the people who have helped with the development of this book: Clifford A. Kottman, Oregon State University; Franz X. Hiergeist, West Virginia University; and Haile D. Perry, Texas A & M University.

November 1976   M.L.K.
                                                       M.L.B.

About Calculators and This Text

To the Student

Small electronic calculators are readily available today, and the chances are good that you already own one. Certain exercises in this text (marked ⊞) are written under the assumption that you have a calculator, but it is not essential that you have one (you can simply skip those exercises).

There are many kinds of small calculators. They do not all operate in the same way, and some of them will do much more than others. We assume that you will read the instructions that accompany your calculator and thus teach yourself to use it. The following points are to be kept in mind, no matter what kind of calculator you may have.

1. *The fact that you have a calculator does not mean that you need to know any less algebra or trigonometry.*

To illustrate this point, let us consider solving a simple equation, first without a calculator.

$3x + 5 = x - 7$
$3x - x = -7 - 5$ (We added $-x$ and -5 on both sides.)
$2x = -12$ (We simplified.)
$x = -6$ (We divided by 2 on both sides.)

Next, consider an equation for which a calculator would be helpful. It is like the equation above, except that the numbers are different.

$$3.14x + 5.012 = 12.5x - 6.89$$

$$3.14x - 12.5x = -6.89 - 5.012$$

$$(3.14 - 12.5)x = -6.89 - 5.012$$

$$x = \frac{-6.89 - 5.012}{3.14 - 12.5}$$

$$\left[= \frac{-(6.89 + 5.012)}{-(12.5 - 3.14)} \right.$$

$$\left. = \frac{6.89 + 5.012}{12.5 - 3.14} \right]$$

Note that we have solved for x, but have left all of the calculations to be done at the end. (The manipulations shown in brackets are optional, depending upon the capability of the calculator.) The calculations are now a simple task using a calculator, but the algebraic knowledge required is just as great as for the simpler equation above, if not greater.

2. *There are times to use a calculator and times not to use it.*

Whenever we get a new toy we tend to play with it a great deal. The calculator may affect us in the same way. That is, you may tend to use your calculator when you do not need to, or when it does not really make sense to do so. For example, you could mentally add 8, 2, 5, and 12 in less time than it would take to get your calculator out of the case. Whenever you can get along without your calculator, try to do so. This brings us to our next point.

3. *Don't let yourself get too dependent upon a calculator.*

If you walk with a crutch constantly, your leg muscles will get weaker. Although the analogy is not perfect, it is also true that if you overuse a calculator you will find it difficult to do calculations without it. So, don't let yourself get too dependent on a calculator.

Your instructor may wish to give some of your tests and quizzes with calculators permitted and some with calculators not permitted, just to encourage you to use your head as well as the little machine.

4. *Practice estimating answers.*

Whenever you do *any* calculation, with or without a calculator, you should make a rough estimate of the answer. This will help detect gross errors. Calculators sometimes get out of order and give incorrect answers. Checking answers by estimating can help detect this. Checking answers with a slide rule now and then is also a good idea. Also, even though a calculator may be in perfect repair and functioning well, you may still on occasion hit the wrong button. If you do, and thereby obtain an unreasonable answer, you may be able to detect it by estimating.

5. *Calculators have a built-in rounding error.*

Suppose your calculator has eight-digit capacity. It will then round all answers accordingly. If your calculator has ten-digit capacity, answers will be rounded to ten digits. There may be small discrepancies in answers because of the way in which answers are rounded. If you use the logarithm tables or the trigonometric tables at the end of the text in working problems, your answers may be slightly different than if you obtain values from a calculator. Don't let this upset you. The answers in the back of the book may also vary slightly from those you obtain. This is to be expected.

About the Study Supplement

To the Student

An (optional) supplement (called a *Study Supplement*) to this text contains the following material.

1. *For each lesson a list of objectives.* These objectives tell you what you should be able to *do* when you have completed the lesson. In other words, they give you a basic list of things for which you are to be responsible. You will find that the homework exercises for each lesson conform quite strictly to these objectives, except for those designed for the calculator and those marked ▶. Exercises marked ▶ are designed to stretch your mind a bit and may require you to do a little beyond that which is stated in the objectives.

2. *Exercises to help you understand the text material.* As concepts and techniques are developed in the reading material in the text, these exercises will help you in their understanding and in skill development.

If you are using this supplement, when you come to a symbol such as **[4–7]** you should stop reading and do the indicated exercises in the supplement. Check your answers (which are in the back of the supplement) before you continue reading.

3. *Practice tests for each chapter.* These practice tests can be used to help you prepare for a class test.

Contents

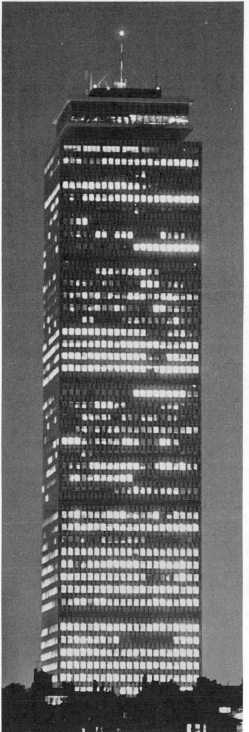

CHAPTER **1**

Review of
Elementary Algebra

1.1 Operations on the Real Numbers

The set of real numbers corresponds to the set of points on a line. On this number line, the numbers to the right of (greater than) 0 are called *positive*. Those to the left of (less than) 0 are called *negative*. The real numbers, 0, 1, −1, 2, −2, 3, −3, and so on, are called *integers*. Those real numbers that can be named by a fractional symbol with integer numerator and denominator are called *rational*. Those that cannot be so named are called *irrational*. The numbers $\frac{3}{7}$, $-\frac{9}{25}$, and 5 are rational. The numbers $\sqrt{2}$ and π are irrational. The distance of a number from 0 is called its *absolute value*. The absolute value of a number x is denoted $|x|$. Thus $|3| = 3$ and $|-7| = 7$. Absolute values are never negative. **[1–3]**

ADDITION

To add two negative numbers we can add their absolute values, but remember that the sum is negative.

Example. Add $-5 + (-6)$.

The absolute values are 5 and 6. We add them: $5 + 6 = 11$. The answer will be negative, so $-5 + (-6) = -11$.

To add a negative and a positive number, we find the difference of their absolute values. The answer will have the sign of the addend with the larger absolute value. If the absolute values are the same, then the sum is 0.

Examples

a) $8 + (-5) = 3$ b) $8.6 + (-4.2) = 4.4$

c) $4 + (-10) = -6$ d) $\frac{3}{5} + \left(-\frac{9}{5}\right) = -\frac{6}{5}$

e) $-5 + 3 = -2$ f) $\pi + (-\pi) = 0$ **[4–9]**

MULTIPLICATION

The product of two negative numbers is positive. The product of a negative and a positive number is negative.

Examples

a) $3 \cdot (-4) = -12$ b) $1.5 \cdot (-3.8) = -5.7$

c) $-5 \cdot (-4) = 20$ d) $-\frac{2}{3} \cdot \left(-\frac{4}{5}\right) = \frac{8}{15}$

e) $-3 \cdot (-2) \cdot (-4) = -24$ **[10–12]**

DIVISION

The quotient of two negative numbers is positive. The quotient of a positive and a negative number is negative.

Examples

a) $\frac{-8}{-4} = 2$ b) $\frac{-4.8}{-2.4} = 2$

c) $\frac{-12}{4} = -3$ d) $\frac{-5.5}{5} = -1.1$

e) $\frac{5}{-10} = -\frac{1}{2}$ f) $\frac{3}{4} \div \left(-\frac{2}{3}\right) = -\frac{9}{8}$ **[13–15]**

RECIPROCALS

If the product of two numbers is 1, they are *reciprocals* of each other.

Examples

a) The reciprocal of $\frac{1}{2}$ is 2.

b) The reciprocal of $-\frac{2}{3}$ is $-\frac{3}{2}$.

c) The reciprocal of 0.16 is 6.25.

When fractional notation for a number is given, its reciprocal can be found by inverting. To divide by a number is the same as multiplying by its reciprocal. Every real number except 0 has a reciprocal.

ADDITIVE INVERSES

The *additive inverse* of a number is the number opposite to it on the number line. When a number and its additive inverse are added, the result is always 0. The additive inverse of a number x is symbolized $-x$ or ^-x. Every real number has an additive inverse.

Examples

a) The additive inverse of 3 is negative 3, symbolized -3 or $^-3$.

b) The additive inverse of -5 is 5, symbolized $-(-5)$ or $^-(-5)$, or 5.

c) The additive inverse of 0 is 0, symbolized -0 or $^-0$, or 0.   **[16–20]**

SUBTRACTION

To subtract one number from another, we can add its additive inverse.

Examples

a) $8 - 5 = 8 + (-5) = 3$

b) $10 - (-4) = 10 + 4 = 14$

c) $8.6 - (-2.3) = 8.6 + 2.3 = 10.9$

d) $-15 - (-5) = -15 + 5 = -10$ **[21–24]**

Exercise Set 1.1

Find the additive inverse of each and symbolize it in two ways.

1. 8   **2.** 1.4   **3.** $-\frac{10}{3}$ **4.** -17

5. $3x$ **6.** $4y$ **7.** $(a+b)$ **8.** $(2a+b)$

Simplify.

9. $|12|$ **10.** $|2.56|$ **11.** $|-47|$ **12.** $|-5.6|$

Find the reciprocal of each.

13. 3   **14.** 5   **15.** $-\frac{2}{3}$ **16.** $-\frac{5}{9}$

Add.

17. $-3.1 + {}^-7.2$

18. $-5.2 + {}^-8.3$

19. $-34 + {}^-76$

20. $-42 + {}^-64$

21. $-\dfrac{7}{5} + \dfrac{3}{5}$

22. $-\dfrac{8}{3} + \dfrac{5}{3}$

23. $-412 + 186$

24. $-735 + 319$

25. $6 + {}^-10$

26. $8 + {}^-12$

27. $\dfrac{9}{2} + \dfrac{-3}{5}$

28. $\dfrac{11}{3} + \dfrac{-5}{2}$

29. $-5 + {}^-7 + {}^-12$

30. $-6 + {}^-4 + {}^-10$

31. $-8 + 12 + {}^-5$

32. $-10 + 13 + {}^-6$

Multiply.

33. $5 \cdot (-6)$

34. $7 \cdot (-4)$

35. $\dfrac{12}{5} \cdot \left(-\dfrac{17}{7}\right)$

36. $\dfrac{13}{2} \cdot \left(-\dfrac{15}{4}\right)$

37. $(-7.1) \cdot 8$

38. $(-8.2) \cdot 6$

39. $-\dfrac{8}{3} \cdot \left(-\dfrac{5}{2}\right)$

40. $-\dfrac{7}{5} \cdot \left(-\dfrac{6}{7}\right)$

41. $-7(-2)(-3)$

42. $-6(-2)(-4)$

43. $-\dfrac{14}{3}\left(-\dfrac{17}{5}\right)\left(-\dfrac{21}{2}\right)$

44. $-\dfrac{13}{4}\left(-\dfrac{16}{5}\right)\left(-\dfrac{23}{2}\right)$

Divide.

45. $\dfrac{-20}{-4}$

46. $\dfrac{-30}{-5}$

47. $\dfrac{36}{-6}$

48. $\dfrac{49}{-7}$

49. $\dfrac{-35}{7}$

50. $\dfrac{-40}{8}$

51. $\dfrac{-11}{55}$

52. $\dfrac{-10}{70}$

Subtract.

53. $11 - 15$

54. $12 - 17$

55. $12 - {}^-6$

56. $13 - {}^-4$

57. $-\dfrac{10}{3} - \dfrac{-17}{3}$

58. $-\dfrac{11}{5} - \dfrac{-18}{5}$

59. $-12 - 8$

60. $-14 - 5$

Simplify.

61. $17.53 + {}^-31.25$

62. $3.175 + {}^-10.861$

63. $-14.12 + {}^-3.74 + 7.43$

64. $-105.81 + 41.32 + {}^-83.45$

65. $0.0751(-3.12)$

66. $-13.715(4.001)$

67. $-12.35(-4.12)$

68. $-14.37(-4.212)$

69. $9.435 - 12.486$

70. $18.931 - 11.874$

71. $17.506 - {}^-21249$

72. $18.312 - {}^-41.365$

73. $-1.415 - {}^-2.148$

74. $-11.541 - {}^-2.415$

1.2 Exponential Notation

INTEGERS AS EXPONENTS

The set of integers is as follows:

$$\{\ldots, -3, -2, -1, 0, 1, 2, 3, \ldots\}.$$

The braces indicate that a *set* is being named. When an integer greater than 1 is used as an exponent, the integer gives the number of times the base is used as a factor. For example, 5^3 means $5 \cdot 5 \cdot 5$. An exponent of 1 does not change the meaning of an expression. For example, $(-3)^1 = -3$. When 0 occurs as the exponent of a nonzero expression, we agree that the expression is equal to 1. For example, $37^0 = 1$. When a minus sign occurs with exponential notation, a certain caution is in order. For example, $(-4)^2$ means that -4 is to be raised to the second power. Hence $(-4)^2 = (-4)(-4) = 16$. On the other hand, -4^2 represents the additive inverse of 4^2. Thus $-4^2 = -16$.

[25–34]

Negative integers as exponents have meaning as follows:

> **Definition.** If n is any positive integer, then a^{-n} means $1/a^n$ for $a \neq 0$. In other words, a^n and a^{-n} are reciprocals of each other.

Examples

a) $\dfrac{1}{5^2} = 5^{-2}$

b) $7^{-3} = \dfrac{1}{7^3}$

c) $5^{-4} = \dfrac{1}{5^4} = \dfrac{1}{5 \cdot 5 \cdot 5 \cdot 5} = \dfrac{1}{625}$

[35–37]

PROPERTIES OF EXPONENTS

Let us consider an example involving multiplication.

$$b^5 \cdot b^{-2} = (b \cdot b \cdot b \cdot b \cdot b) \cdot \frac{1}{b \cdot b} = \frac{b \cdot b}{b \cdot b} \cdot (b \cdot b \cdot b)$$
$$= 1 \cdot (b \cdot b \cdot b) = b^3$$

Note that the result can be obtained by adding the exponents. This is true in general.

> **Theorem.** For any number a, and any integers m and n, $a^m \cdot a^n = a^{m+n}$.

Examples

a) $x^4 \cdot x^{-2} = x^{4+(-2)} = x^2$

b) $5^4 \cdot 5^6 = 5^{10}$

c) $c^{-3} \cdot c^{-2} = c^{-5}$

d) $a^4 \cdot a^3 = a^7$

[38–43]

Let us consider an example involving division:

$$\frac{8^5}{8^3} = 8^5 \cdot \frac{1}{8^3} = 8^5 \cdot 8^{-3} = 8^{5-3} = 8^2.$$

Note that the result could also be obtained by subtracting the exponents. Here is another example:

$$\frac{7^{-2}}{7^3} = 7^{-2} \cdot 7^{-3} = 7^{-2-3} = 7^{-5}.$$

Again, the result could be obtained by subtracting the exponents. This is true in general.

> **Theorem.** For any nonzero a, and any integers m and n, $a^m/a^n = a^{m-n}$.

Examples

a) $\dfrac{9^{-2}}{9^5} = 9^{-2-5} = 9^{-7}$

b) $\dfrac{7^{-4}}{7^{-5}} = 7^{-4-(-5)} = 7^1 = 7$

This property can be used to show why a^0 is not defined when $a = 0$. Consider the following:

$$a^0 = a^{3-3} = \frac{a^3}{a^3}.$$

If a were 0, we would then have 0/0, which is meaningless. **[44–50]**

RAISING A POWER TO A POWER

Consider this example:

$$(5^2)^4 = 5^2 \cdot 5^2 \cdot 5^2 \cdot 5^2 = 5^8.$$

The result can be obtained by multiplying the exponents. This is true in general.

> **Theorem.** For any number a, and any integers m and n, $(a^m)^n = a^{m \cdot n}$.

Examples

a) $(8^{-2})^3 = 8^{-2} \cdot 8^{-2} \cdot 8^{-2} = 8^{-6}$

b) $(x^{-5})^4 = x^{-20}$

c) $(3x^2y^{-2})^3 = 3^3(x^2)^3(y^{-2})^3 = 3^3x^6y^{-6} = 27x^6y^{-6}$

d) $(5x^3y^{-5}z^2)^4 = 5^4x^{12}y^{-20}z^8 = 625x^{12}y^{-20}z^8$

e) $(4x^2y^{-3})^{-4} = 4^{-4}x^{-8}y^{12} = \frac{1}{256}x^{-8}y^{12}$ **[51–57]**

SCIENTIFIC NOTATION

Scientific notation is particularly useful for naming very large or very small numbers. It also has uses for our later study of logarithms. Some examples are:

$$7.8 \times 10^{13} = 78{,}000{,}000{,}000{,}000,$$
$$5.64 \times 10^{-8} = 0.0000000564.$$

> **Definition.** *Scientific notation* for a positive number consists of exponential notation for a power of 10 and decimal notation for a number greater than or equal to 1 and less than 10, and a multiplication sign.

We can convert to scientific notation by multiplying by 1, choosing an appropriate symbol $10^k/10^k$ for 1.

Example 1. Convert to scientific notation.

$96{,}000 = 96{,}000 \times \dfrac{10^4}{10^4}$ We use 10^4 in order to "move the decimal point" between 9 and 6.

$\quad = \dfrac{96{,}000}{10^4} \times 10^4$

$\quad = 9.6 \times 10^4$

With practice such conversions can be done mentally, and you should try to do this as much as possible. **[58, 59]**

Example 2. Convert to scientific notation.

$0.00000478 = 0.00000478 \times \dfrac{10^6}{10^6}$

$\quad = (0.00000478 \times 10^6) \times 10^{-6}$

$\quad = 4.78 \times 10^{-6}$

We use 10^6 in order to "move the decimal point" between 4 and 7.

Again you should try to make conversions mentally as much as possible.

Examples. Convert to decimal notation.

a) $6.043 \times 10^5 = 604{,}300$

b) $4.7 \times 10^{-8} = 0.000000047$ **[60–63]**

Exercise Set 1.2

Simplify.

1. $2^3 \cdot 2^{-4}$ **2.** $3^4 \cdot 3^{-5}$ **3.** $b^2 \cdot b^{-2}$ **4.** $c^3 \cdot c^{-3}$

5. $4^2 \cdot 4^{-5} \cdot 4^6$ **6.** $5^2 \cdot 5^{-4} \cdot 5^5$ **7.** $2x^3 \cdot 3x^2$ **8.** $3y^4 \cdot 4y^3$

9. $(5a^2b)(3a^{-3}b^4)$ **10.** $(4xy^2)(3x^{-4}y^5)$ **11.** $(2x)^3(3x)^2$ **12.** $(4y)^2(3y)^3$

13. $(6x^5y^{-2}z^3)(-3x^2y^3z^{-2})$ **14.** $(5x^4y^{-3}z^2)(-2x^2y^4z^{-1})$ **15.** $\dfrac{b^{40}}{b^{37}}$ **16.** $\dfrac{a^{39}}{a^{32}}$

17. $\dfrac{x^2y^{-2}}{x^{-1}y}$ **18.** $\dfrac{x^3y^{-3}}{x^{-1}y^2}$ **19.** $\dfrac{9a^2}{(-3a)^2}$ **20.** $\dfrac{16y^2}{(-4y)^2}$

21. $\dfrac{24a^5b^3}{8a^4b}$ **22.** $\dfrac{30x^6y^4}{5x^3y^2}$ **23.** $\dfrac{12x^2y^3z^{-2}}{21xy^2z^3}$ **24.** $\dfrac{15x^3y^4z^{-3}}{45xyz^5}$

25. $(2ab^2)^3$ **26.** $(4xy^3)^2$ **27.** $(-2x^3)^4$ **28.** $(-3x^2)^4$

29. $-(2x^3)^4$ **30.** $-(3x^2)^4$ **31.** $(6a^2b^3c)^2$ **32.** $(5x^3y^2z)^2$

33. $(-5c^{-1}d^{-2})^{-2}$ **34.** $(-4x^{-1}z^{-2})^{-2}$ **35.** $\dfrac{4^{-2} + 2^{-4}}{8^{-1}}$ **36.** $\dfrac{3^{-2} + 2^{-3}}{7^{-1}}$

37. $\dfrac{(-2)^4 + (-4)^2}{(-1)^8}$ **38.** $\dfrac{(-3)^2 + (-2)^4}{(-1)^6}$ **39.** $\dfrac{(3a^2b^{-2}c^4)^3}{(2a^{-1}b^2c^{-3})^2}$ **40.** $\dfrac{(2a^3b^{-3}c^3)^3}{(3a^{-1}b^{-3}c^{-5})^2}$

41. $\dfrac{6^{-2}x^{-3}y^2}{3^{-3}x^{-4}y}$ **42.** $\dfrac{5^{-2}x^{-4}y^3}{2^{-3}x^{-5}y}$

Convert to scientific notation.

43. 58,000,000   **44.** 27,000   **45.** 365,000   **46.** 3645

47. 0.0000027   **48.** 0.0000658   **49.** 0.027   **50.** 0.0038

51. 0.05

Convert to decimal notation.

52. 4×10^5 **53.** 5×10^{-4} **54.** 6.2×10^{-3} **55.** 7.8×10^6

56. 7.69×10^{12} **57.** 8.54×10^{-7}

1.3 Polynomials, Addition and Subtraction

Expressions such as $3x^2 - 5x + 4$ and $5x^2y^3 + 17x^2y - 2$ are called *polynomials*. A polynomial has one or more terms. Each term has a *coefficient*, which is a constant, and possibly one or more variables raised to positive integral powers.

Example

The polynomial $5x^3y - 7xy^2 + 2$ has three terms.

They are $5x^3y$, $-7xy^2$, and 2.

The coefficients of the terms are 5, −7, and 2.

The *degree of a term* is the sum of the exponents of the variables. The *degree of a polynomial* is the degree of the term of highest degree.

Example. In the polynomial $5x^3y - 7xy^2 + 2$, the degrees of the terms are 4, 3, and 0. The polynomial is of degree 4.

A polynomial with just one term is called a *monomial*. If there are just two terms, a polynomial is called a *binomial*. If there are just three terms, it is called a *trinomial*.

Much of the algebraic manipulation we do with polynomials can also be done with expressions that are not polynomials. Here are some examples of expressions that are not polynomials.

Examples

a) $3\sqrt{x} + 4y$

b) $\dfrac{3x^2 + 2}{x - 1}$

c) $4x^{\frac{1}{2}} - 5y^{\frac{3}{2}}$

If two terms of an expression have the same letters raised to the same powers, the terms are called *similar*.

This is true even if the expression is not a polynomial. Similar terms can be "combined" using the distributive properties.

Examples

a)
$$3x^2 - 4y + 2x^2 = 3x^2 + 2x^2 - 4y$$
$$= (3 + 2)x^2 - 4y$$
$$= 5x^2 - 4y$$

b) $4x^{\frac{1}{2}}y + 7x^{\frac{1}{2}}y = 11x^{\frac{1}{2}}y$

c) $-2x^2\sqrt{y^3} + 5x^2\sqrt{y^3} = 3x^2\sqrt{y^3}$ **[64–66]**

ADDITION

The sum of two polynomials can be found by writing a plus sign between them and then combining similar terms.

Example. Add $-3x^3 + 2x - 4$ and $4x^3 + 3x^2 + 2$.

$$(-3x^3 + 2x - 4) + (4x^3 + 3x^2 + 2)$$
$$= x^3 + 3x^2 + 2x - 2$$
     [67, 68]

ADDITIVE INVERSES

The additive inverse of a polynomial can be found by changing the sign of every term.

Example. The additive inverse of $-3xy^2 + 4x^2y - 5x - 3$ is

$$3xy^2 - 4x^2y + 5x + 3.$$

To check this we can add the two polynomials, observing that the sum is 0.

Example. The additive inverse of $7xy^2 - 6xy - 4y + 3$ can be symbolized as

$$^-(7xy^2 - 6xy - 4y + 3).$$

Thus,

$$^-(7xy^2 - 6xy - 4y + 3) = -7xy^2 + 6xy + 4y - 3.$$

The preceding example may recall a rule that says: To remove parentheses preceded by an additive inverse (minus) sign, we change the sign of every term inside the parentheses.   **[69,70]**

SUBTRACTION

Recall that we can subtract by adding an inverse. Thus to subtract one polynomial from another, we add its additive inverse. We change the sign of each term of the subtrahend and then add.

Example

$$(-9x^5 - x^3 + 2x^2 + 4) - (2x^5 - x^4 + 4x^3 - 3x^2)$$

$$= (-9x^5 - x^3 + 2x^2 + 4) + {}^-(2x^5 - x^4 + 4x^3 - 3x^2)$$
$$= (-9x^5 - x^3 + 2x^2 + 4) + (-2x^5 + x^4 - 4x^3 + 3x^2)$$
$$= -11x^5 + x^4 - 5x^3 + 5x^2 + 4$$

On occasion, it may be helpful to write polynomials to be subtracted with similar terms in columns.

Example. Subtract the second polynomial from the first.

$$\begin{array}{l} 4x^2y - 6x^3y^2 \qquad\qquad\; + x^2y^2 - \;\;5y \\ 4x^2y + \;\,x^3y^2 + 3x^2y^3 \qquad\qquad + \;\;6y \\ \hline \;\;\; - 7x^3y^2 - 3x^2y^3 + x^2y^2 - 11y \end{array}$$

[71,72]

Exercise Set 1.3

Add.

1. $5x^2y - 2xy^2 + 3xy - 5$ and
$-2x^2y - 3xy^2 + 4xy + 7$

2. $6x^2y - 3xy^2 + 5xy - 3$ and
$-4x^2y - 4xy^2 + 3xy + 8$

3. $-3pq^2 - 5p^2q + 4pq + 3$ and
$-7pq^2 + 3pq - 4p + 2q$

4. $-5pq^2 - 3p^2q + 6pq + 5$ and
$-4pq^2 + 5pq - 6p + 4q$

5. $2x + 3y + z \;\; 7$ and
$4x - 2y - z + 8$ and
$-3x + y - 2z - 4$

6. $2x^2 + 12xy - 11$ and
$6x^2 - 2x + 4$ and
$-x^2 - y - 2$

7. $7x\sqrt{y} - 3y\sqrt{x} + \dfrac{1}{5}$ and

$-2x\sqrt{y} - y\sqrt{x} - \dfrac{3}{5}$

8. $10x\sqrt{y} - 4y\sqrt{x} + \dfrac{4}{3}$ and

$-3x\sqrt{y} - y\sqrt{x} - \dfrac{1}{3}$

Rename each additive inverse without parentheses.

9. $^-(5x^3 - 7x^2 + 3x - 6)$

10. $^-(-4y^4 + 7y^2 - 2y - 1)$

Subtract.

11. $(3x^2 - 2x - x^3 + 2)$

    $- (5x^2 - 8x - x^3 + 4)$

12. $(5x^2 + 4xy - 3y^2 + 2)$

    $- (9x^2 - 4xy + 2y^2 - 1)$

13. $(4a - 2b - c + 3d)$

    $- (-2a + 3b + c - d)$

14. $(5a - 3b - c + 4d)$

    $- (-3a + 5b + c - 2d)$

15. $(x^4 - 3x^2 + 4x)$

    $- (3x^3 + x^2 - 5x + 3)$

16. $(2x^4 - 5x^2 + 7x)$

    $- (5x^3 + 2x^2 - 3x + 5)$

17. $(7x\sqrt{y} - 4y\sqrt{x} + 7.5)$

    $-(-2x\sqrt{y} - y\sqrt{x} - 1.6)$

18. $\left(10x\sqrt{y} - 4y\sqrt{x} + \frac{4}{3}\right) - \left(-3x\sqrt{y} + y\sqrt{x} - \frac{1}{3}\right)$

 Simplify.

19. $(0.565p^2q - 2.167pq^2 + 16.02pq - 17.1)$

    $+ (-1.612p^2q - 0.312pq^2 - 7.141pq - 87.044)$

20. $(675.3xy^2 + 1003.2x^2y - 75.33x + 47.55y + 35)$

    $+ (37.1xy^2 - 375.4x^2y + 107.7x - 175.45)$

21. $(0.512p^2\sqrt{q} + 1.215\sqrt[3]{pq} + 0.0753\sqrt{p})$

    $+ (-37.56p^2\sqrt{q} - 1.152\sqrt[3]{pq} + 0.1345\sqrt{p})$

22. $(0.06031xy^{-2} - 0.3142xy + 0.0404\sqrt{xy} - 5.142)$

    $+ (0.07062xy^{-2} + 0.5143xy - 6.003\sqrt{xy})$

23. $(3.1051xy^{-2} + 2.0143\sqrt{xy} - 1.1011)$

    $- (-5.0121xy^{-2} + 2.1057xy + 5.0101\sqrt{xy})$

24. $(5003.2xy^{-2} + 3102.4\sqrt{xy} - 5280)$

    $- (2143.6xy^{-2} + 6153.8xy - 4141\sqrt{xy})$

1.4 Multiplication of Polynomials

Multiplication of polynomials is based on the distributive properties. To multiply two polynomials, we multiply each term of one by every term of the other and then add the results.

Example. Multiply $4x^4y - 7x^2y + 3y$ by $2y - 3x^2y$.

$$
\begin{array}{l}
4x^4y - 7x^2y + 3y \\
\underline{\quad\quad 2y - 3x^2y} \\
8x^4y^2 - 14x^2y^2 + 6y^2 \quad \text{(multiplying by } 2y) \\
-12x^6y^2 + 21x^4y^2 - 9x^2y^2 \quad \text{(multiplying by } -3x^2y) \\
\hline
-12x^6y^2 + 29x^4y^2 - 23x^2y^2 + 6y^2 \quad \text{(adding)}
\end{array}
$$

[73, 74]

PRODUCTS OF TWO BINOMIALS

We can find a product of two binomials mentally. We multiply the first terms, then the outside terms, then the inside terms, then the last terms (this procedure is sometimes abbreviated FOIL), and then add the results. This also works for expressions that are not polynomials.

Examples. Multiply:

a) $(3xy + 2x)(x^2 + 2xy^2)$

    $= 3x^3y + 6x^2y^3 + 2x^3 + 4x^2y^2$

b) $(x + \sqrt{2})(y - \sqrt{2}) = xy + \sqrt{2}\,y - \sqrt{2}\,x - 2$

c) $(2x - \sqrt{3})(y + 2) = 2xy - \sqrt{3}\,y + 4x - 2\sqrt{3}$

d) $(2x + 3y)(x - 4y) = 2x^2 - 5xy - 12y^2$ **[75–77]**

SQUARES OF BINOMIALS

Multiplying a binomial by itself, we obtain the following:

$$(a + b)^2 = a^2 + 2ab + b^2$$

and

$$(a - b)^2 = a^2 - 2ab + b^2.$$

Thus, to square a binomial we square the first term, add twice the product of the terms, and then add the square of the second term.

Examples. Multiply:

a) $(2x + 9y^2)^2 = (2x)^2 + 2(2x)(9y^2) + (9y^2)^2$
$$= 4x^2 + 36xy^2 + 81y^4$$

b) $(3x^2 - 5xy^2)^2 = (3x^2)^2 - 2(3x^2)(5xy^2) + (5xy^2)^2$
$$= 9x^4 - 30x^3y^2 + 25x^2y^4$$
$$[78, 79]$$

PRODUCTS OF SUMS AND DIFFERENCES

The following multiplication gives a result to be remembered:

$$(a + b)(a - b) = (a + b) \cdot a - (a + b) \cdot b$$
$$= a^2 + ab - ab - b^2$$
$$= a^2 - b^2.$$

The result to be remembered is as follows:

$$(a + b)(a - b) = a^2 - b^2.$$

The product of a sum and a difference of the same two terms is the difference of their squares. Thus to find such a product, we square the first term, square the second term, and write a minus sign between the results.

Examples. Multiply:

a) $(y + 5)(y - 5) = y^2 - 25$

b) $(3x + 2)(3x - 2) = (3x)^2 - 2^2$
$$= 9x^2 - 4$$

c) $(2xy^2 + 3x)(2xy^2 - 3x) = (2xy^2)^2 - (3x)^2$
$$= 4x^2y^4 - 9x^2$$

d) $(5x + \sqrt{2})(5x - \sqrt{2}) = (5x)^2 - (\sqrt{2})^2$
$$= 25x^2 - 2$$

e) $(5y + 4 + 3x)(5y + 4 - 3x)$
$$= (5y + 4)^2 - (3x)^2$$
$$= 25y^2 + 40y + 16 - 9x^2$$

f) $(3xy^2 + 4y)(-3xy^2 + 4y) = -(3xy^2)^2 + (4y)^2$
$$= 16y^2 - 9x^2y^4$$
$$[80-84]$$

In the following exercises you should do as much of the calculating mentally as you can. If possible, write only the answer. Work for speed with accuracy.

Exercise Set 1.4

Multiply.

1. $2x^2 + 4x + 16$ and $3x - 4$

2. $3y^2 - 3y + 9$ and $2y + 3$

3. $4a^2b - 2ab + 3b^2$ and $ab - 2b + 1$

4. $2x^2 + y^2 - 2xy$ and $x^2 - 2y^2 - xy$

5. $(2y + 3)(3y - 2)$

6. $(5y - 4)(3y + 7)$

7. $(2x + 3y)(2x + y)$

8. $(2a - 3b)(2a - b)$

9. $\left(4x^2 - \frac{1}{2}y\right)\left(3x + \frac{1}{4}y\right)$

10. $\left(2y^3 + \frac{1}{5}x\right)\left(3y - \frac{1}{4}x\right)$

11. $(\sqrt{2}\,x^2 - y^2)(\sqrt{2}\,x - 2y)$

12. $(\sqrt{3}\,y^2 - 2)(\sqrt{3}\,y - x)$

13. $(2x + 3y)^2$

14. $(5x + 2y)^2$

15. $(2x^2 - 3y)^2$

16. $(4x^2 - 5y)^2$

17. $(2x^3 + 3y^2)^2$

18. $(5x^3 + 2y^2)^2$

19. $\left(\frac{1}{2}x^2 - \frac{3}{5}y\right)^2$

20. $\left(\frac{1}{4}x^2 - \frac{2}{3}y\right)^2$

21. $(0.5x + 0.7y^2)^2$

22. $(0.3x + 0.8y^2)^2$

23. $(3x - 2y)(3x + 2y)$

24. $(3x + 5y)(3x - 5y)$

25. $(x^2 + yz)(x^2 - yz)$

26. $(2x^2 + 5xy)(2x^2 - 5xy)$

27. $(3x^2 - \sqrt{2})(3x^2 + \sqrt{2})$

28. $(5x^2 - \sqrt{3})(5x^2 + \sqrt{3})$

29. $(2x + 3y + 4)(2x + 3y - 4)$

30. $(5x + 2y + 3)(5x + 2y - 3)$

31. $(x^2 + 3y + y^2)(x^2 + 3y - y^2)$

32. $(2x^2 + y + y^2)(2x^2 + y - y^2)$

33. $(x + 1)(x - 1)(x^2 + 1)$

34. $(y - 2)(y + 2)(y^2 + 4)$

35. $(2x + y)(2x - y)(4x^2 + y^2)$

36. $(5x + y)(5x - y)(25x^2 + y^2)$

⊞ Multiply.

37. $(0.051x + 0.04y)^2$

38. $(1.032x - 2.512y)^2$

39. $(37.86x + 1.42)(65.03x - 27.4)$

40. $(3.601x - 17.5)(47.105x + 31.23)$

41. $(0.412x + 1.352y)(0.0165x + 2.176y)$

42. $(6.514x + 7.914y)(3.201x - 7.016y)$

1.5 Factoring

To factor a polynomial we do the reverse of multiplying; that is, we find an expression that is a product. Facility in factoring is an important algebraic skill.

TERMS WITH COMMON FACTORS

When an expression is to be factored, we should always look first for a possible factor that is common to all terms.

Examples. Factor:

a) $4x^2 + 8 = 4(x^2 + 2)$

b) $12x^2y - 20x^3y = 4x^2y(3 - 5x)$

c) $7x\sqrt{y} + 14x^2\sqrt{y} - 21\sqrt{y} = 7\sqrt{y}(x + 2x^2 - 3)$

d) $(a - b)(x + 5) + (a - b)(x - y^2)$

   $= (a - b)[(x + 5) + (x - y^2)]$

   $= (a - b)(2x + 5 - y^2)$

In some polynomials pairs of terms have a common factor that can be removed, as in the following examples. This process is called *factoring by grouping*.

Examples. Factor:

a) $y^2 + 3y + 4y + 12 = y(y + 3) + 4(y + 3)$

   $= (y + 4)(y + 3)$

b) $ax^2 + ay + bx^2 + by = a(x^2 + y) + b(x^2 + y)$

   $= (a + b)(x^2 + y)$

   [85–87]

DIFFERENCES OF SQUARES

Recall that $(a + b)(a - b) = a^2 - b^2$. We can use this equation in reverse to factor an expression that is the difference of two squares.

Examples. Factor:

a) $x^2 - 9 = (x + 3)(x - 3)$

b) $y^2 - 2 = (y + \sqrt{2})(y - \sqrt{2})$

c) $9a^2 - 16x^4 = (3a + 4x^2)(3a - 4x^2)$

d) $9y^4 - 9x^4 = 9(y^4 - x^4)$

   $= 9(y^2 + x^2)(y^2 - x^2)$

   $= 9(y^2 + x^2)(y + x)(y - x)$ **[88–91]**

TRINOMIAL SQUARES

You should recall that $a^2 + 2ab + b^2 = (a + b)^2$ and $a^2 - 2ab + b^2 = (a - b)^2$. We can use these equations to factor trinomials that are squares. To factor a trinomial, you should check to see if it is a square. For this to be the case, two of the terms must be squares and the other term must be twice the product of the square roots.

Examples. Factor:

a) $x^2 - 10x + 25 = (x - 5)^2$

b) $16y^2 + 56y + 49 = (4y + 7)^2$

c) $-4y^2 - 144y^8 + 48y^5$

   $= -4y^2(1 + 36y^6 - 12y^3)$ (We first removed

   $= -4y^2(1 - 12y^3 + 36y^6)$ the common factor).

   $= -4y^2(1 - 6y^3)^2$ **[92–94]**

TRINOMIALS THAT ARE NOT SQUARES

Certain trinomials that are not squares can be factored into two binomials. To do this, we can use the equation $acx^2 + (ad + bc)x + bd = (ax + b)(cx + d)$.

Example. Factor $2x^2 + 11x + 12$.

We look for binomials $(ax + b)$ and $(cx + d)$. The product of the first terms must be $2x^2$. The product of the last terms must be 12. When we multiply the inside terms, then the outside terms, and add, we must get $11x$. By trial, we thus determine the factors to be as follows: $(x + 4)(2x + 3)$.   **[95–97]**

SUMS OR DIFFERENCES OF CUBES

We can use the following equations to factor a sum or a difference of two cubes:

$$a^3 + b^3 = (a + b)(a^2 - ab + b^2),$$
$$a^3 - b^3 = (a - b)(a^2 + ab + b^2).$$

Examples. Factor:

a) $27x^3 + y^3 = (3x + y)(9x^2 - 3xy + y^2)$

b) $64y^6 - 125x^6 = (4y^2 - 5x^2)$
$$\times (16x^4 + 20y^2x^2 + 25x^4)$$
[98, 99]

TO FIND SQUARE ROOTS ON A CALCULATOR

Some calculators have a square root key. If yours does not you can use Table 1 if the number in question occurs there, or you can use the following method for finding square roots. The method amounts to making successive guesses and then checking them with the calculator. We illustrate with an example, in which we approximate the square root of 27.

First, we make a guess. Let's guess 4. Using the calculator we find 4^2, which is 16. This is less than 27, so the square root is at *least* 4.

Next we try 5. We find 5^2, which is 25. This is also less than 27, so the square root is at least 5.

Next we try 6. We find 6^2, which is 36. This is greater than 27, so we know that $\sqrt{27}$ is between 5 and 6. $\sqrt{27}$ is 5, plus some fraction.

We now find the tenths digit by trying 5.1, 5.2, 5.3, etc.

$5.1^2 = 26.01$ (this is less than 27)
$5.2^2 = 27.04$ (this is greater than 27)

Thus, the tenths digit is 1.

We now find the hundredths digit by trying 5.11, 5.12, etc.

$5.11^2 = 26.1121$
$5.12^2 = 26.2144$
.   .   (All of these are less than 27,
.   .   so the hundredths digit is 9.)
.   .
$5.18^2 = 26.8324$
$5.19^2 = 26.9361$

To find the thousandths digit we would try 5.191, 5.192, etc. The process can be shortened by some estimating or clever guessing. It should be carried out until the required number of decimal places is obtained.

Exercise Set 1.5

Factor.

1. $18a^2b - 15ab^2$

2. $4x^2y + 12xy^2$

3. $a(b - 2) + c(b - 2)$

4. $a(x^2 - 3) - 2(x^2 - 3)$

5. $x^2 + 3x + 6x + 18$

6. $3x^3 + x^2 - 18x - 6$

7. $9x^2 - 25$

8. $16x^2 - 9$

9. $4xy^4 - 4xz^2$

10. $5xy^4 - 5xz^4$

11. $y^2 - 6y + 9$

12. $x^2 + 8x + 16$

13. $1 - 8x + 16x^2$

14. $1 + 10x + 25x^2$

15. $4x^2 - 5$

16. $16x^2 - 7$

17. $x^2y^2 - 14xy + 49$

18. $x^2y^2 - 16xy + 64$

19. $4ax^2 + 20ax - 56a$

20. $21x^2y + 2xy - 8y$

21. $a^2 + 2ab + b^2 - c^2$

22. $x^2 - 2xy + y^2 - z^2$

23. $x^2 + 2xy + y^2 - a^2 - 2ab - b^2$

24. $r^2 + 2rs + s^2 - t^2 + 2tv - v^2$

25. $5y^4 - 80x^4$

26. $6y^4 - 96x^4$

27. $x^3 + 8$

28. $y^3 - 64$

29. $3x^3 - \dfrac{3}{8}$

30. $5y^3 + \dfrac{5}{27}$

31. $x^3 + 0.001$

32. $y^3 - 0.125$

33. $3z^3 - 24$

34. $4t^3 + 108$

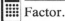 Factor.

35. $x^2 - 17.6$

36. $x^2 - 8.03$

37. $37x^2 - 14.5y^2$
(*Hint:* First remove the common factor 37.)

38. $1.96x^2 - 17.4y^2$
(*Hint:* First remove the common factor 1.96.)

1.6 Solving Equations and Inequalities

A *solution* of an equation is any number that makes the equation true when that number is substituted for the variable. The set of all solutions of an equation is called its *solution set*. When we find all the solutions of an equation (find its solution set), we say we have *solved* it.

THE ADDITION AND MULTIPLICATION PRINCIPLES

Two simple principles allow us to solve a great many equations. The first of these is as follows:

> **The *addition principle*. If an equation $a = b$ is true, then $a + c = b + c$ is true for any number *c*.**

The second principle is similar to the first.

> **The *multiplication principle*. If an equation $a = b$ is true, then $a \cdot c = b \cdot c$ is true for any number c.**

These principles may be used together as needed to solve an equation.

Example 1. Solve $3x + 4 = 15$.

$3x + 4 + {}^-4 = 15 + {}^-4$ Here we used the addition principle, adding $^-4$.

$\qquad\qquad 3x = 11$ Here we simplified.

$\dfrac{1}{3} \cdot 3x = \dfrac{1}{3} \cdot 11$ Here we used the multiplication principle, multiplying by $\frac{1}{3}$.

$\qquad\qquad x = \dfrac{11}{3}$ Here we simplified.

Check:

$$\begin{array}{c|c} \multicolumn{2}{c}{3x + 4 = 15} \\ \hline 3 \cdot \dfrac{\mathbf{11}}{\mathbf{3}} + 4 & 15 \\ 11 + 4 & \\ 15 & \end{array}$$

The only solution is the number $\frac{11}{3}$.

The solution set can be indicated $\{\frac{11}{3}\}$, but for brevity we shall most often omit the braces.

In Example 1 we used the addition and multiplication principles. Thus we know that if $3x + 4 = 15$ is true, then $x = \frac{11}{3}$ is true. This does not guarantee that if $x = \frac{11}{3}$ is true, then $3x + 4 = 15$ is true. Thus it is important to check by substituting $\frac{11}{3}$ in the original equation.

Example 2. Solve $3(7 - 2x) = 14 - 8(x - 1)$.

$21 - 6x = 14 - 8x + 8$ Here we multiplied to remove parentheses.

$21 - 6x = 22 - 8x$ Here we simplified.

$8x - 6x = 22 - 21$ Here we added -21 and also $8x$.

$\qquad 2x = 1$ Here we combined like terms and simplified.

$\qquad x = \dfrac{1}{2}$ Here we multiplied by $\dfrac{1}{2}$.

Check:

$$\begin{array}{c|c} 3(7 - 2x) & = 14 - 8(x - 1) \\ \hline 3\left(7 - 2 \cdot \dfrac{\mathbf{1}}{\mathbf{2}}\right) & 14 - 8\left(\dfrac{\mathbf{1}}{\mathbf{2}} - 1\right) \\ 3(7 - 1) & 14 - 8\left(-\dfrac{1}{2}\right) \\ 3 \cdot 6 & 14 + 4 \\ 18 & 18 \end{array}$$

The number $\frac{1}{2}$ checks. Thus the solution is $\frac{1}{2}$.

Example 3. Solve $x + 3 = x$.

$^-x + x + 3 = {}^-x + x$ Here we added ^-x.

$\qquad\qquad 3 = 0$ Here we simplified.

In Example 3 we get a false equation. No replacement for x will make the equation true. Thus there are no solutions. The solution set is the *empty set*, denoted $\emptyset$.

[100–104]

A third principle for solving equations is called the *principle of zero products*. It is as follows:

> **Principle of zero products.** For any numbers a and b, if $ab = 0$, then $a = 0$ or $b = 0$, and if $a = 0$ or $b = 0$, then $ab = 0$.

To solve an equation using this principle, there must be 0 on one side of the equation and a product on the other. The solutions are then obtained by setting the factors equal to 0 separately.

Example 4. Solve $x^2 + x - 12 = 0$.

$(x + 4)(x - 3) = 0$ Here we factored.

$x + 4 = 0$ or $x - 3 = 0$ Here we used the principle of zero products.

$x = -4$ or $x = 3$

The solutions are -4 and 3. The solution set is $\{-4, 3\}$.

[105, 106]

SOLVING INEQUALITIES

Principles for solving inequalities are similar to those for solving equations. We can add the same number to both sides of an inequality. We can also multiply both sides by the same nonzero number, but if that number is negative, we must reverse the inequality sign.

Example 5. Solve $3x < 11 - 2x$.

$3x + 2x < 11$ Here we added $2x$.

$5x < 11$ Here we combined similar terms.

$x < \dfrac{11}{5}$ Here we multiplied by $\dfrac{1}{5}$.

Any number less than $\frac{11}{5}$ is a solution.

The solution set is the set of all x such that $x < \frac{11}{5}$.

We abbreviate this using *set-builder* notation as follows:

$$\left\{ x \mid x < \frac{11}{5} \right\}.$$

For brevity we often write merely $x < \frac{11}{5}$.

Example 6. Solve $16 - 7y \geqslant 10y - 4$.

$-16 + 16 - 7y \geqslant -16 + 10y - 4$ We added -16.

$-7y \geqslant 10y - 20$ We have simplified.

$-17y \geqslant -20$ We added $-10y$ and simplified.

$y \leqslant \dfrac{20}{17}$ We multiplied by $-\dfrac{1}{17}$ and reversed the inequality sign.

Any number less than or equal to $\frac{20}{17}$ is a solution. The solution set is $\{y \mid y \leqslant \frac{20}{17}\}$.   **[107–112]**

Exercise Set 1.6

Solve.

1. $4x + 12 = 60$

2. $2y - 11 = 37$

3. $4 + \dfrac{1}{2}x = 1$

4. $4.1 - 0.2y = 1.3$

5. $y + 1 = 2y - 7$

6. $5 - 4x = x - 13$

7. $5x - 2 + 3x = 2x + 6 - 4x$

8. $5x - 17 - 2x = 6x - 1 - x$

9. $1.9x - 7.8 + 5.3x = 3.0 + 1.8x$

10. $2.2y - 5 + 4.5y = 1.7y - 20$

11. $7(3x + 6) = 11 - (x + 2)$

12. $4(5y + 3) = 3(2y - 5)$

13. $2x - (5 + 7x) = 4 - [x - (2x + 3)]$

14. $y - (9y - 8) = [5 - 2y - 3(2y - 3)] + 29$

15. $(2x - 3)(3x - 2) = 0$

16. $(5x - 2)(2x + 3) = 0$

17. $x(x - 1)(x + 2) = 0$

18. $x(x + 2)(x - 3) = 0$

19. $3x^2 + x - 2 = 0$

20. $10x^2 - 16x + 6 = 0$

21. $(x - 1)(x + 1) = 5(x - 1)$

22. $6(y - 3) = (y - 3)(y - 2)$

23. $x + 6 < 5x - 6$

24. $3 - x < 4x + 7$

25. $3x - 3 + 2x \geqslant 1 - 7x - 9$

26. $5y - 5 + y \leqslant 2 - 6y - 8$

 Solve.

27. $2.905x - 3.214 + 6.789x = 3.012 + 1.805x$

28. $13.14x + 17.152 + 8.001x = 15.15 - 7.616x$

29. $1.52(6.51x + 7.3) = 11.2 - (7.2x + 13.52)$

30. $4.73(5.16y + 3.62) = 3.005(2.75y - 6.31)$

(1.7) Fractional Expressions

Expressions like the following are called *fractional expressions*:

$$\frac{8}{5}, \quad \frac{5}{x - 2}, \quad \frac{3x^2 + 5\sqrt{x} - 2}{x^2 - y^2}.$$

Fractional expressions represent division. Certain substitutions are not sensible in such expressions. Since division by 0 is not defined, any number that makes a denominator 0 is not a sensible replacement.

MULTIPLICATION AND DIVISION

To multiply two fractional expressions, we multiply their numerators and also their denominators. When we divide, we multiply by the reciprocal of the divisor, which can be obtained by inverting the divisor.

Examples

a) Multiply.

$$\frac{x + 3}{y - 4} \cdot \frac{x^3}{y + 5} = \frac{(x + 3)x^3}{(y - 4)(y + 5)}$$

$$= \frac{x^4 + 3x^3}{y^2 + y - 20}$$

b) Divide.

$$\frac{x - 2}{x + 1} \div \frac{x + 5}{x - 3} = \frac{x - 2}{x + 1} \cdot \frac{x - 3}{x + 5} \quad \text{(inverting)}$$

$$= \frac{(x - 2)(x - 3)}{(x + 1)(x + 5)} \quad \text{(multiplying)}$$

$$= \frac{x^2 - 5x + 6}{x^2 + 6x + 5} \quad \textbf{[113, 114]}$$

SIMPLIFYING

The basis of simplifying fractional expressions rests on the fact that certain expressions are equal to 1 for all sensible replacements. Such expressions have the same numerator and denominator. Here are some examples:

$$\frac{x-2}{x-2}, \qquad \frac{3x^2-4x+2}{3x^2-4x+2}, \qquad \frac{4x-5}{4x-5}.$$

When we multiply by such an expression we obtain an equivalent expression. This means that the new expression will name the same number as the first for all sensible replacements. The set of sensible replacements may not be the same for the two expressions.

Example. Multiply:

$$\frac{y+4}{y-3} \cdot \frac{y-2}{y-2} = \frac{(y+4)(y-2)}{(y-3)(y-2)}$$

$$= \frac{y^2+2y-8}{y^2-5y+6}$$

The expressions $(y+4)/(y-3)$ and $(y^2+2y-8)/(y^2-5y+6)$ are equivalent. That is, they will name the same number for all sensible replacements. The only nonsensible replacement in the first expression is 3. For the second expression the nonsensible replacements are 2 and 3.   **[115]**

Simplification can be accomplished by reversing the procedure in the above example; that is, we try to factor the fractional expression in such a way that one of the factors is equal to 1 and then "remove" that factor.

Examples. Simplify:

a) $\dfrac{15x^3y^2}{20x^2y} = \dfrac{(5x^2y)3xy}{(5x^2y)4}$ (factoring numerator and denominator)

$\qquad = \dfrac{5x^2y}{5x^2y} \cdot \dfrac{3xy}{4}$ (factoring the expression)

$\qquad = \dfrac{3xy}{4}$ ("removing" a factor of 1)

Note that in the original expression neither x nor y can be 0. In the simplified expression, however, all replacements are sensible.

b) $\dfrac{x^2-1}{2x^2-x-1} = \dfrac{(x-1)(x+1)}{(2x+1)(x-1)} = \dfrac{x-1}{x-1} \cdot \dfrac{x+1}{2x+1}$

$\qquad = \dfrac{x+1}{2x+1}$

In the original expression the nonsensible replacements are 1 and $-\frac{1}{2}$. In the simplified expression the only nonsensible replacement is $-\frac{1}{2}$.   **[116, 117]**

CANCELING

Canceling is a shortcut for part of the procedure in the preceding examples. Canceling gives rise to a great many errors, particularly when it is not well understood. It should therefore be used with caution.

Example. Simplify:

$$\frac{x^3-27}{x^2+x-12} = \frac{(x-3)(x^2+3x+9)}{(x+4)(x-3)}$$

$$= \frac{x^2+3x+9}{x+4}$$

Note that the canceling is a shortcut for "removing" a factor of 1. When fractional expressions are multiplied or divided, they should be simplified when possible.

Examples

a) Multiply and simplify:

$$\frac{x + 2}{x - 2} \cdot \frac{x^2 - 4}{x^2 + x - 2}$$

$$= \frac{(x + 2)(x^2 - 4)}{(x - 2)(x^2 + x - 2)} \quad \text{(multiplying)}$$

$$= \frac{(x + 2)(x + 2)(x - 2)}{(x - 2)(x + 2)(x - 1)} \quad \text{(factoring)}$$

$$= \frac{x + 2}{x - 1} \quad \text{(``removing'' a factor of 1)}$$

b) Divide and simplify:

$$\frac{a^2 - 1}{a + 1} \div \frac{a^2 - 2a + 1}{a + 1} = \frac{a^2 - 1}{a + 1} \cdot \frac{a + 1}{a^2 - 2a + 1}$$

$$= \frac{(a + 1)(a - 1)(a + 1)}{(a + 1)(a - 1)(a - 1)}$$

$$= \frac{a + 1}{a - 1}$$

[118, 119]

ADDITION AND SUBTRACTION

When fractional expressions have the same denominator, we can add or subtract them by adding or subtracting the numerators and retaining the common denominator. If denominators are not the same, we then find equivalent expressions with the same denominator and add. If one denominator is the additive inverse of another, we can find a common denominator by multiplying by $\frac{-1}{-1}$.

Examples. Add:

a) $\dfrac{3x^2 + 4x - 8}{x^2 + y^2} + \dfrac{-5x^2 + 5x + 7}{x^2 + y^2} = \dfrac{-2x^2 + 9x - 1}{x^2 + y^2}$

In the following example, one denominator is the additive inverse of the other.

b) $\dfrac{3x^2 + 4}{x - y} + \dfrac{5x^2 - 11}{y - x}$

$$= \frac{3x^2 + 4}{x - y} + \frac{-1}{-1} \cdot \frac{5x^2 - 11}{y - x}$$

$$= \frac{3x^2 + 4}{x - y} + \frac{-1(5x^2 - 11)}{-1(y - x)} = \frac{3x^2 + 4}{x - y} + \frac{11 - 5x^2}{x - y}$$

$$= \frac{-2x^2 + 15}{x - y}$$

[120, 121]

When denominators are different, but not additive inverses of each other, we find a common denominator by factoring the denominators. Then we multiply by 1 to get the common denominator in each expression.

Example. Add $\dfrac{1}{2x} + \dfrac{5x}{x^2 - 1} + \dfrac{3}{x + 1}$.

We first find the *Least Common Multiple* (L.C.M.) of the denominators. The denominators are (factored)

$$2x, \qquad (x + 1)(x - 1), \qquad x + 1.$$

The L.C.M. is $2x(x + 1)(x - 1)$.

Now we multiply each fractional expression by 1 appropriately.

$$\frac{1}{2x} \cdot \frac{(x + 1)(x - 1)}{(x + 1)(x - 1)} + \frac{5x}{(x + 1)(x - 1)} \cdot \frac{2x}{2x}$$

$$+ \frac{3}{(x + 1)} \cdot \frac{2x(x - 1)}{2x(x - 1)}$$

$$= \frac{(x + 1)(x - 1) + 10x^2 + 6x(x - 1)}{2x(x + 1)(x - 1)}$$

$$= \frac{17x^2 - 6x - 1}{2x(x + 1)(x - 1)} \quad \text{or} \quad \frac{17x^2 - 6x - 1}{2x^3 - 2x}$$

[122, 123]

COMPLEX FRACTIONAL EXPRESSIONS

A complex fractional expression is one that has a fractional expression in its numerator or denominator, or both. To simplify such an expression, we can combine as necessary in numerator and denominator in order to obtain a single fractional expression for each. Then we divide the numerator by the denominator.

Example 1. Simplify:

$$\frac{x + \dfrac{1}{5}}{x - \dfrac{1}{3}} = \frac{x \cdot \dfrac{5}{5} + \dfrac{1}{5}}{x \cdot \dfrac{3}{3} - \dfrac{1}{3}}$$

$$= \frac{\dfrac{5x + 1}{5}}{\dfrac{3x - 1}{3}}$$

Now we have a single fractional expression for both numerator and denominator.

$$= \frac{5x + 1}{5} \cdot \frac{3}{3x - 1}$$

Here we divided by multiplying by the reciprocal of the denominator.

$$= \frac{15x + 3}{15x - 5}$$

Example 2. Simplify:

$$\frac{\dfrac{1}{a^2} - \dfrac{1}{b^2}}{\dfrac{1}{a} + \dfrac{1}{b}} = \frac{\dfrac{b^2}{b^2} \cdot \dfrac{1}{a^2} - \dfrac{a^2}{a^2} \cdot \dfrac{1}{b^2}}{\dfrac{b}{b} \cdot \dfrac{1}{a} + \dfrac{a}{a} \cdot \dfrac{1}{b}} = \frac{\dfrac{b^2 - a^2}{a^2 b^2}}{\dfrac{b + a}{ab}}$$

$$= \frac{b^2 - a^2}{a^2 b^2} \cdot \frac{ab}{b + a}$$

$$= \frac{(b - a)(b + a)ab}{(b + a)a^2 b^2}$$

$$= \frac{ab(b + a)}{ab(b + a)} \cdot \frac{b - a}{ab} = \frac{b - a}{ab}$$

Example 3. Simplify:

$$\frac{\dfrac{3}{x} + \dfrac{1}{2x^2}}{\dfrac{1}{3x} - \dfrac{3}{4x^2}} = \frac{\dfrac{3}{x} \cdot \dfrac{2x}{2x} + \dfrac{1}{2x^2}}{\dfrac{1}{3x} \cdot \dfrac{4x}{4x} - \dfrac{3}{4x^2} \cdot \dfrac{3}{3}} = \frac{\dfrac{6x + 1}{2x^2}}{\dfrac{4x - 9}{12x^2}}$$

$$= \frac{6x + 1}{2x^2} \cdot \frac{12x^2}{4x - 9} = \frac{12x^2(6x + 1)}{2x^2(4x - 9)}$$

$$= \frac{2x^2}{2x^2} \cdot \frac{6(6x + 1)}{4x - 9}$$

$$= \frac{6(6x + 1)}{4x - 9} \qquad\qquad \mathbf{[124, 125]}$$

Exercise Set 1.7

In Exercises 1–3, determine the nonsensible replacements.

1. $\dfrac{3x - 2}{x(x - 1)}$

2. $\dfrac{(x^2 - 4)(x + 1)}{(x + 2)(x^2 - 1)}$

3. $\dfrac{7y^2 - 2y + 4}{x(x^2 - x - 6)}$

In Exercises 4–6, simplify. Then determine the replacements that are not sensible in the simplified expression.

4. $\dfrac{25x^2 y^2}{10xy^2}$

5. $\dfrac{x^2 - 4}{x^2 + 5x + 6}$

6. $\dfrac{x^2 - 3x + 2}{x^2 + x - 2}$

Multiply or divide, and simplify.

7. $\dfrac{x^2 - y^2}{(x - y)^2} \cdot \dfrac{1}{x + y}$

8. $\dfrac{r - s}{r + s} \cdot \dfrac{r^2 - s^2}{(r - s)^2}$

9. $\dfrac{x^2 - 2x - 35}{2x^3 - 3x^2} \cdot \dfrac{4x^3 - 9x}{7x - 49}$

10. $\dfrac{x^2 + 2x - 35}{3x^3 - 2x^2} \cdot \dfrac{9x^3 - 4x}{7x + 49}$

11. $\dfrac{a^2 - a - 6}{a^2 - 7a + 12} \cdot \dfrac{a^2 - 2a - 8}{a^2 - 3a - 10}$

12. $\dfrac{a^2 - a - 12}{a^2 - 6a + 8} \cdot \dfrac{a^2 + a - 6}{a^2 - 2a - 24}$

13. $\dfrac{m^2 - n^2}{r + s} \div \dfrac{m - n}{r + s}$

14. $\dfrac{a^2 - b^2}{x - y} \div \dfrac{a + b}{x - y}$

15. $\dfrac{3x + 12}{2x - 8} \div \dfrac{(x + 4)^2}{(x - 4)^2}$

16. $\dfrac{a^2 - a - 2}{a^2 - a - 6} \div \dfrac{a^2 - 2a}{2a + a^2}$

17. $\dfrac{x^2 - y^2}{x^3 - y^3} \cdot \dfrac{x^2 + xy + y^2}{x^2 + 2xy + y^2}$

18. $\dfrac{c^3 + 8}{c^2 - 4} \div \dfrac{c^2 - 2c + 4}{c^2 - 4c + 4}$

19. $\dfrac{(x - y)^2 - z^2}{(x + y)^2 - z^2} \div \dfrac{x - y + z}{x + y - z}$

20. $\dfrac{(a + b)^2 - 9}{(a - b)^2 + 9} \cdot \dfrac{a - b - 3}{a + b + 3}$

Add or subtract, and simplify.

21. $\dfrac{3}{2a + 3} + \dfrac{2a}{2a + 3}$

22. $\dfrac{a - 3b}{a + b} + \dfrac{a + 5b}{a + b}$

23. $\dfrac{y}{y - 1} + \dfrac{2}{1 - y}$

24. $\dfrac{a}{a - b} + \dfrac{b}{b - a}$

25. $\dfrac{x}{2x - 3y} - \dfrac{y}{3y - 2x}$

26. $\dfrac{3a}{3a - 2b} - \dfrac{2a}{2b - 3a}$

27. $\dfrac{3}{x + 2} + \dfrac{2}{x^2 - 4}$

28. $\dfrac{5}{a - 3} - \dfrac{2}{a^2 - 9}$

29. $\dfrac{y}{y^2 - y - 20} + \dfrac{2}{y + 4}$

30. $\dfrac{6}{y^2 + 6y + 9} - \dfrac{5}{y + 3}$

31. $\dfrac{3}{x + y} + \dfrac{x - 5y}{x^2 - y^2}$

32. $\dfrac{a^2 + 1}{a^2 - 1} - \dfrac{a - 1}{a + 1}$

33. $\dfrac{9x + 2}{3x^2 - 2x - 8} + \dfrac{7}{3x^2 + x - 4}$

34. $\dfrac{3y}{y^2 - 7y + 10} - \dfrac{2y}{y^2 - 8y + 15}$

35. $\dfrac{5a}{a-b} + \dfrac{ab}{a^2-b^2} + \dfrac{4b}{a+b}$

36. $\dfrac{6a}{a-b} - \dfrac{3b}{b-a} + \dfrac{5}{a^2-b^2}$

37. $\dfrac{7}{x+2} - \dfrac{x+8}{4-x^2} + \dfrac{3x-2}{4-4x+x^2}$

38. $\dfrac{6}{x+3} - \dfrac{x+4}{9-x^2} + \dfrac{2x-3}{9-6x+x^2}$

39. $\dfrac{1}{x+1} - \dfrac{x}{x-2} + \dfrac{x^2+2}{x^2-x-2}$

40. $\dfrac{x-1}{x-2} - \dfrac{x+1}{x+2} + \dfrac{x-6}{x^2-4}$

Simplify.

41. $\dfrac{\dfrac{x^2-y^2}{xy}}{\dfrac{x-y}{y}}$

42. $\dfrac{\dfrac{a-b}{b}}{\dfrac{a^2-b^2}{ab}}$

43. $\dfrac{x-\dfrac{1}{x}}{x+\dfrac{1}{x}}$

44. $\dfrac{a-\dfrac{a}{b}}{b-\dfrac{b}{a}}$

45. $\dfrac{c+\dfrac{8}{c^2}}{1+\dfrac{2}{c}}$

46. $\dfrac{1-\dfrac{2}{3x}}{x-\dfrac{4}{9x}}$

47. $\dfrac{x^2+xy+y^2}{\dfrac{x^2}{y}-\dfrac{y^2}{x}}$

48. $\dfrac{\dfrac{a^2}{b}+\dfrac{b^2}{a}}{a^2-ab+b^2}$

49. $\dfrac{\dfrac{x}{y}-\dfrac{y}{x}}{\dfrac{1}{y}+\dfrac{1}{x}}$

50. $\dfrac{\dfrac{a}{b}-\dfrac{b}{a}}{\dfrac{1}{a}-\dfrac{1}{b}}$

51. $\dfrac{\dfrac{x^2}{y^2}-\dfrac{y^2}{x^2}}{\dfrac{x}{y}+\dfrac{y}{x}}$

52. $\dfrac{\dfrac{a^2}{b^2}\cdot\dfrac{b^2}{a^2}}{\dfrac{a}{b}-\dfrac{b}{a}}$

53. $\dfrac{\dfrac{a}{1-a}+\dfrac{1+a}{a}}{\dfrac{1-a}{a}+\dfrac{a}{1+a}}$

54. $\dfrac{\dfrac{1-x}{x}+\dfrac{x}{1+x}}{\dfrac{1+x}{x}+\dfrac{x}{1-x}}$

55. $\dfrac{\dfrac{1}{a^2}+\dfrac{2}{ab}+\dfrac{1}{b^2}}{\dfrac{1}{a^2}-\dfrac{1}{b^2}}$

56. $\dfrac{\dfrac{1}{x^2}-\dfrac{1}{y^2}}{\dfrac{1}{x^2}-\dfrac{2}{xy}+\dfrac{1}{y^2}}$

1.8 Radical Notation and Absolute Value

The symbol $\sqrt{a}$ denotes the nonnegative square root of the number a. The symbol $\sqrt[3]{a}$ denotes the cube root of a, and $\sqrt[4]{a}$ denotes the nonnegative fourth root of a. In general, $\sqrt[n]{a}$ denotes the nth root of a; that is, a number whose nth power is a. The symbol $\sqrt[n]{}$ is called a *radical* and the symbol under the radical is called the *radicand.* The number n (which is omitted when it is 2) is called the *index.*

ODD AND EVEN ROOTS

Any positive real number has two square roots, one positive and one negative. The same is true for fourth roots, or roots of any even index. The positive root is called the *principal* root. When a radical such as $\sqrt{4}$ or

$\sqrt[4]{18}$ is used, it is understood to represent the principal (nonnegative) root. To denote a nonpositive root we use $-\sqrt{2}$, $-\sqrt[4]{18}$, and so on.

> **Definition. A radical expression $\sqrt[n]{a}$, where n is even, represents the principal (nonnegative) nth root of a. The nonpositive root is denoted $-\sqrt[n]{a}$.**

Since negative numbers do not have even roots in the system of real numbers, any replacement that makes a radicand negative when the index is even is a nonsensible replacement.

Every real number, positive, negative, or zero, has just one cube root, and the same is true for any odd root. Thus $\sqrt[n]{a}$, where n is odd, represents the (only) nth root of a. In this case there are no nonsensible replacements in the radicand.

Example. What are the nonsensible replacements in $\sqrt{x-4}$?

Since any replacement for x less than 4 will make the radicand negative, the nonsensible replacements consist of the set of all real numbers less than 4.

[126–129]

ABSOLUTE VALUE

The absolute value of a nonnegative real number is that number itself. The absolute value of a negative number is its additive inverse. We make our definition as follows.

> **Definition. For any real number x,**
> $$|x| = x \quad \text{if} \quad x \geq 0,$$
> **and**
> $$|x| = -x \quad \text{if} \quad x < 0.$$

Certain properties of absolute value notation follow at once. For example, the absolute value of a product is the product of absolute values.

Examples

a) $|-3 \cdot 5| = |-15| = 15$ and $|-3| \cdot |5| = 3 \cdot 5 = 15$,

so $|-3 \cdot 5| = |-3| \cdot |5|$.

Similarly,

b) $|-4 \cdot (-3)| = |12| = 12$

and $|-4| \cdot |-3| = 4 \cdot 3 = 12$,

so $|-4 \cdot (-3)| = |-4| \cdot |-3|$.

The absolute value of a quotient is similarly the quotient of the absolute values.

Example

$$\left|\frac{25}{-5}\right| = |-5| = 5 \quad \text{and} \quad \frac{|25|}{|-5|} = \frac{25}{5} = 5,$$

so $\left|\dfrac{25}{-5}\right| = \dfrac{|25|}{|-5|}$.

The absolute value of an even power can be simplified by leaving off the absolute value signs, because no even power can be negative.

The absolute value of the additive inverse of a number is the same as the absolute value of the number. Their distances from 0 are the same.

Examples

a) $|(-3)^2| = |9| = 9$ and $(-3)^2 = 9$,

so $|(-3)^2| = (-3)^2$.

b) $|-3| = 3$ and $|3| = 3$,

so $|-3| = |3|$.

Theorem. For any real numbers a and b and any nonzero number c,

1. $|ab| = |a| \cdot |b|$,

2. $\left|\dfrac{a}{c}\right| = \dfrac{|a|}{|c|}$,

3. $|a^n| = a^n$ if n is an even integer,

4. $|-a| = |a|$.

Examples. Simplify, leaving as little as possible inside absolute value signs:

a) $|3x| = |3| \cdot |x| = 3|x|$

b) $|x^2| = x^2$

c) $|x^2 y^3| = |x^2| \cdot |y^3| = x^2|y^3| = x^2 y^2 |y|$

d) $\left|\dfrac{x^2}{y}\right| = \dfrac{|x^2|}{|y|} = \dfrac{x^2}{|y|}$

e) $|-3x| = 3|x|$ **[130–133]**

PROPERTIES OF RADICALS

Consider the expression $\sqrt{(-3)^2}$. This is equivalent to $\sqrt{9}$, which simplifies to 3. Similarly, $\sqrt{3^2} = 3$. This illustrates an important general principle for simplifying radicals of even index.

Theorem. For any radicand R, $\sqrt{R^2} = |R|$. Similarly, for any even index n, $\sqrt[n]{R^n} = |R|$.

Examples. Simplify:

a) $\sqrt{x^2} = |x|$

b) $\sqrt{x^2 - 2ax + a^2} = \sqrt{(x-a)^2} = |x - a|$

c) $\sqrt{x^2 y^6} = \sqrt{(xy^3)^2} = |xy^3|$ or $|x| \cdot |y^3|$

If an index is odd, no absolute value signs are necessary.

Theorem. For any radicand R and any odd index n, $\sqrt[n]{R^n} = R$.

[134–138]

A second property of radicals enables us to multiply. We illustrate it with an example.

Example. Compare $\sqrt{4} \cdot \sqrt{9}$ and $\sqrt{4 \cdot 9}$.

$\sqrt{4} \cdot \sqrt{9} = 2 \cdot 3 = 6$ and $\sqrt{4 \cdot 9} = \sqrt{36} = 6$,

so $\sqrt{4} \cdot \sqrt{9} = \sqrt{4 \cdot 9}$.

Theorem. For any nonnegative real numbers a and b and any index n, $\sqrt[n]{a} \cdot \sqrt[n]{b} = \sqrt[n]{a \cdot b}$.

Examples. Multiply:

a) $\sqrt{3} \cdot \sqrt{5} = \sqrt{3 \cdot 5} = \sqrt{15}$

b) $\sqrt{x + 2} \cdot \sqrt{x - 2} = \sqrt{(x + 2)(x - 2)} = \sqrt{x^2 - 4}$

c) $\sqrt[3]{4} \cdot \sqrt[3]{5} = \sqrt[3]{4 \cdot 5} = \sqrt[3]{20}$ **[139–141]**

The foregoing property also enables us to simplify radical expressions. The idea is to factor the radicand, obtaining factors that are perfect nth powers.

Examples. Simplify:

a) $\sqrt{50} = \sqrt{25 \cdot 2} = \sqrt{25} \cdot \sqrt{2} = 5\sqrt{2}$

b) $\sqrt{5x^2} = \sqrt{x^2 \cdot 5} = \sqrt{x^2} \cdot \sqrt{5} = |x|\sqrt{5}$

c) $\sqrt[3]{32} = \sqrt[3]{8 \cdot 4} = \sqrt[3]{8} \cdot \sqrt[3]{4} = 2\sqrt[3]{4}$

d) $\sqrt{216 x^5 y^3} = \sqrt{36 \cdot 6 \cdot x^4 \cdot x \cdot y^2 \cdot y}$

$\qquad = |6x^2 y| \sqrt{6xy} = 6x^2 |y| \sqrt{6xy}$

e) $\sqrt{2x^2 - 4x + 2} = \sqrt{2(x - 1)^2} = |x - 1|\sqrt{2}$

[142–146]

A third fundamental property of radicals is as follows.

> For any nonnegative number a and any positive number b, and any index n, $\sqrt[n]{\dfrac{a}{b}} = \dfrac{\sqrt[n]{a}}{\sqrt[n]{b}}$.

This property can be used to divide and to simplify radical expressions.

Examples. Simplify:

a) $\sqrt{\dfrac{16x^3}{y^4}} = \dfrac{\sqrt{16x^3}}{\sqrt{y^4}} = \dfrac{\sqrt{16x^2 \cdot x}}{\sqrt{y^4}} = \dfrac{4\,|x|\,\sqrt{x}}{y^2}$

b) $\sqrt{\dfrac{27y^5}{343x^3}} = \dfrac{\sqrt[3]{27y^5}}{\sqrt[3]{343x^3}} = \dfrac{\sqrt[3]{27y^3 \cdot y^2}}{\sqrt[3]{343x^3}} = \dfrac{3y\sqrt[3]{y^2}}{7x}$

Fractional expressions are often considered simpler when the denominator is free of radicals. Thus in simplifying, it is usual to remove the radicals in a denominator. This is called *rationalizing the denominator.*

Examples. Simplify:

a) $\sqrt{\dfrac{1}{2}} = \sqrt{\dfrac{1}{2} \cdot \dfrac{2}{2}} = \sqrt{\dfrac{2}{4}} = \dfrac{\sqrt{2}}{\sqrt{4}} = \dfrac{\sqrt{2}}{2}$

b) $\sqrt[3]{\dfrac{7}{9}} = \sqrt[3]{\dfrac{7}{9} \cdot \dfrac{3}{3}} = \sqrt[3]{\dfrac{21}{27}} = \dfrac{\sqrt[3]{21}}{\sqrt[3]{27}} = \dfrac{\sqrt[3]{21}}{3}$

Examples. Divide and simplify:

a) $\dfrac{18\sqrt{72}}{6\sqrt{6}} = 3\sqrt{\dfrac{72}{6}} = 3\sqrt{12} = 3\sqrt{4 \cdot 3}$
$\qquad = 3 \cdot 2\sqrt{3} = 6\sqrt{3}$

b) $\dfrac{\sqrt[3]{32}}{\sqrt[3]{2}} = \sqrt[3]{\dfrac{32}{2}} = \sqrt[3]{16} = \sqrt[3]{8 \cdot 2} = \sqrt[3]{8} \cdot \sqrt[3]{2} = 2\sqrt[3]{2}$

[147–153]

A fourth fundamental principle of radicals involves an exponent under the radical. We illustrate with an example.

Example. Compare $\sqrt{3^4}$ and $(\sqrt{3})^4$.

$$\sqrt{3^4} = \sqrt{81} = 9,$$
$$(\sqrt{3})^4 = \sqrt{3} \cdot \sqrt{3} \cdot \sqrt{3} \cdot \sqrt{3} = 3 \cdot 3 = 9$$

Thus $\sqrt{3^4} = (\sqrt{3})^4$.

The general principle is as follows.

> **Theorem.** For any nonnegative number a and any index n and any natural number m, $\sqrt[n]{a^m} = (\sqrt[n]{a})^m$.

This principle sometimes facilitates radical simplification.

Examples. Simplify:

a) $\sqrt[3]{8^5} = (\sqrt[3]{8})^5 = 2^5 = 32$

b) $(\sqrt{2})^6 = \sqrt{2^6} = 2^3 = 8$ **[154, 155]**

Exercise Set 1.8

What are the nonsensible replacements in each of the following?

1. $\sqrt{x - 3}$ **2.** $\sqrt{2x - 5}$ **3.** $\sqrt{3 - 4x}$ **4.** $\sqrt{x^2 + 3}$

Simplify.

5. $\sqrt{(-11)^2}$ **6.** $\sqrt{(-7)^2}$ **7.** $\sqrt{16x^2}$ **8.** $\sqrt{36t^2}$

9. $\sqrt{(b+1)^2}$ **10.** $\sqrt{(2c-3)^2}$ **11.** $\sqrt[3]{-27x^3}$ **12.** $\sqrt[3]{-8y^3}$

13. $\sqrt{x^2-4x+4}$ **14.** $\sqrt{y^2+16y+64}$ **15.** $\sqrt[5]{32}$ **16.** $\sqrt[5]{-32}$

17. $\sqrt{180}$ **18.** $\sqrt{48}$ **19.** $\sqrt[3]{54}$ **20.** $\sqrt[3]{135}$

21. $\sqrt{128c^2d^{-4}}$ **22.** $\sqrt{162c^4d^{-6}}$ **23.** $\sqrt{3}\cdot\sqrt{6}$ **24.** $\sqrt{6}\cdot\sqrt{8}$

In the following exercises simplify, assuming that all letters represent positive numbers and that all radicands are positive. Thus no absolute value signs will be needed.

25. $\sqrt{2x^3y}\sqrt{12xy}$ **26.** $\sqrt{3y^4z}\sqrt{20z}$ **27.** $\sqrt[3]{3x^2y}\sqrt[3]{36x}$

28. $\sqrt[5]{8x^3y^4}\sqrt[5]{4x^4y}$ **29.** $\sqrt[3]{2(x+4)}\sqrt[3]{4(x+4)^4}$ **30.** $\sqrt[3]{4(x+1)^2}\sqrt[3]{18(x+1)^2}$

31. $\dfrac{\sqrt{21ab^2}}{\sqrt{3ab}}$ **32.** $\dfrac{\sqrt{128ab^2}}{\sqrt{16a^2b}}$ **33.** $\dfrac{\sqrt[3]{40m}}{\sqrt[3]{5m}}$ **34.** $\dfrac{\sqrt{40xy}}{\sqrt{8x}}$

35. $\dfrac{\sqrt[3]{3x^2}}{\sqrt[3]{24x^5}}$ **36.** $\dfrac{\sqrt[3]{40xy^3}}{\sqrt[3]{8x}}$ **37.** $\dfrac{\sqrt{a^2-b^2}}{\sqrt{a-b}}$ **38.** $\dfrac{\sqrt{x^3-y^3}}{\sqrt{x-y}}$

39. $\sqrt{\dfrac{9a^2}{8b}}$ **40.** $\sqrt{\dfrac{5b^2}{12a}}$ **41.** $\sqrt[3]{\dfrac{2x^2 2y^3}{25z^4}}$ **42.** $\sqrt[3]{\dfrac{24x^3y}{3y^4}}$

43. $\dfrac{(\sqrt[3]{32x^4}y)^2}{(\sqrt[3]{xy})^2}$ **44.** $\dfrac{(\sqrt[3]{16x^2}y)^2}{(\sqrt[3]{xy})^2}$ **45.** $\dfrac{3\sqrt{a^2b^2}\sqrt{4xy}}{2\sqrt{a^{-1}b^{-2}}\sqrt{9x^{-3}y^{-1}}}$ **46.** $\dfrac{4\sqrt{xy^2}\sqrt{9ab}}{3\sqrt{x^{-1}y^{-2}}\sqrt{16a^{-5}b^{-1}}}$

 Simplify, assuming that all letters represent positive numbers.

47. $\sqrt{8.2x^3y}\sqrt{12.5xy}$ **48.** $\sqrt{0.012y^4z}\sqrt{1.305z}$ **49.** $\sqrt{\dfrac{6.03a^2}{17.13b}}$ **50.** $\sqrt{\dfrac{3.2b^2}{82.1a}}$

▶ **51.** For what integer values of n is $|a^n| = |a|^n$ for all a?

52. For what values of x and y is $|x| = |y|$?

53. For what values of x and y is $|x+y| = |x|+|y|$?

1.9 Further Calculations with Radical Notation

Various calculations with radicals can be carried out using the properties of radicals and the properties of numbers, such as the distributive property. The following examples illustrate.

Examples. Simplify:

a) $3\sqrt{8} - 5\sqrt{2} = 3\sqrt{4\cdot2} - 5\sqrt{2} = 3\cdot2\sqrt{2} - 5\sqrt{2}$

$\qquad = (6-5)\sqrt{2}$ (Here we used the distributive property.)

$\qquad = \sqrt{2}$

b) $(4\sqrt{3} + \sqrt{2})(\sqrt{3} - 5\sqrt{2}) = 4(\sqrt{3})^2 - 20\sqrt{3}\sqrt{2}$
$\qquad + \sqrt{2}\sqrt{3} - 5(\sqrt{2})^2$
$\qquad = 4\cdot3 - 20\sqrt{6}$
$\qquad + \sqrt{6} - 5\cdot2$
$\qquad = 12 - 19\sqrt{6} - 10$
$\qquad = 2 - 19\sqrt{6}$

[156–158]

RATIONALIZING DENOMINATORS OR NUMERATORS

When a fractional symbol contains radicals, we ordinarily rationalize the denominator, but on occasion we prefer to rationalize the numerator. In either case, we can accomplish the rationalization by multiplying by 1, as in the following examples.

Examples. Rationalize the denominator:

a) $\dfrac{\sqrt{7}}{\sqrt{5}} = \dfrac{\sqrt{7}}{\sqrt{5}}\cdot\dfrac{\sqrt{5}}{\sqrt{5}} = \dfrac{\sqrt{35}}{\sqrt{25}} = \dfrac{\sqrt{35}}{5}$

b) $\dfrac{\sqrt{2a}}{\sqrt{5b}} = \dfrac{\sqrt{2a}}{\sqrt{5b}}\cdot\dfrac{\sqrt{5b}}{\sqrt{5b}} = \dfrac{\sqrt{10ab}}{\sqrt{(5b)^2}} = \dfrac{\sqrt{10ab}}{|5b|}$

c) $\dfrac{\sqrt{27x^3}}{\sqrt{8y^5}} = \sqrt{\dfrac{27x^3}{8y^5}\cdot\dfrac{2y}{2y}} = \sqrt{\dfrac{54x^3y}{16y^6}}$

$\qquad = \dfrac{\sqrt{9x^2\cdot6xy}}{\sqrt{16y^6}} = \dfrac{|3x|\sqrt{6xy}}{|4y^3|}$

When a numerator or denominator to be rationalized has two terms, we must choose the symbol for 1 a little differently. The symbol for 1 will have two terms in its numerator and denominator. The following examples illustrate.

Examples. Rationalize the denominator. Assume all letters represent positive numbers.

a) $\dfrac{1}{\sqrt{2}+\sqrt{3}} = \dfrac{1}{\sqrt{2}+\sqrt{3}}\cdot\dfrac{\sqrt{2}-\sqrt{3}}{\sqrt{2}-\sqrt{3}}$

$\qquad = \dfrac{\sqrt{2}-\sqrt{3}}{(\sqrt{2}+\sqrt{3})(\sqrt{2}-\sqrt{3})}$

$\qquad = \dfrac{\sqrt{2}-\sqrt{3}}{(\sqrt{2})^2 - (\sqrt{3})^2} = \dfrac{\sqrt{2}-\sqrt{3}}{2-3}$

$\qquad = \dfrac{\sqrt{2}-\sqrt{3}}{-1} = \sqrt{3}-\sqrt{2}$

b) $\dfrac{\sqrt{x}+\sqrt{y}}{\sqrt{x}-\sqrt{y}} = \dfrac{\sqrt{x}+\sqrt{y}}{\sqrt{x}-\sqrt{y}}\cdot\dfrac{\sqrt{x}+\sqrt{y}}{\sqrt{x}+\sqrt{y}}$

$\qquad = \dfrac{(\sqrt{x}+\sqrt{y})^2}{(\sqrt{x})^2 - (\sqrt{y})^2}$

$\qquad = \dfrac{x + 2\sqrt{x}\sqrt{y} + y}{x - y}$

Examples. Rationalize the numerator. Assume all letters represent positive numbers.

a) $\dfrac{1-\sqrt{2}}{5} = \dfrac{1-\sqrt{2}}{5}\cdot\dfrac{1+\sqrt{2}}{1+\sqrt{2}} = \dfrac{(1-\sqrt{2})(1+\sqrt{2})}{5(1+\sqrt{2})}$

$\qquad = \dfrac{1-2}{5(1+\sqrt{2})} = \dfrac{-1}{5+5\sqrt{2}}$

b) $\dfrac{\sqrt{x+h}-\sqrt{x}}{h} = \dfrac{\sqrt{x+h}-\sqrt{x}}{h}\cdot\dfrac{\sqrt{x+h}+\sqrt{x}}{\sqrt{x+h}+\sqrt{x}} = \dfrac{(x+h)-x}{h(\sqrt{x+h}+\sqrt{x})}$

$$= \dfrac{h}{h(\sqrt{x+h}+\sqrt{x})} = \dfrac{1}{\sqrt{x+h}+\sqrt{x}} \qquad\qquad \textbf{[159–162]}$$

Exercise Set 1.9

In this exercise set assume that all letters represent positive numbers and that all radicands are positive. Thus, absolute value signs will not be necessary.

Simplify.

1. $8\sqrt{2} - 6\sqrt{20} - 5\sqrt{8}$

2. $\sqrt{12} - \sqrt{27} + \sqrt{75}$

3. $2\sqrt[3]{8x^2} + 5\sqrt[3]{27x^2} - 3\sqrt[3]{x^3}$

4. $5a\sqrt{(a+b)^3} - 2ab\sqrt{a+b} - 3b\sqrt{(a+b)^3}$

5. $3\sqrt{3y^2} - \dfrac{y\sqrt{48}}{\sqrt{2}} + \sqrt{\dfrac{12}{4y^{-2}}}$

6. $\sqrt[3]{x^5} - \dfrac{2\sqrt[3]{x}}{\sqrt[3]{x^{-1}}} + \sqrt[3]{\dfrac{8}{x^{-5}}}$

7. $(\sqrt{3} - \sqrt{2})(\sqrt{3} + \sqrt{2})$

8. $(\sqrt{8} + 2\sqrt{5})(\sqrt{8} - 2\sqrt{5})$

9. $(\sqrt{m^2 y} - 2\sqrt{x})(3m\sqrt{y} + \sqrt{x})$

10. $(\sqrt{a^2 b} + 3\sqrt{y})(2a\sqrt{b} - \sqrt{y})$

11. $(\sqrt{x+3} - \sqrt{3})(\sqrt{x+3} + \sqrt{3})$

12. $(\sqrt{x+h} - \sqrt{x})(\sqrt{x+h} + \sqrt{x})$

Rationalize the denominator.

13. $\dfrac{6}{3+\sqrt{5}}$

14. $\dfrac{2}{\sqrt{3}-1}$

15. $\sqrt[3]{\dfrac{16}{9}}$

16. $\dfrac{\sqrt[3]{3}}{\sqrt[3]{6}}$

17. $\dfrac{4\sqrt{x} - 3\sqrt{xy}}{2\sqrt{x} + 5\sqrt{y}}$

18. $\dfrac{5\sqrt{x} + 2\sqrt{xy}}{3\sqrt{x} - 2\sqrt{y}}$

Rationalize the numerator.

19. $\dfrac{\sqrt{2} + \sqrt{5a}}{6}$

20. $\dfrac{\sqrt{3} + \sqrt{5y}}{4}$

21. $\dfrac{\sqrt{x+1} + 1}{\sqrt{x+1} - 1}$

22. $\dfrac{\sqrt{x+4} - 2}{\sqrt{x+4} + 2}$

23. $\dfrac{\sqrt{a+3} - \sqrt{3}}{3}$

24. $\dfrac{\sqrt{a+h} - \sqrt{a}}{h}$

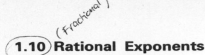

1.10 Rational Exponents

We are motivated to define fractional exponents so that the same rules, or laws, hold for them as for integer exponents. For example, if the laws of exponents are to hold, we would have

$$a^{\frac{1}{2}} \cdot a^{\frac{1}{2}} = a^{\frac{1}{2}+\frac{1}{2}} = a^1 = a.$$

Thus we are led to define $a^{\frac{1}{2}}$ to mean $\sqrt{a}$. Similarly, $a^{\frac{1}{n}}$ would mean $\sqrt[n]{a}$. Again, if the usual laws of exponents are to hold, we would have

$$(a^{\frac{1}{n}})^m = (a^m)^{\frac{1}{n}} = a^{\frac{m}{n}}.$$

Thus we are led to define $a^{\frac{m}{n}}$ to mean $(\sqrt[n]{a})^m$ or $\sqrt[n]{a^m}$.

> **Definition.** An expression $a^{m/n}$, where a is positive and m and n are natural numbers, is defined to mean $(\sqrt[n]{a})^m$ or $\sqrt[n]{a^m}$. An expression $a^{-m/n}$ is defined to mean $1/a^{m/n}$.

Note that in this definition we require *a to be positive*. Thus in manipulations with fractional exponents we assume that all letters represent positive numbers and that all radicands are positive. No absolute value signs need be used.

Once the definition of rational exponents is made, the question arises whether the usual laws of exponents actually do hold. We shall not prove it, but the answer is that they do. Thus we can simplify or otherwise manipulate expressions containing rational exponents using those laws and the usual arithmetic of rational numbers.

Examples. Convert to exponential notation and simplify.

a) $(\sqrt[4]{7xy})^5 = (7xy)^{\frac{5}{4}}$

b) $\sqrt[3]{8^4} = 8^{\frac{4}{3}} = (8^{\frac{1}{3}})^4 = 2^4 = 16$

c) $\sqrt[6]{x^3} = x^{\frac{3}{6}} = x^{\frac{1}{2}}$ (or $\sqrt{x}$)

d) $\sqrt[6]{4} = 4^{\frac{1}{6}} = (4^{\frac{1}{2}})^{\frac{1}{3}} = 2^{\frac{1}{3}}$ (or $\sqrt[3]{2}$)

e) $\sqrt[3]{\sqrt{7}} = \sqrt[3]{7^{\frac{1}{2}}} = (7^{\frac{1}{2}})^{\frac{1}{3}} = 7^{\frac{1}{6}}$ (or $\sqrt[6]{7}$)

f) $\sqrt{6}\sqrt[3]{6} = 6^{\frac{1}{2}} \cdot 6^{\frac{1}{3}} = 6^{\frac{1}{2}+\frac{1}{3}} = 6^{\frac{5}{6}}$ (or $\sqrt[6]{6^5}$)

[163–167]

Examples. Simplify and then write radical notation.

a) $x^{\frac{5}{6}} \cdot x^{\frac{2}{3}} = x^{\frac{5}{6}+\frac{2}{3}} = x^{\frac{9}{6}} = x^{\frac{3}{2}} = \sqrt{x^3}$

b) $(a^5)^{-\frac{2}{3}} = a^{-\frac{10}{3}} = \dfrac{1}{a^{\frac{10}{3}}} = \dfrac{1}{\sqrt[3]{a^{10}}}$

c) $(3^{\frac{1}{3}} - 3^{-\frac{5}{3}}) \cdot 3^{\frac{1}{3}} = 3^{\frac{1}{3}} \cdot 3^{\frac{1}{3}} - 3^{-\frac{5}{3}} \cdot 3^{\frac{1}{3}}$

$$= 3^{\frac{2}{3}} - 3^{-\frac{4}{3}}$$

$$= \sqrt[3]{3^2} - \dfrac{1}{\sqrt[3]{3^4}}$$

[168–170]

In certain expressions containing radicals or fractional exponents, it is possible to simplify in such a way that there is a single radical.

Examples. Write an expression containing a single radical.

a) $a^{\frac{1}{2}}b^{-\frac{1}{2}}c^{\frac{5}{6}} = a^{\frac{3}{6}}b^{-\frac{3}{6}}c^{\frac{5}{6}} = (a^3b^{-3}c^5)^{\frac{1}{6}} = \sqrt[6]{a^3b^{-3}c^5}$

b) $\dfrac{a^{\frac{1}{4}}b^{\frac{3}{8}}}{a^{\frac{1}{2}}b^{\frac{1}{8}}} = a^{-\frac{1}{4}}b^{\frac{1}{4}} = (a^{-1}b)^{\frac{1}{4}} = \sqrt[4]{a^{-1}b}$

c) $\sqrt[4]{7}\sqrt{3} = 7^{\frac{1}{4}} \cdot 3^{\frac{1}{2}} = 7^{\frac{1}{4}} \cdot 3^{\frac{2}{4}} = (7 \cdot 3^2)^{\frac{1}{4}} = \sqrt[4]{63}$

d) $\dfrac{\sqrt[4]{(x+2)^3}\,\sqrt[5]{x+2}}{\sqrt{x+2}} = \dfrac{(x+2)^{\frac{3}{4}}(x+2)^{\frac{1}{5}}}{(x+2)^{\frac{1}{2}}}$

$$= (x+2)^{\frac{3}{4}+\frac{1}{5}-\frac{1}{2}}$$

$$= (x+2)^{\frac{9}{20}} = \sqrt[20]{(x+2)^9}$$

[171–173]

Exercise Set 1.10

Convert to radical notation and simplify.

1. $x^{\frac{3}{4}}$

2. $y^{\frac{2}{5}}$

3. $16^{\frac{3}{4}}$

4. $4^{\frac{7}{2}}$

5. $x^{\frac{5}{4}}y^{-\frac{3}{4}}$

6. $x^{\frac{2}{3}}y^{-\frac{1}{3}}$

7. $a^{\frac{2}{3}}b^{-\frac{1}{2}}$

8. $x^{\frac{2}{5}}y^{-\frac{1}{5}}$

Convert to exponential notation and simplify.

9. $\sqrt[3]{20^2}$

10. $\sqrt[5]{17^3}$

11. $(\sqrt[4]{13})^5$

12. $(\sqrt[5]{12})^4$

13. $\sqrt[3]{\sqrt{11}}$

14. $\sqrt[3]{\sqrt[4]{7}}$

15. $\sqrt{5}\sqrt[3]{5}$

16. $\sqrt[3]{2}\sqrt{2}$

17. $\sqrt[5]{32^2}$

18. $\sqrt[4]{16^3}$

19. $\sqrt[3]{8y^6}$

20. $\sqrt[5]{32c^{10}d^{15}}$

21. $\sqrt[3]{a^2+b^2}$

22. $\sqrt[4]{a^3-b^3}$

23. $\sqrt[3]{27a^3b^9}$

24. $\sqrt[4]{81x^8y^8}$

25. $\sqrt[6]{\dfrac{m^{12}n^{24}}{64}}$

26. $\sqrt[8]{\dfrac{m^{16}n^{24}}{2^8}}$

Simplify and then write radical notation, unless inappropriate.

27. $(2a^{\frac{3}{2}})(4a^{\frac{1}{2}})$

28. $(3a^{\frac{5}{6}})(8a^{\frac{2}{3}})$

29. $\left(\dfrac{x^6}{9b^{-4}}\right)^{-\frac{1}{2}}$

30. $\left(\dfrac{x^{\frac{2}{3}}}{4y^{-2}}\right)^{-\frac{1}{2}}$

31. $\dfrac{x^{\frac{2}{3}}y^{\frac{5}{6}}}{x^{-\frac{1}{3}}y^{\frac{1}{2}}}$

32. $\dfrac{a^{\frac{1}{2}}b^{\frac{5}{8}}}{a^{\frac{1}{4}}b^{\frac{3}{8}}}$

Write an expression containing a single radical and simplify.

33. $\sqrt[3]{6}\sqrt{2}$

34. $\sqrt{2}\sqrt[4]{8}$

35. $\sqrt[4]{xy}\sqrt[3]{x^2y}$

36. $\sqrt[3]{ab^2}\sqrt{ab}$

37. $\sqrt[3]{a^4}\sqrt{a^3}$

38. $\sqrt{a^3}\sqrt[3]{a^2}$

39. $\dfrac{\sqrt{(a+x)^3}\sqrt[3]{(a+x)^2}}{\sqrt[4]{a+x}}$

40. $\dfrac{\sqrt[4]{(x+y)^2}\sqrt[3]{(x+y)}}{\sqrt{(x+y)^3}}$

Simplify. (*Note:* Since $x^{\frac{1}{4}} = (x^{\frac{1}{2}})^{\frac{1}{2}}$ you can take a fourth root by taking a square root, and then the square root of the result.)

41. $(\sqrt[4]{13})^5$

42. $\sqrt[4]{17^3}$

43. $12.3^{\frac{3}{2}}$

44. $1.345^{\frac{5}{2}}$

45. $105.6^{\frac{3}{4}}$

46. $7.14^{\frac{5}{4}}$

1.11 Handling Dimension Symbols

SPEED

Speed is often measured by measuring a distance and a time and then dividing the distance by the time (this is *average* speed):

$$\text{Speed} = \frac{\text{distance}}{\text{time}}.$$

If a distance is measured in kilometers and the time required to travel that distance is measured in hours, the speed will be computed in *kilometers per hour* (km/h). For example, if a car travels 100 km in 2 hr, the average speed is

$$\frac{100 \text{ km}}{2 \text{ hr}}, \quad \text{or} \quad 50 \frac{\text{km}}{\text{hr}}. \quad \textbf{[174, 175]}$$

DIMENSION SYMBOLS

The symbol 100 km/2 hr makes it look as if we are dividing 100 km by 2 hr. It may be argued that we cannot divide 100 km by 2 hr (we can only divide 100 by 2). Nevertheless, it is convenient to treat dimension symbols such as *kilometers, hours, feet, seconds,* and *pounds* much like numerals or variables, for the reason that correct results can thus be obtained mechanically. Compare, for example,

$$\frac{100x}{2y} = \frac{100}{2} \cdot \frac{x}{y} = 50 \frac{x}{y}$$

with

$$\frac{100 \text{ km}}{2 \text{ hr}} = \frac{100}{2} \cdot \frac{\text{km}}{\text{hr}} = 50 \frac{\text{km}}{\text{hr}}.$$

The analogy holds in other situations, as shown in the following examples.

Example 1. Compare

$$3 \text{ ft} + 2 \text{ ft} = (3 + 2) \text{ ft} = 5 \text{ ft}$$

with

$$3x + 2x = (3 + 2)x = 5x.$$

This looks like the distributive law in use. **[176–178]**

Example 2. Compare

$$4 \text{ m} \cdot 3 \text{ m} = 3 \cdot 4 \cdot \text{m} \cdot \text{m} = 12 \text{ m}^2 \quad \text{(sq m)}$$

with

$$4x \cdot 3x = 4 \cdot 3 \cdot x \cdot x = 12x^2.$$

Example 3. Compare

$$5 \text{ men} \cdot 8 \text{ hr} = 5 \cdot 8 \cdot \text{man-hr} = 40 \text{ man-hr}$$

with

$$5x \cdot 8y = 5 \cdot 8 \cdot x \cdot y = 40xy.$$

In each of the above examples, dimension symbols are treated as if they were variables or numerals, and as if a symbol such as "3 m" represents a product 3 times m. A symbol like km/h is treated as if it represents a division of km by h (*kilometers* by *hours*). Any two measures can be "multiplied" or "divided." **[179–183]**

CHANGES OF UNIT

Changes of unit can be achieved by substitutions.

Example 4. Change to inches: 25 yd.

$$25 \text{ yd} = 25 \cdot 1 \text{ yd}$$
$$= 25 \cdot 3 \text{ ft} \quad \text{(substituting } 3 \text{ ft for } 1 \text{ yd)}$$
$$= 25 \cdot 3 \cdot 1 \text{ ft}$$
$$= 25 \cdot 3 \cdot 12 \text{ in.} \quad \text{(substituting } 12 \text{ in. for } 1 \text{ ft)}$$
$$= 900 \text{ in.}$$

The notion of "multiplying by one" can also be used to change units. **[184–186]**

Example 5. Change to yd: 7.2 in.

$$7.2 \text{ in.} = 7.2 \text{ in.} \cdot \frac{1 \text{ ft}}{12 \text{ in.}} \cdot \frac{1 \text{ yd}}{3 \text{ ft}}$$

Both of these are equal to 1.

$$= \frac{7.2}{12 \cdot 3} \frac{\text{in. ft}}{\text{in. ft}} \text{yd}$$
$$= 0.2 \text{ yd} \quad \textbf{[187–189]}$$

Example 6. Change to $\dfrac{m}{sec}$: $60\,\dfrac{km}{hr}$. *

$$60\,\frac{km}{hr} = 60\,\frac{km}{hr}\cdot\frac{1000\ m}{1\ km}\cdot\frac{1\ hr}{60\ min}\cdot\frac{1\ min}{60\ sec} = \frac{60\cdot1000}{60\cdot60}\,\frac{km\ hr\ min\ m}{km\ hr\ min\ sec} = 16.67\,\frac{m}{sec} = 16.67\ m/s \qquad \textbf{[190–193]}$$

Exercise Set 1.11

Perform these calculations and simplify if possible. Do not make any unit changes.

1. $36\ ft\cdot\dfrac{1\ yd}{3\ ft}$ **2.** $6\ lb\cdot\dfrac{16\ oz}{1\ lb}$ **3.** $6\ kg\cdot8\,\dfrac{hr}{kg}$ **4.** $9\,\dfrac{km}{hr}\cdot3\ hr$

5. $3\ cm\cdot\dfrac{2\ g}{2\ cm}$ **6.** $\dfrac{9\ km}{3\ days}\cdot6\ days$ **7.** $6\ m+2\ m$ **8.** $10\ tons+6\ tons$

9. $5\ ft^3+7\ ft^3$ **10.** $10\ yd^3+17\ yd^3$ **11.** $\dfrac{3\ kg}{5\ m}\cdot\dfrac{7\ kg}{6\ m}$ **12.** $3\ acres\times60\,\dfrac{1}{acre}$

13. $\dfrac{2000\ lb\cdot(6\ mi/hr)^2}{100\ ft}$ **14.** $\dfrac{7\ m\cdot8\ kg/sec}{4\ sec}$

15. $\dfrac{6\ cm^2\cdot5\ cm/sec}{2\ sec^2/cm^2\cdot2\,\dfrac{1}{kg}}$ **16.** $\dfrac{320\ lb\cdot(5\ ft/sec)^2}{2\cdot32\,\dfrac{ft}{sec^2}}$

Perform the following changes of unit, using substitution or multiplying by one.

17. 72 in., change to ft.

18. 17 hr, change to min.

19. 2 days, change to sec.

20. 360 sec, change to hr.

21. $60\,\dfrac{kg}{m}$, change to g/cm.

22. $44\,\dfrac{ft}{sec}$, change to mi/hr.

23. $216\ m^2$, change to cm^2.

24. $60\,\dfrac{lb}{ft^3}$, change to ton/yd^3.

25. $\dfrac{\$36}{day}$, change to $\dfrac{\cancel{c}}{hr}$.

26. 1440 man-hr, change to man-days.

---

* The standard abbreviation for meters per second is m/s and for kilometers per hour is km/h. For present purposes it is better to write m/sec and km/hr.

27. $186,000 \dfrac{\text{mi}}{\text{sec}}$ (speed of light), change to $\dfrac{\text{mi}}{\text{yr}}$. Let 365 days = 1 yr.

28. $1100 \dfrac{\text{ft}}{\text{sec}}$ (speed of sound), change to $\dfrac{\text{mi}}{\text{yr}}$. Let 365 days = 1 yr.

Use Table 6 at the back of the book to do the following unit changes.

29. $89.2 \dfrac{\text{ft}}{\text{sec}}$, change to m/min.

30. 1013 yd^3, change to m^3.

31. 640 mi^2, change to km^2.

32. $312.2 \dfrac{\text{kg}}{\text{m}}$, change to lb/ft.

Chapter 1 Test, or Review

Add.

1. $5 + |-9|$

2. $-12 + {}^-(-4)$

Multiply.   Divide.   Subtract.

3. $(-7)(-9)$

4. $\dfrac{-15}{-5}$

5. $17 - {}^-7$

Convert to decimal notation.

6. 9.724×10^4

7. 3.21×10^{-4}

Convert to scientific notation.

8. 43,210

9. 0.00002

Simplify.

10. $(3x^2y^3)(2x^{-3}y^2)$

11. $\dfrac{18xy^3z^{-5}}{27x^{-2}y^2z^2}$

12. $\sqrt[4]{81}$

13. $\sqrt[5]{-32}$

14. $\dfrac{\dfrac{x^2}{y} + \dfrac{y^2}{x}}{y^2 - yx + x^2}$

15. $(\sqrt{7} - \sqrt{5})(\sqrt{7} + \sqrt{5})$

Write an expression containing a single radical.

16. $\dfrac{\sqrt{(a+b)^3} \cdot \sqrt[3]{(a+b)}}{\sqrt[9]{(a+b)^7}}$

Convert to radical notation.

Write rational exponents and simplify.

17. $a^{\frac{3}{5}}$

18. $\sqrt[8]{\dfrac{m^{32}n^{16}}{3^8}}$

Solve.

19. $y^2 - 3y = 18$ **20.** $12 - 3y > 21$ **21.** $(x - 2)(x + 3) + 4 = 0$

22. Divide and simplify.

$$\frac{3x^2 - 12}{x^2 + 4x + 4} \div \frac{x - 2}{x + 2}$$

23. Subtract and simplify.

$$\frac{a^2 + 1}{a^2 - 1} - \frac{a - 1}{a + 1}$$

24. Rationalize the denominator.

$$\frac{\sqrt{x} - \sqrt{y}}{\sqrt{x} + \sqrt{y}}$$

25. Change $10\dfrac{km}{hr}$ to $\dfrac{m}{min}$.

CHAPTER **2**

Equations

2.1 Solving Equations

EQUIVALENT EQUATIONS

Equations that have the same solution set are called *equivalent equations*. The following pairs of equations are equivalent.

Example 1.

$$3x = 6 \qquad\qquad 3x + 5 = 11$$
Solution set {2}.   Solution set {2}.

Example 2.

$$3x = 6 \qquad\qquad -12x = -24$$
Solution set {2}.   Solution set {2}.

The following pairs of equations are *not* equivalent.

Example 3.

$$3x = 4x \qquad\qquad \frac{3}{x} = \frac{4}{x}$$

Solution set {0}.   The solution set is Ø, the empty set (no solution, since division by 0 is not defined).

Example 4.

$$x = 1 \qquad\qquad x^2 = x$$
Solution set {1}.   Solution set {0, 1}.

[1–6]

EQUATION-SOLVING PRINCIPLES

In Chapter 1 we reviewed some equation-solving principles. Let us consider them in more detail.

> **The addition principle.** If an equation $a = b$ is true, then $a + c = b + c$ is true for any number c.

Let us look at a simple example illustrating this principle.

$$
\begin{aligned}
x + 5 &= 9 \\
x + 5 + (-5) &= 9 + (-5) \qquad \text{(adding } -5 \text{ on} \\
x &= 4 \qquad\qquad\quad \text{both sides)}
\end{aligned}
$$

According to the principle, if $x + 5 = 9$ is true, then $x = 4$ is true. In other words, any number that makes the first equation true also makes the last equation true. To say this still another way, any solution of the first equation is a solution of the last one. Obviously the only solution of the last equation is 4. Is it a solution of the first equation? We can check by substituting in the first equation. We could also reverse the above steps, as follows:

$$
\begin{aligned}
x &= 4 \\
x + 5 &= 4 + 5 \\
x + 5 &= 9.
\end{aligned}
$$

This tells us that any number making $x = 4$ true will also make $x + 5 = 9$ true.

In this example the original equation and the last equation had exactly the same solutions. They were equivalent. Whenever the steps in an argument are reversible, this will be the case. When we use the addition principle, this will always be the case. To see this, note that we start with an equation $a = b$ and obtain $a + c = b + c$. By adding $-c$ we can always obtain $a = b$ again, so the steps are reversible.

> **The use of the addition principle produces an equation equivalent to the original. Checking by substituting is therefore not necessary except to detect errors in solving.**

[7, 8]

Now let us consider the multiplication principle.

> **The multiplication principle.** If an equation $a = b$ is true, then $a \cdot c = b \cdot c$ is true for any number c.

Does the multiplication principle yield equivalent equations? In other words, are the steps reversible? If the number c by which we multiply is not 0, then we can reverse the step by multiplying by $1/c$, but if we multiply by 0, then $1/c$ does not exist and the step is not reversible.

The use of the multiplication principle produces an equation equivalent to the original, only if we multiply by a nonzero number.

Now let us consider multiplying by expressions with variables, as in the following example.

$$\frac{3}{x} = \frac{4}{x}$$

$$\frac{3}{x} \cdot x^2 = \frac{4}{x} \cdot x^2 \qquad \text{Here we multiplied by } x^2.$$

$$3x = 4x$$

$$0 = x$$

The number 0 is a solution of the last equation but is not a solution of the first. Hence we did not obtain equivalent equations. What can we do in practice?

When we use the multiplication principle and multiply by an expression with a variable, we may not obtain equivalent equations. We must check possible solutions by substituting in the original equation.

Example 5. Solve $\dfrac{x-3}{x-7} = \dfrac{4}{x-7}$.

$$(x-7) \cdot \frac{x-3}{x-7} = (x-7) \cdot \frac{4}{x-7}$$

$$x - 3 = 4$$

$$x = 7$$

Caution! Here we multiplied by an expression with a variable. Thus we must check.

The possible solution is 7. We check:

$$\frac{x-3}{x-7} = \frac{4}{x-7}$$

$$\frac{\boxed{7}-3}{\boxed{7}-7} \mid \frac{4}{\boxed{7}-7}$$

$$\frac{4}{0} \mid \frac{4}{0}$$

Division by 0 is undefined; 7 is not a solution.

The equation has no solutions. The solution set is ∅.

[9–11]

Now let us consider the principle of zero products.

The principle of zero products. **For any numbers *a* and *b*, if *ab* = 0, then *a* = 0 or *b* = 0; and if *a* = 0 or *b* = 0, then *ab* = 0.**

According to this principle, if we start with an equation $ab = 0$, we obtain $a = 0$ or $b = 0$. Also, if we start with $a = 0$ or $b = 0$, we can obtain $ab = 0$. Thus when we use this principle, that step is reversible and we have equivalent statements.

The use of the principle of zero products yields the solutions of the original equation. Checking by substituting is not necessary except to detect errors in solving.

Example 6. Solve $2x^3 - x^2 = 3x$.

$$2x^3 - x^2 - 3x = 0 \qquad \text{(addition principle)}$$

$$x(2x^2 - x - 3) = 0 \qquad \text{(factoring)}$$

$$x(2x - 3)(x + 1) = 0$$

$$x = 0 \text{ or } 2x - 3 = 0 \text{ or } x + 1 = 0 \qquad \text{(principle of zero products)}$$

$$x = 0 \quad \text{or} \quad x = \frac{3}{2} \quad \text{or} \quad x = -1$$

The solution set is $\left\{0, \dfrac{3}{2}, -1\right\}$.   **[12–16]**

In the following example we use the multiplication principle, multiplying by an expression with a variable, before we use the principle of zero products. Thus we must check possible solutions.

Example 7. Solve $\dfrac{x^2}{x-3} = \dfrac{9}{x-3}$.

$$(x - 3) \cdot \frac{x^2}{x - 3} = (x - 3) \cdot \frac{9}{x - 3}$$

$$x^2 = 9$$

$$x^2 - 9 = 0$$

$$(x + 3)(x - 3) = 0$$

$$x + 3 = 0 \quad \text{or} \quad x - 3 = 0$$

$$x = -3 \quad \text{or} \quad x = 3$$

Caution! Here we multiplied by an expression with a variable. Thus we must check.

The possible solutions are 3 and -3. We must check since we multiplied by an expression with a variable.

For 3:

$$\frac{x^2}{x - 3} = \frac{9}{x - 3}$$

$$\frac{\boxed{3}^2}{\boxed{3} - 3} \quad \frac{9}{\boxed{3} - 3}$$

$$\frac{9}{0} \quad \frac{9}{0}$$

3 does not check.

For -3:

$$\frac{x^2}{x - 3} = \frac{9}{x - 3}$$

$$\frac{\boxed{(-3)}^2}{\boxed{-3} - 3} \quad \frac{9}{\boxed{-3} - 3}$$

$$\frac{9}{-6} \quad \frac{9}{-6}$$

-3 checks.

Thus the solution set is $\{-3\}$.   **[17, 18]**

A *fractional equation* is an equation that contains fractional expressions. A procedure for solving fractional equations involves multiplying by the L.C.M. of all the denominators. It is called "clearing of fractions."

Example 8. Solve $\dfrac{14}{x + 2} - \dfrac{1}{x - 4} = 1$.

We multiply by the L.C.M. of all the denominators: $(x + 2)(x - 4)$.

$$(x + 2)(x - 4) \cdot \frac{14}{x + 2} - (x + 2)(x - 4) \cdot \frac{1}{x - 4}$$
$$= (x + 2)(x - 4) \cdot 1$$

$$14(x - 4) - (x + 2) = (x + 2)(x - 4)$$

$$14x - 56 - x - 2 = x^2 - 2x - 8$$

$$0 = x^2 - 15x + 50$$

$$0 = (x - 10)(x - 5)$$

$$x = 10 \quad \text{or} \quad x = 5$$

The possible solutions are 10 and 5. These check, so the solution set is $\{10, 5\}$.   **[19]**

Exercise Set 2.1

Decide which pairs of equations are equivalent.

1. $3x + 5 = 12$
$3x = 7$

2. $x = -7$
$x^2 = -7x$

3. $x = -7$
$x^2 = 49$

4. $2y + 1 = -3$
$8y + 4 = -12$

Solve.

5. $2x^2 - 6x = 0$

6. $9x^2 + 18x = 0$

7. $3y^3 - 5y^2 - 2y = 0$

8. $3t^3 - 5t^2 + 2t = 0$

9. $(2x - 3)(3x + 2)(x - 1) = 0$

10. $(y - 4)(4y + 12)(2y + 1) = 0$

11. $(2 - 4y)(y^2 + 3y) = 0$

12. $(y^2 - 9)(y^2 - 36) = 0$

13. $y^3 + 2y^2 - y - 2 = 0$

14. $t^3 + t^2 - 25t - 25 = 0$

15. $\dfrac{x + 2}{2} + \dfrac{3x + 1}{5} = \dfrac{x - 2}{4}$

16. $\dfrac{2x - 1}{3} - \dfrac{x - 2}{5} = \dfrac{x}{2}$

17. $\dfrac{1}{2} + \dfrac{2}{x} = \dfrac{1}{3} + \dfrac{3}{x}$

18. $\dfrac{1}{t} + \dfrac{1}{2t} + \dfrac{1}{3t} = 5$

19. $\dfrac{4}{x^2 - 1} - \dfrac{2}{x - 1} = \dfrac{3}{x + 1}$

20. $\dfrac{3y + 5}{y^2 + 5y} + \dfrac{y + 4}{y + 5} = \dfrac{y + 1}{y}$

21. $\dfrac{1}{2t} - \dfrac{2}{5t} = \dfrac{1}{10t} - 3$

22. $\dfrac{3}{m + 2} + \dfrac{2}{m - 2} = \dfrac{4m - 4}{m^2 - 4}$

23. $1 - \dfrac{3}{x} = \dfrac{40}{x^2}$

24. $1 - \dfrac{15}{y^2} = \dfrac{2}{y}$

25. $\dfrac{11 - t^2}{3t^2 - 5t + 2} = \dfrac{2t + 3}{3t - 2} - \dfrac{t - 3}{t - 1}$

26. $\dfrac{1}{3y^2 - 10y + 3} = \dfrac{6y}{9y^2 - 1} + \dfrac{2}{1 - 3y}$

 Solve.

27. $3.12x^2 - 6.715x = 0$

28. $9.25x^2 + 18.03x = 0$

29. $\dfrac{2.315}{y} - \dfrac{12.6}{17.4} = \dfrac{6.71}{y} + 0.763$

30. $\dfrac{6.034}{x} - 43.17 = \dfrac{0.793}{x} + 18.15$

31. $\dfrac{2.35x - 1.05}{3.1} - \dfrac{7.2x - 5.3}{5.3} = \dfrac{x}{8.4}$

32. $\dfrac{85.6y + 17.6}{8.3} + \dfrac{13.7y - 16.8}{0.12} = \dfrac{y}{1.1}$

33. $(6.08x - 17.3)(75.7x + 0.42)(1.67x - 8.95) = 0$

34. $(0.0003y + 1.005)(1.05y - 1.414)(67.35y - 8.105) = 0$

2.2 Formulas and Applied Problems

FORMULAS

A formula is a recipe for doing a calculation. An example is $A = \pi rs + \pi r^2$, which gives the area A of a cone in terms of the slant height s and radius of the base r.

Suppose we wanted to find the slant height s when the area A and radius r are known. Our knowledge of equations allows us to get s alone on one side, or as we say, "solve the formula for s."

Example 1. Solve $A = \pi rs + \pi r^2$, for s.

$A - \pi r^2 = \pi rs$

$\dfrac{A - \pi r^2}{\pi r} = s$ $\left(\dfrac{A - \pi r^2}{\pi r} \text{ could also be expressed} \right.$

$\left. \text{as } \dfrac{A}{\pi r} - r. \right)$

Example 2. Solve $\dfrac{1}{R} = \dfrac{1}{r_1} + \dfrac{1}{r_2}$, for R. (This is a formula from electricity.)

We first multiply by Rr_1r_2:

$$Rr_1r_2 \cdot \frac{1}{R} = Rr_1r_2 \cdot \left[\frac{1}{r_1} + \frac{1}{r_2} \right]$$

$$Rr_1r_2 \cdot \frac{1}{R} = Rr_1r_2 \cdot \frac{1}{r_1} + Rr_1r_2 \cdot \frac{1}{r_2}$$

$$r_1r_2 = Rr_2 + Rr_1$$

$$r_1r_2 = (r_2 + r_1)R$$

$$\frac{r_1r_2}{r_2 + r_1} = R.$$ [20, 21]

APPLIED PROBLEMS

By an *applied problem* we mean a problem in which mathematical techniques are used to answer some question. Problems like this may be posed orally. They may come about in the course of a conversation, or they can be hatched within the mind of one person. Thus to call them "word problems" or "story problems" is misleading.

There is no rule that will enable us to solve applied problems, because they are of many different kinds. We can, however, describe an overall, or general, strategy.

The idea is to translate the problem situation to mathematical language and then calculate to find a solution.

GENERAL STRATEGY FOR SOLVING APPLIED PROBLEMS

1. Become familiar with the problem situation. If the problem is presented to you in written words, then of course this means to read carefully.
   a) Make a drawing, if it makes sense to do so. It is difficult to overemphasize the importance of this!
   b) Make a written list of the known facts and a list of what you wish to find out.
2. Translate the problem situation to mathematical language or symbolism. For most of the problems you will encounter in algebra this means to write one or more equations. You will of course also assign certain variables to represent unknown quantities.
3. Use your mathematical knowledge to find a possible solution. In algebra this usually means to solve an equation, or system of equations.
4. Check to see if your possible solution actually fits the problem situation, and is thus really a solution of the problem.

Problems stated in textbooks are of necessity somewhat contrived. Problems that you encounter in nonclassroom situations will almost invariably contain insufficient information to obtain a firm, or exact, answer. They also usually contain a good deal of extraneous, useless information. Here is an example that illustrates this point.

Example. There are 145 persons in the junior class at Notown College. The prom committee wishes to know how much they will have to charge each person who attends the spring prom, to be held May 19 in the College Gymnasium at 8:00 PM.

The above problem is typical of problems encountered in real life. There is insufficient information to obtain an answer. To get an answer we need to know:

1. The cost of holding the prom. This would include such things as cost of music, refreshments, and hall rent.

2. The number of persons who will attend.

The committee will need to find out information about costs, and in the course of finding it, they may revise their formulation of the problem. For example, if a band costs too much, they may have to settle for using records. In any event, they may find that they can determine costs only approximately; in other words, they must estimate.

The number 145 may help in estimating the number who will attend, but at best this number will be an estimate. Thus, on the basis of the best information and/or estimates available, the committee will do its arithmetic.

Note that the date, time, and place, while they are interesting information, do not contribute to the solution of the problem. Thus this is extraneous information.

In the following examples we illustrate how a problem situation can be translated to mathematical language. In certain simple situations, the translation is easy because certain words translate directly to mathematical symbols. Note how the word "is" translates to an equals sign, the word "what" translates to a variable, and the word "of" translates to a multiplication sign.

Example 1. What percent of 84 is 11.76?

Translate: $\qquad x\% \qquad \cdot \ 84 = 11.76$

Solve: $\qquad x \cdot 0.01 \quad \cdot \ 84 = 11.76$

$$x \cdot 0.84 = 11.76$$

$$x = \frac{11.76}{0.84} = 14$$

Check: $14\% \cdot 84 = 0.14 \cdot 84 = 11.76$

Example 2. 14% of what is 11.76?

Translate: $\quad 14\% \ \cdot \quad y \ = 11.76$

Solve: $\qquad 0.14 \quad \cdot \quad y \ = 11.76$

$$y \ = \frac{11.76}{0.14} = 84$$

Check: $14\% \cdot 84 = 0.14 \cdot 84 = 11.76$ **[22–24]**

In the remainder of this section we consider applied problems of various types. Although there is no rule for solving applied problems because they can be so different, it does help somewhat to consider a few different types of problems. The best way to learn to solve applied problems is to solve a lot of them.

COMPOUND INTEREST PROBLEMS

Example 1. An investment is made at 8%, compounded annually. It grows to $783 at the end of one year. How much was originally invested?

There is more than one way to translate the problem situation to mathematical language. The following is one method.

We first restate the situation as follows:

The invested amount
plus the interest
amounts to
$783.

Now the interest is 8% of the invested amount, so we have the following, which translates directly.

Invested amount	plus	8%	of	Invested amount	is	$783
x	+	8%	·	x	=	783

Now we solve the equation:

$$x + 8\% x = 783$$

$$x + 0.08x = 783$$

$$(1 + 0.08)x = 783$$

$$1.08x = 783$$

$$x = \frac{783}{1.08} = 725.$$

The number 725 checks in the problem situation, so the answer is $725.   [25]

Let us now consider an investment over a period longer than one year. If we invest P dollars at an interest rate i, compounded annually, we will have an amount in the account at the end of a year that we will call A_1. Now $A_1 = P + Pi$, or

$$A_1 = P(1 + i), \quad \text{or}$$

$$A_1 = Pr, \quad \text{where we have let } r = 1 + i.$$

Going into the second year we have Pr dollars. By the end of the second year we will have A_2 dollars, given by

$$A_2 = A_1 \cdot r.$$

But $A_1 = Pr$, so $A_2 = (Pr)r$, or

$$A_2 = Pr^2.$$

Similarly, the amount A_3 in the account at the end of three years is given by

$$A_3 = Pr^3,$$

and so on. In general, the following applies.

If an amount P is invested at an interest rate of i, compounded annually, in t years it will grow to an amount A given by

$$A = P(1 + i)^t.$$

Example 2. Suppose $1000 is invested at 8%, compounded annually. What amount will be in the account at the end of two years?

We use the equation $A = P(1 + i)^t$. We get

$$A = 1000(1 + 0.08)^2 = 1000(1.08)^2 = 1166.4.$$

The answer is $1166.40.   [26]

Interest may be compounded more often than once a year. Suppose it is compounded four times a year, or *quarterly*. The formula derived above can be altered to apply. We consider one-fourth of a year to be an *interest period*. The rate of interest for such a period is then $i/4$. The number of periods will be four times the number of years. This is shown in the following diagram.

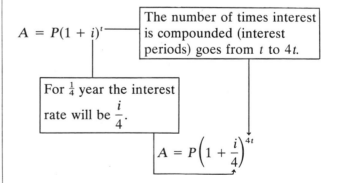

Now suppose the number of interest periods per year is something other than 4, say n. Using the reasoning of the example above, we obtain a general formula.

If an amount P is invested at an interest rate i, compounded n times per year, in t years it will grow to an amount A given by

$$A = P\left(1 + \frac{i}{n}\right)^{nt}.$$

When problems involving compound interest are translated to mathematical language, the above formula is almost always used.

Example 3. Suppose $1000 is invested at 8%, compounded quarterly. How much will be in the account at the end of two years?

In this case $n = 4$ and $t = 2$. We substitute into the formula:

$$A = P\left(1 + \frac{i}{n}\right)^{nt} = 1000\left(1 + \frac{0.08}{4}\right)^{4 \cdot 2}$$

$$= 1000(1.02)^8$$

$$= 1171.66.$$

The answer is $1171.66.   [27]

AREA PROBLEMS

Example. The radius of a circular swimming pool is 10 ft. A sidewalk of uniform width is constructed around the outside and has an area of 44π ft². How wide is the sidewalk?

First make a drawing:

Let x represent the width of the walk. Then, recalling that a formula for the area of a circle is $A = \pi r^2$, we have

Area of pool $= \pi \cdot 10^2 = 100\pi$,

Area of sidewalk plus pool $= \pi \cdot (10 + x)^2$

$$= \pi(100 + 20x + x^2).$$

Thus

$$\underbrace{\text{(Area of sidewalk}}_{} \underbrace{\text{(Area of}}_{} \underbrace{\text{Area of}}_{}$$
$$\text{plus pool)} - \text{pool)} = \text{sidewalk}$$
$$\pi(100 + 20x + x^2) - 100\pi = 44\pi$$

$$100 + 20x + x^2 - 100 = 44 \qquad \left(\text{multiplying by } \frac{1}{\pi}\right)$$

$$x^2 + 20x = 44$$
$$x^2 + 20x - 44 = 0$$
$$(x + 22)(x - 2) = 0$$
$$x = -22 \quad \text{or} \quad x = 2$$

We see that -22 ft is not a solution of the original problem since width has to be positive. The number 2 checks; that is, when the sidewalk is 2 ft wide, the area of the pool is 100π ft², the area of the pool plus sidewalk is $\pi \cdot 12^2$, or 144π ft², so the area of the sidewalk is 44π ft².   [28]

MOTION PROBLEMS

For problems that deal with distance, time, and speed, we almost always need to recall the definition of speed, or something equivalent to it.

Speed = distance/time   or $r = d/t$,   where r = speed, d = distance, and t = time.

If you memorize $r = d/t$, you can easily obtain either of the two equivalent equations $d = rt$ or $t = d/r$, as needed.

When translating these problems to mathematical language it is often helpful to look for some quantity that is constant in the problem. For example, two cars may travel for the same length of time, or two boats may travel the same distance. Such facts often provide the basis for setting up an equation.

Example 1. A boat travels 246 km downstream in the same time that it takes to travel 180 km upstream. The speed of the current in the stream is 5.5 km/h. Find the speed of the boat in still water.

We first make a drawing and lay out the known facts, and any other information that is pertinent.

————————————→ Downstream		
$d_1 = 246$	t_1 unknown	r_1 unknown, but equals speed of boat plus speed of current
←———————————— Upstream		
$d_2 = 180$	t_2 unknown, but same as t_1	r_2 unknown, but equals speed of boat minus speed of current

In this problem the times are the same, so we have an equation

$$t_1 = t_2.$$

Now, remembering that $t = d/r$, we substitute to obtain

$$\frac{d_1}{r_1} = \frac{d_2}{r_2}.$$

Now d_1, the distance downstream, is 246, and d_2 is 180.

The speed downstream is the speed of the boat *plus* that of the current.

Let's call the boat's speed in still water r.

Then r_1, the speed downstream, is $r + 5.5$, and r_2, the speed upstream, is $r - 5.5$. This gives us the equation

$$\frac{246}{r + 5.5} = \frac{180}{r - 5.5}.$$

Solving for r we get 35.5 km/h. This checks. Thus the speed of the boat in still water is 35.5 km/h.   [29]

In the following example, although the distance is the same in two cases, an additional piece of information is given that is the key to the translation.

Example 2. The speed of a boat in still water is 10 mph. It travels 24 miles upstream and 24 miles downstream in a total time of 5 hr. What is the speed of the current?

We first make a drawing and write out pertinent information.

————————————→ Downstream		
$d_1 = 24$ mi	t_1 unknown	r_1 unknown, but is 10 mph plus speed of current
←———————————— Upstream		
$d_2 = 24$ mi	t_2 unknown, but $t_1 + t_2 = 5$ hr	r_2 unknown, but is 10 mph minus speed of current.

This time the basis of our translation is the equation involving times:

$$t_1 + t_2 = 5.$$

This then leads to

$$\frac{d_1}{r_1} + \frac{d_2}{r_2} = 5,$$

and then

$$\frac{24}{10 + r} + \frac{24}{10 - r} = 5,$$

where r is the speed of the current. Solving for r we get $r = -2$ or $r = 2$. Since speed cannot be negative in this problem, -2 cannot be a solution. But 2 checks, so the speed of the current is 2 mph.   **[30, 31]**

WORK PROBLEMS

Suppose a man can do a certain job in 4 hr. Then he can do $\frac{1}{4}$ of it in 1 hr and $\frac{3}{4}$ of it in 3 hr. The basic principle for translating work problems follows.

✓ **If a job can be done in time t, then $1/t$ of it can be done in 1 unit of time.**

Example 1. Man A can do a certain job in 3 hr. Man B can do the same job in 5 hr. How long would it take both men, working together, to do the same job?

a) Make a guess at a solution. Does 4 hr seem reasonable? Sometimes our intuition can fool us. Clearly the answer is less than 3 hr because one man can do the job alone in 3 hr.

b) Man A can do the job in 3 hr. Thus he can do $\frac{1}{3}$ of it in 1 hr. Similarly, man B can do $\frac{1}{5}$ of the job in 1 hr. Thus together they can do $\frac{1}{3} + \frac{1}{5}$ of it in 1 hr.

Let t represent the amount of time it takes to do the job if they work together. Then together they can do $1/t$ of the job in 1 hr. Thus

$$\frac{1}{3} + \frac{1}{5} = \frac{1}{t}$$

$$5t + 3t = 5 \cdot 3 \qquad \text{(multiplying by } 3 \cdot 5 \cdot t)$$

$$8t = 15$$

$$t = \frac{15}{8}, \text{ or } 1\frac{7}{8} \text{ hr.}$$

And $t = 1\frac{7}{8}$ hr checks. Thus it takes the men $1\frac{7}{8}$ hr to do the job if they work together.   **[32]**

Example 2. It takes Red 9 hrs longer to build a wall than Mort. If they work together they can build the wall in 20 hr. How long would it take each, working alone, to build the wall?

Let t = the amount of time it takes Mort working alone. Then $t + 9$ = the amount of time it takes Red working alone.

Then Mort can do $1/t$ of the work in 1 hr and Red can do $1/(t + 9)$ of it in 1 hr. Together they can do $1/t + 1/(t + 9)$ of the work in 1 hr. We also know that they can do $\frac{1}{20}$ of the work in 1 hr. Thus,

$$\frac{1}{t} + \frac{1}{t + 9} = \frac{1}{20}.$$

Solving the equation, we get $t = -5$ or $t = 36$. Since negative time has no meaning in the problem, -5 is not a solution of the original problem. The number 36 checks in the original problem. Thus it would take Mort 36 hr and Red 45 hr.   **[33]**

Exercise Set 2.2

1. Solve $P = 2l + 2w$, for w.

2. Solve $F = ma$, for a.

3. Solve $E = IR$, for I.

4. Solve $F = \frac{km_1 m_2}{d^2}$, for m_2.

5. Solve $\dfrac{P_1 V_1}{T_1} = \dfrac{P_2 V_2}{T_2}$, for T_1.

6. Solve $\dfrac{P_1 V_1}{T_1} = \dfrac{P_2 V_2}{T_2}$, for V_2.

7. Solve $S = \dfrac{H}{m(v_1 - v_2)}$, for v_1.

8. Solve $S = \dfrac{H}{m(v_1 - v_2)}$, for v_2.

9. Solve $\dfrac{1}{F} = \dfrac{1}{m} + \dfrac{1}{p}$, for p.

10. Solve $\dfrac{1}{F} = \dfrac{1}{m} + \dfrac{1}{p}$, for F.

Solve for x.

11. $(x + a)(x - b) = x^2 + 5$

12. $(c + d)x + (c - d)x = c^2$

13. $10(a + x) = 8(a - x)$

14. $4(a + b + x) + 3(a + b - x) = 8a$

Applied problems

15. 79.2 is what percent of 180?

16. 6% of what number is 480?

17. What percent of 28 is 1.68?

18. What is 7% of 45.3?

19. A man gets a 6% raise which is \$480. What was his old salary? his new salary?

20. A man gets a 5% raise, which is \$430. What was his old salary? his new salary?

21. An investment is made at 9%, compounded annually. It grows to \$708.50 at the end of one year. How much was originally invested?

22. An investment is made at 7%, compounded annually. It grows to \$856 at the end of one year. How much was originally invested?

23. In triangle ABC, Angle B is five times as large as angle A. The measure of angle C is 2° less than that of angle A. Find the measures of the angles. (*Hint*: The sum of the angle measures is 180°.)

24. In triangle ABC, angle B is twice as large as angle A. Angle C measures 20° more than angle A. Find the measures of the angles.

25. The perimeter of a rectangle is 322 m. The length is 25 m more than the width. Find the dimensions.

26. The length of a rectangle is twice the width. The perimeter is 39 m. Find the dimensions.

27. A student's scores on three tests are 87%, 64%, and 78%. What must he score on the fourth test so that his average will be 80%?

28. A student's scores on three tests are 74%, 55%, and 68%. What must he score on the fourth test so that his average will be 70%?

29. An open box is made from a 10-cm by 20-cm piece of tin by cutting a square from each corner and folding up the edges. The area of the resulting base is 96 cm². What is the length of the sides of the squares?

30. The frame of a picture is 28 cm by 32 cm outside and is of uniform width. What is the width of the frame if 192 cm² of the picture shows?

31. After a 2% increase, the population of a city is 826,200. What was the former population?

32. After a 3% increase, the population of a city is 741,600. What was the former population?

33. A motorist drove 144 mi. If he had gone 4 mph faster he could have made his trip in $\frac{1}{2}$ hr less time. What was his speed?

34. A motorist drove 280 mi. If he had gone 5 mph faster he could have made his trip in 1 hr less time. What was his speed?

35. A boat goes 50 km downstream in the same time that it takes to go 30 km upstream. The speed of the stream is 3 km/h. Find the speed of the boat in still water.

36. A boat goes 50 km downstream in the same time that it takes to go 30 km upstream. The speed of the boat in still water is 16 km/h. Find the speed of the stream.

37. Man A can do a certain job in 3 hr, man B can do the same job in 5 hr, and man C can do the same job in 7 hr. How long would the job take with all working together?

38. Pipe A can fill a tank in 4 hr, pipe B can fill it in 10 hr, and pipe C can fill it in 12 hr. The pipes are connected to the same tank. How long does it take to fill the tank if all three are running together?

39. Woman A can do a certain job, working alone, in 3.15 hr less time than woman B working alone. Together they can do the job in 2.09 hr. How long would each take working alone to do the job?

40. At a factory, smokestack A pollutes the air 2.13 times as fast as smokestack B. When both stacks operate together they yield a certain amount of pollution in 16.3 hr. Find the amount of time it would take each to yield the same amount of pollution if it operated alone.

41. Suppose $1000 is invested at 8%. How much is in the account at the end of one year if interest is compounded (a) annually? (b) semiannually? (c) quarterly? (d) daily (use 365 days per yr)?

42. Suppose $1000 is invested at 10%. How much is in the account at the end of one year, if interest is compounded (a) annually? (b) semiannually? (c) quarterly? (d) daily (use 365 days per yr)?

▶ **43.** A woman drives home at 45 km/hr and arrives 5 minutes early. If she drives home at 40 km/hr she arrives 5 minutes late. How far does she drive home?

2.3 Quadratic Equations

A *quadratic* equation, also known as an equation of *second degree*, is any equation equivalent to the following:

$$ax^2 + bx + c = 0, \quad \text{where } a \neq 0.$$

You have solved such equations by factoring. We now consider other methods. Let us first consider an equation $x^2 = p$, where p is not negative. We shall solve this equation in two ways.

1.
$$x^2 = p$$
$$x^2 - p = 0$$
$$(x - \sqrt{p})(x + \sqrt{p}) = 0 \quad \text{(factoring)}$$
$$x - \sqrt{p} = 0 \quad \text{or} \quad x + \sqrt{p} = 0 \quad \text{(principle of zero products)}$$
$$x = \sqrt{p} \quad \text{or} \quad x = -\sqrt{p}$$

2.
$$x^2 = p$$
$$\sqrt{x^2} = \sqrt{p} \quad \text{(taking principal square root)}$$
$$|x| = \sqrt{p}$$

$x = \sqrt{p}$ or $-x = \sqrt{p}$ (definition of absolute value)

$x = \sqrt{p}$ or $x = -\sqrt{p}$

With either method we obtain $\sqrt{p}$ and $-\sqrt{p}$, abbreviated $\pm\sqrt{p}$. If $p > 0$, there are two solutions. If $p = 0$, there is just one solution. If $p < 0$, there are no real number solutions. [34–37]

We now use this method in another example.

Example. Solve $(x + 5)^2 = 3$.

Taking the principal square root,
$$|x + 5| = \sqrt{3}.$$

Then,
$$x + 5 = \pm\sqrt{3}$$
$$x = -5 \pm \sqrt{3}.$$
The solution set is $\{-5 -\sqrt{3}, -5 + \sqrt{3}\}$. [38–40]

COMPLETING THE SQUARE

Now let us consider the equation $x^2 - 6x - 12 = 0$:
$$x^2 - 6x - 12 = 0$$
$$x^2 - 6x = 12.$$

We know that $x^2 - 6x + 9$ is a perfect square $(x - 3)^2$. So if we add 9 we can solve as follows:

$$x^2 - 6x + 9 = 12 + 9 \quad \text{(adding 9 makes the left side a perfect square)}$$
$$(x - 3)^2 = 21$$
$$x - 3 = \pm\sqrt{21}$$
$$x = 3 \pm \sqrt{21}$$

The solution set is $\{3 + \sqrt{21}, 3 - \sqrt{21}\}$, which we often abbreviate as $3 \pm \sqrt{21}$.

Note that we can determine the number to add to make a perfect square as follows.

> **To complete the square on $x^2 + bx$, we take half the coefficient of x and square it. Then we add that number, $\left(\dfrac{b}{2}\right)^2$.**

Example 1. Solve by completing the square.
$$x^2 + 3x - 5 = 0$$
$$x^2 + 3x = 5$$

$$x^2 + 3x + \frac{9}{4} = 5 + \frac{9}{4}$$

> Take half of 3: $\dfrac{1}{2} \cdot 3 = \dfrac{3}{2}$;
> square it: $\left(\dfrac{3}{2}\right)^2 = \dfrac{9}{4}$; and add.

$$\left(x + \frac{3}{2}\right)^2 = \frac{20}{4} + \frac{9}{4} = \frac{29}{4}$$

$$x + \frac{3}{2} = \pm\sqrt{\frac{29}{4}} = \pm\frac{\sqrt{29}}{2}$$

$$x = -\frac{3}{2} \pm \frac{\sqrt{29}}{2} = \frac{-3 \pm \sqrt{29}}{2}$$

The solution set is $\left\{\dfrac{-3 + \sqrt{29}}{2}, \dfrac{-3 - \sqrt{29}}{2}\right\}$, or $\dfrac{-3 \pm \sqrt{29}}{2}$.

In the previous examples we were solving $ax^2 + bx + c = 0$ with $a = 1$. For cases where $a \neq 1$, we first mutiply by $1/a$ to get an equation whose x^2 coefficient is 1.

Example 2. Solve by completing the square.

$$2x^2 - 3x - 1 = 0$$

$$x^2 - \frac{3}{2}x - \frac{1}{2} = 0 \qquad \left(\text{multiplying by } \frac{1}{2}\right)$$

$$x^2 - \frac{3}{2}x = \frac{1}{2}$$

$$x^2 - \frac{3}{2}x + \frac{9}{16} = \frac{1}{2} + \frac{9}{16}$$

$$\left(x - \frac{3}{4}\right)^2 = \frac{8}{16} + \frac{9}{16} = \frac{17}{16}$$

$$x - \frac{3}{4} = \pm\sqrt{\frac{17}{16}} = \pm\frac{\sqrt{17}}{4}$$

$$x = \frac{3}{4} \pm \frac{\sqrt{17}}{4} = \frac{3 \pm \sqrt{17}}{4}$$

The solution set is $\left\{\dfrac{3 + \sqrt{17}}{4}, \dfrac{3 - \sqrt{17}}{4}\right\}$, or $\dfrac{3 \pm \sqrt{17}}{4}$.

[41–51]

THE QUADRATIC FORMULA

To facilitate the solving of quadratic equations, we shall derive a formula. To do this, we will consider the standard form of the quadratic equation, with unspecified coefficients. Solving that equation gives us the formula we seek. We begin with

$$ax^2 + bx + c = 0.$$

We multiply on both sides by $4a$, to obtain

$$4a^2x^2 + 4abx + 4ac = 0.$$

Next we add $b^2 - b^2$ on the left and rearrange, as follows:

$$(4a^2x^2 + 4abx + b^2) - (b^2 - 4ac) = 0,$$

or

$$(2ax + b)^2 - (b^2 - 4ac) = 0.$$

The left side can be factored as a difference of squares, after which we use the principle of zero products.

$$[(2ax + b) - \sqrt{b^2 - 4ac}][(2ax + b) + \sqrt{b^2 - 4ac}]$$

$$2ax + b - \sqrt{b^2 - 4ac} = 0$$

or

$$2ax + b + \sqrt{b^2 - 4ac} = 0,$$

$$x = \frac{-b + \sqrt{b^2 - 4ac}}{2a}$$

or

$$x = \frac{-b - \sqrt{b^2 - 4ac}}{2a}.$$

We can abbreviate the last lines using the sign $\pm$. This gives us the quadratic formula.

> **The quadratic formula.** If a quadratic equation has solutions, they are given by
> $$x = \frac{-b \pm \sqrt{b^2 - 4ac}}{2a}.$$

When using the quadratic formula it is helpful to first find the standard form so that the coefficients a, b, and c can be determined.

Example. Solve $3x^2 + 2x = 7$.

First find the standard form and determine a, b, and c:

$$3x^2 + 2x - 7 = 0,$$

$$a = 3, b = 2, c = -7.$$

Then use the quadratic formula:

$$x = \frac{-b \pm \sqrt{b^2 - 4ac}}{2a}$$

$$x = \frac{-2 \pm \sqrt{2^2 - 4 \cdot 3 \cdot (-7)}}{2 \cdot 3}$$

(To prevent careless mistakes it helps to write out *all* the steps.)

$$x = \frac{-2 \pm \sqrt{4 + 84}}{6}$$

$$x = \frac{-2 \pm \sqrt{88}}{6} = \frac{-2 \pm \sqrt{4 \cdot 22}}{6}$$

$$= \frac{-2 \pm 2\sqrt{22}}{6} = \frac{2(-1 \pm \sqrt{22})}{2 \cdot 3} = \frac{-1 \pm \sqrt{22}}{3}.$$

Should such solutions arise in an applied problem, we can find approximations using Table 1 at the end of the text:

$$\frac{-1 + \sqrt{22}}{3} \approx \frac{-1 + 4.69}{3}$$

$$\approx \frac{3.69}{3} \approx 1.2 \qquad \text{(rounded to the nearest tenth)}$$

$$\frac{-1 - \sqrt{22}}{2} \approx \frac{-1 - 4.69}{3}$$

$$\approx \frac{-5.69}{3} \approx -1.9 \qquad \text{(rounded to the nearest tenth)}$$

[52, 53]

The expression $b^2 - 4ac$, called the *discriminant*, determines the nature of the solutions. If x_1 and x_2 represent the solutions, then

$$x_1 = \frac{-b + \sqrt{b^2 - 4ac}}{2a}, \qquad x_2 = \frac{-b - \sqrt{b^2 - 4ac}}{2a}.$$

Note that if $b^2 - 4ac = 0$, then both x_1 and x_2 are the same, $-b/2a$.

If $b^2 - 4ac > 0$, then the expression $\sqrt{b^2 - 4ac}$ represents a positive real number that is to be added to or subtracted from $-b$. In this case the solutions are different. If $b^2 - 4ac < 0$, the expression $\sqrt{b^2 - 4ac}$ does not represent a real number. Thus there are no real number solutions. In a later chapter we will consider a number system in which such solutions exist.

> If $b^2 - 4ac = 0$, $ax^2 + bx + c = 0$ has just one real number solution.
> If $b^2 - 4ac > 0$, $ax^2 + bx + c = 0$ has two real number solutions.
> If $b^2 - 4ac < 0$, $ax^2 + bx + c = 0$ has no real number solution.

[54–56]

WRITING EQUATIONS FROM SOLUTIONS

We can use the principle of zero products to write a quadratic equation whose solutions are known.

Example. Write a quadratic equation whose solutions are 3 and $-\frac{2}{5}$.

$$x = 3 \qquad \text{or} \qquad x = -\frac{2}{5}$$

$$x - 3 = 0 \qquad \text{or} \qquad x + \frac{2}{5} = 0$$

$$(x - 3)\left(x + \frac{2}{5}\right) = 0 \qquad \text{(multiplying)}$$

$$x^2 - \frac{13}{5}x - \frac{6}{5} = 0 \qquad \text{or} \qquad 5x^2 - 13x - 6 = 0$$

[57–59]

Exercise Set 2.3

Solve for x.

1. $2x^2 = 14$

2. $6x^2 = 36$

3. $9x^2 = 5$

4. $4x^2 = 3$

5. $ax^2 = b$

6. $\pi x^2 = k$

7. $(x - 7)^2 = 5$

8. $(x + 3)^2 = 2$

9. $(x - h)^2 = a$

10. $(x + h)^2 = a$

Solve by completing the square. (It is important to practice this method since we will need it later.)

11. $x^2 + 6x + 4 = 0$

12. $x^2 - 6x - 4 = 0$

13. $y^2 + 7y - 30 = 0$

14. $y^2 - 7y - 30 = 0$

15. $5x^2 - 4x - 2 = 0$

16. $12y^2 - 14y + 3 = 0$

17. $2x^2 + 7x - 15 = 0$

18. $9x^2 - 30x = -25$

Solve, using the quadratic formula.

19. $x^2 + 4x - 5 = 0$

20. $x^2 - 2x = 15$

21. $2y^2 - 3y - 2 = 0$

22. $5m^2 + 3m - 2 = 0$

23. $3t^2 + 8t + 5 = 0$

24. $3u^2 = 18u - 6$

25. $u^2 = 12u - 3$

26. $5p^2 + 30p + 40 = 0$

Solve, using any method. (In general, try factoring first. Then use the quadratic formula if factoring is not possible.)

27. $2x^2 - x - 6 = 0$

28. $3x^2 + 5x + 2 = 0$

29. $x^2 + 3x = 8$

30. $x^2 - 6x = 4$

31. $x + \dfrac{1}{x} = \dfrac{13}{6}$

32. $\dfrac{3}{x} + \dfrac{x}{3} = \dfrac{5}{2}$

33. $t^2 + 0.2t - 0.3 = 0$

34. $p^2 + 0.3p - 0.2 = 0$

35. $x^2 + x - \sqrt{2} = 0$

36. $x^2 - x - \sqrt{3} = 0$

37. $x^2 + \sqrt{5}x - \sqrt{3} = 0$

38. $2x^2 + \sqrt{3}x - \pi = 0$

39. $\sqrt{2}x^2 - \sqrt{3}x - \sqrt{5} = 0$

40. $\sqrt{2}x^2 + 5x + \sqrt{2} = 0$

41. $(2t - 3)^2 + 17t = 15$

42. $2y^2 - (y + 2)(y - 3) = 12$

43. $(x + 3)(x - 2) = 2(x + 11)$

44. $9t(t + 2) - 3t(t - 2) = 2(t + 4)(t + 6)$

45. $2x^2 + (x - 4)^2 = 5x(x - 4) + 24$

46. $(c + 2)^2 + (c - 2)(c + 2) = 44 + (c - 2)^2$

Determine the nature of the solutions of each equation. Do not solve.

47. $x^2 - 2x + 10 = 0$

48. $4x^2 - 4\sqrt{3}x + 3 = 0$

49. $9x^2 - 6x = 0$

Write quadratic equations whose solutions are as follows.

50. $-11, 9$

51. $-4, 4$

52. 7, only solution

53. -5, only solution

54. $-\dfrac{2}{5}, \dfrac{6}{5}$ **55.** $-\dfrac{1}{4}, -\dfrac{1}{2}$ **56.** $\dfrac{c}{2}, \dfrac{d}{2}$ **57.** $\dfrac{k}{3}, \dfrac{m}{4}$

58. $\sqrt{2}, \ 3\sqrt{2}$ **59.** $-\sqrt{3}, \ 2\sqrt{3}$ **60.** $\pi, \ -2\pi$

Solve.

61. $x^2 - 0.75x - 0.5 = 0$ **62.** $2.2x^2 + 0.5x - 1 = 0$

63. $5.33x^2 - 8.23x - 3.24 = 0$ **64.** $0.034x^2 + 7.01x - 0.0356 = 0$

65. Solve for x in terms of y.

$$3x^2 + xy + 4y^2 - 9 = 0$$

66. Derive the quadratic formula by completing the square.

67. One solution of $kx^2 + 3x - k = 0$ is -2. Find the other.

68. Find k so that the following equation has (a) two real number solutions; (b) one solution; and (c) no real number solutions.

$$3x^2 + 4x = k - 5$$

69. Prove that the solutions of $ax^2 + bx + c = 0$ are the reciprocals of the solutions of the equation $cx^2 + bx + a = 0$, $c \neq 0$.

70. Prove that the solutions of $ax^2 + bx + c = 0$ are the additive inverses of the solutions of the equation $ax^2 - bx + c = 0$.

2.4 Formulas and Applied Problems

FORMULAS

To solve a formula for a certain variable, we use the principles of equation solving we have developed until we have an equation with the variable alone on one side. In most formulas the variables represent nonnegative numbers, so we usually do not need to use absolute values when taking principal square roots.

Example 1. Solve $V = \pi r^2 h$, for r.

$$\frac{V}{\pi h} = r^2$$

$$\sqrt{\frac{V}{\pi h}} = r \qquad \text{[60]}$$

Example 2. Solve $A = \pi r s + \pi r^2$, for r.

$$\pi r^2 + \pi r s - A = 0$$

Then $a = \pi$, $b = \pi s$, $c = -A$, and we use the quadratic formula:

$$r = \frac{-b \pm \sqrt{b^2 - 4ac}}{2a} = \frac{-\pi s \pm \sqrt{(\pi s)^2 - 4 \cdot \pi \cdot (-A)}}{2\pi}$$

$$= \frac{-\pi s \pm \sqrt{\pi^2 s^2 + 4\pi A}}{2\pi}$$

or just

$$\frac{-\pi s + \sqrt{\pi^2 s^2 + 4\pi A}}{2\pi},$$

since the negative square root would result in a negative solution. **[61]**

APPLIED PROBLEMS

Example 1. A ladder 10 ft long leans against a wall. The bottom of the ladder is 6 ft from the wall. The bottom of the ladder is then pulled out 3 ft farther. How much does the top end move down the wall?

The first thing to do is to make a drawing and label it, with the known and unknown data. The dotted line shows the ladder in its original position, with the lower end 6 ft from the wall.

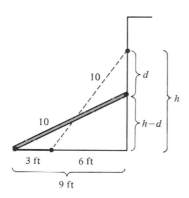

In the figure there are right triangles. This is a clue that we may wish to use the Pythagorean theorem. We use that theorem and begin to write equations. From the taller triangle, we get

$$h^2 + 6^2 = 10^2.$$

We solve this for h and find that $h = 8$ ft.

From the other triangle, we get

$$9^2 + (h - d)^2 = 10^2$$

but we know that $h = 8$, so we have

$$9^2 + (8 - d)^2 = 10^2$$

or

$$d^2 - 16d + 45 = 0.$$

Using the quadratic formula we get

$$d = \frac{16 \pm \sqrt{76}}{2} = \frac{16 \pm 2\sqrt{19}}{2} = 8 \pm \sqrt{19}.$$

The length $8 + \sqrt{19}$ is not a solution since it exceeds the original length. Thus the solution is $8 - \sqrt{19} \approx 8 - 4.359 = 3.641$. Therefore the top moves down 3.641 ft when the bottom is moved out 3 ft. **[62]**

When an object is dropped or thrown downward, the distance, in meters, that it falls in t seconds is given by the following formula:

$$s = 4.9t^2 + v_0 t.$$

In this formula v_0 is the initial velocity.

Example 2

a) An object is dropped from the top of the Gateway Arch in St. Louis, which is 195 meters high. How long does it take to reach the ground?

Since the object was *dropped* its initial velocity was 0. So we substitute 0 for v_0 and 195 for s and then solve for t:

$$195 = 4.9t^2 + 0 \cdot t$$
$$195 = 4.9t^2$$
$$t^2 = 39.8$$
$$t = \sqrt{39.8}.$$

Thus it takes about 6.31 seconds to reach the ground.

b) An object is thrown downward from the arch at an initial velocity of 16 m/sec. How long does it take to reach the ground?

We substitute 195 for s and 16 for v_0 and solve for t:

$$195 = 4.9t^2 + 16t$$
$$0 = 4.9t^2 + 16t - 195.$$

By the quadratic formula we obtain

$$t = -8.15 \quad \text{or} \quad t = 4.88.$$

The negative answer is meaningless in this problem, so the answer is 4.88 sec.

c) How far will an object fall in 3 seconds if it is thrown downward from the arch at an initial velocity of 16 m/sec?

We substitute 16 for v_0 and 3 for t and solve for s:

$$s = 4.9t^2 + v_0 t$$
$$= 4.9(3)^2 + 16 \cdot 3 = 92.1.$$

Thus the object falls 92.1 meters in 3 seconds.

[63]

Exercise Set 2.4

Solve each formula for the given variable, assuming all variables represent nonnegative numbers.

1. $F = \dfrac{kM_1 M_2}{d^2}$, for d

2. $E = mc^2$, for c

3. $S = \dfrac{1}{2} at^2$, for t

4. $V = 4\pi r^2$, for r

5. $s = -16t^2 + v_0 t$, for t

6. $A = 2\pi r^2 + 3\pi rh$, for r

7. $Ls^2 + Rs = c$, for s

8. $\sqrt{2} t^2 + 3k = \pi t$, for t

Solve for x.

9. $kx^2 + (3 - 2k)x - 6 = 0$

10. $mnx^2 + mn = (m^2 + n^2)x$

11. $(m + n)^2 x^2 + (m + n)x = 2$

12. $kx^2 - m(k + 1)x + m^2 = 0$

13. $x^2 - 2x + kx + 1 = kx^2$

14. $mx^2 - 2mx + 3x = 6$

15. Solve $x^2 - 3xy - 4y^2 = 0$
(a) for x; (b) for y.

16. Solve $3x^2 + 4xy + y^2 = 0$
(a) for x; (b) for y.

Applied problems

17. A ladder 10 ft long leans against a wall. The bottom of the ladder is 6 ft from the wall. How much would the lower end of the ladder have to be pulled away so that the top end would be pulled down the same amount?

18. A ladder 13 ft long leans against a wall. The bottom of the ladder is 5 ft from the wall. How much would the lower end of the ladder have to be pulled away so that the top end would be pulled down the same amount?

19. The area of a triangle is 18 cm². The base is 3 cm longer than the height. Find the height.

20. A baseball diamond is a square 90 ft on a side. How far is it directly from second base to home?

21. Trains A and B leave the same city at right angles at the same time. Train B travels 5 mph faster than train A. After 2 hr they are 50 mi apart. Find the speed of each train.

22. Trains A and B leave the same city at right angles at the same time. Train A travels 14 km/h faster than train B. After 5 hr they are 130 km apart. Find the speed of each train.

For Exercises 23 and 24 use the formula $s = 4.9t^2 + v_0 t$.

23. a) An object is dropped 75 m from a plane. How long does it take to reach the ground?
   b) An object is thrown downward from the plane at an initial velocity of 30 m/s. How long does it take to reach the ground?
   c) How far will an object fall in 2 sec, thrown downward at an initial velocity of 30 m/s?

24. a) An object is dropped 500 m from a plane. How long does it take to reach the ground?
   b) An object is thrown downward from the plane at an initial velocity of 30 m/s. How long does it take to reach the ground?
   c) How far will an object fall in 5 sec, thrown downward at an initial velocity of 30 m/s?

The following formula will be helpful in Exercises 25 through 28:

$$T = c \cdot N.$$

Total cost = (cost per item) · (number of items)

Total cost = (cost per person) · (number of persons)

25. A group of women share equally in the $140 cost of a boat. At the last minute 3 women drop out and this raises the share of each remaining woman $15. How many women were in the group at the outset?

26. A woman bought a group of lots for $8400. She sold all but 4 of them for the same price. The selling price for each lot was $350 greater than the cost. How many lots did she buy?

27. A man buys some stock for $720. If each share had cost $15 less he could have bought 4 more shares for the same $720. How many shares of stock did he buy?

28. A sorority is going to spend $112 for a party. When 14 new pledges join the sorority, this reduces each student's cost by $4. How much did it cost each student before?

29. The diagonal of a square is 1.341 cm longer than a side. Find the length of the side.

30. The hypotenuse of a right triangle is 8.312 cm long. The sum of the lengths of the legs is 10.23 cm. Find the lengths of the legs.

31. A rectangle of 12 cm² area is inscribed in the right triangle *ABC* as shown in the drawing. What are its dimensions?

32. A rectangle of 1500 m² area is inscribed in the right triangle *ABC* as shown in the drawing. What are its dimensions?

2.5 Radical Equations

A *radical equation* is an equation in which variables occur in one or more radicands. For example, $\sqrt[3]{x} + \sqrt[3]{4x - 7} = 2$. To solve such equations we need a new principle.

> *The principle of powers.* **For any number** n**, if an equation** $a = b$ **is true, then** $a^n = b^n$ **is true.**

This principle does *not* always yield equivalent equations. For example, the solution of $x = 3$ is 3. If we square both sides, we get $x^2 = 9$, which has solutions -3 and 3. As another example, consider $\sqrt{x} = -3$. At the outset we should note that this equation has no solution because, by definition, $\sqrt{x}$ must be a *nonnegative number*. Suppose, though, that we should try to solve by squaring both sides. We would get $(\sqrt{x})^2 = (-3)^2$, or $x = 9$. The number 9 does not check.

> **It is imperative when using the principle of powers to check possible solutions in the original equation.**

Example 1. Solve $x - 5 = \sqrt{x + 7}$.

$$(x - 5)^2 = (\sqrt{x + 7})^2 \qquad \text{(principle of powers; squaring both sides)}$$

$$x^2 - 10x + 25 = x + 7$$

$$x^2 - 11x + 18 = 0$$

$$(x - 9)(x - 2) = 0$$

$$x = 9 \qquad \text{or} \qquad x = 2$$

The possible solutions are 9 and 2. We check:

For 9:
$$\begin{array}{c|c} x - 5 = \sqrt{x + 7} \\ \hline 9 - 5 & \sqrt{9 + 7} \\ 4 & 4 \end{array}$$

For 2:
$$\begin{array}{c|c} x - 5 = \sqrt{x + 7} \\ \hline 2 - 5 & \sqrt{2 + 7} \\ -3 & 3 \end{array}$$

Since 9 checks but 2 does not, the only solution is 9.

[64, 65]

Example 2. Solve $\sqrt[3]{4x^2 + 1} = 5$.

$$(\sqrt[3]{4x^2 + 1})^3 = 5^3 \qquad \text{(principle of powers; cubing both sides)}$$

$$4x^2 + 1 = 125$$

$$4x^2 = 124$$

$$x^2 = 31$$

$$x = \pm\sqrt{31}$$

Both $\sqrt{31}$ and $-\sqrt{31}$ check. These are the solutions.

[66]

Sometimes we have to use the principle of powers more than once.

Example 3. Solve $\sqrt{2x - 5} = 1 + \sqrt{x - 3}$.

$$(\sqrt{2x - 5})^2 = (1 + \sqrt{x - 3})^2$$

$$2x - 5 = 1 + 2\sqrt{x - 3} + (x - 3)$$

$$x - 3 = 2\sqrt{x - 3}$$

$$(x - 3)^2 = (2\sqrt{x - 3})^2 \quad \text{(Get the radical alone, then square.)}$$

$$x^2 - 6x + 9 = 4(x - 3)$$

$$x^2 - 6x + 9 = 4x - 12$$

$$x^2 - 10x + 21 = 0$$

$$(x - 7)(x - 3) = 0$$

$$x = 7 \quad \text{or} \quad x = 3$$

The numbers 7 and 3 check. Thus the solutions are 7 and 3.

[67]

Example 4. Solve $A = \sqrt{1 + \dfrac{a^2}{b^2}}$, for a. Assume the variables represent nonnegative numbers.

$$A^2 = 1 + \frac{a^2}{b^2}$$

$$b^2 A^2 = b^2 + a^2$$

$$b^2 A^2 - b^2 = a^2$$

$$\sqrt{b^2 A^2 - b^2} = a$$

$$b\sqrt{A^2 - 1} = a$$

[68]

Exercise Set 2.5

Solve.

1. $\sqrt{3x - 4} = 1$

2. $\sqrt[3]{2x + 1} = -5$

3. $\sqrt[4]{x^2 - 1} = 1$

4. $\sqrt{m + 1} - 5 = 8$

5. $\sqrt{y - 1} + 4 = 0$

6. $5 + \sqrt{3x^2 + \pi} = 0$

7. $\sqrt{x - 3} + \sqrt{x + 5} = 4$

8. $\sqrt{x} - \sqrt{x - 5} = 1$

9. $\sqrt{3x - 5} + \sqrt{2x + 3} + 1 = 0$

10. $\sqrt{2m - 3} = \sqrt{m + 7} - 2$

11. $\sqrt[3]{6x + 9} + 8 = 5$

12. $\sqrt[3]{3x + 4} = 2$

13. $\sqrt{6x + 7} = x + 2$

14. $\sqrt{6x + 7} - \sqrt{3x + 3} = 1$

15. $\sqrt{20 - x} = \sqrt{9 - x} + 3$

16. $\sqrt{n + 2} + \sqrt{3n + 4} = 2$

17. $(x - 5)^{\frac{2}{3}} = 2$

18. $(x - 3)^{\frac{2}{3}} = 2$

19. $\dfrac{x + \sqrt{x + 1}}{x - \sqrt{x + 1}} = \dfrac{5}{11}$

20. $\sqrt{\sqrt{x + 25} - \sqrt{x}} = 5$

For Exercises 21 and 22 assume that the variables represent nonnegative numbers.

21. Solve $T = 2\pi\sqrt{\dfrac{m}{g}}$, for m; for g.

22. Solve $H = \sqrt{c^2 + d^2}$, for c.

Solve.

23. $\sqrt{7.35x + 8.051} = 0.345x + 0.067$

24. $\sqrt{1.213x + 9.333} = 5.343x + 2.312$

2.6 Equations Quadratic in Form

Look for a pattern.

a) $x + 3\sqrt{x} - 10 = 0$, let $u = \sqrt{x}$.
   Then $u^2 + 3u - 10 = 0$.

b) $x^4 - 6x^2 + 7 = 0$, let $u = x^2$.
   Then $u^2 - 6u + 7 = 0$.

c) $(x^2 - x)^2 - 14(x^2 - x) + 24 = 0$, let $u = x^2 - x$.
   Then $u^2 - 14u + 24 = 0$.

The original equations are not quadratic, but after an appropriate substitution of an expression in another variable, we get a quadratic equation. Equations like the original ones are said to be *quadratic in form*.

> **To solve equations quadratic in form we first make a substitution, solve for the new variable, then solve for the original variable.**

Example 1. Solve $x + 3\sqrt{x} - 10 = 0$.

Let $u = \sqrt{x}$. Then we solve the equation resulting from substituting u for $\sqrt{x}$:

$$u^2 + 3u - 10 = 0$$
$$(u + 5)(u - 2) = 0$$
$$u = -5 \quad \text{or} \quad u = 2$$

Now we substitute $\sqrt{x}$ for u and solve these equations:

$$\sqrt{x} = -5 \quad \text{or} \quad \sqrt{x} = 2$$
$$\text{(no solution)} \quad \text{or} \quad x = 4$$

The solution is 4. **[69]**

Example 2. Solve $x^4 - 6x^2 + 7 = 0$.

Let $u = x^2$. Then we solve the equation resulting from substituting u for x^2.

$$u^2 - 6u + 7 = 0$$
$$a = 1, b = -6, c = 7$$

$$u = \frac{-b \pm \sqrt{b^2 - 4ac}}{2a} = \frac{-(-6) \pm \sqrt{(-6^2) - 4 \cdot 1 \cdot 7}}{2 \cdot 1}$$

$$u = \frac{6 \pm \sqrt{8}}{2} = \frac{2 \cdot 3 \pm 2\sqrt{2}}{2 \cdot 1} = 3 \pm \sqrt{2}$$

Now we substitute x^2 for u and solve for x:

$$x^2 = 3 + \sqrt{2} \qquad \text{or} \qquad x^2 = 3 - \sqrt{2}$$
$$x = \pm\sqrt{3 + \sqrt{2}} \qquad \text{or} \qquad x = \pm\sqrt{3 - \sqrt{2}}$$

Thus we have the four solutions: $\sqrt{3 + \sqrt{2}}$, $-\sqrt{3 + \sqrt{2}}$, $\sqrt{3 - \sqrt{2}}$, and $-\sqrt{3 - \sqrt{2}}$.   **[70]**

Example 3. Solve $(x^2 - x)^2 - 14(x^2 - x) + 24 = 0$.

Let $u = x^2 - x$. Then we solve the equation resulting from substituting u for $x^2 - x$:

$$u^2 - 14u + 24 = 0$$
$$(u - 12)(u - 2) = 0$$
$$u = 12 \qquad \text{or} \qquad u = 2.$$

Now we substitute $x^2 - x$ for u and solve:

$$x^2 - x = 12 \qquad \text{or} \qquad x^2 - x = 2$$
$$x^2 - x - 12 = 0 \qquad \text{or} \qquad x^2 - x - 2 = 0$$
$$(x - 4)(x + 3) = 0 \qquad \text{or} \qquad (x - 2)(x + 1) = 0$$
$$x = 4 \text{ or } x = -3 \qquad \text{or} \qquad x = 2 \text{ or } x = -1.$$

The solutions are $4, -3, 2, -1$.   **[71]**

Example 4. Solve $t^{\frac{2}{5}} - t^{\frac{1}{5}} - 2 = 0$.

Let $u = t^{\frac{1}{5}}$. Then we solve the equation resulting from substituting u for $t^{\frac{1}{5}}$:

$$u^2 - u - 2 = 0$$
$$(u - 2)(u + 1) = 0$$
$$u = 2 \qquad \text{or} \qquad u = -1$$

Now we substitute $t^{\frac{1}{5}}$ for u and solve:

$$t^{\frac{1}{5}} = 2 \qquad \text{or} \qquad t^{\frac{1}{5}} = -1$$
$$t = 32 \quad \text{or} \quad t = -1 \qquad \text{(principle of powers;}$$
raising to the 5th power)

The solutions are 32 and -1.   **[72]**

AN APPLIED PROBLEM

Example. (*A well problem*). An object is dropped into a well. Two seconds later the sound of the splash is heard at the top. The speed of sound is 1100 ft/sec. How deep is the well?

a) Let s = the depth of the well. The formula for falling objects (p. 55) when the distance is in feet becomes

$$s = 16t^2 + v_0 t.$$

Since the object is dropped, $v_0 = 0$. The time t_1 that it takes for the object to reach the bottom of the well can be found as follows:

$$s = 16 t_1{}^2, \qquad \text{or} \qquad t_1 = \frac{\sqrt{s}}{4}.$$

b) Now how long does it take the sound of the splash to reach the top of the well? We can use the formula $d = rt$, and let $d = s$, $r = 1100$, and $t = t_2$, the time it takes the sound to get to the top. Then

$$s = 1100 \cdot t_2, \qquad \text{or} \qquad t_2 = \frac{s}{1100}.$$

c) The total time for the object to fall and the sound to get back to the top is given by

$$t_1 + t_2 = 2,$$

or

$$\frac{\sqrt{s}}{4} + \frac{s}{1100} = 2.$$

Then multiplying by 1100, we get

$$275\sqrt{s} + s = 2200$$

and

$$s + 275\sqrt{s} - 2200 = 0.$$

$$t_1 = \frac{\sqrt{s}}{4} \qquad s \qquad t_2 = \frac{s}{1100}$$

This equation is quadratic in form with $u = \sqrt{s}$. Substituting, we get

$$u^2 + 275u - 2200 = 0.$$

Using the quadratic formula we can solve for u:

$$u = \frac{-275 + \sqrt{275^2 + 8800}}{2} \quad \text{(We want the positive solution.)}$$

$$= \frac{-275 + \sqrt{84,425}}{2} \approx \frac{-275 + \sqrt{840 \cdot 100}}{2}$$

$$u = \frac{-275 + 10\sqrt{840}}{2}$$

$$\approx \frac{-275 + 10 \cdot 29}{2}$$

$$= \frac{15}{2} = 7.5.$$

Thus $u = 7.5 = \sqrt{s}$, so $s = 56.25$; that is, the well is about 56.25 ft deep.   [73]

Exercise Set 2.6

Solve.

1. $x - 10\sqrt{x} + 9 = 0$

2. $2x - 9\sqrt{x} + 4 = 0$

3. $x^4 - 10x^2 + 25 = 0$

4. $x^4 - 3x^2 + 2 = 0$

5. $t^{\frac{2}{3}} + t^{\frac{1}{3}} - 6 = 0$

6. $w^{\frac{2}{3}} - 2w^{\frac{1}{3}} - 8 = 0$

7. $z^{\frac{1}{2}} - z^{\frac{1}{4}} - 2 = 0$

8. $m^{\frac{1}{3}} - m^{\frac{1}{6}} - 6 = 0$

9. $(x^2 - 6x)^2 - 2(x^2 - 6x) - 35 = 0$

10. $(1 + \sqrt{x})^2 + (1 + \sqrt{x}) - 6 = 0$

11. $(y^2 - 5y)^2 + (y^2 - 5y) - 12 = 0$

12. $(2t^2 + t)^2 - 4(2t^2 + t) + 3 = 0$

13. $w^4 - 4w^2 - 2 = 0$

14. $t^4 - 5t^2 + 5 = 0$

15. $x^{-2} - x^{-1} - 6 = 0$

16. $4x^{-2} - x^{-1} - 5 = 0$

17. $2x^{-2} + x^{-1} - 1 = 0$

18. $m^{-2} + 9m^{-1} - 10 = 0$

19. $\left(\dfrac{x^2 - 2}{x}\right)^2 - 7\left(\dfrac{x^2 - 2}{x}\right) - 18 = 0$

20. $\left(\dfrac{x^2 + 1}{x}\right)^2 - 8\left(\dfrac{x^2 + 1}{x}\right) + 15 = 0$

21. $\dfrac{x}{x - 1} - 6\sqrt{\dfrac{x}{x - 1}} - 40 = 0$

22. $\dfrac{2x + 1}{x} - 7\sqrt{\dfrac{2x + 1}{x}} - 3 = 0$

23. $5\left(\dfrac{x + 2}{x - 2}\right)^2 - 3\left(\dfrac{x + 2}{x - 2}\right) - 2 = 0$

24. $\left(\dfrac{x + 1}{x + 3}\right)^2 + \left(\dfrac{x + 1}{x + 3}\right) - 6 = 0$

25. A stone is dropped from a cliff. In 3 sec the sound of the stone striking the ground reaches the top of the cliff. Assuming the speed of sound is 1100 ft/sec, how high is the cliff?

26. A stone is dropped from a cliff. In 4 sec the sound of the stone striking the ground reaches the top of the cliff. Assuming the speed of sound is 1100 ft/sec, how high is the cliff?

 Solve. Check possible solutions by substituting into the original equation.

27. $6.75x - \sqrt{35x} - 5.36 = 0$

28. $\pi x^4 - \pi^2 x^2 - \sqrt{99.3} = 0$

2.7 Variation

DIRECT VARIATION

There are many situations that yield linear equations like $y = kx$, where k is some positive number. Note that as x increases, y increases. In such a situation we say we have *direct variation*, and k is called the *variation constant*. Usually only positive values of x and y are considered.

> **Definition. If two variables x and y are related as in the equation $y = kx$, where k is a positive constant, we say that "y varies directly as x," or that "y is directly proportional to x."**

For example, the circumference C of a circle varies directly as its diameter D: $C = \pi D$. A car moves at a constant speed of 65 mph. The distance d it travels varies directly as the time t: $d = 65t$.

Example 1. Find an equation of variation where y varies directly as x, and $y = 5.6$ when $x = 8$.

We know $y = kx$, so $5.6 = k \cdot 8$ and $0.7 = k$. Thus $y = 0.7x$.   **[74]**

Suppose y varies directly as x. Then we have $y = kx$. When (x_1, y_1) and (x_2, y_2) are solutions of the equation, we have $y_1 = kx_1$ and $y_2 = kx_2$, and

$$\frac{y_2}{y_1} = \frac{kx_2}{kx_1} = \frac{k}{k} \cdot \frac{x_2}{x_1} = \frac{x_2}{x_1}.$$

The equation $y_2/y_1 = x_2/x_1$ is called a *proportion*. Such equations are helpful in solving applied problems.

Example 2. (*A spring problem*). *Hooke's law* states that the distance d an elastic object such as a spring is stretched by placing a certain weight on it varies directly as the weight w of the object. If the distance is 40 cm when the weight is 3 kg, what is the distance stretched when a 2-kg weight is attached?

Method 1. First find k using the first set of data. Then solve for d_2 using the second set of data.

$$d_1 = kw_1 \qquad d_2 = \frac{40}{3} \cdot w_2$$

$$40 = k \cdot 3 \qquad d_2 = \frac{40}{3} \cdot 2$$

$$\frac{40}{3} = k \qquad d_2 = \frac{80}{3}, \text{ or } 26.7 \text{ cm}$$

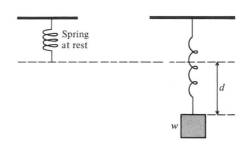

Method 2. Use a proportion to solve for d_2 without first finding the variation constant.

$$\frac{d_2}{d_1} = \frac{w_2}{w_1}$$

$$\frac{d_2}{40} = \frac{2}{3}$$

$$3 \cdot d_2 = 40 \cdot 2$$

$$d_2 = 26.7 \text{ cm} \qquad \textbf{[75–77]}$$

INVERSE VARIATION

Note that the graph of an equation of the type $y = k/x$, or $xy = k$, where k is a positive constant, looks like the figure below. As positive values of x increase, y decreases. In such a situation we say we have *inverse variation*, and k is called the *variation constant*. In applications we are usually only considering positive values of x and y.

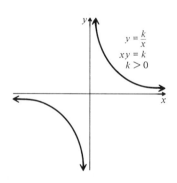

$y = \frac{k}{x}$
$xy = k$
$k > 0$

> **Definition.** If two variables x and y are related according to the equation $y = k/x$, where k is a positive constant, we say that "y varies inversely as x," or that "y is inversely proportional to x."

$$\textbf{[78]}$$

Suppose y varies inversely as x. Then we have $y = k/x$. When (x_1, y_1) and (x_2, y_2) are solutions of the equation, we have $y_1 = k/x_1$ and $y_2 = k/x_2$. Then

$$\frac{y_2}{y_1} = \frac{\dfrac{k}{x_2}}{\dfrac{k}{x_1}} = \frac{k}{x_2} \cdot \frac{x_1}{k} = \frac{k}{k} \cdot \frac{x_1}{x_2} = \frac{x_1}{x_2}.$$

The equation $y_2/y_1 = x_1/x_2$ is a proportion that also can be helpful in solving applied problems. Compare it to the proportion for direct variation. Note how the variables are interchanged.

Example 3. The length l of rectangles of fixed area is inversely proportional to the width w. (In other words, as the length is increased the width must be decreased to maintain the fixed area, and conversely.) Suppose the length is 64 cm when the width is 3 cm. Find the length when the width is 12 cm.

Method 1. First find k using the first set of data. Then solve for l_2.

$$l_1 = \frac{k}{w_1}$$

$$64 = \frac{k}{3}$$

$$k = 64 \cdot 3 = 192$$

$$l_2 = \frac{k}{w_2}$$

$$= \frac{192}{12} = 16 \text{ cm}$$

Method 2. Use a proportion to solve for l_2 without first finding the variation constant.

$$\frac{l_2}{l_1} = \frac{w_1}{w_2}$$

$$\frac{l_2}{64} = \frac{3}{12}$$

$$12 \cdot l_2 = 3 \cdot 64$$

$$l_2 = 16 \text{ cm} \qquad \textbf{[79]}$$

OTHER KINDS OF VARIATION

There are many other types of variation.

> **Definition.** *y* **varies directly as the square of** *x* **if there is some positive number** *k* **such that** $y = kx^2$.

For example, consider the equation for the area of a circle: $A = \pi r^2$. [80, 81]

> **Definition.** *y* **varies inversely as the square of** *x* **if there is some positive number** *k* **such that** $y = k/x^2$.

For example, the weight W of a body varies inversely as the square of the distance d from the center of the earth: $W = k/d^2$. [82, 83]

> **Definition.** *y* **varies** *jointly* **as** *x* **and** *z* **if there is some positive number** *k* **such that** $y = kxz$.

For example, consider the equation for the area of a triangle: $A = \frac{1}{2}bh$. The area varies jointly as b and h. The variation constant is $\frac{1}{2}$. [84, 85]

Several kinds of variation can occur together. For example, if $y = k \cdot xz^3/w^2$, then y varies jointly as x and the cube of z and inversely as the square of w. [86]

APPLIED PROBLEMS

Example 1. (*The volume of a tree*). The volume of wood V in a tree varies jointly as the height h and the square of the girth g (girth is distance around). If the volume is $7750 \, \text{ft}^3$ when the height is $100 \, \text{ft}$ and the girth is $5 \, \text{ft}$, what is the height when the volume is $37,975 \, \text{ft}^3$ and the girth is $7 \, \text{ft}$?

Method 1. First find k using the first set of data. Then solve for h_2 using the second set of data.

$$V_1 = k \cdot h_1 \cdot g_1^2$$
$$7750 = k \cdot 100 \cdot 5^2$$
$$3.1 = k$$

$$37,975 = 3.1 \cdot h_2 \cdot 7^2$$
$$250 = h_2$$
$$h_2 = 250 \, \text{ft}$$

Method 2. Use a proportion to solve for h_2 without first finding the variation constant.

$$\frac{V_2}{V_1} = \frac{h_2 \cdot g_2^2}{h_1 \cdot g_1^2}$$

$$\frac{37,975}{7750} = \frac{h_2 \cdot 7^2}{100 \cdot 5^2}$$

$$h_2 = 250 \, \text{ft} \qquad [87]$$

Example 2. (*The weight of an astronaut*). The weight W of an object varies inversely as the square of the distance d from the object to the center of the earth. At sea level (4000 mi from the center of the earth) an astronaut weighs 200 lb. Find his weight when he is 100 mi above the surface of the earth, and the spacecraft is not in motion.

We use the proportion

$$\frac{W_2}{W_1} = \frac{d_1^2}{d_2^2}$$

$$\frac{W_2}{200} = \frac{4000^2}{4100^2}$$

$$16,810,000 \cdot W_2 = 200 \cdot 16,000,000$$

$$W_2 = 190 \, \text{lb (to the nearest pound)}$$

$$[88]$$

Exercise Set 2.7

Find an equation of variation where:

1. y varies directly as x, and $y = 0.6$ when $x = 0.4$.

2. y varies inversely as x, and $y = 0.4$ when $x = 0.8$.

3. y varies inversely as the square of x, and $y = 0.15$ when $x = 0.1$.

4. y varies jointly as x and z, and $y = 56$ when $x = 7$ and $z = 10$.

5. y varies jointly as x and z and inversely as w, and $y = \frac{3}{2}$ when $x = 2$, $z = 3$, and $w = 4$.

6. y varies jointly as x and the square of z, and $y = 105$ when $x = 14$ and $z = 5$.

7. y varies jointly as x and z and inversely as the square of w, and $y = \frac{12}{5}$ when $x = 16$, $z = 3$, and $w = 5$.

8. y varies jointly as x and z and inversely as the product of w and p, and $y = \frac{3}{28}$ when $x = 3$, $z = 10$, $w = 7$, and $p = 8$.

9. Suppose y varies directly as x and x is doubled. What is the effect on y?

10. Suppose y varies inversely as x and x is tripled. What is the effect on y?

11. Suppose y varies inversely as the square of x and x is multiplied by n. What is the effect on y?

12. Suppose y varies directly as the square of x and x is multiplied by n. What is the effect on y?

13. The amount of pollution A entering the atmosphere varies directly as the amount of people N living in an area. If 60,000 people cause 42,600 tons of pollutants, how many tons entered the atmosphere in a city with a population of 750,000?

14. The volume V of a given mass of gas varies directly as the temperature T and inversely as the pressure P. If $V = 231$ in^3 when $T = 420°$ and $P = 20$ lb/sq in., what is the volume when $T = 300°$ and $P = 15$ lb/sq in.?

15. (*The strength of a beam*). The safe load (amount it supports without breaking) L of a beam varies jointly as its width w and the square of its height h and inversely as its length l. If the width and height are doubled at the same time the length is halved, what is the effect on L?

16. For a chord $\overline{PQ}$ through a fixed point A in a circle, the length of $\overline{PA}$ is inversely proportional to the length of $\overline{AQ}$. If the length of $\overline{PA} = 64$ when the length $\overline{AQ} = 16$, what is the length of $\overline{AQ}$ when the length of $\overline{PA} = 4$?

 17. (*A sighting problem*). The distance d that one can see to the horizon varies directly as the square root of the height above sea level. If a person 19.5 m above sea level can see 28.97 km, how high above sea level must one be to see 54.32 km?

18. (*Electrical resistance*). At a fixed temperature and chemical composition, the resistance of a wire varies directly as the length l and inversely as the square of the diameter d. If the resistance of a certain kind of wire is 0.112 ohms when the diameter is 0.254 cm and the length is 15.24 m, what is the resistance of a wire whose length is 608.7 m and whose diameter is 0.478 cm?

▶ **19.** Show that if u varies inversely as v, then $1/u$ varies directly as v.

20. The area of a circle varies as the square of the length of a diameter. What is the variation constant?

Chapter 2 Test, or Review

Solve.

1. $\dfrac{3x + 2}{7} - \dfrac{5x}{3} = \dfrac{32}{21}$

2. $(p - 3)(3p + 2)(p + 2) = 0$

3. $3x^2 + 2x - 8 = 0$

4. $\dfrac{6}{y} - \dfrac{1}{y} + \dfrac{1}{4y} = 10.5$

5. The sum of an odd integer and the next two even integers is 61. What are the integers?

6. Marlon can mow the lawn in 4 hr. His father can mow it in 2 hr. How long would it take if they worked together?

7. What is 9 percent of 50?

8. Solve by completing the square: $4z^2 + 8z - 64 = 0$.

9. Determine the nature of the solutions of $4y^2 + 5y + 1 = 0$.

10. Solve using the quadratic formula: $r^2 + 3r - 1 = 0$.

11. Write a quadratic equation whose solutions are -3 and $-\dfrac{1}{2}$.

12. Solve $v = \sqrt{2gh}$ for h.

13. Two airplanes leave the same airport at the same time flying at right angles to each other. In 2 hr they are 1300 km apart. The speed of one plane is 100 km/h more than twice the speed of the other plane. What is the speed of each plane?

14. Solve $y^4 - 3y^2 + 1 = 0$.

15. Solve $\sqrt{5x + 1} - 1 = \sqrt{3x}$.

16. Find an equation of variation where y varies inversely as the square of x, and $y = 0.005$ when $x = 10$.

17. For a body falling freely from rest, the distance (s ft) that the body falls varies directly as the square of the time (t sec). Given that $s = 64$ when $t = 2$, find a formula for s in terms of t. How long will it take the body to fall 900 ft?

CHAPTER **3**

Relations, Functions, and Transformations

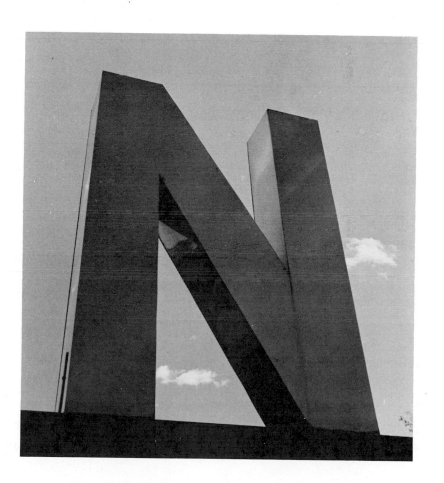

3.1 Relations and Ordered Pairs

For certain relations it is easy to determine a set of ordered pairs.

Example 1. Consider the set $\{2, 3, 5\}$ and the relation $<$ (is less than).

This gives rise to the following ordered pairs, in which the first member is less than the second:

$$(2, 3), \quad (2, 5), \quad (3, 5).$$

For certain sets of ordered pairs it is easy to determine a relation.

Example 2. Consider the set $\{2, 3, 5\}$ and the following set of ordered pairs:

$$\{(2, 2), (3, 3), (5, 5)\}.$$

In each ordered pair the first member is the same as the second.

This set of ordered pairs determines the relation $=$ (is equal to). **[1–3]**

Since relations and ordered pairs are so closely associated, we shall actually *define* a relation to *be* a set of ordered pairs. We shall do this after another concept is developed.

CARTESIAN PRODUCTS

The *Cartesian product* of two sets is a set of ordered pairs. It is the set of *all* ordered pairs having the first member from the first set and the second member from the second set. The Cartesian product of two sets A and B is symbolized $A \times B$.

Example 3. Consider sets A and B, where $A = \{1, 2, 3\}$ and $B = \{a, b\}$.

The Cartesian product, $A \times B$, is as follows:

$$(1, b) \quad (2, b) \quad (3, b)$$
$$(1, a) \quad (2, a) \quad (3, a)$$

Note that in each ordered pair of $A \times B$ the first member is taken from A and the second member is taken from B. **[4]**

The sets A and B may be the same set.

Example 4. Consider the set $\{2, 3, 4, 5\}$. The Cartesian product of this set by itself (this is called a *Cartesian square*) is as follows:

5	(2, 5)	(3, 5)	(4, 5)	(5, 5)
4	(2, 4)	(3, 4)	(4, 4)	(5, 4)
3	(2, 3)	(3, 3)	(4, 3)	(5, 3)
2	(2, 2)	(3, 2)	(4, 2)	(5, 2)
	2	3	4	5

The headings at the bottom and at the left are only for reference. The Cartesian square consists only of the ordered pairs. **[5]**

In a Cartesian product we can pick out ordered pairs that make up a common relation, such as $=$ or $<$ in the next examples.

Examples 5 and 6.

(2, 5)	(3, 5)	(4, 5)	**(5, 5)**
(2, 4)	(3, 4)	**(4, 4)**	(5, 4)
(2, 3)	**(3, 3)**	(4, 3)	(5, 3)
(2, 2)	(3, 2)	(4, 2)	(5, 2)

This is the relation $=$ (all ordered pairs in which the first member is equal to the second).

(2, 5)	**(3, 5)**	**(4, 5)**	(5, 5)
(2, 4)	**(3, 4)**	(4, 4)	(5, 4)
(2, 3)	(3, 3)	(4, 3)	(5, 3)
(2, 2)	(3, 2)	(4, 2)	(5, 2)

This is the relation < (all ordered pairs in which the first member is less than the second).

There are also many relations that do not have common names and relations with which we are not already familiar. Any time we select a set of ordered pairs from a Cartesian product, we have selected some relation. This is true even if we make the selection at random.

Example 7. The following set of ordered pairs is a relation, but is not a familiar one. It has no common name.

(2, 5)	(3, 5)	(4, 5)	**(5, 5)**
(2, 4)	(3, 4)	(4, 4)	(5, 4)
(2, 3)	(3, 3)	**(4, 3)**	(5, 3)
(2, 2)	(3, 2)	(4, 2)	**(5, 2)**

We shall now make our definition of relation.

> A *relation* from a set *A* to a set *B* is defined to be any set of ordered pairs in *A* × *B*.
>
> The set of all first members in a relation is called its *domain*.
>
> The set of all second members in a relation is called its *range*.

GRAPHS OF RELATIONS

To graph a relation from a set *A* to set *B*, we first lay out a diagram of the Cartesian product *A* × *B*. Then we show which of the ordered pairs are in the relation.

Examples. Examples 5, 6, and 7 are graphs of relations. In Example 6 the domain is {2, 3, 4}. The range is {3, 4, 5}. In Example 7 the domain is {2, 4, 5}. The range is {2, 3, 5}.   **[6]**

RELATIONS IN REAL NUMBERS

We shall be most interested in relations from *R*, the set of real numbers, to itself. To graph such relations, we picture *R* × *R* and then indicate which ordered pairs are in the relation. This is a familiar process. We draw an *x*-axis and a *y*-axis. Then each point of the plane corresponds to an ordered pair of real numbers.

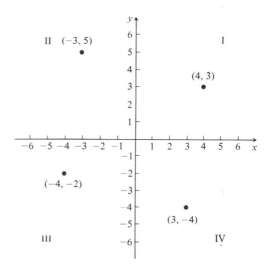

This is called a Cartesian coordinate system. The first member of an ordered pair is called the *first coordinate*. The second member is called the *second coordinate*.* Together these are called the *coordinates of a*

---
* The first coordinate is sometimes called the *abscissa* and the second coordinate the *ordinate*.

point. The axes divide the plane into four *quadrants,* indicated by the Roman numerals.

Following are some relations in real numbers.

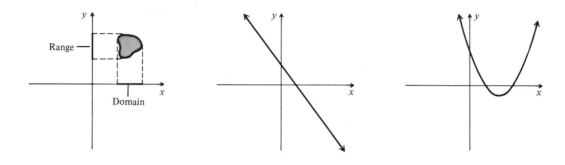

[7–9]

Exercise Set 3.1

For Exercises 1–6, consider the set $\{-1, 0, 1, 2\}$.

1. Find the set of ordered pairs determined by the relation $<$ (is less than).

2. Find the set of ordered pairs determined by the relation $>$ (is greater than).

3. Find the set of ordered pairs determined by the relation $\leq$ (is less than or equal to).

4. Find the set of ordered pairs determined by the relation $\geq$ (is greater than or equal to).

5. Find the set of ordered pairs determined by the relation $=$.

6. Find the set of ordered pairs determined by the relation $\neq$.

7. List all ordered pairs in the Cartesian product $A \times B$, where $A = \{0, 2, 4, 5\}$ and $B = \{a, b, c\}$. Remember that first coordinates come from A and second coordinates from B.

8. List all ordered pairs in the Cartesian product $A \times B$, where $A = \{1, 3, 5, 9\}$ and $B = \{d, e, f\}$. Remember that first coordinates come from A and second coordinates from B.

9. a) List all the ordered pairs in the Cartesian square $D \times D$, where $D = \{-1, 0, 1, 2\}$.

b) Graph the relation whose ordered pairs are $(0, 0)$, $(1, 1)$, $(0, 1)$, and $(1, 2)$.

c) List the domain and the range of this relation.

10. a) List all the ordered pairs in the Cartesian square $E \times E$, where $E = \{-1, 1, 3, 5\}$.

b) Graph the relation whose ordered pairs are $(-1, 1)$, $(1, 1)$, $(-1, 3)$, and $(1, 3)$.

c) List the domain and the range of this relation.

Use graph paper for the following exercises. For each, draw and label an x-axis and a y-axis, and label the quadrants. All relations to be considered are in $R \times R$, where R is the set of all real numbers.

11. Graph the relation in which the second coordinate is always 2 and the first coordinate may be any real number.

12. Graph the relation in which the first coordinate is always -3, and the second coordinate may be any real number.

13. Graph the relation in which the second coordinate is always 1 more than the first coordinate, and the first coordinate may be any real number.

14. Graph the relation in which the second coordinate is always 1 less than the first coordinate, and the first coordinate may be any real number.

15. Graph the relation in which the second coordinate is always twice the first coordinate, and the first coordinate may be any real number.

16. Graph the relation in which the second coordinate is always half the first coordinate, and the first coordinate may be any real number.

17. Graph the relation in which the second coordinate is always the square of the first coordinate, and the first coordinate may be any real number.

18. Graph the relation in which the first coordinate is always the square of the second coordinate, and the second coordinate may be any real number.

19. Graph a relation as follows:

a) Draw a circle with radius of length 2, centered at $(4, 3)$. Shade the circle and its interior.

b) Shade (on the x-axis) the domain. Describe the domain.

c) Shade (on the y-axis) the range. Describe the range.

20. Graph a relation as follows:

a) Draw a triangle with vertices at $(1, 1)$, $(4, 2)$, and $(3, 6)$. Shade the triangle and its interior.

b) Shade (on the x-axis) the domain. Describe the domain.

c) Shade (on the y-axis) the range. Describe the range.

3.2 Graphs of Equations

If an equation has two variables, its solutions arc pairs of numbers. We usually take the variables in alphabetical order, and hence get ordered pairs of numbers. Thus the solutions of an equation with two variables constitute a relation.

Example 1. The equation $y = 3x - 1$ has an infinite (unending) set of ordered pairs for solutions. Some of them are $(-1, -4)$, $(0, -1)$, and $(2, 5)$. The graph of this relation is also called the *graph of the equation,* and is a straight line, as shown. Thus the relation consists of all pairs (x, y) such that $y = 3x - 1$ is true. That is, $\{(x, y) \mid y = 3x - 1\}$.

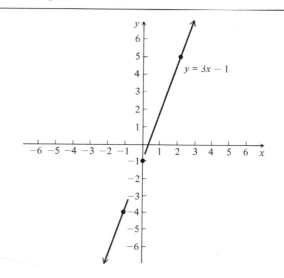

Example 2. Graph the equation $y = x^2 - 5$.

We select numbers for x and find the corresponding values for y. The table gives us the ordered pairs $(0, -5)$, $(-1, -4)$, and so on.

x	0	-1	1	-2	2	-3	3
y	-5	-4	-4	-1	-1	4	4

Next we plot these points. We note that as the absolute value of x increases, also x^2-5 increases. Thus the graph is a curve that rises gradually on either side of the y-axis, as follows.

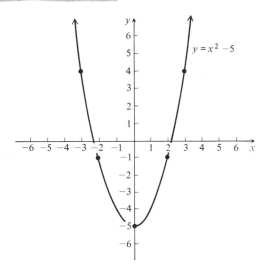

This graph shows the relation $\{(x, y) \mid y = x^2 - 5\}$.

Example 3. Graph the equation $x = y^2 + 1$.

Here we shall select numbers for y and then find the corresponding values for x.

x	2	2	1	5	5
y	-1	1	0	-2	2

We must remember that x is the first coordinate and y is the second coordinate. Thus the table gives us the ordered pairs $(2, -1)$, $(2, 1)$, $(1, 0)$, and so on. We note that as the absolute value of y gradually increases, the value of x also gradually increases. Thus the graph is a curve that stretches farther and farther to the right as it gets farther from the x-axis.

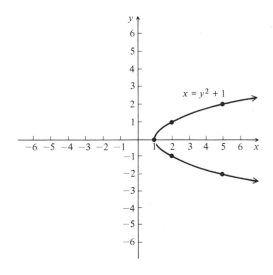

This graph shows the relation $\{(x, y) \mid x = y^2 + 1\}$.

[10]

Example 4. Graph the equation $xy = 12$.

We find numbers that satisfy the equation.

x	1	-1	2	-2	3	-3	4	-4	6	-6	12	-12
y	12	-12	6	-6	4	-4	3	-3	2	-2	1	-1

We plot these points, and connect them. To see how to do this, note that neither x nor y can be 0. Thus the graph does not cross either axis. As the absolute value of x gets small, the absolute value of y must get large, and conversely. Thus the graph consists of two curves, as follows.

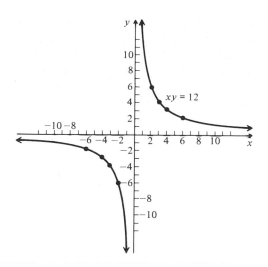

$xy = 12$

Example 5. Graph the equation $y = |x|$.

We find numbers that satisfy the equation.

x	0	1	−1	2	−2	3	−3	4	−4
y	0	1	1	2	2	3	3	4	4

We plot these points and connect them. To see how to do this, note that as we get farther from the origin, to the left or right, the absolute value of x increases. Thus the graph is a curve that rises to the left and right of the y-axis. It actually consists of parts of two straight lines, as follows.

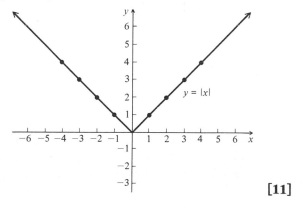

$y = |x|$

[11]

GRAPHS OF LINEAR EQUATIONS

An equation of the type $Ax + By + C = 0$ is called a *linear* equation because its graph is a straight line. In the above, A, B, and C are constants, but A and B cannot both be 0. Any equation that is equivalent to one of this form has a straight line graph.

Examples
a) The equation $5x + 8y = 3$ is linear because it is equivalent to $5x + 8y − 3 = 0$. Here, $A = 5$, $B = 8$, and $C = −3$.

b) The equation $3x^2 − 4y + 5 = 0$ is not linear because x is squared.

c) The equation $4x + 3xy = 25$ is not linear because the product xy occurs. [12]

Since two points determine a line, we can graph a linear equation by finding two of its points. Then we draw a line through those points.

A third point should always be used as a check. The easiest points to find are often the intercepts (the points where the line crosses the axes).

Example. Graph $4x + 5y = 20$.

We set $x = 0$ and find that $y = 4$. Thus $(0, 4)$ is a point of the graph (the y-intercept).

We set $y = 0$ and find that $x = 5$. Thus $(5, 0)$ is a point of the graph (the x-intercept). The graph is as follows.

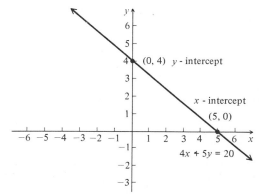

$(0, 4)$ y-intercept

x-intercept
$(5, 0)$

$4x + 5y = 20$

If an equation has a missing variable ($A = 0$ or $B = 0$), then its graph is parallel to one of the axes.

Examples

a)

b)

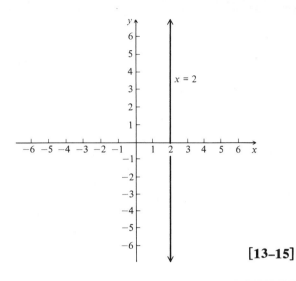

[13–15]

Exercise Set 3.2

In Exercises 1–12, graph the equations.

1. $y = x^2 + 2$ **2.** $y = x^2 - 2$ **3.** $x = y^2 + 2$ **4.** $x = y^2 - 2$

5. $xy = 10$ **6.** $xy = 18$ **7.** $xy = -10$ **8.** $xy = -18$

9. $y = |x + 1|$ **10.** $y = |x - 1|$ **11.** $x = |y + 1|$ **12.** $x = |y - 1|$

13. Which of the following are linear equations?

  a) $3y = 2x - 5$ b) $5x + 3 = 4y$ c) $3y = x^2 + 2$ d) $y = 3$

  e) $xy = 5$ f) $3x^2 + 2y = 4$ g) $3x + \dfrac{1}{y} = 4$ h) $5x - 2 = 4y$

14. Which of the following are linear equations?

  a) $5y = 3x - 4$ b) $3x + 5 = 7y$ c) $4y = 3x^2 - 4$ d) $x = -4$

  e) $2xy = 4$ f) $5x^2 + 3y = -4$ g) $4x - \dfrac{2}{y} = 3$ h) $6x - 7 = 3y$

Graph the following equations.

15. $8x - 3y = 24$ **16.** $5x - 10y = 50$ **17.** $3x + 12 = 4y$ **18.** $4x - 20 = 5y$

19. $y = -2$ **20.** $y = 6$ **21.** $x = 3$ **22.** $x = -7$

Graph and compare.

23. $y = x^2 + 1$ and $y = (-x)^2 + 1$ **24.** $y = x^2 - 2$ and $y = (-x)^2 - 2$

 Graph these equations.

25. $y = 3.21x^2 - 5.03x + 2.168$ **26.** $-1.055x^2 + 3.001x + 1.444$

▶ Graph these equations.

27. $y = |x^3|$ **28.** $y = \sqrt{x}$

3.3 Symmetry and Inverses

Two points are said to be *symmetric* with respect to a line if they are situated as shown below. That is, the points are the same distance from the line, measured along a perpendicular to the line. Another way to say this is that P and P_1 are symmetric with respect to the line l in a case where l is the perpendicular bisector of the segment $\overline{PP_1}$. The line l is known as a *line of symmetry*.

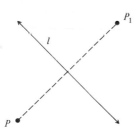

We say, too, that the two points above are *reflections* of each other across the line. The line is also, then, known as a *line of reflection*.

Now consider a set of points (geometric figure). We say that a figure, or set of points, is symmetric with respect to a line when each point in the set is symmetric with *some* point in the set. This is illustrated below. Imagine picking this figure up and flipping it over.

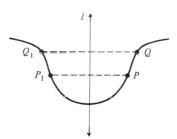

Points P and P_1 would be interchanged. Points Q and Q_1 would be interchanged. These are, then, pairs of symmetric points. The entire figure would look exactly like it did before flipping. This means that each point of the figure is symmetric with *some* point of the figure. Thus the figure is symmetric with respect to the line. A point and its reflection are known as *images* of each other. Thus P_1 is the image of P, for example. The line l is known as an *axis* of symmetry.

[16, 17]

SYMMETRY WITH RESPECT TO THE AXES

There are special and interesting kinds of symmetry in which the x-axis or the y-axis are lines of symmetry. The following example shows figures that are symmetric with an axis and a figure that is not.

Example 1.

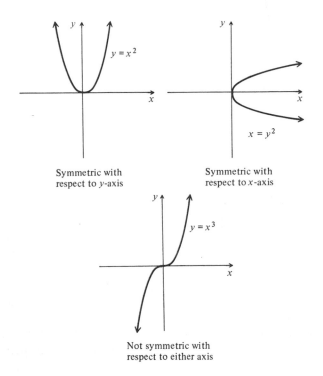

Symmetric with
respect to y-axis

Symmetric with
respect to x-axis

Not symmetric with
respect to either axis

In the first graph, flipping the figure about the y-axis would not change the figure. In the second graph, flipping about the x-axis would not change the figure. In the third case, flipping about either axis would change the figure.

Let us consider a figure like the first one, symmetric with respect to the y-axis. For every point of the figure there is another point the same distance across the y-axis. The first coordinates of such a pair of points are additive inverses of each other.

Example 2. In the relation $y = x^2$ there are points $(2, 4)$ and $(-2, 4)$. The first coordinates, 2 and -2, are additive inverses of each other, while the second coordinates are the same. For every point of the figure (x, y), there is another point $(-x, y)$.

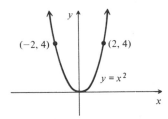

Let us consider a figure symmetric with respect to the x-axis. For every point of such a figure there is another point the same distance across the x-axis. The second coordinates of such a pair of points are additive inverses of each other.

Example 3. In the relation $x = y^2$ there are points $(4, 2)$ and $(4, -2)$. The second coordinates, 2 and -2, are additive inverses of each other, while the first coordinates are the same. For every point of the figure (x, y), there is another point $(x, -y)$.

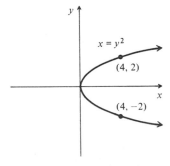

Let us consider a figure symmetric with respect to the y-axis, as in Example 2. Suppose it is defined by an equation. If in this equation we replace x by $-x$, we obtain a new equation, but we get the same figure. This is true because any number x gives us the same y-value as its additive inverse, $-x$.

Let us consider a figure symmetric with respect to the x-axis, as in Example 3. Suppose it is defined by an equation. If we replace y by $-y$ in this equation, we obtain a new equation, but we get the same figure. This is true because any number y gives us the same x-value as $-y$. We thus have a means of testing a relation for symmetry, when it is defined by an equation.

When a relation is defined by an equation:

1. **If replacing x by $-x$ produces an equivalent equation, then the graph is symmetric with respect to the y-axis.**
2. **If replacing y by $-y$ produces an equivalent equation, then the graph is symmetric with respect to the x-axis.**

Example 4. Test $y = x^2 + 2$ for symmetry with respect to the axes.

We replace x by $-x$, and obtain $y = (-x)^2 + 2$, which is equivalent to $y = x^2 + 2$. Therefore the graph is symmetric with respect to the y-axis.

We replace y by $-y$ and obtain $-y = x^2 + 2$, which is not equivalent to $y = x^2 + 2$. Therefore the graph is not symmetric with respect to the x-axis.

Example 5. Test $x^2 + y^4 - 5 = 0$ for symmetry with respect to the axes.

We replace x by $-x$, and obtain $(-x)^2 + y^4 - 5 = 0$, which is equivalent to the original equation. Therefore the graph is symmetric with respect to the y-axis.

We replace y by $-y$ and obtain $x^2 + (-y)^4 - 5 = 0$, which is equivalent to the original equation. Therefore the graph is symmetric with respect to the x-axis.

[18]

SYMMETRY WITH RESPECT TO A POINT

Two points are symmetric with respect to a point when they are situated as shown below. That is, the points are the same distance from that point, and all three points are on a line. Another way to say this is that the point Q (the point of symmetry) is the midpoint of segment $\overline{PP_1}$.

A *set* of points is symmetric with respect to a point when each point in the set is symmetric with some point in the set. This is illustrated below. Imagine sticking a pin in this figure at O and then rotating the figure 180°. Points P and P_1 would be interchanged. Points Q and Q_1 would be interchanged. These are pairs of symmetric points. The entire figure would look exactly as it did before rotating. This means that each point of the figure is symmetric with *some* point of the figure. Thus the figure is symmetric with respect to the point O.

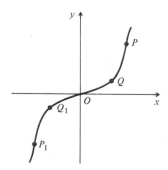

SYMMETRY WITH RESPECT TO THE ORIGIN

A special kind of symmetry with respect to a point is symmetry with respect to the origin.

Example 6. In the first two graphs, rotating the figure about the origin 180° would not change it. In the third graph such a rotation would change the figure.

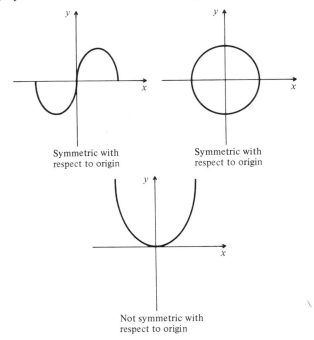

Symmetric with respect to origin

Symmetric with respect to origin

Not symmetric with respect to origin

Let us consider a figure like the first two above, symmetric with respect to the origin. For every point of the figure there is another point the same distance across the origin. The first coordinates of such a pair are additive inverses of each other, and the second coordinates are additive inverses of each other. **[19]**

Example 7. The relation $y = x^3$ is symmetric with respect to the origin. In this relation are the points $(2, 8)$ and $(-2, -8)$. The first coordinates are additive inverses of each other. The second coordinates are additive inverses of each other. For every point of the figure (x, y), there is another point $(-x, -y)$.

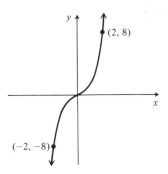

In a relation symmetric with respect to the origin, as in Example 7, if we replace x by $-x$ and y by $-y$, we obtain a new equation, but we will get the same figure. This is true because whenever a point (x, y) is in the relation, the point $(-x, -y)$ is also in the relation. This gives us a means for testing a relation for symmetry when it is defined by an equation.

> When a relation is defined by an equation, if replacing x by $-x$ and replacing y by $-y$ produces an equivalent equation, then the graph is symmetric with respect to the origin.

Example 8. Test $x^2 = y^2 + 2$ for symmetry with respect to the origin.

We replace x by $-x$ and y by $-y$, and obtain $(-x)^2 = (-y)^2 + 2$, which is equivalent to $x^2 = y^2 + 2$, the original equation. Therefore the graph is symmetric with respect to the origin. **[20]**

INVERSES OF RELATIONS

If in a relation we interchange first and second members in each ordered pair, we obtain a new relation. The new relation is called the *inverse* of the original relation. A relation is shown here; its inverse is shaded.

(1, 4)   **(2, 4)**   (3, 4)   (4, 4)

(1, 3)   (2, 3)   (3, 3)   (4, 3)

(1, 2)   (2, 2)   (3, 2)   (4, 2)

(1, 1)   (2, 1)   (3, 1)   (4, 1)   **[21]**

> **When a relation is defined by an equation, interchanging x and y produces an equation of the inverse relation.**

Example 9. Find an equation of the inverse of $y = x^2 - 5$.

We interchange x and y, and obtain $x = y^2 - 5$. This is an equation of the inverse relation.   **[22]**

Interchanging first and second coordinates in each ordered pair of a relation has the effect of interchanging the x-axis and the y-axis.   **[23]**

Interchanging the x-axis and the y-axis has the effect of reflecting across the diagonal line whose equation is $y = x$, as shown below. Thus the graphs of a relation and its inverse are always reflections of each other across the line $y = x$. (This assumes, of course, that the same scale is used on both axes.)

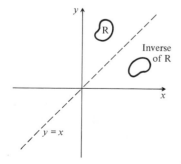

Here are some graphs of relations and their inverses.

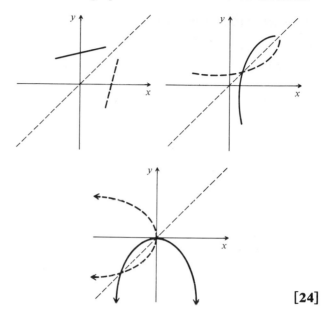

[24]

It can happen that a relation is its own inverse; that is, when x and y are interchanged, or the relation is reflected across the line $y = x$, there is no change. Such a relation is symmetric with respect to the line $y = x$.

> **When a relation is defined by an equation:**
>
> 1. **If interchanging x and y produces an equivalent equation, the relation is its own inverse, and**
> 2. **The graph of the equation is symmetric with respect to the line $y = x$.**

Example 10. Test the relation $3x + 3y = 5$ for symmetry with respect to the line $y = x$.

We interchange x and y in the equation, obtaining $3y + 3x = 5$. This is equivalent to the original equation, so the graph is symmetric with respect to the line $y = x$.   **[25]**

Exercise Set 3.3

Use graph paper for Exercises 1–6.

1. Plot $(3, -7)$ and the point symmetric to it with respect to the x-axis. List the coordinates of that point.

2. Plot $(-5, 2)$ and the point symmetric to it with respect to the x-axis. List the coordinates of that point.

3. Plot $(-4, 3)$ and the point symmetric to it with respect to the y-axis. List the coordinates of that point.

4. Plot $(1, -6)$ and the point symmetric to it with respect to the y-axis. List the coordinates of that point.

5. Plot $(-3, -6)$ and the point symmetric to it with respect to the origin. List the coordinates of that point.

6. Plot $(4, -5)$ and the point symmetric to it with respect to the origin. List the coordinates of that point.

In Exercises 7–18, test for symmetry with respect to the x-axis, the y-axis, and the origin.

7. $3y = x^2 + 4$ **8.** $5y = 2x^2 - 3$ **9.** $y^3 = 2x^2$ **10.** $3y^3 = 4x^2$

11. $2x^4 + 3 = y^2$ **12.** $3y^2 = 2x^4 - 5$ **13.** $2y^2 = 5x^2 + 12$ **14.** $3x^2 - 2y^2 = 7$

15. $2x - 5 = 3y$ **16.** $5y = 4x + 5$ **17.** $3y^3 = 4x^3 + 2$ **18.** $x^3 - 4y^3 = 12$

In Exercises 19–30, test for symmetry with respect to the origin.

19. $3x^2 - 2y^2 = 3$ **20.** $5y^2 = -7x^2 + 4$ **21.** $5x - 5y = 0$ **22.** $3x = 3y$

23. $3x + 3y = 0$ **24.** $7x = -7y$ **25.** $3x = \dfrac{5}{y}$ **26.** $3y = \dfrac{7}{x}$

27. $y = |2x|$ **28.** $3x = |y|$ **29.** $3x^2 + 4x = 2y$ **30.** $5y = 7x^2 - 2x$

In Exercises 31–42, test for symmetry with respect to the line $y = x$.

31. $3x + 2y = 4$ **32.** $5x - 2y = 7$ **33.** $4x + 4y = 3$ **34.** $5x + 5y = -1$

35. $xy = 10$ **36.** $xy = 12$ **37.** $3x = \dfrac{4}{y}$ **38.** $4y = \dfrac{5}{x}$

39. $y = |2x|$ **40.** $3x = |2y|$ **41.** $4x^2 + 4y^2 = 3$ **42.** $3x^2 + 3y^2 = 5$

In Exercises 43–49, write an equation of the inverse relation.

43. $y = 4x - 5$ **44.** $y = 3x + 5$ **45.** $x^2 - 3y^2 = 3$ **46.** $2x^2 + 5y^2 = 4$

47. $y = 3x^2 + 2$ **48.** $y = 5x^2 - 4$ **49.** $xy = 7$ **50.** $xy = -5$

51. Graph $y = x^2 + 1$. Then by reflection across the line $y = x$, graph its inverse.

52. Graph $y = x^2 - 3$. Then by reflection across the line $y = x$, graph its inverse.

53. Graph $y = |x|$. Then by reflection across the line $y = x$, graph its inverse.

54. Graph $x = |y|$. Then by reflection across the line $y = x$, graph its inverse.

---

55. Carefully graph $y = x^2$, using a large scale. Then use the graph to approximate $\sqrt{3.1}$.

56. Carefully graph $y = x^3$, using a large scale. Then use the graph to approximate $\sqrt[3]{-5.2}$.

3.4 Functions

A *function* is a special kind of relation. It is defined as follows.

> A *function* is a relation in which no two ordered pairs have the same first coordinate and different second coordinates.

In a function, given a member of the domain, there is one and only one member of the range that goes with it (the second coordinate). Thus each member of the domain *determines* a member of the range, but only one member. It is easy to recognize the graph of a relation which is a function. If there are two or more points of the graph on the same vertical line, then the relation is not a function. Otherwise it is. Here are some graphs of functions.

a)   b)

c)

In graph (c), the solid dot indicates that $(-1, 1)$ belongs to the graph. The open dot indicates that $(-1, -2)$ does not belong to the graph. Thus no vertical line crosses the graph more than once.

The following are not graphs of functions, because they fail the so-called *vertical line test*. That is, we can find a vertical line that meets the graph in more than one point.

a)   b)

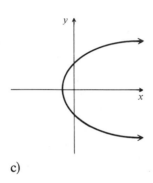

c)

✓ Every function has an inverse, but that inverse may not be a function, as the following example shows.

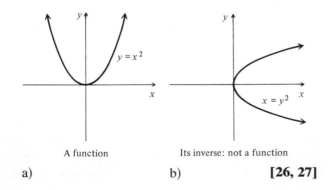

$y = x^2$

$x = y^2$

A function   Its inverse: not a function

a)   b)   [26, 27]

NOTATION FOR FUNCTIONS

Functions are often named by letters, such as f or g. A function f is thus a set of ordered pairs. If we represent the first coordinate of a pair by x, then we may represent the second coordinate by $f(x)$. The symbol $f(x)$ is read "f of x" or "f at x." The number represented by $f(x)$ is called the "value" of the function at x. [*Note:* "$f(x)$" does *not* mean "f times x."]

Example 1. Let us call the function shaded below g.

(1, 4)	(2, 4)	(3, 4)	**(4, 4)**
(1, 3)	**(2, 3)**	(3, 3)	(4, 3)
(1, 2)	(2, 2)	**(3, 2)**	(4, 2)
(1, 1)	(2, 1)	(3, 1)	(4, 1)

Here $g(1) = 4$, $g(2) = 3$, $g(3) = 2$, and $g(4) = 4$.

Example 2. Let us call this function f. To find function values, we locate x on the x-axis, and then find $f(x)$ on the y-axis.

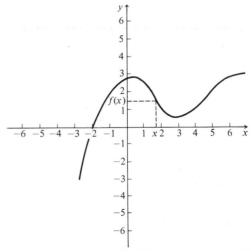

From this graph we can see that $f(-2) = 0$, and that $f(0)$ is about 2.7, and $f(3)$ is about 0.6.   **[28, 29]**

Some functions in real numbers can be defined by formulas, or equations. Here are some examples:

$$g(s) = 3,$$

$$p(t) = \frac{1}{t},$$

$$f(x) = 3x^2 + 4x - 5,$$

$$u(y) = |y| + 3.$$

A function such as g above is called a *constant function* because all of its function values are the same. The range contains only one number, 3.

Example 3. Let $f(x) = 2x^2 - 3$. We can find function values as follows:

a) $\quad f(0) = 2 \cdot 0^2 - 3 = -3$

b) $\quad f(-1) = 2(-1)^2 - 3 = 2 \cdot 1 - 3 = -1$

c) $\quad f(5a) = 2(5a)^2 - 3 = 2 \cdot 25a^2 - 3 = 50a^2 - 3$

d) $\quad f(a - 4) = 2(a - 4)^2 - 3 = 2(a^2 - 8a + 16) - 3$

$$= 2a^2 - 16a + 29$$

e) $\quad \dfrac{f(a + h) - f(a)}{h} = \dfrac{[2(a + h)^2 - 3] - [2a^2 - 3]}{h}$

$$= \dfrac{2a^2 + 4ah + 2h^2 - 3 - 2a^2 + 3}{h}$$

$$= \dfrac{4ah + 2h^2}{h} = 4a + 2h$$

When a function is defined by a formula, its domain is understood to be the set of all real numbers for which the formula makes sense.

Examples

a) If $g(x) = x/(x - 1)$, the domain of g is the set of all real numbers except 1 (because 1 makes the denominator 0).

b) If $t(s) = \sqrt{s}$, the domain of t is the set of all nonnegative real numbers (no negative number has a square root).   **[30]**

FUNCTIONS, MAPPINGS, MACHINES, AND INVERSES

Functions can be thought of as mappings. A function f *maps* the set of first coordinates (the domain) to the set of second coordinates (the range).

As in this diagram, each x in the domain corresponds to (or is mapped onto) just one y in the range. That y is the second coordinate of the ordered pair (x, y).

Example 4. Consider the function f for which $f(x) = 2x + 3$.

Since $f(0)$ is 3, this function maps 0 to 3.
Since $f(3) = 9$, this function maps 3 to 9.

The concept of function is illuminated somewhat by considering a so-called "function machine." In this drawing we see a function machine designed, or programmed, to do the mapping (function) f. The acceptable inputs to the machine are the members of the domain of f. The outputs are, of course, members of the range of f.

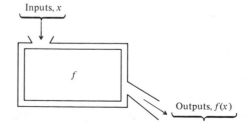

All functions have inverses, but in only some cases is the inverse also a function. If the inverse of a function f is also a function, we denote it by f^{-1} (read "f inverse"). [*Caution:* This is *not* exponential notation!] Recall we obtain the inverse of any relation by reversing the coordinates in each ordered pair. In terms of mappings, let us see what this means. Compare the following with the preceding diagram. The inverse mapping f^{-1} maps the range of f onto the domain of f. Each y in R is mapped onto just one x in D, provided f^{-1} is a function. That x is the first coordinate of the ordered pair (x, y). Note that the domain of f is the range of f^{-1} and the range of f is the domain of f^{-1}.

Let us consider inverses of functions in terms of function machines. Suppose that the function f programmed into the above machine has an inverse that is also a function. Suppose then that the function machine has a reverse switch. When the switch is thrown the machine is then programmed to do the inverse mapping f^{-1}. Inputs then enter at the opposite end and the entire process is reversed.

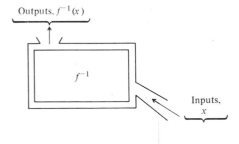

When a function is defined by a formula, we can sometimes find a formula for its inverse by thinking of interchanging x and y.

Example 5. Given $f(x) = x + 1$, find a formula for $f^{-1}(x)$.

a) Let us think of this as $y = x + 1$.

b) To find the inverse we interchange x and y:
$x = y + 1$.

c) Now we solve for y: $y = x - 1$.

d) Thus $f^{-1}(x) = x - 1$.

Note in Example 5 that f maps any x onto $x + 1$ (this function adds 1 to each number of the domain). Its inverse, f^{-1}, maps any number x onto $x - 1$ (this inverse function subtracts 1 from each member of its domain). Thus the function and its inverse do opposite things.

Example 6. Let $g(x) = 2x + 3$. Find a formula for $g^{-1}(x)$.

a) Let us think of this as $y = 2x + 3$.

b) To find the inverse we interchange x and y:
$x = 2y + 3$.

c) Now we solve for y: $y = (x - 3)/2$.

d) Thus $g^{-1}(x) = (x - 3)/2$.

Note in Example 6 that g maps any x onto $2x + 3$ (this function doubles each input and then adds 3). Its inverse, g^{-1}, maps any input onto $(x - 3)/2$ (this inverse function subtracts 3 from each input and then divides it by 2). Thus the function and its inverse do opposite things.

Example 7. Let $S(x) = \sqrt{x}$. Find a formula for $S^{-1}(x)$.

a) Let us think of this as $y = \sqrt{x}$. Note that the domain and range both consist of just nonnegative numbers.

b) To find the inverse we interchange x and y:
$x = \sqrt{y}$.

c) Now we solve for y, squaring both sides: $y = x^2$.

d) Thus $S^{-1}(x) = x^2$, with the understanding that x cannot be negative.

Note in Example 7 that S maps any x onto $\sqrt{x}$ (this function takes the square root of any input). Its inverse, S^{-1}, maps any number x onto x^2 (this function squares each input; thus the function and its inverse do opposite things).   **[31, 32]**

Suppose the inverse of a function f is also a function. Let us suppose that we do the mapping f and then do the inverse mapping f^{-1}. We will be back where we started. In other words, if we find $f(x)$ for some x and then find f^{-1} for this number, we will be back at x. In function notation the statement looks like this:

$$f^{-1}(f(x)) = x.$$

This is read "f inverse of f of x equals x." It means, working from the inside out, to take x, then find $f(x)$, and then find f^{-1} for that number. When we do, we will be back where we started, at x. For similar reasons, the following is also true:

$$f(f^{-1}(x)) = x.$$

For the above statements to be true, x must of course be in the domain of the function being considered.

Let us consider function machines. To find $f^{-1}(f(x))$ we use x as an input, when the machine is set on f. We then use the output for an input, running the machine backward. The last output is the same as the first input. The first output must of course be an acceptable input when the machine is set on f^{-1}. Following is a precise statement of the property.

> **Theorem.** For any function f whose inverse is a function, $f^{-1}(f(a)) = a$ for any a in the domain of f. Also, $f(f^{-1}(a)) = a$ for any a in the domain of f^{-1}.

Example 8. For the function g of Example 6, find $g(4)$. Then find $g^{-1}(g(4))$.

$$g(x) = 2x + 3, \qquad \text{so} \qquad g(4) = 11$$

Now
$$g^{-1}(x) = \frac{x - 3}{2},$$

so
$$g^{-1}(11) = \frac{11 - 3}{2} = 4.$$

Thus
$$g^{-1}(g(4)) = 4. \qquad \text{[33]}$$

Example 9. For the function g of Example 6, find $g^{-1}(g(283))$. Find also $g(g^{-1}(-12,045))$.

We note that every real number is in the domain of both g and g^{-1}. Thus we may immediately write the answers, without calculating.

$$g^{-1}(g(283)) = 283,$$
$$g(g^{-1}(-12,045)) = -12,045. \qquad \text{[34]}$$

COMPOSITION OF FUNCTIONS

Functions can be combined in a way called *composition* of functions. Consider, for example,

$$f(x) = x^2 \qquad \text{(This function squares each input.)}$$

and

$$g(x) = x + 1. \qquad \text{(This function adds 1 to each input.)}$$

We define a new function that first does what g does (adds 1) and then does what f does (squares). The new function is called the *composition* of f and g, and is symbolized $f \circ g$. Let us think of hooking two function

A composition machine for
$f \circ g$

machines f and g together to get the resultant function machine $f \circ g$.

> **Definition.** The composed function $f \circ g$ is defined as follows: $f \circ g(x) = f(g(x))$.

Now let us see how to find a formula for $f \circ g$, and also the reverse composition $g \circ f$.

Example 1. Given that $f(x) = x^2$ and $g(x) = x + 1$, find formulas for $f \circ g(x)$ and $g \circ f(x)$.

By definition of $\circ$,

$$f \circ g(x) = f(g(x)).$$

Now

$$f(g(x)) = f(x + 1) \qquad \text{(substituting } x + 1 \text{ for } g(x)\text{)}$$
$$= (x + 1)^2 \qquad \text{(substituting } x + 1 \text{ for } x \text{ in the formula for } f(x)\text{)}$$
$$= x^2 + 2x + 1.$$

Similarly,

$$g \circ f(x) = g(x^2) \qquad \text{(substituting } x^2 \text{ for } f(x)\text{)}$$
$$= x^2 + 1. \qquad \text{(substituting } x^2 \text{ for } x \text{ in the formula for } g(x)\text{)}$$

Note that the function $f \circ g$ is not the same as the function $g \circ f$.

In order for functions to be composable, such as f and g above, the outputs of g must be acceptable as inputs for f. In other words, if any number $g(x)$ is not in the domain of f, then x is not in the domain of $f \circ g$. Note also the order of happenings in $f \circ g$. The function $f \circ g$ does *first* what g does, then what f does. **[35]**

Example 2. Let $f(x) = 2x$ and $g(x) = x^2 + 1$. Find $f \circ g(x)$ and $g \circ f(x)$.

By definition of $\circ$,

$$f \circ g(x) = f(g(x))$$
$$= f(x^2 + 1) \qquad \text{(substituting } x^2 + 1 \text{ for } g(x)\text{)}$$
$$= 2(x^2 + 1) \qquad \text{(substituting } x^2 + 1 \text{ for } x \text{ in the formula for } f(x)\text{)}$$
$$= 2x^2 + 2$$

Similarly,

$$g \circ f(x) = g(f(x))$$
$$= g(2x) \qquad \text{(substituting } 2x \text{ for } f(x)\text{)}$$
$$= (2x)^2 + 1 \qquad \text{(substituting } 2x \text{ for } x \text{ in the formula for } g(x)\text{)}$$
$$= 4x^2 + 1.$$

The following diagram helps to show how substitutions are made. We find $f \circ g(x)$.

$$g(x) = x^2 + 1$$

$$f \circ g(x) = f(g(x)) = f(x^2 + 1)$$

$$f(x) = 2x \qquad = 2(x^2 + 1) = 2x^2 + 2 \quad \textbf{[36]}$$

Exercise Set 3.4

1. Which of the following are graphs of functions?

a)   b)

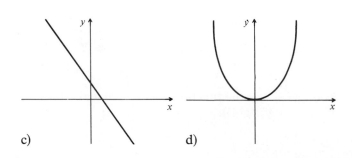

c)   d)

2. Which of the following are graphs of functions?

a)

b)

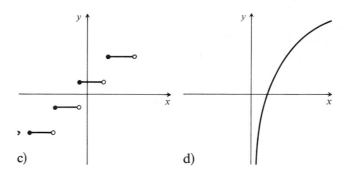

c)

d)

3. Which of the relations of Exercise 1 have inverses that are functions?

4. Which of the relations of Exercise 2 have inverses that are functions?

5. From this graph, find approximately $g(-2)$, $g(-3)$, $g(0)$, and $g(2)$.

6. From this graph, find approximately, $h(-2)$, $h(0)$, $h(3)$, and $h(-3)$.

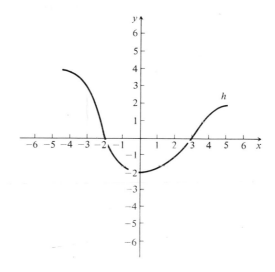

7. $f(x) = 5x^2 + 4x$. Find:

   a) $f(0)$

   b) $f(-1)$

   c) $f(3)$

   d) $f(t)$

   e) $f(t - 1)$

   f) $\dfrac{f(a + h) - f(a)}{h}$

8. $g(x) = 3x^2 - 2x$. Find:

   a) $g(0)$

   b) $g(-1)$

   c) $g(3)$

   d) $g(t)$

   e) $g(a + h)$

   f) $\dfrac{g(a + h) - g(a)}{h}$

9. $f(x) = 2|x| + 3x$. Find:

a) $f(1)$ b) $f(-2)$

c) $f(-4)$ d) $f(2y)$

e) $f(a + h)$ f) $\dfrac{f(a + h) - f(a)}{h}$

10. $g(x) = 3|x| - 2x$. Find:

a) $g(1)$ b) $g(-2)$

c) $g(-4)$ d) $g(3y)$

e) $g(2 + h)$ f) $\dfrac{g(2 + h) - g(2)}{h}$

11. $f(x) = 2x + 5$. Find a formula for $f^{-1}(x)$.

12. $g(x) = 3x - 1$. Find a formula for $g^{-1}(x)$.

13. $f(x) = \sqrt{x + 1}$. Find a formula for $f^{-1}(x)$.

14. $g(x) = \sqrt{x - 1}$. Find a formula for $g^{-1}(x)$.

15. $f(x) = 35x - 173$. Find $f^{-1}(f(3))$.
Find $f(f^{-1}(-125))$.

16. $g(x) = \dfrac{-173x + 15}{3}$. Find $g^{-1}(g(5))$.
Find $g(g^{-1}(-12))$.

17. $f(x) = x^3 + 2$. Find $f^{-1}(f(12{,}053))$.
Find $f(f^{-1}(-17{,}243))$.

18. $g(x) = x^3 - 486$. Find $g^{-1}(g(489))$.
Find $g(g^{-1}(-17{,}422))$.

In Exercises 19–24, find $f \circ g(x)$ and $g \circ f(x)$.

19. $f(x) = 3x^2 + 2,$ $g(x) = 2x - 1$

20. $f(x) = 4x + 3,$ $g(x) = 2x^2 - 5$

21. $f(x) = 4x^2 - 1,$ $g(x) = \dfrac{2}{x}$

22. $f(x) = \dfrac{3}{x},$ $g(x) = 2x^2 + 3$

23. $f(x) = x^2 + 1,$ $g(x) = x^2 - 1$

24. $f(x) = \dfrac{1}{x^2},$ $g(x) = x + 2$

25. $f(x) = 4.3x^2 - 1.4x$. Find:

a) $f(1.034)$ b) $f(-3.441)$ c) $f(27.35)$ d) $f(-16.31)$

26. $g(x) = \sqrt{2.2|x| + 3.5}$. Find:

a) $g(17.3)$ b) $g(-64.2)$ c) $g(0.095)$ d) $g(-6.33)$

▶ **27.** Is it ever possible, for functions f and g, for $f \circ g$ to be the same as $g \circ f$?

28. The *greatest integer* function $y = [x]$ is defined as follows: $[x]$ is the greatest integer that is less than or equal to x. Graph the greatest integer function for values of x from -5 to 5.

3.5 Transformations

Given a relation, we can find various ways of altering it to obtain another relation. Such an alteration is called a *transformation*. If such an alteration consists merely of moving the graph without changing its shape or orientation, the transformation is called a *translation*.

VERTICAL TRANSLATIONS

Consider the relation $y = x^2$, whose graph is shown.

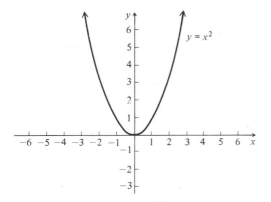

We will compare it with the graph of $y = 1 + x^2$. **[37]**

The graph of $y = 1 + x^2$ has the same shape as that of $y = x^2$, but is moved upward a distance of 1 unit. Consider any equation $y = f(x)$. Adding a constant a to produce $y = a + f(x)$ changes each function value by the same amount, a, hence produces no change in the shape of the graph, but merely translates it upward if the constant is positive. If a is negative, the graph will be moved downward.

Note that $y = 1 + x^2$ is equivalent to $y - 1 = x^2$. Thus the transformation above amounts to replacing y by $y - 1$ in the original equation.

> **Theorem. In an equation of a relation, replacing y by $y - a$, where a is a constant, translates the graph vertically a distance of $|a|$. If a is positive, the translation is upward. If a is negative, the translation is downward.**

If in an equation we replace y by $y + 3$, this is the same as replacing it by $y - (-3)$. In this case the constant a is -3 and the translation is downward. If we replace y by $y - 5$, the constant a is 5 and the translation is upward.

Example 1. Sketch a graph of $y = |x|$ and then $y = -2 + |x|$.

The graph of $y = |x|$ is shown below on the left. Now consider $y = -2 + |x|$. We are subtracting 2 from each function value, so the translation is downward. To see this another way, note that $y = -2 + |x|$ is equivalent to $y + 2 = |x|$ or $y - (-2) = |x|$. This shows the new equation can be obtained by replacing y by $y - (-2)$, so the translation is downward, two units, as shown below on the right.   **[38, 39]**

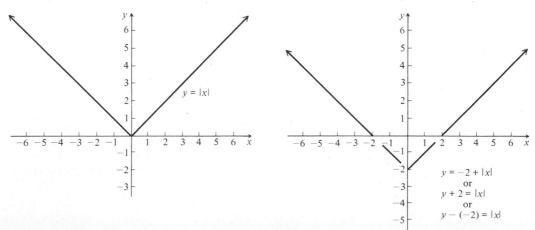

HORIZONTAL TRANSLATIONS

Replacing y by $y - a$ in an equation translates vertically a distance of $|a|$. The translation is in the positive direction (upward) if a is positive. A similar thing happens in the horizontal direction. If we replace x by $x - b$ everywhere it occurs in the equation, we translate a distance of $|b|$ horizontally. If b is positive, we translate in the positive direction (to the right).

> **Theorem. In an equation of a relation, replacing x by $x - b$, where b is a constant, translates the graph horizontally a distance of $|b|$. If b is positive, the translation is to the right. If b is negative, the translation is to the left.**

Example 2. Given a graph of $y = |x|$, sketch a graph of $y = |x + 2|$.

Here we note that x is replaced by $x + 2$, or $x - (-2)$. Thus $b = -2$, and the translated graph will be moved two units in the negative direction (to the left).

[40, 41]

Note that it is not only functions that can be translated. The rules we have just developed hold for any relations.

Example 3. A circle centered at the origin with radius of length 1 has an equation $x^2 + y^2 = 1$. If we replace x by $x - 1$ and y by $y + 2$, we translate the circle so that the center is at the point $(1, -2)$.

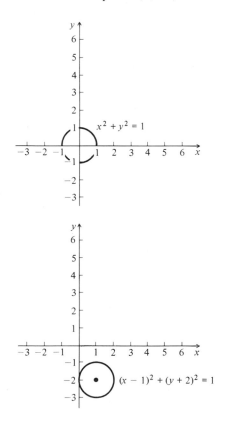

VERTICAL STRETCHINGS AND SHRINKINGS

Consider the function $y = |x|$. We will compare its graph with that of $y = 2|x|$ and $y = (1/2)|x|$.

The graph of $y = 2|x|$ looks like that of $y = |x|$ but is stretched in a vertical direction. The graph of $y = (1/2)|x|$ is flattened or shrunk in a vertical direction.

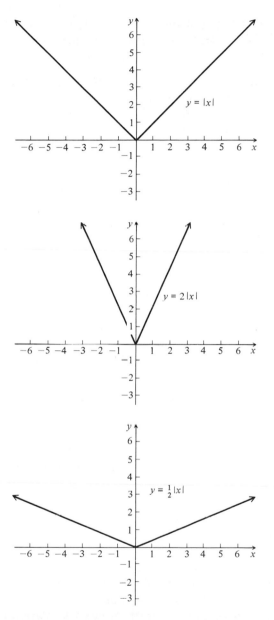

and 1, then the graph will be flattened or shrunk vertically.   [42, 43]

When we multiply by a negative constant, the graph is reflected across the x-axis as well as being stretched or shrunk.

Example 4. Compare the graphs of $y = |x|$, $y = -2|x|$, and $y = -\frac{1}{2}|x|$.

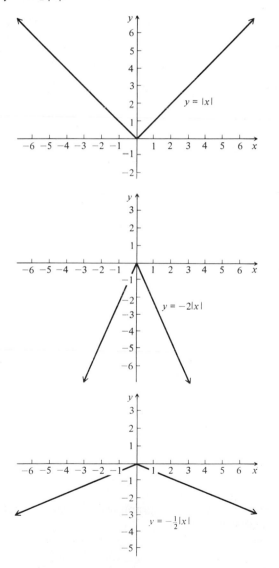

Consider any equation such as $y = f(x)$. Multiplying on the right by the constant 2 will double every function value, thus stretching the graph both ways from the horizontal axis. A similar thing is true for any constant greater than 1. If the constant is between 0

Theorem. In an equation of a function $y = f(x)$, multiplying on the right by a constant c does the following to the graph.
1. **If $|c| > 1$, the graph is stretched vertically.**
2. **If $|c| < 1$, the graph is shrunk vertically.**
3. **If c is negative, the graph is also reflected across the x-axis.**

Note that if $c = -1$, this has the effect of replacing y by $-y$ and we obtain a reflection without stretching or shrinking.

Example 5. Here is a graph of $y = f(x)$. Sketch a graph of $y = 2f(x)$.

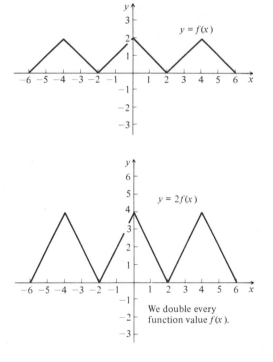

Example 6. Here is a graph of $y = g(x)$. Sketch a graph of $y = -\frac{1}{2}g(x)$.

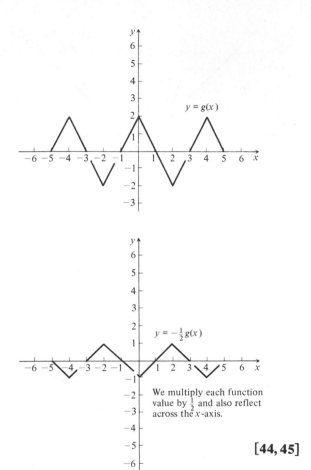

We multiply each function value by $\frac{1}{2}$ and also reflect across the x-axis.

[44, 45]

HORIZONTAL STRETCHINGS AND SHRINKINGS

For vertical stretchings and shrinkings we considered an equation such as $y = f(x)$. We multiplied on the right by a constant c. This would amount to multiplying y by $1/c$ wherever it occurs. Similarly, if we multiply x by a constant wherever it occurs, we will get a horizontal stretching or shrinking. If the constant is greater than 1, a shrinking will occur.

> **Theorem.** In an equation of a relation, replacing x wherever it occurs by dx, where d is a constant, does the following to the graph.
> 1. If $|d| > 1$, the graph is shrunk horizontally.
> 2. If $|d| < 1$, the graph is stretched horizontally.
> 3. If d is negative, the graph is also reflected across the y-axis.

A shrinking. Cut each x-value in half.

Note that if $d = -1$, this has the effect of replacing x by $-x$ and we obtain a reflection without stretching or shrinking.

A stretching. Double each x-value.

Example 7. Here is a graph of $y = f(x)$. Sketch a graph of $y = f(2x)$, a graph of $y = f(\frac{1}{2}x)$, and a graph of $y = f(-\frac{1}{2}x)$.

A stretching and a reflection across the x-axis.

[46–49]

Exercise Set 3.5

Here is a graph of $y = |x|$. In Exercises 1–20 sketch graphs by transforming this one.

1. $y = 2 + |x|$ **2.** $y = 3 + |x|$ **3.** $y = -1 + |x|$ **4.** $y = -2 + |x|$

5. $y = |x - 1|$ **6.** $y = |x - 3|$ **7.** $y = |x + 2|$ **8.** $y = |x + 3|$

9. $y = 4\,|x|$ **10.** $y = 3\,|x|$ **11.** $y = -4\,|x|$ **12.** $y = -3\,|x|$

13. $y = \dfrac{1}{4}|x|$ **14.** $y = \dfrac{1}{3}|x|$ **15.** $y = -\dfrac{1}{4}|x|$ **16.** $y = -\dfrac{1}{3}|x|$

17. $y = |2x|$ **18.** $y = |3x|$ **19.** $y = \left|\dfrac{1}{2}x\right|$ **20.** $y = \left|\dfrac{1}{3}x\right|$

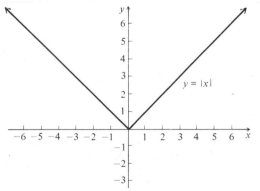

Here is a graph of $y = f(x)$. No formula will be given for this function. In Exercises 21–44, sketch graphs by transforming this one.

21. $y = 2 + f(x)$ **22.** $y = 3 + f(x)$ **23.** $y = -1 + f(x)$

24. $y = -2 + f(x)$ **25.** $y = f(x - 1)$ **26.** $y = f(x - 3)$

27. $y = f(x + 2)$ **28.** $y = f(x + 3)$ **29.** $y = 2f(x)$

30. $y = 3f(x)$ **31.** $y = -2f(x)$ **32.** $y = -3f(x)$

33. $y = \frac{1}{2}f(x)$ **34.** $y = \frac{1}{3}f(x)$ **35.** $y = -\frac{1}{2}f(x)$

36. $y = -\frac{1}{3}f(x)$ **37.** $y = f(2x)$ **38.** $y = f(3x)$

39. $y = f\left(\frac{1}{2}x\right)$ **40.** $y = f\left(\frac{1}{3}x\right)$ **41.** $y = f(-2x)$

42. $y = f(-3x)$ **43.** $y = f\left(-\frac{1}{2}x\right)$ **44.** $y = f\left(-\frac{1}{3}x\right)$

▶ **45.** A *linear* transformation of a coordinatized line is one that takes any point x to the point x', where $x' = ax + b$ (a and b constants). For example, the transformation $x' = 3x + 5$ takes the point 2 to the point $3 \cdot 2 + 5$, or 11. Suppose for a particular linear transformation the point 2 goes to 5 and the point 3 goes to 7.

a) Describe the transformation as $x' = ax + b$.

b) This transformation leaves one point fixed. What point is it?

47. Show that any linear transformation leaves one point fixed.

49. Suppose the average score on the test of Exercise 48 was 60. What will be the average of the transformed scores?

46. Ice melts at 0° Celsius or 32° Fahrenheit. Water boils at 100° Celsius or 212° Fahrenheit.

a) What linear transformation converts Celsius temperature to Fahrenheit?

b) Find the inverse of your answer to (a). Is it a function? What kind of conversion does it accomplish?

c) At what temperature are the Celsius and Fahrenheit scales the same?

48. A professor gives a test with 80 possible points. He decides that a score of 55 should be passing. He performs a linear transformation on the scores so that a perfect paper gets 100 and 70 is passing.

a) Describe the linear transformation that the professor used.

b) What grade remains unchanged under the transformation?

3.6 Some Special Classes of Functions

EVEN AND ODD FUNCTIONS

If the graph of a function is symmetric with respect to the y-axis, it is an *even* function. Recall (Section 3.3) that a function will be symmetric to the y-axis if in its equation we can replace x by $-x$ and obtain an equivalent equation. Thus if we have a function given by $y = f(x)$, then $y = f(-x)$ will give the same function if the function is even. In other words, an even function is one for which $f(x) = f(-x)$ for all x in its domain. This is the definition of even function.

> **Definition.** A function f is an *even* function in case $f(x) = f(-x)$ for all x in the domain of f.

Example 1. Show that $f(x) = x^2 + 1$ is an even function.

$$f(-x) = (-x)^2 + 1 = x^2 + 1 = f(x)$$

Since $f(-x) = f(x)$ for all x in the domain, f is an even function.

Note that the graph is symmetric with respect to the y-axis.

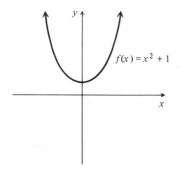

$f(x) = x^2 + 1$

Example 2. Show that $f(x) = x^2 + 3x^4$ is an even function.

$$f(-x) = (-x)^2 + 3(-x)^4 = x^2 + 3x^4 = f(x)$$

Since $f(-x) = f(x)$ for all x in the domain, the function is even.   **[50, 51]**

If the graph of a function is symmetric with respect to the origin, it is an *odd* function. Recall that a function will be symmetric with respect to the origin if in its equation we can replace x by $-x$ and y by $-y$ and obtain an equivalent equation. Thus if we have a function given by $y = f(x)$, then $-y = f(-x)$ will be equivalent if f is an odd function. In other words, an odd function is one for which $f(-x) = -f(x)$ for all x in the domain. Let us make this our definition.

> **Definition.** A function f is an *odd* function when $f(-x) = -f(x)$ for all x in the domain of f.

Example 3. Show that $f(x) = x^3$ is an odd function.

a) $f(-x) = (-x)^3 = -(x)^3$
b) $-f(x) = -x^3$

Since $f(-x) = -f(x)$ for all x in the domain, f is odd. Note that the graph is symmetric with respect to the origin.

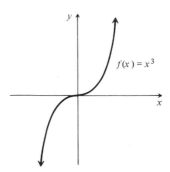

$f(x) = x^3$

Example 4. Show that $f(x) = x^3 + 5x$ is an odd function.

a) $f(-x) = (-x)^3 + 5(-x) = -x^3 - 5x$

b) $-f(x) = -(x^3 + 5x) = -x^3 - 5x$

Since $f(-x) = -f(x)$ for all x in the domain, f is odd.

[52, 53]

PERIODIC FUNCTIONS

Certain functions with a repeating pattern are called *periodic*. Here are some examples.

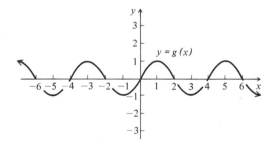

The function values of the function f repeat themselves every two units as we move from left to right. In other words, for any x, we have $f(x) = f(x + 2)$. To see this another way, think of the part of the graph between 0 and 2 and note that the rest of the graph consists of copies of it. In terms of translations, if we translate the graph two units to the left or right, the original graph will be obtained.

In the function g, the function values repeat themselves every four units. Hence $g(x) = g(x + 4)$ for any x, and if the graph is translated four units to the left, or right, it will coincide with itself. Or, think of the part of the graph between 0 and 4. The rest of the graph consists of copies of it.

We say that f has a *period* of 2, and that g has a period of 4.

Definition. If a function f has the property that $f(x + p) = f(x)$ whenever x and $x + p$ are in the domain, where p is a constant, then f is said to be *periodic*. The smallest positive number p (if there is one) for which $f(x + p) = f(x)$ for all x is called the *period* of the function.

[54, 56]

INTERVAL NOTATION

For a and b real numbers such that $a < b$, we define the *open interval* (a, b) as follows:

(a, b) is the set of all numbers x such that $a < x < b$,

or

$$\{x \mid a < x < b\}.$$

Its graph is as follows:

Note that the endpoints are not included. Be careful not to confuse this notation with that of an ordered pair. The context of the writing should make the meaning clear. When we mean intervals, we might say "the interval $(-2, 3)$." When we mean an ordered pair, we might say "the pair $(-2, 3)$." **[57, 58]**

The *closed interval* $[a, b]$ is defined as follows:

$[a, b]$ is the set of all x such that $a \leq x \leq b$,

or

$$\{x \mid a \leq x \leq b\}.$$

Its graph is as follows:

Note that endpoints are included. For example, the graph of $[-2, 3]$ is as follows:

There are two kinds of *half-open intervals* defined as follows:

a) $\qquad (a, b] = \{x \mid a < x \leq b\}.$

This is open on the left. Its graph is as follows:

b) $\qquad [a, b) = \{x \mid a \leq x < b\}.$

This is open on the right. Its graph is as follows:

[59, 60]

CONTINUOUS FUNCTIONS

Some functions have graphs that are continuous curves, without breaks or holes in them. Such functions are called *continuous functions*.

Example. The function f below is continuous because it has no breaks, jumps, or holes in it. The function g has *discontinuities* where $x = -2$ and $x = 5$. The function g is continuous on the interval $[-2, 5)$ or on any interval contained therein. It is also continuous on other intervals, but it is not continuous on an interval such as $[-3, 1]$ or $(3, 7)$.

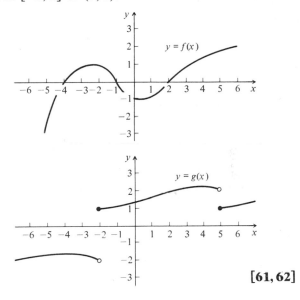

[61, 62]

INCREASING AND DECREASING FUNCTIONS

If the graph of a function rises from left to right it is said to be an *increasing* function. If the graph of a function drops from left to right, it is said to be a *decreasing* function. This can be stated more formally.

Definition.
1. A function f is an *increasing* function when for all a and b in the domain of f, if $a < b$, then $f(a) < f(b)$.
2. A function f is a *decreasing* function when for all a and b in the domain of f, if $a < b$, then $f(a) > f(b)$.

f is an increasing function

g is decreasing

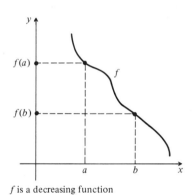

f is a decreasing function

h is neither increasing
nor decreasing

Examples

f is increasing

m is neither increasing
nor decreasing

Note that while the function m is neither increasing nor decreasing, it is increasing on the interval $[0, 2]$ and decreasing on the interval $[-2, 0]$. **[63–65]**

Exercise Set 3.6

1. Which of the following functions are even? odd? neither even nor odd?

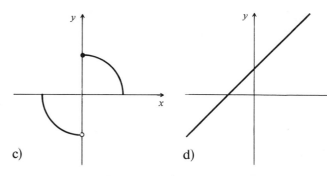

a)   b)   c)   d)

2. Which of the following functions are even? odd? neither even nor odd?

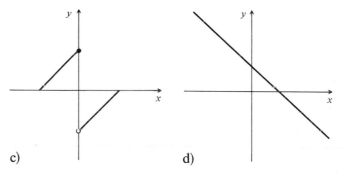

a)   b)   c)   d)

3. Which of the following functions are even? odd? neither even nor odd?

a) $f(x) = 2x^2 + 4x$ b) $f(x) = 5x^2 + 2x^4$

c) $f(x) = |2x|$ d) $f(x) = -4x$

e) $f(x) = 4x^3 - x$ f) $f(x) = -3x^3 + 2x$

4. Which of the following functions are even? odd? neither even nor odd?

a) $f(x) = 3x^2 - 2x$ b) $f(x) = 3x^4 - 4x^2$

c) $f(x) = |3x|$ d) $f(x) = 4x$

e) $f(x) = 2x + 5x^3$ f) $f(x) = 4x^3 - 5x$

5. Which of the following functions are periodic?

a)

b)

c)

d)

6. Which of the following functions are periodic?

a)

b)

c)

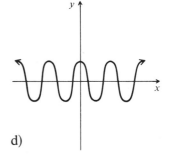

d)

7. What is the period of this function?

8. What is the period of this function?

9. Is this function continuous

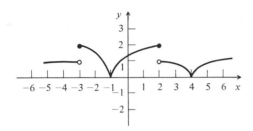

a) in the interval $[0, 2]$?

b) in the interval $(-2, 0)$?

c) in the interval $[0, 3)$?

d) in the interval $[-3, -1]$?

e) in the interval $(-3, -1]$?

10. Is this function continuous

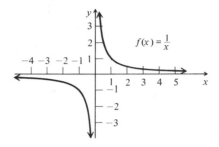

a) in the interval $[-3, -1]$?

b) in the interval $(1, 4)$?

c) in the interval $[-1, 1]$?

d) in the interval $[-2, 4]$?

e) in the interval $(0, 1]$?

11. Where are the discontinuities of the function in Exercise 9?

12. Where are the discontinuities of the function in Exercise 10?

13. Write interval notation for each set pictured.

a)

b)

c)

d)

14. Write interval notation for each set pictured.

a)

b)

c)

d)

15. Write interval notation for each set.

a) $\{x \mid -2 < x < 4\}$

b) $\left\{x \mid -\dfrac{1}{4} < x \leqslant \dfrac{1}{4}\right\}$

c) $\{x \mid 7 \leqslant x < 10\pi\}$

d) $\{x \mid -9 \leqslant x \leqslant -6\}$

16. Write interval notation for each set.

a) $\{x \mid -5 < x < 0\}$

b) $\{x \mid -\sqrt{2} \leqslant x < \sqrt{2}\}$

c) $\left\{x \mid -\dfrac{\pi}{2} < x \leqslant \dfrac{\pi}{2}\right\}$

d) $\left\{x \mid -12 \leqslant x \leqslant -\dfrac{1}{2}\right\}$

17. Which of the following functions are increasing? decreasing? neither increasing nor decreasing?

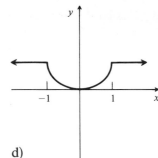

a)   b)   c)   d)

18. Which of the following functions are increasing? decreasing? neither increasing nor decreasing?

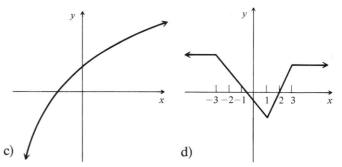

a)   b)   c)   d)

19. For the function in Exercise 17(d), find an interval on which the function is (a) increasing; (b) decreasing.

20. For the function in Exercise 18(d), find an interval on which the function is (a) increasing; (b) decreasing.

21. Which of the following functions are increasing? decreasing? neither increasing nor decreasing?

a) $f(x) = 3x + 4$ b) $f(x) = -3x + 4$

c) $f(x) = x^2 + 1$ d) $f(x) = -2$

e) $f(x) = x^3 + 1$ f) $f(x) = |x|$

22. Which of the following functions are increasing? decreasing? neither increasing nor decreasing?

a) $f(x) = -2x - 3$ b) $f(x) = 2x - 3$

c) $f(x) = 3x^2$ d) $f(x) = \sqrt{3}$

e) $f(x) = |x| + 2$ f) $f(x) = x^3 - 2$

Chapter 3 Test, or Review

1. List all the ordered pairs in the Cartesian product $A \times B$, where $A = \{b, 1, 3\}$, and $B = \{a, 1, 3\}$.

2. Graph the relation in $R \times R$, in which the first coordinate is one less than the second.

3. Graph $x = |y|$.

4. Graph $y = (x + 1)^2$.

5. Which are symmetric with respect to the x-axis?

   a) $y = 7$ b) $x^2 + y^2 = 4$ c) $x^3 = y^3 - y$

   d) $y^2 = x^2 + 3$ e) $x + y = 3$ f) $x = 3$

6. Which of the above are symmetric with respect to the origin?

7. Write an equation of the inverse of $y - 3x^2 + 2x - 1$.

8. Which of the following are graphs of functions?

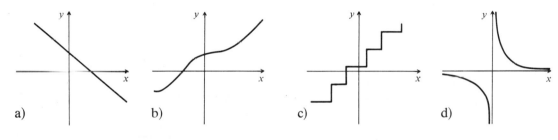

a)   b)   c)   d)

9. Which of the relations in Exercise 8 have inverses that are functions?

Use $f(x) = 2\sqrt{x - 1}$ to answer Exercises 10–12.

10. Find $f(1)$.   11. Find $f(5)$.   12. Find $f(a + 2)$.

13. $g(x) = \dfrac{\sqrt{x}}{2} + 2$. Find a formula for $g^{-1}(x)$.

14. $h(x) = 5x^3 - 1000$. Find $h(h^{-1}(s))$.

15. Here is a graph of $y = f(x)$. Sketch graphs of the following equations: (a) $y = \frac{1}{2}f(x)$; (b) $y = f(x) - 2$; (c) $y = f(x - 1)$.

Use the following to answer Exercises 16–18.

a)

b)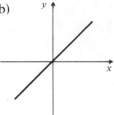

16. Which of these are even?

17. Which of these are odd?

18. Which of these are neither even nor odd?

c) $f(x) = -2x^2 - 2$

d) $f(x) = x^5 + x^2$

e) $f(x) = x + 3$

f) $f(x) = x^5 + x$

19. Which of these functions are periodic?

a)

b)

c)

d)

20. What is the period of this function?

21. Is this function continuous

a) in the interval $[-3, -1]$?

b) in the interval $[-1, 1]$?

Write interval notation for:

22. $\{x \mid -\pi \leqslant x \leqslant 2\pi\}$.

23. $\{x \mid 0 < x \leqslant 1\}$.

Use the following to answer Exercises 24–26.

a) $g(x) = -4x + 2$

b) $t(x) = x^2 - 7$

c) $f(x) = \dfrac{1}{2}x - 4$

d) $g(x) = x^3 + 4$

24. Which of the above are increasing?

25. Which of the above are decreasing?

26. Which of the above are neither increasing nor decreasing?

27. Find $f \circ g(x)$ and $g \circ f(x)$, where $f(x) = \dfrac{4}{x^2}$; $g(x) = 3 - 2x$.

Linear and Quadratic Functions and Inequalities

4.1 Lines and Linear Functions

We saw earlier that the graph of any equation equivalent to one of the type $Ax + By + C = 0$ is a straight line. Such equations are called _linear_. The graph of a linear equation may slant upward or downward in various ways. Let us see how this relates to equations.

SLOPE

Suppose points P_1 and P_2 with coordinates (x_1, y_1) and (x_2, y_2) are two different points on a line not parallel to an axis. Consider a right triangle as shown, with legs parallel to the axes. The point P_3 with coordinates (x_2, y_1) is the third vertex of the triangle. As we move from P_1 to P_2, y changes from y_1 to y_2. The change in y is $y_2 - y_1$. Similarly, the change in x is $x_2 - x_1$. The ratio of these changes is called the _slope_.

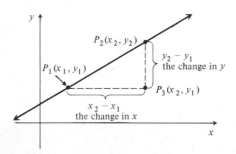

Definition. The _slope_ of a line containing two points (x_1, y_1) and (x_2, y_2) is defined to be

$$\frac{y_2 - y_1}{x_2 - x_1}\left(\frac{\text{change in } y}{\text{change in } x}\right).$$

Example 1. Graph the line through the points $(1, 2)$ and $(3, 6)$ and find its slope.

Let us call the slope m. Then

$$m = \frac{\text{change in } y}{\text{change in } x} = \frac{6 - 2}{3 - 1} = \frac{4}{2} = 2.$$

Note that we can also use the points in the opposite order, so long as we are consistent. We get the same slope:

$$m = \frac{\text{change in } y}{\text{change in } x} = \frac{2 - 6}{1 - 3} = \frac{-4}{-2} = 2.$$

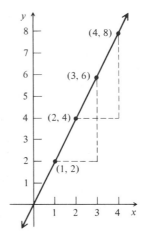

From Example 1 we see that it does not matter in which order we choose the points, so long as we take differences in the same order. From Example 1 we can also see that it does not matter which two points of a line we choose to determine the slope. No matter what points we choose we get the same number for the slope. For example, if we choose $(2, 4)$ and $(4, 8)$, we get for the slope,

$$\frac{8 - 4}{4 - 2} = \frac{4}{2} = 2. \qquad \text{[1–4]}$$

If a line slants upward from left to right, it has a positive slope, as in Example 1. If a line slants downward from left to right, the change in x and the change in y have opposite signs, so the line has a negative slope.

If a line is horizontal, the change in y for any two points is 0. Thus a horizontal line has zero slope.

If a line is vertical, the change in x for any two points is 0. Thus the slope is not defined, because we cannot divide by zero. A vertical line does not have a slope.

[5–9]

POINT-SLOPE EQUATIONS OF LINES

Suppose we have a nonvertical line and that the coordinates of one point P_1 are (x_1, y_1). We think of point P_1 as fixed. Suppose, also, that we have a movable point P on the line with coordinates (x, y). Thus the slope would be given by

$$\frac{(y - y_1)}{(x - x_1)} = m. \qquad (1)$$

Note that this is true only when (x, y) is a point different from (x_1, y_1). If we use the multiplication principle, we get

$$(y - y_1) = m(x - x_1). \quad \textit{Point-slope equation} \quad (2)$$

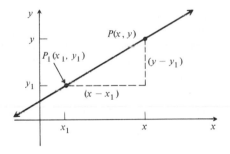

Equation (2) will be true even if $(x, y) = (x_1, y_1)$. Equation (2) is called the *point-slope equation* of a line. Thus if we know the slope of a line and the coordinates of a point on the line, we can find an equation of the line.

Example 2. Find an equation of the line containing the point $(\frac{1}{2}, -1)$ with slope 5.

If we substitute in $(y - y_1) = m(x - x_1)$, we get $y - (\boxed{-1}) = 5(x - \boxed{\tfrac{1}{2}})$, which simplifies to

$$y + 1 = 5\left(x - \frac{1}{2}\right)$$

or

$$y = 5x - \frac{5}{2} - 1$$

or

$$y = 5x - \frac{7}{2}.$$

[10–12]

TWO-POINT EQUATIONS OF LINES

Suppose a nonvertical line contains the points $P_1(x_1, y_1)$ and $P_2(x_2, y_2)$. The slope of the line is

$$\frac{y_2 - y_1}{x_2 - x_1}.$$

If we substitute $(y_2 - y_1)/(x_2 - x_1)$ for m in the point-slope equation,

$$y - y_1 = m(x - x_1),$$

we have

$$y - y_1 = \frac{y_2 - y_1}{x_2 - x_1}(x - x_1). \quad \textit{Two-point equation}$$

This is known as the *two-point equation* of a line. Note that either of the two given points can be called P_1 or P_2 and (x, y) is any point on the line.

Example 3. Find an equation of the line containing the points $(2, 3)$ and $(1, -4)$.

If we take $(2, 3)$ as P_1 and use the two-point equation, we get

$$y - 3 = \frac{-4 - 3}{1 - 2}(x - 2),$$

which simplifies to $y = 7x - 11$.   **[13, 14]**

SLOPE-INTERCEPT EQUATIONS OF LINES

Suppose a nonvertical line has slope m and y-intercept $(0, b)$. We sometimes, for brevity, refer to the number b as the y-intercept. Let us substitute m and $(0, b)$ in the point-slope equation. We get

$$y - y_1 = m(x - x_1)$$
$$y - b = m(x - 0).$$

This simplifies to

$$y = mx + b. \qquad \textbf{\textit{Slope-intercept equation}}$$

This is called the *slope-intercept equation* of a line. The advantage of such an equation is that we can read the slope m and the y-intercept b from the equation.

Example 4. Find the slope and the y-intercept of $y = 5x - \dfrac{1}{4}$.

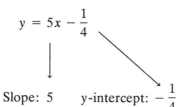

Slope: 5 y-intercept: $-\dfrac{1}{4}$

Example 5. Find the slope and y-intercept of $y = 8$.

We can rewrite this equation as $y = 0x + 8$. We then see that the slope is 0 and the y-intercept is 8.

[15, 16]

To find the slope-intercept equation of a line, when given another equation, we solve for y.

Example 6. Find the slope and y-intercept of the line having the equation $3x - 6y - 7 = 0$.

We solve for y, obtaining $y = \frac{1}{2}x - \frac{7}{6}$. Thus the slope is $\frac{1}{2}$ and the y-intercept is $-\frac{7}{6}$.

If a line is vertical it has no slope. Thus it has no slope-intercept equation. Such a line does have a simple equation, however. All vertical lines have equations $x = c$, where c is some constant.

[17]

LINEAR FUNCTIONS

Any nonvertical straight line is the graph of a function. Such a function is called a *linear function*. Any nonvertical line has an equation $y = mx + b$. Thus a function is a linear function if and only if it has an equation $y = mx + b$. If the slope m is zero, the equation simplifies to $y = b$. A function like this is called a *constant function*.

Exercise Set 4.1

Find the slopes of the lines containing these points.

1. $(6, 2)$ and $(-2, 1)$

2. $(-2, 1)$ and $(-4, -2)$

3. $(2, -4)$ and $(4, -3)$

4. $(5, -3)$ and $(-5, 8)$

5. $(2\pi, 5)$ and $(\pi, 4)$

6. $(\sqrt{2}, -4)$ and $(\pi, -4)$

Find equations of the following lines.

7. Through $(3, 2)$ with $m = 4$

8. Through $(4, 7)$ with $m = -2$

9. With y-intercept -5 and $m = 2$

10. With y-intercept π and $m = \dfrac{1}{4}$

11. Containing $(1, 4)$ and $(5, 6)$

12. Containing $(-2, 0)$ and $(2, 3)$

Find the slope and y-intercept of each line.

13. $y = 2x + 3$

14. $y = 6 - x$

15. $2y = -6x + 10$

16. $-3y = -12x + 9$

17. $3x - 4y = 12$

18. $5x + 2y = -7$

19. $3y + 10 = 0$

20. $y = 7$

 Find equations of the following lines.

21. Through $(3.014, -2.563)$ with slope 3.516.

22. Through $(-173.4, -17.6)$ with slope -0.00014.

23. Through the points $(1.103, 2.443)$ and $(8.114, 11.012)$.

24. Through the points $(473.78, 910.2)$ and $(993.55, 171.43)$.

▶ **25.** Determine whether these three points are on a line. [*Hint:* Compare the slopes of $\overline{AB}$ and $\overline{BC}$. ($\overline{AB}$ refers to the segment from A to B.)]

$$A(9, 4), \qquad B(-1, 2), \qquad C(4, 3)$$

26. Determine whether these three points are on a line. (See hint for Exercise 25.)

$$A(-1, -1), \qquad B(2, 2), \qquad C(-3, -4)$$

27. Use graph paper. Plot the points $A(0, 0)$, $B(8, 2)$, $C(11, 6)$, and $D(3, 4)$. Draw $\overline{AB}$, $\overline{BC}$, $\overline{CD}$, and $\overline{DA}$. Find the slopes of these four segments. Compare the slopes of $\overline{AB}$ and $\overline{CD}$. Compare the slopes of $\overline{BC}$ and $\overline{DA}$. (Figure $ABCD$ is a parallelogram and its opposite sides are parallel.)

28. Use graph paper. Plot the points $E(-2, -5)$, $F(2, -2)$, $G(7, -2)$, and $H(3, -5)$. Draw $\overline{EF}$, $\overline{FG}$, $\overline{GH}$, $\overline{HE}$, $\overline{EG}$, and $\overline{FH}$. Compare the slopes of $\overline{EG}$ and $\overline{FH}$. (Figure $EFGH$ is a rhombus and its diagonals are perpendicular.)

29. (*Fahrenheit temperature as a function of Celsius temperature*). Fahrenheit temperature F is a linear function of Celsius (or Centigrade) temperature C. When C is 0, F is 32. When C is 100, F is 212. Use these data to express F as a linear function of C.

30. (*Celsius temperature as a function of Fahrenheit temperature*). Celsius (Centigrade) temperature C is a linear function of Fahrenheit temperature F. When F is 32, C is 0. When F is 212, C is 100. Use these data to express C as a linear function of F.

31. Suppose P is a nonconstant linear function of Q. Show that Q is a linear function of P.

4.2 Parallel Lines; The Distance and Midpoint Formulas

If two lines are vertical, they are parallel. Thus equations such as $x = c_1$ and $x = c_2$ (where c_1 and c_2 are constants) have graphs that are parallel lines. Now let us consider nonvertical lines. In order that such lines be parallel they must have the same slope, but different y-intercepts. Thus equations such as $y = mx + b_1$ and $y = mx + b_2$ have graphs that are parallel lines.

Vertical lines are parallel. Nonvertical lines are parallel if and only if they have the same slope and different y-intercepts.

If two equations are equivalent, they represent the same line. Thus if two lines have the same slope and the same y-intercept, they are not really two different lines. They are the same line. In such a case we sometimes speak of "coincident lines."

Example 1. Show that the graphs of $3x - y = -5$ and $y - 3x = -2$ are parallel.

We first find the slope-intercept equations:

$$y = 3x + 5 \quad \text{and} \quad y = 3x - 2.$$

These lines have the same slope but different y-intercepts, hence they are parallel. **[18–20]**

THE DISTANCE FORMULA

We will develop a formula for finding the distance between two points whose coordinates are known. Suppose the points are on a horizontal line, thus having the same second coordinates. We can find the distance between them by subtracting their first coordinates. This difference may be negative, depending on the order in which we subtract. So to make sure we

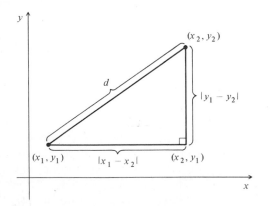

get a positive number, we take the absolute value of this difference. The distance between two points on a horizontal line (x_1, y) and (x_2, y) is thus $|x_1 - x_2|$. Similarly, the distance between two points on a vertical line (x, y_1) and (x, y_2) is $|y_1 - y_2|$.

Now consider any two points not on a horizontal or vertical line (x_1, y_1) and (x_2, y_2). These points are vertices of a right triangle, as shown. The other vertex is (x_2, y_1). The legs of this triangle have the lengths $|x_1 - x_2|$ and $|y_1 - y_2|$. Now by the Pythagorean theorem we obtain a relation between the length of the hypotenuse d, and the lengths of the legs:

$$d^2 = |x_1 - x_2|^2 + |y_1 - y_2|^2.$$

We may now dispense with the absolute value signs because squares of numbers are never negative. Thus we have

$$d^2 = (x_1 - x_2)^2 + (y_1 - y_2)^2.$$

By taking the square root we obtain the distance between the two points.

Theorem. *The distance formula.* **The distance between any two points (x_1, y_1) and (x_2, y_2) is given by**

$$d = \sqrt{(x_1 - x_2)^2 + (y_1 - y_2)^2}.$$

Although we derived the distance formula by considering two points not on a horizontal or vertical line, the formula holds for *any* two points.

Example 2. Find the distance between the points $(8, 7)$ and $(3, -5)$.

Using the distance formula, we have

$$d = \sqrt{(8 - 3)^2 + [7 - (-5)]^2} = \sqrt{5^2 + 12^2}$$

$$= \sqrt{169} = 13. \qquad \textbf{[21–24]}$$

Example 3. Decide whether the points $(1, 4)$, $(2, 1)$, and $(3, 2)$ are vertices of a right triangle.

First we find the squares of the distances between the points:

$$d_1^2 = (1-2)^2 + (4-1)^2 = (-1)^2 + 3^2 \quad = 1 + 9$$
$$= 10,$$
$$d_2^2 = (1-3)^2 + (4-2)^2 = (-2)^2 + 2^2 \quad = 4 + 4$$
$$= 8,$$
$$d_3^2 = (2-3)^2 + (1-2)^2 = (-1)^2 + (-1)^2 = 1 + 1$$
$$= 2.$$

Since $d_2^2 + d_3^2 = d_1^2$, it follows by the converse of the Pythagorean theorem that the points are the vertices of a right triangle.   **[25, 26]**

MIDPOINTS OF SEGMENTS

The distance formula can be used to verify or derive a formula for finding the coordinates of the midpoint of a segment when the coordinates of its endpoints are known. We shall not derive this formula but simply state it.

Theorem. *The midpoint formula.* If the endpoints of a segment are (x_1, y_1) and (x_2, y_2), then the coordinates of the midpoint are

$$\left(\frac{x_1 + x_2}{2}, \frac{y_1 + y_2}{2} \right).$$

Note that we obtain the coordinates of the midpoint by averaging the coordinates of the endpoints. This is an easy way to remember this formula.

Example 4. Find the midpoint of the segment with endpoints $(-3, 5)$ and $(4, -7)$.

Using the midpoint formula, we obtain

$$\left(\frac{-3 + 4}{2}, \frac{5 + (-7)}{2} \right) \quad \text{or} \quad \left(\frac{1}{2}, -1 \right).$$

[27, 28]

Exercise Set 4.2

For each pair of equations, state whether the graphs are parallel.

1. $2x - 5y = -3$
   $2x + 5y = 4$

2. $x + 2y = 5$
   $2x + 4y = 8$

3. $y = 4x - 5$
   $4y = 8 - x$

4. $y = -x + 7$
   $y = x + 3$

Find the distance between the points of each pair.

5. $(-3, -2)$ and $(1, 1)$

6. $(5, 9)$ and $(-1, 6)$

7. $(0, -7)$ and $(3, -4)$

8. $(2, 2)$ and $(-2, -2)$

9. $(a, -3)$ and $(2a, 5)$

10. $(5, 2k)$ and $(-3, k)$

11. $(0, 0)$ and (a, b)

12. $(\sqrt{2}, \sqrt{3})$ and $(0, 0)$

13. $(\sqrt{a}, \sqrt{b})$ and $(-\sqrt{a}, \sqrt{b})$

14. $(c - d, c + d)$ and $(c + d, d - c)$

Decide whether the points are vertices of a right triangle.

15. $(9, 6), (-1, 2)$ and $(1, -3)$

16. $(-5, -8), (1, 6)$ and $(5, -4)$

Find the midpoints of the segments having the following endpoints.

17. $(-4, 7)$ and $(3, -9)$ **18.** $(4, 5)$ and $(6, -7)$ **19.** (a, b) and $(a, -b)$ **20.** $(-c, d)$ and (c, d)

 Find the distance between the points of each pair.

21. $(7.3482, -3.0991)$ and $(18.9431, -17.9054)$ **22.** $(-25.414, 175.31)$ and $(275.34, -95.144)$

Find the midpoints of the segments having the following endpoints.

23. $(-3.895, 8.1212)$ and $(2.998, -8.6677)$ **24.** $(4.1112, 6.9898)$ and $(5.1928, -6.9143)$

25. Find the point on the x-axis that is equidistant from the points $(1, 3)$ and $(8, 4)$.

26. Find the point on the y-axis that is equidistant from the points $(-2, 0)$ and $(4, 6)$.

27. Consider any right triangle with base b and height h, situated as shown. Show that the midpoint of the hypotenuse P is equidistant from the three vertices of the triangle.

28. Consider any quadrilateral situated as shown. Show that the segments joining the midpoints of the sides, in order as shown, form a parallelogram.

4.3 Quadratic Functions

If a function can be described by a second-degree polynomial, it is called *quadratic*. The following is a more precise definition.

> **Definition. A *quadratic* function is one that can be described as follows:**
>
> $$f(x) = ax^2 + bx + c, \qquad \text{where} \qquad a \neq 0.$$

In this definition we insist that $a \neq 0$; otherwise the polynomial would not be of degree two. One or both of the constants b and c can be 0.

Consider $f(x) = x^2$. This is an even function, so the y-axis is a line of symmetry. The graph opens upward, as shown in Fig. 1. If we multiply by a constant a to get $f(x) = ax^2$, we obtain a vertical stretching or shrinking, and a reflection if a is negative. Examples of this are shown in Fig. 1. Bear in mind that if a is negative the graph opens downward.

Graphs of quadratic functions are called *parabolas*. In each parabola (Fig. 1), the point $(0, 0)$ is the *vertex*.

[29, 30]

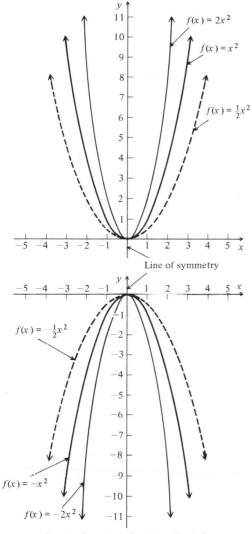

Graphs of quadratic functions. Parabolas.

Figure 1

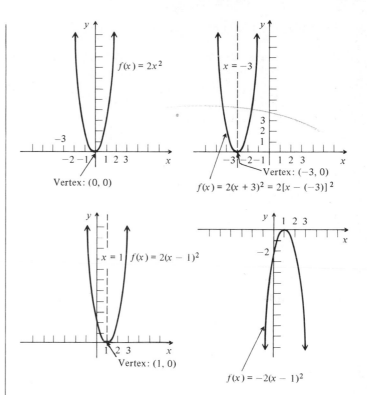

Figure 2

The graph of $f(x) = a(x - h)^2$

a) opens upward if $a > 0$, downward if $a < 0$;

b) has $(h, 0)$ as a vertex;

c) has $x = h$ as a line of symmetry;

d) has a minimum 0 if $a > 0$, a maximum 0 if $a < 0$.

[31, 32]

Let us consider $f(x) = a(x - h)^2$. We have replaced x by $x - h$ in ax^2, and will therefore obtain a horizontal translation. The translation will be to the right if h is positive. The following examples illustrate (see Fig. 2), and a summary is given below.

Now consider $f(x) = a(x - h)^2 + k$, or $f(x) - k = a(x - h)^2$. We have replaced $f(x)$ by $f(x) - k$ in the equation $f(x) = a(x - h)^2$. Thus we have a translation. If k is positive, the translation is upward. If k is negative, the translation is downward. Consider these examples. Note that the vertex has been moved off the x-axis.

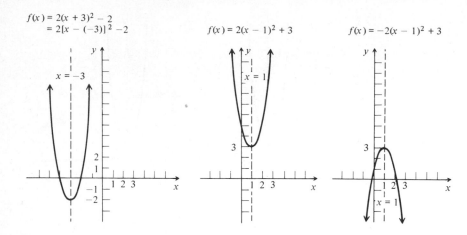

$f(x) = 2(x + 3)^2 - 2$
$= 2[x - (-3)]^2 - 2$

$f(x) = 2(x - 1)^2 + 3$

$f(x) = -2(x - 1)^2 + 3$

The graph of $f(x) = a(x - h)^2 + k$

a) opens upward if $a > 0$, downward if $a < 0$;

b) has (h, k) as a vertex;

c) has $x = h$ as the line of symmetry;

d) has k as a minimum value (output) if $a > 0$, has k as a maximum value (output) if $a < 0$.

Thus without graphing, we can determine a lot of information about a function described by $f(x) = a(x - h)^2 + k$. The following table is an example.

Function	$f(x) = 3(x - \frac{1}{4})^2 - 2$	$g(x) = -3(x + 5)^2 + 7$ $= -3[x - (-5)]^2 + 7$
a) What is the vertex?	$\left(\frac{1}{4}, -2\right)$	$(-5, 7)$
b) What is the line of symmetry?	$x = \frac{1}{4}$	$x = -5$
c) Is there a maximum? What is it?	No; graph extends upward; $3 > 0$	Yes; 7; graph extends downward; $-3 < 0$
d) Is there a minimum? What is it?	Yes; -2; graph extends upward; $3 > 0$	No; graph extends downward; $-3 < 0$

[33–38]

Now let us consider a quadratic function described by $f(x) = ax^2 + bx + c$. Note that it is not in the form $f(x) = a(x - h)^2 + k$. We can get it in this form by completing the square. For example, consider

$$f(x) = x^2 - 6x + 4$$
$$= (x^2 - 6x) + 4.$$

We complete the square using the two terms in parentheses, but we do it in a different way than before. We take half the x coefficient: $\frac{1}{2} \cdot 6 = 3$; square it: $3^2 = 9$; then add and subtract 9 inside the parentheses and proceed as follows:

$$f(x) = (x^2 - 6x + 9 - 9) + 4$$
$$= (x^2 - 6x + 9) + (-9 + 4)$$
$$= (x - 3)^2 - 5$$
$$= 1 \cdot (x - 3)^2 - 5.$$

Vertex: $(3, -5)$,

Line of symmetry: $x = 3$,

Minimum: -5, since the coefficient 1 is positive.

Example 1. For the following function, (a) find the vertex, (b) find the line of symmetry, and (c) determine whether the second coordinate of the vertex is a maximum or a minimum, and find the maximum or minimum.

$$f(x) = -2x^2 + 10x - 7$$
$$= -2(x^2 - 5x) - 7$$
$$= -2\left(x^2 - 5x + \frac{25}{4} - \frac{25}{4}\right) - 7$$
$$= -2\left(x^2 - 5x + \frac{25}{4}\right) - 2\left(-\frac{25}{4}\right) - 7$$
$$= -2\left(x - \frac{5}{2}\right)^2 + \frac{25}{2} - \frac{14}{2}$$
$$= -2\left(x - \frac{5}{2}\right)^2 + \frac{11}{2}$$

Vertex: $\left(\dfrac{5}{2}, \dfrac{11}{2}\right)$,

Line of symmetry: $x = \dfrac{5}{2}$,

Maximum: $\dfrac{11}{2}$, since the coefficient -2 is negative.

[39–41]

Example 2. For the following function, (a) find the vertex, (b) find the line of symmetry, and (c) determine whether the second coordinate of the vertex is a maximum or a minimum, and find the maximum or minimum output.

$$f(x) = \frac{3}{4}x^2 + 6x$$
$$= \frac{3}{4}(x^2 + 8x)$$
$$= \frac{3}{4}(x^2 + 8x + 16 - 16) \quad \left(\left[\frac{1}{2} \cdot 8\right]^2 = 16\right)$$
$$= \frac{3}{4}(x^2 + 8x + 16) + \frac{3}{4}(-16)$$
$$= \frac{3}{4}(x + 4)^2 - 12$$
$$= \frac{3}{4}[x - (-4)]^2 - 12$$

Vertex: $(-4, -12)$,

Line of symmetry: $x = -4$,

Minimum: -12, since the coefficient $\dfrac{3}{4}$ is positive.

The preceding examples illustrate the following.

Theorem. For any quadratic function, we can complete the square and obtain an equivalent equation:

$$f(x) = a(x - h)^2 + k.$$

The function f has

a) vertex: (h, k),
b) line of symmetry: $x = h$,
c) k as a minimum if $a > 0$,
d) k as a maximum if $a < 0$.

[42–44]

x-INTERCEPTS

The x-intercepts of the graph of $y = f(x) = ax^2 + bx + c$ occur where the graph crosses the x-axis; that is, when y, the output, is 0. Thus to find the x-coordinates of such points, we solve the equation $0 = ax^2 + bx + c$.

Example. Find the x-intercepts of the graph of $y = f(x) = x^2 - 2x - 2$. Use these and the vertex to graph the function.

We solve $0 = x^2 - 2x - 2$. Using the quadratic formula, we find the solutions are $1 \pm \sqrt{3}$. Thus the x-intercepts are $(1 + \sqrt{3}, 0)$ and $(1 - \sqrt{3}, 0)$. When we complete the square, we get $f(x) = (x - 1)^2 - 3$, so the vertex is $(1, -3)$. The graph opens upward so we can complete the graph as shown.

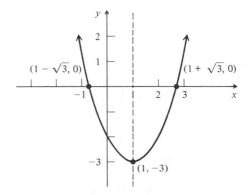

The discriminant of $ax^2 + bx + c$, which is $b^2 - 4ac$, indicates how many x-intercepts there are. Compare the following graphs.

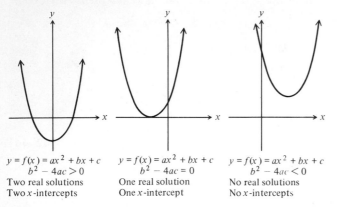

$y = f(x) = ax^2 + bx + c$
$b^2 - 4ac > 0$
Two real solutions
Two x-intercepts

$y = f(x) = ax^2 + bx + c$
$b^2 - 4ac = 0$
One real solution
One x-intercept

$y = f(x) = ax^2 + bx + c$
$b^2 - 4ac < 0$
No real solutions
No x-intercepts

[45–47]

THE GRAPH OF $f(x) = \sqrt{x}$

Recall from Chapter 3 that all functions have inverses, but only in some cases is the inverse also a function. If the inverse is a function, we denote it by f^{-1}.

Example. Consider $f(x) = x^2$. Let us think of this as $y = x^2$.

To find the inverse we interchange x and y: $x = y^2$. Now we solve for y: $y = \pm\sqrt{x}$. Note that for each positive x we get two y's. For example, the pairs $(4, 2)$ and $(4, -2)$ belong to the relation. Note also that the inverse fails the vertical line test.

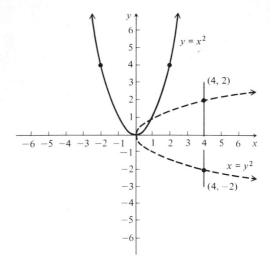

If we restrict the domain of $f(x) = x^2$ to nonnegative numbers, then its inverse is a function, $f^{-1}(x) = \sqrt{x}$.

[48]

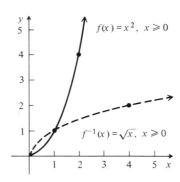

Exercise Set 4.3

For each of the following functions,

a) find the vertex;

b) find the line of symmetry; and

c) determine whether the second coordinate of the vertex is a maximum or a minimum, and find the maximum or minimum.

1. $f(x) = x^2$

2. $f(x) = -x^2$

3. $f(x) = -5x^2$

4. $f(x) = \pi x^2$

5. $f(x) = 2\left(x - \frac{1}{4}\right)^2$

6. $f(x) = 5(x - 7)^2$

7. $f(x) = -2(x - 9)^2$

8. $f(x) = -3\left(x - \frac{1}{2}\right)^2$

9. $f(x) = 2(x + 7)^2$

10. $f(x) = 4(x + 8)^2$

11. $f(x) = -2\left(x + \frac{1}{2}\right)^2$

12. $f(x) = -3(x + \pi)^2$

13. $f(x) = 3(x - 9)^2 + 5$

14. $f(x) = \left(x - \frac{1}{4}\right)^2 + 3$

15. $f(x) = 7(x + 4)^2 + 9$

16. $f(x) = 5\left(x + \frac{1}{4}\right)^2 + \frac{5}{4}$

17. $f(x) = -3(x - 2)^2 - 11$

18. $f(x) = -2(x - \pi)^2 + 31$

19. $f(x) = -\pi(x + 7)^2 + \frac{1}{2}$

20. $f(x) = -\sqrt{3}(x + 5)^2 - 23$

For each of the following functions,

a) find an equation of the type $f(x) = a(x - h)^2 + k$;

b) find the vertex;

c) find the line of symmetry; and

d) determine whether the second coordinate of the vertex is a maximum or a minimum, and find the maximum or minimum.

21. $f(x) = -x^2 + 2x + 3$

22. $f(x) = -x^2 + 8x - 7$

23. $f(x) = x^2 + 3x$

24. $f(x) - x^2 - 9x$

25. $f(x) = -\frac{3}{4}x^2 + 6x$

26. $f(x) = \frac{3}{2}x^2 + 3x$

27. $f(x) = 3x^2 + x - 4$

28. $f(x) = -2x^2 + x - 1$

Find the x-intercepts. Use these and the vertex to graph each function.

29. $f(x) - -x^2 + 2x + 3$

30. $f(x) = x^2 - 3x - 4$

Find the x-intercepts.

31. $f(x) = x^2 - 8x + 5$

32. $f(x) = 2x^2 + x - 6$

33. $f(x) = -x^2 - 3x - 3$

34. $f(x) = 5x^2 - 6x + 5$

Graph.

35. $f(x) = \sqrt{x}$

36. $f(x) = \sqrt{x - 2}$

37. $f(x) = \sqrt{x + 3}$

38. $f(x) = \sqrt{x - 1} + 2$

Find an equation of the type $f(x) = a(x - h)^2 + k$.

39. $f(x) = 3x^2 + mx + m^2$

40. $f(x) = mx^2 - 2x + m^2$

Find the maximum or minimum value for each of the following functions.

41. $f(x) = 2.31x^2 - 3.135x - 5.89$

42. $f(x) = -18.8x^2 + 7.92x + 6.18$

43. What is the minimum product of two numbers whose difference is 4.932? What are the numbers?

44. What is the minimum product of two numbers whose sum is 21.355? What are the numbers?

▶ **45.** Find the dimensions and area of the largest rectangle that can be inscribed as shown in a right triangle ABC whose sides have lengths 9 cm, 12 cm, and 15 cm.

46. A farmer wants to build a rectangular fence near a river. He is going to use 120 ft of fencing. What is the area of the largest region he can enclose? Note that he does not fence the side next to the river.

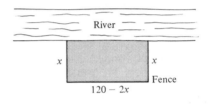

4.4 Mathematical Models

Mathematics is often constructed to fit certain situations. When this is done, we say that we have a *mathematical model.* One of the simplest examples is the natural numbers, i.e., the numbers 1, 2, 3, 4, and so on. These numbers and operations on them were invented so that they would apply to situations in which counting is involved, in some way or other. By working within a mathematical model, we hope to be able to predict what will happen in an actual situation.

Example. Use the mathematical model of the natural numbers to predict how much money a theatre owner will collect if he charges $2 per admission and 147 people attend.

We translate the problem situation to the language of the mathematical model. In this case, the total number of dollars collected will be the product of the admission price and the number of admissions. We multiply, to get an answer of 294. On this basis we predict that when the owner counts his receipts, he will find $294 there.

In an example such as the preceding one, we expect our prediction to be exact. In most situations, mathematical models are not that good. Predictions will be only approximate.

Example. Use the mathematical model of the natural numbers to predict how much mixture will result from mixing one liter of water and one liter of alcohol.

We solve this problem by adding 1 and 1, to get 2. On this basis, the answer is 2 liters.

In the latter example, our result is not exact. The actual result will be something less than 2 liters, because for some reason there is shrinkage when water and alcohol are mixed.

If a mathematical model does not give precise answers, we ordinarily try revising it so that it does, or we may even look for an entirely new model.

FUNCTIONS AS MATHEMATICAL MODELS

As a result of experiment or experience, we often acquire data that indicate that a function of some sort would be a good mathematical model. In the following diagram data have been plotted on a graph. It looks as if the points lie more or less on a straight line, and therefore a linear function would be a good model.

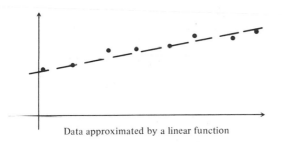

Data approximated by a linear function

We can find a formula for such a function and use it to make predictions. Some sets of data are well approximated by linear functions, while others are well approximated by quadratic functions. Still others are approximated best by other kinds of functions.

Example 1. (*Temperature as a function of frequency of cricket chirps*). It has been shown experimentally that the temperature T, in degrees Fahrenheit, is a linear function of the number of cricket chirps per minute, C. When crickets chirp 60 times per minute the temperature is 55° and when they chirp 88 times per minute the temperature is 62°.

a) Find a linear function that fits the data.

b) Find the temperature when there are 76 chirps per minute; 100 per minute.

To determine T as a function of C we use the two-point equation

$$T - T_1 = \frac{T_2 - T_1}{C_2 - C_1}(C - C_1),$$

and the data (ordered pairs) $(60, 55°)$, $(88, 62°)$.

We substitute and simplify:

$$T - 55 = \frac{62 - 55}{88 - 60}(C - 60)$$

$$T - 55 = \frac{1}{4}(C - 60)$$

$$T = \frac{1}{4}C + 40.$$

Now, using this function, we find that when $C = 76$, we have $T = 59°$. When $C = 100$, we have $T = 65°$.

[49]

Example 2. (*Profit and loss analysis*). Boxowits, Inc., a computer manufacturing firm, is going to produce a new minicalculator. During the first year, the costs for setting up the new production line are \$100,000. These are fixed costs such as rent, tools, etc. These costs must be incurred before any calculators are produced. The additional cost of producing a calculator is \$20. This cost is directly related to production, such as materials, wages, fuel, and so on. It is a variable cost, according to the number of calculators produced. If x calculators are produced, the variable cost is then $20x$ dollars. The *total* cost of producing x calculators is given by a function C:

Total cost = fixed cost plus variable cost
$$C(x) = 100{,}000 + 20x.$$

The firm determines that its revenue (money coming in) from the sales of the calculators is \$45 per calculator, or $45x$ dollars, for x calculators. Thus we have a *revenue* function R:

$$R(x) = 45x.$$

The stockholders are most interested in the *profit* function P:

$$\text{Profit} = \text{Revenue} - \text{Total cost}$$

$$P(x) = 45x - (100{,}000 + 20x)$$

$$P(x) = 25x - 100{,}000.$$

Find those values of x for which (a) the company will break even; (b) the company will make a profit; and (c) the company will suffer a loss.

In this example, we have a model consisting of three linear functions. The function that will provide the answer to the question is the profit function P. When the profit is 0 the company breaks even. When it is positive the company makes money. When it is negative the company loses money.

Let us first find the value(s) of x that make $P(x) = 0$:

$$0 = P(x) = 25x - 100{,}000$$

$$25x = 100{,}000$$

$$x = 4{,}000.$$

The breakeven point occurs when 4000 calculators are sold. When $x > 4000$ there is a profit. When $x < 4000$ there is a loss.

A graph of the profit function in the preceding exam-

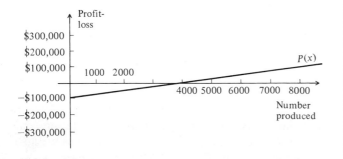

[50]

ple is of interest. In fact, graphs are often of considerable help with mathematical models.

Example 3. (*A projectile problem*). When an object such as a bullet or a ball is shot or thrown upward with an initial velocity v_0, its height is given, approximately, by a quadratic function:

$$s = -4.9t^2 + v_0 t + h.$$

In this function, h is the starting height in meters, s is the actual height (also in meters), and t is the time from projection in seconds.

This model is constructed from theoretical principles, rather than experiment. It is based on the assumption that there is no air resistance, and that the force of gravity pulling the object earthward is constant. Neither of these conditions exists precisely, so this model (as is the case with most mathematical models) gives only approximate results.

A model rocket is fired upward. At the end of the burn it has an upward velocity of 49 m/sec and is 155 m high. Find (a) its maximum height and when it is attained; (b) when it reaches the ground.

We will start counting time at the end of the burn. Thus $v_0 = 49$ and $h = 155$. We will graph the appropriate function, and we begin by completing the square:

$$s = -4.9\left(t^2 - \frac{49}{4.9}t\right) + 155$$

$$= -4.9(t^2 - 10t + 25 - 25) + 155$$

$$= -4.9(t - 5)^2 + 4.9 \times 25 + 155$$

$$= -4.9(t - 5)^2 + 277.5.$$

The vertex of the graph is the point $(5, 277.5)$ and the graph is shown on the following page. The maximum height reached is 277.5 m and it is attained 5 seconds after the end of the burn.

To find when the rocket reaches the ground, we set $s = 0$ in our equation and solve for t:

$$-4.9(t - 5)^2 + 277.5 = 0$$

$$(t - 5)^2 = \frac{277.5}{4.9}$$

$$t - 5 = \sqrt{\frac{277.5}{4.9}} \approx 7.525$$

$$t \approx 12.525.$$

The rocket will reach the ground about 12.525 seconds after the end of the burn. **[51]**

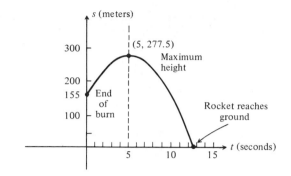

Exercise Set 4.4

1. (*Life expectancy of females in the United States*). In 1950 the life expectancy of females was 72 years. In 1970 it was 75 years. Let E represent the life expectancy and t the number of years since 1950. ($t = 0$ gives 1950 and $t = 10$ gives 1960).

   a) Express E as a linear function of t. [*Hint:* Data points are $(0, 72)$ and $(20, 75)$.]

   b) Use the equation of (a) to predict the life expectancy of females in 1980; in 1985.

2. (*Life expectancy of males in the United States*). In 1950 the life expectancy of males was 65 years. In 1970 it was 68 years. Let E represent life expectancy and t the number of years since 1950.

   a) Express E as a linear function of t.

   b) Use the equation of (a) to predict the life expectancy of males in 1980; in 1985.

3. (*Percentage of the population in college*). In 1940 15% of the population was in college. In 1970 52.5% was in college. Let P represent the percentage of the population in college, and t the number of years since 1940.

   a) Express P as a linear function of t.

   b) Use the equation of (a) to predict the percentage of the population in college in 1980; in 2000.

4. (*Natural gas demand*). In 1950 natural gas demand in the United States was 19 quadrillion BTU. In 1960 the demand was 21 quadrillion BTU. Let D represent the demand for natural gas t years after 1950.

   a) Express D as a linear function of t.

   b) Use the equation of (a) to predict the natural gas demand in 1980; in 2000.

5. A rocket is fired upward from ground level at a velocity of 147 m/sec. Find (a) its maximum height and when it is attained; (b) when it reaches the ground.

6. A rocket is fired upward from ground level at a velocity of 245 m/sec. Find (a) its maximum height and when it is attained; (b) when it reaches the ground.

7. The sum of the base and height of a triangle is 20. Find the dimensions for which the area is a maximum.

8. The sum of the base and height of a triangle is 14. Find the dimensions for which the area is a maximum.

9. (*Maximizing yield*). An orange grower finds that she gets an average yield of 40 bu per tree when she plants 20 trees on an acre of ground. Each time she adds a tree to an acre the yield per tree decreases by 1 bu, due to congestion. How many trees per acre should she plant for maximum yield?

10. (*Maximizing revenue*). When a theatre owner charges $2 for admission he averages 100 people attending. For each 10¢ increase in admission price the average number attending decreases by 1. What should be charge to make the most money?

11. (*Maximizing area*). A farmer wants to enclose two rectangular regions near a river, one for sheep and one for cattle. He is going to use 60 m of fence. What is the area of the largest region he can enclose?

12. (*Profit and loss in the ski business*). A ski manufacturer is planning a new line of skis. For the first year the fixed costs for setting up the new production line are $22,500. Variable costs for producing each pair of skis are estimated to be $40. The sales department projects that 3,000 pairs of skis can be sold the first year. The revenue from each pair is to be $85.

a) Formulate a function $C(x)$ for the total cost of producing x pairs of skis.

b) Formulate a function $R(x)$ for the total revenue from the sale of x pairs of skis.

c) Formulate a function $P(x)$ for the profit from the sale of x pairs of skis.

d) What profit or loss will the company realize if 3,000 pairs are actually sold?

e) Find the breakeven value of x.

f) Find the values of x that will result in a profit.

g) Find the values of x that will result in a loss.

4.5 Sets, Sentences, and Inequalities

The *intersection* of two sets consists of those elements common to the sets. Intersection is illustrated in the following diagram. Note that the intersection of two sets may be the empty set. The intersection of sets A and B is indicated as $A \cap B$.

Graphs are set diagrams. They often show pictorially the solution set of an equation or inequality. We can find intersections of solution sets using graphs. In the following example, we find the intersection of the set of all x greater than 3 and the set of all x less than or equal to 5. These sets are indicated, and the symbolism is read, as follows:

$\{x \mid x > 3\}$ "the set of all x such that x is greater than 3,"

$\{x \mid x \leqslant 5\}$ "the set of all x such that x is less than or equal to 5."

Example 1. Find and graph $\{x \mid x > 3\} \cap \{x \mid x \leqslant 5\}$.

We graph the two solution sets separately and then find the intersection.

$$\{x|x > 3\}$$

$$\{x|x \leqslant 5\}$$

The open circle at 3 indicates that 3 is not in the solution set. The solid circle at 5 indicates that 5 is in the solution set. The intersection is as follows.

$$\{x|3 < x\} \cap \{x|x \leqslant 5\}$$

Example 2. Graph $\{x \mid -3 \leqslant x\} \cap \{x \mid x \leqslant 0\}$.

Again, we graph the solution sets separately and then find the intersection.

$$\{x|-3 \leqslant x\}$$

$$\{x|x \leqslant 0\}$$

$$\{x|-3 \leqslant x\} \cap \{x|x \leqslant 0\}$$

[52–57]

The *union* of two sets consists of the members that are in one or both of the sets. Union is illustrated in the following diagram. The union of sets *A* and *B* is indicated as $A \cup B$.

In the following examples, we find unions of solution sets. Note that we graph the individual sets separately and then combine them.

Example 3. Graph $\{x \mid -1 \leqslant x\} \cup \{x \mid x < 2\}$.

$$\{x|-1 \leqslant x\}$$

$$\{x|x < 2\}$$

$$\{x|-1 \leqslant x\} \cup \{x|x < 2\} = \text{The set of all real numbers}$$

Example 4. Graph $\{x \mid x \leqslant -2\} \cup \{x \mid x > 1\}$.

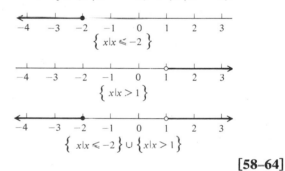

$$\{x|x \leqslant -2\}$$

$$\{x|x > 1\}$$

$$\{x|x \leqslant -2\} \cup \{x|x > 1\}$$

[58–64]

COMPOUND SENTENCES

When two sentences are joined by the word *and*, a compound sentence is formed. Such a sentence is called a *conjunction*. (The word conjunction used in this way is a logical term; the meaning is not the same as in ordinary grammar.) A conjunction of two sentences is true when both parts are true. Thus the solution set is the intersection of the solution sets of the parts. Consider, for example, the conjunction

$$-2 \leqslant x \qquad and \qquad x < 1.$$

Any number that makes this sentence true must make both parts true. We can graph the solution set by graphing the intersection of the two solution sets of the parts.

$-2 \leqslant x$ $x < 1$

Any number in this set   Any number in this set makes
makes the first part true.   the second part true.

Any number in this set (the intersection) makes both
parts true ($-2 \leqslant x$ *and* $x < 1$ are both true).

We often abbreviate certain conjunctions of inequalities. In this case,

$-2 \leqslant x$ *and* $x < 1$ is abbreviated $-2 \leqslant x < 1$.

The latter is read "-2 is less than or equal to x and x is less than 1," or "-2 is less than or equal to x is less than 1." Thus

$$\{x \mid -2 \leqslant x < 1\} = \{x \mid -2 \leqslant x \text{ and } x < 1\}$$
$$= \{x \mid -2 \leqslant x\} \cap \{x \mid x < 1\}.$$

The word *and* corresponds to set *intersection*.

[65–71]

Example 1. Solve and graph $-3 < 2x + 5 < 7$.

Method 1. $-3 < 2x + 5$ *and* $2x + 5 < 7$

                                 (rewriting using *and*)

        $-8 < 2x$ *and* $2x < 2$

                                   (adding -5)

        $-4 < x$ *and* $x < 1$

                                 (multiplying by $\frac{1}{2}$)

Method 2. $-3 < 2x + 5 < 7$
            $-8 < 2x < 2$
            $-4 < x < 1$

The solution set is

$$\{x \mid -4 < x\} \cap \{x \mid x < 1\}, \quad \text{or} \quad \{x \mid -4 < x < 1\}.$$

The graph is as follows:

Example 2. Solve and graph

$$-4 < \frac{5 - 3x}{2} \leqslant 5.$$

$-8 < 5 - 3x \leqslant 10$ (multiplying by 2)

$-13 < -3x \leqslant 5$ (adding -5)

$\dfrac{13}{3} > x \geqslant -\dfrac{5}{3}$ $\left(\text{multiplying by } -\dfrac{1}{3}\right)$

$-\dfrac{5}{3} \leqslant x < \dfrac{13}{3}$ $\left(x \geqslant -\dfrac{5}{3} \text{ means } -\dfrac{5}{3} \leqslant x,\right.$

                 and

           $\left.\dfrac{13}{3} > x \text{ means } x < \dfrac{13}{3}\right)$

The solution set is $\left\{x \mid -\dfrac{5}{3} \leqslant x < \dfrac{13}{3}\right\}$.

The graph is as follows:

[72–74]

When two sentences are joined by the word *or* a compound sentence is formed. Such a sentence is called a *disjunction*. A disjunction of two sentences is true when either part is true. It is also true when both parts are true. The solution set of a disjunction is thus the union of the solution sets of the parts. Consider the disjunction

$$x < -2 \quad or \quad x > \frac{1}{4}.$$

Any number that makes either or both of the parts true makes the disjunction true.

We can graph the solution set by graphing the union of the solution sets of the parts.

$x < -2$

Any number in this set makes the first part true.

Any number in this set makes the second part true.

$x < -2 \ or \ x > \frac{1}{4}$
$\{x \mid x < -2\} \cup \{x \mid x > \frac{1}{4}\}$

Any number in this set makes one or both of the parts true.

The word *or* corresponds to set *union*.

Note that $3x \leqslant 15$ is an abbreviation for $3x < 15$ *or* $3x = 15$.

There is no compact way to abbreviate disjunctions of inequalities, ordinarily. *Be careful about this!* For ex-

ample, if you try to abbreviate $-3 < x$ or $x < 4$ as $-3 < x < 4$ you will be *wrong*, because $-3 < x < 4$ is an abbreviation for the conjunction $-3 < x$ *and* $x < 4$.

Example 1. Solve. Then graph.

$2x - 5 < -7 \ or \ 2x - 5 > 7$

$\quad 2x < -2 \ or \quad 2x > 12$ (adding 5)

$\quad x < -1 \ or \quad \quad x > 6$ (multiplying by $\frac{1}{2}$)

The solution set is $\{x \mid x < -1 \ or \ x > 6\}$ which is the union $\{x \mid x < -1\} \cup \{x \mid x > 6\}$.

The graph is as follows:

Example 2. Solve. Then graph.

$$\frac{4 - 3x}{2} < -1 \ or \ \frac{4 - 3x}{2} \geqslant 1$$

$4 - 3x < -2 \ or \ 4 - 3x \geqslant 2$ (multiplying by 2)

$4 < -2 + 3x \ or \ 4 \geqslant 2 + 3x$ (adding $3x$)

$6 < 3x \quad \quad or \ 2 \geqslant 3x$

$2 < x \quad \quad or \ \dfrac{2}{3} \geqslant x$

The solution set is

$$\left\{ x \mid 2 < x \quad or \quad \frac{2}{3} \geqslant x \right\},$$

which is the union

$$\left\{ x \mid 2 < x \right\} \cup \left\{ x \mid \frac{2}{3} \geqslant x \right\}.$$

The graph is as follows:

[75–78]

Exercise Set 4.5

Find these unions or intersections.

1. $\{3, 4, 5, 8, 10\} \cap \{1, 2, 3, 4, 5, 6, 7\}$ **2.** $\{3, 4, 5, 8, 10\} \cup \{1, 2, 3, 4, 5, 6, 7\}$ **3.** $\{0, 2, 4, 6, 8\} \cup \{4, 6, 9\}$

4. $\{0, 2, 4, 6, 8\} \cap \{4, 6, 9\}$ **5.** $\{a, b, c\} \cap \{c, d\}$ **6.** $\{a, b, c\} \cup \{c, d\}$

Graph.

7. $\{x \mid 7 \leqslant x\} \cup \{x \mid x < 9\}$ **8.** $\left\{x \mid -\frac{1}{2} \leqslant x\right\} \cup \left\{x \mid x < \frac{1}{2}\right\}$ **9.** $\left\{x \mid -\frac{1}{2} \leqslant x\right\} \cap \left\{x \mid x < \frac{1}{2}\right\}$

10. $\left\{x \mid x > \frac{1}{4}\right\} \cap \{x \mid 1 \geqslant x\}$ **11.** $\{x \mid x < -\pi\} \cup \{x \mid x > \pi\}$ **12.** $\{x \mid -\pi \leqslant x\} \cap \{x \mid x < \pi\}$

13. $\{x \mid x < -7\} \cup \{x \mid x = -7\}$ **14.** $\left\{x \mid x > \frac{1}{2}\right\} \cup \left\{x \mid x = \frac{1}{2}\right\}$

Solve. Then graph.

15. $-2 < x + 1$ **16.** $-5 \geqslant x + 3$ **17.** $x - 5 > -7$ **18.** $x - 3 \leqslant 9$

Solve.

19. $2x - 3 \geqslant -6$ **20.** $5x + 7 < -8$ **21.** $7 - 3x < x - 9$ **22.** $5 - 2x \geqslant 7x + 4$

Solve. Then graph.

23. $-2 \leqslant x + 1 < 4$ **24.** $-3 < x + 2 \leqslant 5$ **25.** $5 \leqslant x - 3 \leqslant 7$ **26.** $-1 < x - 4 < 7$

Solve.

27. $-2 < 2x + 1 < 5$ **28.** $-3 \leqslant 5x + 1 \leqslant 3$ **29.** $-4 \leqslant 6 - 2x < 4$ **30.** $-3 < 1 - 2x \leqslant 3$

Solve.

31. $-\frac{1}{4} \leqslant 2x + 1 \leqslant \frac{1}{4}$ **32.** $-\frac{1}{2} < 3x - 4 < \frac{1}{2}$ **33.** $-1 \leqslant \frac{2 - 3x}{2} < 1$ **34.** $-3 \leqslant \frac{4 - 2x}{2} \leqslant 3$

Solve. Then graph.

35. $3x \leqslant -6 \ or \ x - 1 > 0$ **36.** $2x < 8 \ or \ x + 3 \geqslant 1$

37. $x - 1 < -2 \ or \ x - 1 > 2$ **38.** $x - 3 \leqslant -1 \ or \ x - 3 \geqslant 1$

39. $2x + 3 \leqslant -4 \ or \ 2x + 3 \geqslant 4$ **40.** $3x - 1 < -5 \ or \ 3x - 1 > 5$

Solve.

41. $2x - 20 < -0.8$ *or* $2x - 20 > 0.8$

42. $5x + 11 \leqslant -4$ *or* $5x + 11 \geqslant 4$

43. $x + 14 \leqslant -\dfrac{1}{4}$ *or* $x + 14 \geqslant \dfrac{1}{4}$

44. $x - 9 < -\dfrac{1}{2}$ *or* $x - 9 > \dfrac{1}{2}$

 45. The length of a rectangle is 15.23 cm. What widths will give a perimeter greater than 40.23 cm and less than 137.8 cm?

46. The height of a triangle is 15 m. What lengths of the base will keep the area less than or equal to 305.4 m^2 (and, of course, positive)?

▶ **47.** To get an A in a course, a student's average must be greater than or equal to 90%. It will of course be less than or equal to 100%. On the first three tests a student scored 83%, 87%, and 93%. What scores on the fourth test will produce an A? Is an A possible?

48. In Exercise 47, suppose the scores on the first three tests are 75%, 70%, and 83%. What scores on the fourth test will produce an A? Is an A possible?

✗ 4.6 Equations and Inequalities with Absolute Value

Absolute value was defined in Chapter 1 (p. 2). A more informal way of thinking of absolute value is that it is the distance from 0 of a number on a number line. For example $|4|$ is 4 because 4 is 4 units from 0; $|-5|$ is 5 because -5 is 5 units from 0. This idea is helpful in solving equations and inequalities with absolute value.

Example 1. Solve $|x| = 3$.

To solve we look for all numbers x whose distance from 0 is 3. There are two of them, so there are two solutions, 3 and -3. The graph is as follows:

[79, 80]

Example 2. Solve $|x| < 3$.

This time we look for all numbers x whose distance from 0 is less than 3. These are the numbers between -3 and 3. The solution set and its graph are as follows:

$$\{x \mid -3 < x < 3\}$$

[81, 82]

Example 3. Solve $|x| \geqslant 3$.

This time we look for all numbers x whose distance from 0 is 3 or greater. The solution set and its graph are as follows:

$$\{x \mid x \leqslant -3 \ or \ x \geqslant 3\}$$

[83, 84]

The results of the above examples can be generalized as follows.

For any $a > 0$,

  i) $|x| = a$ is equivalent to $x = -a$ or $x = a$.

 ii) $|x| < a$ is equivalent to $-a < x < a$.

iii) $|x| > a$ is equivalent to $x < -a$ or $x > a$.

Similar statements hold true for $|x| \leq a$ and $|x| \geq a$.

Let us now consider the inequality $|x - 2| = 3$. Note that this is a translation of $|x| = 3$, two units to the right. We first graph $|x| = 3$.

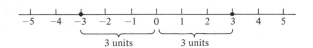

This consists of the numbers that are a distance of 3 from 0. We now translate.

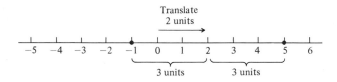

This solution set consists of the numbers that are a distance of 3 from 2 (note that 2 is where 0 went in the translation.)

The solutions of $|x - 2| = 3$ are -1 and 5.

The results of this example can be generalized as follows.

For any a, $|x - a|$ is the distance of x from a.

Examples

a) $|x - 5|$ is the distance of x from 5.

b) $|x + 7|$ is the distance of x from -7 [because $x + 7 = x - (-7)$].

Here are some further examples of solving inequalities.

Example 4. Solve $|x + 2| < 3$.

Method 1. We translate the graph of $|x| < 3$, to the left 2 units.

The solution set is $\{x \,|\, -5 < x < 1\}$.

Method 2. The solutions are those numbers x whose distance from -2 is less than 3. Thus to find the solutions graphically we locate -2. Then we locate those numbers that are less than 3 units to the left and less than 3 units to the right. Thus the solution set is $\{x \,|\, -5 < x < 1\}$.

Method 3. We use Property (ii), replacing x by $x + 2$.

$$|x + 2| < 3$$
$$-3 < x + 2 < 3$$
$$-5 < x < 1$$

The solution set is $\{x \,|\, -5 < x < 1\}$.   **[85–87]**

The sentences in the next examples are more complicated. While we could continue using translations and graphs, this actually gets more difficult than if we use Properties (i) to (iii).

Example 5. Solve $|2x + 3| = 1$.

$2x + 3 = -1$ *or* $2x + 3 = 1$ (Property i)

    $2x = -4$ *or* $2x = -2$ (adding -3)

      $x = -2$ *or* $x = -1$

The solution set is $\{-2, -1\}$.

Example 6. Solve $|2x + 3| \leqslant 1$.

$$-1 \leqslant 2x + 3 \leqslant 1 \qquad \text{(Property ii)}$$
$$-4 \leqslant 2x \leqslant -2 \qquad \text{(adding } -3\text{)}$$
$$-2 \leqslant x \leqslant -1$$

The solution set is $\{x \mid -2 \leqslant x \leqslant -1\}$.

Example 7. Solve $|3 - 4x| > 2$.

$$3 - 4x < -2 \quad or \quad 3 - 4x > 2 \qquad \text{(Property iii)}$$
$$-4x < -5 \quad or \quad -4x > -1 \qquad \text{(adding } -3\text{)}$$
$$x > \frac{5}{4} \quad or \quad x < \frac{1}{4}$$

The solution set is $\{x \mid x > \frac{5}{4} \text{ or } x < \frac{1}{4}\}$.   **[88–90]**

Exercise Set 4.6

Solve and graph.

1. $|x| = 7$

2. $|x| = \pi$

3. $|x| < 7$

4. $|x| \leqslant \pi$

5. $|x| \geqslant \pi$

6. $|x| > 7$

Solve. Use three methods.

7. $|x - 1| = 4$

8. $|x - 7| = 5$

9. $|x + 8| < 9$

10. $|x + 6| \leqslant 10$

11. $|x + 8| \geqslant 9$

12. $|x + 6| > 10$

13. $\left| x - \frac{1}{4} \right| < \frac{1}{2}$

14. $|x - 0.5| \leqslant 0.2$

Solve. Use any method.

15. $|3x| = 1$

16. $|5x| = 4$

17. $|3x + 2| = 1$

18. $|7x - 4| = 8$

19. $|3x| < 1$

20. $|5x| \leqslant 4$

21. $|2x + 3| \leqslant 9$

22. $|2x + 3| < 13$

23. $|x - 5| > 0.1$

24. $|x - 7| \geqslant 0.4$

25. $\left| x + \frac{2}{3} \right| \leqslant \frac{5}{3}$

26. $\left| x + \frac{3}{4} \right| < \frac{1}{4}$

27. $|6 - 4x| \leqslant 8$

28. $|5 - 2x| > 10$

29. $\left| \frac{2x + 1}{3} \right| > 5$

30. $\left| \frac{3x + 2}{4} \right| \leqslant 5$

31. $\left| \frac{13}{4} + 2x \right| > \frac{1}{4}$

32. $\left| \frac{5}{6} + 3x \right| < \frac{7}{6}$

33. $\left| \frac{3 - 4x}{2} \right| \leqslant \frac{3}{4}$

34. $\left| \frac{2x - 1}{3} \right| \geqslant \frac{5}{6}$

35. $|x - a| = e$

36. $|x + a| = e$

37. $|x - a| < e$

38. $|x - a| \geqslant e$

39. $|x - 2.0245| < 0.1011$

40. $|x + 17.217| > 5.0012$

41. $|3.0147x - 8.9912| \leqslant 6.0243$

42. $|-2.1437x + 7.8814| \geqslant 9.1132$

▶ Solve. Explain your answers.

43. $|x| = -3$ **44.** $|x| < -3$ **45.** $|2x - 4| < -5$ **46.** $|3x + 5| < 0$

47. a) Prove that $\left|x - \dfrac{a + b}{2}\right| < \dfrac{b - a}{2}$ is equivalent to $a < x < b$.

Use graphs or the result of (a) to find an inequality with absolute value for each of the following:

b) $-5 < x < 5$ c) $-6 < x < 6$ d) $-1 < x < 7$ e) $-5 < x < 1$

48. Use absolute value to prove that the number halfway between a and b is $\dfrac{a + b}{2}$.

✶ ④.7 Quadratic and Related Inequalities

Inequalities such as the following are called *quadratic* inequalities:

$$x^2 - 2x - 2 > 0, \qquad 3x^2 + 5x + 1 \leq 0.$$

In each case we have a polynomial of degree 2 on the left. One way of solving quadratic inequalities is by graphing.

Example 1. Solve $x^2 + 2x - 3 > 0$.

We consider the function $f(x) = x^2 + 2x - 3$. The inputs that produce positive outputs are the solutions of the inequality. We graph the function (at the right) to see where the outputs (function values) are positive.

We set $f(x) = 0$ and factor to find the intercepts, and graph:

$(x + 3)(x - 1) = 0$ so $x = -3$ or $x = 1$.

The solution set of the inequality is $\{x \mid x > 1$ or $x < -3\}$.   **[91]**

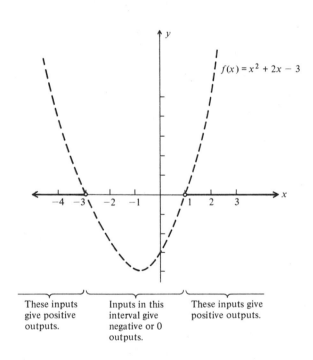

$f(x) = x^2 + 2x - 3$

These inputs give positive outputs.

Inputs in this interval give negative or 0 outputs.

These inputs give positive outputs.

Example 2. Solve $x^2 - 2x \leq 2$.

We first find standard form, with 0 on one side:

$$x^2 - 2x - 2 \leq 0.$$

Now we graph the function $f(x) = x^2 - 2x - 2$. (See the following page.) The quadratic formula is needed to find the intercepts. They are $1 + \sqrt{3}$ and $1 - \sqrt{3}$.

The solution set is $\{x \mid 1 - \sqrt{3} \leq x \leq 1 + \sqrt{3}\}$.   **[92]**

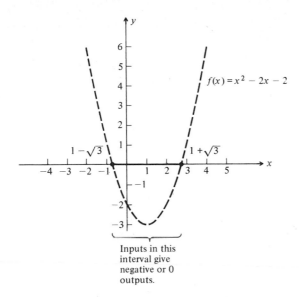

$f(x) = x^2 - 2x - 2$

$1 - \sqrt{3}$ $1 + \sqrt{3}$

Inputs in this interval give negative or 0 outputs.

It should be pointed out that we need not actually draw graphs as in the preceding examples. Merely visualizing the graph will usually suffice.

Let us now consider another method of solving inequalities.

Example 3. Solve $x^2 + 2x - 3 > 0$.

We factor, obtaining $(x + 3)(x - 1) > 0$.

For this inequality to be true, the product $(x + 3) \times (x - 1)$ must be positive. This means either that both of the factors must be positive or that both of the factors must be negative. We state this as follows:

$[x + 3 > 0 \quad \text{and} \quad x - 1 > 0] \qquad \text{or}$

$\qquad\qquad [x + 3 < 0 \quad \text{and} \quad x - 1 < 0].$

From this we obtain the following:

$\qquad [\boldsymbol{x > -3} \qquad \textbf{and} \qquad \boldsymbol{x > 1}]$

or

$\qquad [\boldsymbol{x < -3} \qquad \textbf{and} \qquad \boldsymbol{x < 1}].$

Remember that *and* corresponds to *intersection*. We graph the conjunction at the left.

$x > -3$

$x > 1$

$x > -3 \text{ and } x > 1$

$$\{x | x > -3\} \cap \{x | x > 1\} = \{x | x > 1\}$$

We also graph the conjunction at the right.

$x < -3$

$x < 1$

$x < -3 \text{ and } x < 1$

$$\{x | x < -3\} \cap \{x | x < 1\} = \{x | x < -3\}$$

Thus the sentence in boldface type above is equivalent to

$$x > 1 \qquad \text{or} \qquad x < -3.$$

Now remember that *or* corresponds to *union*. Thus the graph of the solution set is as follows:

The solution set can be described in the following two ways:

$$\{x \mid x > 1\} \cup \{x \mid x < -3\},$$
$$\{x \mid x > 1 \quad \text{or} \quad x < -3\}.$$

Example 4. Solve $x^2 + 2x - 3 < 0$.

We factor: $(x + 3)(x - 1) < 0$. This time we have a product of two factors less than 0, or negative. Thus the factors must have opposite signs. One must be negative and the other positive. We state this as follows:

$$[x + 3 > 0 \quad \text{and} \quad x - 1 < 0]$$

or

$$[x + 3 < 0 \quad \text{and} \quad x - 1 > 0].$$

This simplifies to

$$[x > -3 \quad \text{and} \quad x < 1]$$
$$\text{or} \ [x < -3 \quad \text{and} \quad x > 1].$$

We graph the conjunction at the left.

$$x > -3$$

$$x < 1$$

$$x > -3 \text{ and } x < 1$$

$$\{x \mid x > -3\} \cap \{x \mid x < 1\} = \{x \mid -3 < x < 1\}$$

We graph the conjunction at the right.

$$x < -3$$

$$x > 1$$

The intersection of these is empty:

$$\{x \mid x < -3 \quad \text{and} \quad x > 1\}$$
$$= \{x \mid x < -3\} \cap \{x \mid x > 1\} = \emptyset.$$

Now, remember that *or* corresponds to *union*. Thus the solution set is the following union:

$$\{x \mid -3 < x < 1\} \cup \emptyset,$$

which is simply

$$\{x \mid -3 < x < 1\}. \qquad \textbf{[93, 94]}$$

Although the following inequality is not quadratic, it can be solved by methods similar to those of the preceding examples.

Example 5. Solve $\dfrac{x + 1}{x - 2} \geq 3$.

We add -3, to get 0 on one side:

$$\frac{x + 1}{x - 2} - 3 \geq 0.$$

Next, we obtain a single fractional expression:

$$\frac{x + 1}{x - 2} - 3 \frac{x - 2}{x - 2} = \frac{x + 1 - 3x + 6}{x - 2} \geq 0$$

$$\frac{-2x + 7}{x - 2} \geq 0.$$

Let us consider the equality portion of $\geqslant$:

$$\frac{-2x + 7}{x - 2} = 0.$$

This has the solution $\frac{7}{2}$. Thus $\frac{7}{2}$ is in the solution set.

Next, consider the inequality portion of $\geqslant$:

$$\frac{-2x + 7}{x - 2} > 0.$$

The fractional expression will be positive when the numerator and denominator are both positive, or are both negative. We state this as follows:

$$[-2x + 7 > 0 \quad \text{and} \quad x - 2 > 0] \quad \text{or}$$
$$[-2x + 7 < 0 \quad \text{and} \quad x - 2 < 0].$$

This simplifies to

$$\left[x < \frac{7}{2} \quad \text{and} \quad x > 2 \right]$$

$$\text{or} \left[x > \frac{7}{2} \quad \text{and} \quad x < 2 \right].$$

The solution set of the sentence at the right is empty. The sentence at the left has the nonempty solution set $\{x \mid 2 < x < \frac{7}{2}\}$. The solution set of the original inequality is $\{x \mid 2 < x \leqslant \frac{7}{2}\}$.   **[95, 96]**

APPLIED PROBLEMS

Certain applied problems translate to inequalities, rather than equations. Here is an example.

Example. The height of a triangle is 2 cm greater than the base. Find the base b such that the area of the triangle will be greater than 20 cm².

We first translate to an inequality:

$$\frac{1}{2}bh > 20$$

$$\frac{1}{2}b(b + 2) > 20.$$

Then we solve the inequality:

$$b(b + 2) > 40$$
$$b^2 + 2b - 40 > 0.$$

We solve this inequality by thinking of the graph of $y = b^2 + 2b - 40$. The b-intercepts are the points $(-1 - \sqrt{41}, 0)$ and $(-1 + \sqrt{41}, 0)$. Since this graph opens upward, we know that $b^2 + 2b - 40 > 0$ for those b's such that $b < -1 - \sqrt{41}$ or $b > -1 + \sqrt{41}$. Since the base is not negative, the solutions of the original problem are those numbers b for which $b > -1 + \sqrt{41}$.   **[97]**

Exercise Set 4.7

Solve by graphing.

1. $x^2 - x - 2 < 0$ **2.** $x^2 - x - 2 > 0$ **3.** $x^2 - 4 > 0$ **4.** $x^2 - 4 < 0$

5. $x^2 \leqslant 1$ **6.** $x^2 \geqslant 1$ **7.** $x^2 - 2x > 5$ **8.** $x^2 - 2x < 5$

9. $x^2 - 2x + 1 \geqslant 0$ **10.** $x^2 - 6x + 9 \geqslant 0$ **11.** $x^2 - 6x + 4 < 0$ **12.** $x^2 - 5x + 2 < 0$

Solve without graphing.

13. $x^2 - 8x - 20 \leqslant 0$ **14.** $x^2 - 8x - 20 \geqslant 0$ **15.** $x^2 - 2x < 8$ **16.** $x^2 - 2x > 8$

17. $x^2 - 5x + 6 > 0$ **18.** $x^2 - 5x + 6 < 0$ **19.** $x^2 + 5x \leqslant 3$ **20.** $x^2 + 5x \geqslant 2$

21. $4x^2 + 7x < 15$ **22.** $4x^2 + 7x \geqslant 15$ **23.** $2x^2 + x > 5$ **24.** $2x^2 + x \leqslant 2$

Solve by any method.

25. $\dfrac{x+1}{2x-3} \geq 1$ **26.** $\dfrac{x-1}{x-2} \geq 3$ **27.** $\dfrac{x+1}{x+2} \leq 3$ **28.** $\dfrac{x+1}{2x-3} \leq 1$

29. $(x+1)(x-2) > (x+3)^2$ **30.** $(x-4)(x+3) \leq (x-1)^2$

31. $x^3 - x^2 > 0$ **32.** $x^3 - 4x > 0$ **33.** $x + \dfrac{4}{x} > 4$ **34.** $\dfrac{1}{x^2} \leq \dfrac{1}{x^3}$

35. $\dfrac{1}{x^3} \leq \dfrac{1}{x^2}$ **36.** $x + \dfrac{1}{x} > 2$

37. The base of a triangle is 4 cm greater than the height. Find the possible heights h such that the area of the triangle will be greater than 10 cm^2.

38. The length of a rectangle is 3 m greater than the width. Find the possible widths w such that the area of the rectangle will be greater than 15 m^2.

39. A company has the following total cost and total revenue functions to use in producing and selling x units of a certain product:

$$R(x) = 50x - x^2, \quad C(x) = 5x + 350.$$

(For reference, see p. 123).

a) Find the breakeven values.

b) Find the values of x that produce a profit.

c) Find the values of x that result in a loss.

40. A company has the following total cost and total revenue functions to use in producing and selling x units of a certain product:

$$R(x) = 80x - x^2, \quad C(x) = 10x + 600.$$

a) Find the breakeven values.

b) Find the values of x that produce a profit.

c) Find the values of x that result in a loss.

41. Solve $2.443x^2 + 1.203x > 4.8123$.

42. Solve $4.9132x^2 - 0.1283x \leq 3.3035$.

▶ **43.** Find the numbers k for which the quadratic equation $x^2 + kx + 1 = 0$ has (a) two real number solutions; (b) no real number solution.

44. Find the numbers k for which the quadratic equation $2x^2 - kx + 1 = 0$ has (a) two real number solutions; (b) no real number solution.

Chapter 4 Test, or Review

1. Find the slope of $-2x - y = 7$.

2. Find an equation of the line through $(0, 1)$ with $m = -\frac{1}{2}$.

3. Find an equation of the line containing $(4, 1)$ and $(-2, -1)$.

4. Find the distance between $(3, 7)$ and $(-2, 4)$.

5. Find the midpoint of the segment with endpoints $(3, 7)$ and $(-2, 4)$.

For the functions in Exercises 6–7,
a) find an equation of the type $f(x) = a(x - h)^2 + k$;
b) find the vertex;
c) find the line of symmetry; and
d) determine whether the second coordinate of the vertex is a maximum or a minimum, and find the maximum or minimum.

6. $f(x) = 3x^2 + 6x + 8$ **7.** $f(x) = -2x^2 - 3x + 6$

8. Find the x-intercepts: $y = f(x) = -x^2 - x - 1$.

9. a) Graph $f(x) = \sqrt{x}$.

    b) Graph $f(x) = \sqrt{x - \dfrac{1}{2}}$.

Find these unions or intersections.

10. $\{0, 2, 3, 7, 9\} \cup \{1, 3, 7, 11\}$ **11.** $\{4, 8, 16, 32\} \cap \{2, 8, 32, 64\}$

12. Graph $\{x \mid x \leqslant 7\} \cap \{x \mid x \geqslant 5\}$.

13. Graph $\{x \mid x \leqslant -3\} \cup \{x \mid x > 1\}$.

14. Solve $2x - 3 \leqslant 6$ *and* $x - 1 > 3$.

15. If the height of a triangle is 3 m, what bases b will make the area of the triangle greater than 15 m^2 and less than 27 m^2?

Solve.

16. $|x - 2| < 7$ **17.** $|2x - 3| \leqslant 12$

18. $|12 - x| \geqslant 29$ **19.** $|4x + 2| = 14$

20. Solve by graphing: $x^2 - 2x + 1 > 0$.

21. Solve by factoring: $8x^2 + 15x - 2 < 0$.

22. Solve $\dfrac{x-3}{2x+1} < 3$.

23. The sum of the base and height of a rectangle is 40. Find the dimensions for which the area is a maximum.

24. A company has the following total cost and total revenue functions to use in producing and selling x units of a product:

$$R(x) = 100 + x^2, \qquad C(x) = 15x + 200.$$

a) Find the breakeven values.

b) Find the values of x that produce a profit.

c) Find the values of x that result in a loss.

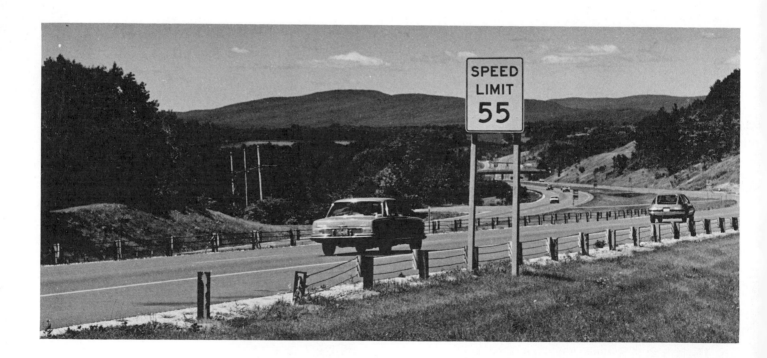

CHAPTER 5

Systems of Linear Equations and Inequalities

5.1 Systems of Equations in Two Variables

Recall that a *conjunction* of sentences is formed by joining sentences with the word *and*. Here is an example:

$$x + y = 11 \quad and \quad 3x - y = 5.$$

A solution of a sentence with two variables such as $x + y = 11$ is an ordered pair. Some pairs in the solution set of $x + y = 11$ are

$$(5, 6), \quad (12, -1), \quad \boxed{(4, 7)}, \quad (8, 3).$$

Some pairs in the solution set of $3x - y = 5$ are

$$(0, -5), \quad \boxed{(4, 7)}, \quad (-2, -11), \quad (9, 22).$$

The solution set of the sentence

$$x + y = 11 \quad and \quad 3x - y = 5$$

consists of all pairs that make *both* sentences true. That is, it is the *intersection* of the solution sets of both sentences. Note that $(4, 7)$ is a solution of the conjunction; in fact, it is the only solution.   [1, 2]

One way to find solutions is through trial and error. Another way is to graph the equations and look for points of intersection.

The graph to the right shows the solution sets of $x + y = 11$ and $3x - y = 5$. Their intersection is the single ordered pair $(4, 7)$.   [3]

We often refer to a conjunction of equations as a *system* of equations. We usually omit the word *and*, and very often write one equation under the other. For example, instead of writing

$$x + y = 11 \quad and \quad 3x - y = 5,$$

we often write

$$x + y = 11$$
$$3x - y = 5.$$

We now consider two algebraic methods for solving systems of linear equations.

THE SUBSTITUTION METHOD

To use the substitution method we solve one of the equations for one of the variables. Then we substitute in the other equation and solve.

Example. Solve the system

$$x + y = 11 \tag{1}$$
$$3x - y = 5. \tag{2}$$

First we solve equation (1) for y (we could just as well solve for x):

$$y = 11 - x.$$

Then we substitute $11 - x$ for y in equation (2). This gives an equation in one variable, which we know how to solve from earlier work. We solve for x:

$$3x - (\boxed{11 - x}) = 5$$
$$x = 4.$$

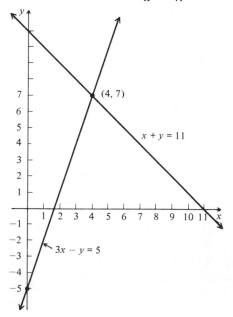

Now substitute 4 for x in either equation (1) or (2) and solve for y. Let us use equation (1):

$$\boxed{4} + y = 11$$
$$y = 7.$$

The solution is $(4, 7)$. Note the alphabetical listing: 4 for x, 7 for y.

Check:

$x + y = 11$	$3x - y = 5$
$\boxed{4} + \boxed{7}$ ∣ 11	$3 \cdot \boxed{4} - \boxed{7}$ ∣ 5
11 ∣	5 ∣ **[4, 5]**

THE ADDITION METHOD

The *addition method* makes use of the addition and multiplication principles for solving equations. Consider the system

$$3x - 4y = -1$$
$$-3x + 2y = \;\;\;0.$$

We add the lefthand sides and obtain $-2y$. We also add the righthand sides and obtain -1. Thus by addition we obtain a new equation: $-2y = -1$. This equation, together with the first one above, makes a new system, equivalent to the original:

$$3x - 4y = -1$$
$$-2y = -1.$$

When we add the lefthand sides and the righthand sides of two equations using the addition principle, as we did above, we often say that we "added the two equations."

In our new system above, if we multiply on both sides of the second equation by $-\frac{1}{2}$ (we may call this "multiplying the equation by $-\frac{1}{2}$") we obtain

$$3x - 4y = -1$$
$$y = \tfrac{1}{2}.$$

This system is equivalent to the original system, but it gives us the value of y, which is $\frac{1}{2}$.

Now let us multiply the second equation by 4 and add it to the first, obtaining

$$3x \quad\;\; = 1$$
$$y = \tfrac{1}{2}.$$

Now multiply the first equation by $\frac{1}{3}$, obtaining

$$x \quad\;\; = \tfrac{1}{3}$$
$$y = \tfrac{1}{2}.$$

We now know that the solution of the original system is $(\frac{1}{3}, \frac{1}{2})$, because the solutions of this last system are obvious and we know that this system is equivalent to the original. We know that the last system is equivalent to the original, because the only computations we did consisted of using the addition principle and multiplying by a nonzero constant, each of which produces results equivalent to the original equations. For this reason we do not need to check results, except to detect errors in computation.

Example 1. Solve

$$5x + 3y = \quad\;\; 7$$
$$3x - 5y = -23.$$

We first multiply the first equation by $\frac{1}{5}$ to make the x-coefficient 1:

$$x + \frac{3}{5}y = \quad \frac{7}{5}$$
$$3x - 5y = -23.$$

Now we look at the coefficient of x in the second equation (3), change the sign, and multiply the first equation by the result:

$$-3x - \frac{9}{5}y = -\frac{21}{5}$$
$$3x - 5y = -23.$$

Now we add the equations, obtaining

$$x + \frac{3}{5}y = \frac{7}{5}$$

(We are retaining the equation in which the x-coefficient is 1.)

$$-\frac{36}{5}y = -\frac{136}{5}.$$

The x-term in the second equation has disappeared. That was our goal at this point. Next we want to make the y-coefficient in the second equation 1, so we multiply by $-\frac{5}{36}$. Then we have

$$x + \frac{3}{5}y = \frac{7}{5}$$
$$y = 4.$$

We now work back up. We look at the coefficient of y in the first equation $(\frac{3}{5})$, change the sign, and multiply the second equation by the result. Then when we add, the y-term will disappear in the first equation. We get

$$x \quad = -1$$
$$y = \quad 4,$$

and the solution of the original system is $(-1, 4)$.

SHORTCUTS

There are various shortcuts possible when using the addition method. One such method is to interchange two equations before beginning. For example, if we have the system

$$3x - 5y = 17$$
$$x + 2y = \quad 4,$$

we may prefer to write the second equation first. Then we will already have an x-coefficient of 1 in the first equation.

Another shortcut consists of multiplying one or more equations by a power of 10 before beginning in order

to eliminate decimal points. For example, if we have the system

$$-0.3x + 0.5y = 0.03$$
$$0.01x - 0.4y = 1.2,$$

we can multiply both equations by 100 to clear of decimal points, obtaining

$$30x + 50y = \quad 3$$
$$x - 40y = 120.$$

Still other shortcuts are possible. However, it is recommended that no others be used at this point, because we are establishing an *algorithm*, which could be done mechanically by a computer.

Example 2. Solve

$$5x - 2y = 1$$
$$x + 3y = 7.$$

We will first interchange the equations, because the x-coefficient of the second equation is 1:

$$x + 3y = 7$$
$$5x - 2y = 1.$$

Next, we look at the coefficient of x in the second equation (5), change the sign, multiply the first equation by the result (-5), and then add the equations:

$$x + 3y = \quad 7$$
$$-17y = -34.$$

Now we multiply the second equation by $-\frac{1}{17}$, to make the y-coefficient 1:

$$x + 3y = 7$$
$$y = 2.$$

Now we work back up. We look at the coefficient of y in the first equation (3), change the sign, multiply the second equation by the result (-3), and then add the equations. This eliminates the y-term in the first equation:

$$x \quad = 1$$
$$y = 2.$$

The solution is $(1, 2)$.

The idea, in using this method, is to get a system of the form

$$x \quad = p$$
$$y = q,$$

where the coefficients of x and y on the left are 1. We can then read off the solution, (p, q). **[6–8]**

Exercise Set 5.1

1. Decide whether $\left(\frac{1}{2}, 1\right)$ is a solution.

$$3x + y = \frac{5}{2}$$

$$2x - y = \frac{1}{4}$$

2. Decide whether $\left(-2, \frac{1}{4}\right)$ is a solution.

$$x + 4y = -1$$

$$2x + 8y = -2$$

Solve graphically.

3. $x + y = 2$

$3x + y = 0$

4. $x + y = 1$

$3x + y = 7$

Solve, using the substitution method.

5. $x - 5y = 4$

$2x + \ y = 7$

6. $3x - y = 5$

$x + y = \frac{1}{2}$

Solve, using the addition method.

7. $x - 3y = 2$
$6x + 5y = -34$

8. $x + \ 3y = 0$
$20x - 15y = 75$

9. $0.3x + 0.2y = -0.9$
$0.2x - 0.3y = -0.6$

10. $0.2x - 0.3y = 0.3$
$0.4x + 0.6y = -0.2$

11. $\frac{1}{5}x + \frac{1}{2}y = 6$
$\frac{3}{5}x - \frac{1}{2}y = 2$

12. $\frac{2}{3}x + \frac{3}{5}y = -17$
$\frac{1}{2}x - \frac{1}{3}y = -1$

13. $2a = 5 - 3b$
$4a = 11 - 7b$

14. $7(a - b) = 14$
$2a = b + 5$

15. $\dfrac{x + y}{4} - \dfrac{x - y}{3} = 1$

$\dfrac{x - y}{2} + \dfrac{x + y}{4} = -9$

16. $\dfrac{x + y}{2} - \dfrac{y - x}{3} = 0$

$\dfrac{x + y}{3} - \dfrac{x + y}{4} = 0$

 Solve. Check by substituting.

17. $2.35x - 3.18y = 4.82$

$1.92x + 6.77y = -3.87$

18. $0.0375x + 0.912y = -1.003$

$463x - 801y = 946$

▶ Each of the following is a system of equations that is *not* linear. But each is *linear in form,* in that an appropriate substitution, say u for $1/x$ and v for $1/y$, yields a linear system. Solve for the new variable and then solve for the original variable.

19. $\dfrac{1}{x} - \dfrac{3}{y} = 2$

$\dfrac{6}{x} + \dfrac{5}{y} = -34$

20. $\dfrac{2}{x} + \dfrac{1}{y} = 0$

$\dfrac{5}{x} + \dfrac{2}{y} = -5$

21. $3\,|x| + 5\,|y| = 30$

$5\,|x| + 3\,|y| = 34$

22. $15\,|x| + 2\,|y| = 6$

$25\,|x| - 2\,|y| = -6$

✩ ⑤.2 Inconsistent and Dependent Equations; Applied Problems

INCONSISTENT EQUATIONS

Some systems of equations have no solution. Such a system is called *inconsistent*. For a system of two linear equations, this means that their graphs are parallel lines and do not intersect.

Example. Solve

$$x - 3y = 1$$
$$-2x + 6y = 5.$$

We multiply the first equation by 2 and add. This gives us

$$x - 3y = 1$$
$$0 = 7.$$

The second equation says that $0 \cdot x + 0 \cdot y = 7$. There are no numbers x and y for which this is true.

Whenever we obtain a statement such as $0 = 7$, which is obviously false, we will know that the system we are trying to solve has no solutions. It is inconsistent. The solution set is ∅.

The graphs of the above equations are as follows.

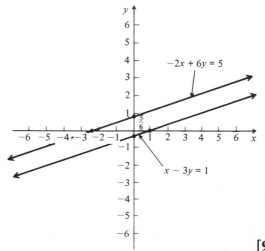

[9, 10]

DEPENDENT EQUATIONS

Consider the following system

$$2x + 3y = 1$$
$$4x + 6y = 2.$$

Note that if we multiply the first equation by 2 we get the second equation. Thus the two equations are equivalent. Or, to put it another way, the conjunction of the *two* equations is equivalent to *one* of the equations. Such equations are called *dependent*. If a system of *three* equations is equivalent to *one* of them or to the conjunction of *two* of them, then it is a dependent system.

> **Definition. If a system of *n* linear equations is equivalent to a system of fewer than *n* of them, then the system is *dependent*.**

Suppose we try to solve a dependent system of two equations:

$$2x + 3y = 1$$
$$4x + 6y = 2.$$

We obtain

$$x + \frac{3}{2}y = \frac{1}{2}$$
$$4x + 6y = 2$$

and then

$$x + \frac{3}{2}y = \frac{1}{2}$$
$$0 + 0 = 0.$$

When, in solving, we get an obviously true statement, such as $0 + 0 = 0$, we know that the system is dependent.

A dependent system of equations always has an infinite number of solutions. We usually describe the solutions by expressing one variable in terms of the other.

Example. Describe the solutions of the system

$$2x + 3y = 1$$
$$4x + 6y = 2.$$

In attempting to solve this system, above, we obtained

$$x + \frac{3}{2}y = \frac{1}{2}$$
$$0 + 0 = 0.$$

The last equation adds nothing, so we consider only the first one. Let us solve it for x. We obtain

$$x = \frac{1}{2} - \frac{3}{2}y, \quad \text{or} \quad \frac{1 - 3y}{2}.$$

We can now describe the ordered pairs in the solution set, in terms of y only, as follows:

$$\left(\frac{1 - 3y}{2}, y \right).$$

Any value we choose for y then gives us a value for x, and thus an ordered pair in the solution set. Some of these solutions are

$$(5, -3), \quad \left(-\frac{5}{2}, 2 \right), \quad \left(\frac{7}{2}, -2 \right). \quad \text{[11, 12]}$$

APPLIED PROBLEMS

Translating problems to equations becomes easier in many cases if we translate to more than one equation in more than one variable.

Example 1. An airplane flies the 3000-mi distance from Los Angeles to New York with a tail wind in 5 hr. On the return trip, against the wind, it makes the trip in 6 hr. Find the speed of the plane and the speed of the wind.

Translate: Let p = speed of the plane, and w = speed of the wind.

Then from $d_1 = r_1 \cdot t_1$, we have

$$3000 = (p + w)5 = 5p + 5w.$$

From $d_2 = r_2 \cdot t_2$, we have

$$3000 = (p - w)6 = 6p - 6w.$$

Then we solve the system:

$$5p + 5w = 3000$$
$$6p - 6w = 3000.$$

The solution is $(550, 50)$; that is, the speed of the plane is 550 mph and the speed of the wind is 50 mph. This checks in the original problem.

Example 2. Wine A is 5% alcohol and wine B is 15% alcohol. How many liters of each should be mixed to get a 10-liter mixture that is 12% alcohol?

a) First consider the amount of wine.

Let x = the amount of wine A, and y = the amount of wine B. The amount of the mixture is to be 10 ℓ. We get the equation

$$x + y = 10.$$

b) Second, consider the amount of alcohol.

The amount of alcohol in wine A is $5\% \cdot x$, and the amount in wine B is $15\% \cdot y$. We know that the amount in the mixture is $12\% \cdot 10$. We get the equation

$$5\% x + 15\% y = 12\% \cdot 10,$$

or

$$0.05x + 0.15y = 1.2,$$

or

$$5x + 15y = 120.$$

c) Now we solve the system:

$$x + \quad y = 10$$
$$5x + 15y = 120.$$

The solution is $(3, 7)$. Thus $3 \, \ell$ of wine A should be mixed with $7 \, \ell$ of wine B.   [13–16]

Exercise Set 5.2

In Exercises 1–6, solve. If a system is dependent, describe the solutions by expressing one variable in terms of the other.

1. $2a = 4 - 3b$
   $4a = 12 - 7b$

2. $7(a - b) = 21$
   $2a = b + 10$

3. $9x - 3y = 15$
   $6x - 2y = 10$

4. $2s - 3t = 9$
   $4s - 6t = 9$

5. $5c + 2d = 24$
   $30c + 12d = 10$

6. $3x + 2y = 18$
   $9x + 6y = 5$

7. Classify the systems in Exercises 1–6 as consistent or inconsistent.

8. Classify the systems in Exercises 1–6 as dependent or independent.

Solve the following systems.

9. $3x + 2y = 5$

$4y = 10 - 6x$

10. $5x + 2 = 7y$

$-14y + 4 = -10x$

11. $12y - 8x = 6$

$4x + 3 = 6y$

12. $16x - 12y = 10$

$6y + 5 = 8x$

Solve the following applied problems.

13. Find two numbers whose sum is -10 and whose difference is 1.

14. Find two numbers whose sum is -1 and whose difference is 10.

15. A boat travels 46 km downstream in 2 hr. It travels 51 km upstream in 3 hr. Find the speed of the boat and the speed of the stream.

16. An airplane travels 3000 km with a tail wind in 3 hr. It travels 3000 km with a head wind in 4 hr. Find the speed of the plane and the speed of the wind.

17. Antifreeze A is 18% alcohol. Antifreeze B is 10% alcohol. How many liters of each should be mixed to get 20 ℓ of a mixture that is 15% alcohol?

18. Beer A is 6% alcohol and beer B is 2% alcohol. How many liters of each should be mixed to get 50 ℓ of a mixture that is 3.2% alcohol?

 Solve.

19. $4.026x - 1.448y = 18.32$

$0.724y = -9.16 + 2.013x$

20. $0.0284y = 1.052 - 8.114x$

$0.0142y + 4.057x = 0.526$

▶ Determine the constant k such that each system is dependent.

21. $6x - 9y = -3$

$-4x + 6y = k$

22. $8x - 16y = 20$

$10x - 20y = k$

5.3 Systems of Equations in Three or More Variables

A solution of an equation in three variables is an ordered triple of numbers. A solution of a system, or conjunction, of equations in three variables is a triple that makes all of them true. Graphical methods of solving linear equations in three variables are unsatisfactory, because a three-dimensional coordinate system is required. The substitution method becomes cumbersome for most systems of more than two equations. Therefore, we will use the addition method. It is essentially the same as for systems of two equations.

Example. Solve

$2x - 4y + 6z = 22$ ①

$4x + 2y - 3z = 4$ ②

$3x + 3y - z = 4.$ ③

These numbers indicate the equations in the first, second, and third positions, respectively.

We begin by making the x-coefficient of equation ① a 1. We multiply by $\frac{1}{2}$:

$$x - 2y + 3z = 11 \qquad ①$$

$$4x + 2y - 3z = 4 \qquad ②$$

$$3x + 3y - z = 4. \qquad ③$$

Next, to eliminate x-terms, we multiply ① by -4 and add it to ②. We also multiply ① by -3 and add it to ③. Then we have the following:

$$
\begin{array}{ll}
x - 2y + 3z = 11 & \text{①} \\
10y - 15z = -40 & \text{②} \\
9y - 10z = -29. & \text{③}
\end{array}
$$

Next, we make the y-coefficient of ② a 1, by multiplying by $\frac{1}{10}$:

$$x - 2y + 3z = 11$$
$$y - \frac{15}{10}z = -4$$
$$9y - 10z = -29.$$

Hereafter we will omit the reference numbers.

Now we multiply ② by -9 and add it to ③:

$$x - 2y + 3z = 11$$
$$y - \frac{3}{2}z = -4$$
$$\frac{7}{2}z = 7.$$

Equation ③ is now multiplied by $\frac{2}{7}$ to make the z-coefficient 1:

$$x - 2y + 3z = 11$$
$$y - \frac{3}{2}z = -4$$
$$z = 2.$$

Now we start working back up. We multiply ③ by $\frac{3}{2}$ and add it to ②. We also multiply ③ by -3 and add it to ①:

$$x - 2y \quad = 5$$
$$y \quad = -1$$
$$z = 2.$$

Finally, we multiply ② by 2 and add it to ①:

$$x \quad = 3$$
$$y \quad = -1$$
$$z = 2.$$

The system has as its only solution $(3, -1, 2)$.

[17, 18]

DEPENDENT AND INCONSISTENT EQUATIONS

If a system of equations is inconsistent, we will obtain, at some stage of our solving, a false equation, such as $1 = 5$. If a system of three equations is dependent, this means that it is equivalent to a system of two of them, or to one of them alone. When we try to solve such a system, we may find that at some stage two of the equations are identical. We may also obtain an obviously true statement, such as $0 = 0$. When a system is dependent, its solutions should be described by expressing two of the variables in terms of one of them.

Example. Solve

$$
\begin{array}{ll}
x + 2y + 3z = 4 & \text{①} \\
2x - y + z = 3 & \text{②} \\
3x + y + 4z = 7. & \text{③}
\end{array}
$$

Since the x-coefficient in ① is already 1, we begin by multiplying ① by -2 and adding it to ②. We also multiply ① by -3 and add it to ③:

$$x + 2y + 3z = 4$$
$$-5y - 5z = -5$$
$$-5y - 5z = -5.$$

Now ② and ③ are identical. We no longer have a system of three equations, but a system of two. Thus we know that the system is dependent. If we were now to multiply ② by -1 and add it to ③ we would obtain $0 = 0$.

We proceed by multiplying ② by $-\frac{1}{5}$:

$$x + 2y + 3z = 4$$
$$y + z = 1.$$

Now we work back up. We multiply ② by -3 and add it to ①:

$$x - y \qquad = 1$$
$$y + z = 1.$$

We will express two of the variables in terms of the other one. Let us choose x.

Then we solve ① for y:

$$y = x - 1.$$

We substitute this value of y in ②, obtaining

$$x - 1 + z = 1.$$

Solving for z, we get

$$z = 2 - x.$$

The solutions, then, are all of the form

$$(x, x - 1, 2 - x).$$

We can obtain the solutions by choosing various values of x. If we let $x = 0$, we obtain the triple $(0, -1, 2)$. If we let $x = 1$, we obtain $(1, 0, 1)$, and so on.

[19, 20]

HOMOGENEOUS EQUATIONS

When all of the terms of a polynomial have the same degree, we say that the polynomial is *homogeneous*. Here are some examples:

$$3x^2 + 5y^2, \qquad 4x + 5y - 2z, \qquad 17x^3 - 4y^3 + 57z^3.$$

An equation formed by a homogeneous polynomial set equal to 0 is called a *homogeneous equation*. Let us now consider a system of homogeneous equations.

Example. Solve
$$4x - 3y + z = 0$$
$$2x - 3z = 0$$
$$-8x + 6y - 2z = 0.$$

Any homogeneous system like this always has a solution (can never be inconsistent), because $(0, 0, 0)$ is a solution. This is called the *trivial* solution. There may or may not be other solutions. To find out, we proceed as in the case of nonhomogeneous equations:

$$x - \frac{3}{4}y + \frac{1}{4}z = 0 \qquad \left(\text{multiplying by } \frac{1}{4}\right)$$

$$2x \phantom{- \frac{3}{4}y} - 3z = 0$$

$$-8x + 6y - 2z = 0$$

Now we multiply ① by -2 and add it to ②. We also multiply ① by 8 and add it to ③:

$$x - \frac{3}{4}y + \frac{1}{4}z = 0$$

$$\frac{3}{2}y - \frac{7}{2}z = 0$$

$$0 = 0.$$

Now we know that the system is dependent, hence it has an infinite set of solutions.

$$x - \frac{3}{4}y + \frac{1}{4}z = 0$$
$$\left(\text{multiplying 2 by } \frac{2}{3}\right)$$
$$y - \frac{7}{3}z = 0$$

Now we solve ② for y:

$$y = \frac{7}{3}z.$$

We substitute this value of y in ① and solve for x:

$$x - \frac{3}{4}\left(\frac{7}{3}z\right) + \frac{1}{4}z = 0$$

$$x = \frac{3}{2}z.$$

We can now describe the members of the solution set as follows:

$$\left(\frac{3}{2}z, \frac{7}{3}z, z\right).$$

Some of the ordered pairs in the solution set are

$$\left(\frac{3}{2}, \frac{7}{3}, 1\right), \qquad \left(3, \frac{14}{3}, 2\right), \qquad \left(-\frac{3}{2}, -\frac{7}{3}, -1\right).$$

[21, 22]

MATHEMATICAL MODELS AND APPLIED PROBLEMS

In a situation where a quadratic function will serve as a mathematical model, we may wish to find an equation, or formula, for the function. Recall that for a linear model, we can find an equation if we know two data points. For a quadratic function we need three data points.

Example 1. In a certain situation, it is believed that a quadratic function will be a good model. Find an equation of the function, given the data points $(1, -4)$, $(-1, -6)$, and $(2, -9)$.

We wish to find a quadratic function

$$f(x) = ax^2 + bx + c$$

containing the three given data points, i.e., a function for which the equation will be true when we substitute any of the ordered pairs of numbers into it. When we substitute, we get,

$$\text{for } (1, -4), \quad -4 = a \cdot 1^2 + b \cdot 1 + c$$
$$\text{for } (-1, -6), \quad -6 = a(-1)^2 + b(-1) + c$$
$$\text{for } (2, -9), \quad -9 = a \cdot 2^2 + b \cdot 2 + c.$$

We now have a system of equations in the three unknowns a, b, and c:

$$a + b + c = -4$$
$$a - b + c = -6$$
$$4a + 2b + c = -9$$

We solve this system of equations, obtaining

$(-2, 1, -3)$. Thus the function we are looking for is as follows:

$$f(x) = -2x^2 + x - 3. \qquad [23]$$

Example 2. (*The cost of operating an automobile at various speeds*). It is found that the cost of operating an automobile as a function of speed is approximated by a quadratic function. Use the data given to find an equation of the function. Then use the equation to determine the cost of operating the automobile at 60 mph and at 80 mph.

Speed in mph	Operating cost per mile, in cents
10	12
20	10
50	10

We use the three data points to obtain a, b, and c in $f(x) = ax^2 + bx + c$:

$$12 = 100a + 10b + c$$
$$10 = 400a + 20b + c \qquad \text{(substituting)}$$
$$10 = 2500a + 50b + c$$

We solve this system of equations, thus obtaining $(0.005, -0.35, 15)$. Thus

$$f(x) = 0.005x^2 - 0.35x + 15.$$

To find the cost of operating at 60 mph, we find $f(60)$:

$$f(60) = 0.005(60)^2 - 0.35(60) + 15$$
$$= 12 \text{¢}.$$

We also find $f(80)$:

$$f(80) = 0.005(80)^2 - 0.35(80) + 15$$
$$= 19 \text{¢}.$$

A graph of the cost function is as follows.

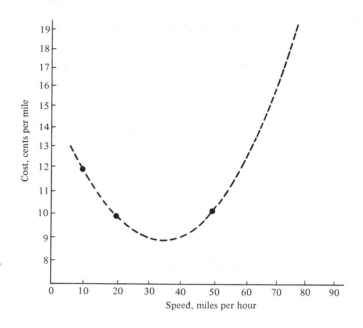

Speed, miles per hour

It should be noted that this cost function can give approximate results only within a certain interval. For example, $f(0) = 15$, meaning that it costs 15¢ per mile to stand still, and this, of course, is absurd.   [24]

Exercise Set 5.3

Consider the system

$$2x + 3y - 5z = 1$$
$$6x - 6y + 10z - 3$$
$$4x - 9y + 5z = 0.$$

1. Decide whether $\left(\dfrac{1}{2}, \dfrac{1}{3}, \dfrac{1}{5}\right)$ is a solution of the system.

2. Decide whether $(-1, 1, 0)$ is a solution of the system.

Solve. If a system has more than one solution, list three of them.

3.
$$x + y + z = 2$$
$$6x - 4y + 5z = 31$$
$$5x + 2y + 2z = 13$$

4.
$$x + 6y + 3z = 4$$
$$2x + y + 2z = 3$$
$$3x - 2y + z = 0$$

5.
$$x - y + 2z = -3$$
$$x + 2y + 3z = 4$$
$$2x + y + z = -3$$

6.
$$x + y + z = 6$$
$$2x - y - z = -3$$
$$x - 2y + 3z = 6$$

7.
$$4a + 9b = 8$$
$$8a + 6c = -1$$
$$ 6b + 6c = -1$$

8.
$$3p + 2r = 11$$
$$ q - 7r = 4$$
$$p - 6q = 1$$

9.
$$x + 2y - z = -8$$
$$2x - y + z = 4$$
$$8x + y + z = 2$$

10.
$$x + 2y - z = 4$$
$$4x - 3y + z = 8$$
$$5x - y = 12$$

11. $2x + y - 3z = 1$
$x - 4y + z = 6$
$4x - 16y + 4z = 24$

12. $4x + 12y + 16z = 4$
$3x + 4y + 5z = 3$
$x + 8y + 11z = 1$

13. $2x + y - 3z = 0$
$x - 4y + z = 0$
$4x - 16y + 4z = 0$

14. $4x + 12y + 16z = 0$
$3x + 4y + 5z = 0$
$x + 8y + 11z = 0$

15. $x + y - z = -3$
$x + 2y + 2z = -1$

16. $x + y + 13z = 0$
$x - y - 6z = 0$

17. $2x + y + z = 0$
$x + y - z = 0$
$x + 2y + 2z = 0$

18. $5x + 4y + z = 0$
$10x + 8y - z = 0$
$x - y - z = 0$

Hint for Exercises 19 and 20: First solve for $\dfrac{1}{x}$, $\dfrac{1}{y}$, and $\dfrac{1}{z}$.

19. $\dfrac{2}{x} - \dfrac{1}{y} - \dfrac{3}{z} = -1$

$\dfrac{2}{x} - \dfrac{1}{y} + \dfrac{1}{z} = -9$

$\dfrac{1}{x} + \dfrac{2}{y} - \dfrac{4}{z} = 17$

20. $\dfrac{2}{x} + \dfrac{2}{y} - \dfrac{3}{z} = 3$

$\dfrac{1}{x} - \dfrac{2}{y} - \dfrac{3}{z} = 9$

$\dfrac{7}{x} - \dfrac{2}{y} + \dfrac{9}{z} = -39$

21. (*Curve fitting*). Find numbers a, b, and c, such that a quadratic function $ax^2 + bx + c$ fits the data points $(1, 4)$, $(-1, -2)$, and $(2, 13)$.

22. (*Curve fitting*). Find numbers a, b, and c, such that a quadratic function $ax^2 + bx + c$ fits the data points $(1, 4)$, $(-1, 6)$, and $(-2, 16)$.

23. (*Predicting earnings*). A business earns \$38 in the first week, \$66 in the second week, and \$86 in the third week. When the manager graphs the points $(1, 38)$, $(2, 66)$, and $(3, 86)$, she finds that a quadratic function might fit the data.

a) Find a quadratic function that fits the data.

b) Using your model, predict the earnings for the fourth week.

24. (*Predicting earnings*). A business earns \$1000 in its first month, \$2000 in the second month, and \$8000 in the third month. The manager plots the points $(1, 1000)$, $(2, 2000)$, and $(3, 8000)$ and finds that a quadratic function might fit the data.

a) Find a quadratic function that fits the data.

b) Using your model, predict the earnings for the fourth month.

25. When man A, man B, and man C are working together, they can do a job in 2 hr. When man B and man C work together they can do the job in 4 hr. When man A and man B work together they can do the job in $\frac{12}{5}$ hr. How long would it take each, working alone, to do the job?

26. Pipes A, B, and C are connected to the same tank. When all three pipes are running, they can fill the tank in 3 hr. When pipes A and C are running, they can fill the tank in 4 hr. When pipes A and B are running, they can fill the tank in 8 hr. How long would it take each, running alone, to fill the tank?

27. Solve.

$$3.12x + 2.14y - 0.988z = 3.79$$

$$3.84x - 3.53y + 1.96z = 7.80$$

$$4.63x - 1.08y + 0.011z = 6.34$$

28. Solve.

$$1.01x - 0.905y + 2.12z = -2.54$$

$$1.32x + 2.05y + 2.97z = 3.97$$

$$2.21x + 1.35y + 0.001z = -3.15$$

▶ Solve.

29. $x + y + z + w = 2$

$2x + 2y + 4z + w = 1$

$x - y - z - w = -6$

$3x + y - z - w = -2$

30. $x - y + z + w = 0$

$2x + 2y + z - w = 5$

$3x + y - z - w = -4$

$x + y - 3z - 2w = -7$

5.4 Matrices and Systems of Equations

In solving systems of equations, we perform computations with the constants. The variables play no important role in the process. We can simplify writing by omitting the variables. For example, the system

$$3x + 4y = 5$$
$$x - 2y = 1$$

simplifies to

$$\begin{array}{rrr} 3 & 4 & 5 \\ 1 & -2 & 1 \end{array}$$

if we leave off the variables and omit the operation and equals signs.

In this example we have written a rectangular array of numbers. Such an array is called a *matrix* (plural, *matrices*). We ordinarily write brackets around matrices, although this is not necessary when calculating with matrices. The following are matrices.

$$\begin{bmatrix} 4 & 1 & 3 & 5 \\ 1 & 0 & 1 & 2 \\ 6 & 3 & -2 & 0 \end{bmatrix} \begin{bmatrix} 6 & 2 & 1 & 4 & 7 \\ 1 & 2 & 1 & 3 & 1 \\ 4 & 0 & -2 & 0 & -3 \end{bmatrix}$$

$$\begin{bmatrix} 1 & 2 \\ 145 & 0 \\ -7 & 9 \\ 8 & 1 \\ 0 & 0 \end{bmatrix}$$

The *rows* of a matrix are horizontal, and the *columns* are vertical.

$$\begin{bmatrix} 5 & -2 & 2 \\ 1 & 0 & 1 \\ 0 & 1 & 2 \end{bmatrix} \begin{array}{l} \longleftarrow \text{row 1} \\ \longleftarrow \text{row 2} \\ \longleftarrow \text{row 3} \end{array}$$

column 1 column 2 column 3

Let us now use matrices to solve systems of linear equations.

Example. Solve

$$x \qquad -4z = 5$$
$$2x - y + 4z = -3$$
$$6x - y + 2z = 10.$$

We first write a matrix, using only the constants. Note that where there are missing terms we must write 0's:

$$\begin{bmatrix} 1 & 0 & -4 & 5 \\ 2 & -1 & 4 & -3 \\ 6 & -1 & 2 & 10 \end{bmatrix}.$$

We do exactly the same calculations using the matrix that we would do if we wrote the entire equations. (Hereafter, we will omit the brackets, to save writing).

The first thing to do is make the first number in the first row 1. In this case, it is already 1. Next, we multiply the first row by -2 and add it to the second row:

1	0	-4	5	This corresponds to multiply-
0	-1	12	-13	ing equation ① by -2 and add-
6	-1	2	10	ing it to the ② equation.

Now we multiply the first row by -6 and add it to the third row:

1	0	-4	5	This corresponds to multiply-
0	-1	12	-13	ing equation ① by -6 and
0	-1	26	-20	adding it to equation ③.

Next we multiply row 2 by -1:

1	0	-4	5	This corresponds to multiply-
0	1	-12	13	ing equation ② by -1 to make
0	-1	26	-20	the y-coefficient 1.

Now we add row 2 to row 3:

$$\begin{array}{cccc} 1 & 0 & -4 & 5 \\ 0 & 1 & -12 & 13 \\ 0 & 0 & 14 & -7 \end{array}$$

Then we multiply row 3 by $\frac{1}{14}$:

1	0	-4	5	
0	1	-12	13	This corresponds to making the
0	0	1	$-\frac{1}{2}$	z-coefficient 1.

Now we work back up. We multiply the third row by 12 and add it to the second row:

$$\begin{array}{cccc} 1 & 0 & -4 & 5 \\ 0 & 1 & 0 & 7 \\ 0 & 0 & 1 & -\frac{1}{2} \end{array}$$

We multiply the third row by 4 and add it to the first row:

$$\begin{array}{cccc} 1 & 0 & 0 & 3 \\ 0 & 1 & 0 & 7 \\ 0 & 0 & 1 & -\frac{1}{2} \end{array}$$

If we now put the variables back we have

$$x \qquad = 3$$
$$y \quad = 7$$
$$z = -\frac{1}{2}.$$

The solution is $(3, 7, -\frac{1}{2})$.   **[25, 26]**

Exercise Set 5.4

Solve, using matrices.

1. $4x + 2y = 11$
   $3x - y = 2$

2. $3x - 3y = 11$
   $9x - 2y = 5$

3. $x + 2y - 3z = 9$
   $2x - y + 2z = -8$
   $3x - y - 4z = 3$

4. $x - y + 2z = 0$
　　$x - 2y + 3z = -1$
　　$2x - 2y + z = -3$

5. $5x - 3y = -2$
　　$4x + 2y = 5$

6. $3x + 4y = 7$
　　$-5x + 2y = 10$

7. $4x - y - 3z = 1$
　　$8x + y - z = 5$
　　$2x + y + 2z = 5$

8. $3x + 2y + 2z = 3$
　　$x + 2y - z = 5$
　　$2x - 4y + z = 0$

9. $p + q + r = 1$
　　$p + 2q + 3r = 4$
　　$p + 3q + 7r = 13$

10. $m + n + t = 9$
　　$m - n - t = -15$
　　$m + n - t = -5$

11. $2x + 2y - 2z - 2w = -10$
　　$x + y + z + w = -5$
　　$x - y + 4z + 3w = -2$
　　$3x - 2y + 2z + w = -6$

12. $2x - 3y + z - w = -8$
　　$x + y - z - w = -4$
　　$x + y + z + w = 22$
　　$x - y - z - w = -14$

13. A collection of 34 coins consists of dimes and nickels. The total value is $1.90. How many dimes and how many nickels are there?

14. A collection of 43 coins consists of dimes and quarters. The total value is $7.60. How many dimes and how many quarters are there?

15. A collection of 22 coins consists of nickels, dimes, and quarters. The total value is $2.90. There are twice as many quarters as dimes, and there are six more nickels than dimes. How many of each type of coin are there?

16. A collection of 18 coins consists of nickels, dimes, and quarters. The total value is $2.55. There is one more nickel than there are dimes. There are two more quarters than there are dimes. How many of each type of coin are there?

17. A tobacco dealer has two kinds of tobacco. One is worth $4.05 per lb and the other is worth $2.70 per lb. He wants to blend the two tobaccos to get a 15-lb mixture worth $3.15 per lb. How much of each kind of tobacco should he use?

18. A grocer mixes candy worth $0.80 per lb with nuts worth $0.70 per lb to get a 20-lb mixture worth $0.77 per lb. How many pounds of candy and how many pounds of nuts did she use?

Recall the formula $I = prt$, for simple interest.

19. One year a man received $4050 in interest from two investments. He has a certain amount invested at $5\frac{1}{2}\%$ and $10,000 more than this invested at 6%. Find the amount of principal invested at each rate.

20. One year a woman had some money invested at $5\frac{1}{2}\%$ and another amount invested at $5\frac{3}{4}\%$. The income from the investments was $1355. The income from the $5\frac{1}{2}\%$ investment was $255 less than from the $5\frac{3}{4}\%$ investment. How much was invested at each rate?

Solve.

21. $4.83x + 9.06y = -39.42$

$-1.35x + 6.67y = -33.99$

22. $3.11x - 2.04y = -24.39$

$7.73x + 5.19y = -35.48$

23. $3.55x - 1.35y + 1.03z = 9.16$

$-2.14x + 4.12y + 3.61z = -4.50$

$5.48x - 2.44y - 5.86z = 0.813$

24. $4.12x - 1.35y - 18.2z = 601.3$

$-3.41x + 68.9y + 38.7z = 1777$

$0.955x - 0.813y - 6.53z = 160.2$

▶ **25.** $\sqrt{2}x + \pi y = 3$

$\pi x - \sqrt{2}y = 1$

26. $ax + by = c$

$dx + ey = f$

5.5 Determinants

If a matrix has the same number of rows and columns, it is called a *square* matrix. With every square matrix is associated a number called its determinant, defined as follows for 2×2 matrices.

Definition. The determinant of the matrix $\begin{bmatrix} a & c \\ b & d \end{bmatrix}$ is denoted $\begin{vmatrix} a & c \\ b & d \end{vmatrix}$ and is defined as follows:

$$\begin{vmatrix} a & c \\ b & d \end{vmatrix} = ad - bc.$$

Example. Evaluate $\begin{vmatrix} \sqrt{2} & -3 \\ -4 & -\sqrt{2} \end{vmatrix}$.

$\begin{vmatrix} \sqrt{2} & -3 \\ -4 & -\sqrt{2} \end{vmatrix}$ (The arrows indicate the products involved.)

$$= \sqrt{2}(-\sqrt{2}) - (-4)(-3) = -2 - 12 = -14$$

[27–29]

Determinants have many uses. One of these is in solving systems of nonhomogeneous linear equations,

where the number of variables is the same as the number of equations. Let us consider a system of two equations:

$$a_1 x + b_1 y = c_1$$
$$a_2 x + b_2 y = c_2.$$

Using the methods of the preceding sections we can solve. We obtain

$$x = \frac{c_1 b_2 - c_2 b_1}{a_1 b_2 - a_2 b_1}, \qquad y = \frac{a_1 c_2 - a_2 c_1}{a_1 b_2 - a_2 b_1}.$$

The numerators and denominators of the expressions for x and y are determinants:

$$x = \frac{\begin{vmatrix} c_1 & b_1 \\ c_2 & b_2 \end{vmatrix}}{\begin{vmatrix} a_1 & b_1 \\ a_2 & b_2 \end{vmatrix}}, \qquad y = \frac{\begin{vmatrix} a_1 & c_1 \\ a_2 & c_2 \end{vmatrix}}{\begin{vmatrix} a_1 & b_1 \\ a_2 & b_2 \end{vmatrix}}.$$

The above equations make sense only if the denominator determinant is not 0. If the denominator *is* 0, then one of two things happens.

1. If the denominator is 0 and the other two determinants are also 0, then the system of equations is dependent.

2. If the denominator is 0 and at least one of the other determinants is not 0, then the system is inconsistent.

The equations with determinants above describe *Cramer's rule* for solving systems of equations. To use this rule, we compute the three determinants and compute as shown above. Note that the denominator in both cases contains the coefficients of x and y, in the same position as in the original equations. For x the numerator is obtained by replacing the x-coefficients (the a's) by the c's. For y, the numerator is obtained by replacing the y-coefficients (the b's) by the c's.

Example. Solve, using Cramer's rule

$$2x + 5y = 7$$
$$5x - 2y = -3.$$

$$x = \frac{\begin{vmatrix} 7 & 5 \\ -3 & -2 \end{vmatrix}}{\begin{vmatrix} 2 & 5 \\ 5 & -2 \end{vmatrix}} = \frac{7(-2) - (-3)5}{2(-2) - 5 \cdot 5} = -\frac{1}{29}$$

$$y = \frac{\begin{vmatrix} 2 & 7 \\ 5 & -3 \end{vmatrix}}{\begin{vmatrix} 2 & 5 \\ 5 & -2 \end{vmatrix}} = \frac{2(-3) - 5 \cdot 7}{-29} = \frac{41}{29}$$

The solution is $\left(-\dfrac{1}{29}, \dfrac{41}{29}\right)$. [30–32]

THREE-BY-THREE DETERMINANTS

Definition. The *determinant* of a three-by-three matrix is defined as follows:

$$\begin{vmatrix} a_1 & b_1 & c_1 \\ a_2 & b_2 & c_2 \\ a_3 & b_3 & c_3 \end{vmatrix}$$

$$= a_1 \cdot \begin{vmatrix} b_2 & c_2 \\ b_3 & c_3 \end{vmatrix} - a_2 \cdot \begin{vmatrix} b_1 & c_1 \\ b_3 & c_3 \end{vmatrix} + a_3 \cdot \begin{vmatrix} b_1 & c_1 \\ b_2 & c_2 \end{vmatrix}.$$

The two-by-two determinants on the right can be found by crossing out the row and column in which the a coefficient occurs.

Example. Evaluate.

$$\begin{vmatrix} -1 & 0 & 1 \\ -5 & 1 & -1 \\ 4 & 8 & 1 \end{vmatrix} = -1 \cdot \begin{vmatrix} 1 & -1 \\ 8 & 1 \end{vmatrix} - (-5) \cdot \begin{vmatrix} 0 & 1 \\ 8 & 1 \end{vmatrix}$$

$$+ 4 \cdot \begin{vmatrix} 0 & 1 \\ 1 & -1 \end{vmatrix}$$

$$= -1(1 + 8) + 5(-8) + 4(-1)$$

$$= -9 - 40 - 4 = -53 \qquad \textbf{[33–35]}$$

Let us consider three equations in three variables. Consider

$$a_1 x + b_1 y + c_1 z = d_1$$
$$a_2 x + b_2 y + c_2 z = d_2$$
$$a_3 x + b_3 y + c_3 z = d_3$$

and the following determinants:

$$D = \begin{vmatrix} a_1 & b_1 & c_1 \\ a_2 & b_2 & c_2 \\ a_3 & b_3 & c_3 \end{vmatrix} \qquad D_x = \begin{vmatrix} d_1 & b_1 & c_1 \\ d_2 & b_2 & c_2 \\ d_3 & b_3 & c_3 \end{vmatrix}$$

$$D_y = \begin{vmatrix} a_1 & d_1 & c_1 \\ a_2 & d_2 & c_2 \\ a_3 & d_3 & c_3 \end{vmatrix} \qquad D_z = \begin{vmatrix} a_1 & b_1 & d_1 \\ a_2 & b_2 & d_2 \\ a_3 & b_3 & d_3 \end{vmatrix}.$$

If we solve the system of equations, we obtain the following:

$$x = \frac{D_x}{D}, \qquad y = \frac{D_y}{D}, \qquad z = \frac{D_z}{D}.$$

Note that we obtain the determinant D_x in the numerator for x from D by replacing the x-coefficients by d_1, d_2, and d_3. A similar thing happens with D_y and D_z. We have thus extended *Cramer's rule* to solve systems of three equations in three variables. As before, when $D = 0$, Cramer's rule cannot be used. If $D = 0$, and D_x, D_y, and D_z are 0, the system is dependent. If $D = 0$ and one of D_x, D_y, or D_z is not zero, then the system is inconsistent.

Example. Solve, using Cramer's rule

$$x - 3y + 7z = 13$$
$$x + y + z = 1$$
$$x - 2y + 3z = 4.$$

$$D = \begin{vmatrix} 1 & -3 & 7 \\ 1 & 1 & 1 \\ 1 & -2 & 3 \end{vmatrix} = -10,$$

$$D_x = \begin{vmatrix} 13 & -3 & 7 \\ 1 & 1 & 1 \\ 4 & -2 & 3 \end{vmatrix} = 20,$$

$$D_y = \begin{vmatrix} 1 & 13 & 7 \\ 1 & 1 & 1 \\ 1 & 4 & 3 \end{vmatrix} = -6,$$

$$D_z = \begin{vmatrix} 1 & -3 & 13 \\ 1 & 1 & 1 \\ 1 & -2 & 4 \end{vmatrix} = -24.$$

Then

$$x = \frac{D_x}{D} = \frac{20}{-10} = -2,$$

$$y = \frac{D_y}{D} = \frac{-6}{10} = \frac{3}{5},$$

$$z = \frac{D_z}{D} = \frac{-24}{-10} = \frac{12}{5}.$$

The solution is $(-2, \frac{3}{5}, \frac{12}{5})$. In practice, it is not necessary to evaluate D_z. When we have found values for x and y we can substitute them into one of the equations and find z.   **[36]**

Exercise Set 5.5

Evaluate.

1. $\begin{vmatrix} -2 & -\sqrt{5} \\ -\sqrt{5} & 3 \end{vmatrix}$

2. $\begin{vmatrix} \sqrt{5} & -3 \\ 4 & 2 \end{vmatrix}$

3. $\begin{vmatrix} x & 4 \\ x & x^2 \end{vmatrix}$

4. $\begin{vmatrix} y^2 & -2 \\ y & 3 \end{vmatrix}$

5. $\begin{vmatrix} 3 & 1 & 2 \\ -2 & 3 & 1 \\ 3 & 4 & -6 \end{vmatrix}$

6. $\begin{vmatrix} 3 & -2 & 1 \\ 2 & 4 & 3 \\ -1 & 5 & 1 \end{vmatrix}$

7. $\begin{vmatrix} x & 0 & -1 \\ 2 & x & x^2 \\ -3 & x & 1 \end{vmatrix}$

8. $\begin{vmatrix} x & 1 & -1 \\ x^2 & x & x \\ 0 & x & 1 \end{vmatrix}$

Solve, using Cramer's rule.

9. $-2x + 4y = 3$
$3x - 7y = 1$

10. $5x - 4y = -3$
$7x + 2y = 6$

11. $\sqrt{3}x + \pi y = -5$
$\pi x - \sqrt{3}y = 4$

12. $\pi x - \sqrt{5}y = 2$
$\sqrt{5}x + \pi y = -3$

13. $3x + 2y - z = 4$
$3x - 2y + z = 5$
$4x - 5y - z = -1$

14. $3x - y + 2z = 1$
$x - y + 2z = 3$
$-2x + 3y + z = 1$

15. $6y + 6z = -1$
$8x + 6z = -1$
$4x + 9y = 8$

16. $3x + 5y = 2$
$2x - 3z = 7$
$4y + 2z = -1$

▶ Verify each of the following.

17. $\begin{vmatrix} 1 & x & x^2 \\ 1 & y & y^2 \\ 1 & z & z^2 \end{vmatrix} = (x - y)(y - z)(z - x)$

18. $\begin{vmatrix} 1 & 1 & 1 \\ a & b & c \\ a^2 & b^2 & c^2 \end{vmatrix} = (a - b)(b - c)(c - a)$

19. If a line contains the points (x_1, y_1) and (x_2, y_2), an equation of the line can be written as follows:

$$\begin{vmatrix} x & y & 1 \\ x_1 & y_1 & 1 \\ x_2 & y_2 & 1 \end{vmatrix} = 0.$$

Prove this.

20. Show that three points (x_1, y_1), (x_2, y_2), and (x_3, y_3) are collinear (on the same straight line) if and only if

$$\begin{vmatrix} x_1 & y_1 & 1 \\ x_2 & y_2 & 1 \\ x_3 & y_3 & 1 \end{vmatrix} = 0.$$

21. Consider a triangle with vertices (x_1, y_1), (x_2, y_2), and (x_3, y_3). The area of this triangle is the absolute value of

$$\frac{1}{2} \cdot \begin{vmatrix} x_1 & y_1 & 1 \\ x_2 & y_2 & 1 \\ x_3 & y_3 & 1 \end{vmatrix}.$$

Prove this. (*Hint:* Look at this drawing. The area of triangle *ABC* is the area of trapezoid *ABDE* plus the area of trapezoid *AEFC* minus the area of trapezoid *BDFC*.)

22. Prove that the lines $a_1x + b_1y = c_1$ and $a_2x + b_2y = c_2$ are parallel when

$$\begin{vmatrix} a_1 & b_1 \\ a_2 & b_2 \end{vmatrix} = 0$$

and either

$$\begin{vmatrix} c_1 & b_1 \\ c_2 & b_2 \end{vmatrix} \neq 0 \quad \text{or} \quad \begin{vmatrix} a_1 & c_1 \\ a_2 & c_2 \end{vmatrix} \neq 0.$$

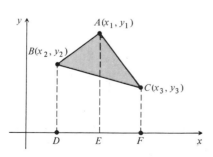

5.6 Systems of Inequalities

A *solution* of an inequality in two variables is an ordered pair of numbers that makes it true.

Example. Decide whether $(-3, 2)$ is a solution of the inequality $5x - 4y \leq 13$.

We replace x by -3 and y by 2:

$$\begin{array}{c|c} 5x - 4y & \leq 13 \\ \hline 5(-3) - 4 \cdot 2 & 13 \\ -15 - 8 & \\ -23 & \end{array}$$

Since -23 is less than 13, this replacement makes the inequality true.   **[37]**

To graph inequalities, we use our knowledge and skill in graphing equations. In fact, the first step in graphing an inequality is usually the graphing of an equation.

Example 1. Graph $y < x + 2$.

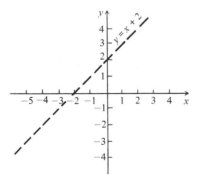

We first graph the equation $y = x + 2$, drawing the line dashed. For any point on the line the value of y is $x + 2$. For any point above the line, y is greater than this; in other words, $y > x + 2$. For any point below the line y is less than $x + 2$, or $y < x + 2$. Thus the graph is the half-plane *below* the line $y = x + 2$. We show this by shading the lower half-plane. The fact that the line is drawn dashed means that points on the line are not in the graph.

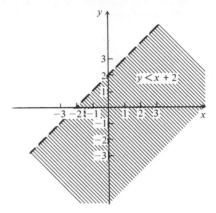

The graph of any linear inequality in two variables is either a half-plane or a half-plane together with the line along the edge.

Example 2. Graph $3y - 2x \geq 1$.

Method 1.   Solve for y: $y \geq \dfrac{2x + 1}{3}$.

Now graph the line $y = (2x + 1)/3$. For any point on the line the value of y is $(2x + 1)/3$. Such values make the inequality true, hence are in the graph. Therefore we draw the line solid this time.

For any point above the line the value of y is greater than $(2x + 1)/3$. Hence any such point is in the graph. The graph of the inequality is the half-plane above the line, together with the line.

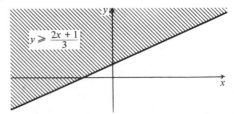

Method 2. We are to graph $3y - 2x \geq 1$.

We graph the line $3y - 2x = 1$, by any method. This time let us find the intercepts. They are $(0, \frac{1}{3})$ and $-\frac{1}{2}, 0)$. We plot them and then use them to draw the line.

Next, we know that the rest of the graph is a half-plane, but we need to determine which one. All we need to do is choose any point on one of the half-planes, substitute it into the inequality, and see if we get a true sentence. The origin is an easy point to use, if the line doesn't contain the origin. We try $(0, 0)$:

$$3 \cdot 0 - 2 \cdot 0 \geq 1, \quad \text{or} \quad 0 \geq 1.$$

This gives us a false sentence, hence $(0, 0)$ is not a solution. Thus we shade the half-plane not containing $(0, 0)$.   **[38–40]**

Example 3. Graph $x \leq 3$.

We first graph the equation $x = 3$, drawing it solid. Then we shade the appropriate half-plane.

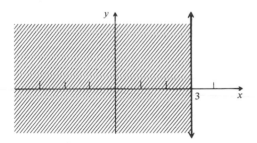

Example 4. Graph $-1 < y \leq 2$.

This is a conjunction of two inequalities,

$$-1 < y \quad \text{and} \quad y \leq 2.$$

It will be true for any y that is both greater than -1 and less than or equal to 2. The graph is as follows.

Since our inequality is a conjunction, the graph is the intersection of the graphs of the parts.

[41–43]

SYSTEMS OF INEQUALITIES

To get a picture of the solution set of a system or *conjunction* of inequalities, we will graph the inequalities separately and find their intersection. A system of linear inequalities may have a graph that is a polygon and its interior. In certain applications it is important to find the vertices.

Example. Graph this system of inequalities. Find the coordinates of any vertices formed.

$$2x + y \geqslant 2$$
$$4x + 3y \leqslant 12$$
$$\frac{1}{2} \leqslant x \leqslant 2$$
$$y \geqslant 0$$

The separate graphs are shown at the left and the graph of the intersection, which is the graph of the system, is shown at the right.

We find the vertex $(\frac{1}{2}, 1)$ by solving the system

$$2x + y = 2$$
$$x = \frac{1}{2}.$$

We find the vertex $(1, 0)$ by solving the system

$$2x + y = 2$$
$$y = 0.$$

We find the vertex $(2, 0)$ from the system

$$x = 2$$
$$y = 0.$$

The vertices $(2, \frac{4}{3})$ and $(\frac{1}{2}, \frac{10}{3})$ were found by solving, respectively, the systems

$$x = 2 \qquad\qquad x = \frac{1}{2}$$
$$\text{and}$$
$$4x + 3y = 12 \qquad\qquad 4x + 3y = 12.$$

[44, 45]

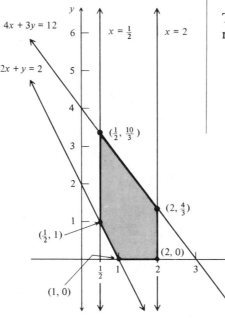

Exercise Set 5.6

Graph.

1. $y < x$ **2.** $y \geqslant x$ **3.** $y + x \geqslant 0$ **4.** $y + x < 0$

5. $3x - 2y < 6$ **6.** $2x - 5y > 10$ **7.** $2x + 3y \geqslant 6$ **8.** $x + 2y \leqslant 4$

9. $3x - 2 \leqslant 5x + y$ **10.** $2x - 6y \geqslant 8 + 4y$ **11.** $x < -4$ **12.** $y \geqslant 5$

13. $0 \leqslant x < 5\frac{1}{2}$ **14.** $-4 < y < -1$ **15.** $y \geqslant |x|$ **16.** $y < |x|$

Graph these systems. Find the coordinates of any vertices formed.

17. $x + y \leqslant 1$
$\quad\ x - y \leqslant 2$

18. $x + y \leqslant 3$
$\quad\ x - y \leqslant 4$

19. $y - 2x > 1$
$\quad\ y - 2x < 3$

20. $y + x > 0$
$\quad\ y + x < 2$

21. $2y - x \leqslant 2$
$\quad\ y - 3x \geqslant -1$

22. $\ x + 3y \geqslant 9$
$\quad\ 3x - 2y \leqslant 5$

23. $y \leqslant 2x + 1$
$\quad\ y \geqslant -2x + 1$
$\quad\ x \leqslant 2$

24. $x - \ y \leqslant 2$
$\quad\ x + 2y \geqslant 8$
$\quad\ y \leqslant 4$

25. $\ x + 2y \leqslant 12$
$\quad 2x + \ y \leqslant 12$
$\quad\ x \geqslant 0$
$\quad\ y \geqslant 0$

26. $8x + 5y \leqslant 40$
$\quad\ x + 2y \leqslant 8$
$\quad\ x \geqslant 0$
$\quad\ y \geqslant 0$

27. $3x + 4y \geqslant 12$
$\quad 5x + 6y \leqslant 30$
$\quad 1 \leqslant x \leqslant 3$

28. $\ y - 2x \geqslant 3$
$\quad\ y - 2x \leqslant 5$
$\quad 6 \leqslant y \leqslant 8$

▶ Graph.

29. $y \geqslant x^2 + 2$ **30.** $y \geqslant 2x^2 - 1$ **31.** $y < x + 1$ **32.** $y \leqslant -x^2 + 5$

                                                                 $y \geqslant x^2$ $y > \frac{1}{2}x^2 - 1$

5.7 Linear Programming

Suppose you are taking a test in which different items are worth different numbers of points. Presumably those with higher point values take more time. How many items of each kind should you do, in order to make the best score? A kind of mathematics called *linear programming* (developed during World War II) may provide an answer. Let us consider an example.

You are taking a test in which items of type A are worth 10 points and items of type B are worth 15 points. It takes three minutes for each item of type A and six minutes for each item of type B. The total time allowed is 60 minutes and you are not allowed to answer more than 16 questions. Assuming that all of your answers are correct, how many items of each type should you answer to get the best score?

Let $x = $ the number of items of type A, and $y = $ the number of items of type B. The total score T is a function of the two variables x and y:

$$T = 10x + 15y.$$

This function has a domain that is a set of ordered pairs of numbers (x, y). This domain is determined by the following conditions, called *constraints*:

Total number of questions allowed, not more than 16	$x + y \leq 16$
Time, not more than 60 min	$3x + 6y \leq 60$
Numbers of items answered will not be negative	$x \geq 0,$ $y \geq 0.$

We now graph the domain of the function T. This is the graph of the system of inequalities above. We will determine the vertices, if any are formed.

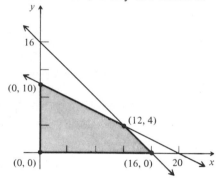

The domain consists of a *convex polygon** and its interior. Under this condition, our linear function does have a maximum value and a minimum value. Moreover, the maximum and minimum values occur at the vertices of the polygon. All we need do to find these values is substitute the coordinates of the vertices in $T = 10x + 15y$.

Vertices (x, y)	Score $T = 10x + 15y$
$(0, 0)$	0
$(16, 0)$	160
$(12, 4)$	180
$(0, 10)$	150

---

* A *convex polygon*, roughly speaking, is one which has no identations, unlike this one:

From this table, we see that the minimum value is 0 and the maximum is 180. To get this maximum you would answer 12 items of type A and 4 items of type B.

We now state the main theorem needed to perform linear programming.

> **Theorem.** If a linear function $F = ax + by + c$ is defined on a domain described by a system of linear inequalities (constraints), then any maximum or minimum value of F will occur at a vertex. If the domain consists of a convex polygon and its interior, then both maximum and minimum values of F actually exist.

Example 1. Find the maximum and minimum values of $F = 9x + 40y$, subject to the constraints

$$y - x \geq 1$$
$$y - x \leq 3$$
$$2 \leq x \leq 5.$$

We graph the system of inequalities, determine the vertices, and find the function values for those ordered pairs.

Vertices (x, y)	$F = 9x + 40y$
$(2, 3)$	138
$(2, 5)$	218
$(5, 6)$	285
$(5, 8)$	365

The maximum value of F is 365 when $x = 5$ and $y = 8$. The minimum value of F is 138 when $x = 2$ and $y = 3$.

Example 2. A company manufactures motorcycles and bicycles. To stay in business it must produce at least 10 motorcycles each month, but it does not have facilities to produce more than 60 motorcycles. It also does not have facilities to produce more than 120 bicycles. The total production of motorcycles and bicycles cannot exceed 160. The profit on a motorcycle is $134 and on a bicycle is $20. Find the number of each that should be manufactured to maximize profit.

Let $x =$ the number of motorcycles to be produced, and $y =$ the number of bicycles to be produced.

The profit P is given by

$$P = \$134x + \$20y,$$

subject to the constraints

$$10 \leqslant x \leqslant 60$$

$$0 \leqslant y \leqslant 120$$

$$x + y \leqslant 160.$$

Vertices (x, y)	Profit $P = \$134x + \$20y$
$(10, 0)$	$ 1,340
$(60, 0)$	$ 8,040
$(60, 100)$	$10,040
$(40, 120)$	$ 7,760
$(10, 120)$	$ 3,740

Thus the company will make a maximum profit of $10,040 by producing 60 motorcycles and 100 bicycles.   **[46–48]**

Exercise Set 5.7

In Exercises 1–4, maximize and also minimize (find maximum and minimum values of the function, and the values of x and y where they occur).

1. $F = 4x + 28y,$

subject to

$5x + 3y \leqslant 34$

$3x + 5y \leqslant 30$

$x \geqslant 0$

$y \geqslant 0.$

2. $G = 14x + 16y,$

subject to

$3x + 2y \leqslant 12$

$7x + 5y \leqslant 29$

$x \geqslant 0$

$y \geqslant 0.$

3. $P = 16x - 2y + 40,$

subject to

$6x + 8y \leqslant 48$

$0 \leqslant y \leqslant 4$

$0 \leqslant x \leqslant 7.$

4. $Q = 24x - 3y + 52,$

subject to

$5x + 4y \geqslant 20$

$0 \leqslant y \leqslant 4$

$0 \leqslant x \leqslant 3.$

5. You are about to take a test that contains questions of type A worth 4 points and questions of type B worth 7 points. You must do at least 5 questions of type A but time restricts doing more than 10. You must do at least 3 questions of type B but time restricts doing more than 10. In total, you can do no more than 18 questions. How many of each type of question must you do to maximize your score? What is this maximum score?

6. You are about to take a test that contains questions of type A worth 10 points and questions of type B worth 25 points. You must do at least 3 questions of type A but time restricts doing more than 12. You must do at least 4 questions of type B but time restricts doing more than 15. In total you can do no more than 20 questions. How many of each type of question must you do to maximize your score? What is this maximum score?

7. A man is planning to invest up to $22,000 in bank X or bank Y or both. He wants to invest at least $2000 but no more than $14,000 in bank X. Bank Y does not insure more than a $15,000 investment so he will invest no more than that in bank Y. The interest in bank X is 6% and in bank Y it is $6\frac{1}{2}\%$ and this will be simple interest for one year. How much should he invest in each bank to maximize his income? What is the maximum income?

8. A woman is planning to invest up to $40,000 in corporate or municipal bonds or both. The least she is allowed to invest in corporate bonds is $6000 and she does not want to invest more than $22,000 in corporate bonds. She also does not want to invest more than $30,000 in municipal bonds. The interest on corporate bonds is 8% and on municipal bonds it is $7\frac{1}{2}\%$. This is simple interest for one year. How much should she invest in each type of bond to maximize her income? What is the maximum income?

9. It takes a tailoring firm 2 hr of cutting and 4 hr of sewing to make a knit suit. To make a worsted suit it takes 4 hr of cutting and 2 hr of sewing. At most, 20 hr per day are available for cutting and, at most, 16 hr per day are available for sewing. The profit on a knit suit is $34 and on a worsted suit is $31. How many of each kind of suit should be made to maximize profit? What is the maximum profit?

10. A pipe tobacco company has 3000 lb of English tobacco, 2000 lb of Virginia tobacco, and 500 lb of Latakia tobacco. To make one batch of SMELLO tobacco it takes 12 lb of English tobacco and 4 lb of Latakia. To make one batch of ROPPO tobacco it takes 8 lb of English and 8 lb of Virginia tobacco. The profit is $10.56 per batch for SMELLO and $6.40 for ROPPO. How many batches of each kind of tobacco should be made to yield maximum profit? What is the maximum profit?

5.8 Operations on Matrices

A matrix of m rows and n columns is called a matrix with *dimensions* $m \times n$ (read "m by n").

Examples. Find the dimensions of each matrix.

$$\begin{bmatrix} 2 & -3 & 4 \\ -1 & \frac{1}{2} & \pi \end{bmatrix},$$

A 2 × 3 matrix

$$\begin{bmatrix} -3 & 8 & 9 \\ \pi & -2 & 5 \\ -6 & 7 & 8 \end{bmatrix},$$

A 3 × 3 matrix

$$[-3 \quad 4],$$

A 1 × 2 matrix

$$\begin{bmatrix} 10 \\ -7 \end{bmatrix}$$

A 2 × 1 matrix

A matrix with the same number of rows as columns is called a *square* matrix. The 3×3 matrix above is a square matrix. **[49–55]**

MATRIX ADDITION

To add matrices, we add the corresponding members. In order to do this the matrices must have the same dimensions.

Examples

a) $\begin{bmatrix} -5 & 0 \\ 4 & \frac{1}{2} \end{bmatrix} + \begin{bmatrix} 6 & -3 \\ 2 & 3 \end{bmatrix} = \begin{bmatrix} -5+6 & 0-3 \\ 4+2 & \frac{1}{2}+3 \end{bmatrix}$

$\qquad = \begin{bmatrix} 1 & -3 \\ 6 & 3\frac{1}{2} \end{bmatrix}.$

b) $\begin{bmatrix} 1 & 3 & 2 \\ -1 & 5 & 4 \\ 6 & 0 & 1 \end{bmatrix} + \begin{bmatrix} -1 & -2 & 1 \\ 1 & -2 & 2 \\ -3 & 1 & 0 \end{bmatrix} = \begin{bmatrix} 0 & 1 & 3 \\ 0 & 3 & 6 \\ 3 & 1 & 1 \end{bmatrix}.$

Addition of matrices is both commutative and associative. **[56, 57]**

ZERO MATRICES

A matrix having zeros for all of its entries is called a *zero matrix* and is often denoted by **0**. When a zero matrix is added to another matrix of the same dimensions, that same matrix is obtained. Thus a zero matrix is an *additive identity*.

Example

$\begin{bmatrix} 2 & -1 & 3 \\ 1 & 0 & -1 \end{bmatrix} + \begin{bmatrix} 0 & 0 & 0 \\ 0 & 0 & 0 \end{bmatrix} = \begin{bmatrix} 2 & -1 & 3 \\ 1 & 0 & -1 \end{bmatrix}.$ **[58]**

INVERSES AND SUBTRACTION

To subtract matrices, we subtract the corresponding members. Of course the matrices must have the same dimensions in order to do this.

Example 1.

$\begin{bmatrix} 1 & 2 \\ -2 & 0 \\ -3 & -1 \end{bmatrix} - \begin{bmatrix} 1 & -1 \\ 1 & 3 \\ 2 & 3 \end{bmatrix} = \begin{bmatrix} 0 & 3 \\ -3 & -3 \\ -5 & -4 \end{bmatrix}.$ **[59, 60]**

The additive inverse of a matrix can be obtained by replacing each member by its additive inverse. Of course, when two matrices that are inverses of each other are added, a zero matrix is obtained.

Example 2.

$\begin{bmatrix} 1 & 0 & 2 \\ 3 & -1 & 5 \end{bmatrix} + \begin{bmatrix} -1 & 0 & -2 \\ -3 & 1 & -5 \end{bmatrix} = \begin{bmatrix} 0 & 0 & 0 \\ 0 & 0 & 0 \end{bmatrix}.$

$\quad \mathbf{A} \qquad + \qquad (-\mathbf{A}) \qquad = \qquad \mathbf{0}.$ **[61, 62]**

With numbers, we can subtract by adding an inverse. This is also true of matrices. If we denote matrices by **A** and **B** and an additive inverse by $-\mathbf{B}$, this fact can be stated as follows:

$$\mathbf{A} - \mathbf{B} = \mathbf{A} + (-\mathbf{B}).$$

Example 3.

$\begin{bmatrix} 3 & -1 \\ -2 & 4 \end{bmatrix} - \begin{bmatrix} 2 & 1 \\ 3 & -2 \end{bmatrix} = \begin{bmatrix} 1 & -2 \\ -5 & 2 \end{bmatrix}$

$\quad \mathbf{A} \qquad - \qquad \mathbf{B}$

$\begin{bmatrix} 3 & -1 \\ -2 & 4 \end{bmatrix} + \begin{bmatrix} -2 & -1 \\ -3 & 2 \end{bmatrix} = \begin{bmatrix} 1 & -2 \\ -5 & 2 \end{bmatrix}.$

$\quad \mathbf{A} \qquad + \qquad (-\mathbf{B})$ **[63]**

MULTIPLYING MATRICES AND NUMBERS

We define a product of a matrix and a number, and call this product a *scalar* product.

> **Definition. The (scalar) product of a number k and a matrix A is the matrix, denoted $k\mathbf{A}$, obtained by multiplying each number in A by the number k.**

Examples. Let

$$A = \begin{bmatrix} -3 & 0 \\ 4 & 5 \end{bmatrix}.$$

a) $\qquad 3A = 3\begin{bmatrix} -3 & 0 \\ 4 & 5 \end{bmatrix} = \begin{bmatrix} -9 & 0 \\ 12 & 15 \end{bmatrix}.$

b) $\qquad (-1)A = -1\begin{bmatrix} -3 & 0 \\ 4 & 5 \end{bmatrix} = \begin{bmatrix} 3 & 0 \\ -4 & 5 \end{bmatrix}.$

[64, 65]

PRODUCTS OF MATRICES

We do not multiply two matrices by multiplying their corresponding members. The motivation for defining matrix products comes from systems of equations. Let us begin by considering one equation,

$$3x + 2y - 2z = 4.$$

We will write the coefficients on the left side in a 1×3 matrix (a *row* matrix) and the variables in a 3×1 matrix (a *column* matrix). The 4 on the right is written in a 1×1 matrix:

$$[3 \quad 2 \quad -2]\begin{bmatrix} x \\ y \\ z \end{bmatrix} = [4].$$

We can return to our original equation by multiplying the members of the row matrix by those of the column matrix, and adding:

$$[3 \quad 2 \quad -2]\begin{bmatrix} x \\ y \\ z \end{bmatrix} = [3x + 2y - 2z].$$

We define multiplication accordingly. In this special case, we have a row matrix **A** and a column matrix **B**. Their product **AB** is a 1×1 matrix, having the single member 4 (also called $3x + 2y - 2z$).

Example. Find the product of these matrices.

$$[3 \quad 2 \quad -1]\begin{bmatrix} 1 \\ -2 \\ 3 \end{bmatrix} = [3 \cdot 1 + 2(-2) + (-1) \cdot 3] = [-4]$$

[66]

Let us continue by considering a system of equations:

$$\begin{aligned} 3x + 2y - 2z &= 4 \\ 2x - y + 5z &= 3 \\ -x + y + 4z &= 7. \end{aligned}$$

Consider the following matrices:

$$\underbrace{\begin{bmatrix} 3 & 2 & -2 \\ 2 & -1 & 5 \\ -1 & 1 & 4 \end{bmatrix}}_{\mathbf{A}} \underbrace{\begin{bmatrix} x \\ y \\ z \end{bmatrix}}_{\mathbf{X}} \underbrace{\begin{bmatrix} 4 \\ 3 \\ 7 \end{bmatrix}}_{\mathbf{B}}.$$

If we multiply the first row of **A** by the (only) column of **X**, as we did above, we get $3x + 2y - 2z$. If we multiply the second row of **A** by the column in **X**, in the same way we get the following:

$$\begin{bmatrix} 3 & 2 & -2 \\ 2 & -1 & 5 \\ -1 & 1 & 4 \end{bmatrix}\begin{bmatrix} x \\ y \\ z \end{bmatrix} \quad 2x - y + 5z.$$

Note that the first members are multiplied, the second members are multiplied, the third members are multiplied, and the results are added, to get the single number $2x - y + 5z$. What do we get when we multiply the third row of **A** by the column in **X**?

$$\begin{bmatrix} 3 & 2 & -2 \\ 2 & -1 & 5 \\ -1 & 1 & 4 \end{bmatrix}\begin{bmatrix} x \\ y \\ z \end{bmatrix} \quad -x + y + 4z$$

We define the product **AX** to be the column matrix

$$\begin{bmatrix} 3x + 2y - 2z \\ 2x - y + 5z \\ -x + y + 4z \end{bmatrix}.$$

Now consider this matrix equation:

$$\begin{bmatrix} 3x + 2y - 2z \\ 2x - y + 5z \\ -x + y + 4z \end{bmatrix} = \begin{bmatrix} 4 \\ 3 \\ 7 \end{bmatrix}.$$

Equality for matrices is the same as for numbers, i.e., a sentence such as $a = b$ says that a and b are two names for the same thing. Thus if the above matrix equation is true, the "two" matrices are really the same one. This means that $3x + 2y - 2z$ is 4, $2x - y + 5z$ is 3, and $-x + y + 4z$ is 7, or that

$$3x + 2y - 2z = 4,$$
$$2x - y + 5z = 3,$$
$$-x + y + 4z = 7.$$

Thus the matrix equation $\mathbf{AX} = \mathbf{B}$ is equivalent to the original system of equations.

Example 1. Write a matrix equation equivalent to this system of equations:

$$4x + 2y - z = 3$$
$$9x + z = 5$$
$$4x + 5y - 2z = 1$$
$$x + y + z = 0.$$

We write the coefficients on the left in a matrix. We multiply that matrix by the column matrix containing the variables, and set this equal to the column matrix containing the constants on the right:

$$\begin{bmatrix} 4 & 2 & -1 \\ 9 & 0 & 1 \\ 4 & 5 & -2 \\ 1 & 1 & 1 \end{bmatrix} \begin{bmatrix} x \\ y \\ z \end{bmatrix} = \begin{bmatrix} 3 \\ 5 \\ 1 \\ 0 \end{bmatrix}. \qquad \textbf{[67]}$$

Example 2. Multiply.

$$\begin{bmatrix} 3 & 1 & -1 \\ 1 & 2 & 2 \\ -1 & 0 & 5 \\ 4 & 1 & 2 \end{bmatrix} \begin{bmatrix} 1 \\ 2 \\ 1 \end{bmatrix} = \begin{bmatrix} 3 \cdot 1 + 1 \cdot 2 - 1 \cdot 1 \\ 1 \cdot 1 + 2 \cdot 2 + 2 \cdot 1 \\ -1 \cdot 1 + 0 \cdot 2 + 5 \cdot 1 \\ 4 \cdot 1 + 1 \cdot 2 + 2 \cdot 1 \end{bmatrix} = \begin{bmatrix} 4 \\ 7 \\ 4 \\ 8 \end{bmatrix} \qquad \textbf{[68]}$$

In all of the examples so far, the second matrix had only one column. If the second matrix has more than one column, we treat it in the same way when multiplying that we treated the single column. The product matrix will have as many columns as the second matrix.

Example 3. Multiply (compare with Example 2).

$$\underbrace{\begin{bmatrix} 3 & 1 & -1 \\ 1 & 2 & 2 \\ -1 & 0 & 5 \\ 4 & 1 & 2 \end{bmatrix}}_{\mathbf{A}} \underbrace{\begin{bmatrix} 1 & 0 \\ 2 & 1 \\ 1 & 3 \end{bmatrix}}_{\mathbf{B}}$$

$$= \begin{bmatrix} 4 & 3 \cdot 0 + 1 \cdot 1 + (-1)3 \\ 7 & 1 \cdot 0 + 2 \cdot 1 + 2 \cdot 3 \\ 4 & -1 \cdot 0 + 0 \cdot 1 + 5 \cdot 3 \\ 8 & 4 \cdot 0 + 1 \cdot 1 + 2 \cdot 3 \end{bmatrix} = \begin{bmatrix} 4 & -2 \\ 7 & 8 \\ 4 & 15 \\ 8 & 7 \end{bmatrix}$$

Same as in Example 2   The rows of $\mathbf{A}$ multiplied by the second column of $\mathbf{B}$

$$\textbf{[69]}$$

Example 4. Multiply.

$$\begin{bmatrix} 3 & 1 & -1 \\ 2 & 0 & 3 \end{bmatrix} \begin{bmatrix} 1 & 4 & 6 \\ 3 & -1 & 9 \\ 2 & 5 & 1 \end{bmatrix}$$

$$= \begin{bmatrix} 3 \cdot 1 + 1 \cdot 3 - 1 \cdot 2 & 3 \cdot 4 + 1(-1) - 1 \cdot 5 & 3 \cdot 6 + 1 \cdot 9 - 1 \cdot 1 \\ 2 \cdot 1 + 0 \cdot 3 + 3 \cdot 2 & 2 \cdot 4 + 0 \cdot (-1) + 3 \cdot 5 & 2 \cdot 6 + 0 \cdot 9 + 3 \cdot 1 \end{bmatrix}$$

$$= \begin{bmatrix} 4 & 6 & 26 \\ 8 & 23 & 15 \end{bmatrix}$$

If matrix $\mathbf{A}$ has n columns and matrix $\mathbf{B}$ has n rows, then we can compute the product $\mathbf{AB}$, regardless of the other dimensions. The product will have as many rows as $\mathbf{A}$ and as many columns as $\mathbf{B}$.

$$\textbf{[70–73]}$$

Exercise Set 5.8

For Exercises 1–16, let

$$A = \begin{bmatrix} 1 & 2 \\ 4 & 3 \end{bmatrix}, \quad B = \begin{bmatrix} -3 & 5 \\ 2 & -1 \end{bmatrix}, \quad C = \begin{bmatrix} 1 & -1 \\ -1 & 1 \end{bmatrix}, \quad D = \begin{bmatrix} 1 & 1 \\ 1 & 1 \end{bmatrix},$$

$$E = \begin{bmatrix} 1 & 3 \\ 2 & 6 \end{bmatrix}, \quad F = \begin{bmatrix} 3 & 3 \\ -1 & -1 \end{bmatrix}, \quad 0 = \begin{bmatrix} 0 & 0 \\ 0 & 0 \end{bmatrix}, \quad \text{and} \quad I = \begin{bmatrix} 1 & 0 \\ 0 & 1 \end{bmatrix}.$$

Find.

1. A + B   **2. B + A**   **3. E + 0**   **4. 2A**

5. 3F   **6. (−1)D**   **7. 3F + 2A**   **8. A − B**

9. B − A   **10. AB**   **11. BA**   **12. 0F**

13. CD   **14. EF**   **15. AI**   **16. IA**

In Exercises 17–20, let

$$A = \begin{bmatrix} 1 & 0 & -2 \\ 0 & -1 & 3 \\ 3 & 2 & 4 \end{bmatrix}, \quad B = \begin{bmatrix} -1 & -2 & 5 \\ 1 & 0 & -1 \\ 2 & -3 & 1 \end{bmatrix}, \quad C = \begin{bmatrix} -2 & 9 & 6 \\ -3 & 3 & 4 \\ 2 & -2 & 1 \end{bmatrix}, \quad \text{and} \quad I = \begin{bmatrix} 1 & 0 & 0 \\ 0 & 1 & 0 \\ 0 & 0 & 1 \end{bmatrix}.$$

Find.

17. AB   **18. BA**   **19. CI**   **20. IC**

Multiply.

21. $[-3 \quad 2]\begin{bmatrix} 4 \\ -2 \end{bmatrix}$ **22.** $[-2 \quad 0 \quad 4]\begin{bmatrix} 8 \\ -6 \\ \frac{1}{2} \end{bmatrix}$ **23.** $[-5 \quad 1 \quad 2]\begin{bmatrix} 1 & 3 \\ -1 & 0 \\ 4 & -2 \end{bmatrix}$ **24.** $\begin{bmatrix} -3 & 2 \\ 0 & 1 \\ -4 & 5 \end{bmatrix}\begin{bmatrix} 4 \\ 2 \end{bmatrix}$

Write a matrix equation equivalent to each of the following systems of equations.

25. $3x - 2y + 4z = 17$
$\quad\ 2x + \ y - 5z = 13$

26. $3x + 2y + 5z = 9$
$\quad\ 4x - 3y + 2z = 10$

27. $\ x - \ y + 2z - 4w = 12$
$\quad 2x - \ y - \ z + \ w = 0$
$\quad\ x + 4y - 3z - \ w = 1$
$\quad 3x + 5y - 7z + 2w = 9$

28. $2x + \ 4y - \ 5z + 12w = 2$
$\quad 4x - \ y + 12z - \ w = 5$
$\quad -x + \ 4y \quad\quad + \ 2w = 13$
$\quad 2x + 10y + \ z \quad\quad = 5$

Compute.

29. $\begin{bmatrix} 3.61 & -2.14 & 16.7 \\ -4.33 & 7.03 & 12.9 \\ 5.82 & -6.95 & 2.34 \end{bmatrix} \begin{bmatrix} 3.05 & 0.402 & -1.34 \\ 1.84 & -1.13 & 0.024 \\ -2.83 & 2.04 & 8.81 \end{bmatrix}$

30. $\begin{bmatrix} -1.23 & 4.51 & -17.4 \\ 61.2 & -8.81 & 0.123 \\ 14.14 & 6.92 & -14.4 \end{bmatrix} \begin{bmatrix} 4.24 & 16.1 & 41.3 \\ 0.146 & -6.06 & -18.9 \\ -8.43 & 1.12 & 0.0245 \end{bmatrix}$

▶ For Exercises 31 and 32, let

$$\mathbf{A} = \begin{bmatrix} -1 & 0 \\ 2 & 1 \end{bmatrix}, \quad \text{and} \quad \mathbf{B} = \begin{bmatrix} 1 & -1 \\ 0 & 2 \end{bmatrix}.$$

31. Show that $(\mathbf{A} + \mathbf{B})(\mathbf{A} - \mathbf{B}) \neq \mathbf{A}^2 - \mathbf{B}^2$, where $\mathbf{A}^2 = \mathbf{AA}$ and $\mathbf{B}^2 = \mathbf{BB}$.

32. Show that $(\mathbf{A} + \mathbf{B})(\mathbf{A} + \mathbf{B}) \neq \mathbf{A}^2 + 2\mathbf{AB} + \mathbf{B}^2$.

Chapter 5 Test, or Review

1. Solve, using the substitution method.

$5x - 3y = -4$

$3x - y = -4$

2. Solve, using Cramer's rule.

$2x + 3y = 2$

$5x - y = -29$

3. The value of 75 coins, consisting of nickels and dimes, is $5.95. How many of each kind of coin are there?

Solve, using matrices. If there is more than one solution, list three of them.

4. $x + 2y = 5$
  $2x - 5y = -8$

5. $3x + 4y + 2z = 3$
  $5x - 2y - 13z = 3$
  $4x + 3y - 3z = 6$

6. $3x + 5y + z = 0$
  $2x - 4y - 3z = 0$
  $x + 3y + z = 0$

Classify as consistent or inconsistent.

7. $3x - 2y = 1$
  $-6x + 4y = -2$

8. $x + 5y = 12$
  $5x + 25y = 12$

Classify as dependent or independent.

9. $3x - 2y = 1$
   $-6x + 4y = -2$

10. $x + 5y = 12$
   $5x + 25y = 12$

11. Find numbers a, b, and c such that the quadratic function $y = ax^2 + bx + c$ fits the data points $(0, 3)$, $(1, 0)$, and $(-1, 4)$. Then write the equation.

12. Graph $x + 2y \leqslant 4$.

13. Maximize and minimize $T = 6x + 10y$ subject to these constraints.

$$x + y \leqslant 10$$
$$5x + 10y \leqslant 50$$
$$x \geqslant 0$$
$$y \geqslant 2$$

14. You are about to take a test that contains questions of type A worth 4 points and questions of type B worth 8 points. You must do a total of at least 8 questions, and you must do at least 5 type A questions and 3 type B questions. If you know that type A questions take 3 min and type B questions take 5 min and that the total time cannot exceed 45 min, how many of each type of question must you do to maximize your score? What is this maximum score?

Let $\quad A = \begin{bmatrix} 1 & 1 & 3 \\ 0 & 2 & -1 \\ 2 & -1 & 0 \end{bmatrix}$, $\quad$ and $\quad B = \begin{bmatrix} -1 & 0 & 2 \\ 1 & -2 & 0 \\ 0 & 1 & -3 \end{bmatrix}$.

Find.

15. $A + B$ $\qquad$ **16.** $-3A$ $\qquad$ **17.** $-A$ $\qquad$ **18.** AB

19. Write a matrix equation equivalent to this system of equations.

$$3x - 2y + 4z = 13$$
$$x + 5y - 3z = 7$$
$$2x - 3y + 7z = -8$$

CHAPTER **6**

Exponential and Logarithmic Functions

6.1 Exponential and Logarithmic Functions

IRRATIONAL EXPONENTS

We have defined exponential notation for cases in which the exponent is a rational number. For example $x^{2.34}$, or $x^{\frac{234}{100}}$, means to take the 100th root of x and raise the result to the 234th power. We will now consider irrational exponents, such as π or $\sqrt{2}$.

Let us consider 2^{π}. We know that π has an unending decimal representation,

$$3.1415926535\ldots.$$

Now consider this sequence of numbers:

$$3, 3.1, 3.14, 3.141, 3.1415, 3.14159, \ldots.$$

Each of these numbers is an approximation to π, the more decimal places the better the approximation. Let us use these (rational) numbers to form a sequence as follows:

$$2^3, 2^{3.1}, 2^{3.14}, 2^{3.141}, 2^{3.1415}, 2^{3.14159}, \ldots.$$

Each of the numbers in this sequence is already defined, the exponent being rational. The numbers in this sequence get closer and closer to some real number. We define that number to be 2^{π}.

We can define any irrational exponent in a similar way. Thus any exponential expression a^x now has meaning, whether the exponent is rational or irrational. The usual laws of exponents still hold, in case exponents are irrational. We will not attempt to prove that fact here, however.

EXPONENTIAL FUNCTIONS

An exponential function is one that can be defined using exponential notation. Here is a precise definition.

Definition. The function $f(x) = a^x$, where a is some positive constant, is called _the exponential function, base a._

Example 1. Graph $y = 2^x$. Use the graph to approximate 2^{π}.

We find some solutions, plot them and then draw the graph.

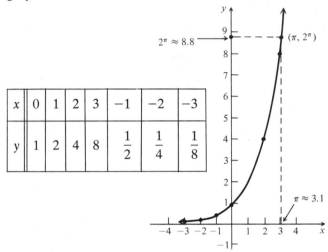

x	0	1	2	3	−1	−2	−3
y	1	2	4	8	$\frac{1}{2}$	$\frac{1}{4}$	$\frac{1}{8}$

Note that as x increases, the function values increase. As x decreases, the function values decrease toward 0.

To approximate 2^{π}, we locate π on the x-axis, at about 3.1. Then we find the corresponding function value. It is about 8.8.   **[1, 2]**

Let us now look at some other exponential functions. We will make comparisons, using transformations.

Example 2. Graph $y = 4^x$.

We could plot points and connect them, but we will

be more clever. We note that $4^x = (2^2)^x = 2^{2x}$. Thus the function we wish to graph is

$$y = 2^{2x}.$$

Compare this with $y = 2^x$, graphed above. The graph of $y = 2^{2x}$ is a compression, in the x-direction, of the graph of $y = 2^x$. Knowing this allows us to graph $y = 2^{2x}$ at once. Each point on the graph of 2^x is moved half the distance to the y-axis.

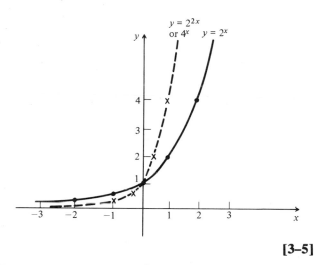

[3–5]

Example 3. Graph $y = (\frac{1}{2})^x$.

We could plot points and connect them, but we will be more clever. We note that $(\frac{1}{2})^x = 1/2^x = 2^{-x}$. Thus the function we wish to graph is

$$y = 2^{-x}.$$

Compare this with the graph of $y = 2^x$ in Example 1. The graph of $y = 2^{-x}$ is a reflection, across the y-axis, of the graph of $y = 2^x$. Knowing this allows us to graph $y = 2^{-x}$ at once.   [6]

The preceding examples and exercises illustrate exponential functions of various bases. If $a = 1$ in $f(x) = a^x$, then the graph is a horizontal line $y = 1$. For other positive values of a, the graphs are interesting.

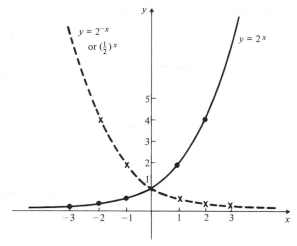

We summarize.

1. **When $a > 1$, the function $f(x) = a^x$ is an increasing function. The greater the value of a, the faster the function increases.**
2. **When $a < 1$, the function $f(x) = a^x$ is a decreasing function. The greater the value of a, the more slowly the function decreases.**

It should be noted that for any value of a, the y-intercept is 1.

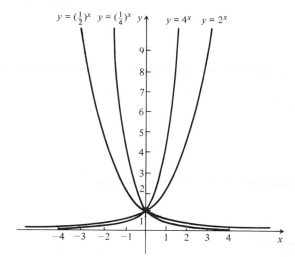

LOGARITHMIC FUNCTIONS

The inverse of an exponential function, for $a > 0$ and $a \neq 1$, is called a *logarithmic function*, or *logarithm function*. Thus one way to describe a logarithm function is to interchange variables in $y = a^x$:

$$x = a^y.$$

The most useful and interesting logarithmic functions are those for which $a > 1$. The graph of such a function is as follows (a reflection of $y = a^x$ across the line $y = x$). Note that the domain of a logarithm function is the set of all positive real numbers.

For logarithm functions we use the notation $\log_a (x)$ or $\log_a x$.* That is, we use the symbol $\log_a x$ to denote the second coordinates of a function $x = a^y$. To say this another way, a logarithmic function can be described as $y = \log_a x$.

> **The following are equivalent:**
> 1. $x = a^y$; and $\quad x = a^{\log_a x}$
> 2. $y = \log_a x$ (read "y equals the logarithm, base a, of x").

Thus $\log_a x$ represents the exponent in the equation $x = a^y$, so the logarithm, base a, of a number x is the power to which a is raised to get x. [7, 8]

It is important to be able to convert from an exponential equation to a logarithmic equation.

---

*The parentheses in $\log_a (x)$ are like those in $f(x)$. In the case of logarithm functions we usually omit the parentheses.

Examples. Convert to logarithmic equations.

a) $8 = 2^x \rightarrow x = \log_2 8$
b) $y^{-1} = 4 \rightarrow -1 = \log_y 4$
c) $a^b = c \rightarrow b = \log_a c$

It helps, in such conversions, to remember that the *logarithm is the exponent.*

[9–12]

It is also important to be able to convert from a logarithmic equation to an exponential equation.

Examples. Convert to exponential equations.

a) $y = \log_3 5 \rightarrow 3^y = 5$
b) $-2 = \log_a 7 \rightarrow a^{-2} = 7$
c) $a = \log_b d \rightarrow b^a = d$

Again, it helps to remember that the *logarithm is the exponent.*

[13–16]

Certain equations containing logarithmic notation can be solved by first converting to exponential notation.

Examples

1. Solve $\log_2 x = -3$.

   If $\log_2 x = -3$, then $2^{-3} = x$. So $x = \frac{1}{8}$.

2. Find $\log_{27} 3$.

   Let $x = \log_{27} 3$. Then $27^x = 3$. Also $27^{\frac{1}{3}} = 3$ so $x = \frac{1}{3}$.

3. Solve $\log_x 4 = \frac{1}{2}$.

   Now $\log_x 4 = \frac{1}{2}$ means $x^{\frac{1}{2}} = 4$. Then $(x^{\frac{1}{2}})^2 = 4^2$, or $x = 16$. [17–21]

Recall that exponential and logarithm functions are inverses of each other. Let us also recall an important fact about functions and their inverses (p. 87). If the domains are suitable, then for any x,

$$f(f^{-1}(x)) = x$$

and

$$f^{-1}(f(x)) = x.$$

We apply this fact to exponential and logarithm functions. Suppose f is the exponential function, base a:

$$f(x) = a^x.$$

Then f^{-1} is the logarithm function, base a:

$$f^{-1}(x) = \log_a x. \quad x = a^y$$

Now let us find $f(f^{-1}(x))$:

$$f(f^{-1}(x)) = a^{f^{-1}(x)} = a^{\log_a x}.$$

Thus for any suitable base a, $a^{\log_a x} = x$ for any positive number x (negative numbers and 0 do not have logarithms).

Next, let us find $f^{-1}(f(x))$:

$$f^{-1}(f(x)) = \log_a f(x) \log_a a^x.$$

Thus for any suitable base a, $\log_a a^x = x$ for any number x whatever.

These facts are important in simplification and should be learned well.

> For any number a, suitable as a logarithm base,
> 1. $a^{\log_a x} = x$, for any positive number x; and
> 2. $\log_a a^x = x$, for any number x.

Examples. Simplify:

a) $2^{\log_2 5} = 5$

b) $10^{\log_{10} t} = t$

c) $\log_e e^{-3} = -3$

d) $\log_{10} 10^{5.6} = 5.6$ **[22–27]**

Exercise Set 6.1

Graph. Where possible, use transformations.

1. a) $y = 5^x$ b) $y = \log_5 x$ c) $y = 5^{x-2}$ d) $y = \log_5 (x - 2)$

2. a) $y = 4^{x+1}$ b) $y = \log_4 (x + 1)$

Write equivalent exponential equations.

3. $\log_5 25 = 2$ **4.** $\log_2 \dfrac{1}{2} = -1$ **5.** $\log_6 6 = 1$

6. $\log_8 \dfrac{1}{4} = -\dfrac{2}{3}$ **7.** $\log_b M = N$ **8.** $\log_k A = c$

Write equivalent logarithmic equations.

9. $10^0 = 1$ **10.** $5^4 = 625$ **11.** $5^{-2} = \dfrac{1}{25}$

12. $8^{\frac{1}{3}} = 2$ **13.** $10^{0.3010} = 2$ **14.** $10^{0.4771} = 3$

15. $a^{-b} = c$ **16.** $a^b = c$

Solve.

17. $\log_3 x = 2$

18. $\log_x \dfrac{1}{32} = 5$

19. $\log_x 16 = 2$

20. $\log_x 64 = 3$

21. $\log_2 x = -1$

22. $\log_8 x = \dfrac{1}{3}$

Find.

23. $\log_2 64$

24. $\log_4 2$

25. $\log_{10} 10^2$

26. $\log_3 3^4$

27. $\log_\pi \pi$

28. $\log_a a$

29. $\log_9 3$

30. $\log_{10} 0.01$

31. $\log_{10} 0.001$

32. $\log_{10} 1000$

Simplify.

33. $3^{\log_3(4x)}$

34. $5^{\log_5(4x-5)}$

35. $\log_4 4^{3.2}$

36. $\log_{3.7} 3.7^{(x^2-1)}$

37. $\log_m m^\pi$

38. $\log_Q Q^{\sqrt{5}}$

39. $(a + 2)^{\log_{(a+2)}7.5}$

40. $(3x^2)^{\log_{(3x^2)}8.9}$

41. $\pi^{\log_\pi(x^2+3)}$

42. $e^{\log_e(3x^2+1)}$

43. $\log_{10} 10^{\sqrt{x^2+y^2}}$

44. $\log_e e^{|x-4|}$

▶ Graph.

45. $y = \log_2 |x|$

46. $y = \log_3 |x|$

47. $y = 2^x + 2^{-x}$

48. $y = 3^x + 3^{-x}$

6.2 Properties of Logarithmic Functions

Logarithm functions are important in many applications of mathematics. We now establish some of their basic properties.

> **Theorem 1. For any positive numbers x and y,**
> $$\log_a (x \cdot y) = \log_a x + \log_a y,$$
> **where a is any positive number different from 1.**

Theorem 1 says that the logarithm of a *product* is the *sum* of the logarithms of the factors. Note that the base a must remain constant. The logarithm of a sum is *not* the sum of the logarithms of the summands.

Proof of Theorem 1. Since a is positive and different from 1, it can serve as a logarithm base. Since x and y are assumed positive, they are in the domain of the function $y = \log_a x$. Now let $b = \log_a x$ and $c = \log_a y$.

Writing equivalent exponential equations, we have

$$x = a^b \quad \text{and} \quad y = a^c.$$

Next we multiply, to obtain

$$xy = a^b a^c = a^{b+c}.$$

Now writing an equivalent logarithmic equation, we obtain

$$\log_a (xy) = b + c, \quad \text{or}$$
$$\log_a (xy) = \log_a x + \log_a y,$$

which was to be shown.

Example 1. Express as a sum of logarithms and simplify.

$$\log_2 (4 \cdot 16) = \log_2 4 + \log_2 16$$
$$\log_2 64 = 2 + 4 = 6$$

Theorem 2. For any positive number x and any number p,

$$\log_a x^p = p \cdot \log_a x,$$

where a is any logarithm base.

[28–31]

Theorem 2 says that the logarithm of a power of a number is the exponent times the logarithm of the number.

Proof of Theorem 2. Let $b = \log_a x$. Then, writing an equivalent exponential equation we have $x = a^b$. Next we raise both sides of the latter equation to the pth power. This gives us

$$x^p = (a^b)^p, \quad \text{or} \quad a^{bp}.$$

Now we write an equivalent logarithmic equation,

$$\log_a x^p = \log_a a^{bp} = bp.$$

But $b = \log_a x$, so we have

$$\log_a x^p = p \cdot \log_a x,$$

which was to be shown.

Examples. Express as products.

a) $\log_b 9^{-5} = -5 \cdot \log_b 9$

b) $\log_a \sqrt[4]{5} = \log_a 5^{\frac{1}{4}} = \frac{1}{4} \log_a 5$ [32, 33]

Theorem 3. For any positive numbers x and y,

$$\log_a \frac{x}{y} = \log_a x - \log_a y,$$

where a is any logarithm base.

Theorem 3 says that the logarithm of a quotient is the difference of the logarithms (i.e., the logarithm of the dividend minus the logarithm of the divisor).

Proof of Theorem 3. $x/y = x \cdot y^{-1}$, so

$$\log_a \frac{x}{y} = \log_a (xy^{-1}).$$

By Theorem 1,

$$\log_a (xy^{-1}) = \log_a x + \log_a y^{-1},$$

and by Theorem 2,

$$\log_a y^{-1} = -1 \cdot \log_a y,$$

so we have

$$\log_a \frac{x}{y} = \log_a x - \log_a y,$$

which was to be shown.

Example 1. Express as sums and differences of logarithms and without exponential notation or radicals.

$$\log_a \frac{\sqrt{17}}{5\pi} = \log_a \sqrt{17} - \log_a 5\pi$$
$$= \log_a 17^{\frac{1}{2}} - (\log_a 5 + \log_a \pi)$$
$$= \frac{1}{2} \log_a 17 - \log_a 5 - \log_a \pi$$

Example 2. Express in terms of logarithms of x, y, and z.

$$\log_a \sqrt[4]{\frac{xy}{z^3}} = \log_a \left(\frac{xy}{z^3}\right)^{\frac{1}{4}} = \frac{1}{4} \cdot \log_a \frac{xy}{z^3}$$

$$= \frac{1}{4}\left[\log_a xy - \log_a z^3\right]$$

$$= \frac{1}{4}\left[\log_a x + \log_a y - 3\log_a z\right]$$

Example 3. Express as a single logarithm.

$$\frac{1}{2}\log_a x - 7\log_a y + \log_a z$$

$$= \log_a \sqrt{x} - \log_a y^7 + \log_a z$$

$$= \log_a \frac{\sqrt{x}}{y^7} + \log_a z$$

$$= \log_a \frac{z\sqrt{x}}{y^7}$$

[34–37]

Example 4. Given that $\log_a 2 = 0.301$ and $\log_a 3 = 0.477$, find:

1. $\log_a 6 = \log_a 2 \cdot 3 = \log_a 2 + \log_a 3$
   $= 0.301 + 0.477 = 0.778$

2. $\log_a \sqrt{3} = \log_a 3^{\frac{1}{2}} = \frac{1}{2} \cdot \log_a 3 = \frac{1}{2} \cdot 0.477$
   $= 0.2385$

3. $\log_a \frac{2}{3} = \log_a 2 - \log_a 3 = 0.301 - 0.477$
   $= -0.176$

4. $\log_a 5$; *No way to find, using these properties.*
   ($\log_a 5 \neq \log_a 2 + \log_a 3$)

5. $\frac{\log_a 2}{\log_a 3} = \frac{0.301}{0.477} = 0.63$. Note that we could not use any of the properties; we simply divided. **[38]**

For any base a, $\log_a a = 1$. This is easily seen by writing an equivalent exponential equation, $a^1 = a$. Similarly, for any base a, $\log_a 1 = 0$. These facts are important and should be remembered well.

> **For any base a,**
>
> $$\log_a a = 1 \quad \text{and} \quad \log_a 1 = 0.$$

[39–42]

Exercise Set 6.2

Express in terms of logarithms of x, y, and z.

1. $\log_a x^2 y^3 z$ **2.** $\log_a 5xy^4 z^3$ **3.** $\log_b \frac{xy^2}{z^3}$ **4.** $\log_c \sqrt[3]{\frac{x^4}{y^3 z^2}}$

Express as a single logarithm and simplify if possible.

5. $\frac{2}{3}\log_b 64 - \frac{1}{2}\log_b 16$ **6.** $\frac{1}{2}\log_a x + 3\log_a y - 2\log_a x$

7. $\log_a 2x + 3(\log_a x - \log_a y)$ **8.** $\log_a x^2 - 2\log_a \sqrt{x}$

9. $\log_a \frac{a}{\sqrt{x}} - \log_a \sqrt{ax}$ **10.** $\log_a (x^2 - 4) - \log_a (x - 2)$

Express as a sum and/or difference of logarithms.

11. $\log_a \sqrt{1 - x^2}$

12. $\log_a \dfrac{x + t}{\sqrt{x^2 - t^2}}$

Given $\log_{10} 2 = \underline{0.301}$, $\log_{10} 3 = \underline{0.477}$, and $\log_{10} 10 = \underline{1}$, find:

13. $\log_{10} 4$

14. $\log_{10} 5$

$\left(Hint:\ 5 = \dfrac{10}{2} \right)$

15. $\log_{10} 50$

$\left(Hint:\ 50 = \dfrac{100}{2} \right)$

16. $\log_{10} 12$

17. $\log_{10} 60$

18. $\log_{10} \dfrac{1}{3}$

19. $\log_{10} \sqrt{\dfrac{2}{3}}$

20. $\log_{10} \sqrt[5]{12}$

21. $\log_{10} 90$

22. $\log_{10} \dfrac{9}{8}$

23. $\log_{10} \dfrac{9}{10}$

24. $\log_{10} \dfrac{1}{4}$

Which of the following are false?

25. $\dfrac{\log_a M}{\log_a N} = \log_a M - \log_a N$

26. $\dfrac{\log_a M}{\log_a N} = \log_a \dfrac{M}{N}$

27. $\dfrac{\log_a M}{c} = \log_a M^{1/c}$

28. $\log_N (M \cdot N)^x = x \log_N M + x$

29. $\log_a 2x = 2 \log_a x$

30. $\log_a 2x = \log_a 2 + \log_a x$

Solve.

31. $\log_\pi \pi^{2x+3} = 4$

32. $3^{\log_3 (8x-4)} = 5$

33. $4^{2\log_4 x} = 7$

34. $8^{2\log_8 x + \log_8 x} = 27$

35. If $\log_a x = 2$, what is $\log_a \left(\dfrac{1}{x} \right)$?

36. If $\log_a x = 2$, what is $\log_{1/a} x$?

37. Compare $\log_a 1/x$ and $\log_{1/a} x$. Prove your conjecture.

38. Graph and compare.

$y = \log_2 |x| \quad$ and $\quad y = |\log_2 x|$

6.3 Common Logarithms

Base ten logarithms are known as *common logarithms.* Tables for these logarithms are readily available (Table 2 at the end of this book).

LOGARITHMS IN COMPUTATION

Before calculators and computers became so readily available, common logarithms were used extensively to do certain kinds of calculations. In fact, this is why logarithms were developed. Today, computations with logarithms are mainly of historical interest; the logarithm *functions* are of modern importance. The study of computations with logarithms can, however, help the student to fix his or her ideas with respect to properties of logarithm functions.

The following is a table of powers of 10, or *logarithms* base 10.

$1 = 10^{0.0000}$,	or	$\log_{10} 1 \ = 0.0000$
$2 = 10^{0.3010}$,	or	$\log_{10} 2 \ = 0.3010$
$3 = 10^{0.4771}$,	or	$\log_{10} 3 \ = 0.4771$
$4 = 10^{0.6021}$,	or	$\log_{10} 4 \ = 0.6021$
$5 = 10^{0.6990}$,	or	$\log_{10} 5 \ = 0.6990$
$6 = 10^{0.7782}$,	or	$\log_{10} 6 \ = 0.7782$
$7 = 10^{0.8451}$,	or	$\log_{10} 7 \ = 0.8451$
$8 = 10^{0.9031}$,	or	$\log_{10} 8 \ = 0.9031$
$9 = 10^{0.9542}$,	or	$\log_{10} 9 \ = 0.9542$
$10 = 10^{1.0000}$,	or	$\log_{10} 10 = 1.0000$
$11 = 10^{1.0414}$,	or	$\log_{10} 11 = 1.0414$
$12 = 10^{1.0792}$,	or	$\log_{10} 12 = 1.0792$
$13 = 10^{1.1139}$,	or	$\log_{10} 13 = 1.1139$
$14 = 10^{1.1461}$,	or	$\log_{10} 14 = 1.1461$
$15 = 10^{1.1761}$,	or	$\log_{10} 15 = 1.1761$
$16 = 10^{1.2041}$,	or	$\log_{10} 16 = 1.2041$

The exponents are approximate, but accurate to four decimal places. To illustrate how logarithms can be used for computation we will use the above table and do some easy calculations.

Example 1. Find 3×4 using the table of exponents.

$$3 \times 4 = 10^{0.4771} \times 10^{0.6021}$$
$$= 10^{1.0792} \text{ (adding exponents)}$$

From the table we see that $10^{1.0792} = 12$, so

$$3 \times 4 = 12. \qquad \text{[43]}$$

Note from example 1 that we can find a product by adding the logarithms of the factors and then finding the number having the result as its logarithm. That is, we found the number $10^{1.0792}$. This number is often referred to as the *antilogarithm* of 1.0792. To state this another way, if

$$f(x) = \log_{10} x,$$

then

$$f^{-1}(x) = \text{antilog}_{10} x = 10^x.$$

In other words, an antilogarithm function is simply an exponential function.

Example 2. Find 3×5, using base 10 logarithms.

$$\log_{10} (3 \times 5) = \log_{10} 3 + \log_{10} 5$$
$$= 0.4771 + 0.6990$$
$$\log_{10} (3 \times 5) = 1.1761$$
$$3 \times 5 = \text{antilog}_{10} 1.1761 = 15$$

Example 3. Find $\frac{14}{2}$, using base 10 logarithms.

$$\log_{10} \frac{14}{2} = \log_{10} 14 - \log_{10} 2$$
$$= 1.1461 - 0.3010$$
$$\log_{10} \frac{14}{2} = 0.8451$$
$$\frac{14}{2} = \text{antilog}_{10} 0.8451 = 7$$

Example 4. Find $\sqrt[4]{16}$, using base 10 logarithms.

$$\log_{10} \sqrt[4]{16} = \log_{10} 16^{\frac{1}{4}} = \frac{1}{4} \cdot \log_{10} 16 = \frac{1}{4} \cdot 1.2041$$

$$\log_{10} \sqrt[4]{16} = 0.3010 \text{ (rounded to four decimal places)}$$
$$\sqrt[4]{16} = \text{antilog}_{10} 0.3010 = 2$$

Example 5. Find 2^3, using base 10 logarithms.

$$\log_{10} 2^3 = 3 \cdot \log_{10} 2 = 3 \cdot 0.3010 = 0.9030$$
$$\log_{10} 2^3 = 0.9030$$
$$2^3 = \text{antilog}_{10} 0.9030 \approx 8$$

Note the rounding error. \qquad **[44–47]**

We will often omit the base, 10, when working with common logarithms.

Table 2 contains logarithms of numbers from 1 to 10. Part of that table is shown on the following page.

x	0	1	2	3	4	5	6	7	8	9
5.0	0.6990	0.6998	0.7007	0.7016	0.7024	0.7033	0.7042	0.7050	0.7059	0.7067
5.1	0.7076	0.7084	0.7093	0.7101	0.7110	0.7118	0.7126	0.7135	0.7143	0.7152
5.2	0.7160	0.7168	0.7177	0.7185	**0.7193**	0.7202	0.7210	0.7218	0.7226	0.7235
5.3	0.7234	0.7251	0.7259	0.7267	0.7275	0.7284	0.7292	0.7300	0.7308	0.7316
5.4	0.7324	0.7332	0.7340	0.7348	0.7356	0.7364	0.7372	0.7380	0.7388	0.7396

To illustrate the use of the table, let us find log 5.24. We locate the row headed 5.2, then move across to the column headed 4. We find log 5.24 as the shaded entry in the table.

We can find antilogarithms by reversing this process. For example, antilog $0.7193 = 10^{0.7193} = 5.24$. Similarly, antilog $0.7292 = 5.36$.   **[48–53]**

Using Table 2 and scientific notation* we can find logarithms of numbers that are not between 1 and 10. First recall the following:

$$\log_a a^k = k \text{ for any number } k.$$

Thus

$$\log_{10} 10^k = k \text{ for any number } k.$$

Examples

a) $\log 52.4 = \log (5.24 \times 10^1)$
  $= \log 5.24 + \log 10^1$
  $= 0.7193 + 1$

b) $\log 0.524 = \log (5.24 \times 10^{-1})$
  $= \log 5.24 + \log 10^{-1}$
  $= 0.7193 + (-1)$

c) $\log 52{,}400 = \log (5.24 \times 10^4)$
  $= \log 5.24 + \log 10^4$
  $= 0.7193 + 4$

d) $\log 0.00524 = \log (5.24 \times 10^{-3})$
  $= \log 5.24 + \log 10^{-3}$
  $= 0.7193 + (-3)$ **[54, 55]**

_____
* It may be helpful to review scientific notation in Chapter 1.

The preceding examples illustrate the importance of using the base 10 for computation. It allows great economy in the printing of tables. If we know the logarithm of a number from 1 to 10 we can multiply that number by any power of ten and easily determine the logarithm of the resulting number. For any base other than 10 this would not be the case. In each of these examples, the integer part of the logarithm is the exponent in the scientific notation. This integer is called the *characteristic* of the logarithm. The other part of the logarithm, a number between 0 and 1, is called the *mantissa* of the logarithm. Table 2 contains only mantissas.

Example. Find log 0.0538, indicating the characteristic and mantissa.

We first write scientific notation for the number:

$$5.38 \times 10^{-2}.$$

Then we find log 5.38. This is the mantissa:

$$\log 5.38 = 0.7308.$$

The characteristic is the exponent -2.

Now $\log 0.0538 = 0.7308 + (-2)$, or -1.2692.

When negative characteristics occur, it is usually best to name the logarithm in such a way that the characteristic and mantissa are preserved. In the preceding example, we have

$$\log 0.0538 = -1.2692,$$

but this notation displays neither the characteristic nor

the mantissa. We can name the characteristic, -2, as $8 - 10$, and then add the mantissa, to obtain

$$8.7308 - 10,$$

thus preserving both mantissa and characteristic.

Example. Find $\log 0.00687$.

We write scientific notation (or at least visualize it):

$$0.00687 = 6.87 \times 10^{-3}.$$

The characteristic is -3, or $7 - 10$. The mantissa, from the table, is 0.8370. Thus $\log 0.00687 = 7.8370 - 10$. **[56–62]**

ANTILOGARITHMS

To find antilogarithms, we reverse the procedure for finding logarithms.

Example 1. Find antilog 2.6085.

$$\text{antilog } 2.6085 = 10^{2.6085} = 10^{(2+0.6085)}$$
$$= 10^2 \cdot 10^{0.6085}$$

From the table we can find $10^{0.6085}$, or antilog 0.6085. It is 4.06. Hence we have

$$\text{antilog } 2.6085 = 10^2 \times 4.06, \quad \text{or} \quad 406.$$

Note in this example, we in effect separate the number 2.6085 into an integer and a number between 0 and 1. We use the latter with the table, after which we have scientific notation for our answer.

Example 2. Find antilog 3.7118.

From the table we find antilog $0.7118 = 5.15$. Thus

$$\text{antilog } 3.7118 = 5.15 \times 10^3 \quad \text{(Note that 3 is the characteristic.)}$$
$$= 5150.$$

Example 3. Find antilog $(7.7143 - 10)$.

The characteristic is -3 and the mantissa is 0.7143.

From the table we find that antilog $0.7143 = 5.18$. Thus

$$\text{antilog } (7.7143 - 10) = 5.18 \times 10^{-3}$$
$$= 0.00518. \quad \textbf{[63–67]}$$

CALCULATIONS WITH LOGARITHMS

The kinds of calculations in which logarithms may be helpful are multiplication, division, taking powers, and taking roots.

Example 1. Find $\dfrac{0.0578 \times 32.7}{8460}$.

We write a *plan* for the use of logarithms, then look up all of the mantissas at one time.

Let

$$N = \frac{0.0578 \times 32.7}{8460}$$

Then

$$\log N = \log 0.0578 + \log 32.7 - \log 8460.$$

This gives us the plan.

We use a straight line to indicate addition and a wavy line to indicate subtraction.

Completion of plan:

$$\log 0.0578 = 8.7619 - 10$$
$$\log 32.7 = 1.5145$$

$$\log \text{numerator} = 10.2764 - 10$$
$$\log 8460 = 3.9274$$

〰〰〰〰〰〰〰

$$\log \text{fraction} = 6.3490 - 10$$
$$\text{fraction} = 0.000223 \quad \text{(taking antilog)}$$

$$\textbf{[68]}$$

Example 2. Use logarithms to find $\sqrt[4]{0.325} \times (4.23)^2$.

If
$$N = \sqrt[4]{0.325} \times (4.23)^2,$$
then
$$\log N = \frac{1}{4}\log 0.325 + 2\log 4.23;$$

this yields the plan.

Note that powers and roots are involved. In such cases it is easier to first find the following logs:
$$\log 0.325 = 9.5119 - 10$$
$$\log 4.23 = 0.6263.$$

Consider $9.5119 - 10$. Since we will be dividing this number by 4, but -10 is not divisible by 4, we rename this number:
$$\log 0.325 = 39.5119 - 40.$$

Now the negative term is divisible by 4. We divide $\log 0.325$ by 4 and multiply $\log 4.23$ by 2. Then we have

$$\log \sqrt[4]{0.325} = 9.8780 - 10$$
$$\log (4.23)^2 = 1.2526$$
$$\overline{\hspace{3cm}}$$
$$\log \text{product} = 11.1306 - 10$$
$$= 1.1306$$
$$\text{product} = 13.5. \qquad \textbf{[69]}$$

Exercise Set 6.3

Use Table 2 to find each of the following. Where appropriate, write so that (positive) mantissas are preserved.

1. $\log 2.46$
2. $\log 7.56$
3. $\log 5.31$
4. $\log 8.57$

5. $\log 347$
6. $\log 8720$
7. $\log 52.5$
8. $\log 20.6$

9. $\log 624,000$
10. $\log 13,400$
11. $\log 0.0702$
12. $\log 0.640$

13. $\log 0.000216$
14. $\log 0.173$
15. $\log 0.00347$
16. $\log 0.0000404$

17. antilog 2.3674
18. antilog 1.9222
19. antilog 3.2553
20. antilog 2.6294

21. $10^{1.4014}$
22. $10^{8.9881-10}$
23. $10^{7.5391-10}$
24. $10^{3.6590}$

25. antilog $(9.8156 - 10)$ **26.** antilog $(8.1239 - 10)$

Use logarithms to compute. When exact values do not occur in the table, use the nearest values.

27. 3.14×60.4
28. 541×0.0152
29. $286 \div 1.05$
30. $12.8 \div 81.6$

31. $\sqrt{76.9}$
32. $\sqrt[3]{56.9}$
33. $(1.36)^{4.2}$
34. $(0.727)^{3.6}$

35. $\dfrac{70.7 \times (10.6)^2}{18.6 \times \sqrt{276}}$
36. $\sqrt[3]{\dfrac{3.24 \times (3.16)^2}{78.4 \times 24.6}}$

6.4 Interpolation

In the previous section we developed procedures for using Table 2 using three-digit precision. By using a procedure called *interpolation* we can find values between those listed in the table, obtaining four-digit precision. Interpolation can be done in various ways, the simplest and most common being *linear* interpolation. We describe it now. What we say applies to a table for any continuous function.

Let us consider how a table of values for any function is made. We select members of the domain x_1, x_2, x_3, and so on. Then we compute or somehow determine the corresponding function values, $f(x_1)$, $f(x_2)$, $f(x_3)$, and so on. Then we tabulate the results. We might also graph the results.

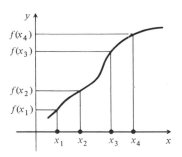

x	x_1	x_2	x_3	x_4	$\cdots$
$f(x)$	$f(x_1)$	$f(x_2)$	$f(x_3)$	$f(x_4)$	$\cdots$

Suppose we want to find the function value $f(x)$ for an x not in the table. If x is halfway between x_1 and x_2, then we can take the number halfway between $f(x_1)$ and $f(x_2)$ as an approximation to $f(x)$. If x is one-fifth of the way between x_2 and x_3, we take the number that is one-fifth of the way between $f(x_2)$ and $f(x_3)$ as an approximation to $f(x)$. What we do is divide the length from x_2 to x_3 in a certain ratio, and then divide the length from $f(x_2)$ to $f(x_3)$ in the same ratio. This is *linear interpolation*.

We can show this geometrically. The length from x_1 to x_2 is divided in a certain ratio by x. The length from $f(x_1)$ to $f(x_2)$ is divided in the same ratio by y. The number y approximates $f(x)$ with the noted error.

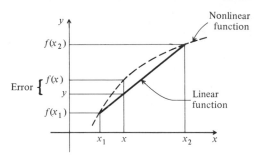

Note the slanted line in the figure. The approximation y comes from this line. This explains the use of the term *linear interpolation*. Let us apply linear interpolation to Table 2 of common logarithms.

Example 1. Find $\log 34870$.

a) Find the characteristic. Since $34870 = 3.487 \times 10^4$, the characteristic is 4.

b) Find the mantissa. From Table 2 we have:

$$0.01 \begin{cases} 0.007 \begin{cases} \log 3.480 = 0.5416 \\ \log 3.487 = 0.54?? \end{cases} \\ \log 3.490 = 0.5428 \end{cases} \left.\begin{matrix} \\ \\ \\ \\ \end{matrix}\right\} \begin{matrix} \text{Tabular} \\ \text{difference} \\ \text{is } 0.0012 \end{matrix}$$

The tabular difference (difference between consecutive values in the table) is 0.0012. Now 3.487 is $\frac{7}{10}$ of the way from 3.480 to 3.490. So we take 0.7 of 0.0012, which is 0.00084, and round it to 0.0008. We add this to 0.5416. The mantissa is 0.5424.

c) Add the characteristic and mantissa:

$$\log 34870 = 4.5424.$$

With practice you will take 0.7 of 12, forgetting the zeros, but adding in the same way.   **[70]**

Example 2. Find $\log 0.009543$.

a) Find the characteristic. Since $0.009543 = 9.543 \times 10^{-3}$, the characteristic is -3, or $7 - 10$.

b) Find the mantissa. From Table 2 we have:

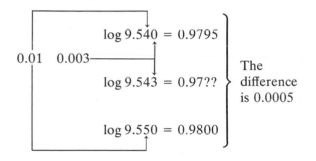

$$\begin{matrix} \log 9.540 = 0.9795 \\ \log 9.543 = 0.97?? \\ \log 9.550 = 0.9800 \end{matrix} \quad \left.\begin{matrix} \\ \\ \end{matrix}\right\} \begin{matrix} \text{The} \\ \text{difference} \\ \text{is } 0.0005 \end{matrix}$$

Now 9.543 is $\frac{3}{10}$ of the way from 9.540 to 9.550, so we take 0.3 of 0.005, which is 0.00015, and round it to 0.0002. We add this to 0.9795. The mantissa that results is 0.9797.

c) Add the characteristic and the mantissa:

$$\log 0.009543 = 7.9797 - 10.$$ **[71]**

ANTILOGARITHMS

We interpolate when finding antilogarithms, using the table in reverse.

Example 1. Find antilog 4.9164.

a) The characteristic is 4. The mantissa is 0.9164.

b) Find the antilog of the mantissa, 0.9164. From Table 2 we have

$$\begin{matrix} \text{antilog } 0.9159 = 8.240 \\ 0.0006 \quad 0.0005 \\ \text{antilog } 0.9164 = 8.24? \\ \text{antilog } 0.9165 = 8.250 \end{matrix} \quad \left.\begin{matrix} \\ \\ \\ \end{matrix}\right\} \begin{matrix} \text{Difference} \\ \text{is } 0.010 \end{matrix}$$

The difference between 0.9159 and 0.9165 is 0.0006. Thus 0.9164 is $\frac{0.0005}{0.0006}$, or $\frac{5}{6}$, of the way between 0.9159 and 0.9165. Then antilog 0.9164 is $\frac{5}{6}$ of the way between 8.240 and 8.250, or $\frac{5}{6}$ (0.010), which is $0.00833\ldots$, and round it to 0.008. Thus the antilog of the mantissa is 8.248.

Thus antilog $4.9164 = 8.248 \times 10^4 = 82{,}480$.   **[72]**

Example 2. Find antilog $(7.4122 - 10)$.

a) The characteristic is -3. The mantissa is 0.4122.

b) Find the antilog of the mantissa, 0.4122. From Table 2 we have

$$\begin{matrix} \text{antilog } 0.4116 = 2.580 \\ 0.0017 \quad 0.0006 \\ \text{antilog } 0.4122 = 2.58? \\ \text{antilog } 0.4133 = 2.590 \end{matrix} \quad \left.\begin{matrix} \\ \\ \\ \end{matrix}\right\} \begin{matrix} \text{Difference} \\ \text{is } 0.010 \end{matrix}$$

The difference between 0.4116 and 0.4133 is 0.0017. Thus 0.4122 is $\frac{0.0006}{0.0017}$, or $\frac{6}{17}$ of the way between 0.4116 and 0.4133. Then antilog 0.4122 is $\frac{6}{17}$ of the way between 2.580 and 2.590, or $\frac{6}{17}$ (0.010), which is 0.0035, to four places. We round it to 0.004. Thus the antilog of the mantissa is 2.584.

So antilog $(7.4122 - 10) = 2.584 \times 10^{-3} = .002584$.   **[73]**

CALCULATIONS

Calculations with logarithms, using Table 2, can be done with four-digit precision when interpolation is used, in finding both logarithms and antilogarithms.

Exercise Set 6.4

Find each of the following logarithms using interpolation.

1. log 41.63	**2.** log 472.1	**3.** log 2.944	**4.** log 21.76
5. log 650.2	**6.** log 37.37	**7.** log 0.1425	**8.** log 0.0904
9. log 0.004257	**10.** log 4518	**11.** log 0.1776	**12.** log 0.08356
13. log 600.6	**14** log (log 3)	**15.** log (log 5)	

Find each of the following antilogarithms using interpolation.

16. antilog 1.6350	**17.** antilog 2.3512	**18.** antilog 0.6478	**19.** antilog 1.1624
20. antilog 0.0342	**21.** antilog 4.8453	**22.** antilog 9.8561 − 10	**23.** antilog 8.9659 − 10
24. antilog 7.4128 − 10	**25.** antilog 9.7278 − 10	**26.** antilog 8.2010 − 10	**27.** antilog 7.8630 − 10

Use logarithms and interpolation to do the following calculations. Use four-digit precision. Answers may be checked using a calculator.

28. $\dfrac{35.24 \times (16.77)^3}{12.93 \times \sqrt{276.2}}$

29. $\sqrt[5]{\dfrac{16.79 \times (4.234)^3}{18.81 \times 175.3}}$

6.5 Exponential and Logarithmic Equations

An equation with variables in exponents, such as $3^{2x-1} = 4$, is called an *exponential equation*. We can often solve such equations by taking the logarithm on both sides and then using Theorem 3, p. 181.*

---

*The use of a calculator (if it will do arithmetic, it will suffice) is recommended for the rest of this chapter.

Example 1. Solve $3^x = 8$.

$$\log 3^x = \log 8 \qquad \text{(taking log on both sides)}$$

$$x \log 3 = \log 8 \qquad \text{(using Theorem 3)}$$

$$x = \frac{\log 8}{\log 3}$$

$$x \approx \frac{0.9031}{0.4771} \qquad \text{(we look up the logs and divide)}$$

$$x \approx 1.8929 \qquad\qquad\qquad \textbf{[74]}$$

Example 2. Solve $2^{3x-5} = 16$.

Method 1.

$$\log 2^{3x-5} = \log 16 \qquad \text{(taking log on both sides)}$$

$$(3x - 5)\log 2 = \log 16 \qquad \text{(using Theorem 3)}$$

$$3x - 5 = \frac{\log 16}{\log 2}$$

$$x = \frac{\dfrac{\log 16}{\log 2} + 5}{3}$$

$$x = \frac{\dfrac{1.2041}{0.3010} + 5}{3}$$

$$x \approx 3.0001$$

The answer is approximate because the logarithms are approximate.

Method 2. Note that $16 = 2^4$. Then we have

$$2^{3x-5} = 2^4.$$

Since the base is the same, 2, on both sides, the exponents must be the same. Thus

$$3x - 5 = 4.$$

We solve this equation to get

$$x = 3.$$

This answer is exact. **[75]**

Example 3. Solve $\dfrac{e^x + e^{-x}}{2} = t$, for x.

$$e^x + e^{-x} = 2t \qquad \text{(multiplying by 2)}$$

$$e^x + \frac{1}{e^x} = 2t \qquad \begin{array}{l}\text{(rewriting to elimi-}\\\text{nate the minus sign in}\\\text{an exponent)}\end{array}$$

$$e^{2x} + 1 = 2t \cdot e^x \qquad \begin{array}{l}\text{(multiplying on both}\\\text{sides by } e^x)\end{array}$$

$$(e^x)^2 - 2t \cdot e^x + 1 = 0$$

This equation is quadratic in form, with $u = e^x$. Using the quadratic formula, we obtain

$$e^x = \frac{2t \pm \sqrt{4t^2 - 4}}{2} = t \pm \sqrt{t^2 - 1}$$

$$\log e^x = \log\left(t \pm \sqrt{t^2 - 1}\right) \qquad \begin{array}{l}\text{(taking log on both}\\\text{sides)}\end{array}$$

$$x \log e = \log\left(t \pm \sqrt{t^2 - 1}\right) \qquad \text{(using Theorem 3)}$$

$$x = \frac{\log\left(t \pm \sqrt{t^2 - 1}\right)}{\log e}$$

If e should be a number suitable as a logarithm base, we might also take base e logarithms on both sides. The denominator would then be $\log_e e$, or 1, and we would have

$$x = \log_e\left(t \pm \sqrt{t^2 - 1}\right). \qquad \textbf{[76]}$$

LOGARITHMIC EQUATIONS

Equations that contain logarithmic expressions are called *logarithmic equations*. To solve such equations we try to obtain a single logarithmic expression on one side of the equation and then take the antilogarithm on both sides.

Example. Solve $\log x + \log(x - 3) = 1$.

$$\log x(x - 3) = 1 \qquad \begin{array}{l}\text{(using Theorem 1, p.}\\\text{180, to obtain a}\\\text{single logarithm)}\end{array}$$

$$x(x - 3) = 10^1 \qquad \begin{array}{l}\text{(taking the antilog on}\\\text{both sides)}\end{array}$$

$$x^2 - 3x - 10 = 0$$

$$(x + 2)(x - 5) = 0 \qquad \begin{array}{l}\text{(factoring and princi-}\\\text{ple of zero products)}\end{array}$$

$$x = -2 \quad \text{or} \quad x = 5$$

Check:

$$\frac{\log x + \log (x - 3) = 1}{\log (-2) + \log (-2 - 3) \mid 1}$$

The number -2 is not a solution because negative numbers do not have logarithms.

$$\frac{\log x + \log (x - 3) = 1}{\log 5 + \log (5 - 3) \quad \bigg| \quad 1}$$
$$\log 5 + \log 2$$
$$\log 10$$
$$1$$

[77]

APPLICATIONS

Exponential and logarithmic functions and equations have many applications. We shall consider a few of them.

Example 1. (*Compound interest*). The amount A that principal p will be worth after t years at $r\%$ interest compounded annually is given by the formula $A = p(1 + r\%)^t$. Suppose \$4000 principal is invested at 6% interest and yields \$5353. How many years was it invested?

Using the formula $A = p(1 + r\%)^t$, we have

$$5353 = 4000(1 + .06)^t, \quad \text{or} \quad 5353 = 4000(1.06)^t.$$

Solving for t, we have

$$\log 5353 = \log 4000 \, (1.06)^t$$
$$\log 5353 = \log 4000 + t \log 1.06$$
$$\frac{\log 5353 - \log 4000}{\log 1.06} = t$$
$$\frac{3.7286 - 3.6021}{0.0253} = t$$
$$5 = t.$$

The money was invested for 5 years. **[78]**

Example 2. ((*Loudness of sound*). The sensation of loudness of sound is not proportional to the energy intensity, but rather is a logarithmic function. *Loudness*, in Bels (after Alexander Graham Bell), of a sound of intensity I is defined to be

$$L = \log \frac{I}{I_0},$$

where I_0 is the minimum intensity detectable by the human ear (such as the tick of a watch at 20 ft under quiet conditions). When a sound is 10 times as intense as another, its loudness is 1 Bel greater. If a sound is 100 times as intense as another, it is louder by 2 Bels, and so on. The Bel is a large unit, so a subunit, a *decibel*, is usually used. For L in decibels, the formula is as follows:

$$L = 10 \log \frac{I}{I_0}.$$

a) Find the loudness, in decibels, of the sound in a radio studio, for which the intensity I is 199 times I_0.

We substitute into the formula and calculate, using Table 2:

$$L = 10 \log \frac{199 \cdot I_0}{I_0} = 10 \log 199$$
$$= 10 \, (2.2989)$$
$$= 23 \text{ decibels.}$$

b) Find the loudness of the sound of a heavy truck, for which the intensity is 10^9 times I_0.

$$L = 10 \log \frac{10^9 \cdot I_0}{I_0} = 10 \log 10^9$$
$$= 10 \cdot 9$$
$$= 90 \text{ decibels}$$

[79, 80]

Example 3. (*Earthquake magnitude*). The magnitude R (on the Richter scale) of an earthquake of intensity I is defined as follows:

$$R = \log \frac{I}{I_0},$$

where I_0 is a minimum intensity used for comparison.

An earthquake has an intensity $10^{8.6}$ times I_0. What is its magnitude on the Richter scale?

We substitute into the formula:

$$R = \log \frac{10^{8.6} \cdot I_0}{I_0} = \log 10^{8.6} = 8.6. \qquad \textbf{[81]}$$

Example 4. (*Forgetting*). Here is a mathematical model for psychology. A group of people take a test and make an average score of S. After a time t they take an equivalent form of the same test. At that time the average score is $S(t)$. According to this model, $S(t)$ is given by the following function,

$$S(t) = A - B \log (t + 1),$$

where t is in months and the constants A and B are determined by experiment in various kinds of learning situations.

Students in a zoology class took a final exam, and took equivalent forms of the test at monthly intervals thereafter. The average scores were found to be given by the function

$$S(t) = 78 - 15 \log (t + 1).$$

What was the average score (a) when they took the test originally? (b) after 4 months?

We substitute into the equation defining the function:

a) $S(0) = 78 - 15 \log (0 + 1)$
   $= 78 - 15 \log 1 = 78 - 0 = 78.$

b) $S(4) = 78 - 15 \log (4 + 1)$
   $= 78 - 15 \log 5 = 78 - 15 \cdot 0.6990$
   $= 78 - 10.49 = 67.51. \qquad \textbf{[82]}$

Exercise Set 6.5

Solve.

1. $2^x = 32$

2. $3^{x-1} + 3 = 30$

3. $4^{2x} = 8^{3x-4}$

4. $3^{x^2+4x} = \dfrac{1}{27}$

5. $3^{5x} \cdot 9^{x^2} = 27$

6. $4^x = 7$

7. $2^x = 3^{x-1}$

8. $3^{x+2} = 5^{x-1}$

9. $\log x + \log (x - 9) = 1$

10. $\log x - \log (x + 3) = -1$

11. $\log (x + 9) - \log x = 1$

12. $\log (2x + 1) - \log (x - 2) = 1$

13. $\log_4 (x + 3) + \log_4 (x - 3) = 2$

14. $\log_8 (x + 1) - \log_8 x = \log_8 4$

15. $\log x^2 = (\log x)^2$

16. $(\log_3 x)^2 - \log_3 x^2 = 3$

17. $\log \sqrt{x} = \sqrt{\log x}$

18. $\log(\log x) = 2$

19. $\log_5 \sqrt{x^2 + 1} = 1$

20. $\log \sqrt[3]{x^2} + \log \sqrt[3]{x^4} = \log 2^{-3}$

21. Solve for x. Use $\log_3$.

$$\frac{3^x + 3^{-x}}{2} = t$$

22. Solve for x. Use $\log_3$.

$$\frac{3^x - 3^{-x}}{2} = t$$

23. Solve for x. Use $\log_5$.

$$\frac{5^x - 5^{-x}}{5^x + 5^{-x}} = t$$

24. Solve for x. Use $\log_e$.

$$\frac{e^x + e^{-x}}{e^x - e^{-x}} = t$$

25. Solve $y = ax^n$, for n. Use $\log_x$.

26. Solve $y = ke^{at}$, for t. Use $\log_e$.

27. Solve for t. Use $\log_e$.

$$P = P_0 e^{rt/100}$$

28. Solve for t. Use $\log_e$.

$$I = \frac{E}{R}(1 - e^{-(Rt/L)})$$

29. Solve for t.

$$T = T_0 + (T_1 - T_0)10^{-kt}$$

30. Solve for n. Use $\log_V$.

$$PV^n = c$$

31. (*Doubling time*). How many years will it take an investment of $1000 to double itself when interest is compounded annually at 6%?

32. (*Tripling time*). How many years will it take an investment of $1000 to triple itself when interest is compounded annually at 5%?

33. Find the loudness of the sound of an automobile, having an intensity 3,100,000 times I_0.

34. Find the loudness of the sound of a dishwasher, having an intensity 2,500,000 times I_0.

35. Find the loudness of the threshold of sound pain, for which the intensity is 10^{14} times I_0.

36. Find the loudness of a jet aircraft, having an intensity 10^{12} times I_0.

37. The Los Angeles earthquake of 1971 had an intensity $10^{6.7}$ times I_0. What was its magnitude on the Richter scale?

38. The San Francisco earthquake of 1906 had an intensity $10^{8.25}$ times I_0. What was its magnitude on the Richter scale?

39. An earthquake has a magnitude of 5 on the Richter scale. What is its intensity?

40. An earthquake has a magnitude of 7 on the Richter scale. What is its intensity?

41. Students in an industrial mathematics course take a final exam and are then retested at monthly intervals. The forgetting function is given by $S(t) = 82 - 18 \log (t + 1)$.

a) What was the average score on the final exam?

b) What was the average score after 5 months had elapsed?

43. Refer to Exercise 41. How much time will elapse before the average score has decreased to 64?

45. In chemistry, pH is defined as follows:

$$pH = -\log [H^+],$$

where $[H^+]$ is the hydrogen ion concentration in moles per liter. For example, the hydrogen ion concentration in milk is 4×10^{-7} moles per liter, so $pH = -\log(4 \times 10^{-7}) = -[\log 4 + (-7)] \approx 6.4$. For tomatoes, $[H^+]$ is about 6.3×10^{-5}. Find the pH.

42. Students graduating from a cosmetology curriculum take a final exam and are then retested at monthly intervals. The forgetting function is given by $S(t) = 75 - 20 \log (t + 1)$.

a) What was the average score on the final exam?

b) What was the average score after 6 months had elapsed?

44. Refer to Exercise 42. How much time will elapse before the average score has decreased to 61?

46. For eggs, $[H^+]$ is about 1.6×10^{-8}. Find the pH.

▶ Solve these systems of equations.

47. $y = 5^{2x}$
$y = 5^x + 2$
(*Hint:* Let $u = 5^x$).

48. $y = 3^{2x}$
$y = 3^x + 6$

49. $y = \log x$
$x = \log y$
(*Hint:* Draw a graph.)

50. $y = 3^x$
$x = 3^y$

51. $4^x = 5^y$
$2(4^x) = 7^y$

52. $2^x = 3^y$
$3(2^x) = 6^y$

6.6 The Number *e*; Change of Base

THE NUMBER *e*

One of the most important numbers is a certain irrational number, with a nonrepeating decimal representation. This number is usually named *e*, and it arises in a number of different ways. One of these is the following.

Consider the compound interest formula

$$A = p(1 + r)^t,$$

where A is the amount that the investment is worth, p is the principal, r is the rate of interest, and t is the time in years. Interest is usually compounded more often than once a year, say n times per year. In this event we alter the formula. The rate of interest for an *interest period* is r/n and the number of interest periods is $n \cdot t$, for t years. Thus we have

$$A = p\left(1 + \frac{r}{n}\right)^{nt}.$$

Suppose you invest one dollar for one year at 100%. This makes the formula simple:

$$A = \left(1 + \frac{1}{n}\right)^n.$$

The amount A is now a function of n. The more often interest is compounded, the greater A becomes. Let us look at some values of this function.

8760   525,600

Compounding	n	A
annually	1	$(1 + \frac{1}{1})^1 = 2$
semiannually	2	$(1 + \frac{1}{2})^2 = 2.25$
quarterly	4	$(1 + \frac{1}{4})^4 = 2.44\ldots$

According to this table, for semiannual compounding the dollar grows to $2.25 in one year. For quarterly compounding it grows to $2.44. What would you expect to happen if interest were compounded daily, or once each minute?   **[83, 84]**

Let us look at some more function values.

Compounding	n	A
daily	365	$2.71456\ldots$
once per hour	8,760	$2.71812\ldots$
once per minute	525,600	$2.71828\ldots$

This result may be surprising. The function values approach a limit as n increases. No matter how often interest is compounded your investment will not amount to more than $2.72 for the year. The limit that these function values approach is the number called e:

$$e = 2.71828182\ldots.$$

NATURAL LOGARITHMS AND EXPONENTIAL FUNCTIONS

The exponential function, base e, is important in many applications, and its inverse, the logarithm function base e, is also important in mathematical theory and in applications as well. Logarithms to the base e are called *natural* logarithms. Table 4 at the end of the book gives function values for e^x and e^{-x}.   **[85, 86]**

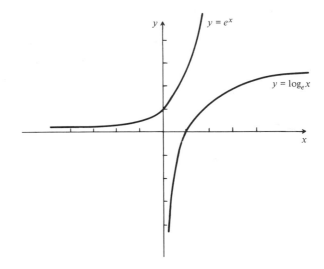

One interesting property of the function $y = e^x$ is the following: At any point on the curve, the slope of the curve is equal to the y-coordinate. This fact, strange as it may seem at this point, is important in many applications.

LOGARITHM TABLES

It is only common (base ten) logarithms that have characteristic and mantissa and therefore have compact tables. There are tables of natural logarithms, but they require rather extensive space. Fortunately we can use tables of common logarithms to find natural logarithms. The following theorem shows how we can change from base ten, or any base, to base e, or any other base.

Theorem. For any bases a and b, and any positive number M,

$$\log_b M = \frac{\log_a M}{\log_a b}.$$

Proof. Let $x = \log_b M$. Then $b^x = M$, so that

$$\log_a M = \log_a b^x, \quad \text{or} \quad x \log_a b.$$

We now solve for x:

$$x = \log_b M = \frac{\log_a M}{\log_a b}.$$

This is the desired formula.

Example 1. Find $\log_3 81$.

$$\log_3 81 = \frac{\log_{10} 81}{\log_{10} 3} = \frac{1.9085}{0.4771} \approx 4$$

Example 2. Find $\log_5 346$.

$$\log_5 346 = \frac{\log_{10} 346}{\log_{10} 5} = \frac{2.5391}{0.6990} \approx 3.6324$$

[87–89]

If, in the preceding theorem, we let $a = 10$ and $b = e$, we obtain a formula for changing from common to natural logarithms:

$$\log_e M = \frac{\log_{10} M}{\log_{10} e}.$$

Now $\log_{10} e \approx 0.4343$, so we have

$$\log_e M = \frac{\log_{10} M}{0.4343}$$

Example 3. Find $\log_e 257$.

$$\log_e 257 = \frac{\log_{10} 257}{0.4343} = \frac{2.4099}{0.4343} = 5.5489$$

[90, 91]

APPLICATIONS

There are many applications of exponential functions, base e. We consider a few.

Example 1. (*Population growth*). One mathematical model for describing population growth is the formula

$$P = P_0 e^{kt},$$

where P_0 is the number of people at time 0, P is the number of people at time t, and k is a positive constant depending on the situation.

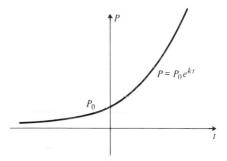

The population of the United States in 1970 was 208 million. In 1980 it is expected to be 250 million. Use these data to find the value of k and then use the model to predict the population in the year 2000.

Substituting the data into the formula, we get

$$250 = 208 e^{k \cdot 10}$$

We solve for k.

Method 1.

$$\log 250 = \log 208 e^{10k} \qquad \text{(taking logs on both sides)}$$

$$= \log 208 + 10k \log e$$

$$k = \frac{\log 250 - \log 208}{10 \log e} = 0.018.$$

Method 2. $\quad e^{10k} = \dfrac{250}{208} \approx 1.2019$

We look in Table 4, and find that

$$e^{0.18} = 1.1972,$$

$$e^{0.19} = 1.2092.$$

Thus $10k$ is between 0.18 and 0.19, so k is about 0.018.

To find the population in 2000, we will use $P_0 = 208$ (population in the year 1970). We then have

$$P = 208 e^{0.02t}.$$

We have rounded k to 0.02. In 2000, t will be 30, so we have

$$P = 208 e^{0.6}.$$

From Table 4, we find $e^{0.6} = 1.8221$. Multiplying by 208 gives us about 379 million. This is our prediction for the population of the United States in the year 2000. **[92]**

Example 2. (*Radioactive decay*). In a radioactive substance such as radium, some of the atoms are always ceasing to become radioactive. Thus the amount of a radioactive substance decreases. This is called radioactive *decay*. A model for radioactive decay is as follows:

$$N = N_0 e^{-kt},$$

where N_0 is the amount of a radioactive substance at time 0, N is the amount at time t, and k is a positive constant depending upon the situation.

$$N = N_0 e^{-kt}$$

Strontium 90 has a *half-life* of 25 years. This means that half of a sample of the substance will cease to become radioactive in 25 yr. Find k in the formula and then use the formula to find how much of a 36-gram sample will remain after 100 years.

When $t = 25$ (half-life), N will be half of N_0, so we have

$$\tfrac{1}{2}N_0 = N_0 e^{-25k} \qquad \text{or} \qquad \tfrac{1}{2} = e^{-25k}.$$

We take the natural log on both sides:

$$\log_e \tfrac{1}{2} = \log_e e^{-25k} = -25k.$$

Thus

$$k = -\frac{\log_e 0.5}{25} = -\frac{\log_{10} 0.5}{25 \log e} \approx 0.0277.$$

Now to find the amount remaining after 100 years, we use the formula:

$$N = 36 e^{-0.0277 \cdot 100}$$

$$= 36 e^{-2.77}.$$

From Table 4 we find that $e^{-2.8} = 0.0608$, and thus

$$N \approx 2.2 \text{ grams.} \qquad \textbf{[93]}$$

Example 3. (*Atmospheric pressure*). Under standard conditions of temperature, the atmospheric pressure at height h is given by

$$P = P_0 e^{-kh},$$

where P is the pressure, P_0 is the pressure where $h = 0$, and k is a positive constant.

Standard sea level pressure is 1013 millibars. Suppose that the pressure at 18,000 ft is half that at sea level. Then find k and find the pressure at 1000 ft.

At 18,000 ft P is half of P_0, so we have

$$\frac{P_0}{2} = P_0 e^{-18,000k}.$$

Taking natural logarithms on both sides, we obtain

$$\log_e \tfrac{1}{2} = -18,000k, \qquad \text{or} \qquad -\log_e 2 = -18,000k.$$

Then

$$k = \frac{\log_e 2}{18,000} = 3.85 \times 10^{-5}.$$

To find the pressure at 1000 ft we use the fact that $P_0 = 1013$ and we let $h = 1000$:

$$P = 1013 e^{-3.85 \times 10^{-5} \times 1000}$$
$$= 1013 e^{-0.0385}.$$

Rounding the exponent to -0.04 and using Table 4, we calculate the pressure to be 973 millibars at 1000 ft.   **[94]**

Exercise Set 6.6

Find the following.

1. $\log_4 7$ **2.** $\log_4 5$ **3.** $\log_4 20$ **4.** $\log_4 80$

5. $\log_{12} 10$ **6.** $\log_{12} 120$ **7.** $\log_{12} 1440$ **8.** $\log_{12} 15{,}000$

9. $\log_7 1$ **10.** $\log_8 1$ **11.** $\log_4 0.57$ **12.** $\log_4 0.78$

13. $\log_8 0.99$ **14.** $\log_8 0.88$ **15.** $\log_e 10$ **16.** $\log_e 12$

17. $\log_e 0.77$ **18.** $\log_e 0.55$ **19.** $\log_e 1$ **20.** $\log_e 0$

21. (*Population growth*). The population of Dallas was 680,000 in 1960. In 1969 it was 815,000. Find k in the growth formula and estimate the population in 1990.

22. (*Population growth*). The population of Kansas City was 475,000 in 1960. In 1970 it was 507,000. Find k in the growth formula and estimate the population in 2000.

23. (*Radioactive decay*). The half-life of polonium is 3 minutes. After 30 minutes, how much of a 410-gram sample will remain radioactive?

24. (*Radioactive decay*). The half-life of a lead isotope is 22 yr. After 66 yr, how much of a 1000-gram sample will remain radioactive?

25. (*Radioactive decay*). A certain radioactive substance decays from 66,560 grams to 6.5 grams in 16 days. What is its half-life?

26. Ten grams of uranium will decay to 2.5 grams in 496,000 years. What is its half-life?

27. (*Radiocarbon dating*). Carbon-14, an isotope of carbon, has a half-life of 5750 years. Organic objects contain carbon-14 as well as nonradioactive carbon, in known proportions. When a living organism dies, it takes in no more carbon. The carbon-14 decays, thus changing the proportions of the kinds of carbon in the organism. By determining the amount of carbon-14 it is possible to determine how long the organism has been dead, hence how old it is.

a) How old is an animal bone that has lost 30% of its carbon-14?

b) A mummy discovered in the pyramid Khufu in Egypt had lost 46% of its carbon-14. Determine its age.

28. (*Radiocarbon dating*).

a) How old is an animal bone that has lost 20% of its carbon-14?

b) The Statue of Zeus at Olympia in Greece is one of the seven wonders of the world. It is made of gold and ivory. The ivory was found to have lost 35% of its carbon-14. Determine the age of the statue.

29. (*Atmospheric pressure*). What is the pressure at the top of Mt. Shasta in California, 14,162 ft high?

30. (*Atmospheric pressure*). Blood will boil when atmospheric pressure goes below about 62 millibars. At what altitude, in an unpressurized vehicle, will a pilot's blood boil?

▶ **31.** Find a (simple) formula for radioactive decay involving H, the half-life.

32. The time required for a population to double is called the *doubling time*.

a) Find an expression relating T, the doubling time, to k, the constant in the growth equation.

b) Find a (simple) formula for population growth involving T.

33. Prove the following theorem: For any logarithm bases a and b, $(\log_a b)(\log_b a) = 1$.

Chapter 6 Test, or Review

1. Graph $y = \log_2 x$.

2. Graph $y = e^{2x}$.

3. Graph $y = e^{-2x}$.

4. Write an exponential equation equivalent to $\log_8 \frac{1}{4} = -\frac{2}{3}$.

5. Write a logarithmic equation equivalent to $7^{2.3} = 2x$.

Solve.

6. $\log_x 64 = 3$

7. $\log_{16} 4 = x$

8. Write an equivalent expression containing a single logarithm.

$\frac{1}{2}\log_b a + \frac{3}{2}\log_b c - 4\log_b d$

9. Solve for x: $\log_a a^{x^2-x-4} = 2$.

Given that $\log_a 2 = 0.301$, $\log_a 3 = 0.477$, and $\log_a 7 = 0.845$, find.

10. $\log_a 18$ **11.** $\log_a \left(\frac{7}{2}\right)$ **12.** $\log_a \frac{1}{4}$ **13.** $\log_a \sqrt{3}$

14. Express in terms of logarithms of M and N: $\log \sqrt[3]{M^2/N}$.

Using Table 2, find.

15. $\log 26.3$ **16.** $\log 0.00806$ **17.** $10^{1.8686}$

18. $\log_5 290$ (round to nearest tenth)

19. antilog $(8.4409 - 10)$

20. Use logarithms to compute: $(0.0524)^2 \cdot \sqrt{0.0638}$.

Simplify.

21. $\log_{12} 12^{x^2+1}$ **22.** $8^{\log_8 13y}$

Solve.

23. $3^{1-x} = 9^{2x}$ **24.** $\log(x^2 - 1) - \log(x - 1) = 1$

25. How many years will it take an investment of \$1000 to double if interest is compounded annually at 5%?

26. Find $\log_e 27$.

27. What is the loudness, in decibels, of a sound whose intensity is 1000 times I_0?

28. The half-life of a radioactive substance is 15 days. How much of a 25-gram sample will remain radioactive after 30 days?

The Circular Functions

7.1 Triangles (Optional)*

In this chapter we will consider an important class of functions called *trigonometric* functions, or *circular* functions. They are based, historically, on certain properties of triangles. In this section we consider some of those properties. We focus our attention on right triangles.

The angles and sides of a right triangle are often labeled as shown, with $\angle C$ a right angle and c the length of the hypotenuse. Side a is opposite $\angle A$ and side b is opposite $\angle B$.

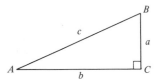

In any triangle the sum of the angle measures is 180°. Thus in a right triangle the measures of the two acute angles add up to 90°.

Example 1. In this triangle, find $m \angle B$ (the measure of $\angle B$).

We know that $m \angle A + m \angle B = 90°$ and that $m \angle A = 32°$, so

$$m \angle B = 90° - 32° = 58°. \qquad [1]$$

---

* The reader who wishes to approach trigonometry from the functional point of view first, and then consider triangles, should skip this lesson. The reader who wishes a brief introduction to triangles before going on to the study of the functions should read this section and then proceed. If a thorough treatment of triangles is desired before considering functions in general, the reader should read this section and then the following ones before returning to this chapter: 8.3 (last part), 8.5, 10.1, 10.2, 10.3, and possibly 10.4, 10.5 and 10.7.

SIMILAR TRIANGLES

Triangles are similar if their corresponding angles have the same measure. In the following triangles, if we know that $\angle A$ and $\angle A'$ are the same size then we know that *all* corresponding angles have the same measure, hence the triangles are similar.

In similar triangles corresponding sides are in the same ratio (are proportional). For the triangles above, this means the following:

$$\frac{a}{a'} = \frac{b}{b'} = \frac{c}{c'}.$$

Similar triangles can be used to determine distances without measuring directly.

Example 2. Find the height of the flagpole using a rod and a measuring device as shown.

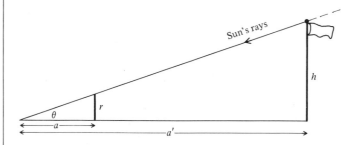

Place the rod of length r so that the top of its shadow coincides with the shadow of the top of the flagpole. We know that we have similar triangles, because the acute angle θ at the ground is the same in both triangles. We measure and find that $a = 3$ ft, that $a' = 30$ ft, and that $r = 2$ ft.

Now $\dfrac{h}{r} = \dfrac{a'}{a}$ by similar triangles, so

$$h = r\frac{a'}{a} = 2\,\frac{30}{3} = 20\,\text{ft}. \qquad\qquad \textbf{[2, 3]}$$

TRIGONOMETRIC RATIOS

In a right triangle as shown, the ratio a/c of the side *opposite* θ to the hypotenuse depends on the size of θ. In other words, <u>this ratio is a *function* of θ.</u>

This function is called the *sine* function. Another such function, called the *cosine* function, is the ratio b/c, the ratio of the side *adjacent* to θ to the hypotenuse. There are other such ratios, or functions, defined as follows.

Function	Abbreviation for function value	Defining ratio
sine	$\sin(\theta)^*$ or $\sin\theta$	$\dfrac{\text{side opposite }\theta}{\text{hypotenuse}}$
cosine	$\cos(\theta)$ or $\cos\theta$	$\dfrac{\text{side adjacent }\theta}{\text{hypotenuse}}$
tangent	$\tan(\theta)$ or $\tan\theta$	$\dfrac{\text{side opposite }\theta}{\text{side adjacent }\theta}$
cotangent	$\cot(\theta)$ or $\cot\theta$	$\dfrac{\text{side adjacent }\theta}{\text{side opposite }\theta}$

Note that the function values do not depend on the size of a triangle, but only on <u>the size of the angle θ.</u>

---

* For function values we generally write $f(x)$. For these functions we often omit parentheses, as in $\sin\theta$.

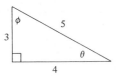

Example 3. In this triangle find

a) $\sin\theta$, $\cos\theta$, $\tan\theta$, and $\cot\theta$;

$$\sin\theta = \frac{\text{side opposite }\theta}{\text{hypotenuse}} = \frac{3}{5}$$

$$\cos\theta = \frac{\text{side adjacent }\theta}{\text{hypotenuse}} = \frac{4}{5}$$

$$\tan\theta = \frac{\text{side opposite }\theta}{\text{side adjacent }\theta} = \frac{3}{4}$$

$$\cot\theta = \frac{\text{side adjacent }\theta}{\text{side opposite }\theta} = \frac{4}{3}$$

b) $\sin\phi$, $\cos\phi$, $\tan\phi$, and $\cot\phi$.

$$\sin\phi = \frac{\text{side opposite }\phi}{\text{hypotenuse}} = \frac{4}{5}$$

$$\cos\phi = \frac{\text{side adjacent }\phi}{\text{hypotenuse}} = \frac{3}{5}$$

$$\tan\phi = \frac{\text{side opposite }\phi}{\text{side adjacent }\phi} = \frac{4}{3}$$

$$\cot\phi = \frac{\text{side adjacent }\phi}{\text{side opposite }\phi} = \frac{3}{4} \qquad \textbf{[4]}$$

Values for the trigonometric functions have been worked out in great detail and are given in tables. When these values are available we can use them to help determine distances or angles without actually measuring them directly.

Example 4. A man stands on level ground, 200 meters from the base of a TV tower. He finds he must look up at an angle of 26.5° to see the top of the tower. How high is the tower?

We draw a diagram and see that a right triangle is formed. We use one of the trigonometric functions. This time the tangent function is most convenient.

From the definition of the tangent function, we have

$$\frac{h}{200} = \tan 26.5°.$$

Then $h = 200 \tan 26.5°$. We find, from a table, that $\tan 26.5° = 0.499$, approximately. Thus

$$h = 200 \times 0.499 = 99.8 \text{ m.} \qquad [5]$$

Example 5. A kite flies at a height of 60 ft when 130 ft of string is out. Assuming that the string is in a straight line, what is the angle that it makes with the ground?

We draw a diagram and then use the most convenient trigonometric function. A portion of a sine table is given.

$\sin 26.5° = 0.4462$	$\sin 28.5° = 0.4772$
$\sin 27° = 0.4540$	$\sin 29° = 0.4848$
$\sin 27.5° = 0.4615$	$\sin 29.5° = 0.4924$
$\sin 28° = 0.4695$	$\sin 30° = 0.5000$

From the definition of the sine function, we have

$$\frac{60}{130} = \sin \theta = 0.4615.$$

From the table, we find that θ is about 27.5°. [6]

Exercise Set 7.1

1. Find $m\angle B$.

2. Find $m\angle A$.

3. Find b.

4. Find c.

5. Find $\sin\theta$, $\cos\theta$, $\tan\theta$, and $\cot\theta$.

6. Find $\sin\phi$, $\cos\phi$, $\tan\phi$, and $\cot\phi$.

7. Find $\sin\theta$, $\cos\theta$, $\tan\theta$, and $\cot\theta$.

8. Find $\sin\phi$, $\cos\phi$, $\tan\phi$, and $\cot\phi$.

For Exercises 9–12, use the following function values.

$\sin 36° = 0.5878$	$\cos 36° = 0.8090$	$\tan 36° = 0.7265$	$\cot 36° = 1.376$
$\sin 36.5° = 0.5948$	$\cos 36.5° = 0.8039$	$\tan 36.5° = 0.7400$	$\cot 36.5° = 1.351$
$\sin 37° = 0.6018$	$\cos 37° = 0.7986$	$\tan 37° = 0.7536$	$\cot 37° = 1.327$
$\sin 37.5° = 0.6088$	$\cos 37.5° = 0.7934$	$\tan 37.5° = 0.7673$	$\cot 37.5° = 1.303$
$\sin 38° = 0.6157$	$\cos 38° = 0.7880$	$\tan 38° = 0.7813$	$\cot 38° = 1.280$

9. a) Find $\angle B$.*

    b) Find a.

    c) Find b.

10. a) Find $\angle B$.

    b) Find a.

    c) Find b.

11. a) Find $\angle A$.

    b) Find a.

    c) Find c.

12. a) Find $\angle A$.

    b) Find a.

    c) Find c.

---

* Instead of saying "find $m\ \angle B$," we often say "find $\angle B$."

7.2 The Unit Circle

To develop the important circular functions we will use a circle with a radius of length 1. Such a circle is called a *unit circle*. When its center is at the origin of a coordinate system, its equation is

$$x^2 + y^2 = 1.$$

Any circle centered at the origin is symmetric with respect to the x-axis, the y-axis, and the origin.

Example 1. Suppose the point $(1, 2)$ is on a circle centered at the origin. Find its reflection across the x-axis, the y-axis, and the origin.

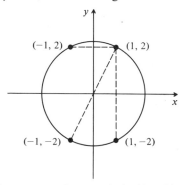

The reflection across the x-axis is $(1, -2)$.
The reflection across the y-axis is $(-1, 2)$.
The reflection across the origin is $(-1, -2)$.
By symmetry, all these points are on the circle. **[7,8]**

The intercepts (points of intersection with the axes) of the unit circle A, B, C, and D have coordinates as shown below. Let us find the coordinates of point E, which is the intersection of the circle with the line

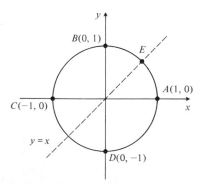

$y = x$. Note that this point divides the arc in the first quadrant in half.

Since for any point (x, y) on the circle $x^2 + y^2 = 1$, and for point E we have $y = x$, we know that the coordinates of E satisfy $x^2 + x^2 = 1$ (substituting x for y in the equation of the circle). Let us solve this equation:

$$x^2 + x^2 = 1, \quad \text{or} \quad 2x^2 = 1$$

$$x^2 = \frac{1}{2}$$

$$x = \sqrt{\frac{1}{2}}, \quad \text{or} \quad \frac{\sqrt{1}}{\sqrt{2}}, \quad \text{or} \quad \frac{1}{\sqrt{2}}.$$

Now

$$\frac{1}{\sqrt{2}} = \frac{1}{\sqrt{2}} \cdot \frac{\sqrt{2}}{\sqrt{2}} = \frac{\sqrt{2}}{2}.$$

Thus the coordinates of point E are $\left(\frac{\sqrt{2}}{2}, \frac{\sqrt{2}}{2}\right)$. **[9]**

DISTANCES ON THE UNIT CIRCLE

The circumference of a circle of radius r is $2\pi r$. Thus for the unit circle the circumference is 2π. If a point starts at A and travels counterclockwise around the circle, it will travel a distance of 2π. If it travels halfway around the circle, it will travel a distance of π.

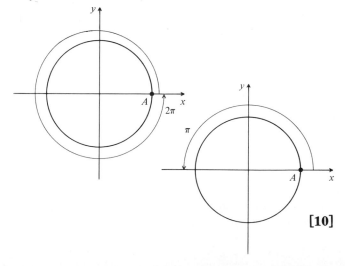

[10]

If a point travels $\frac{1}{8}$ of the way around the circle, it will travel a distance of $(\frac{1}{8}) \cdot 2\pi$, or $\pi/4$. Note that the stopping point is $\frac{1}{4}$ of the way from A to C and $\frac{1}{2}$ of the way from A to B.

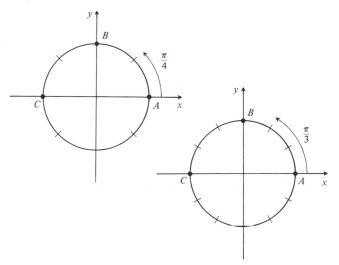

If a point travels $\frac{1}{6}$ of the way around the circle ($\frac{2}{12}$ of the way, as shown above), it will travel a distance of $(\frac{1}{6}) \cdot 2\pi$, or $\pi/3$. Note that the stopping point is $\frac{1}{3}$ of the way from A to C and $\frac{2}{3}$ of the way from A to B.

[11, 12]

A point may travel completely around the circle and then continue. For example, if it goes around once and then continues $\frac{1}{4}$ of the way around, it will have traveled a distance of $2\pi + (\pi/2)$, or $(\frac{5}{2})\pi$.

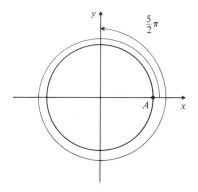

Any positive number thus determines a point on the unit circle. For the number 35, for example, we start at A and travel counterclockwise a distance of 35. The point at which we stop is the point "determined" by the number 35.   **[13, 14]**

Negative numbers also determine points on the unit circle. For a negative number, we move clockwise around the circle. Points for $-\pi/4$ and $-3\pi/2$ are shown. Any negative number thus determines a point on the unit circle. The same is true for any positive number. The number 0 determines the point A. Hence there is a point on the unit circle for every real number.   **[15]**

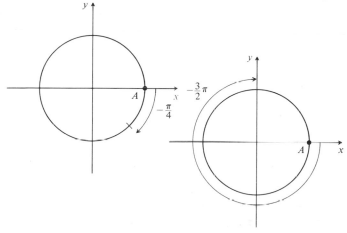

Points on the unit circle determined by two numbers that are additive inverses are situated as shown. The points are reflections of each other across the x-axis. Thus their first coordinates are the same and their second coordinates are additive inverses of each other.

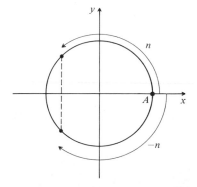

Exercise Set 7.2

1. The point $(-5, 2)$ is on a circle centered at the origin. Find the coordinates of its reflection across (a) the x-axis, (b) the y-axis, and (c) the origin. (d) Are these points on the circle? Why?

2. The point $(3, -5)$ is on a circle centered at the origin. Find the coordinates of its reflection across (a) the x-axis, (b) the y-axis, and (c) the origin. (d) Are these points on the circle? Why?

3. Find the coordinates of these points on a unit circle.

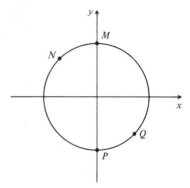

4. Find the coordinates of these points on a unit circle.

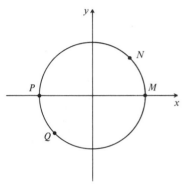

For each of Exercises 5–10, sketch a unit circle such as the one shown below.

5. Mark the points determined by (a) $\dfrac{\pi}{4}$, (b) $\dfrac{3}{2}\pi$, (c) $\dfrac{3}{4}\pi$, (d) π, (e) $\dfrac{11}{4}\pi$, and (f) $\dfrac{17}{4}\pi$.

6. Mark the points determined by (a) $\dfrac{\pi}{2}$, (b) $\dfrac{5}{4}\pi$, (c) 2π, (d) $\dfrac{9}{4}\pi$, (e) $\dfrac{13}{4}\pi$, and (f) $\dfrac{23}{4}\pi$.

7. Mark the points determined by (a) $\dfrac{\pi}{6}$, (b) $\dfrac{2}{3}\pi$, (c) $\dfrac{7}{6}\pi$, (d) $\dfrac{10}{6}\pi$, (e) $\dfrac{14}{6}\pi$, and (f) $\dfrac{23}{4}\pi$.

8. Mark the points determined by (a) $\dfrac{\pi}{3}$, (b) $\dfrac{5}{6}\pi$, (c) $\dfrac{11}{6}\pi$, (d) $\dfrac{13}{6}\pi$, (e) $\dfrac{23}{6}\pi$, and (f) $\dfrac{33}{6}\pi$.

9. Mark the points determined by (a) $-\dfrac{\pi}{2}$, (b) $-\dfrac{3}{4}\pi$, (c) $-\dfrac{5}{6}\pi$, (d) $-\dfrac{5}{2}\pi$, (e) $-\dfrac{17}{6}\pi$, and (f) $-\dfrac{9}{4}\pi$.

10. Mark the points determined by (a) $-\dfrac{3}{2}\pi$, (b) $-\dfrac{\pi}{3}$, (c) $-\dfrac{7}{6}\pi$, (d) $-\dfrac{13}{6}\pi$, (e) $-\dfrac{19}{6}\pi$, and (f) $-\dfrac{11}{4}\pi$.

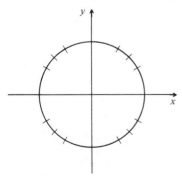

11. Find two real numbers between -2π and 2π that determine each of these points.

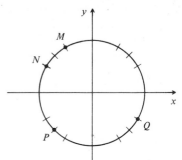

12. Find two real numbers between -2π and 2π that determine each of these points.

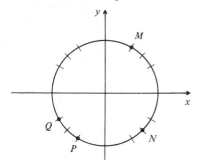

13. A certain real number r determines a point on the unit circle with coordinates

$$\left(\frac{\sqrt{3}}{2}, \frac{1}{2}\right).$$

What are the coordinates of the point determined by $-r$?

14. A certain real number q determines a point on the unit circle with coordinates

$$\left(\frac{1}{2}, \frac{\sqrt{3}}{2}\right).$$

What are the coordinates of the point determined by $-q$?

7.3 The Sine and Cosine Functions

THE SINE FUNCTION

Every real number s determines a point T on the unit circle, as shown. To the real number s we will assign the second coordinate of point T as a function value. The function thus defined is called the *sine function*. Function values are denoted by "sine s" or, more briefly, "sin s".* By considering the unit circle, we see that

$$\sin 0 = 0,$$

$$\sin \frac{\pi}{2} = 1. \qquad\qquad \textbf{[16]}$$

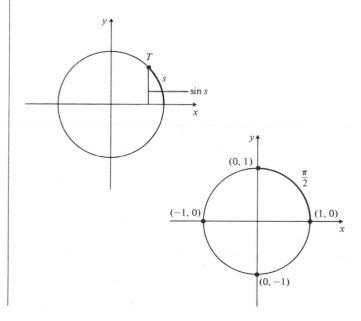

---

* The sine function, as we develop it here, is a generalization of what was done in Section 7.1. To help visualize this, we could draw a triangle as shown here. Its hypotenuse has length 1, so $\sin \theta = y/1$, or y. Note also that the arc length s determines the angle θ, so we think of $\sin s$ rather than $\sin \theta$. For the cosine function, we note that $\cos s = x/1$, or x.

+decrease to a maximum of -1. Picture the unit circle and the possibilities of sine value.

Function values increase to a maximum of 1 at $\pi/2$, then decrease to 0 at π, decrease further to -1 at $(\frac{3}{2})\pi$, then increase to 0 at 2π, and so on. The graph of the sine function is shown here.

The sine function

[17–21]

From the graph of the sine function, certain properties are apparent.

1. **The sine function is periodic, with period 2π.**
2. **It is an odd function, by symmetry with respect to the origin. Thus we know that $\sin(-s) = -\sin s$ for all real numbers s.**
3. **It is continuous everywhere.**
4. **The domain is the set of all real numbers. The range is the set of all real numbers from -1 to 1, inclusive.**

The unit circle can be used to verify some of the above, as well as to determine other important properties of the sine function.

Let us verify that the period is 2π. Consider any real number s and its point T on the unit circle. Now we increase s by 2π. The point for $s + 2\pi$ is again the point T. Hence for any real number s, $\sin s = \sin(s + 2\pi)$. There is no number smaller than 2π for which this is true. Hence the period is 2π. Actually, we know that $\sin s = \sin(s + 2k\pi)$, where k is any integer.

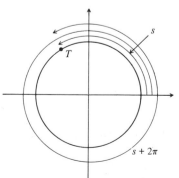

Consider any real number s and its additive inverse $-s$. These numbers determine points on the unit circle that are symmetric with respect to the x-axis, hence their second coordinates are additive inverses of each other. Thus we know for any number s that $\sin(-s) = -\sin s$. Thus the sine function is odd.

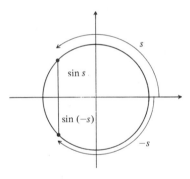

[22]

Consider any real number s and its point T on the unit circle. Then $s + \pi$ and $s - \pi$ both determine a point T_1 symmetric with T with respect to the origin. Thus the sines of $s + \pi$ and $s - \pi$ are the same, and are the additive inverse of $\sin s$. This gives us another important property.

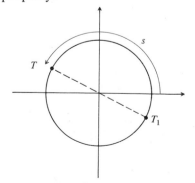

For any real number s, $\sin(s + \pi) = -\sin s$, and $\sin(s - \pi) = -\sin s$.

Let us add to this list a property concerning $\sin(\pi - s)$. Since $\pi - s$ is the additive inverse of $s - \pi$, $\sin(\pi - s) = \sin[-(s - \pi)]$. Since the sine function is odd, this is equal to $-\sin(s - \pi)$. By the second property above, this is equal to $-(-\sin s)$ or $\sin s$. Thus our last property is

$$\sin(\pi - s) = \sin s.$$

Equations that hold for all sensible replacements for the variables are known as *identities*. We shall use the sign $\equiv$ instead of $=$ to indicate that an equation is an identity. We now have the following identities concerning the sine function.

> $\sin s \equiv \sin(s + 2k\pi),\ k$ **any integer**
>
> $\sin(-s) \equiv -\sin s$
>
> $\sin(s \pm \pi) \equiv -\sin s$
>
> $\sin(\pi - s) \equiv \sin s$

The *amplitude* of a periodic function is half the difference between its maximum and minimum function values. It is always positive. The maximum value of the sine function can be seen to be 1, either from the graph or the unit circle, while the minimum value is -1. Thus the amplitude of the sine function is 1.

THE COSINE FUNCTION

Every real number s determines a point T on the unit circle. To the real number s we will assign the first coordinate of point T as a function value. This defines the function known as the *cosine function*. Function values are denoted by "cosine s" or, more briefly, "cos s." By considering the unit circle, we see that

$$\cos 0 = 1$$

$$\cos \frac{\pi}{2} = 0.$$

[23]

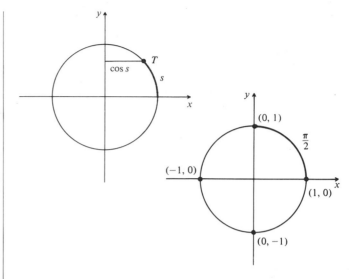

The graph of the cosine function is as follows:

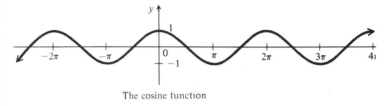

The cosine function

[24–28]

It should be noted that for any point on the unit circle, the coordinates are $(\cos s, \sin s)$.

From the graph of the cosine function, certain properties are apparent.

> 1. **The cosine function is periodic, with period 2π.**
> 2. **It is an even function, by symmetry with respect to the y-axis. Thus we know that $\cos(-s) = \cos s$ for all real numbers s.**
> 3. **It is continuous everywhere.**
> 4. **The domain is the set of all real numbers. The range is the set of all real numbers from -1 to 1 inclusive.**
> 5. **The amplitude is 1.**

The unit circle can be used to verify that the period is 2π and, in fact, that $\cos s = \cos (s + 2k\pi)$ for any integer k.

Consider any real number s and its additive inverse. They determine points symmetric with respect to the x-axis, hence their first coordinates are the same. Thus

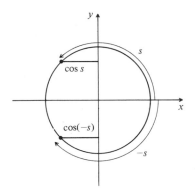

we know that for any number s, $\cos (-s) = \cos s$, and that the cosine function is even.

Let us consider $\cos s$ and $\cos (s \pm \pi)$. Recall that s and $s \pm \pi$ determine points symmetric with respect to the origin. Thus their coordinates are additive inverses of each other. This verifies that $\cos (s \pm \pi) = -\cos s$ for all real numbers s.

Let us consider $\cos (\pi - s)$. This is equal to $\cos [-(s - \pi)]$. Since the cosine function is even, this is equal to $\cos (s - \pi)$, and by the above this is in turn equal to $-\cos s$. Hence we have $\cos (\pi - s) = -\cos s$. We now list the identities that we have developed for the cosine function.

$$\cos s \equiv \cos (s + 2k\pi), \ k \text{ any integer}$$

$$\cos (-s) \equiv \cos s$$

$$\cos (s \pm \pi) \equiv -\cos s$$

$$\cos (\pi - s) \equiv -\cos s$$

Exercise Set 7.3

1. Construct a graph of the sine function. The lower set of axes is shown here at half size, so on other paper, copy the figure at twice the size shown here. Then from the unit circle (shown full size here) transfer vertical distances with a compass.

2. Construct a graph of the cosine function. Follow the instructions for Exercise 1, except that horizontal distances on the unit circle will be transferred with a compass.

3. a) Sketch a graph of $y = \sin x$.

    b) By reflecting the graph in (a), sketch a graph of $y = \sin(-x)$.

    c) By reflecting the graph in (a), sketch a graph of $y = -\sin x$.

    d) How do the graphs in (b) and (c) compare?

4. a) Sketch a graph of $y = \cos x$.

    b) By reflecting the graph in (a), sketch a graph of $y = \cos(-x)$.

    c) By reflecting the graph in (a), sketch a graph of $y = -\cos x$.

    d) How do the graphs in (a) and (b) compare?

5. a) Sketch a graph of $y = \sin x$.

    b) By translating, sketch a graph of $y = \sin(x + \pi)$.

    c) By reflecting the graph of (a), sketch a graph of $y = -\sin x$.

    d) How do the graphs of (b) and (c) compare?

6. a) Sketch a graph of $y = \sin x$.

    b) By translating, sketch a graph of $y = \sin(x - \pi)$.

    c) By reflecting the graph of (a), sketch a graph of $y = -\sin x$.

    d) How do the graphs of (b) and (c) compare?

7. a) Sketch a graph of $y = \cos x$.

    b) By translating, sketch a graph of $y = \cos(x + \pi)$.

    c) By reflecting the graph of (a), sketch a graph of $y = -\cos x$.

    d) How do the graphs in (b) and (c) compare?

8. a) Sketch a graph of $y = \cos x$.

    b) By translating, sketch a graph of $y = \cos(x - \pi)$.

    c) By reflecting the graph of (a), sketch a graph of $y = -\cos x$.

    d) How do the graphs in (b) and (c) compare?

Complete.

9. $\cos(-x) \equiv$ _____

10. $\sin(-x) \equiv$ _____

11. $\sin(x + \pi) \equiv$ _____

12. $\sin(x - \pi) \equiv$ _____

13. $\cos(\pi - x) \equiv$ _____

14. $\sin(\pi - x) \equiv$ _____

15. $\cos(x + 2k\pi) \equiv$ _____

16. $\sin(x + 2k\pi) \equiv$ _____

17. $\cos(x - \pi) \equiv$ _____

18. $\cos(x + \pi) \equiv$ _____

19. Find.

a) $\sin\dfrac{\pi}{4}$ $\dfrac{\sqrt{2}}{2}$

b) $\sin\pi$ 0

c) $\sin\dfrac{5}{4}\pi$ $-\dfrac{\sqrt{2}}{2}$

d) $\sin\dfrac{3}{2}\pi$ -1

e) $\sin\left(-\dfrac{\pi}{4}\right)$ $-\dfrac{\sqrt{2}}{2}$

f) $\sin(-\pi)$ 0

g) $\sin\left(-\dfrac{5}{4}\pi\right)$ $\dfrac{\sqrt{2}}{2}$

h) $\sin\left(-\dfrac{3}{2}\pi\right)$ 1

20. Find.

a) $\sin \dfrac{\pi}{2}$ 　　　　　　　 b) $\sin \dfrac{3}{4}\pi$ 　　　　　　　 c) $\sin \dfrac{7}{4}\pi$ 　　　　　　　 d) $\sin 2\pi$

e) $\sin\left(-\dfrac{\pi}{2}\right)$ 　　　 f) $\sin\left(-\dfrac{3}{4}\pi\right)$ 　　　 g) $\sin\left(-\dfrac{7}{4}\pi\right)$ 　　　 h) $\sin(-2\pi)$

21. Find.

a) $\cos \dfrac{\pi}{4}$ $\dfrac{\sqrt{2}}{2}$ 　　 b) $\cos \pi$ -1 　　 c) $\cos \dfrac{5}{4}\pi$ $-\dfrac{\sqrt{2}}{2}$ 　　 d) $\cos \dfrac{3}{2}\pi$ 0

e) $\cos\left(-\dfrac{\pi}{4}\right)$ $\dfrac{\sqrt{2}}{2}$ 　　 f) $\cos(-\pi)$ -1 　　 g) $\cos\left(-\dfrac{5}{4}\pi\right)$ $-\dfrac{\sqrt{2}}{2}$ 　　 h) $\cos\left(-\dfrac{3}{2}\pi\right)$ 0

22. Find.

a) $\cos \dfrac{\pi}{2}$ 　　　　　　　 b) $\cos \dfrac{3}{4}\pi$ 　　　　　　　 c) $\cos \dfrac{7}{4}\pi$ 　　　　　　　 d) $\cos 2\pi$

e) $\cos\left(-\dfrac{\pi}{2}\right)$ 　　　 f) $\cos\left(-\dfrac{3}{4}\pi\right)$ 　　　 g) $\cos\left(-\dfrac{7}{4}\pi\right)$ 　　　 h) $\cos(-2\pi)$

7.4 The Other Circular Functions

There are four other circular functions, all defined in terms of the sine and cosine functions. Their definitions are as follows.

Definitions.

The tangent function:	$\tan s \equiv \dfrac{\sin s}{\cos s}$
The cotangent function:	$\cot s \equiv \dfrac{\cos s}{\sin s}$
The secant function:	$\sec s \equiv \dfrac{1}{\cos s}$
The cosecant function:	$\csc s \equiv \dfrac{1}{\sin s}$

THE TANGENT FUNCTION

The tangent of a number is the quotient of its sine by its cosine. For example,

$$\tan 0 = \frac{\sin 0}{\cos 0} = \frac{0}{1} = 0,$$

$$\tan \frac{\pi}{4} = \frac{\sin \dfrac{\pi}{4}}{\cos \dfrac{\pi}{4}} = \frac{\dfrac{\sqrt{2}}{2}}{\dfrac{\sqrt{2}}{2}} = 1.$$

[29–31]

Not every real number has a tangent. For example,

$$\tan \frac{\pi}{2} = \frac{\sin \dfrac{\pi}{2}}{\cos \dfrac{\pi}{2}} = \frac{1}{0},$$

but division by 0 is undefined. Hence tan $(\pi/2)$ is meaningless, and $\pi/2$ is not in the domain of the tangent function.   **[32]**

The tangent function is undefined for any number whose cosine is 0. Thus it is undefined for $(\pi/2) + k\pi$, where k is any integer. In the first quadrant the function values are positive. In the second quadrant, however, the sine and cosine values have opposite signs, so the tangent values are negative. Tangent values are also negative in the fourth quadrant, and they are positive in quadrant three.

A graph of the tangent function is shown. Note that the function value is 0 when $x = 0$, and the values increase as x increases toward $\pi/2$. As we approach $\pi/2$, the denominator becomes very small, so the tangent values become very large. In fact, they increase without bound. The dashed vertical line at $\pi/2$ is not a part of the graph. The graph approaches this vertical line closely, however. The vertical dashed lines are known as *asymptotes* to the curve.

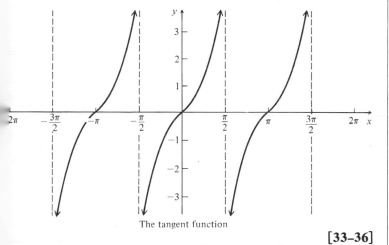

The tangent function

[33–36]

The tangent function is periodic, with a period of π. Its domain is the set of all real numbers except $\frac{\pi}{2} + k\pi$, k any integer. Its range is the set of all real numbers.

THE COTANGENT FUNCTION

The cotangent of a number is the quotient of its cosine by its sine. Thus the cotangent function is undefined for any number whose sine is 0.   **[37]**

The cotangent function is undefined for $k\pi$, where k is any integer. The graph of this function is shown here.

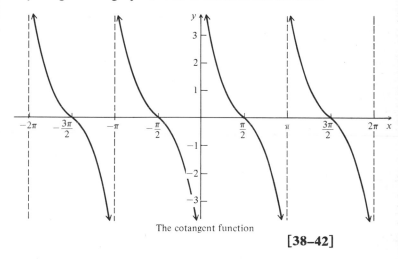

The cotangent function

[38–42]

The cotangent function is periodic, with a period of π. Its domain is the set of all real numbers except $k\pi$, k any integer. Its range is the set of all real numbers. Like the tangent function, the cotangent has function values positive in quadrants I and III and negative in quadrants II and IV. It should be noted that the tangent and cotangent are reciprocal functions. Hence the following identities hold.

Theorem.

$$\tan x \equiv \frac{1}{\cot x} \quad \text{or} \quad \cot x \equiv \frac{1}{\tan x}$$

THE SECANT FUNCTION

The secant and cosine functions are reciprocals. For example,

$$\sec 0 = \frac{1}{\cos 0} = \frac{1}{1} = 1.$$

This function will be undefined for those numbers for which cos $x = 0$. **[43–45]**

A graph of the secant function is shown below. The cosine graph is dotted in for reference, since these functions are reciprocals. Note that this function is periodic, with a period of 2π. Its domain is the set of all real numbers except $(\pi/2) + k\pi$, k any integer. Its range consists of all real numbers 1 and greater, in addition to all real numbers -1 and less.

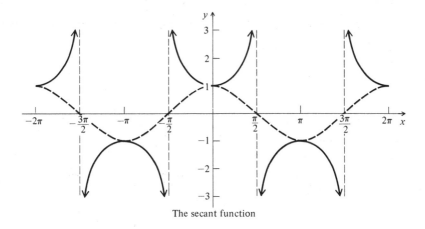

The secant function

THE COSECANT FUNCTION

Since the cosecant and sine functions are reciprocals, the cosecant will be undefined wherever the sine function is 0. The functions will be positive together and negative together. A graph of the cosecant function is shown below. The sine graph is dotted in for reference, since these functions are reciprocals.

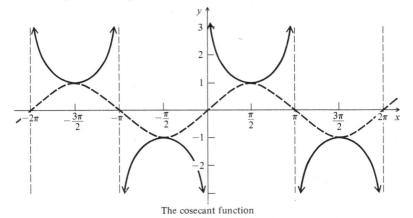

The cosecant function

[46–50]

Like the secant function, this function is periodic, with a period of 2π. Its domain is the set of all real numbers except $k\pi$, k any integer. The range is the same as for the secant function.

SIGNS OF THE FUNCTIONS

Suppose a real number s determines a point on the unit circle in the first quadrant. Since both coordinates are positive there, the function values for all the circular functions will be positive. In the second quadrant the first coordinate is negative and the second coordinate is positive. Thus the sine function has positive values and the cosine has negative values. The secant, being the reciprocal of the cosine, also has negative values, and the cosecant, being the reciprocal of the sine, has positive values. The tangent and cotangent both have negative values in the second quadrant.

[51]

The following diagram summarizes, showing the quadrants in which the circular function values are positive. This diagram need not be memorized, because the signs can readily be determined by reference to a unit circle.

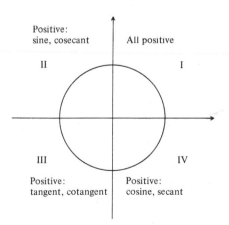

SOME IDENTITIES

The tangent function appears to be odd. Let us investigate by finding $\tan(-x)$. By definition of the tangent function,

$$\tan(-x) \equiv \frac{\sin(-x)}{\cos(-x)}.$$

But we know that $\sin(-x) \equiv -\sin x$ and $\cos(-x) \equiv \cos x$. Hence

$$\tan(-x) \equiv \frac{\sin(-x)}{\cos(-x)} \equiv \frac{-\sin x}{\cos x} \equiv -\tan x.$$

Thus the tangent function is indeed odd. Similarly, it can be shown that the cotangent function is odd, the secant function is even, and the cosecant function is odd. Each such demonstration gives us an identity.

[52]

By use of the previously developed identities involving the sine and cosine functions we can develop a number of other identities.

Example. Show that $\tan(x + \pi) \equiv \tan x$.

$$\tan(x + \pi) \equiv \frac{\sin(x + \pi)}{\cos(x + \pi)} \quad \text{(by definition of tangent function)}$$

$$\equiv \frac{-\sin x}{-\cos x} \quad \text{(using } \sin(x + \pi) \equiv -\sin x \text{ and } \cos(x + \pi) \equiv -\cos x\text{)}$$

$$\equiv \frac{\sin x}{\cos x} \equiv \tan x$$

Example. Show that $\sec(\pi - x) \equiv -\sec x$.

$$\sec(\pi - x) \equiv \frac{1}{\cos(\pi - x)} \quad \text{(by definition of secant function)}$$

$$\equiv \frac{1}{-\cos x} \quad \text{(using } \cos(\pi - x) \equiv -\cos x\text{)}$$

$$\equiv -\frac{1}{\cos x}$$

$$\equiv -\sec x$$

Example. Show that $\csc(x - \pi) \equiv -\csc x$.

$\csc(x - \pi) \equiv \dfrac{1}{\sin(x - \pi)}$ (by definition of cosecant function)

$\csc(x - \pi) \equiv \dfrac{1}{-\sin x}$ (using $\sin(x - \pi) \equiv -\sin x$)

$\equiv -\csc x$ **[53, 54]**

Exercise Set 7.4

Here is a table of approximate values of functions.

	$\dfrac{\pi}{16}$	$\dfrac{\pi}{8}$	$\dfrac{\pi}{6}$	$\dfrac{\pi}{4}$	$\dfrac{\pi}{3}$	$\dfrac{3}{8}\pi$	$\dfrac{7}{16}\pi$	$-\dfrac{\pi}{16}$	$-\dfrac{\pi}{8}$	$-\dfrac{\pi}{6}$	$-\dfrac{\pi}{4}$
Tan	0.2	0.4	0.6	1	1.7	2.4	5.03	−0.2	−0.4	−0.6	−1
Cot	5.03	2.4	1.7	1	0.6	0.4	0.2	−5.03	−2.4	−1.7	−1
Sec	1.02	1.1	1.2	1.4	2	2.6	5.13	1.02	1.1	1.2	1.4
Csc	5.13	2.6	2	1.4	1.2	1.08	1.02	−5.13	−2.6	−2	−1.4

In Exercises 1–4, use graph paper. Use the table above, plus your other knowledge of the functions, to make graphs.

1. Graph the tangent function between -2π and 2π.

2. Graph the cotangent function between -2π and 2π.

3. Graph the secant function between -2π and 2π.

4. Graph the cosecant function between -2π and 2π.

5. Of the six circular functions, which are even?

6. Of the six circular functions, which are odd?

7. Which of the six circular functions have period 2π?

8. Which of the six circular functions have period π?

9. In which quadrants is the tangent function positive? negative?

10. In which quadrants is the cotangent function positive? negative?

11. In which quadrants is the secant function positive? negative?

12. In which quadrants is the cosecant function positive? negative?

Verify the following identities.

13. $\sec(-x) \equiv \sec x$ **14.** $\csc(-x) \equiv -\csc x$ **15.** $\cot(x + \pi) \equiv \cot x$ **16.** $\cot(x - \pi) \equiv \cot x$

17. $\sec(x + \pi) \equiv -\sec x$ **18.** $\sec(x - \pi) \equiv -\sec x$ **19.** $\tan(\pi - x) \equiv -\tan x$ **20.** $\cot(\pi - x) \equiv -\cot x$

7.5 Some Relations Among the Circular Functions

We have already seen that there are some relations among the six circular functions. In fact the sine and cosine functions are used to define the others. There are certain other important relations among these functions. These are given by identities.

THE PYTHAGOREAN IDENTITIES

Recall that the equation of the unit circle is

$$x^2 + y^2 = 1.$$

For any point on the unit circle, the coordinates x and y satisfy this equation. Suppose a real number s determines a point T on the unit circle, with coordinates (x, y). Then $x = \cos s$ and $y = \sin s$. Substituting these in the equation of the unit circle gives us the identity

$$\sin^2 s + \cos^2 s \equiv 1.$$

This is true because the coordinates of a point on the unit circle are $(\cos s, \sin s)$. When exponents are used with the circular functions, we write $\sin^2 s$ instead of $(\sin s)^2$. This identity relates the sine and cosine of any real number s. It is an important identity, known as one of the *Pythagorean* identities. We now develop another. We will divide the above identity by $\sin^2 s$:

$$\frac{\sin^2 s}{\sin^2 s} + \frac{\cos^2 s}{\sin^2 s} \equiv \frac{1}{\sin^2 s}.$$

This simplifies to

$$1 + \cot^2 s \equiv \csc^2 s.$$

This relation is valid for any number s for which $\sin^2 s \neq 0$, since we divided by $\sin^2 s$. But the numbers for which $\sin^2 s = 0$ (or $\sin s = 0$) are exactly the ones for which the cotangent and cosecant functions are undefined. Hence our new equation holds for all numbers s for which $\cot s$ and $\csc s$ are defined, and is thus an identity.   [55]

The third Pythagorean identity, obtained by dividing the first by $\cos^2 s$, is

$$1 + \tan^2 s \equiv \sec^2 s.$$

The Pythagorean identities should be memorized. Certain variations of them, although most useful, need not be memorized, because they are so easily obtained from these three.

Example 1. Derive identities that give $\cos^2 x$ and $\cos x$ in terms of $\sin x$.

We begin with $\sin^2 x + \cos^2 x \equiv 1$, and solve for $\cos^2 x$. We have $\cos^2 x \equiv 1 - \sin^2 x$. This gives $\cos^2 x$ in terms of $\sin x$. If we now take the principal square root, we obtain

$$|\cos x| \equiv \sqrt{1 - \sin^2 x}.$$

We can also express this as

$$\cos x \equiv \pm\sqrt{1 - \sin^2 x},$$

with the understanding that the sign must be determined by the quadrant in which the point for x lies.   [56, 57]

Example 2. From the identity $1 + \cot^2 x \equiv \csc^2 x$, we readily obtain

$$\csc^2 x - \cot^2 x \equiv 1$$

and also

$$\cot^2 x \equiv \csc^2 x - 1.   [58]$$

THE COFUNCTION IDENTITIES

The sine and cosine are called *cofunctions* of each other. Similarly, the tangent and cotangent are cofunctions and the secant and cosecant are cofunctions. Another class of identities gives functions in terms of

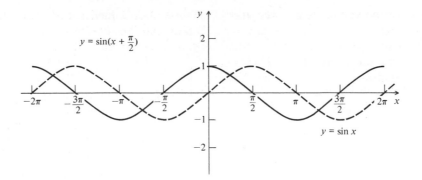

their cofunctions at numbers differing by $\pi/2$. We consider first the sine and cosine. Consider this graph.

The graph of $y = \sin x$ has been translated to the left a distance of $\pi/2$, to obtain the graph of $y = \sin(x + \pi/2)$. The latter is also a graph of the cosine function. Thus we obtain the identity

$$\sin\left(x + \frac{\pi}{2}\right) \equiv \cos x. \qquad [59]$$

By a means similar to that above, we obtain the identity

$$\cos\left(x - \frac{\pi}{2}\right) \equiv \sin x.$$

Consider the following graph. The graph of $y = \sin x$ has been translated to the right a distance of $\pi/2$, to obtain the graph of $y = \sin(x - \pi/2)$. The latter is a reflection of the cosine function across the x-axis. In other words, it is a graph of $y = -\cos x$. We thus obtain the following identity:

$$\sin\left(x - \frac{\pi}{2}\right) \equiv -\cos x. \qquad [60]$$

By a means similar to that above, we obtain the identity

$$\cos\left(x + \frac{\pi}{2}\right) \equiv -\sin x.$$

The preceding identities can be established more rigorously by considering the unit circle. A point T, determined by a number s, is shown, as well as points T_1 and T_2, determined by $s + (\pi/2)$ and $s - (\pi/2)$, respectively. Angle TOT_1 is a right angle. Hence the measure of angle θ_2 is $90° - \alpha$. Similarly, the measure of angle θ_1 is $90° - \alpha$. Thus these angles are congruent. Since the right triangles that are shown each have hypotenuse of length 1 and have an acute angle congruent, the triangles are congruent. Angles θ_2 and θ_3 are vertical angles and hence are congruent. Therefore the right triangle in the fourth quadrant is congruent to the other two. The lengths of the legs of

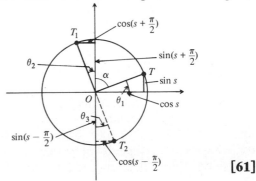

[61]

these triangles are the absolute values of the sine and cosine values. From this diagram we see that $-\sin s \equiv \cos[s + \pi/2]$. Similarly, we can deduce the other identities.

We now consider function values at $(\pi/2) - x$. Since the sine function is odd, we know that

$$\sin\left(\frac{\pi}{2} - x\right) \equiv \sin -\left(x - \frac{\pi}{2}\right) \equiv -\sin\left(x - \frac{\pi}{2}\right).$$

Now consider the identity already established,

$$\sin\left(x - \frac{\pi}{2}\right) \equiv -\cos x.$$

This is equivalent to

$$-\sin\left(x - \frac{\pi}{2}\right) \equiv \cos x.$$

We now have the following identity:

$$\sin\left(\frac{\pi}{2} - x\right) \equiv \cos x.$$

Similarly, we can establish the identity $\cos\left(\frac{\pi}{2} - x\right) \equiv \sin x.$
[62]

We have established the following cofunction identities.

$$\sin\left(x + \frac{\pi}{2}\right) \equiv \cos x$$

$$\cos\left(x + \frac{\pi}{2}\right) \equiv -\sin x$$

$$\sin\left(x - \frac{\pi}{2}\right) \equiv -\cos x$$

$$\cos\left(x - \frac{\pi}{2}\right) \equiv \sin x$$

$$\sin\left(\frac{\pi}{2} - x\right) \equiv \cos x$$

$$\cos\left(\frac{\pi}{2} - x\right) \equiv \sin x$$

These should be learned. The other cofunction identities can be obtained easily, using these and the definitions of the other circular functions.

Example 3. Find an identity for $\tan\left(x + \frac{\pi}{2}\right)$.

By definition of the tangent function,

$$\tan\left(x + \frac{\pi}{2}\right) \equiv \frac{\sin\left(x + \frac{\pi}{2}\right)}{\cos\left(x + \frac{\pi}{2}\right)}.$$

Using the first two identities in the above list, we obtain

$$\frac{\sin\left(x + \frac{\pi}{2}\right)}{\cos\left(x + \frac{\pi}{2}\right)} \equiv \frac{\cos x}{-\sin x} \equiv -\frac{\cos x}{\sin x} \equiv -\cot x.$$

Thus the identity we seek is

$$\tan\left(x + \frac{\pi}{2}\right) \equiv -\cot x.$$

Example 4. Find an identity for $\sec\left(\frac{\pi}{2} - x\right)$. By definition of the secant function,

$$\sec\left(\frac{\pi}{2} - x\right) \equiv \frac{1}{\cos\left(\frac{\pi}{2} - x\right)}.$$

Using the last identity in the above list, we obtain

$$\frac{1}{\cos\left(\frac{\pi}{2} - x\right)} \equiv \frac{1}{\sin x} \equiv \csc x.$$

Thus the identity we seek is

$$\sec\left(\frac{\pi}{2} - x\right) \equiv \csc x.$$
[63]

Exercise Set 7.5

1. From the identity $1 + \cot^2 x \equiv \csc^2 x$, obtain two other identities.

2. From the identity $1 + \tan^2 x \equiv \sec^2 x$, obtain two other identities.

3. a) Derive an identity for csc x in terms of cot x.

b) Derive an identity for cot x in terms of csc x.

4. a) Derive an identity for tan x in terms of sec x.

b) Derive an identity for sec x in terms of tan x.

5. Draw a unit circle diagram like that on page 214, with point T in the second quadrant. Write all of the identities that are apparent from your diagram.

6. Draw a unit circle diagram like that on page 214, with point T in the fourth quadrant. Write all of the identities that are apparent from your diagram.

7. Find an identity for $\tan\left(x - \dfrac{\pi}{2}\right)$.

8. Find an identity for $\cot\left(x + \dfrac{\pi}{2}\right)$.

9. Find an identity for $\sec\left(\dfrac{\pi}{2} - x\right)$.

10. Find an identity for $\csc\left(\dfrac{\pi}{2} - x\right)$.

11. For the six circular functions, list the cofunction identities involving $\pi/2 - x$.

12. Describe the pattern you see in the list of Exercise 11.

▶ **13.** The coordinates of a point on the unit circle are $(\cos s, \sin s)$, for some suitable s. Show that for a circle with center at the origin of radius r, the coordinates of any point on the circle are $(r \cos s, r \sin s)$.

14. Using sines and cosines and a determinant, write an equation of the unit circle.

7.6 Graphs

We will consider graphs of some variations of the sine and cosine functions. In particular, we are interested in the following:

$$y = A + B \sin (Cx - D),$$

and

$$y = A + B \cos (Cx - D),$$

where A, B, C, and D are constants, some of which may be 0. These constants have the effect of translating, stretching, reflecting, or shrinking the basic graphs. Let us examine an equation to see what each

of these constants does.* We first change the form a bit.

$$y - A = B \sin C\left(x - \dfrac{D}{C}\right).$$

Translates, upward if positive.	Stretches, vertically if greater than 1.	Stretches, horizontally if between 0 and 1.	Translates, to the right if positive.

---

* You may wish to review pp. 91–95.

The amplitude of the sine or cosine function is multiplied by B, when that constant is present. The period will be affected by the constant C. If $C = 2$, for example, the period will be divided by 2. If $C = \frac{1}{2}$, the period will be multiplied by 2.

Example 1. The graph of $y = 3 + \sin x$ is a translation of $y = \sin x$ upward 3 units ($A = 3$, $B = C = 1$, and $D = 0$).

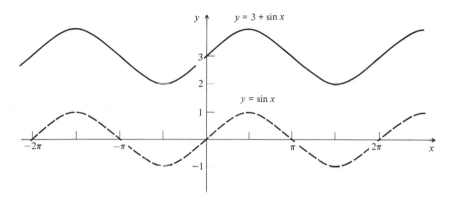

[64]

Example 2. The graph of $y = 2 \sin x$ is a vertical stretching of the graph of $y = \sin x$. The amplitude of this function is 2 ($A = 0$, $B = 1$, $C = 2$, and $D = 0$).

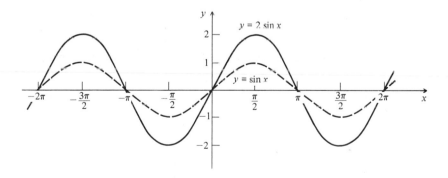

If the constant B in $y = B \sin x$ is negative, there will also be a reflection across the x-axis. If the absolute value of B is less than 1, then there will be a vertical shrinking. $|B|$ will be the amplitude.

Example 3. The graph of $y = -(\frac{1}{2}) \sin x$ is a vertical shrinking and a reflection of the graph of $y = \sin x$. The amplitude is $\frac{1}{2}$.

[65]

Example 4. The graph of $y = \sin 2x$ is a horizontal shrinking of the graph of $y = \sin x$. The period of this function is π (half the period of $y = \sin x$).

[66, 67]

Example 5. The graph of $y = \sin(2x - \pi)$ is the same as that of $y = \sin 2(x - \pi/2)$. We merely factored the 2 out of the parentheses. The $\pi/2$ translates the graph of $y = \sin 2x$ a distance of $\pi/2$ to the right. The 2 in front of the brackets shrinks by half, making the period π.

The quantity D/C translates to the right or left, and is called the *phase shift*. In Example 5, the phase shift is $\pi/2$. This means that the graph of $\sin 2x$ has been shifted forward a distance of $\pi/2$. [68]

Example 6. The graph of $y = 3 \sin[2x + (\pi/2)]$ has an amplitude of 3.

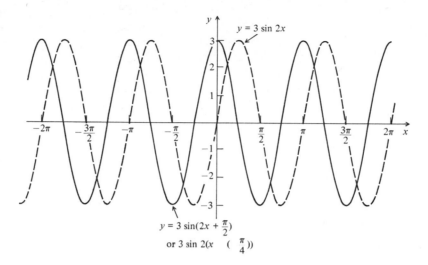

$$y = 3 \sin 2x$$

$$y = 3 \sin(2x + \frac{\pi}{2})$$
$$\text{or } 3 \sin 2(x \ (\ \frac{\pi}{4}))$$

The period is π and the phase shift is $-\pi/4$. This means that the graph of $3 \sin 2x$ has been shifted back a distance of $\pi/4$. **[69]**

GRAPHS OF SUMS

A function that is a sum of two functions can often be graphed by a method called *addition of ordinates*. We graph the two functions separately and then add the second coordinates (called *ordinates*) graphically. A compass may be helpful.

Example 7. Graph $y = 2 \sin x + \sin 2x$.

We graph $y = 2 \sin x$ and $y = \sin 2x$ using the same axes.

Now we graphically add some ordinates to obtain points on the graph we seek. At $x = \pi/4$ we transfer the distance h, which is the value of $\sin 2x$, upward to add it to the value of $2 \sin x$. Point P_1 is on the graph we seek. At $x = -\pi/4$ we do a similar thing, but the distance m is negative. Point P_2 is on our graph. At $x = -(\frac{5}{4})\pi$ the distance n is negative, so we in effect subtract it from the value of $2 \sin x$. Point P_3 is on the graph we seek. We continue to plot points in this fashion and then connect them to get the desired graph, shown here.

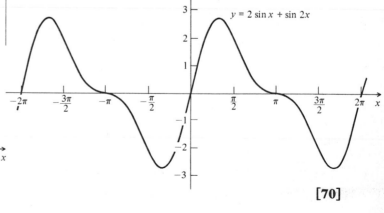

[70]

Exercise Set 7.6

In Exercises 1–28, use graph paper. Sketch graphs of the functions.

1. $y = 2 + \sin x$ **2.** $y = -3 + \cos x$ **3.** $y = \frac{1}{2}\sin x$ **4.** $y = \frac{1}{3}\cos x$

5. $y = 2\cos x$ **6.** $y = 3\cos x$ **7.** $y = -\frac{1}{2}\cos x$ **8.** $y = -2\sin x$

9. $y = \cos 2x$ **10.** $y = \cos 3x$ **11.** $y = \cos(-2x)$ **12.** $y = \cos(-3x)$

13. $y = \sin\frac{1}{2}x$ **14.** $y = \cos\frac{1}{3}x$ **15.** $y = \sin\left(-\frac{1}{2}x\right)$ **16.** $y = \cos\left(-\frac{1}{3}x\right)$

17. $y = \cos(2x - \pi)$ **18.** $y = \sin(2x + \pi)$ **19.** $y = 2\cos(2x - \pi)$ **20.** $y = 2\sin(2x + \pi)$

21. $y = -2\cos\left(2x - \frac{\pi}{2}\right)$ **22.** $y = -2\sin\left(2x + \frac{\pi}{2}\right)$ **23.** $y = 2\cos x + \cos 2x$ **24.** $y = 3\cos x + \cos 3x$

25. $y = \sin x + \cos 2x$ **26.** $y = 2\sin x + \cos 2x$ **27.** $y = 3\cos x - \sin 2x$ **28.** $y = 3\sin x - \cos 2x$

In Exercises 29–32, determine the amplitude, period, and phase shift.

29. $y = 3\cos\left(3x - \frac{\pi}{2}\right)$ **30.** $y = 4\sin\left(4x - \frac{\pi}{3}\right)$ **31.** $y = -5\cos\left(4x + \frac{\pi}{3}\right)$

32. $y = -4\sin\left(5x + \frac{\pi}{2}\right)$ **33.** $y = \frac{1}{2}\sin(2\pi x + \pi)$ **34.** $y = -\frac{1}{4}\cos(\pi x - 4)$

7.7 Algebraic and Trigonometric Manipulations

The circular functions and variations of them are called *trigonometric functions*. Trigonometric expressions such as $\sin 2x$ or $\tan(x - \pi)$ represent numbers, just as algebraic expressions such as $3x$ or $3x^2 - 2$ represent numbers. Thus we can manipulate expressions containing trigonometric expressions in much the same way as we manipulate purely algebraic expressions.

Example 1. Multiply and simplify $\cos y\,(\tan y - \sec y)$.

$$\cos y\,(\tan y - \sec y) = \cos y \tan y - \cos y \sec y$$

The multiplication has now been accomplished, but we can simplify:

$$\cos y \tan y - \cos y \sec y = \cos y\frac{\sin y}{\cos y} - \cos y\frac{1}{\cos y}$$
$$= \sin y - 1.$$

In Example 1 it has been illustrated how we can use certain identities to accomplish simplification. There is no rule for doing this, but it is often helpful to put everything in terms of sines and cosines, as we did in Example 1.

Example 2. Factor and simplify $\sin^2 x \cos^2 x + \cos^4 x$.

$$\sin^2 x \cos^2 x + \cos^4 x = \cos^2 x\,(\sin^2 x + \cos^2 x)$$

The factoring has been accomplished, but we can now simplify, using the Pythagorean identity $\sin^2 x + \cos^2 x \equiv 1$:

$$\cos^2 x \, (\sin^2 x + \cos^2 x) = \cos^2 x.$$

Example 3. Factor and simplify $\tan x + \cos\left(\dfrac{\pi}{2} - x\right)$.

$$\tan x + \cos\left(\frac{\pi}{2} - x\right) = \sin x \frac{1}{\cos x} + \sin x.$$

Here we have used the identity $\cos\left(\pi/2 - x\right) \equiv \sin x$, as well as the definition of the tangent function. Now we factor as follows:

$$\sin x \left(\frac{1}{\cos x} + 1\right) \quad \text{or} \quad \sin x(\sec x + 1).$$

[71–73]

Example 4. Simplify $\dfrac{\sin x - \sin x \cos x}{\sin x + \sin x \tan x}$.

$$\frac{\sin x - \sin x \cos x}{\sin x + \sin x \tan x} = \frac{\sin x(1 - \cos x)}{\sin x(1 + \tan x)} \quad \text{(factoring)}$$

$$= \frac{1 - \cos x}{1 + \tan x} \quad \text{(simplifying)}$$

Example 5. Subtract and simplify

$$\frac{2}{\sin x - \cos x} - \frac{3}{\sin x + \cos x}.$$

$$\frac{2}{\sin x - \cos x} - \frac{3}{\sin x + \cos x}$$

$$= \frac{2}{\sin x - \cos x} \cdot \frac{\sin x + \cos x}{\sin x + \cos x}$$

$$\quad - \frac{3}{\sin x + \cos x} \cdot \frac{\sin x - \cos x}{\sin x - \cos x}$$

$$= \frac{2(\sin x + \cos x) - 3(\sin x - \cos x)}{\sin^2 x - \cos^2 x}$$

$$= \frac{-\sin x + 5 \cos x}{\sin^2 x - \cos^2 x}$$

Example 6. Add and simplify

$$\frac{2}{\tan^3 x - 2 \tan^2 x} + \frac{2}{\tan x - 2}.$$

$$\frac{2}{\tan^3 x - 2 \tan^2 x} + \frac{2}{\tan x - 2}$$

$$= \frac{2}{\tan^2 x(\tan x - 2)} + \frac{2}{\tan x - 2} \cdot \frac{\tan^2 x}{\tan^2 x}$$

$$= \frac{2 + 2 \tan^2 x}{\tan^2 x(\tan x - 2)} = \frac{2(1 + \tan^2 x)}{\tan^2 x(\tan x - 2)}$$

Now we use the Pythagorean identity $1 + \tan^2 x \equiv \sec^2 x$ in the numerator, and obtain for that numerator,

$$2 \sec^2 x, \quad \text{or} \quad 2\frac{1}{\cos^2 x}.$$

Thus we have

$$\frac{2}{\cos^2 x \dfrac{\sin^2 x}{\cos^2 x} (\tan x - 2)},$$

and finally

$$\frac{2}{\sin^2 x(\tan x - 2)}. \qquad \text{[74–76]}$$

Example 7. Multiply and simplify $\sqrt{\sin^3 x \cos x} \cdot \sqrt{\cos x}$.

$$\sqrt{\sin^3 x \cos x} \cdot \sqrt{\cos x} = \sqrt{\sin^3 x \cos^2 x}$$

$$= |\sin x \cos x| \sqrt{\sin x}$$

Example 8. Rationalize the denominator $\sqrt{\dfrac{2}{\tan x}}$.

$$\sqrt{\frac{2}{\tan x}} = \sqrt{\frac{2}{\tan x} \cdot \frac{\tan x}{\tan x}} = \sqrt{\frac{2 \tan x}{\tan^2 x}}$$

$$= \frac{\sqrt{2 \tan x}}{|\tan x|} \qquad \text{[77, 78]}$$

Example 9. Solve for tan x: $\tan^2 x + \tan x = 56$.

$\tan^2 x + \tan x - 56 = 0$ (quadratic, let u = $\tan x$)

$(\tan x + 8)(\tan x - 7) = 0$ (factoring)

$\tan x + 8 = 0$ or $\tan x - 7 = 0$

$\tan x = -8$ or $\tan x = 7$

Example 10. Solve for sec x: $\sec^2 x - \dfrac{3}{4}\sec x = \dfrac{1}{2}$.

$$\sec^2 x - \frac{3}{4}\sec x - \frac{1}{2} = 0$$

We now use the quadratic formula, and obtain

$$\sec x = \frac{\dfrac{3}{4} \pm \sqrt{\dfrac{9}{16} - 4\cdot 1 \cdot\left(-\dfrac{1}{2}\right)}}{2} = \frac{\dfrac{3}{4} \pm \sqrt{\dfrac{41}{16}}}{2}$$

$$\sec x = \frac{\dfrac{3}{4} \pm \dfrac{\sqrt{41}}{4}}{2} = \frac{3 \pm \sqrt{41}}{8}.$$

Example 11. Solve for sin x:

$$8\sin^2 x + 2\cos\left(x + \frac{\pi}{2}\right) - 3 = 0.$$

We first use the identity $\cos(x + \pi/2) \equiv -\sin x$, to get everything in terms of $\sin x$:

$$8\sin^2 x - 2\sin x - 3 = 0.$$

Now we factor: $(4\sin x - 3)(2\sin x + 1) = 0$

$4\sin x - 3 = 0$ or $2\sin x + 1 = 0$

$\sin x = \dfrac{3}{4}$ or $\sin x = -\dfrac{1}{2}.$

[79–81]

Exercise Set 7.7A

In Exercises 1–20, multiply and simplify.

1. $(\sin x - \cos x)(\sin x + \cos x)$

2. $(\tan y - \cot y)(\tan y + \cot y)$

3. $\tan x(\cos x - \csc x)$

4. $\cot x(\sin x + \sec x)$

5. $\cos y \sin y(\sec y + \csc y)$

6. $\tan y \sin y(\cot y - \csc y)$

7. $(\sin x + \cos x)(\csc x - \sec x)$

8. $(\sin x + \cos x)(\sec x + \csc x)$

9. $(\sin y - \cos y)^2$

10. $(\sin y + \cos y)^2$

11. $(1 + \tan x)^2$

12. $(1 + \cot x)^2$

13. $(\sin y - \csc y)^2$

14. $(\cos y + \sec y)^2$

15. $(\cos x - \sec x)(\cos^2 x + \sec^2 x + 1)$

16. $(\sin x + \csc x)(\sin^2 x + \csc^2 x - 1)$

17. $(\cot x - \tan x)(\cot^2 x + 1 + \tan^2 x)$

18. $(\cot y + \tan y)(\cot^2 y - 1 + \tan^2 y)$

19. $\sin\left(\dfrac{\pi}{2} - x\right)[\sec x - \cos x]$

20. $\cos\left(\dfrac{\pi}{2} - x\right)[\csc x - \sin x]$

In Exercises 21–40, factor and simplify.

21. $\sin x \cos x + \cos^2 x$

22. $\sec x \csc x - \csc^2 x$

23. $\sin^2 y - \cos^2 y$

24. $\tan^2 y - \cot^2 y$

25. $\tan x + \sin(\pi - x)$

26. $\cot x - \cos(\pi - x)$

27. $\sin^4 x - \cos^4 x$

28. $\tan^4 x - \sec^4 x$

29. $3 \cot^2 y + 6 \cot y + 3$

30. $4 \sin^2 y + 8 \sin y + 4$

31. $\csc^4 x + 4 \csc^2 x - 5$

32. $8 + \tan^4 x - 2 \tan^2 x$

33. $\sin^3 y + 27$

34. $1 - 125 \tan^3 y$

35. $\sin^3 y - \csc^3 y$

36. $\cos^3 x - \sec^3 x$

37. $\sin x \cos y - \cos\left(x + \dfrac{\pi}{2}\right) \tan y$

38. $\cos\left(x - \dfrac{\pi}{2}\right) \tan y + \sin x \cot y$

39. $\cos(\pi - x) + \cot x \sin\left(x - \dfrac{\pi}{2}\right)$

40. $\sin(\pi - x) - \tan x \cos\left(\dfrac{\pi}{2} - x\right)$

Exercise Set 7.7B

Simplify.

1. $\dfrac{\sin^2 x \cos x}{\cos^2 x \sin x}$

2. $\dfrac{\cos^2 x \sin x}{\sin^2 x \cos x}$

3. $\dfrac{4 \sin x \cos^3 x}{18 \sin^2 x \cos x}$

4. $\dfrac{30 \sin^3 x \cos x}{6 \cos^2 x \sin x}$

5. $\dfrac{\cos^2 x - 2 \cos x + 1}{\cos x - 1}$

6. $\dfrac{\sin^2 x + 2 \sin x + 1}{\sin x + 1}$

7. $\dfrac{\cos^2 x - 1}{\cos x - 1}$

8. $\dfrac{\sin^2 x - 1}{\sin x + 1}$

9. $\dfrac{4 \tan x \sec x + 2 \sec x}{6 \sin x \sec x + 2 \sec x}$

10. $\dfrac{6 \tan x \sin x - 3 \sin x}{9 \sin^2 x + 3 \sin x}$

11. $\dfrac{\cos^2 x - 1}{\sin\left(\dfrac{\pi}{2} - x\right) - 1}$

12. $\dfrac{\sin^2 x - 1}{\cos\left(\dfrac{\pi}{2} - x\right) + 1}$

13. $\dfrac{\sin x - \cos\left(x - \dfrac{\pi}{2}\right)\cos x}{-\sin x - \cos\left(x - \dfrac{\pi}{2}\right)\tan x}$

14. $\dfrac{\cos x - \sin\left(\dfrac{\pi}{2} - x\right)\sin x}{\cos x - \cos(\pi - x)\tan x}$

15. $\dfrac{\sin^4 x - \cos^4 x}{\sin^2 x - \cos^2 x}$

16. $\dfrac{\sec^4 x - \tan^4 x}{\sec^2 x + \tan^2 x}$

17. $\dfrac{\cos^2 x + 2\sin\left(x - \dfrac{\pi}{2}\right) + 1}{\sin\left(\dfrac{\pi}{2} - x\right) - 1}$

18. $\dfrac{\sin^2 x - 2\cos\left(x - \dfrac{\pi}{2}\right) + 1}{\cos\left(\dfrac{\pi}{2} - x\right) - 1}$

19. $\dfrac{\sin^2 y \cos\left(y + \dfrac{\pi}{2}\right)}{\cos^2 y \cos\left(\dfrac{\pi}{2} - y\right)}$

20. $\dfrac{\cos^2 y \sin\left(y + \dfrac{\pi}{2}\right)}{\sin^2 y \sin\left(\dfrac{\pi}{2} - y\right)}$

21. $\dfrac{2\sin^2 x}{\cos^3 x} \cdot \left(\dfrac{\cos x}{2\sin x}\right)^2$

22. $\dfrac{4\cos^3 x}{\sin^2 x} \cdot \left(\dfrac{\sin x}{4\cos x}\right)^2$

23. $\dfrac{3\sin x}{\cos^2 x} \cdot \dfrac{\cos^2 x + \cos x \sin x}{\cos^2 x - \sin^2 x}$

24. $\dfrac{5\cos x}{\sin^2 x} \cdot \dfrac{\sin^2 x - \sin x \cos x}{\sin^2 x - \cos^2 x}$

25. $\dfrac{\tan^2 y}{\sec y} \div \dfrac{3\tan^3 y}{\sec y}$

26. $\dfrac{\cot^3 y}{\csc y} \div \dfrac{4\cot^2 y}{\csc y}$

27. $\dfrac{1}{\sin^2 y - \cos^2 y} - \dfrac{2}{\cos y + \sin y}$

28. $\dfrac{3}{\cos y - \sin y} - \dfrac{2}{\sin^2 y - \cos^2 y}$

29. $\left(\dfrac{\sin x}{\cos x}\right)^2 - \dfrac{1}{\cos^2 x}$

30. $\left(\dfrac{\cot x}{\csc x}\right)^2 + \dfrac{1}{\csc^2 x}$

31. $\dfrac{\sin^2 x - 9}{2\cos x + 1} \cdot \dfrac{10\cos x + 5}{3\sin x + 9}$

32. $\dfrac{9\cos^2 x - 25}{2\cos x - 2} \cdot \dfrac{\cos^2 x - 1}{6\cos x - 10}$

Exercise Set 7.7C

In Exercises 1–10, simplify.

1. $\sqrt{\sin^2 x \cos x} \cdot \sqrt{\cos x}$

2. $\sqrt{\cos^2 x \sin x} \cdot \sqrt{\sin x}$

3. $\sqrt{\sin^3 y} + \sqrt{\sin y \cos^2 y}$

4. $\sqrt{\cos y \sin^2 y} - \sqrt{\cos^3 y}$

5. $\sqrt{\sin^2 x + 2 \cos x \sin x + \cos^2 x}$

6. $\sqrt{\tan^2 x - 2 \tan x \sin x + \sin^2 x}$

7. $(1 - \sqrt{\sin y})(\sqrt{\sin y} + 1)$

8. $(2 - \sqrt{\tan y})(\sqrt{\tan y} + 2)$

9. $\sqrt{\sin x} \, (\sqrt{2 \sin x} + \sqrt{\sin x \cos x})$

10. $\sqrt{\cos x} \, (\sqrt{3 \cos x} - \sqrt{\sin x \cos x})$

In Exercises 11–18, rationalize the denominator.

11. $\sqrt{\dfrac{\sin x}{\cos x}}$

12. $\sqrt{\dfrac{\cos x}{\sin x}}$

13. $\sqrt{\dfrac{\sin x}{\cot x}}$

14. $\sqrt{\dfrac{\cos x}{\tan x}}$

15. $\sqrt{\dfrac{\cos^2 x}{2 \sin^2 x}}$

16. $\sqrt{\dfrac{\sin^2 x}{3 \cos^2 x}}$

17. $\sqrt{\dfrac{1 + \sin x}{1 - \sin x}}$

18. $\sqrt{\dfrac{1 - \cos x}{1 + \cos x}}$

19. Solve for tan x.
$\tan^2 x + 4 \tan x = 21$

20. Solve for sec x.
$\sec^2 x - 7 \sec x = -10$

21. Solve for sin x.
$8 \sin^2 x - 2 \sin x = 3$

22. Solve for cos x.
$6 \cos^2 x + 17 \cos x = -5$

23. Solve for cot x.
$\cot^2 x + 9 \cot x - 10 = 0$

24. Solve for csc x.
$\csc^2 x + 3 \csc x - 10 = 0$

25. Solve for sin x.
$\sin^2 x - \cos\left(x + \dfrac{\pi}{2}\right) = 6$

26. Solve for sin x.
$2 \cos^2\left(x - \dfrac{\pi}{2}\right) - 3 \cos\left(x + \dfrac{\pi}{2}\right) - 2 = 0$

27. Solve for tan x.

$\tan^2 x - 6 \tan x = 4$

28. Solve for cot x.

$\cot^2 x + 8 \cot x = 5$

29. Solve for sec x.

$6 \sec^2 x - 5 \sec x - 2 = 0$

30. Solve for csc x.

$2 \csc^2 x - 3 \csc x - 4 = 0$

Chapter 7 Test, or Review

The point $(3, -2)$ is on a circle centered at the origin. Find the coordinates of its reflections across:

1. The y-axis **2.** The origin **3.** The x-axis

On a unit circle, mark the points determined by

4. $\dfrac{7\pi}{6}$ **5.** $\dfrac{3\pi}{4}$ **6.** $\dfrac{\pi}{6}$ **7.** $\dfrac{9\pi}{4}$

8. Sketch a graph of $y = \sin x$.

9. What is the domain of the sine function?

10. Sketch a graph of $y = \cos x$.

11. What is the period of the cosine function?

12. Sketch a graph of $y = \sin\left(x + \dfrac{\pi}{2}\right)$. Use the axes of Exercise 8.

13. Complete the following table.

	$\pi/4$	$\pi/2$	$3\pi/4$	$5\pi/4$
$\sin x$				
$\cos x$				

14. Sketch a graph of $y = \csc x$.

15. What is the period of the cosecant function?

16. What is the range of the cosecant function?

17. In which quadrants are the signs of the sine and the tangent the same?

18. Verify the following identity: $\cot(x - \pi) \equiv \cot x$.

Complete these Pythagorean identities.

19. $\sin^2 x + \cos^2 x \equiv$ _____   **20.** $1 + \cot^2 x \equiv$ _____

Complete these cofunction identities.

21. $\cos\left(x + \dfrac{\pi}{2}\right) \equiv$ _____   **22.** $\cos\left(\dfrac{\pi}{2} - x\right) \equiv$ _____

23. $\sin\left(x - \dfrac{\pi}{2}\right) \equiv$ _____

24. Express $\tan x$ in terms of $\sec x$.

25. Sketch a graph of $y = 3 + \cos\left(x - \dfrac{\pi}{4}\right)$.

26. What is the phase shift of the function in Exercise 25?

27. What is the period of the function in Exercise 25?

28. Sketch a graph of $y = 3\cos x + \sin x$ for values of x between 0 and 2π.

Simplify.

29. $\cos x(\tan x + \cot x)$ **30.** $\dfrac{\csc x(\sin^2 x + \cos^2 x \tan x)}{\sin x + \cos x}$

Rationalize the denominator.

31. $\sqrt{\dfrac{\tan x}{\sec x}}$

32. Solve for $\tan x$: $3\tan^2 x - 2\tan x - 2 = 0$.

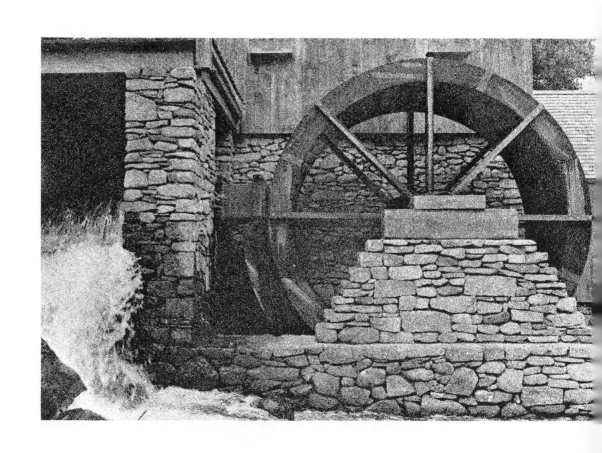

CHAPTER **8**

Trigonometric Functions of Rotations or Angles

8.1 Rotations and Angles

We shall consider rotations abstractly. That is, instead of considering a specific rotating object, such as a wheel or part of a machine, we will consider a rotating ray, with its endpoint at the origin of an *xy*-plane. The ray starts in position along the positive half of the *x*-axis. A counterclockwise rotation will be called positive. Clockwise rotations will be called negative.

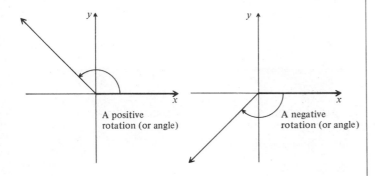

A positive rotation (or angle)

A negative rotation (or angle)

Note that the rotating ray and the positive half of the *x*-axis form an angle. Thus we often speak of "rotations" and "angles" interchangeably. The rotating ray is often called the *terminal side* of the angle, and the positive half of the *x*-axis is called the *initial side*.

MEASURES OF ROTATIONS OR ANGLES

The measure of an angle, or rotation, may be given in degrees. For example, a complete revolution has a measure of 360°, half a revolution has a measure of 180°, and so on. We also speak of an *angle* of 90°, or 720°, or −240°, and so on. An angle between 0° and 90° has its terminal side in the first quadrant. An angle between 90° and 180° has its terminal side in the second quadrant. An angle between 0° and −90° has its terminal side in the fourth quadrant, and so on.

[1, 2]

RADIAN MEASURE

Consider a unit circle with its center at the origin, as was done in Chapter 7. The distance around this circle from the initial side of an angle to the terminal side can be used as a measure of the rotation. This kind of angle measure is very useful. The unit is called a *radian*.

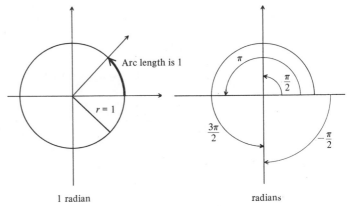

1 radian

radians

A rotation of 360° (1 revolution) thus has a measure of 2π radians. Half a revolution is a rotation of 180° or π radians. A quarter revolution is a rotation of 90°, or $\pi/2$ radians, and so on. To convert between degrees and radians we can use the notion of "multiplying by one" (see Section 1.11). Note the following:

$$\frac{1 \text{ revolution}}{1 \text{ revolution}} = 1 = \frac{2\pi \text{ radians}}{360 \text{ degrees}} = \frac{\pi \text{ radians}}{180 \text{ degrees}}.$$

Also

$$\frac{180 \text{ degrees}}{\pi \text{ radians}} = 1.$$

When a rotation is given in radians, the word "radians" is optional and is most often omitted. Thus if no unit is given for a rotation, it is understood to be in radians.

Example 1.　Convert 60° to radians.

$$60° = 60° \cdot \frac{\pi \text{ radians}}{180°} = \frac{60°}{180°} \pi \text{ radians}$$

$$= \frac{\pi}{3} \text{ radians, or } \frac{\pi}{3}$$

Using 3.14 for π, we find $\pi/3$ is about 1.047.

Example 2.　Convert $3\pi/4$ radians to degrees.

$$\frac{3\pi}{4} \text{ radians} = \frac{3\pi}{4} \text{ radians} \cdot \frac{180°}{\pi \text{ radians}}$$

$$= \frac{3\pi}{4\pi} \cdot 180° = 135° \qquad \text{[3–6]}$$

ARC LENGTH AND CENTRAL ANGLES

Radian measure can be determined using a circle other than a unit circle. In the following drawing, a unit circle is shown as well as another circle. The angle shown is a central angle of both circles, hence the arcs that it intercepts have their lengths in the same ratio as the radii of the circles. The radii of the circles are r and 1.

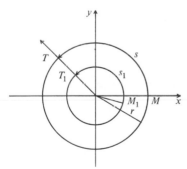

The corresponding arc lengths are MT and $M_1 T_1$, or more simply, s and s_1. We therefore have the proportion

$$\frac{s}{r} = \frac{s_1}{1}.$$

Now s_1 is the radian measure of the rotation in question. It is more common to use a Greek letter, such as θ, for the measure of an angle or rotation. We commonly use the letter s for arc length. Adopting this convention, the above proportion becomes $\theta = s/r$. In any circle, arc length, central angle, and length of radius are related in this fashion. Or, in general, the following is true.

> **The radian measure θ of a rotation is the ratio of the distance s traveled by a point at a radius r from the center of rotation, to the length of the radius r:**
>
> $$\theta = \frac{s}{r}.$$

Example 3.　Find the length of an arc of a circle of 5-cm radius associated with a central angle of $\pi/3$ radians.

$$\theta = \frac{s}{r}, \qquad \text{or} \qquad s = r\theta$$

Therefore, $s = 5 \cdot \dfrac{\pi}{3}$ cm or, using 3.14 for π, about 5.23 cm.

Example 4.　Find the measure of a rotation in radians where a point 2 m from the center of rotation travels 4 m.

$$\theta = \frac{s}{r} = \frac{4 \text{ m}}{2 \text{ m}} = 2 \qquad \text{(The unit is understood to be radians.)}$$

A look at Examples 3 and 4 will show why the word "radian" is most often omitted. In Example 4, we have the division 4 m/2 m, which simplifies to 2, since m/m = 1. From this point of view it would seem preferable to omit the word "radians." In Example 3, had we used the word "radians" all the way through, our answer would have come out to be 5.23 cm-radians. It is a distance we seek, hence we know the unit should be centimeters. Thus we must omit the word "radians." Usually it is preferable to omit the word.

[7–9]

Exercise Set 8.1

For angles of the following measures, state in which quadrant the terminal side lies.

1. 34°   **2.** 320°   **3.** −120°   **4.** 175°

5. $\dfrac{\pi}{3}$ **6.** $-\dfrac{3}{4}\pi$ **7.** $\dfrac{11}{4}\pi$ **8.** $\dfrac{19}{4}\pi$

Convert to radian measure. Leave answers in terms of π.

9. 30°   **10.** 15°   **11.** 60°

12. 200°   **13.** 75°   **14.** 300°

Convert to radian measure. Do not leave answers in terms of π. Use 3.14 for π.

15. 120°   **16.** 240°   **17.** 320°

18. 75°   **19.** 200°   **20.** 300°

Convert to degree measure.

21. 1 radian   **22.** 2 radians   **23.** 8π

24. -12π **25.** $\dfrac{3}{4}\pi$ **26.** $\dfrac{5}{4}\pi$

27. In a circle with 120-cm radius, an arc 132 cm long subtends a central angle of how many radians? how many degrees, to the nearest degree?

28. In a circle with 200-cm radius, an arc 65 cm long subtends a central angle of how many radians? how many degrees, to the nearest degree?

29. Through how many radians does the minute hand of a clock rotate in 50 min?

30. A wheel on a car has a 14-in. radius. Through what angle (in radians) does the wheel turn while the car travels 1 mi?

31. In a circle with 10-m radius, how long is an arc associated with a central angle of 1.6 radians?

32. In a circle with 5-m radius, how long is an arc associated with a central angle of 2.1 radians?

 If your calculator has a key for radians to degrees, or vice versa, it is best not to use that key for these exercises, except as a check. Convert to radian measure. Leave answers in terms of π.

33. 37.71°   **34.** 12.73°   **35.** 214.6°   **36.** 73.87°

Convert to radian measure. Do not leave answers in terms of π.

37. $117.8°$ **38.** $231.2°$ **39.** $1.354°$ **40.** $327.9°$

Convert these radian measures to degree measure.

41. 1.303 **42.** 2.347 **43.** 37.89 **44.** 7.005

45. 8.206π **46.** -14.13π **47.** 0.7532π **48.** -1.205π

▶ **49.** What is the angle between the hands of a clock at 2:30?

50. What is the angle between the hands of a clock at 7:45?

8.2 Angular Speed

Speed is defined to be distance traveled per unit of time. Similarly, *angular speed* is defined to be amount of rotation per unit of time. For example, we might speak of the angular speed of a wheel as 150 revolutions per minute or the angular speed of the earth as 2π radians per day. The Greek letter ω (omega) is usually used for angular speed. Thus angular speed is defined as

$$\omega = \frac{\theta}{t}.$$

For many applications it is important to know a relationship between angular speed and linear speed. For example, we might wish to find the linear speed of a point on the earth, knowing its angular speed. Or, we might wish to know the linear speed of an earth satellite, knowing its angular speed. To develop the relationship we seek, we recall the relation between angle and distance from the preceding section, $\theta = s/r$. This is equivalent to

$$s = r\theta.$$

We now divide by the time, t, to obtain

$$\frac{s}{t} = r\frac{\theta}{t}.$$

Now s/t is linear speed v, and θ/t is angular speed ω. We thus have the relation we seek.

> The linear speed v of a point a distance of r from the center of rotation is given by
>
> $$v = r\omega,$$
>
> where ω is the angular speed, in radians per unit of time.

In deriving this formula we used the equation $s = r\theta$, in which the units for s and r must be the same and θ must be in radians. So, for our new formula $v = r\omega$, the units of distance for v and r must be the same, ω must be in radians per unit of time, and the units of time must be the same for v and ω.   [10, 11]

Example 1. An earth satellite in a circular orbit 1200 km high makes one complete revolution every 90 min. What is its linear speed? Use 6400 km for the length of a radius of the earth.

We will use the formula $v = r\omega$; thus we shall need r and ω.

$r = 6400 \text{ km} + 1200 \text{ km}$ (radius of earth plus height of satellite)

$\quad = 7600 \text{ km}$

$\omega = \dfrac{2\pi \text{ radians}}{90 \text{ min}} = \dfrac{\pi}{45 \text{ min}}$ (We have, as usual, omitted the word "radians.")

Now, using $v = r\omega$, we have

$$v = 7600 \text{ km} \cdot \frac{\pi}{45 \text{ min}} = \frac{7600\pi}{45} \cdot \frac{\text{km}}{\text{min}}.$$

Using 3.14 for π, we obtain $v = 530 \dfrac{\text{km}}{\text{min}}$.

Example 2. A car is traveling 45 mph. Its tires have a 20-in. radius. Find the angle through which a wheel turns in 5 sec.

Recall that $\omega = \theta/t$ or $\theta = \omega t$. Thus we can find θ if we know ω and t.

To find ω we use $v = r\omega$. For convenience we will first convert 45 mph to ft/sec:

$$v = 45 \frac{\text{mi}}{\text{hr}} \cdot \frac{1 \text{ hr}}{60 \text{ min}} \cdot \frac{1 \text{ min}}{60 \text{ sec}} \cdot \frac{5280 \text{ ft}}{1 \text{ mi}} = 66 \frac{\text{ft}}{\text{sec}}.$$

Now $r = 20$ in. We shall convert to ft, since v is in ft/sec:

$$r = 20 \text{ in.} \cdot \frac{1 \text{ ft}}{12 \text{ in.}} = \frac{20}{12} \text{ ft} = \frac{5}{3} \text{ ft.}$$

Using $v = r\omega$, we have

$$66 \frac{\text{ft}}{\text{sec}} = \frac{5}{3} \text{ ft} \cdot \omega, \qquad \text{so } \omega = 39.6 \frac{\text{radians}}{\text{sec}}.$$

Then

$$\theta = \omega t = 39.6 \frac{\text{radians}}{\text{sec}} \cdot 5 \text{ sec} = 198 \text{ radians.*}$$

[12, 13]

_____

* If you had trouble working with the units, review Section 1.11.

Exercise Set 8.2

1. A flywheel is rotating 7 radians/sec. It has a 15-cm diameter. What is the speed of a point on its rim, in cm/min?

2. A wheel is rotating at 3 radians/sec. The wheel has a 30-cm radius. What is the speed of a point on its rim, in m/min?

3. A $33\frac{1}{3}$-rpm record has a radius of 15 cm. What is the linear velocity of a point on the rim, in cm/sec?

4. A 45-rpm record has a radius of 8.7 cm. What is the linear velocity of a point on the rim, in cm/sec?

5. The earth has a 4000-mile radius and rotates one revolution every 24 hours. What is the linear speed of a point on the equator, in mph?

6. The earth is 93,000,000 miles from the sun and traverses its orbit, which is nearly circular, every 365.25 days. What is the linear velocity of the earth in its orbit, in mph?

7. The wheels of a bicycle have a 24-in. diameter. When the bike is being ridden so that the wheels make 12 rpm, how far will the bike travel in 1 min?

8. The wheels of a car have a 15-in. radius. When the car is being driven so that the wheels make 10 revolutions/sec, how far will the car travel in one minute?

9. A wheel has a 32-cm diameter. The speed of a point on its rim is 11 m/s. What is its angular speed?

10. A horse on a merry-go-round is 7 m from the center and travels at 10 km/h. What is its angular speed?

11. A car is traveling 30 mph. Its wheels have a 14-in. radius. Find the angle through which a wheel rotates in 10 sec.

12. A car is traveling 40 mph. Its wheels have a 15-in. radius. Find the angle through which a wheel rotates in 12 sec.

13. (*Determining the speed of a river*). A water wheel has a 10-ft radius. To get a good approximation to the speed of the river, you count the revolutions of the wheel and find that it makes 14 revolutions per minute. What is the speed of the river?

14. (*Determining the speed of a river*). A water wheel has a 10-ft radius. To get a good approximation to the speed of the river, you count the revolutions of the wheel and find that it makes 16 rpm. What is the speed of the river?

15. Two pulleys, 50 cm and 30 cm in diameter, respectively, are connected by a belt. The larger pulley makes 12 revolutions per minute. Find the angular speed of the smaller pulley in radians/sec.

16. One gear wheel turns another, the teeth being on the rims. The wheels have 40-cm and 50-cm radii and the smaller wheel rotates at 20 rpm. Find the angular speed of the larger wheel in radians/sec.

8.3 Trigonometric Functions of Angles or Rotations

In Chapter 7 the trigonometric functions were developed. The domains of those functions are sets of real numbers. We can very easily define these functions so that their domains are sets of angles or rotations. If a rotation is given in radians, the numbers in the two kinds of functions are identical. For example, we define the sine of $\pi/2$ radians to be the same as $\sin \pi/2$, and so on. If a rotation is given in degrees, we merely change to radians to determine the trigonometric function values. The diagrams below show unit circles marked in both radians and degrees. These relationships should be memorized.

From these diagrams and from the facts in Chapter 7, we can immediately determine such things as the following:

$$\sin \frac{\pi}{2} = \sin 90° = 1,$$

$$\tan \frac{3\pi}{4} = 135° = -1,$$

$$\cos \left(-\frac{5\pi}{4}\right) = \cos\left(-225°\right) = -\frac{\sqrt{2}}{2}. \quad \textbf{[14–18]}$$

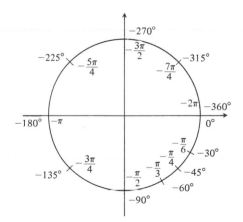

FUNCTION VALUES AND TRIANGLES

Let us consider a circle of radius r other than a unit circle, as shown below.

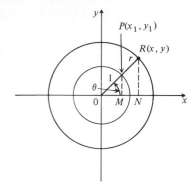

Also shown is a unit circle and a rotation θ. The triangles OMP and ONR are similar, being right triangles with the same acute angle. Thus we know that certain sides have the same ratio. For example,

$$\frac{MP}{OP} = \frac{NR}{OR}.$$

But $MP = y_1$ and $OP = 1$; $NR = y$ and $OR = r$. Thus we have

$$\frac{y_1}{1} = \frac{y}{r}.$$

Since P is a point on the unit circle, we know that $y_1 = \sin \theta$. Thus $\sin \theta = y/r$.   **[19, 20]**

All of the trigonometric function values can be considered to be ratios of sides of triangles, placed as in the preceding diagram. A triangle placed that way is said to be *in standard position*. The point R can be anywhere on the circle of radius r. Its coordinates may be positive, negative, or zero, depending on its location. The length of the radius (hypotenuse of the triangle) is always considered positive. Then, regardless of the position of point R, we have

$$\sin \theta = \frac{y}{r}.$$

The following diagram shows R in quadrants II and III. In quadrant II y and r are both positive, so $\sin \theta$ is positive. In quadrant III y is negative (and r is positive) so $\sin \theta$ is negative.

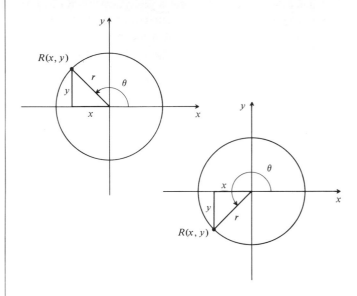

The values of the six trigonometric functions are as follows:

$$\sin \theta = \frac{y}{r} \left(\frac{\text{second coordinate}}{\text{radius}} \right),$$

$$\cos \theta = \frac{x}{r} \left(\frac{\text{first coordinate}}{\text{radius}} \right),$$

$$\tan \theta = \frac{y}{x} \left(\frac{\text{second coordinate}}{\text{first coordinate}} \right),$$

$$\cot \theta = \frac{x}{y} \left(\frac{\text{first coordinate}}{\text{second coordinate}} \right),$$

$$\sec \theta = \frac{r}{x} \left(\frac{\text{radius}}{\text{first coordinate}} \right),$$

$$\csc \theta = \frac{r}{y} \left(\frac{\text{radius}}{\text{second coordinate}} \right).$$

Example 1. Find the six trigonometric function values for the angle shown.

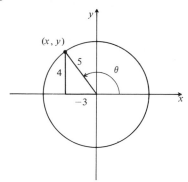

$$\sin \theta = \frac{y}{r} = \frac{4}{5} = 0.8,$$

$$\cos \theta = \frac{x}{r} = \frac{-3}{5} = -0.6,$$

$$\tan \theta = \frac{y}{x} = \frac{4}{-3} \approx -1.33,$$

$$\cot \theta = \frac{x}{y} = \frac{-3}{4} = -0.75,$$

$$\sec \theta = \frac{r}{x} = \frac{5}{-3} \approx -1.67,$$

$$\csc \theta = \frac{r}{y} = \frac{5}{4} = 1.25.$$

[21]

FUNCTION VALUES FOR SOME SPECIAL ANGLES

Our knowledge of triangles enables us to determine function values for certain angles. Let us first recall the Pythagorean theorem about right triangles. It says that in any right triangle, as shown, $a^2 + b^2 = c^2$, where c is the length of the hypotenuse.

A 45° right triangle is half of a square, so its legs are the same length. Let us consider such a triangle whose legs have length 1. Then its hypotenuse has length c given by

$$1^2 + 1^2 = c^2, \quad \text{or} \quad c^2 = 2, \quad \text{or} \quad c = \sqrt{2}.$$

Such a triangle is shown below. From this diagram we can easily determine the function values for 45° or $\pi/4$:

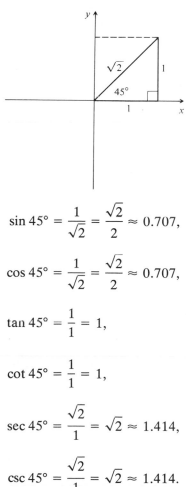

$$\sin 45° = \frac{1}{\sqrt{2}} = \frac{\sqrt{2}}{2} \approx 0.707,$$

$$\cos 45° = \frac{1}{\sqrt{2}} = \frac{\sqrt{2}}{2} \approx 0.707,$$

$$\tan 45° = \frac{1}{1} = 1,$$

$$\cot 45° = \frac{1}{1} = 1,$$

$$\sec 45° = \frac{\sqrt{2}}{1} = \sqrt{2} \approx 1.414,$$

$$\csc 45° = \frac{\sqrt{2}}{1} = \sqrt{2} \approx 1.414.$$

These function values should be memorized. The decimal values need not be, and it is sufficient to memorize the first three, since the others are their reciprocals.

The following should be memorized:

$$\sin 45° = \frac{\sqrt{2}}{2}, \qquad \cos 45° = \frac{\sqrt{2}}{2}, \qquad \tan 45° = 1.$$

Next we consider an equilateral triangle, each of whose sides has length 2. If we take half of it as shown, we obtain a right triangle having a hypotenuse of length 2 and a leg of length 1. The other leg has length *a*, given by the Pythagorean theorem as follows:

$$a^2 + 1^2 = 2^2, \quad \text{or} \quad a^2 = 3, \quad \text{or} \quad a = \sqrt{3}.$$

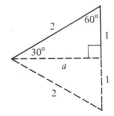

The acute angles of this triangle have measures of 30° and 60°. We can now determine function values for 30° and 60°. The function values for 30° are as follows:

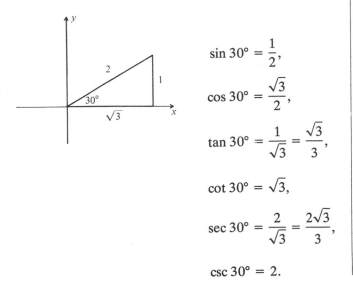

$$\sin 30° = \frac{1}{2},$$

$$\cos 30° = \frac{\sqrt{3}}{2},$$

$$\tan 30° = \frac{1}{\sqrt{3}} = \frac{\sqrt{3}}{3},$$

$$\cot 30° = \sqrt{3},$$

$$\sec 30° = \frac{2}{\sqrt{3}} = \frac{2\sqrt{3}}{3},$$

$$\csc 30° = 2.$$

We can now determine the function values for 60°, or, $\pi/3$, by repositioning the 30°-60° triangle:

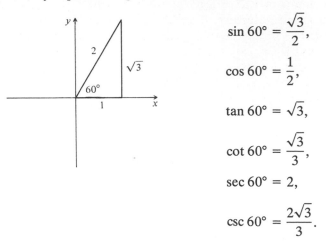

$$\sin 60° = \frac{\sqrt{3}}{2},$$

$$\cos 60° = \frac{1}{2},$$

$$\tan 60° = \sqrt{3},$$

$$\cot 60° = \frac{\sqrt{3}}{3},$$

$$\sec 60° = 2,$$

$$\csc 60° = \frac{2\sqrt{3}}{3}.$$

These function values for 30° and 60° should also be memorized, but again it is sufficient to learn only those for the sine, cosine, and tangent, since the others are their reciprocals.

The following should be memorized:

$$\sin 30° = \frac{1}{2}, \qquad \cos 30° = \frac{\sqrt{3}}{2}, \qquad \tan 30° = \frac{\sqrt{3}}{3},$$

$$\sin 60° = \frac{\sqrt{3}}{2}, \qquad \cos 60° = \frac{1}{2}, \qquad \tan 60° = \sqrt{3}.$$

We are now in a position to be able to determine easily the trigonometric function values for a number of special angles. If the terminal side of an angle falls on one of the axes, the function values are 0 or 1 or −1 or else are undefined. Thus we can determine function values for any multiple of 90°. We can also determine the function values for any angle whose terminal side makes a 30°, 45°, or 60° angle with the x-axis. Consider, for example, an angle of 150°, or $5\pi/6$. The terminal side makes a 30° angle with the x-axis, since 180° − 150° = 30°. As the next diagram shows, triangle *ONR* is congruent to triangle *ON'R'*, hence the ratios of the sides of the two triangles are the same except perhaps for sign. We could determine the function values directly from triangle *ONR*, but this is not necessary. If we remember that the sine is positive in quadrant II and that the cosine and tangent are negative, we can simply use the values for 30°, prefixing the appropriate sign. The triangle *ONR* is called a *reference* triangle and its acute angle at the origin is called a *reference* angle.

> **In general, to find the function values of an angle, we find them for the reference angle and prefix the appropriate sign.**

Example 2. Find the sine, cosine, and tangent of 600°, or $10\pi/3$.

We find the multiple of 180° nearest 600°:

$$180° \times 2 = 360°,$$
$$180° \times 3 = 540°,$$

and

$$180° \times 4 = 720°.$$

The nearest multiple is 540°. The difference between 600° and 540° is 60°. This gives us the reference angle.

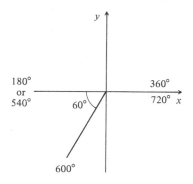

We recall that $\sin 60° = \sqrt{3}/2$, $\cos 60° = \frac{1}{2}$, and $\tan 60° = \sqrt{3}$. We also recall that the sine and cosine are negative in the third quadrant, and that the tangent is positive. Hence we have

$$\sin 600° = -\frac{\sqrt{3}}{2},$$

$$\cos 600° = -\frac{1}{2},$$

$$\tan 600° = \sqrt{3}. \qquad \textbf{[22–24]}$$

Exercise Set 8.3

Before beginning, make a list of the function values of 30°, 60°, and 45°. Then memorize your list. In Exercises 1–4, find the six trigonometric function values for the angle θ as shown.

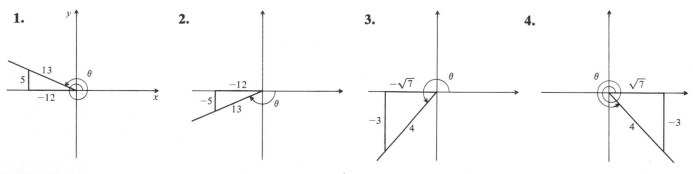

In Exercises 5 and 6, use the fact that $\sqrt{2} \approx 1.414$ and $\sqrt{3} \approx 1.732$.

5. Find decimal values for the six trigonometric functions of 30°.

6. Find decimal values for the six trigonometric functions of 60°.

Find the following if they exist.

7. cos 180°	**8.** sin 360°	**9.** tan 90°	**10.** cot 180°
11. sec 720°	**12.** csc 720°	**13.** sin (−270°)	**14.** cos 270°
15. sin 150°	**16.** cos 150°	**17.** tan 240°	**18.** cot 240°
19. sec 315°	**20.** csc 315°	**21.** tan (−315°)	**22.** cot (−315°)
23. sin (−210°)	**24.** cos (−210°)	**25.** tan 210°	**26.** cot 210°
27. $\sin \dfrac{11\pi}{4}$	**28.** $\cos \dfrac{11\pi}{4}$	**29.** $\tan \dfrac{11\pi}{6}$	**30.** $\cot \dfrac{11\pi}{6}$

8.4 More About Functions of Angles

GRAPHS

We have already graphed the trigonometric functions. In many applications it is helpful to consider these graphs, but with the horizontal axis marked in degrees. Such a graph for the sine function is shown here.

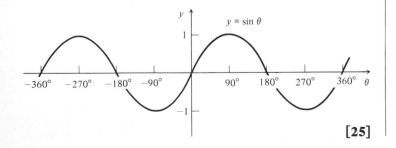

[25]

IDENTITIES

In Chapter 7 we developed several trigonometric identities. All of these hold, whether we are using radians or degrees. When we are using degrees, some of them of course look a little different. For example, the identity

$$\sin\left(x + \frac{\pi}{2}\right) \equiv \cos x$$

becomes

$$\sin (x + 90°) \equiv \cos x. \qquad \textbf{[26, 27]}$$

RELATIONSHIPS AMONG FUNCTION VALUES

When we know one of the trigonometric function values for an angle, we can find the other five if we know the quadrant in which the terminal side lies. The idea is to sketch a triangle in the appropriate quadrant, use the Pythagorean theorem to find the lengths of its sides as needed, and then read off the ratios of its sides.

Example 1. Given that $\tan \theta = -\frac{2}{3}$ and that θ is in the second quadrant, find the other function values.

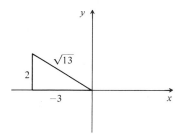

We first sketch a second quadrant triangle. Since $\tan \theta = -\frac{2}{3}$, we make the legs of lengths 2 and 3. The hypotenuse must then have length $\sqrt{13}$. Now we can read off the appropriate ratios:

$$\sin \theta = \frac{2}{\sqrt{13}}, \qquad \cos \theta = -\frac{3}{\sqrt{13}},$$

$$\tan \theta = -\frac{2}{3}, \qquad \cot \theta = -\frac{3}{2},$$

$$\sec \theta = -\frac{\sqrt{13}}{3}, \qquad \csc \theta = \frac{\sqrt{13}}{2}.$$

Example 2. Given that $\cot \theta = 2$ and θ is in the third quadrant, find $\sin \theta$, $\cos \theta$, and $\tan \theta$.

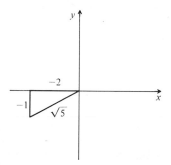

Again, we sketch a triangle and label the sides, then read off the appropriate ratios:

$$\sin \theta = -\frac{1}{\sqrt{5}}, \qquad \cos \theta = -\frac{2}{\sqrt{5}}, \qquad \tan \theta = \frac{1}{2}.$$

[28, 29]

COFUNCTIONS AND COMPLEMENTS

Recall that $\sin (90° - \theta) \equiv \cos \theta$. If θ is less than 90°, then $90° - \theta$ is its complement. Thus the sine of an acute angle is the cosine of its complement. A similar thing is true for all of the trigonometric functions. That is, a function value for an acute angle is the cofunction of its complement. The complete list of these relations is as follows:

$$\sin \theta \equiv \cos (90° - \theta), \qquad \cos \theta \equiv \sin (90° - \theta),$$

$$\tan \theta \equiv \cot (90° - \theta), \qquad \cot \theta \equiv \tan (90° - \theta),$$

$$\sec \theta \equiv \csc (90° - \theta), \qquad \csc \theta \equiv \sec (90° - \theta).$$

The names of three of these functions actually arose from these relations. The *co*sine was so named to mean the sine of the complement. The *co*tangent's name means tangent of the complement, and the *co*secant means the secant of the complement.

Example 3. Given that

$$\sin 18° = 0.3090, \qquad \cos 18° = 0.9511,$$

$$\tan 18° = 0.3249, \qquad \cot 18° = 3.078,$$

$$\sec 18° = 1.051, \qquad \csc 18° = 3.236,$$

find the six function values for 72°.

Since 72° and 18° are complements, we have $\sin 72° = \cos 18°$, etc., and the function values are

$$\sin 72° = 0.9511, \qquad \cos 72° = 0.3090,$$

$$\tan 72° = 3.078, \qquad \cot 72° = 0.3249,$$

$$\sec 72° = 3.236, \qquad \csc 72° = 1.051. \qquad [30]$$

Exercise Set 8.4

In Exercises 1 and 2, use graph paper.

1. Draw a graph of the tangent function with the horizontal axis marked in degrees.

2. Draw a graph of the cotangent function with the horizontal axis marked in degrees.

In Exercises 3–10, rewrite the identity in terms of degrees.

3. $\sin (x \pm \pi) \equiv -\sin x$

4. $\cos (x \pm \pi) \equiv -\cos x$

5. $\sin x \equiv \sin (x + 2k\pi)$

6. $\cos x \equiv \cos (x + 2k\pi)$

7. $\sin \left(x + \dfrac{\pi}{2} \right) \equiv \cos x$

8. $\cos \left(x + \dfrac{\pi}{2} \right) \equiv -\sin x$

9. $\sin \left(\dfrac{\pi}{2} - x \right) \equiv \cos x$

10. $\cos \left(\dfrac{\pi}{2} - x \right) \equiv \sin x$

11. Recall an identity for $\tan (x + \pi)$ and express it in terms of degrees.

12. Recall an identity for $\cot (x - \pi)$ and express it in terms of degrees.

13. Recall an identity for $\tan \left(x + \dfrac{\pi}{2} \right)$ and express it in terms of degrees.

14. Recall an identity for $\cot \left(x - \dfrac{\pi}{2} \right)$ and express it in terms of degrees.

15. Given that $\sin \theta = -\frac{1}{3}$ and that the terminal side is in quadrant III, find the other five function values of θ.

16. Given that $\cot \theta = -2$ and that the terminal side is in quadrant IV, find the other five function values of θ.

17. Given that $\cos \theta = -\frac{2}{3}$ and that the terminal side is in quadrant II, find the other five function values of θ.

18. Given that $\tan \theta = 5$ and that the terminal side is in quadrant I, find the other five function values of θ.

19. Given that

$\sin 65° = 0.9063, \quad \cos 65° = 0.4226,$

$\tan 65° = 2.145, \quad \cot 65° = 0.4663,$

$\sec 65° = 2.366 \quad \csc 65° = 1.103,$

find the six function values for 25°.

20. Given that

$\sin 32° = 0.5299, \quad \cos 32° = 0.8480,$

$\tan 32° = 0.6249, \quad \cot 32° = 1.600,$

$\sec 32° = 1.179, \quad \csc 32° = 1.887,$

find the six function values for 58°.

8.5 Tables of Trigonometric Functions

By use of certain formulas, theoretically determined, tables of values for the trigonometric functions have been constructed. Table 3 at the back of the book is such a table. A portion of it is shown below. This table gives the function values for angles from 0° to 90° only. Values for other angles can always be determined from these, since any angle has an acute reference angle. Note that angle measures are given in degrees and minutes (60 minutes = 1°) as well as radians. Values in the table are given for intervals of 10′ (10 minutes) and are correct to four digits.

Degrees	Radians	Sin	Cos	Tan	Cot	Sec	Csc		
36° 00′	.6283	.5878	.8090	.7265	1.376	1.236	1.701	.9425	54° 00′
10	312	901	073	310	368	239	695	396	50
20	341	925	056	355	360	241	688	367	40
30	.6370	.5948	.8039	.7400	1.351	1.244	1.681	.9338	30
40	400	972	021	445	343	247	675	308	20
50	429	995	004	490	335	249	668	279	10
37° 00′	.6458	.6018	.7986	.7536	1.327	1.252	1.662	.9250	53° 00′
10	487	041	969	581	319	255	655	221	50
20	516	065	951	627	311	258	649	192	40
30	.6545	.6088	.7934	.7673	1.303	1.260	1.643	.9163	30
40	574	111	916	720	295	263	636	134	20
50	603	134	898	766	288	266	630	105	10
44° 00′	.7679	.6947	.7193	.9657	1.036	1.390	1.440	.8029	46° 00′
10	709	967	173	713	030	394	435	999	50
20	738	988	153	770	024	398	431	970	40
30	.7767	.7009	.7133	.9827	1.018	1.402	1.427	.7941	30
40	796	030	112	884	012	406	423	912	20
50	825	050	092	942	006	410	418	883	10
45° 00′	.7854	.7071	.7071	1.000	1.000	1.414	1.414	.7854	45° 00′
		Cos	Sin	Cot	Tan	Csc	Sec	Radians	Degrees

The headings on the left of Table 3 range from 0° to 45° only. Thus the table may seem to be only half of what it should be. Function values from 45° to 90° are the cofunction values of their complements, however. Hence these can be found without further entries. For angles from 45° to 90° the headings on the right are used, together with the headings at the bottom. For example, sin 37° is found to be 0.6018 using the top and left headings. The cosine of 53° (the complement of 37°) is found also to be 0.6018, using the bottom and right headings.

Example 1. Find cos 37°20′.

We find 37°20′ in the left column and then *cos* at the top. At the intersection of this row and column we find the entry we seek:

$$\cos 37°20' = 0.7951.$$

Example 2. Find cot 0.9192.

Since no degree symbol is given, we know that the angle is in radians. We do not find 0.9192 on the left, under radians. This is because the angle is greater than 45° or π/4 radians. Therefore, we will use the right and bottom headings. At the right, under radians, we find 0.9192. Next we find *cot* at the bottom. At the intersection of this row and column we find the entry we seek:

$$\cot 0.9192 = 0.7627. \qquad [31\text{--}36]$$

FUNCTION VALUES FOR SMALL ANGLES

Consider the following diagram showing a unit circle and a small angle.

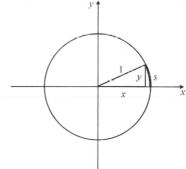

Since we are assuming *s* to be small, the length of arc *s* is very nearly the same as *y*. Also *x* is very nearly 1. Since $y = \sin s$, we see that $s \approx \sin s$. Since $\tan s = y/x$ and $x \approx 1$, we see that $\tan s \approx s$. These relations also hold if *s* is negative with small absolute value, and are useful in certain applications.

If $|s|$ is a small number, $s \approx \sin s \approx \tan s$ (a small angle—in radians—is approximately equal to its sine and its tangent).

[37]

MINUTES VERSUS TENTHS AND HUNDREDTHS

It is usual to express the measure of an angle in degrees and minutes, but it is often useful to have the measure in degrees, tenths, hundredths, etc. Thus we will need to know how to convert between these.

Examples

a) Convert 16.35° to degrees and minutes.

$$16.35° = 16° + 0.35 \times 1°$$

Now

$$0.35 \times 1° = 0.35 \times 60' = 21'.$$

So

$$16.35° = 16°21'.$$

b) Convert 34°37′ to degrees and decimal parts of degrees.

$$34°37' = 34° + \frac{37°}{60},$$

$$\frac{37}{60} = 0.617$$

so

$$34°37' = 34.617°. \qquad [38, 39]$$

INTERPOLATION

The process of linear interpolation, described in Section 6.4, can be applied to tables of any function. In particular, we can use it with tables of the trigonometric functions.

Example 1. Find $\tan 27°43'$.

The tabular difference is 0.0037, and 43′ is $\frac{3}{10}$ of the way from 40′ to 50′, so we take $\frac{3}{10}$ of 0.0037. This is 0.0011. Thus

$$\tan 27°43' = 0.5243 + 0.0011, \text{ or } 0.5254.$$

Interpolation for decreasing functions is about the same as for increasing functions, but there is a slight difference as the next example shows.

Example 2. Find $\cot 29°44'$.

We take 0.4 of the tabular difference, 0.012, and obtain 0.0048, or 0.005. Because the cotangent function is *decreasing* in the interval (0°, 90°], we *subtract* 0.005 from 1.756. Thus $\cot 29°44' = 1.751$.

Once the process of interpolation is understood, it will not be necessary to write as much as we did in the above examples. After a bit of practice, you will find that interpolation is rather easy, and you can accomplish some of the steps without writing.   [40, 41]

Let us look at an example of using the tables in reverse, that is, given a function value, to find the measure of an angle.

Example 3. Given $\tan B = 0.3727$, find B (between 0° and 90°).

$$\tan 20°20' = 0.3706$$
$$10' \quad \tan B \quad\ = 0.3727 \Big\} \ {-}0.0021$$
$$\tan 20°30' = 0.3739$$

Tabular difference is 0.0033.

We find that B is $\frac{21}{33}$ or $\frac{7}{11}$ of the way from $20°20'$ to $20°30'$. The tabular difference is $10'$, so we take $\frac{7}{11}$ of $10'$ and obtain $6'$. Thus $B = 20°26'$.   **[42, 43]**

FUNCTION VALUES FOR ANGLES OF ANY SIZE

Table 3 gives function values for angles from $0°$ to $90°$. For any other angle we can still use the table to find the function values. To do this, we first find the reference angle, which is the angle that the terminal side makes with the x-axis. We then look up the function values for the reference angle in the table and use the appropriate sign, depending on the quadrant in which the terminal side lies.

Example. Find $\sin 285°40'$.

We first find the reference angle. To do this we find the multiple of $180°$ that is nearest $285°40'$. The multiples of $180°$ are $180°$, $360°$, and so on. Now $285°40'$ is nearest $360°$. We subtract to find the reference angle.

$$\begin{array}{r} 359°60' \\ -285°40' \\ \hline 74°20' \end{array}$$

Now we find that $\sin 74°20' = 0.9628$. The terminal side is in quadrant IV, where the sine is negative. Hence

$$\sin 285°40' = -0.9628.$$

It is helpful to make a diagram like the one below showing the reference angle.

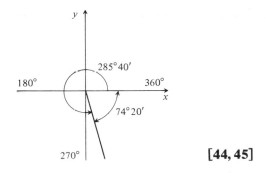

[44, 45]

Exercise Set 8.5

In Exercises 1 and 2, use Table 3 at the back of the book.

1. How big must an angle be in order that it first differs from its tangent in the fourth decimal place?

2. How big must an angle be in order that it first differs from its tangent in the third decimal place?

Convert to degrees and minutes.

3. $46.38°$ **4.** $85.21°$ **5.** $67.84°$ **6.** $38.48°$

Convert to degrees and decimal parts of degrees.

7. $45°45'$ **8.** $36°17'$ **9.** $76°53'$ **10.** $12°23'$

Use Table 3 to find the following.

11. $\sin 13°20'$ **12.** $\sin 41°40'$ **13.** $\cos 56°30'$ **14.** $\cos 71°50'$

15. $\tan 0.3956$ **16.** $\tan 0.7010$ **17.** $\cot 0.9134$ **18.** $\cot 1.0443$

19. $\sin 292°40'$ **20.** $\sin 283°20'$ **21.** $\cos 472°40'$ **22.** $\cos 514°30'$

23. $\tan(-237°50')$ **24.** $\tan(-423°10')$ **25.** $\sec 701°40'$ **26.** $\sec 653°50'$

27. $\sin 28°13'$ **28.** $\sin 36°42'$ **29.** $\cos 53°53'$ **30.** $\cos 80°33'$

31. $\tan 349°28'$ **32.** $\cot 253°34'$ **33.** $\sin 17.43°$ **34.** $\sin 38.72°$

35. $\cos 75.15°$ **36.** $\cos 81.91°$

For each of the following, find θ in degrees and minutes between 0° and 90°.

37. $\sin \theta = 0.2363$ **38.** $\sin \theta = 0.3854$ **39.** $\cos \theta = 0.3719$

40. $\cos \theta = 0.6361$ **41.** $\cos \theta = 0.3538$ **42.** $\cos \theta = 0.9678$

For each of the following, find θ in radians between 0 and $\pi/2$.

43. $\tan \theta = 0.4699$ **44.** $\cot \theta = 1.621$

45. $\sec \theta = 1.457$ **46.** $\csc \theta = 1.173$

Chapter 8 Test, or Review

For angles of the following measures, state in which quadrant the terminal side lies, convert to radian measure in terms of π, and convert to radian measure not in terms of π. Use 3.14 for π.

1. $87°$ **2.** $145°$ **3.** $30°$ **4.** $-30°$

Convert to degree measure.

5. $\dfrac{3\pi}{2}$ **6.** 4π

7. Find the length of an arc of a circle, given a central angle of $\pi/4$ and a radius of 7 cm.

8. An arc 18 m long on a circle of radius 8 m subtends an angle of how many radians? how many degrees, to the nearest degree?

9. A phonograph record revolves at 45 rpm. What is the linear velocity in cm/min of a point 4 cm from the center?

10. An automobile wheel has a diameter of 26 in. If the car travels 30 mph, what is the angular velocity in radians/hr of a point on the edge of the wheel?

11. Find the six trigonometric function values for the angle θ as shown.

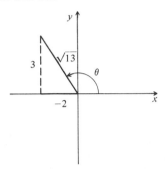

12. Complete the following table.

θ	0°	30°	45°	60°	90°	270°
$\sin \theta$						
$\cos \theta$						
$\tan \theta$						
$\cot \theta$						
$\sec \theta$						
$\csc \theta$						

Find the following exactly. Do not use the table.

13. $\sin 495°$

14. $\tan -315°$

15. $\cot 210°$

16. Draw a graph of the cosine function with the horizontal axis marked in degrees.

Given that $\tan \theta = 2/\sqrt{5}$ and that the terminal side is in quadrant III, find the following.

17. $\sin \theta$ **18.** $\cos \theta$ **19.** $\cot \theta$ **20.** $\sec \theta$ **21.** $\csc \theta$

Given $\sin \theta = 0.6820$, $\cos \theta = 0.7314$, $\tan \theta = 0.9325$, $\cot \theta = 1.0724$, $\sec \theta = 1.3673$, and $\csc \theta = 1.4663$, find the following.

22. $\sin (90° - \theta)$ **23.** $\cos (90° - \theta)$ **24.** $\tan (90° - \theta)$

25. $\cot (90° - \theta)$ **26.** $\sec (90° - \theta)$ **27.** $\csc (90° - \theta)$

28. Convert to degrees and minutes: 22.20°.

29. Convert to degrees and decimal parts of degrees: 47°33′.

Use Table 3 to find the following.

30. $\cos 8°20'$ **31.** $\tan 27°14'$ **32.** $\sec 44°30'$

33. $\cot \theta = 3.450$ and $0° < \theta < 90°$. Find θ.

34. $\sin \theta = 0.6293$ and $0° < \theta < 90°$. Find θ.

Trigonometric Identities, Inverse Functions, and Equations

9.1 Sum and Difference Formulas

We will now develop some important identities involving sums or differences of two numbers (or angles), first an identity for the cosine of the difference of two numbers. We shall use the Greek letters α (alpha) and β (beta) for these numbers. Let us consider a real number α in the interval $[\pi/2, \pi]$ and a real number β in the interval $[0, \pi/2]$. These determine points A and B on the unit circle as shown. The arc length s is $\alpha - \beta$, and we know that $0 \leqslant s \leqslant \pi$. Recall that the coordinates of A are $(\cos \alpha, \sin \alpha)$, and the coordinates of B are $(\cos \beta, \sin \beta)$.

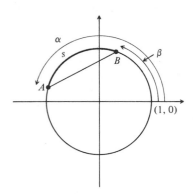

Using the distance formula, we can write an expression for the square of the distance AB:

$$AB^2 = (\cos \alpha - \cos \beta)^2 + (\sin \alpha - \sin \beta)^2.$$

This can be simplified as follows:

$$\begin{aligned} AB^2 &= \cos^2\alpha - 2\cos \alpha \cos \beta + \cos^2\beta \\ &\quad + \sin^2 \alpha - 2\sin \alpha \sin \beta + \sin^2 \beta \\ &= (\sin^2\alpha + \cos^2\alpha) + (\sin^2\beta + \cos^2 \beta) \\ &\quad - 2(\cos \alpha \cos \beta + \sin \alpha \sin \beta) \\ &= 2 - 2(\cos \alpha \cos \beta + \sin \alpha \sin \beta). \end{aligned}$$

Now let us imagine rotating the circle above so that point B is at $(1, 0)$. The coordinates of point A are now $(\cos s, \sin s)$. The distance AB has not changed.

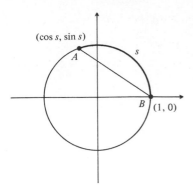

Again we use the distance formula to write an expression for the square of AB:

$$AB^2 = (\cos s - 1)^2 + (\sin s - 0)^2.$$

This simplifies as follows:

$$\begin{aligned} AB^2 &= \cos^2 s - 2\cos s + 1 + \sin^2 s \\ &= (\sin^2 s + \cos^2 s) + 1 - 2\cos s = 2 - 2\cos s. \end{aligned}$$

Equating our two expressions for AB^2 and simplifying, we obtain

$$\cos s = \cos \alpha \cos \beta + \sin \alpha \sin \beta. \qquad (1)$$

But $s = \alpha - \beta$, so we have the equation

$$\cos (\alpha - \beta) = \cos \alpha \cos \beta + \sin \alpha \sin \beta. \qquad (2)$$

This formula holds for any numbers α and β for which $\alpha - \beta$ is the length of the shortest arc from A to B; in other words, when $0 \leqslant \alpha - \beta \leqslant \pi$.

Example 1. Find $\cos \left(\dfrac{3\pi}{4} - \dfrac{\pi}{3} \right)$.

$$\begin{aligned} \cos \left(\frac{3\pi}{4} - \frac{\pi}{3} \right) &= \cos \frac{3\pi}{4} \cos \frac{\pi}{3} + \sin \frac{3\pi}{4} \sin \frac{\pi}{3} \\ &= -\frac{\sqrt{2}}{2} \cdot \frac{1}{2} + \frac{\sqrt{2}}{2} \cdot \frac{\sqrt{3}}{2} \\ &= \frac{\sqrt{2}}{4} (\sqrt{3} - 1) \quad \text{or} \quad \frac{\sqrt{6} - \sqrt{2}}{4} \end{aligned}$$

Example 2. Find $\cos 15°$.

$$\cos 15° = \cos(45° - 30°)$$
$$= \cos 45° \cos 30° + \sin 45° \sin 30°$$
$$= \frac{\sqrt{2}}{2} \cdot \frac{\sqrt{3}}{2} + \frac{\sqrt{2}}{2} \cdot \frac{1}{2}$$
$$= \frac{\sqrt{2}}{4}(\sqrt{3} + 1) \quad \text{or} \quad \frac{\sqrt{6} + \sqrt{2}}{4} \qquad [1,2]$$

Formula (1) above holds when s is the length of the shortest arc from A to B. Given any real numbers α and β, the length of the shortest arc from A to B is not always $\alpha - \beta$. However, $\cos s$ is always equal to $\cos(\alpha - \beta)$. We will not prove this in detail, but the following diagrams help to show how a proof would be done. The length of the shortest arc from A to B always turns out to be $\alpha - \beta$ or $\beta - \alpha$, plus some multiple of 2π.

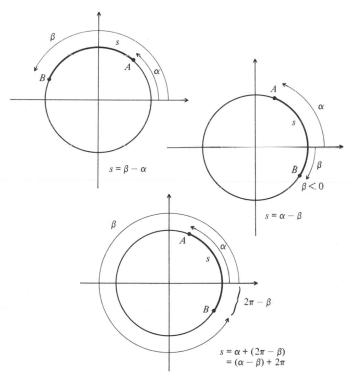

Since $s = |\alpha - \beta| + 2k\pi$, where k is an integer, we have

$$\cos s = \cos(|\alpha - \beta| + 2k\pi)$$
$$= \cos|\alpha - \beta|,$$

since the cosine function has a period of 2π. Now let us recall the identity $\cos(-s) \equiv \cos s$.

From this identity we see that we can drop the absolute value signs and then we know that $\cos s = \cos(\alpha - \beta)$ for any real numbers α and β. Thus Formula (2) holds for all real numbers α and β. That formula is thus the identity we sought.

$$\cos(\alpha - \beta) \equiv \cos \alpha \cos \beta + \sin \alpha \sin \beta$$

Example 3. Simplify

$$\sin\left(-\frac{5\pi}{2}\right)\sin\frac{\pi}{2} + \cos\frac{\pi}{2}\cos\left(-\frac{5\pi}{2}\right).$$

This is equal to

$$\cos\frac{\pi}{2}\cos\left(-\frac{5\pi}{2}\right) + \sin\frac{\pi}{2}\sin\left(-\frac{5\pi}{2}\right).$$

By the identity above we can simplify to

$$\cos\left[\frac{\pi}{2} - \left(-\frac{5\pi}{2}\right)\right], \quad \text{or} \quad \cos\frac{6\pi}{2}, \quad \text{or} \quad \cos 3\pi,$$

which is -1. $[3\text{--}5]$

OTHER FORMULAS

The other sum and difference formulas we seek follow easily from the one we have just derived. Let us consider $\cos(\alpha + \beta)$. This is equal to $\cos[\alpha - (-\beta)]$, and by the identity above, we have

$$\cos(\alpha + \beta) \equiv \cos \alpha \cos(-\beta) + \sin \alpha \sin(-\beta).$$

But $\cos(-\beta) \equiv \cos \beta$ and $\sin(-\beta) \equiv -\sin \beta$, so the identity we seek is the following.

$$\cos(\alpha + \beta) \equiv \cos \alpha \cos \beta - \sin \alpha \sin \beta.$$

To develop an identity for the sine of a sum, we recall the cofunction identity $\sin \theta \equiv \cos (\pi/2 - \theta)$. In this identity we shall substitute $\alpha + \beta$ for θ, obtaining $\sin (\alpha + \beta) \equiv \cos [\pi/2 - (\alpha + \beta)]$. We can now use the identity for the cosine of a difference. We get

$$\sin (\alpha + \beta) \equiv \cos \left[\frac{\pi}{2} - (\alpha + \beta) \right]$$

$$\equiv \cos \left[\left(\frac{\pi}{2} - \alpha \right) - \beta \right]$$

$$\equiv \cos \left(\frac{\pi}{2} - \alpha \right) \cos \beta + \sin \left(\frac{\pi}{2} - \alpha \right) \sin \beta$$

$$\equiv \sin \alpha \cos \beta + \cos \alpha \sin \beta.$$

Thus the identity we seek is

$$\sin (\alpha + \beta) \equiv \sin \alpha \cos \beta + \cos \alpha \sin \beta.$$

[6, 7]

To find a formula for the sine of a difference, we can use the identity just derived, substituting $-\beta$ for β. We obtain

$$\sin (\alpha - \beta) \equiv \sin \alpha \cos \beta - \cos \alpha \sin \beta.$$

A formula for the tangent of a sum can be derived as follows, using identities already established:

$$\tan (\alpha + \beta) \equiv \frac{\sin (\alpha + \beta)}{\cos (\alpha + \beta)}$$

$$\equiv \frac{\sin \alpha \cos \beta + \cos \alpha \sin \beta}{\cos \alpha \cos \beta - \sin \alpha \sin \beta} \cdot \frac{\dfrac{1}{\cos \alpha \cos \beta}}{\dfrac{1}{\cos \alpha \cos \beta}}$$

$$\equiv \frac{\dfrac{\sin \alpha \cos \beta}{\cos \alpha \cos \beta} + \dfrac{\cos \alpha \sin \beta}{\cos \alpha \cos \beta}}{\dfrac{\cos \alpha \cos \beta}{\cos \alpha \cos \beta} - \dfrac{\sin \alpha \sin \beta}{\cos \alpha \cos \beta}}$$

$$\equiv \frac{\dfrac{\sin \alpha}{\cos \alpha} + \dfrac{\sin \beta}{\cos \beta}}{1 - \dfrac{\sin \alpha \sin \beta}{\cos \alpha \cos \beta}} \equiv \frac{\tan \alpha + \tan \beta}{1 - \tan \alpha \tan \beta}.$$

Similarly, a formula for the tangent of a difference can be established. Following is a list of the sum and difference formulas. These should be memorized.

$$\cos (\alpha - \beta) \equiv \cos \alpha \cos \beta + \sin \alpha \sin \beta$$

$$\cos (\alpha + \beta) \equiv \cos \alpha \cos \beta - \sin \alpha \sin \beta$$

$$\sin (\alpha - \beta) \equiv \sin \alpha \cos \beta - \cos \alpha \sin \beta$$

$$\sin (\alpha + \beta) \equiv \sin \alpha \cos \beta + \cos \alpha \sin \beta$$

$$\tan (\alpha - \beta) \equiv \frac{\tan \alpha - \tan \beta}{1 + \tan \alpha \tan \beta}$$

$$\tan (\alpha + \beta) \equiv \frac{\tan \alpha + \tan \beta}{1 - \tan \alpha \tan \beta}$$

[8]

The identities involving sines and tangents can be used in the same way as those involving cosines in the earlier examples.

Example 4. Find $\tan 15°$.

$$\tan 15° = \tan (45° - 30°) = \frac{\tan 45° - \tan 30°}{1 + \tan 45° \tan 30°}$$

$$= \frac{1 - \sqrt{3}/3}{1 + \sqrt{3}/3} = \frac{3 - \sqrt{3}}{3 + \sqrt{3}}$$

Example 5. Simplify $\sin \dfrac{\pi}{3} \cos \pi + \sin \pi \cos \dfrac{\pi}{3}$.

This is equal to

$$\sin \frac{\pi}{3} \cos \pi + \cos \frac{\pi}{3} \sin \pi.$$

Thus by the fourth identity in the list above, we can simplify to

$$\sin \left(\frac{\pi}{3} + \pi \right), \quad \text{or} \quad \sin \frac{4\pi}{3}, \quad \text{or} \quad -\frac{\sqrt{3}}{2}.$$

[9, 10]

Exercise Set 9.1

In Exercises 1–8, use the sum and difference identities to write equivalent expressions.

1. $\sin (P + Q)$

2. $\sin (P - Q)$

3. $\cos (A - B)$

4. $\cos (A + B)$

5. $\tan (P - Q)$

6. $\tan (P + Q)$

7. $\sin (45° + 30°)$

8. $\cos (45° - 30°)$

In Exercises 9–24, simplify.

9. $\cos A \cos B - \sin A \sin B$

10. $\cos A \cos B + \sin A \sin B$

11. $\sin P \cos Q + \sin Q \cos P$

12. $\cos Q \sin P - \cos P \sin Q$

13. $\dfrac{\tan A - \tan B}{1 + \tan A \tan B}$

14. $\dfrac{\tan A + \tan B}{1 - \tan A \tan B}$

15. $\sin 37° \cos 22° + \cos 37° \sin 22°$

16. $\cos 37° \cos 22° - \sin 22° \sin 37°$

17. $\dfrac{\tan 20° + \tan 32°}{1 - \tan 20° \tan 32°}$

18. $\dfrac{\tan 35° - \tan 12°}{1 + \tan 35° \tan 12°}$

19. $\sin (\alpha + \beta) + \sin (\alpha - \beta)$

20. $\sin (\alpha + \beta) - \sin (\alpha - \beta)$

21. $\cos (\alpha + \beta) + \cos (\alpha - \beta)$

22. $\cos (\alpha + \beta) - \cos (\alpha - \beta)$

23. $\cos (u + v) \cos v + \sin (u + v) \sin v$

24. $\sin (u - v) \cos v + \cos (u - v) \sin v$

25. Find an identity for $\sin 2\theta$.
   [*Hint:* $2\theta = \theta + \theta.$]

26. Find an identity for $\cos 2\theta$.
   [*Hint:* $2\theta = \theta + \theta.$]

27. Derive an identity for $\cot (\alpha + \beta)$ in terms of $\cot \alpha$ and $\cot \beta$.

28. Derive an identity for $\cot (\alpha - \beta)$ in terms of $\cot \alpha$ and $\cot \beta$.

The cofunction identities can be derived from the sum and difference formulas. Derive identities for the following.

29. $\sin \left(\dfrac{\pi}{2} - x \right)$

30. $\cos \left(\dfrac{\pi}{2} - x \right)$

31. Find $\sin 45° + \sin 30°$ and compare with $\sin 75°$. (Use Table 3.)

32. Find $\cos 45° - \cos 30°$ and compare with $\cos 15°$. (Use Table 3.)

Given $\sin u = \frac{3}{5}$ and $\sin v = \frac{4}{5}$, and that u and v are between 0 and $\pi/2$, evaluate the following.

33. $\sin(u + v)$ **34.** $\sin(u - v)$ **35.** $\cos(u + v)$

36. $\cos(u - v)$ **37.** $\tan(u + v)$ **38.** $\tan(u - v)$

 Given that $\sin \theta = 0.6249$ and $\cos \phi = 0.1102$, and that θ and ϕ are both first-quadrant angles, find

39. $\sin(\theta + \phi)$ **40.** $\cos(\theta + \phi)$

▶ **41.** Find a formula for $\sin(\sin x + \sin y)$.   **42.** Find a formula for $\cos(\cos x + \cos y)$.

9.2 Half-Angle and Double-Angle Identities

Two important classes of trigonometric identities are known as the half-angle identities and the double-angle identities.

DOUBLE-ANGLE IDENTITIES

To develop these identities we shall use the sum formulas from the preceding section. We first develop a formula for $\sin 2\theta$. Recall that

$$\sin(\alpha + \beta) \equiv \sin \alpha \cos \beta + \cos \alpha \sin \beta.$$

We shall consider a number θ and substitute it for both α and β in this identity. We obtain

$$\sin(\theta + \theta) \equiv \sin 2\theta \equiv \sin \theta \cos \theta + \cos \theta \sin \theta$$
$$\equiv 2 \sin \theta \cos \theta.$$

The identity we seek is

$$\mathbf{\sin 2\theta \equiv 2 \sin\theta \cos\theta}.$$

Example 1. If $\sin \theta = \frac{3}{8}$ and θ is in the first quadrant, what is $\sin 2\theta$?

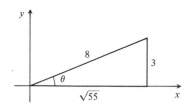

From the diagram, we see that $\cos \theta = \sqrt{55}/8$. Thus,

$$\sin 2\theta = 2 \sin \theta \cos \theta = 2 \cdot \frac{3}{8} \cdot \frac{\sqrt{55}}{8} = \frac{3\sqrt{55}}{32}.$$

[11]

Double-angle identities for the cosine and tangent functions can be derived in much the same way as the above identity:

$$\cos(\alpha + \beta) \equiv \cos \alpha \cos \beta - \sin \alpha \sin \beta$$
$$\cos 2\theta \equiv \cos(\theta + \theta) \equiv \cos \theta \cos \theta - \sin \theta \sin \theta$$
$$\equiv \cos^2\theta - \sin^2\theta$$
$$\mathbf{\cos 2\theta \equiv \cos^2\theta - \sin^2\theta}.$$

Now we derive an identity for $\tan 2\theta$.

$$\tan(\alpha + \beta) \equiv \frac{\tan \alpha + \tan \beta}{1 - \tan \alpha \tan \beta}$$

$$\tan 2\theta \equiv \tan(\theta + \theta) \equiv \frac{\tan \theta + \tan \theta}{1 - \tan \theta \tan \theta} \equiv \frac{2 \tan \theta}{1 - \tan^2\theta}$$

$$\mathbf{\tan 2\theta \equiv \frac{2 \tan \theta}{1 - \tan^2\theta}}$$

Example 2. Given that $\tan \theta = -\frac{3}{4}$ and θ is in the second quadrant, find $\sin 2\theta$, $\cos 2\theta$, $\tan 2\theta$, and the quadrant in which 2θ lies.

By drawing a diagram as shown, we find that $\sin \theta = \frac{3}{5}$ and $\cos \theta = -\frac{4}{5}$.

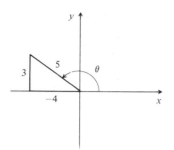

Now,

$$\sin 2\theta = 2 \sin \theta \cos \theta$$

$$= 2 \cdot \frac{3}{5} \cdot \left(-\frac{4}{5}\right) = -\frac{24}{25}$$

$$\cos 2\theta = \cos^2\theta - \sin^2\theta = \left(-\frac{4}{5}\right)^2 - \left(\frac{3}{5}\right)^2$$

$$= \frac{16}{25} - \frac{9}{25} = \frac{7}{25}$$

$$\tan 2\theta = \frac{2 \tan \theta}{1 - \tan^2\theta} = \frac{2 \cdot \left(-\frac{3}{4}\right)}{1 - \left(-\frac{3}{4}\right)^2}$$

$$= -\frac{\frac{3}{2}}{1 - \frac{9}{16}} = -\frac{24}{7}.$$

Since $\sin 2\theta$ is negative and $\cos 2\theta$ is positive, we know that 2θ is in quadrant IV. Note that $\tan 2\theta$ could have been found more easily in this case by dividing the values of $\sin 2\theta$ and $\cos 2\theta$.   [12]

Two other useful identities for $\cos 2\theta$ can easily be derived, as follows:

$$\cos 2\theta \equiv \cos^2\theta - \sin^2\theta$$

$$\equiv (1 - \sin^2\theta) - \sin^2\theta$$

$$\text{(using } \sin^2\theta + \cos^2\theta \equiv 1)$$

$$\equiv 1 - 2\sin^2\theta.$$

Similarly,

$$\cos 2\theta \equiv \cos^2\theta - \sin^2\theta$$

$$\equiv \cos^2\theta - (1 - \cos^2\theta)$$

$$\equiv 2\cos^2\theta - 1.$$

Solving these two identities for $\sin^2\theta$ and $\cos^2\theta$, respectively, we obtain two more identities that are often useful. Following is a list of double-angle identities. It should be memorized.

$$\sin 2\theta \equiv 2 \sin \theta \cos \theta$$

$$\cos 2\theta \equiv \cos^2\theta - \sin^2\theta$$

$$\cos 2\theta \equiv 1 - 2\sin^2\theta$$

$$\cos 2\theta \equiv 2\cos^2\theta - 1$$

$$\tan 2\theta \equiv \frac{2 \tan \theta}{1 - \tan^2\theta}$$

$$\sin^2\theta \equiv \frac{1 - \cos 2\theta}{2}$$

$$\cos^2\theta \equiv \frac{1 + \cos 2\theta}{2}$$

By division and the last two identities, it is always easy to deduce the following identity, which is also often useful:

$$\tan^2\theta \equiv \frac{1 - \cos 2\theta}{1 + \cos 2\theta}.$$

From the basic identities (in the lists to be memorized), others can be obtained.

Example 3. Find a formula for $\sin 3\theta$ in terms of function values of θ.

$$\sin 3\theta \equiv \sin(2\theta + \theta) \equiv \sin 2\theta \cos \theta + \cos 2\theta \sin \theta$$

$$\equiv (2 \sin \theta \cos \theta)\cos \theta + (2\cos^2\theta - 1)\sin \theta$$

$$\equiv 2 \sin \theta \cos^2\theta + 2 \sin \theta \cos^2\theta - \sin \theta$$

$$\sin 3\theta \equiv 4 \sin \theta \cos^2\theta - \sin \theta$$

Example 4. Find a formula for $\cos^3 x$ in terms of function values of x or $2x$, raised only to the first power.

$$\cos^3 x \equiv \cos^2 x \cos x \equiv \frac{1 + \cos 2x}{2} \cos x$$

[13, 14]

HALF-ANGLE IDENTITIES

To develop these identities, we use three of the previously developed ones. As shown below, we take square roots and replace θ by $\phi/2$.

$$\sin^2 \theta \equiv \frac{1 - \cos 2\theta}{2} \rightarrow \left|\sin \frac{\phi}{2}\right| \equiv \sqrt{\frac{1 - \cos \phi}{2}}$$

$$\cos^2 \theta \equiv \frac{1 + \cos 2\theta}{2} \rightarrow \left|\cos \frac{\phi}{2}\right| \equiv \sqrt{\frac{1 + \cos \phi}{2}}$$

$$\tan^2 \theta \equiv \frac{1 - \cos 2\theta}{1 + \cos 2\theta} \rightarrow \left|\tan \frac{\phi}{2}\right| \equiv \sqrt{\frac{1 - \cos \phi}{1 + \cos \phi}}$$

The half-angle formulas are those on the right above. We can eliminate the absolute value signs by introducing $\pm$ signs, with the understanding that we use + or − depending on the quadrant in which the angle lies. We thus obtain these formulas in the following form.

$$\sin \frac{\phi}{2} \equiv \pm \sqrt{\frac{1 - \cos \phi}{2}}$$

$$\cos \frac{\phi}{2} \equiv \pm \sqrt{\frac{1 + \cos \phi}{2}}$$

$$\tan \frac{\phi}{2} \equiv \pm \sqrt{\frac{1 - \cos \phi}{1 + \cos \phi}}$$

These formulas should be memorized. There are two other formulas for $\tan (\phi/2)$ that are often useful. They can be obtained as follows:

$$\left|\tan \frac{\phi}{2}\right| \equiv \sqrt{\frac{1 - \cos \phi}{1 + \cos \phi}} \equiv \sqrt{\frac{1 - \cos \phi}{1 + \cos \phi} \cdot \frac{1 + \cos \phi}{1 + \cos \phi}}$$

$$\equiv \sqrt{\frac{1 - \cos^2 \phi}{(1 + \cos \phi)^2}}$$

$$\equiv \sqrt{\frac{\sin^2 \phi}{(1 + \cos \phi)^2}} \equiv \frac{|\sin \phi|}{|1 + \cos \phi|}.$$

Now $1 + \cos \phi$ cannot be negative because $\cos \phi$ is never less than −1. Hence the absolute value signs are not necessary in the denominator. As the following graph shows, $\tan (\phi/2)$ and $\sin \phi$ have the same sign for all ϕ for which $\tan (\phi/2)$ is defined.

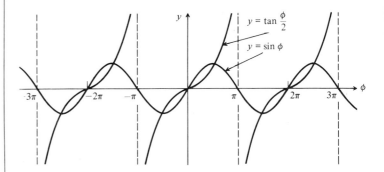

Thus we can dispense with the other absolute value signs, and obtain the formula we seek. A second formula can be obtained similarly.

$$\tan \frac{\phi}{2} \equiv \frac{\sin \phi}{1 + \cos \phi}, \qquad \tan \frac{\phi}{2} \equiv \frac{1 - \cos \phi}{\sin \phi}$$

These formulas have the advantage that they give the sign of $\tan (\phi/2)$ directly.

Example 5. Find $\sin 15°$.

$$\sin 15° = \sin \frac{30°}{2} = \pm\sqrt{\frac{1 - \cos 30°}{2}}$$

$$= \pm\sqrt{\frac{1 - (\sqrt{3}/2)}{2}}$$

$$= \pm\sqrt{\frac{2 - \sqrt{3}}{4}} = \frac{\sqrt{2 - \sqrt{3}}}{2}$$

(The expression is positive, because 15° is in the first quadrant.)

Example 6. Find $\tan \frac{\pi}{8}$.

$$\tan \frac{\pi}{8} = \tan \frac{\frac{\pi}{4}}{2} = \frac{\sin \frac{\pi}{4}}{1 + \cos \frac{\pi}{4}} = \frac{\frac{\sqrt{2}}{2}}{1 + \frac{\sqrt{2}}{2}}$$

$$= \frac{\sqrt{2}}{2 + \sqrt{2}}$$

$$= \sqrt{2} - 1 \qquad \text{(rationalizing the denominator)}$$

[15, 16]

Exercise Set 9.2

In Exercises 1–6, find $\sin 2\theta$, $\cos 2\theta$, $\tan 2\theta$, and the quadrant in which 2θ lies.

1. $\sin \theta = \dfrac{4}{5}$ (θ in quadrant I)

2. $\sin \theta = \dfrac{5}{13}$ (θ in quadrant I)

3. $\cos \theta = -\dfrac{4}{5}$ (θ in quadrant III)

4. $\cos \theta = -\dfrac{3}{5}$ (θ in quadrant III)

5. $\tan \theta = \dfrac{4}{3}$ (θ in quadrant III)

6. $\tan \theta = \dfrac{3}{4}$ (θ in quadrant III)

7. Find a formula for $\sin 4\theta$ in terms of function values of θ.

8. Find a formula for $\cos 4\theta$ in terms of function values of θ.

9. Find a formula for $\sin^4\theta$ in terms of function values of θ or 2θ or 4θ, raised only to the first power.

10. Find a formula for $\cos^4\theta$ in terms of function values of θ or 2θ or 4θ, raised only to the first power.

11. Find $\sin 75°$ without using tables. [*Hint:* $75 = 150/2$]

12. Find $\cos 75°$ without using tables.

13. Find $\tan 75°$ without using tables.

14. Find $\tan 67.5°$ without using tables. [*Hint:* $67.5 = 135/2$]

15. Find $\sin \dfrac{5\pi}{8}$ without using tables.

16. Find $\cos \dfrac{5\pi}{8}$ without using tables.

Simplify.

17. $\dfrac{\sin 2x}{2 \sin x}$

18. $\dfrac{\sin 2x}{2 \cos x}$

19. $1 - 2 \sin^2 \dfrac{x}{2}$

20. $2 \cos^2 \dfrac{x}{2} - 1$

21. $2 \sin \dfrac{x}{2} \cos \dfrac{x}{2}$

22. $2 \sin 2x \cos 2x$

23. $\cos^2 \dfrac{x}{2} - \sin^2 \dfrac{x}{2}$

24. $\cos^4 x - \sin^4 x$

25. $(\sin x + \cos x)^2 - \sin 2x$

26. $(\sin x - \cos x)^2 + \sin 2x$

27. $2 \sin^2 \dfrac{x}{2} + \cos x$

28. $2 \cos^2 \dfrac{x}{2} - \cos x$

29. $(-4 \cos x \sin x + 2 \cos 2x)^2 + (2 \cos 2x + 4 \sin x \cos x)^2$

30. $(-4 \cos 2x + 8 \cos x \sin x)^2 + (8 \sin x \cos x + 4 \cos 2x)^2$

31. $2 \sin x \cos^3 x + 2 \sin^3 x \cos x$

32. $2 \sin x \cos^3 x - 2 \sin^3 x \cos x$

Given that $\sin \theta = 0.3416$ and that θ is in the first quadrant, find

33. $\sin 2\theta$

34. $\cos 2\theta$

35. $\sin 4\theta$

36. $\cos 4\theta$

37. $\sin \dfrac{\theta}{2}$

38. $\cos \dfrac{\theta}{2}$

9.3 Proving Identities

One should remember certain trigonometric identities. Then as the occasion arises, other identities can be proved using those memorized. Following is a minimal list of identities that should be learned. Note that formulas involving cotangents, secants, and cosecants are not in this list. This is because these functions are reciprocals of the sine, cosine, and tangent, and thus formulas for the former can easily be derived from those for the latter.

A list of basic identities

$$\sin(-x) \equiv -\sin x,$$
$$\cos(-x) \equiv \cos x,$$
$$\tan(-x) \equiv -\tan x$$

Pythagorean identities

$$\sin^2 x + \cos^2 x \equiv 1,$$
$$1 + \tan^2 x \equiv \sec^2 x,$$
$$1 + \cot^2 x \equiv \csc^2 x$$

Cofunction identities

$$\sin\left(\frac{\pi}{2} - x\right) \equiv \cos x,$$

$$\cos\left(\frac{\pi}{2} - x\right) \equiv \sin x,$$

$$\tan\left(\frac{\pi}{2} - x\right) \equiv \cot x$$

Note: The other cofunction identities, as well as identities involving function values at $\pi \pm x$ or $x \pm \pi$, can easily be obtained from the sum and difference formulas.

Sum and difference formulas

$$\sin(\alpha \pm \beta) \equiv \sin\alpha\cos\beta \pm \cos\alpha\sin\beta,$$

$$\cos(\alpha \pm \beta) \equiv \cos\alpha\cos\beta \mp \sin\alpha\sin\beta,$$

$$\tan(\alpha \pm \beta) \equiv \frac{\tan\alpha \pm \tan\beta}{1 \mp \tan\alpha\tan\beta}$$

Note: In the above, where $\pm$ or $\mp$ appear, select either the top signs throughout a formula or the bottom signs throughout.

Double-angle formulas

$$\sin 2x \equiv 2\sin x\cos x,$$

$$\cos 2x \equiv \cos^2 x - \sin^2 x \equiv 1 - 2\sin^2 x$$

$$\equiv 2\cos^2 x - 1,$$

$$\tan 2x \equiv \frac{2\tan x}{1 - \tan^2 x},$$

$$\sin^2 x \equiv \frac{1 - \cos 2x}{2},$$

$$\cos^2 x \equiv \frac{1 + \cos 2x}{2}$$

Half-angle formulas

$$\sin\frac{x}{2} \equiv \pm\sqrt{\frac{1 - \cos x}{2}},$$

$$\cos\frac{x}{2} \equiv \pm\sqrt{\frac{1 + \cos x}{2}},$$

$$\tan\frac{x}{2} \equiv \pm\sqrt{\frac{1 - \cos x}{1 + \cos x}} \equiv \frac{\sin x}{1 + \cos x} \equiv \frac{1 - \cos x}{\sin x}$$

In proving other identities, using these, it is wise to consult the list to gain an idea of how to proceed. It is usually helpful to express all function values in terms of sines and cosines. *It is most important* in proving an identity to work with one side at a time. The idea is to simplify each side separately until the same expression is obtained in the two cases.

Example 1. Prove the following identity.

$$\tan^2 x - \sin^2 x \equiv \sin^2 x \tan^2 x$$

$\dfrac{\sin^2 x}{\cos^2 x} - \sin^2 x$	$\sin^2 x \dfrac{\sin^2 x}{\cos^2 x}$
$\dfrac{\sin^2 x - \sin^2 x\cos^2 x}{\cos^2 x}$	$\dfrac{\sin^4 x}{\cos^2 x}$
$\dfrac{\sin^2 x(1 - \cos^2 x)}{\cos^2 x}$	
$\dfrac{\sin^2 x \sin^2 x}{\cos^2 x}$	
$\dfrac{\sin^4 x}{\cos^2 x}$	

In this proof, a vertical line has been drawn as a reminder to work separately with the two sides. Everything has been expressed in terms of sines and cosines and then the two sides are simplified.

We work with each side separately because, as we saw in Chapter 2, "doing the same thing to both sides of an equation" does not always yield equivalent equations.

Example 2. Prove the following identity.

$$\frac{\sin 2\theta}{\sin \theta} - \frac{\cos 2\theta}{\cos \theta} \equiv \sec \theta$$

$\dfrac{2 \sin \theta \cos \theta}{\sin \theta} - \dfrac{\cos^2\theta - \sin^2\theta}{\cos \theta}$	$\dfrac{1}{\cos \theta}$
$\dfrac{2 \cos^2\theta - \cos^2\theta + \sin^2\theta}{\cos \theta}$	
$\dfrac{\cos^2\theta + \sin^2\theta}{\cos \theta}$	
$\dfrac{1}{\cos \theta}$	[17,18]

Note how the double-angle formulas are used in the above proof.

AN IDENTITY FOR $c \sin ax + d \cos ax$

An expression $c \sin ax + d \cos ax$, where a, c, and d are constants, is equivalent to an expression $A \sin (ax + b)$, where A and b are also constants. To prove this we shall look for the numbers A and b. First, let us consider the numbers $c/\sqrt{c^2 + d^2}$ and $d/\sqrt{c^2 + d^2}$. These numbers are the coordinates of a point on the unit circle because

$$\left(\frac{c}{\sqrt{c^2 + d^2}}\right)^2 + \left(\frac{d}{\sqrt{c^2 + d^2}}\right)^2 = 1.$$

Thus there is a number b for which these numbers are the cosine and sine, respectively. In other words,

$$\frac{c}{\sqrt{c^2 + d^2}} = \cos b,$$

and

$$\frac{d}{\sqrt{c^2 + d^2}} \equiv \sin b,$$

for some number b. Now we will consider the expression $c \sin ax + d \cos ax$, and multiply it by 1, as follows:

$$\frac{\sqrt{c^2 + d^2}}{\sqrt{c^2 + d^2}}[c \sin ax + d \cos ax]$$

$$\equiv \sqrt{c^2 + d^2}\left[(\sin ax) \cdot \frac{c}{\sqrt{c^2 + d^2}} + (\cos ax)\frac{d}{\sqrt{c^2 + d^2}}\right]$$

$$\equiv \sqrt{c^2 + d^2}\,[\sin ax \cos b + \cos ax \sin b].$$

Now, by the formula for the sine of a sum, we obtain

$$\sqrt{c^2 + d^2}\,\sin (ax + b).$$

Thus we have an identity as follows.

> **Theorem.** $c \sin ax + d \cos ax \equiv A \sin (ax + b)$, where $A = \sqrt{c^2 + d^2}$ and b is a number whose cosine is c/A and whose sine is d/A.

Example 3. Find an expression equivalent to $\sqrt{3} \sin x + \cos x$ that involves only the sine function.

In this expression, referring to the theorem above, we see that $c = \sqrt{3}$, $d = 1$, and $a = 1$. From this we find A and b:

$$A = \sqrt{c^2 + d^2} = \sqrt{3 + 1} = 2,$$

$$\cos b = \frac{\sqrt{3}}{2}, \quad \text{and} \quad \sin b = \frac{1}{2}.$$

Thus we can use 30° or $\pi/6$ for b. Thus,

$$\sqrt{3} \sin x + \cos x \equiv 2 \sin \left(x + \frac{\pi}{6}\right).$$

Example 4. Find an expression equivalent to $\sqrt{3}\sin(\pi/4)t + \cos(\pi/4)t$ involving only the sine function.

In this case $c = \sqrt{3}$, $d = 1$, and $a = \dfrac{\pi}{4}$.

$$A = \sqrt{3 + 1} = 2,$$

$$\cos b = \frac{\sqrt{3}}{2}, \quad \text{and} \quad \sin b = \frac{1}{2}.$$

Thus we have

$$\sqrt{3}\sin\frac{\pi}{4}t + \cos\frac{\pi}{4}t \equiv 2\sin\left(\frac{\pi}{4}t + \frac{\pi}{6}\right).$$

Example 5. Find an expression equivalent to $3\sin 2x - 4\cos 2x$ involving only the sine function.

In this case $c = 3$, $d = -4$, and $a = 2$.

$$A = \sqrt{3^2 + (-4)^2} = 5,$$

$$\cos b = \frac{3}{5}, \quad \text{and} \quad \sin b = -\frac{4}{5}.$$

Thus we have $3\sin 2x - 4\cos 2x \equiv 5\sin(2x + b)$, where b is a number whose cosine is $\frac{3}{5}$ and whose sine is $-\frac{4}{5}$. **[19, 20]**

Example 6. Graph $y = \sin x - \cos x$.

We first transform the righthand side to an expression involving only the sine function. Since $c = 1$ and $d = -1$, we have

$$A = \sqrt{1^2 + (-1)^2} = \sqrt{2},$$

$$\cos b = \frac{1}{\sqrt{2}}, \quad \text{and} \quad \sin b = -\frac{1}{\sqrt{2}}.$$

So $b = -\pi/4$ and we have $y = \sqrt{2}\sin(x - \pi/4)$. This can be graphed (see below) by translating the sine graph $\pi/4$ units to the right and stretching it vertically.

Skill in making graphs like this is important in such fields as engineering, electricity, and physics. **[21]**

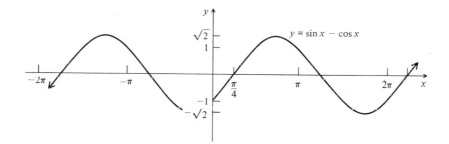

Exercise Set 9.3

In Exercises 1–32, prove the identities.

1. $\csc x - \cos x \cot x \equiv \sin x$

2. $\sec x - \sin x \tan x \equiv \cos x$

3. $\dfrac{1 + \cos\theta}{\sin\theta} + \dfrac{\sin\theta}{\cos\theta} \equiv \dfrac{\cos\theta + 1}{\sin\theta\cos\theta}$

4. $\dfrac{1}{\sin\theta\cos\theta} - \dfrac{\cos\theta}{\sin\theta} \equiv \dfrac{\sin\theta\cos\theta}{1 - \sin^2\theta}$

5. $\dfrac{1 - \sin x}{\cos x} \equiv \dfrac{\cos x}{1 + \sin x}$

6. $\dfrac{1 - \cos x}{\sin x} \equiv \dfrac{\sin x}{1 + \cos x}$

7. $\dfrac{1 + \tan \theta}{1 + \cot \theta} \equiv \dfrac{\sec \theta}{\csc \theta}$

8. $\dfrac{\cot \theta - 1}{1 - \tan \theta} \equiv \dfrac{\csc \theta}{\sec \theta}$

9. $\dfrac{\sin x + \cos x}{\sec x + \csc x} \equiv \dfrac{\sin x}{\sec x}$

10. $\dfrac{\sin x + \cos x}{\sec x + \csc x} \equiv \dfrac{\cos x}{\csc x}$

11. $\dfrac{1 + \tan \theta}{1 - \tan \theta} + \dfrac{1 + \cot \theta}{1 - \cot \theta} \equiv 0$

12. $\dfrac{\cos^2 \theta + \cot \theta}{\cos^2 \theta - \cot \theta} \equiv \dfrac{\cos^2 \theta \tan \theta + 1}{\cos^2 \theta \tan \theta - 1}$

13. $\dfrac{1 + \cos 2\theta}{\sin 2\theta} \equiv \cot \theta$

14. $\dfrac{2 \tan \theta}{1 + \tan^2 \theta} \equiv \sin 2\theta$

15. $\sec 2\theta \equiv \dfrac{\sec^2 \theta}{2 - \sec^2 \theta}$

16. $\cot 2\theta \equiv \dfrac{\cot^2 \theta - 1}{2 \cot \theta}$

17. $\dfrac{\sin (\alpha + \beta)}{\cos \alpha \cos \beta} \equiv \tan \alpha + \tan \beta$

18. $\dfrac{\cos (\alpha - \beta)}{\cos \alpha \sin \beta} \equiv \tan \alpha + \cot \beta$

19. $1 - \cos 5\theta \cos 3\theta - \sin 5\theta \sin 3\theta \equiv 2 \sin^2 \theta$

20. $2 \sin \theta \cos^3 \theta + 2 \sin^3 \theta \cos \theta \equiv \sin 2\theta$

21. $\dfrac{\tan \theta + \sin \theta}{2 \tan \theta} \equiv \cos^2 \dfrac{\theta}{2}$

22. $\dfrac{\tan \theta - \sin \theta}{2 \tan \theta} \equiv \sin^2 \dfrac{\theta}{2}$

23. $\cos^4 x - \sin^4 x \equiv \cos 2x$

24. $\dfrac{\cos^4 x - \sin^4 x}{1 - \tan^4 x} \equiv \cos^4 x$

25. $\dfrac{\tan 3\theta - \tan \theta}{1 + \tan 3\theta \tan \theta} \equiv \dfrac{2 \tan \theta}{1 - \tan^2 \theta}$

26. $\left(\dfrac{1 + \tan \theta}{1 - \tan \theta} \right)^2 \equiv \dfrac{1 + \sin 2\theta}{1 - \sin 2\theta}$

27. $\dfrac{\cos^3 x - \sin^3 x}{\cos x - \sin x} \equiv \dfrac{2 + \sin 2x}{2}$

28. $\dfrac{\sin^3 t + \cos^3 t}{\sin t + \cos t} \equiv \dfrac{2 - \sin 2t}{2}$

29. $\sin (\alpha + \beta) \sin (\alpha - \beta) \equiv \sin^2 \alpha - \sin^2 \beta$

30. $\cos (\alpha + \beta) \cos (\alpha - \beta) \equiv \cos^2 \alpha - \sin^2 \beta$

31. $\cos (\alpha + \beta) + \cos (\alpha - \beta) \equiv 2 \cos \alpha \cos \beta$

32. $\sin (\alpha + \beta) + \sin (\alpha - \beta) \equiv 2 \sin \alpha \cos \beta$

In Exercises 33–38, find an equivalent expression involving the sine function only.

33. $\sin 2x + \sqrt{3} \cos 2x$

34. $\sqrt{3} \sin 3x - \cos 3x$

35. $4 \sin x + 3 \cos x$

36. $4 \sin 2x - 3 \cos 2x$

37. Graph $y = \sin 2x - \cos 2x$

38. Graph $y = \sin x + \sqrt{3} \cos x$

Find equivalent expressions involving the sine function only.

39. $6.75 \sin 0.374x + 4.08 \cos 0.374x$

40. $97.81 \sin 0.8081x - 4.89 \cos 0.8081x$

▶ **41.** Show that

$$\begin{vmatrix} \cos x & \sin x \\ -\sin x & \cos x \end{vmatrix} = \begin{vmatrix} \cos x & -\sin x \\ \sin x & \cos x \end{vmatrix} = 1.$$

42. Show that

$$\log(\cos x - \sin x) + \log(\cos x + \sin x) = \log \cos 2x.$$

43. Show that

$$\begin{bmatrix} \cos x & \sin x \\ -\sin x & \cos x \end{bmatrix} \begin{bmatrix} \cos y & \sin y \\ -\sin y & \cos y \end{bmatrix} = \begin{bmatrix} \cos(x+y) & \sin(x+y) \\ -\sin(x+y) & \cos(x+y) \end{bmatrix}.$$

9.4 Inverses of the Trigonometric Functions

Recall that to obtain the inverse of any relation we interchange the first and second members of each ordered pair in the relation. If a relation is defined by an equation, say in x and y, interchanging x and y produces an equation of the inverse relation. The graphs of a relation and its inverse are reflections of each other across the line $y = x$. The x- and y-axes are interchanged in such a reflection. Let us consider the inverse of the sine function, $y = \sin x$. The inverse may be denoted several ways, as follows:

$$x = \sin y, \qquad y = \sin^{-1}x, \qquad y = \arcsin x.$$

Thus $\sin^{-1}x$ is a number whose sine is x.

The notation arcsin x arises because it is the length of an arc on the unit circle for which the sine is x. The notation $\sin^{-1}x$ is not exponential notation. It does *not* mean $1/\sin x$! Either of the latter two kinds of notation above can be read "the inverse sine of x" or "the arc sine of x" or "the number (or angle) whose sin is x." Notation is chosen similarly for the inverses of the other trigonometric functions: $\cos^{-1}x$ or arccos x, $\tan^{-1}x$ or arctan x, and so on.

Graphs of $y = \sin^{-1}x$ and $y = \tan^{-1}x$ are shown at the right. Note how they compare with the graphs of the sine function and tangent function.

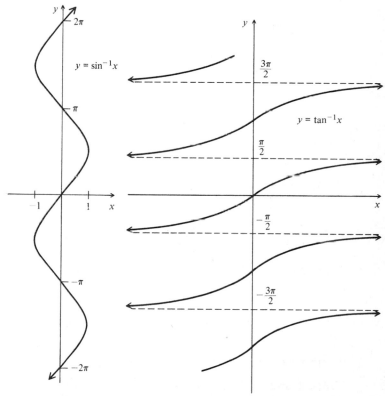

Note that these relations are not functions. **[22, 23]**

FINDING INVERSE VALUES

We shall illustrate finding inverse values using both a graph and the unit circle. In practice the unit circle is easier to use.

Example 1. Find all values of arcsin $\frac{1}{2}$.

On the graph of $y = \arcsin x$, we draw a vertical line at $x = \frac{1}{2}$ (see the figure). It intersects the graph at points whose y-value is arcsin $\frac{1}{2}$. Some of the numbers whose sine is $\frac{1}{2}$ are seen to be $\pi/6$, $5\pi/6$, $-7\pi/6$, and so on. From the graph we can see that $\pi/6$ plus any multiple of 2π is such a number. Also $5\pi/6$ plus any multiple of 2π is such a number. The complete set of values is given by $\pi/6 + 2k\pi$, k an integer, and $5\pi/6 + 2k\pi$, k an integer.

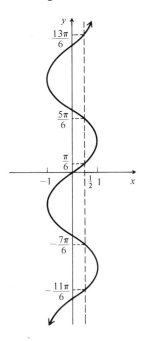

Example 2. Find all values of arcsin $\frac{1}{2}$.

On the unit circle there are two points at which the sine is $\frac{1}{2}$. The arc length for the point in the first quadrant is $\pi/6$ plus any multiple of 2π. The arc length for the point in the second quadrant is $5\pi/6$ plus any multiple of 2π. Hence we obtain all values of arcsin $\frac{1}{2}$ as follows:

$$\frac{\pi}{6} + 2k\pi \quad \text{or} \quad \frac{5\pi}{6} + 2k\pi, \quad k \text{ an integer.}$$

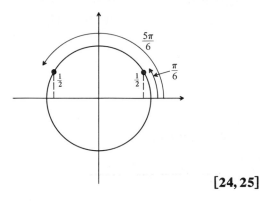

[24, 25]

Example 3. Find all values of $\cos^{-1}(-0.9397)$ in degrees.

From Table 3 we find that the angle whose cosine is 0.9397 is 20°. This is the reference angle. We sketch this on a unit circle to find the two points where the cosine is −0.9397. The angles are 160° and 200°, plus any multiple of 360°. Thus the values of $\cos^{-1}(-0.9397)$ are

$$160° + k \cdot 360° \quad \text{and} \quad 200° + k \cdot 360°,$$

where k is any integer.

Example 4. Find all values of arctan 1 (see the figure at the right).

We find the two points on the unit circle at which the tangent is 1. These points are opposite ends of a diameter. Hence the arc lengths differ by π. Thus we have for all values of arctan 1,

$$\frac{\pi}{4} + k\pi, \qquad k \text{ an integer.}$$

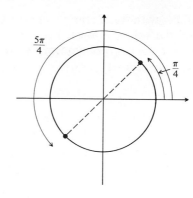

[26, 27]

PRINCIPAL VALUES

The inverses of the trigonometric functions are not themselves functions. However, if we restrict the ranges of these relations, we can obtain functions. The following graphs show how this restriction is made.

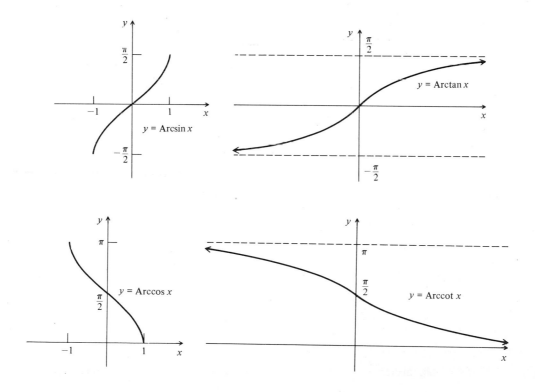

These relations with their ranges so restricted are functions, and the values in these restricted ranges are called *principal values*. To denote principal values we shall capitalize, as follows:

Arcsin x, $\text{Sin}^{-1}x$,   Arccos x, $\text{Cos}^{-1}x$,

and so on.

Thus, whereas arcsin $(\frac{1}{2})$ represents an infinite set of numbers, Arcsin $(\frac{1}{2})$ represents the single number $\pi/6$.

Note that for the function $y = $ Arcsin x the range is the interval $[-\pi/2, \pi/2]$. For the function $y = $ Arctan x the range is $(-\pi/2, \pi/2)$. For the function $y = $ Arccos x the range is $[0, \pi]$, and for $y = $ Arccot x the range is $(0, \pi)$. The diagrams at the right show where principal values are found on the unit circle.

Example 5. Find Arcsin $\sqrt{2}/2$ and $\text{Cos}^{-1}(-\frac{1}{2})$.

In the restricted range as shown in the figure, the only number whose sine is $\sqrt{2}/2$ is $\pi/4$. Hence Arcsin $\sqrt{2}/2 = \pi/4$.

The only number whose cosine is $-\frac{1}{2}$ in the restricted range is $2\pi/3$. Hence $\text{Cos}^{-1}(-\frac{1}{2}) = 2\pi/3$.   **[28–31]**

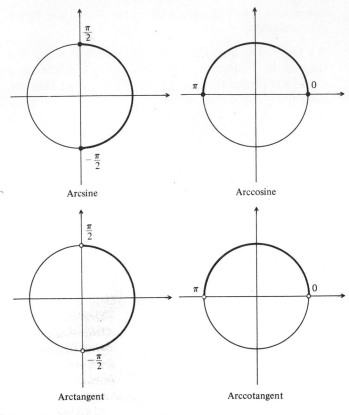

Arcsine   Arccosine

Arctangent   Arccotangent

Range restriction for principal values

Exercise Set 9.4

Find all values of the following without using tables.

1. $\arcsin \dfrac{\sqrt{2}}{2}$

2. $\arcsin \dfrac{\sqrt{3}}{2}$

3. $\cos^{-1} \dfrac{\sqrt{2}}{2}$

4. $\cos^{-1} \dfrac{\sqrt{3}}{2}$

5. $\sin^{-1}\left(-\dfrac{\sqrt{2}}{2}\right)$

6. $\sin^{-1}\left(-\dfrac{\sqrt{3}}{2}\right)$

7. $\arccos\left(-\dfrac{\sqrt{2}}{2}\right)$

8. $\arccos\left(-\dfrac{\sqrt{3}}{2}\right)$

9. $\arctan \sqrt{3}$

10. $\arctan \dfrac{\sqrt{3}}{3}$

11. $\cot^{-1}1$

12. $\cot^{-1}\sqrt{3}$

13. $\arctan\left(-\dfrac{\sqrt{3}}{3}\right)$ **14.** $\arctan(-\sqrt{3})$ **15.** $\operatorname{arccot}(-1)$ **16.** $\operatorname{arccot}(-\sqrt{3})$

17. $\operatorname{arcsec} 1$ **18.** $\operatorname{arcsec} 2$ **19.** $\csc^{-1} 1$ **20.** $\csc^{-1} 2$

Use tables to find, in degrees, all values of the following.

21. $\arcsin 0.3907$ **22.** $\arcsin 0.9613$ **23.** $\sin^{-1} 0.6293$ **24.** $\sin^{-1} 0.8746$

25. $\arccos 0.7990$ **26.** $\arccos 0.9265$ **27.** $\cos^{-1} 0.9310$ **28.** $\cos^{-1} 0.2735$

29. $\tan^{-1} 0.3673$ **30.** $\tan^{-1} 1.091$ **31.** $\cot^{-1} 1.265$ **32.** $\cot^{-1} 0.4770$

33. $\sec^{-1} 1.167$ **34.** $\sec^{-1} 1.440$ **35.** $\operatorname{arccsc} 6.277$ **36.** $\operatorname{arccsc} 1.111$

Find the following without using tables.

37. $\operatorname{Arcsin} \dfrac{\sqrt{2}}{2}$ **38.** $\operatorname{Arcsin} \dfrac{1}{2}$ **39.** $\operatorname{Cos}^{-1} \dfrac{1}{2}$ **40.** $\operatorname{Cos}^{-1} \dfrac{\sqrt{2}}{2}$

41. $\operatorname{Sin}^{-1}\left(-\dfrac{\sqrt{3}}{2}\right)$ **42.** $\operatorname{Sin}^{-1}\left(-\dfrac{1}{2}\right)$ **43.** $\operatorname{Arccos}\left(-\dfrac{\sqrt{2}}{2}\right)$ **44.** $\operatorname{Arccos}\left(-\dfrac{\sqrt{3}}{2}\right)$

45. $\operatorname{Tan}^{-1}\left(-\dfrac{\sqrt{3}}{3}\right)$ **46.** $\operatorname{Tan}^{-1}(-\sqrt{3})$ **47.** $\operatorname{Arccot}\left(-\dfrac{\sqrt{3}}{3}\right)$ **48.** $\operatorname{Arccot}(-\sqrt{3})$

Find the following, in degrees, using tables.

49. $\operatorname{Arcsin} 0.2334$ **50.** $\operatorname{Arcsin} 0.4514$ **51.** $\operatorname{Sin}^{-1}(-0.6361)$ **52.** $\operatorname{Sin}^{-1}(-0.8192)$

53. $\operatorname{Arccos}(-0.8897)$ **54.** $\operatorname{Arccos}(-0.2924)$ **55.** $\operatorname{Tan}^{-1}(-0.4074)$ **56.** $\operatorname{Tan}^{-1}(-0.2401)$

57. $\operatorname{Cot}^{-1}(-5.396)$ **58.** $\operatorname{Cot}^{-1}(-1.319)$

9.5 Combinations of Trigonometric Functions and Their Inverses

In practice, various combinations of trigonometric functions and their inverses arise. We shall discuss evaluating and simplifying such expressions. Let us consider, for example,

sin Arcsin x (the sine of a number whose sine is x).

Recall, from Chapter 3, that if a function f has an inverse that is also a function, then $f(f^{-1}(x)) = x$ and also $f^{-1}(f(x)) = x$ for all x in the domains of the functions. Since the sine and arcsine relations are inverses of each other, we might suspect that

$$\sin \operatorname{Arcsin} x = x$$

for all x in the domain of the Arcsin relation. However, we cannot apply the result of Chapter 3 here because the inverse of the sine function is not a function. Let us study sin Arcsin x using a unit circle. Consider a number a in the domain of the Arcsine function (a number from -1 to 1). Then Arcsin a is the length of an arc s as shown. Its sine is a. In other words.

$$s = \text{Arcsin } a.$$

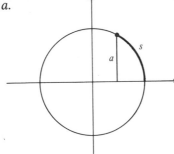

From the drawing, we see that $\sin s = a$. Substituting for s in the last equation, we get

$$\sin \text{Arcsin } a = a.$$

Thus it is true that sin Arcsin $x \equiv x$.

Similar identities hold for the other trigonometric functions.

sin Arcsin $x \equiv x$,	**cot Arccot $x \equiv x$,**
cos Arccos $x \equiv x$,	**sec Arcsec $x \equiv x$,**
tan Arctan $x \equiv x$,	**csc Arccsc $x \equiv x$.**

Now let us consider

$$\text{Arcsin } \sin x.$$

We might also suspect that this is always equal to x for any x, but this is not true unless x is in the range of the Arcsine function.

Example 1. Find Arcsin sin $3\pi/4$.

We first find sin $3\pi/4$. It is $\sqrt{2}/2$.

Next we find Arcsin $\sqrt{2}/2$. It is $\pi/4$.

So Arcsin sin $3\pi/4 = \pi/4$.   **[32–36]**

For any x in the range of the Arcsine function, we do have Arcsin sin $x = x$. Similar conditions hold for the other functions.

Theorem. The following are true if x is in the range of the inverse function. Otherwise they are not.

$$\text{Arcsin sin } x = x, \qquad \text{Arccot cot } x = x,$$

$$\text{Arccos cos } x = x, \qquad \text{Arcsec sec } x = x,$$

$$\text{Arctan tan } x = x, \qquad \text{Arccsc csc } x = x.$$

Now we shall consider some other kinds of combinations.

Example 2. Find sin Arctan (-1).

We first find Arctan (-1). It is $-\pi/4$.

Now we find the sine of this, $\sin(-\pi/4) = -\sqrt{2}/2$, so, sin Arctan $(-1) = -\sqrt{2}/2$.

Example 3. Find $\text{Cos}^{-1} \sin \pi/2$.

We first find sin $\pi/2$. It is 1.

Now we find $\text{Cos}^{-1}1$. It is 0, so $\text{Cos}^{-1} \sin \pi/2 = 0$.

                                        [37–40]

Now let us consider

$$\cos \text{Arcsin } \frac{3}{5}.$$

Without using tables, we cannot find Arcsin $\frac{3}{5}$. However, we can still evaluate the entire expression without using tables. In a case like this we sketch a triangle as follows. The angle θ in this triangle is an angle whose sine is $\frac{3}{5}$ (it is Arcsin $\frac{3}{5}$). We wish to find the cosine of this angle. Since the triangle is a right triangle, we can find the length of the base, b. It is 4. Thus we know that $\cos \theta = b/5$ or $\frac{4}{5}$. Therefore,

$$\cos \text{Arcsin } \frac{3}{5} = \frac{4}{5}.$$

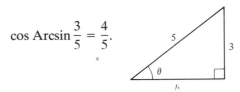

Example 4. Find sin Arccot $x/2$.

We draw a right triangle whose sides have lengths x and 2, so that $\cot \theta = x/2$. We find the length of the hypotenuse and then read off the sine ratio.

$$\sin \text{Arccot} \frac{x}{2} = \frac{2}{\sqrt{x^2 + 2^2}}$$

[41, 42]

In some cases the use of certain identities is needed to evaluate expressions.

Example 5. Evaluate $\sin (\text{Sin}^{-1} \frac{1}{2} + \text{Cos}^{-1} \frac{4}{5})$.

To simplify the use of an identity we shall make substitutions. Let

$$u = \text{Sin}^{-1} \frac{1}{2},$$

and

$$v = \text{Cos}^{-1} \frac{4}{5}.$$

Then we have $\sin (u + v)$. By a sum formula, this is equivalent to

$$\sin u \cos v + \cos u \sin v.$$

Now we make the reverse substitutions and obtain

$$\sin \text{Sin}^{-1} \frac{1}{2} \cdot \cos \text{Cos}^{-1} \frac{4}{5} + \cos \text{Sin}^{-1} \frac{1}{2} \cdot \sin \text{Cos}^{-1} \frac{4}{5}.$$

This immediately simplifies to

$$\frac{1}{2} \cdot \frac{4}{5} + \cos \text{Sin}^{-1} \frac{1}{2} \cdot \sin \text{Cos}^{-1} \frac{4}{5}.$$

Now $\cos \text{Sin}^{-1} \frac{1}{2}$ readily simplifies to $\sqrt{3}/2$.

To find $\sin \text{Cos}^{-1} \frac{4}{5}$, we shall need a triangle.

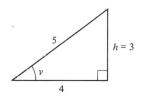

We find that $\sin \text{Cos}^{-1} \frac{4}{5} = \frac{3}{5}$. Our expression is now simplified to

$$\frac{1}{2} \cdot \frac{4}{5} + \frac{\sqrt{3}}{2} \cdot \frac{3}{5},$$

which simplifies to

$$\frac{4 + 3\sqrt{3}}{10}. \qquad \text{[43, 44]}$$

Exercise Set 9.5

Evaluate or simplify.

1. sin Arcsin 0.3

2. cos Arccos 0.2

3. $\tan \text{Tan}^{-1}(-4.2)$

4. $\cot \text{Cot}^{-1}(-1.5)$

5. $\text{Arcsin} \sin \frac{2\pi}{3}$

6. $\text{Arccos} \cos \frac{3\pi}{2}$

7. $\text{Sin}^{-1} \sin \left(-\frac{3\pi}{4}\right)$

8. $\text{Cos}^{-1} \cos \left(-\frac{\pi}{4}\right)$

9. $\text{Sin}^{-1} \sin \frac{\pi}{5}$

10. $\text{Cos}^{-1} \cos \dfrac{\pi}{7}$

11. $\text{Tan}^{-1} \tan \dfrac{2\pi}{3}$

12. $\text{Cot}^{-1} \cot \dfrac{2\pi}{3}$

13. $\sin \text{Arctan } \sqrt{3}$

14. $\sin \text{Arctan } \dfrac{\sqrt{3}}{3}$

15. $\cos \text{Arcsin } \dfrac{\sqrt{3}}{2}$

16. $\cos \text{Arcsin } \dfrac{\sqrt{2}}{2}$

17. $\tan \text{Cos}^{-1} \dfrac{\sqrt{2}}{2}$

18. $\tan \text{Cos}^{-1} \dfrac{\sqrt{3}}{2}$

19. $\text{Cos}^{-1} \sin \dfrac{\pi}{3}$

20. $\text{Cos}^{-1} \sin \pi$

21. $\text{Arcsin } \cos \dfrac{\pi}{6}$

22. $\text{Arcsin } \cos \dfrac{\pi}{4}$

23. $\text{Sin}^{-1} \tan \dfrac{\pi}{4}$

24. $\text{Sin}^{-1} \tan \left(-\dfrac{\pi}{4}\right)$

25. $\sin \text{Arctan } \dfrac{x}{2}$

26. $\sin \text{Arctan } \dfrac{a}{3}$

27. $\cos \text{Tan}^{-1} \dfrac{\sqrt{2}}{3}$

28. $\cos \text{Tan}^{-1} \dfrac{\sqrt{3}}{4}$

29. $\tan \text{Arcsin } 0.1$

30. $\tan \text{Arcsin } 0.2$

31. $\cot \text{Cos}^{-1}(-0.2)$

32. $\cot \text{Cos}^{-1}(-0.3)$

33. $\sin \text{Arccot } y$

34. $\sin \text{Arccot } x$

35. $\tan \left(\dfrac{1}{2} \text{Arcsin } \dfrac{4}{5}\right)$

36. $\tan \left(\dfrac{1}{2} \text{Arcsin } \dfrac{1}{2}\right)$

37. $\cos \left(\dfrac{1}{2} \text{Arcsin } \dfrac{1}{2}\right)$

38. $\cos \left(\dfrac{1}{2} \text{Arcsin } \dfrac{\sqrt{3}}{2}\right)$

39. $\sin \left(2 \text{Cos}^{-1} \dfrac{3}{5}\right)$

40. $\sin \left(2 \text{Cos}^{-1} \dfrac{1}{2}\right)$

41. $\cos \left(2 \text{Sin}^{-1} \dfrac{5}{13}\right)$

42. $\cos \left(2 \text{Cos}^{-1} \dfrac{4}{5}\right)$

43. $\sin \left(\text{Sin}^{-1} \dfrac{1}{2} + \text{Cos}^{-1} \dfrac{3}{5}\right)$

44. $\sin \left(\text{Sin}^{-1} \dfrac{1}{2} - \text{Cos}^{-1} \dfrac{4}{5}\right)$

45. $\cos \left(\text{Sin}^{-1} \dfrac{\sqrt{2}}{2} + \text{Cos}^{-1} \dfrac{3}{5}\right)$

46. $\cos \left(\text{Sin}^{-1} \dfrac{4}{5} - \text{Cos}^{-1} \dfrac{1}{2}\right)$

47. Find $\sin (\text{Sin}^{-1} 0.6032 + \text{Cos}^{-1} 0.4621)$.

48. Find $\cos (\text{Sin}^{-1} 0.7325 - \text{Cos}^{-1} 0.4838)$.

9.6 Angles Between Lines

Recall that a nonvertical line has an equation $y = mx + b$, where m is the slope. Note that such a line forms an angle with the positive half of the x-axis whose tangent is the slope of the line. As in this drawing,

$$\tan \theta = m.$$

One of the identities developed in Section 9.1 gives us an easy way to find an angle formed by two lines. We shall first consider the case in which neither line is vertical. Thus we shall consider two lines with equations:

$$l_1 : y = m_1 x + b_1,$$
$$l_2 : y = m_2 x + b_2.$$

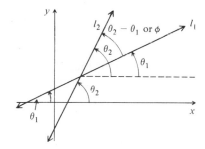

The slopes m_1 and m_2 are the tangents of the angles θ_1 and θ_2 that the lines form with the positive half of the x-axis. Thus we have $m_1 = \tan \theta_1$ and $m_2 = \tan \theta_2$. We wish to find the measure of the smallest angle through which l_1 can be rotated in the positive direc-

tion to get to l_2. In this case that angle is $\theta_2 - \theta_1$, or ϕ. We proceed as follows:

$$\tan \phi = \tan(\theta_2 - \theta_1) = \frac{\tan \theta_2 - \tan \theta_1}{1 + \tan \theta_2 \tan \theta_1}$$

$$= \frac{m_2 - m_1}{1 + m_2 m_1}.$$

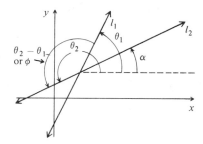

Suppose we had taken the lines in the reverse order. Then the smallest *positive* angle from l_1 to l_2 would be ϕ, as shown here. Note that $\tan \theta_1 = m_1$. Since $\theta_2 = \alpha + 180°$, $\tan \theta_2 = \tan \alpha$ and $\tan \theta_2 = m_2$. Thus the same formula for $\tan \phi$ derived above would hold. In the first case ϕ is an acute angle, so $\tan \phi$ will be positive. In the second case ϕ is obtuse, so $\tan \phi$ will be negative. Thus we have a general formula for finding the angle from one line to another.

Theorem. The smallest positive angle ϕ from a line l_1 to a line l_2 (where neither line is vertical) can be obtained from

$$\tan \phi = \frac{m_2 - m_1}{1 + m_2 m_1},$$

where m_1 and m_2 are the slopes of l_1 and l_2, respectively. If tan ϕ is positive, ϕ is acute. If tan ϕ is negative, then ϕ is obtuse.

Example 1. Two lines have slopes as follows: l_1 has slope $\sqrt{3}/3$, l_2 has slope $\sqrt{3}$. How large is the smallest positive angle from l_1 to l_2?

We have $m_1 = \sqrt{3}/3$ and $m_2 = \sqrt{3}$. Then

$$\tan \phi = \frac{\sqrt{3} - \dfrac{\sqrt{3}}{3}}{1 + \sqrt{3} \cdot \dfrac{\sqrt{3}}{3}} = \frac{\dfrac{3\sqrt{3} - \sqrt{3}}{3}}{\dfrac{3 + 3}{3}} = \frac{2\sqrt{3}}{6} = \frac{\sqrt{3}}{3}.$$

Since $\tan \phi$ is positive, ϕ is acute. Hence

$$\phi = \frac{\pi}{6} \quad \text{or} \quad 30°.$$

Example 2. Find the smallest positive angle from l_1 to l_2:

$$l_1 : 2y = x + 3, \qquad l_2 : 3y + 4x + 6 = 0.$$

We first solve for y to obtain the slopes.

$$l_1 : y = \frac{1}{2}x + \frac{3}{2}, \qquad \text{so } m_1 = \frac{1}{2}$$

$$l_2 : y = -\frac{4}{3}x - 2, \qquad \text{so } m_2 = -\frac{4}{3}$$

$$\tan \phi = \frac{-\dfrac{4}{3} - \dfrac{1}{2}}{1 + \left(-\dfrac{4}{3}\right)\left(\dfrac{1}{2}\right)} = \frac{\dfrac{-8 - 3}{6}}{\dfrac{6 - 4}{6}} = -\frac{11}{2} = -5.5$$

Since $\tan \phi$ is negative, we know that ϕ is obtuse. From the table we find an angle whose tangent is 5.5 to about $79°50'$. This is a reference angle. Subtracting from $180°$, we obtain

$$\phi = 100°10', \qquad \text{approximately.}$$

[45, 46]

PARALLEL AND PERPENDICULAR LINES

If two nonvertical lines are parallel, they make the same angle with the x-axis. Thus they have the same slope. Conversely, if they have the same slope, then

our formula for the angle between two lines will have a zero numerator and we have $\tan \phi = 0$. In this case the angle between the two lines is 0 and the lines are parallel.

> **Theorem. Nonvertical lines are parallel if and only if they have the same slope.**

If two nonvertical lines are perpendicular, then the angle ϕ between them is $90°$, and $\tan \phi$ is undefined. In the formula for $\tan \phi$ this means that the denominator must be 0, in which case $m_2 m_1 = -1$. Conversely, if $m_2 m_1 = -1$, the denominator will be 0, in which case $\tan \phi$ will be undefined and $\phi = 90°$.

> **Theorem. Nonvertical lines are perpendicular if and only if the product of their slopes is −1.**

Example 3. Determine whether the following lines are parallel, perpendicular, or neither.

a) $l_1 : y + 2 = 5x, \quad l_2 : 5y + x = -15.$

We solve for y:

$$l_1 : y = 5x - 2, \qquad l_2 : y = -\frac{1}{5}x - 3.$$

The slopes are 5 and $-\frac{1}{5}$. Their product is -1, so the lines are perpendicular.

b) $l_1 : 2y + 4x = 8, \quad l_2 : 5 + 2x = -y.$

By solving for y we determine that $m_1 = -2$ and $m_2 = -2$, so the lines are parallel.

c) $l_1 : 2x + 1 = y, \quad l_2 : y + 3x = 4.$

By solving for y we determine that $m_1 = 2$ and $m_2 = -3$, so the lines are neither parallel nor perpendicular. [47–49]

Example 4. Write equations of the lines perpendicular and parallel to the line $4y - x = 20$ and containing the point $(2, -3)$.

We first solve for y: $y = \frac{1}{4}x + 5$, so the slope is $\frac{1}{4}$. The slope of the perpendicular line is -4.

Now we use the point-slope equation to write an equation with slope -4 and containing the point $(2, -3)$:

$$y - y_1 = m(x - x_1)$$
$$y - (-3) = -4(x - 2).$$

This simplifies to $y = -4x + 5$.

The line parallel to the given line will have slope $\frac{1}{4}$. The equation is

$$y - (-3) = \frac{1}{4}(x - 2).$$

This simplifies to $y = \frac{1}{4}x - \frac{7}{2}$ or $4y + 14 = x$. **[50]**

VERTICAL LINES

If a line is vertical, it has no slope. Every vertical line has an equation $x = c$, where c is a constant. Any line parallel to a vertical line must also be vertical, hence must also have an equation $x = k$, where k is a constant.

A line will be perpendicular to a vertical line if and only if that line is horizontal. Every horizontal line has zero slope and has an equation $y = c$, where c is a constant. Thus if a line is vertical, it is simple to determine whether another line is parallel to it or perpendicular to it.

Example 5. Find equations of the lines parallel and perpendicular to the line $x = 4$ and containing the point $(-2, 3)$.

The line $x = 4$ is vertical, so any line parallel to it must be vertical. The line we seek has one x-coordinate which is -2, so all x-coordinates on the line must be -2. The equation is $x = -2$.

The perpendicular line has a y-coordinate which is 3, so all y-coordinates must be 3. The equation is $y = 3$.
[51]

Exercise Set 9.6

In Exercises 1–10, find the angle from l_1 to l_2.

1. $l_1: 3y = \sqrt{3}\,x + 2,$
$l_2: 3y + \sqrt{3}\,x = -3$

2. $l_1: 3y = \sqrt{3}\,x + 3,$
$l_2: y = \sqrt{3}\,x + 2$

3. $l_1: 2x = 3 - 2y,$
$l_2: x + y = 5$

4. $l_1: 2x = 3 + 2y,$
$l_2: x - y = 5$

5. $l_1: 2x - 5y + 1 = 0,$
$l_2: 3x + y - 7 = 0$

6. $l_1: 2x + y - 4 = 0,$
$l_2: y - 2x + 5 = 0$

7. $l_1: y = 3,$
$l_2: x + y = 5$

8. $l_1: y = 5,$
$l_2: x - y = 2$

9. $l_1: x + y = -3,$
$l_2: x - y = 2$

10. $l_1: 2x - 2y = 3,$
$l_2: 3x + 3y = 5$

In Exercises 11–14, determine whether the lines are parallel, perpendicular, or neither.

11. $2x - 5y = -3,$
$2x + 5y = 4$

12. $x + 2y = 5,$
$2x + 4y = 8$

13. $y = 4x - 5,$
$4y = 8 - x$

14. $y = -x + 7,$
$y = x + 3$

In Exercises 15–20, find an equation of the line containing the given point and parallel to the given line.

15. $(0, 3)$, $3x - y = 7$ **16.** $(-4, -5)$, $2x + y = -4$ **17.** $(3, 8)$, $x = 2$

18. $(3, -3)$, $x = -1$ **19.** $(-2, -3)$, $y = 4$ **20.** $(-3, 2)$, $y = -3$

In Exercises 21–26, find an equation of the line containing the given point and perpendicular to the given line.

21. $(-3, -5)$, $5x - 2y = 4$ **22.** $(3, -2)$, $3x + 4y = 5$ **23.** $(0, 3)$, $x = 1$

24. $(-2, -2)$, $x = 3$ **25.** $(-3, -7)$, $y = 2$ **26.** $(4, -5)$, $y = -1$

27. Find an equation of the line containing the point $(4, -2)$ and parallel to the line containing $(-1, 4)$ and $(2, -3)$.

28. Find an equation of the line containing the point $(-1, 3)$ and parallel to the line containing $(3, -5)$ and $(-2, -7)$.

Find the slope of line l_1, where m_2 is the slope of line l_2 and ϕ is the smallest positive angle from l_1 to l_2.

29. $m_2 = \dfrac{4}{3}$, $\phi = 45°$.

30. $m_2 = \dfrac{2}{3}$, $\phi = \text{Arctan}\,\dfrac{5}{2}$.

31. Line l_1 contains the points $(-2, 4)$ and $(5, -1)$. Find the slope of line l_2 such that the angle from l_1 to l_2 is $45°$.

32. Line l_1 contains $(3, -1)$ and $(-4, 2)$. Find the slope of line l_2 such that the angle from l_1 to l_2 is $-45°$.

33. Find an equation of the line parallel to the one given, and containing the given point.

$$4.323x - 7.071y = 16.61, \qquad (-2.603, 1.818)$$

34. Find an equation of the line containing the given point and perpendicular to the given line.

$$6.232x + 4.001y = 4.881, \qquad (3.149, -2.908)$$

35. Line l_1 contains the points $(-2.123, 3.899)$ and $(-4.892, -0.9012)$ and line l_2 contains $(0, -3.814)$ and $(5.925, 4.013)$. Find the smallest positive angle from l_1 to l_2.

9.7 Trigonometric Equations

When an equation contains a trigonometric expression with a variable such as sin x, it is called a *trigonometric equation.* To solve such an equation, we find all replacements for the variable that make the equation true.

Example 1. Solve $2 \sin x = 1$.

We first solve for sin x:

$$\sin x = \frac{1}{2}.$$

Now we note that the solutions are those numbers having a sine of $\frac{1}{2}$. We look for them. The unit circle is helpful. There are just two points on it for which the sine is $\frac{1}{2}$, as shown. They are the points for $\pi/6$ and $5\pi/6$. These numbers, plus any multiple of 2π, are the solutions

$$\frac{\pi}{6} + 2k\pi \qquad \text{or} \qquad \frac{5\pi}{6} + 2k\pi,$$

where k is any integer.

In degrees, the solutions are

$$30° + k \cdot 360° \qquad \text{or} \qquad 150° + k \cdot 360°,$$

where k is any integer.

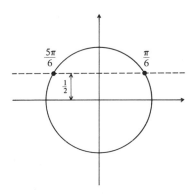

[52]

Example 2. Solve $4 \cos^2 x = 1$.

We first solve for $\cos x$:

$$\cos^2 x = \frac{1}{4}$$

$$|\cos x| = \frac{1}{2} \qquad \text{(taking principal square root)}$$

$$\cos x = \pm\frac{1}{2}.$$

Now we use the unit circle to find those numbers having a cosine of $\pm\frac{1}{2}$. The solutions are $\pi/3$, $2\pi/3$, $4\pi/3$, $5\pi/3$, plus any multiple of 2π.

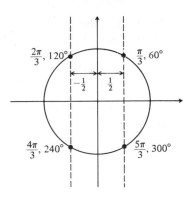

In solving trigonometric equations, it is usually sufficient to find just the solutions from 0 to 2π. We then remember that any multiple of 2π may be added to obtain the rest of the solutions.   **[53]**

The following example illustrates that when we look for solutions in the interval $[0, 2\pi)$ we must be cautious.

Example 3. Solve $2 \sin 2x = 1$ in the interval $[0, 2\pi)$.

We first solve for $\sin 2x$: $\sin 2x = \frac{1}{2}$.

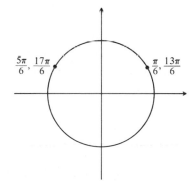

Using the unit circle we find points for which $\sin 2x = \frac{1}{2}$. However, since x is to run from 0 to 2π, we must let $2x$ run from 0 to 4π. These values of $2x$ are $\pi/6$,

$5\pi/6$, $13\pi/6$, and $17\pi/6$. Thus the desired values of x in $[0, 2\pi)$ are half of these. Therefore,

$$x = \frac{\pi}{12}, \frac{5\pi}{12}, \frac{13\pi}{12}, \frac{17\pi}{12}. \qquad \textbf{[54]}$$

In solving some trigonometric equations, it is necessary to use tables. In such cases, we usually find answers in degrees.

Example 4. Solve $2 + \sin x = 2.5299$.

We first solve for $\sin x$:

$$\sin x = 0.5299.$$

From the table we find the reference angle, $x = 32°$. Since $\sin x$ is positive, the solutions are to be found in the first and second quadrants. The solutions are

$$32° \quad \text{and} \quad 148°.$$

Example 5. Solve $\sin x - 1 = -1.5299$.

We first solve for $\sin x$:

$$\sin x = -0.5299.$$

From the table we find the reference angle, $32°$.

Since $\sin x$ is negative, the solutions are to be found in the third and fourth quadrants. The solutions are

$$212° \quad \text{and} \quad 328°. \qquad \textbf{[55, 56]}$$

In solving trigonometric equations, we can expect to apply some algebra before concerning ourselves with the trigonometric part. In the next examples, we begin by factoring.

Example 6. Solve $8 \cos^2\theta - 2 \cos \theta = 1$.

Since we will be using the principle of zero products, we first obtain a 0 on one side of the equation.

$$8 \cos^2\theta - 2 \cos \theta - 1 = 0$$

$$(4 \cos \theta + 1)(2 \cos \theta - 1) = 0 \quad \text{(factoring)}$$

$$4 \cos \theta + 1 = 0 \quad \text{or} \quad 2 \cos \theta - 1 = 0 \quad \text{(principle of zero products)}$$

$$\cos \theta = -\frac{1}{4} = -0.25 \quad \text{or} \quad \cos \theta = \frac{1}{2}$$

$$\theta = 104°30', 255°30' \quad \text{or} \quad \theta = 60°, 300° \left[\text{or } \frac{\pi}{3}, \frac{5\pi}{3}\right]$$

The solutions in $[0, 360°)$ are $104°30'$, $255°30'$, $60°$, and $300°$.

Example 7. Solve $2 \sin^2\phi + \sin \phi = 0$.

$$\sin \phi (2 \sin \phi + 1) = 0 \quad \text{(factoring)}$$

$$\sin \phi = 0 \quad \text{or} \quad 2 \sin \phi + 1 = 0 \quad \text{(principle of zero products)}$$

$$\sin \phi = 0 \quad \text{or} \quad \sin \phi = -\frac{1}{2}$$

$$\phi = 0, \pi \quad \text{or} \quad \phi = \frac{7\pi}{6}, \frac{11\pi}{6}$$

The solutions in $[0, 2\pi)$ are 0, π, $7\pi/6$, and $11\pi/6$.
$$\textbf{[57, 58]}$$

In case a trigonometric equation is quadratic but difficult or impossible to factor, we must use the quadratic formula.

Example 8. Solve $10 \sin^2 x - 12 \sin x - 7 = 0$.

$$\sin x = \frac{12 \pm \sqrt{144 + 280}}{20} \quad \text{(using the quadratic formula)}$$

$$= \frac{12 \pm \sqrt{424}}{20} = \frac{12 \pm 2\sqrt{106}}{20} = \frac{6 \pm \sqrt{106}}{10}$$

$$= \frac{6 \pm 10.296}{10}$$

$$\sin x = 1.6296 \quad \text{or} \quad \sin x = -0.4296$$

Since sines are never greater than 1, the first of the above equations has no solution. We look up the other number and find the reference angle to be $25°30'$ to the nearest $10'$. Thus the solutions are $205°30'$ and $334°30'$.
$$\textbf{[59]}$$

Exercise Set 9.7

Solve, finding all solutions.

1. $\sin x = \dfrac{\sqrt{3}}{2}$ **2.** $\cos x = \dfrac{\sqrt{3}}{2}$ **3.** $\cos x = \dfrac{1}{\sqrt{2}}$

4. $\tan x = \sqrt{3}$ **5.** $\sin x = 0.3448$ **6.** $\cos x = 0.6406$

Solve, finding all solutions in $[0, 2\pi)$ or $[0°, 360°)$.

7. $\cos x = -0.5495$ **8.** $\sin x = -0.4279$

9. $2 \sin x + \sqrt{3} = 0$ **10.** $\sqrt{3} \tan x + 1 = 0$

11. $2 \tan x + 3 = 0$ **12.** $4 \sin x - 1 = 0$

13. $4 \sin^2 x - 1 = 0$ **14.** $2 \cos^2 x = 1$

15. $\cot^2 x - 3 = 0$ **16.** $\csc^2 x - 4 = 0$

17. $2 \sin^2 x + \sin x = 1$ **18.** $2 \cos^2 x + 3 \cos x = -1$

19. $\cos^2 x + 2 \cos x = 3$ **20.** $2 \sin^2 x - \sin x = 3$

21. $4 \sin^3 x - \sin x = 0$ **22.** $2 \cos^2 x - \sqrt{3} \cos x = 0$

23. $2 \sin^2 \theta + 7 \sin \theta = 4$ **24.** $2 \sin^2 \theta - 5 \sin \theta + 2 = 0$

25. $6 \cos^2 \phi + 5 \cos \phi + 1 = 0$ **26.** $2 \sin^2 \phi + \sin \phi - 1 = 0$

27. $2 \sin t \cos t + 2 \sin t - \cos t - 1 = 0$ **28.** $2 \sin t \tan t + \tan t - 2 \sin t - 1 = 0$

29. $\cos 2x \sin x + \sin x = 0$ **30.** $\sin 2x \cos x - \cos x = 0$

9.8 Identities in Solving Equations

When a trigonometric equation involves more than one function, we may use identities to put it in terms of a single function. This can usually be done in several ways. In the following three examples, we illustrate by solving the same equation three different ways.

Example 1. Solve the equation $\sin x + \cos x = 1$.

To express $\cos x$ in terms of $\sin x$, we use the identity

$$\sin^2 x + \cos^2 x \equiv 1.$$

From this we obtain $\cos x \equiv \pm\sqrt{1 - \sin^2 x}$. Now we substitute:

$$\sin x \pm \sqrt{1 - \sin^2 x} = 1.$$

This is a radical equation. We get the radical alone on one side and then square both sides:

$$1 - \sin^2 x = 1 - 2 \sin x + \sin^2 x.$$

This simplifies to

$$-2 \sin^2 x + 2 \sin x = 0.$$

Now we factor:

$$-2 \sin x (\sin x - 1) = 0.$$

Using the principle of zero products,

$$-2 \sin x = 0 \quad \text{or} \quad \sin x - 1 = 0,$$
$$\sin x = 0 \quad \text{or} \quad \sin x = 1.$$

The values of x in $[0, 2\pi)$ satisfying these are

$$x = 0, \quad x = \pi, \quad \text{and} \quad x = \frac{\pi}{2}.$$

Now we check these in the original equation. We find that π does not check but the other values do. Thus the solutions are 0 and $\pi/2$.

It is important to check in examples such as these. Values are often obtained that are not solutions of the original equation.   **[60]**

Example 2. Solve $\sin x + \cos x = 1$.

This time we will square both sides, obtaining

$$\sin^2 x + 2 \sin x \cos x + \cos^2 x = 1.$$

Since $\sin^2 x + \cos^2 x \equiv 1$, we can simplify to

$$2 \sin x \cos x = 0.$$

Now we use the identity $2 \sin x \cos x \equiv \sin 2x$, and obtain

$$\sin 2x = 0.$$

The values in $[0, 2\pi)$ satisfying this equation are 0, $\pi/2$, π, and $3\pi/2$. Only 0 and $\pi/2$ check.   **[61]**

Example 3. Solve $\sin x + \cos x = 1$.

We recall that $c \sin ax + d \cos ax \equiv A \sin(ax + b)$, where $A = \sqrt{c^2 + d^2}$ and b is a number whose cosine is c/A and whose sine is d/A. In this case $c = d = a = 1$, so $A = \sqrt{2}$ and $b = \pi/4$. Thus our equation is equivalent to

$$\sqrt{2} \sin\left(x + \frac{\pi}{4}\right) = 1.$$

Then

$$\sin\left(x + \frac{\pi}{4}\right) = \frac{1}{\sqrt{2}} = \frac{\sqrt{2}}{2}$$

$$x + \frac{\pi}{4} = \frac{\pi}{4} \quad \text{or} \quad x + \frac{\pi}{4} = \frac{3\pi}{4}$$

$$x = 0 \quad \text{or} \quad x = \frac{\pi}{2}.$$

Both values check.   **[62]**

Example 4. Solve $2 \cos^2 x \tan x - \tan x = 0$.

First, we factor:

$$\tan x (2 \cos^2 x - 1) = 0.$$

Now we use the identity $2 \cos^2 x - 1 \equiv \cos 2x$.

$$\tan x \cos 2x = 0$$

$$\tan x = 0 \quad \text{or} \quad \cos 2x = 0 \qquad \text{(using principle of zero products)}$$

$$x = 0, \pi \quad \text{or} \quad 2x = \frac{\pi}{2}, \frac{3\pi}{2}, \frac{5\pi}{2}, \frac{7\pi}{2}$$

$$x = 0, \pi \quad \text{or} \quad x = \frac{\pi}{4}, \frac{3\pi}{4}, \frac{5\pi}{4}, \frac{7\pi}{4}$$

All values check. The solutions in $[0, 2\pi)$ are 0, π, $\pi/4$, $3\pi/4$, $5\pi/4$, and $7\pi/4$.   **[63]**

Example 5. Solve $\cos 2x + \sin x = 1$.

We first use the identity $\cos 2x \equiv 1 - 2\sin^2 x$, to get

$$1 - 2\sin^2 x + \sin x = 1$$

$$-2\sin^2 x + \sin x = 0$$

$$\sin x(1 - 2\sin x) = 0 \qquad \text{(factoring)}$$

$\sin x = 0$ or $1 - 2\sin x = 0$ (principle of zero products)

$\sin x = 0$ or $\sin x = \dfrac{1}{2}$

$x = 0, \pi$ or $x = \dfrac{\pi}{6}, \dfrac{5\pi}{6}$.

All values check. The solutions in $[0, 2\pi)$ are $0, \pi, \pi/6$, and $5\pi/6$. **[64]**

Example 6. Solve $\sin 5\theta \cos 2\theta - \cos 5\theta \sin 2\theta = \dfrac{\sqrt{2}}{2}$.

We use the identity

$$\sin(\alpha - \beta) \equiv \sin\alpha\cos\beta - \cos\alpha\sin\beta$$

to get $\sin 3\theta = \sqrt{2}/2$. Then

$$3\theta = \frac{\pi}{4}, \frac{3\pi}{4}, \frac{9\pi}{4}, \frac{11\pi}{4}, \frac{17\pi}{4}, \frac{19\pi}{4}$$

and

$$\theta = \frac{\pi}{12}, \frac{\pi}{4}, \frac{3\pi}{4}, \frac{11\pi}{12}, \frac{17\pi}{12}, \frac{19\pi}{12}.$$

Let us check $\pi/12$.

$$\sin\frac{5\pi}{12}\cos\frac{\pi}{6} - \cos\frac{5\pi}{12}\sin\frac{\pi}{6}.$$

We again use the above identity to obtain $\sin(5\pi/12 - \pi/6)$. This is equal to $\sin 3\pi/12$ or $\sin \pi/4$, and this is equal to $\sqrt{2}/2$. Hence $\pi/12$ checks. All of the above answers check. **[65]**

Example 7. Solve $\tan^2 x + \sec x - 1 = 0$.

We use the identity $1 + \tan^2 x \equiv \sec^2 x$. Substituting, we get

$$\sec^2 x - 1 + \sec x - 1 = 0,$$

or

$$\sec^2 x + \sec x - 2 = 0$$

$$(\sec x + 2)(\sec x - 1) = 0 \qquad \text{(factoring)}$$

$\sec x = -2$ or $\sec x = 1$ (principle of zero products)

$x = \dfrac{2}{3}\pi, \dfrac{4}{3}\pi$ or $x = 0$.

All of these values check. The solutions in $[0, 2\pi)$ are $0, 2\pi/3, 4\pi/3$.

Example 8. Solve $\sin x = \sin(2x - \pi)$.

We can use the identity $\sin(y - \pi) \equiv -\sin y$ or the identity $\sin(\alpha - \beta) \equiv \sin\alpha\cos\beta - \cos\alpha\sin\beta$ with the righthand side. We get

$$\sin x = -\sin 2x.$$

Next we use the identity $\sin 2x = 2\sin x \cos x$, and obtain

$\sin x = -2\sin x\cos x$, or $2\sin x\cos x + \sin x = 0$

$\sin x(2\cos x + 1) = 0$ (factoring)

$\sin x = 0$ or $\cos x = -\dfrac{1}{2}$ (principle of zero products)

$x = 0, \pi$ or $x = \dfrac{2\pi}{3}, \dfrac{4\pi}{3}$.

All of these values check, so the solutions in $[0, 2\pi)$ are $0, \pi, 2\pi/3$, and $4\pi/3$. **[66]**

Exercise Set 9.8

Find all solutions of the following equations in $[0, 2\pi)$.

1. $\tan x \sin x - \tan x = 0$

2. $2 \sin x \cos x + \sin x = 0$

3. $2 \sec x \tan x + 2 \sec x + \tan x + 1 = 0$

4. $2 \csc x \cos x - 4 \cos x - \csc x + 2 = 0$

5. $\sin 2x - \cos x = 0$

6. $\cos 2x - \sin x = 1$

7. $\sin 2x \sin x - \cos x = 0$

8. $\sin 2x \cos x - \sin x = 0$

9. $\sin 2x + 2 \sin x \cos x = 0$

10. $\cos 2x \sin x + \sin x = 0$

11. $\cos 2x \cos x + \sin 2x \sin x = 1$

12. $\sin 2x \sin x - \cos 2x \cos x = -\cos x$

13. $\sin 4x - 2 \sin 2x = 0$

14. $\sin 4x + 2 \sin 2x = 0$

15. $\sin 2x + 2 \sin x - \cos x - 1 = 0$

16. $\sin 2x + \sin x + 2 \cos x + 1 = 0$

17. $\sec^2 x = 4 \tan^2 x$

18. $\sec^2 x - 2 \tan^2 x = 0$

19. $\sec^2 x + 3 \tan x - 11 = 0$

20. $\tan^2 x + 4 = 2 \sec^2 x + \tan x$

21. $\cot x = \tan (2x - 3\pi)$

22. $\tan x = \cot (2x + \pi)$

23. $\cos (\pi - x) + \sin \left(x - \dfrac{\pi}{2} \right) = 1$

24. $\sin (\pi - x) + \cos \left(\dfrac{\pi}{2} - x \right) = 1$

25. $\dfrac{\cos^2 x - 1}{\sin \left(\dfrac{\pi}{2} - x \right) - 1} = \dfrac{\sqrt{2}}{2} + 1$

26. $\dfrac{\sin^2 x - 1}{\cos \left(\dfrac{\pi}{2} - x \right) + 1} = \dfrac{\sqrt{2}}{2} - 1$

27. $2 \cos x + 2 \sin x = \sqrt{6}$

28. $2 \cos x + 2 \sin x = \sqrt{2}$

29. $\sqrt{3} \cos x - \sin x = 1$

30. $\sqrt{2} \cos x - \sqrt{2} \sin x = 2$

Chapter 9 Test, or Review

Use the sum and difference formulas to write equivalent expressions. You need not simplify.

1. $\cos (X + Y)$

2. $\tan (45° - 30°)$

Simplify.

3. $\cos 27° \cos 16° + \sin 27° \sin 16°$

4. Given $\tan \alpha = \sqrt{3}$, $\sin \beta = \sqrt{2}/2$, and α and β are between 0 and $\pi/2$, evaluate $\tan(\alpha - \beta)$ exactly.

5. Find $\sin \dfrac{\pi}{8}$.

6. Simplify $\dfrac{\sin 2\theta}{\sin^2 \theta}$.

7. Prove the identity: $\tan 2\theta \equiv \dfrac{2 \tan \theta}{1 - \tan^2 \theta}$.

8. Find, in radians, all values of $\sin^{-1} \dfrac{1}{2}$.

9. Use a table to find, in degrees, all values of $\cot^{-1} 0.1584$.

10. Find $\mathrm{Sin}^{-1}\left(-\dfrac{\sqrt{2}}{2}\right)$.

11. Evaluate or simplify $\tan\left(\mathrm{Arctan} \dfrac{7}{8}\right)$.

12. Find the angle, to the nearest 10 minutes, from l_1 to l_2, given the equations

$$l_1: y = 2x - 4 \quad \text{and} \quad l_2: x - y = 2.$$

Determine whether the lines are parallel, perpendicular, or neither.

13. $3x - 2y = 8$
$6x - 4y = 2$

14. $y - 2x = 4$
$2y - 3x = -7$

15. $y = \dfrac{3}{2}x + 7$
$y = -\dfrac{2}{3}x - 4$

16. Find an equation of the line containing $(1, 4)$ and perpendicular to $y = x - 4$.

17. Solve: $\sin^2 x - 7 \sin x = 0$. Solutions in $[0, 2\pi)$.

18. Find an equivalent expression involving the sine function only: $6 \sin 3x + 2 \cos 3x$

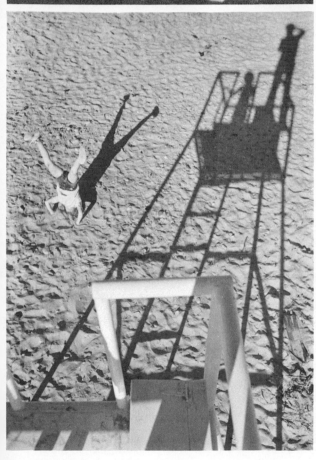

CHAPTER **10**

Triangles, Vectors, and Applications

10.1 Solving Right Triangles

The trigonometric functions are ratios of sides of triangles, as developed in Chapter 8. Triangles need not, however, be in standard position on a coordinate system, as in Chapter 8. In the right triangle shown below, the sine of angle A is a/c, the length of the side opposite A divided by the length of the hypotenuse.

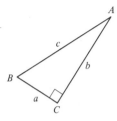

Similarly, $\cos A = b/c$, the length of the side adjacent to A, divided by the length of the hypotenuse. The other trigonometric ratios can be considered in a similar manner, as shown here. These relationships should be memorized.

$$\sin \theta = \frac{\text{opposite}}{\text{hypotenuse}}, \quad \cos \theta = \frac{\text{adjacent}}{\text{hypotenuse}},$$

$$\tan \theta = \frac{\text{opposite}}{\text{adjacent}}, \quad \cot \theta = \frac{\text{adjacent}}{\text{opposite}},$$

$$\sec \theta = \frac{\text{hypotenuse}}{\text{adjacent}}, \quad \csc \theta = \frac{\text{hypotenuse}}{\text{opposite}}.$$

As before, memorizing the first three of these is sufficient, because the other three are their reciprocals.

Example 1. In this triangle, find $\cos A$. Find $\tan B$.

$$\cos A = \frac{\text{adjacent}}{\text{hypotenuse}} = \frac{4}{5}$$

$$\tan B = \frac{\text{opposite}}{\text{adjacent}} = \frac{4}{3} \qquad \text{[1, 2]}$$

SOLVING TRIANGLES

A triangle has three sides and three angles. When the measures of certain of these parts are known, it is possible to find the measures of the rest. Doing this is called *solving* a triangle. Solving triangles is important in many applications of trigonometry. In fact, such applications were the beginnings of trigonometry. The word *trigonometry* actually means "triangle measurement."

Example 2. Find the measures of the acute angles of this triangle.

$$\cot A = \frac{18.00}{7.000} = 2.571, \qquad \text{correct to 4 digits*}$$

$$A = 21°15', \qquad \text{from the table}$$

$$B = 90° - A = 68°45'$$

In Example 2 the tangent function could also have been used. Both the tangent and cotangent functions involve the sides opposite and adjacent to angle A. Whenever an angle is to be found, we should choose a function that involves the known sides.

---

* We have written 18.00 and 7.000 to emphasize that we have four-digit precision. It is not essential that we always do this.

The precision to which we can find an angle, as in Example 2, depends on how precisely we know the lengths of the sides. In this case we determine the cotangent ratio to 4 digits, and this gives the angle measure to the nearest minute. The following table shows the precision in other cases.

Number of digits in ratio	Precision of angle measure
4	To nearest minute
3	To nearest ten minutes
2	To nearest degree

[3]

Example 3. Find the length b in this triangle. Use four-digit precision.

The known side is the hypotenuse. The side we seek is adjacent to the known angle. Thus we shall use the cosine: $\cos A = b/70$. Thus,

$$b = 70 \times \cos 19° = 70 \times 0.9455$$
$$b = 66.18. \qquad\qquad\qquad [4, 5]$$

When we solve a triangle, we find the *measures* of its sides and angles not already known. Note that we sometimes shorten this to saying that we "find the angles" or "find the sides."

APPLICATIONS OF SOLVING TRIANGLES

In many applied problems, unknown parts of right triangles are to be found.

Example 4. A device for measuring cloud height at night consists of a vertical beam of light, which makes a spot on the clouds. The spot is viewed from a point 135 ft away. The angle of elevation is 67°40′. (The angle between the horizontal and a line of sight is called an *angle of elevation* or an *angle of depression*, the latter if the line of sight is below the horizontal.) Find the height of the clouds.

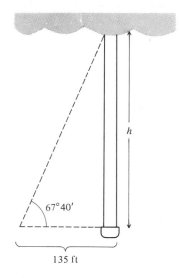

From the drawing we have

$$\frac{h}{135} = \tan 67°40′$$
$$h = 135 \times \tan 67°40′$$
$$= 135 \times 2.434 = 329 \text{ ft.}$$

In the preceding example, it should be noted that distances are precise to three digits and the angle is precise to the nearest ten minutes.   [6]

Example 5. From an observation tower two markers are viewed on the ground. The markers and the base of the tower are on a line and the observer's eye is 65.3 ft above the ground. The angles of depression to the markers are 53°10′ and 27°50′. How far is it from one marker to the other?

From the drawing on the following page, we see that the distance we seek is d, which is $d_1 - d_2$.

From the right triangles in the drawing, we have

$$\frac{d_1}{65.3} = \cot\theta_1 \quad \text{and} \quad \frac{d_2}{65.3} = \cot\theta_2.$$

Then

$$d_1 = 65.3\cot 27°50' \quad \text{and} \quad d_2 = 65.3\cot 53°10'.$$

$$\begin{aligned}d = d_1 - d_2 &= 65.3\cot 27°50' - 65.3\cot 53°10'\\ &= 65.3\,(\cot 27°50' - \cot 53°10')\\ &= 65.3\,(1.894 - 0.7490)\\ &= 74.8\text{ ft}\end{aligned}$$ [7]

Example 6. In aerial navigation, directions are given in degrees, clockwise from north. Thus east is 90°, south is 180°, and so on. An airplane leaves an airport and travels for 100 mi in a direction 300°. How far north of the airport is the plane then? How far west?

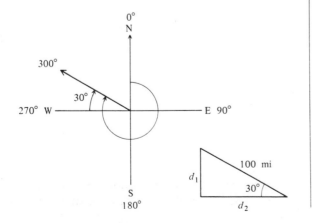

The direction of flight is as shown in the figure. Thus in the accompanying triangle above, d_1 is the northerly distance and d_2 is the westerly distance. Then

$$\frac{d_1}{100} = \sin 30° \quad \text{and} \quad \frac{d_2}{100} = \cos 30°,$$

$$\begin{aligned}d_1 &= 100\sin 30° = 100\times 0.5\\ &= 50\text{ mi (to the nearest mile)},\\ d_2 &= 100\cos 30° = 100\times 0.866\\ &= 87\text{ mi.}\end{aligned}$$

Example 7. In some applications directions, or *bearings*, are given by reference to north or south using an acute angle. For example, N 40°W means 40° west of north and S 30°E means 30° east of south. A forest ranger at point A sights a fire directly south of him. A second ranger at a point B, 7 miles east, sights the fire at a bearing of S 27°20'W. How far from A is the fire?

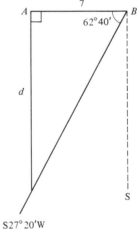

From the drawing we see that the desired distance d is part of a right triangle, as shown. We have

$$\frac{d}{7} = \tan 62°40'$$

$$\begin{aligned}d &= 7\tan 62°40'\\ &= 7\times 1.935\\ &= 13.5\text{ mi.}\end{aligned}$$ [8,9]

Exercise Set 10.1

In Exercises 1–18, standard lettering for a right triangle will be used: A, B, and C are the angles, C being the right angle. The sides opposite A, B, and C are a, b, and c, respectively. Solve the triangles, using three-digit precision.

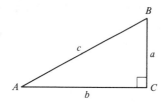

1. $A = 36°10'$, $a = 27.2$

2. $A = 87°40'$, $a = 9.73$

3. $B = 12°40'$, $b = 98.1$

4. $B = 69°50'$, $b = 127$

5. $A = 17°20'$, $b = 13.6$

6. $A = 78°40'$, $b = 1340$

7. $B = 23°10'$, $a = 0.0345$

8. $B = 69°20'$, $a = 0.00488$

9. $A = 47°30'$, $c = 48.3$

10. $A = 88°50'$, $c = 3950$

11. $B = 82°20'$, $c = 0.982$

12. $B = 56°30'$, $c = 0.0447$

13. $a = 12.0$, $b = 18.0$

14. $a = 10.0$, $b = 20.0$

15. $a = 16.0$, $c = 20.0$

16. $a = 15.0$, $c = 45.0$

17. $b = 1.80$, $c = 4.00$

18. $b = 100$, $c = 450$

19. A guy wire to a pole makes an angle of $73°10'$ with the level ground, and is 14.5 ft from the pole at the ground. How far above the ground is the wire attached to the pole?

20. A kite string makes an angle of $31°40'$ with the (level) ground and 455 ft of string is out. How high is the kite?

21. A road rises 3 m per 100 horizontal m. What angle does it make with the horizontal?

22. A kite is 120 ft high when 670 ft of string is out. What angle does the kite make with the ground?

23. What is the angle of elevation of the sun when a 6-ft man casts a 10.3-ft shadow?

24. What is the angle of elevation of the sun when a 35-ft mast casts a 20-ft shadow?

25. From a balloon 2500 ft high, a command post is seen with an angle of depression of $7°40'$. How far is it from a point on the ground below the balloon to the command post?

26. From a lighthouse 55 ft above sea level, the angle of depression to a small boat is $11°20'$. How far from the foot of the lighthouse is the boat?

27. An airplane travels at 120 km/h for 2 hr in a direction of 243° from Chicago. At the end of this time, how far south of Chicago is the plane?

28. An airplane travels at 150 km/h for 2 hr in a direction of 138° from Omaha. At the end of this time, how far east of Omaha is the plane?

29. Ship A is due west of a lighthouse. Ship B is 12 km south of ship A. From ship B the bearing to the lighthouse is N 63°20′E. How far is ship A from the lighthouse?

30. Lookout station A is 15 km west of station B. The bearing from A to a fire directly south of B is S 37°50′E. How far is the fire from B?

31. From a balloon two km high, the angles of depression to two towns in line with the balloon are 81°20′ and 13°40′. How far apart are the towns?

32. From a balloon 1000 m high, the angles of depression to two artillery posts, in line with the balloon, are 11°50′ and 84°10′. How far apart are the artillery posts?

33. A weather balloon is directly west of two observing stations 10 km apart. The angles of elevation of the balloon from the two stations are 17°50′ and 78°10′. How high is the balloon?

34. From two points south of a hill on level ground and 1000 ft apart, the angles of elevation of the hill are 12°20′ and 82°40′. How high is the hill?

▶ **35.** The base of this tetrahedron is an equilateral triangle. The other faces are isosceles triangles. Find b, s, and θ (a vertex angle).

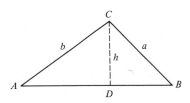

10.2 The Law of Sines

The trigonometric functions can be used to solve triangles that are not right triangles (oblique triangles). In order to solve oblique triangles we need to derive some properties, one of which is called the *law of sines*. We shall consider any oblique triangle. It may or may not have an obtuse angle. We will consider both cases, but the derivations are essentially the same.

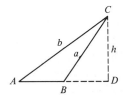

The triangles are lettered in the standard way, with angles A, B, and C and the sides opposite them a, b, and c, respectively. We have drawn an altitude from vertex C. It has length h. In either triangle we now have, from triangle ADC,

$$\frac{h}{b} = \sin A \qquad \text{or} \qquad h = b \sin A.$$

From triangle DBC on the left we have $h/a = \sin B$, or $h = a \sin B$. On the right we have $h/a = \sin(180° - B) = \sin B$. So in either kind of triangle we now have

$$h = b \sin A \qquad \text{and} \qquad h = a \sin B.$$

Thus it follows that

$$b \sin A = a \sin B.$$

We divide by $\sin A \sin B$ to obtain

$$\frac{a}{\sin A} = \frac{b}{\sin B}.$$

There is no danger of dividing by 0 here because we are dealing with triangles whose angles are never 0° or 180°.

If we were to consider an altitude from vertex A in the triangles shown above, the same argument would give us

$$\frac{b}{\sin B} = \frac{c}{\sin C}.$$

We combine these results to obtain the law of sines, which holds for right triangles as well as oblique triangles.

> **Theorem. (The law of sines.) In any triangle ABC,**
>
> $$\frac{a}{\sin A} = \frac{b}{\sin B} = \frac{c}{\sin C}$$
>
> **(the sides are proportional to the sines of the opposite angles).**

SOLVING TRIANGLES (AAS)

When two angles and a side of any triangle are known, the law of sines can be used to solve the triangle.

Example 1. In triangle ABC, $a = 4.56$, $A = 43°$, and $C = 57°$. Solve the triangle.

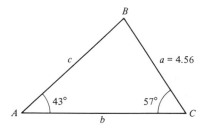

We first draw a sketch. We find B, as follows:

$$B = 180° - (43° + 57°)$$
$$= 80°.$$

We can now find the other two sides, using the law of sines:

$$\frac{c}{\sin C} = \frac{a}{\sin A}$$

$$c = \frac{a \sin C}{\sin A} = \frac{4.56 \sin 57°}{\sin 43°}$$

$$= \frac{4.56 \times 0.8387}{0.6820} = 5.61,$$

$$\frac{b}{\sin B} = \frac{a}{\sin A}$$

$$b = \frac{a \sin B}{\sin A} = \frac{4.56 \sin 80°}{0.6820}$$

$$= \frac{4.56 \times 0.9848}{0.6820} = 6.58.$$

We have now found the unknown parts of the triangle, $B = 80°$, $c = 5.61$, and $b = 6.58$.

A calculator or slide rule is of great help in doing calculations like this.

THE AMBIGUOUS CASE (SSA)

When two sides of a triangle and an angle opposite one of them are known, the law of sines can be used to solve the triangle. However, there may be more than one solution. Thus this is known as the ambiguous case. Suppose a, b, and A are given. Then the various possibilities are as shown in the four cases below.

Case 1

No solution, side a is too short to reach the base.

Case 2

One solution, side a just reaches the base and is perpendicular to it.

Case 3

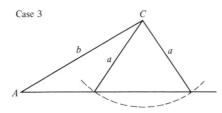

Two solutions, an arc of radius a meets the base at two points.

Case 4

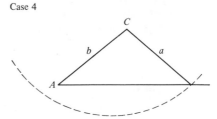

$a \geqslant b$. One solution, an arc of radius a meets the base at just one point, other than A.

The following examples correspond to the four possibilities described above.

Example 2. In triangle ABC, $a = 15$, $b = 25$, and $A = 47°$. Solve the triangle. We look for B:

$$\frac{a}{\sin A} = \frac{b}{\sin B}.$$

Then

$$\sin B = \frac{b \sin A}{a} = \frac{25 \sin 47°}{15} = \frac{25 \times 0.7314}{15} = 1.219.$$

Since there is no angle having a sine greater than 1, there is no solution.

Example 3. In triangle ABC, $a = 12$, $b = 5$, and $B = 24°38'$. Solve the triangle.

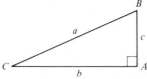

We look for A:

$$\frac{a}{\sin A} = \frac{b}{\sin B}$$

$$\sin A = \frac{a \sin B}{b} = \frac{12 \sin 24°38'}{5}$$

$$= \frac{12 \times 0.4168}{5} = 1.000$$

$$A = 90°.$$

Then $C = 90° - 24°38' = 65°22'$. Since $c/a = \cos B$,

$$c = a \cos B = 12 \times 0.9090 = 10.9.$$

Example 4. In triangle ABC, $a = 20$, $b = 15$, and $B = 30°$. Solve the triangle.

We look for A:

$$\frac{a}{\sin A} = \frac{b}{\sin B}$$

$$\sin A = \frac{a \sin B}{b} = \frac{20 \sin 30°}{15}$$

$$= \frac{20 \times 0.5}{15} = 0.6667.$$

There are two angles less than 180° having a sine of 0.6667. They are 42° and 138°. This gives us two possible solutions.

Possible solution 1. We know that $A = 42°$. Then $C = 180° - (30° + 42°) = 108°$.

We now find c:

$$\frac{c}{\sin C} = \frac{b}{\sin B}$$

$$c = \frac{b \sin C}{\sin B} = \frac{15 \sin 108°}{\sin 30°}$$

$$= \frac{15 \times 0.9511}{0.5} = 28.5.$$

These parts make a triangle, as shown; hence we have a solution

Possible solution 2. $A = 138°$. Then $C = 12°$.

We now find c:

$$c = \frac{b \sin C}{\sin B} = \frac{15 \sin 12°}{\sin 30°}$$

$$= \frac{15 \times 0.2079}{0.5} = 6.2.$$

These parts make a triangle; hence we have a second solution.

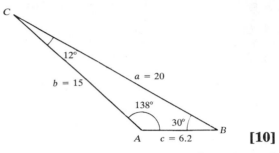

[10]

Example 5. In triangle ABC, $a = 25$, $b = 10$, and $A = 42°$. Solve the triangle.

We look for B:

$$\frac{b}{\sin B} = \frac{a}{\sin A}$$

$$\sin B = \frac{b \sin A}{a} = \frac{10 \sin 42°}{25}$$

$$= \frac{10 \times 0.6691}{25} = 0.2676.$$

Then $B = 15°30'$ or $B = 164°30'$.

Since $a > b$, we know there is only one solution. If we had not noticed this, we could tell it now. An angle of 164°30' cannot be an angle of this triangle because it already has an angle of 42°, and these two would total more than 180°.

$$C = 180° - (42° + 15°30') = 122°30',$$

$$\frac{c}{\sin C} = \frac{a}{\sin A},$$

so

$$c = \frac{a \sin C}{\sin A}$$

$$= \frac{25 \sin 122°30'}{\sin 42°}$$

$$c = \frac{25 \times 0.8434}{0.6691} = 31.5$$

[11]

Exercise Set 10.2

In Exercises 1–12, solve the triangle *ABC*.

1. $A = 133°,$ $B = 30°,$ $b = 18$

2. $B = 120°,$ $C = 30°,$ $a = 16$

3. $B = 38°,$ $C = 21°,$ $b = 24$

4. $A = 131°,$ $C = 23°,$ $b = 10$

5. $A = 68°30',$ $C = 42°40',$ $c = 23.5$

6. $B = 118°20',$ $C = 45°40',$ $b = 42.1$

7. $A = 36°,$ $a = 24,$ $b = 34$

8. $C = 43°,$ $c = 28,$ $b = 27$

9. $A = 116°20',$ $a = 17.2,$ $c = 13.5$

10. $A = 47°50',$ $a = 28.3,$ $b = 18.2$

11. $C = 61°10',$ $c = 30.3,$ $b = 24.2$

12. $B = 58°40',$ $a = 25.1,$ $b = 32.6$

13. Points *A* and *B* are on opposite sides of a lunar crater. A point *C* is 50 meters from *A*. The measure of $\angle BAC$ is determined to be 112° and the measure of $\angle ACB$ is determined to be 42°. What is the width of the crater?

14. A guy wire to a pole makes a 71° angle with level ground. At a point 25 ft farther from the pole than the guy wire, the angle of elevation of the top of the pole is 37°. How long is the guy wire?

15. A pole leans away from the sun at an angle of 7° to the vertical. When the angle of elevation of the sun is 51°, the pole casts a shadow 47 ft long on level ground. How long is the pole?

16. A vertical pole stands by a road that is inclined 10° to the horizontal. When the angle of elevation of the sun is 23°, the pole casts a shadow 38 ft long directly downhill along the road. How long is the pole?

17. A reconnaissance airplane leaves its airport on the east coast of the United States and flies in a direction of 085°. Because of bad weather it returns to another airport 230 km to the north of its home base. For the return it flies in a direction of 283°. What was the total distance it flew?

18. Lookout station *B* is 10.2 km east of station *A*. The bearing of a fire from *A* is S 10°40'W. The bearing of the fire from *B* is S 31°20'W. How far is the fire from *A*? from *B*?

19. A boat leaves a lighthouse *A* and sails 5.1 km. At this time it is sighted from lighthouse *B*, 7.2 km west of *A*. The bearing of the boat from *B* is N 65°10'E. How far is the boat from *B*?

20. An airplane leaves airport *A* and flies 200 km. At this time its bearing from airport *B*, 250 km to the west, is 120°. How far is the airplane from *B*?

10.3 The Law of Cosines

A second property of triangles important in solving oblique triangles is called the *law of cosines*. To derive this property we shall consider any triangle *ABC* placed on a coordinate system. We will place the origin at one of the vertices, say *C*, and the positive half of the *x*-axis along one of the sides, say *CB*. Then the coordinates of B are $(a, 0)$, and the coordinates of A are $(b \cos C, b \sin C)$.

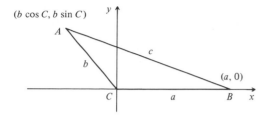

We will next use the distance formula to determine c^2:

$$c^2 = (b \cos C - a)^2 + (b \sin C - 0)^2.$$

Now we multiply and simplify:

$$c^2 = b^2 \cos^2 C - 2ab \cos C + a^2 + b^2 \sin^2 C$$

$$c^2 = a^2 + b^2(\sin^2 C + \cos^2 C) - 2ab \cos C$$

$$c^2 = a^2 + b^2 - 2ab \cos C.$$

Had we placed the origin at one of the other vertices, we would have obtained

$$a^2 = b^2 + c^2 - 2bc \cos A$$

or

$$b^2 = a^2 + c^2 - 2ac \cos B.$$

This result can be summarized as follows.

> **Theorem. (The law of cosines.) In any triangle ABC,**
>
> $$a^2 = b^2 + c^2 - 2bc \cos A,$$
> $$b^2 = a^2 + c^2 - 2ac \cos B, \text{ and}$$
> $$c^2 = a^2 + b^2 - 2ab \cos C.$$
>
> **(In any triangle, the square of a side is the sum of the squares of the other two sides, minus twice the product of those sides and the cosine of the included angle.)**

Only one of the above formulas need be memorized. The other two can be obtained by a change of letters.

SOLVING TRIANGLES (SAS)

When two sides of a triangle and the included angle are known, we can use the law of cosines to find the third side. The law of sines can then be used to finish solving the triangle.

Example 1. In triangle ABC, $a = 24$, $c = 32$, and $B = 115°$. Solve the triangle.

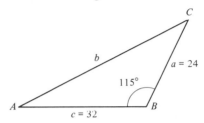

We first find the third side. From the law of cosines,

$$b^2 = a^2 + c^2 - 2ac \cos B$$
$$= 24^2 + 32^2 - 2 \cdot 24 \cdot 32(-0.4226)$$
$$= 2249.$$

Then $b = \sqrt{2249} = 47.4$.

Next, we use the law of sines to find a second angle:

$$\frac{a}{\sin A} = \frac{b}{\sin B}, \quad \text{and} \quad \sin A = \frac{a \sin B}{b}$$

$$\sin A = \frac{24 \sin 115°}{47.4} = \frac{24 \times 0.9063}{47.4} = 0.4589.$$

Thus

$$A = 27°20'.$$

The third angle is now easy to find:

$$C = 180° - (115° + 27°20') = 37°40'. \quad \textbf{[12]}$$

SOLVING TRIANGLES (SSS)

When all three sides of a triangle are known, the law of cosines can be used to solve the triangle.

Example 2. In triangle ABC, $a = 18$, $b = 25$, and $c = 12$. Solve the triangle.

Let us first find angle B. We select the formula from the law of cosines that contains $\cos B$; in other words, $b^2 = a^2 + c^2 - 2ac \cos B$. We solve this for $\cos B$ and substitute:

$$\cos B = \frac{a^2 + c^2 - b^2}{2ac} = \frac{18^2 + 12^2 - 25^2}{2 \cdot 18 \cdot 12} = -0.3634.$$

Then $B = 111°20'$.

Similarly, we shall find angle A:

$$a^2 = b^2 + c^2 - 2bc \cos A$$

$$\cos A = \frac{b^2 + c^2 - a^2}{2bc} = \frac{25^2 + 12^2 - 18^2}{2 \cdot 25 \cdot 12} = 0.7417.$$

Thus $A = 42°10'$.

Then $C = 180° - (111°20' + 42°10') = 26°30'$.

[13]

Exercise Set 10.3

In Exercises 1–12, solve the triangles.

1. $A = 30°$,　$b = 12$,　$c = 24$

2. $C = 60°$,　$a = 15$,　$b = 12$

3. $A = 133°$,　$b = 12$,　$c = 15$

4. $B = 116°$,　$a = 31$,　$c = 25$

5. $B = 72°40'$,　$c = 16$,　$a = 78$

6. $A = 24°30'$,　$b = 68$,　$c = 14$

7. $a = 12$,　$b = 14$,　$c = 20$

8. $a = 22$,　$b = 22$,　$c = 35$

9. $a = 3.3$,　$b = 2.7$,　$c = 2.8$

10. $a = 16$,　$b = 20$,　$c = 32$

11. $a = 2.2$,　$b = 4.1$,　$c = 2.4$

12. $a = 3.6$,　$b = 6.2$,　$c = 4.1$

13. A ship leaves a harbor and sails 15 nautical mi east. It then sails 18 nautical mi in a direction of S 27°E. How far is it, then, from the harbor and in what direction?

14. An airplane leaves an airport and flies west 147 km. It then flies 200 km in a direction of 220°. How far is it, then, from the airport and in what direction?

15. Two ships leave harbor at the same time. The first sails N 15°W at 25 knots (a knot is one nautical mile per hour). The second sails N 32°E at 20 knots. After 2 hr, how far apart are the ships?

16. Two airplanes leave an airport at the same time. The first flies 150 km/h in a direction of 320°. The second flies 200 km/h in a direction of 200°. After 3 hr, how far apart are the planes?

17. A hill is inclined 5° to the horizontal. A 45-ft pole stands at the top of the hill. How long a rope will it take to reach from the top of the pole to a point 35 ft downhill from the base of the pole?

18. A hill is inclined 15° to the horizontal. A 40-ft pole stands at the top of the hill. How long a rope will it take to reach from the top of the pole to a point 68 ft downhill from the base of the pole?

19. A piece of wire 5.5 m long is bent into a triangular shape. One side is 1.5 m long and another is 2 m long. Find the angles of the triangle.

20. A triangular lot has sides 120 ft long, 150 ft long, and 100 ft long. Find the angles of the lot.

▶ **21.** Show that in any triangle ABC,

$$a^2 + b^2 + c^2 = 2(bc \cos A + ac \cos B + ab \cos C).$$

22. Show that in any triangle ABC,

$$\frac{\cos A}{a} + \frac{\cos B}{b} + \frac{\cos C}{c} = \frac{a^2 + b^2 + c^2}{2abc}.$$

10.4 Vectors

In many applications there arise certain quantities in which a direction is specified. Any such quantity having a *direction* and a *magnitude* is called a *vector quantity*, or *vector*. Here are some examples of vector quantities.

Displacement.   An object moves a certain distance in a certain direction.

A train travels 100 mi to the northeast.
A man takes 5 steps to the west.
A batter hits a ball 100 m along the left-field foul line.

Velocity.   An object travels at a certain speed in a certain direction.

The wind is blowing 15 mph from the northwest.
An airplane is traveling 450 km/h in a direction of 243°.

Force.   A push or pull is exerted on an object in a certain direction.

A 15-kg force is exerted downward on the handle of a jack.
A 25-lb upward force is required to lift a box.
A wagon is being pulled up a 30° incline, requiring an effort of 200 kg.

We shall represent vectors abstractly by directed line segments, or arrows. The length is chosen, according to some scale, to represent the magnitude of the vector, and the direction of the arrow represents the direction of the vector. For example, if we let 1 cm represent 5 km/h, then a 15-km/h wind from the northwest would be represented by an arrow 3 cm long, as follows.

VECTOR ADDITION

To "add" vectors, we find a single vector that would have the same effect as the vectors combined. We shall illustrate vector addition for displacements, but it is done the same way for any vector quantities. Suppose a man takes 4 steps east and then 3 steps north. He will then be 5 steps from the starting point in the direction shown. The *sum* of the two vectors is the vector 5 steps in magnitude and in the direction of the drawing. The sum is also called the *resultant* of the two vectors.

In general, if we have two vectors *a* and *b*, we can add them as in the above example. That is, we place the tail of one arrow at the head of the other and then find the vector that forms the third side of a triangle. Or, we can place the tails of the arrows together, complete a parallelogram, and find the diagonal of the parallelogram.

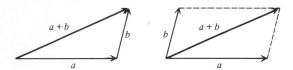

Example 1. Forces of 15 kg and 25 kg act on an object at right angles to each other. Find their *sum*, or *resultant*, giving the angle that it makes with the larger force.

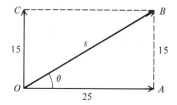

We make a drawing, this time a rectangle. Since *OAB* is a right triangle, we have

$$\tan \theta = \frac{15}{25} = 0.6.$$

Thus θ, the angle the resultant makes with the larger force, is 31°. Now $s/15 = \csc \theta$, or $s = 15 \csc \theta = 15 \times 1.942 = 29.1$. Thus the resultant has a magnitude of 29.1 kg and makes an angle of 31° with the larger force.   **[14]**

Example 2. An airplane heads in a direction of 100° at 180 km/h airspeed while a wind is blowing 40 km/h from 220°. Find the speed of the airplane over the ground and the direction of its track over the ground.

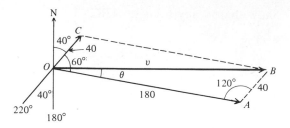

We first make a drawing. The wind is represented by $\overline{OC}$ and the velocity vector of the airplane by $\overline{OA}$. The resultant velocity is *v*, the sum of the two vectors.

By the law of cosines in $\triangle OAB$, we have

$$v^2 = 40^2 + 180^2 - 2 \cdot 40 \cdot 180 \cos 120°$$
$$= 41{,}200.$$

Thus the magnitude of *v* is 203 km/h.

By the law of sines in the same triangle,

$$\frac{40}{\sin \theta} = \frac{203}{\sin 120°},$$

or

$$\sin \theta = \frac{40 \sin 120°}{203} = 0.1706.$$

Thus $\theta = 10°$ to the nearest degree.

Therefore the ground speed of the airplane is 203 km/h and its track is in a direction of 90°.   **[15]**

Exercise Set 10.4

In Exercises 1–8, magnitudes of vectors *a* and *b* are given and the angle between the vectors θ. Find the resultant, giving the direction by specifying to the nearest degree the angle it makes with vector *a*.

1. $a = 45$, $b = 35$, $\theta = 90°$

2. $a = 54$, $b = 43$, $\theta = 90°$

3. $a = 10$, $\quad b = 12$, $\quad \theta = 67°$

4. $a = 25$, $\quad b = 30$, $\quad \theta = 75°$

5. $a = 20$, $\quad b = 20$, $\quad \theta = 117°$

6. $a = 30$, $\quad b = 30$, $\quad \theta = 123°$

7. $a = 23$, $\quad b = 47$, $\quad \theta = 27°$

8. $a = 32$, $\quad b = 74$, $\quad \theta = 72°$

9. Two forces of 5 kg and 12 kg act on an object at right angles. Find the magnitude of the resultant and the angle it makes with the smaller force.

10. Two forces of 30 kg and 40 kg act on an object at right angles. Find the magnitude of the resultant and the angle it makes with the smaller force.

11. Forces of 420 kg and 300 kg act on an object. The angle between the forces is 50°. Find the resultant, giving the angle it makes with the larger force.

12. Forces of 410 kg and 600 kg act on an object. The angle between the forces is 47°. Find the resultant, giving the angle it makes with the smaller force.

13. A balloon is rising 12 ft/sec while a wind is blowing 18 ft/sec. Find the speed of the balloon and the angle it makes with the horizontal.

14. A balloon is rising 10 ft/sec while a wind is blowing 5 ft/sec. Find the speed of the balloon and the angle it makes with the horizontal.

15. A boat heads 35°, propelled by a force of 750 lb. A wind from 320° exerts a force of 150 lb on the boat. How large is the resultant force and in what direction is the boat moving?

16. A boat heads 220°, propelled by a 650-lb force. A wind from 080° exerts a force of 100 lb on the boat. How large is the resultant force, and in what direction is the boat moving?

17. A ship sails N 80°E for 120 nautical mi, then S 20°W for 200 nautical mi. How far is it then from the starting point, and in what direction?

18. An airplane flies 032° for 210 km, then 280° for 170 km. How far is it, then, from the starting point, and in what direction?

19. A motorboat has a speed of 15 km/h. It crosses a river whose current has a speed of 3 km/h. In order to cross the river at right angles, the boat should be pointed in what direction?

20. An airplane has an airspeed of 150 km/h. It is to make a flight in a direction of 080° while there is a 25-km/h wind from 350°. What should be the airplane's heading?

10.5 Components of Vectors

Given a vector, it is often convenient to reverse the addition procedure, that is, to find two vectors whose sum is the given vector. Usually the two vectors we seek will be perpendicular. The two vectors we find are called *components* of the given vector.

Example 1. A certain vector has a magnitude of 130 and is inclined 40° with the horizontal. Resolve the vector into horizontal and vertical components.

We first make a drawing, showing horizontal and vertical vectors whose sum is the given vector. From $\triangle OAB$, we see

$$h = 130 \cos 40° = 99.6,$$

$$v = 130 \sin 40° = 83.6.$$

These are the components we seek.

Example 2. An airplane is flying at 200 km/h in a direction of 305°. Find the westerly and northerly components of its velocity.

We first make a drawing, showing westerly and northerly vectors whose sum is the given velocity. From △ *OAB*, we see

$$n = 200 \cos 55° = 115 \text{ km/h},$$
$$w = 200 \sin 55° = 164 \text{ km/h}. \qquad \textbf{[16, 17]}$$

Given a vector, we can resolve it into components. Given components of a vector, we can find the vector. We simply find the vector sum of the components.

Example 3. A certain vector has a westerly component of 12 and a southerly component of 16. Find the vector.

From the drawing we see that $\tan \theta = \frac{12}{16} = 0.75$. Thus $\theta = 36°50'$.

Then $v = 12 \csc 36°50' = 20$.

Thus the vector has a magnitude of 20 and a direction of S 36°50′W. **[18]**

ADDING VECTORS USING COMPONENTS

When we have two vectors resolved into components, we can add the two vectors by adding the components.

Example 4. A vector has a westerly component of 3 and a northerly component of 5. A second vector has an easterly component of 8 and a northerly component of 4. Find the components of the sum. Find the sum.

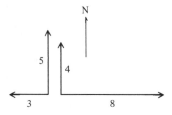

Adding the east-west components, we obtain 5 east. Adding the north-south components, we obtain 9 north. The components of the sum are 5 east and 9 north.

We now add these components:

$$\tan \theta = \frac{9}{5} = 1.8,$$
$$\theta = 61°,$$
$$s = 9 \csc 61° = 10.3.$$

The sum has a magnitude of 10.3 and a direction of N 29°E. **[19]**

VECTORS ON A COORDINATE SYSTEM

If we place a coordinate system so that the origin is at the tail of an arrow representing a vector, we say that the vector is in *standard position*. Then if we know the coordinates of the other end of the vector, we know the vector. The coordinates will be the x-component and the y-component of the vector. Thus we can consider an ordered pair (a, b) to be a vector. When vectors are given in this form, it is easy to add them. We simply add the respective components.

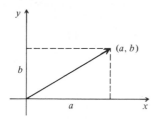

Example 5. Add the vectors $(3, -7)$ and $(4, 2)$.

The sum is found by adding the x-components and then adding the y-components: $(3, -7) + (4, 2) = (7, -5)$.   **[20, 21]**

If we wish, we can also specify a vector by giving its length and its direction. When this is done, we say we have the vector in *polar form*. An example of polar form is $(15, 260°)$. The angle is measured from the positive half of the x-axis counterclockwise.

Example 6. Find polar form for the vector $(7, -2)$.

From the diagram (at top right) we see the reference angle ϕ.

$$\tan \phi = \frac{-2}{7} = -0.2857,$$

$$\phi = -16°,$$

$$v = \sqrt{(-2)^2 + 7^2} = 7.28.$$

Thus polar form for the vector is

$$(7.28, 344°) \quad \text{or} \quad (7.28, -16°). \quad \textbf{[22]}$$

Given polar form for a vector we can also find the ordered pair notation (rectangular form).

Example 7. Find rectangular form for the vector $(14, 155°)$.

From the drawing we have

$$x = 14 \cos 155° = -12.7,$$

$$y = 14 \sin 155° = 5.92.$$

Thus rectangular form for this vector is $(-12.7, 5.92)$.   **[23]**

Exercise Set 10.5

In Exercises 1–22, all vectors are to be considered in standard form on a coordinate system.

In Exercises 1–6, add, giving the result in rectangular form.

1. $(3, 7) + (2, 9)$

2. $(5, -7) + (-3, 2)$

3. $(17, 7.6) + (-12.2, 6.1)$

5. $(-650, -750) + (-12, 324)$

4. $(-15.2, 37.1) + (7.9, -17.8)$

6. $(-354, -973) + (-75, 256)$

In Exercises 7–14, find polar form.

7. $(3, 4)$

8. $(4, 3)$

9. $(10, -15)$

10. $(17, -10)$

11. $(-3, -4)$

12. $(-4, -3)$

13. $(-10, 15)$

14. $(-17, 10)$

In Exercises 15–22, find rectangular form.

15. $(4, 30°)$

16. $(8, 60°)$

17. $(10, 235°)$

18. $(15, 210°)$

19. $(20, 330°)$

20. $(20, 200°)$

21. $(100, -45°)$

22. $(150, -60°)$

23. A vector with magnitude 150 is inclined 52° with the horizontal. Find its horizontal and vertical components.

24. A vector of magnitude 170 is inclined 63° with the horizontal. Find its horizontal and vertical components.

25. An airplane is flying 220° at 250 km/h. Find the southerly and the westerly components of its velocity.

26. A wind is blowing from 310° at 25 mph. Find the southerly and the easterly components.

27. A force has a westerly component of 25 kg and a southerly component of 35 kg. Find the magnitude and direction of the force.

28. A force has an upward component of 65 kg and a component to the left of 90 kg. Find the magnitude and direction of the force.

29. Vector 1 has a westerly component of 15 and a northerly component of 22. Vector 2 has a northerly component of 6 and an easterly component of 8. Find (a) the components of the sum of 1 and 2, and (b) the magnitude and direction of the sum.

30. Vector 1 has a component of 18 upward and a component of 12 to the left. Vector 2 has a component of 5 downward and a component of 35 to the right. Find (a) the components of the sum; (b) the magnitude and direction of the sum.

10.6 Polar Coordinates

In graphing we locate a point with an ordered pair of numbers (a, b). We may consider any such ordered pair to be a vector. From our work with vectors we know that we could also locate a point with a vector in polar form, if given a length and a direction. When we use vectors in rectangular form to locate points, we describe the coordinate system as *rectangular*.* When

we use vectors in polar form to locate points, we describe the coordinate system as *polar*.

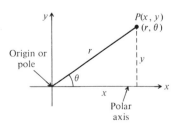

---

* Also called *Cartesian*, after the French mathematician René Descartes.

As this diagram shows, any point has rectangular coordinates (x, y) and has polar coordinates (r, θ). On a polar graph the origin is called the *pole* and the positive half of the x-axis is called the *polar axis*.

To plot points on a polar graph, we usually locate θ first, then move a distance r from the pole in that direction. If r is negative, we move in the opposite direction. Polar-coordinate graph paper, shown in the examples below, facilitates plotting.

Examples

Examples (a) and (b) at the bottom of the page illustrate that θ may be given in degrees or in radians. They also show (see point E below) that the polar coordinates of a point are not unique.   **[24–27]**

POLAR AND RECTANGULAR EQUATIONS

Some curves have simpler equations in polar coordinates than in rectangular coordinates. For others the reverse is true. The following relationships between the two kinds of coordinates allow us to convert an equation from rectangular to polar coordinates.

$$x = r \cos \theta, \qquad y = r \sin \theta$$

Example 1. Convert to a polar equation: $x^2 + y^2 = 25$.

$$(r \cos \theta)^2 + (r \sin \theta)^2 = 25 \quad \text{(substituting for } x \text{ and } y\text{)}$$
$$r^2 \cos^2 \theta + r^2 \sin^2 \theta = 25$$
$$r^2(\cos^2 \theta + \sin^2 \theta) = 25$$
$$r^2 = 25$$
$$r = 5$$

a)

b)

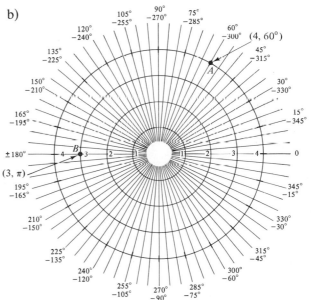

Example 1 illustrates that the polar equation of a circle centered at the origin is much simpler than the rectangular equation.

Example 2. Convert to a polar equation: $2x - y = 5$.

$$2(r \cos \theta) - (r \sin \theta) = 5$$
$$r(2 \cos \theta - \sin \theta) = 5 \qquad \textbf{[28, 29]}$$

The relationships that we need to convert from polar equations to rectangular equations can easily be determined from the triangle in the diagram on p. 300. They are as follows.

$$r = \pm\sqrt{x^2 + y^2},$$

$$\sin \theta = \frac{\pm y}{\sqrt{x^2 + y^2}},$$

$$\cos \theta = \frac{\pm x}{\sqrt{x^2 + y^2}},$$

$$\tan \theta = \frac{y}{x}$$

To convert to rectangular notation, we substitute as needed from either of the two lists, choosing the + or − signs as appropriate in each case.

Example 1. Convert to a rectangular (Cartesian) equation: $r = 4$.

$$+\sqrt{x^2 + y^2} = 4 \qquad \text{(substituting for } r)$$
$$x^2 + y^2 = 16 \qquad \text{(squaring)}$$

In squaring like this, we must be careful not to introduce solutions of the equation that are not already present. In this example we did not, because the graph is a circle of radius 4 centered at the origin, in both cases.

Example 2. Convert to a rectangular equation: $r \cos \theta = 6$.

From our first list we know that $x = r \cos \theta$, so we have

$$x = 6.$$

Example 3. Convert to a rectangular equation: $r = 2 \cos \theta + 3 \sin \theta$.

Let us first multiply on both sides by r:

$$r^2 = 2r \cos \theta + 3r \sin \theta$$
$$x^2 + y^2 = 2x + 3y \qquad \text{(substituting)}$$
$$\textbf{[30--32]}$$

Exercise Set 10.6

Use polar coordinate paper. Graph the following points.

1. $(4, 30°)$

2. $(5, 45°)$

3. $(0, 37°)$

4. $(0, 48°)$

5. $(-6, 150°)$

6. $(-5, 135°)$

7. $(-8, 210°)$

8. $(-5, 270°)$

9. $(3, -30°)$

10. $(6, -45°)$

11. $(7, -315°)$

12. $(4, -270°)$

13. $(-3, -30°)$

14. $(-6, -45°)$

15. $(-3.2, 27°)$

16. $(-6.8, 34°)$

17. $\left(6, \frac{\pi}{4}\right)$

18. $\left(5, \frac{\pi}{6}\right)$

19. $\left(4, \frac{3\pi}{2}\right)$

20. $\left(3, \frac{3\pi}{4}\right)$

21. $\left(-6, \dfrac{\pi}{4}\right)$ **22.** $\left(-5, \dfrac{\pi}{6}\right)$ **23.** $\left(-4, -\dfrac{3\pi}{2}\right)$ **24.** $\left(-3, -\dfrac{3\pi}{4}\right)$

Find polar coordinates of the following points.

25. $(4, 4)$ **26.** $(5, 5)$ **27.** $(0, 5)$ **28.** $(0, -3)$

29. $(4, 0)$ **30.** $(-5, 0)$ **31.** $(3, 3\sqrt{3})$ **32.** $(-3, -3\sqrt{3})$

33. $(\sqrt{3}, 1)$ **34.** $(-\sqrt{3}, 1)$ **35.** $(3\sqrt{3}, 3)$ **36.** $(4\sqrt{3}, -4)$

Find Cartesian coordinates of the following points.

37. $(4, 45°)$ **38.** $(5, 60°)$ **39.** $(0, 23°)$ **40.** $(0, -34°)$

41. $(-3, 45°)$ **42.** $(-5, 30°)$ **43.** $(6, -60°)$ **44.** $(3, -120°)$

45. $\left(10, \dfrac{\pi}{6}\right)$ **46.** $\left(12, \dfrac{3\pi}{4}\right)$ **47.** $\left(-5, \dfrac{5\pi}{6}\right)$ **48.** $\left(-6, \dfrac{3\pi}{4}\right)$

Convert to polar equations.

49. $3x + 4y = 5$ **50.** $5x + 3y = 4$ **51.** $x = 5$ **52.** $y = 4$

53. $x^2 + y^2 = 36$ **54.** $x^2 + y^2 = 16$ **55.** $x^2 - 4y^2 = 4$ **56.** $x^2 - 5y^2 = 5$

Convert to rectangular equations.

57. $r = 5$ **58.** $r = 8$ **59.** $\theta = \dfrac{\pi}{4}$ **60.** $\theta = \dfrac{3\pi}{4}$

61. $r \sin \theta = 2$ **62.** $r \cos \theta = 5$ **63.** $r = 4 \cos \theta$ **64.** $r = -3 \sin \theta$

65. $r - r \sin \theta = 2$ **66.** $r + r \cos \theta = 3$ **67.** $r - 2 \cos \theta = 3 \sin \theta$ **68.** $r + 5 \sin \theta = 7 \cos \theta$

▶ **69.** Convert to a rectangular equation: $r = \sec^2 \dfrac{\theta}{2}$.

70. The center of a regular hexagon is at the origin and one vertex is the point $(4, 0°)$. Find the coordinates of the other vertices.

71. Show that $(2, 90°)$, $(2, 210°)$, and $(2, 330°)$ are vertices of an equilateral triangle. Then find the length of a side.

10.7 Forces in Equilibrium

When several forces act through the same point on an object, their vector sum must be 0 in order for a balance to occur. When a balance occurs, then the object is either stationary or moving in a straight line without acceleration. The fact that the vector sum must be 0 for a balance and conversely, allows us to solve many applied problems involving forces. In these problems we usually resolve vectors into components. For a balance, the sum of the components must be 0 separately.

Example 1. A 200-lb sign is hanging from the end of a horizontal hinged boom, supported by a cable from the end of the boom and inclined 35° with the horizontal. Find the force (tension) in the cable and the force (compression) in the boom.

At the end of the boom we have three forces acting at a point: the weight of the sign acting down, the cable pulling up and to the right, and the boom pushing to the left. We shall draw a force diagram showing these.

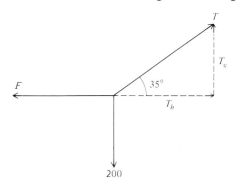

We have called the tension in the cable T and the compression in the boom F. We resolve the tension in the cable into horizontal and vertical components.

We have a balance, so the vector sum of the forces must be 0. In fact, the sum of the horizontal components must be 0; the sum of the vertical components

must also be 0. Thus we know that $T_v = 200$ lb and that $F = T_h$. Then we have

$$T_v = 200 = T \sin 35°$$

$$T = \frac{T_v}{\sin 35°} = \frac{200}{0.5736} = 349 \text{ lb.}$$

Then $F = T_h = 349 \cos 35° = 286$ lb.

The answer is that the tension in the cable is 349 lb and the compression in the boom is 286 lb.　　**[33]**

Example 2. A block weighing 100 kg rests on a 25° incline. Find the components of its weight perpendicular and parallel to the incline.

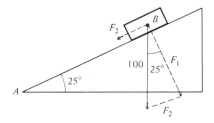

The weight of 100 kg acts downward as shown. We draw F_1 and F_2, the components. The angle at B has the same measure as the angle at A because their sides are respectively perpendicular. Thus we have

$$F_1 = 100 \cos 25° = 90.6 \text{ kg,}$$

$$F_2 = 100 \sin 25° = 42.3 \text{ kg.} \qquad \textbf{[34]}$$

In a situation like that of Example 2, the force necessary to hold the block on the incline is a force the size of F_2 but opposite in direction. The force with which the block pushes on the incline is F_1.

Example 3. A 500-kg block is suspended by two ropes as shown in Fig. 1 on the following page. Find the tension in each rope.

At point A there are three forces acting: the block is pulling down, and the two ropes are pulling upward and outward. We draw a force diagram (see Fig. 2 on the following page) showing these.

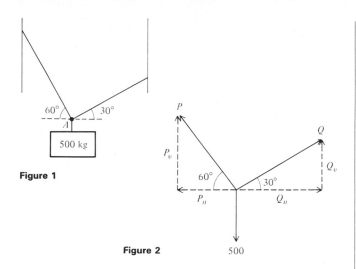

Figure 1

Figure 2

We have called the forces exerted by the ropes P and Q. Their horizontal components are $P \cos 60°$ and $Q \cos 30°$. Since there is a balance, these must be the same:

$$P \cos 60° = Q \cos 30°.$$

The vertical components in the ropes are $P \sin 60°$ and $Q \sin 30°$. Since there is a balance, these must total 500 lb, the weight of the block:

$$P \sin 60° + Q \sin 30° = 500.$$

We now have two equations with unknowns P and Q:

$$P \cos 60° - Q \cos 30° = 0, \tag{1}$$
$$P \sin 60° + Q \sin 30° = 500. \tag{2}$$

To solve, we begin by solving equation (1) for P:

$$P = Q \frac{\cos 30°}{\cos 60°}. \tag{3}$$

Next, we substitute in equation (2):

$$Q \frac{\cos 30° \sin 60°}{\cos 60°} + Q \sin 30° = 500$$

$$Q \frac{\cos 30° \sin 60°}{\cos 60°} + Q \frac{\sin 30° \cos 60°}{\cos 60°} = 500$$

$$Q(\cos 30° \sin 60° + \sin 30° \cos 60°) = 500 \cos 60°$$

$$Q(\sin 90°) = 500 \cos 60° \quad \text{(using an identity)}$$

$$Q = 500 \cdot \frac{1}{2} = 250 \text{ kg.}$$

Then substituting in equation (3), we obtain

$$P = 250 \frac{\cos 30°}{\cos 60°} = 250 \frac{\sqrt{3}/2}{1/2} = 250\sqrt{3} = 433 \text{ kg.}$$

[35]

Exercise Set 10.7

1. A 150-lb sign is hanging from the end of a hinged boom, supported by a cable inclined 42° with the horizontal. Find the tension in the cable and the compression in the boom.

2. A 300-lb sign is hanging from the end of a hinged boom, supported by a cable inclined 51° from the horizontal. Find the tension in the cable and the compression in the boom (see figure for Exercise 1).

3. A weight of 200 kg is supported by a frame made of two rods and hinged at *A*, *B*, and *C* (see the figure on the right). Find the forces exerted by the two rods.

4. A weight of 300 kg is supported by the hinged frame of Exercise 3, but where the angle shown is 50°. Find the forces exerted by the two rods.

5. The force due to air movement on an airplane wing in flight is 2800 lb, acting at an angle of 28° with the vertical. What is the lift (vertical component) and what is the drag (horizontal component)?

6. The force due to air movement on an airplane wing in flight is 3500 lb, acting at an angle of 32° with the vertical. What is the lift (vertical component) and what is the drag (horizontal component)?

7. A 100-kg block of ice rests on a 37° incline. What force parallel to the incline is necessary to keep it from sliding down?

8. What force is necessary to pull a 6500-kg truck up a 7° incline?

9. The moon's gravity is $\frac{1}{6}$ that of the earth. To simulate the moon's gravity an incline is used, as shown in the figure on the right. The astronaut is suspended in a sling and is free to move horizontally. The component of his weight perpendicular to the incline should be $\frac{1}{6}$ of his weight. What must the angle θ be?

10. To simulate gravity on a planet having $\frac{3}{8}$ of the earth's gravity, what should the angle θ be? (See figure and explanation for Exercise 9.)

11. A 400-kg block is suspended by two ropes, as shown. Find the tension in each rope.

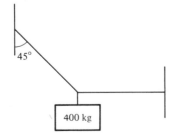

12. A 1000-lb block is suspended by two ropes, as shown. Find the tension in each rope.

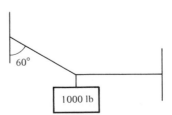

13. A 2000-kg block is suspended by two ropes, as shown. Find the tension in each rope.

14. A 1500-lb block is suspended by two ropes as shown. Find the tension in each rope.

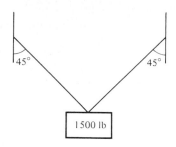

15. A 2500-kg block is suspended by two ropes, as shown. Find the tension in each rope.

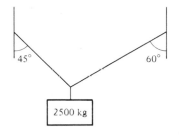

16. A 2000-kg block is suspended by two ropes as shown. Find the tension in each rope.

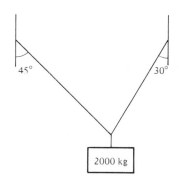

Chapter 10 Test, or Review

In Exercises 1 and 2 solve the triangles. Angle C is a right angle. Use three-digit precision.

1. $a = 7.3$, $c = 8.6$

2. $a = 30.5$, $B = 51°10'$.

3. One leg of a right triangle bears east. The hypotenuse is 734 cm long and bears N 57°20′E. Find the perimeter.

4. Solve triangle ABC, where $B = 118°20'$, $C = 27°30'$, and $b = 0.974$.

5. In an isosceles triangle, the base angles each measure 52°20′ and the base is 513 cm long. Find the lengths of the other two sides.

6. In triangle ABC, $a = 3.7$, $c = 4.9$, and $B = 135°$. Find b.

7. A car is moving north at 45 mph. A ball is thrown from the car at 37 mph in a direction of N 45°E. Find the speed and direction of the ball over the ground.

8. A block weighing 150 lb rests on an inclined plane. The plane makes an angle of 45° with the ground. Find the components of the weight parallel and perpendicular to the plane.

9. Find polar form for the vector $(-2, 3)$.

10. Convert to a polar equation: $x^2 + y^2 + 2x - 3y = 0$.

11. A crane is supporting a 500-kg steel beam. The boom of the crane is inclined 30° from the vertical. Find the compression in the boom of the crane.

CHAPTER 11

Complex Numbers

11.1 Imaginary and Complex Numbers

Negative numbers do not have square roots in the system of real numbers. Certain equations have no solutions. A new kind of number, called *imaginary*, was invented so that negative numbers would have square roots and certain equations would have solutions. These numbers were devised, starting with an imaginary unit, named i, with the agreement that $i^2 = -1$ or $i = \sqrt{-1}$. All other imaginary numbers can be expressed as a product of i and a real number.

Example 1. Express $\sqrt{-5}$ and $-\sqrt{-7}$ in terms of i.

$$\sqrt{-5} = \sqrt{-1 \cdot 5} = \sqrt{-1}\sqrt{5} = i\sqrt{5}$$

$$-\sqrt{-7} = -\sqrt{-1 \cdot 7} = -\sqrt{-1}\sqrt{7} = -i\sqrt{7}$$

It is also to be understood that the imaginary unit obeys the familiar laws of real numbers, such as the commutative and associative laws.

Example 2. Simplify $\sqrt{-3}\sqrt{-7}$.

Important. We first express the two imaginary numbers in terms of i:

$$\sqrt{-3}\sqrt{-7} = i\sqrt{3} \cdot i\sqrt{7}.$$

Now, rearranging and combining, we have

$$i^2\sqrt{3}\sqrt{7} = -1 \cdot \sqrt{21} = -\sqrt{21}.$$

It is important, as in Example 2, to express imaginary numbers in terms of i before simplifying. Had we not done this in Example 2, we would have obtained $\sqrt{(-3)(-7)}$, or $\sqrt{21}$, instead of $-\sqrt{21}$. **[1–5]**

Example 3. Simplify $\dfrac{\sqrt{-20}}{\sqrt{5}}$.

$$\frac{\sqrt{-20}}{\sqrt{-5}} = \frac{i\sqrt{20}}{i\sqrt{5}} = \frac{\sqrt{20}}{\sqrt{5}} = \sqrt{4} = 2$$

Example 4. Simplify $\sqrt{-9} + \sqrt{-25}$.

$$\sqrt{-9} + \sqrt{-25} = i\sqrt{9} + i\sqrt{25} = 3i + 5i$$
$$= (3 + 5)i = 8i$$

[6–10]

POWERS OF i

Let us look at the powers of i.

$$i^2 = -1 \qquad\qquad i^5 = i^4 \cdot i = 1 \cdot i = i$$
$$i^3 = i^2 \cdot i = -1 \cdot i = -i \qquad i^6 = i^5 \cdot i = i \cdot i = -1$$
$$i^4 = i^2 \cdot i^2 = -1(-1) = 1 \qquad i^7 = i^6 \cdot i = -1 \cdot i = -i$$

The first four powers of i are all different, but thereafter there is a repeating pattern, in cycles of four. Note that $i^4 = 1$ and that all powers of i^4, such as i^8, i^{16}, and so on, are 1. To find a higher power we express it in terms of the nearest power of 4 less than the given one.

Example 5. Simplify i^{17} and i^{23}.

$$i^{17} = i^{16} \cdot i$$

Since i^{16} is a power of i^4 and $i^4 = 1$, we know $i^{16} = 1$ so

$$i^{17} = 1 \cdot i = i,$$
$$i^{23} = i^{20} \cdot i^3.$$

Since i^{20} is a power of i^4, $i^{20} = 1$, so $i^{23} = 1 \cdot i^3 = 1 \cdot (-i) = -i$.

[11, 12]

COMPLEX NUMBERS

The equation $x^2 + 1 = 0$ has no solution in real numbers, but it has the imaginary solutions i and $-i$. There are equations that do not have real or imaginary solutions. For example, $x^2 - 2x + 2 = 0$ does not. If we allow sums of real and imaginary numbers, this equation does have a solution, $1 + i$. Let us verify this by substitution:

$$x^2 - 2x + 2 = 0$$
$$(1 + i)^2 - 2(1 + i) + 2 =$$
$$1 + 2i + i^2 - 2 - 2i + 2 =$$
$$1 + 2i - 1 - 2 - 2i + 2 = 0. \qquad \textbf{[13]}$$

In order that more equations will have solutions, we invent a new number system called the *system of complex numbers*.* A complex number is a sum of a real number and an imaginary number.

> **The set of complex numbers consists of all numbers**
> $a + bi$, **where** a **and** b **are real numbers.**

For the complex number $a + bi$ we say that the *real part* is a and the *imaginary part* is bi. It is understood that all of the familiar properties of real numbers hold for complex numbers.†

AN EXTENSION OF THE REAL NUMBERS

The complex number system is an extension of the real number system. Any number $a + bi$, where a and b are real numbers, is a complex number. The number b can be 0, in which case we have $a + 0i$, which simplifies to the real number a. Thus the complex numbers include all of the real numbers. They also include all of the imaginary numbers, because any imaginary number bi is equal to $0 + bi$.

---

*One may wonder why we do not invent a system of imaginary numbers. Since we do not even have closure ($i^2 = -1$, a real number) this would not make sense.

† In a more rigorous treatment, addition and multiplication are defined for complex numbers. It is then proved that the familiar properties hold.

The additive identity in the new system is $0 + 0i$, or 0. The multiplicative identity is $1 + 0i$, or 1. Every complex number $a + bi$ has the additive inverse $-a - bi$.

Example 6. Simplify $(8 + 6i) + (3 + 2i)$.

$$(8 + 6i) + (3 + 2i) = 8 + 3 + 6i + 2i$$
$$= 11 + 8i$$

Example 7. Simplify $(1 + 2i)(1 + 3i)$.

$$(1 + 2i)(1 + 3i) = 1 + 6i^2 + 2i + 3i$$
$$= 1 - 6 + 2i + 3i \qquad (i^2 = -1)$$
$$= -5 + 5i$$

Example 8. Simplify $(3 + 2i) - (5 - 2i)$.

$$(3 + 2i) - (5 - 2i) = (3 + 2i) - 5 + 2i$$
$$= 3 - 5 + 2i + 2i$$
$$= -2 + 4i \qquad \textbf{[14–19]}$$

EQUALITY FOR COMPLEX NUMBERS

An equation $a + bi = c + di$ will be true if and only if the real parts are equal and the imaginary parts are equal. In other words, we have the following.

> $a + bi = c + di$ **if and only if** $a = c$ **and** $b = d.$

Example 9. Suppose that $3x + yi = 5x + 1 + 2i$. Find x and y.

We equate the real parts: $3x = 5x + 1$. Solving this equation, we obtain $x = -\frac{1}{2}$. We equate the imaginary parts: $yi = 2i$. Thus $y = 2$. **[20]**

Exercise Set 11.1

In Exercises 1–6, express in terms of i.

1. $\sqrt{-15}$ **2.** $\sqrt{-17}$ **3.** $\sqrt{-16}$

4. $\sqrt{-25}$ **5.** $-\sqrt{-12}$ **6.** $-\sqrt{-20}$

In Exercises 7–20, simplify. Leave answers in terms of i in Exercises 7–10.

7. $\sqrt{-16} + \sqrt{-25}$ **8.** $\sqrt{-36} - \sqrt{-4}$ **9.** $\sqrt{-7} - \sqrt{-10}$

10. $\sqrt{-5} + \sqrt{-7}$ **11.** $\sqrt{-5}\sqrt{-11}$ **12.** $\sqrt{-7}\sqrt{-8}$

13. $-\sqrt{-4}\sqrt{-5}$ **14.** $-\sqrt{-9}\sqrt{-7}$ **15.** $\dfrac{\sqrt{-5}}{\sqrt{-2}}$ **16.** $\dfrac{\sqrt{-7}}{\sqrt{-5}}$

17. $\dfrac{\sqrt{-9}}{\sqrt{-4}}$ **18.** $\dfrac{\sqrt{-25}}{\sqrt{-16}}$ **19.** $\dfrac{-\sqrt{-36}}{\sqrt{-9}}$ **20.** $\dfrac{\sqrt{-25}}{-\sqrt{-16}}$

In Exercises 21–50, simplify.

21. $(2 + 3i) + (4 + 2i)$ **22.** $(2 + 5i) + (-7 + 3i)$ **23.** $(5 - 2i) + (6 + 3i)$

24. $(3 - 6i) + (1 - 4i)$ **25.** $(4 + 3i) + (4 - 3i)$ **26.** $(5 + 6i) + (5 - 6i)$

27. $(2 + 3i) + (-2 - 3i)$ **28.** $(6 + 2i) + (-6 - 2i)$ **29.** $(8 + 11i) - (6 + 7i)$

30. $(12 + 14i) - (5 + 2i)$ **31.** $(9 - 5i) - (4 + 2i)$ **32.** $(10 - 12i) - (6 + 3i)$

33. $2i - (4 + 3i)$ **34.** $3i - (5 + 2i)$ **35.** $(1 + 2i)(1 + 3i)$

36. $(1 + 4i)(1 + 2i)$ **37.** $(1 + 4i)(1 - 3i)$ **38.** $(1 + 2i)(1 - 3i)$

39. $(2 + 3i)(2 - 3i)$ **40.** $(5 + 2i)(5 - 2i)$ **41.** $3i(4 + 2i)$

42. $5i(3 - 4i)$ **43.** $(2 + 3i)^2$ **44.** $(4 + 2i)^2$

45. $(3 - 2i)^2$ **46.** $(5 - 2i)^2$ **47.** i^{13}

48. i^{22} **49.** i^{57} **50.** i^{72}

51. Determine whether $1 + 2i$ is a solution of $x^2 - 2x + 5 = 0$.

52. Determine whether $1 - 2i$ is a solution of $x^2 - 2x + 5 = 0$.

53. Determine whether $1 + 3i$ is a solution of $x^2 - 3x + 5 = 0$.

54. Determine whether $1 - i$ is a solution of $x^2 + 3x + 5 = 0$.

In Exercises 55–58, solve for x and y.

55. $4x + 7i = -6 + yi$

56. $8 + 8yi = 4x - 2i$

57. $3x + 4y - 7i = 18 + (x - 3y)i$

58. $-4 + (x + y)i = 2x - 5y + 5i$

 Simplify.

59. $(56.4325 + 789.5097i) + (-456.892 + 809.0568i)$

60. $(76.5773 - 567.9076i) - (907.238 - 7890.67i)$

61. $(43.21 - 5.674i)^2$

62. $i^{56,469}$

63. $i^{342,674}$

64. $(45.23 - 56.1i)(45.23 + 56.1i)$

11.2 Conjugates and Division

We shall define the conjugate of a complex number as follows.

> **Definition.** The *conjugate* of a complex number $a + bi$ is $a - bi$, and the conjugate of $a - bi$ is $a + bi$.

Examples

The conjugate of $3 + 4i$ is $3 - 4i$.

The conjugate of $5 - 7i$ is $5 + 7i$.

The conjugate of $5i$ is $-5i$.

The conjugate of 6 is 6.   [21–26]

DIVISION

Fractional notation is useful for division of complex numbers. We also use the notion of conjugates.

Example. Divide $4 + 5i$ by $1 + 4i$.

We shall write fractional notation and then multiply by 1.

$$\frac{4 + 5i}{1 + 4i} = \frac{4 + 5i}{1 + 4i} \cdot \frac{1 - 4i}{1 - 4i}$$

(Here we have multiplied by 1. Note that $1 - 4i$ is the conjugate of the divisor.)

$$= \frac{(4 + 5i)(1 - 4i)}{1^2 - 4^2 i^2}$$

$$= \frac{24 - 11i}{1 + 16} = \frac{24 - 11i}{17} \quad (i^2 = -1)$$

$$= \frac{24}{17} - \frac{11}{17}i$$

The procedure of the last example allows us always to find a quotient of two numbers and express it in the form $a + bi$. This is true because the product of a number and its conjugate is always a real number (we will prove this later), giving us a real number denominator.   [27, 28]

RECIPROCALS

We can find the reciprocal, or multiplicative inverse, of a complex number by division. The reciprocal of a complex number z is $1/z$.

Example. Find the reciprocal of $2 - 3i$ and express it in the form $a + bi$.

a) The reciprocal of $2 - 3i$ is $\dfrac{1}{2 - 3i}$.

b) We can express it in the form $a + bi$ as follows:

$$\frac{1}{2 - 3i} = \frac{1}{2 - 3i} \cdot \frac{2 + 3i}{2 + 3i} = \frac{2 + 3i}{2^2 - 3^2 i^2}$$

$$= \frac{2 + 3i}{4 + 9} = \frac{2}{13} + \frac{3}{13} i. \qquad [29]$$

PROPERTIES OF CONJUGATES

We may use a single letter for a complex number. For example, we could shorten $a + bi$ to z. To denote the conjugate of a number, we use a bar. The conjugate of z is $\bar{z}$. Or, the conjugate of $a + bi$ is $\overline{a + bi}$. Of course, by definition of conjugates, $\overline{a + bi} = a - bi$ and $\overline{a - bi} = a + bi$. We have already noted that the product of a number and its conjugate is always a real number. Let us state this formally and prove it.

Theorem. For any complex number z, $z \cdot \bar{z}$ is a real number.

Proof. Let $z = a + bi$. Then

$$z \cdot \bar{z} = (a + bi)(a - bi) = a^2 - b^2 i^2 = a^2 + b^2.$$

Since a and b are real numbers, so is $a^2 + b^2$. Thus $z \cdot \bar{z}$ is real.

The sum of a number and its conjugate is also always real. We state this as the second property.

Theorem. For any complex number z, $z + \bar{z}$ is a real number.

Proof. Let $z = a + bi$. Then

$$z + \bar{z} = (a + bi) + (a - bi) = 2a.$$

Since a is a real number, $2a$ is real. Thus $z + \bar{z}$ is real.

Now we consider the conjugate of a sum and compare it with the sum of the conjugates.

Example. Compare

$$\overline{(2 + 4i) + (5 + i)} \quad \text{and} \quad \overline{(2 + 4i)} + \overline{(5 + i)}.$$

a) $\overline{(2 + 4i) + (5 + i)} = \overline{7 + 5i}$ (adding the complex numbers)

$$= 7 - 5i \text{ (taking the conjugate)}$$

b) $\overline{(2 + 4i)} + \overline{(5 + i)} = (2 - 4i) + (5 - i)$ (taking conjugates)

$$= 7 - 5i \text{ (adding)} \qquad [30]$$

Taking the conjugate of a sum gives the same result as adding the conjugates. Let us state and prove this.

Theorem. For any complex numbers z and w, $\overline{z + w} = \bar{z} + \bar{w}$.

Proof. Let $z = a + bi$ and $w = c + di$. Then

$$\overline{z + w} = \overline{(a + bi) + (c + di)} = \overline{(a + c) + (b + d)i},$$

by adding. We now take the conjugate and obtain $(a + c) - (b + d)i$.

Now

$$\bar{z} + \bar{w} = \overline{(a + bi)} + \overline{(c + di)} = (a - bi) + (c - di),$$

taking the conjugates. We will now add to obtain $(a + c) - (b + d)i$, the same result as before. Thus $\overline{z + w} = \bar{z} + \bar{w}$.

Let us next consider the conjugate of a product.

Example. Compare $\overline{(3 + 2i)(4 - 5i)}$ and $\overline{(3 + 2i)} \cdot \overline{(4 - 5i)}$.

$\overline{(3 + 2i)(4 - 5i)} = \overline{22 - 7i}$ (multiplying)

$$= 22 + 7i \text{ (taking the conjugate)}$$

$\overline{(3 + 2i)} \cdot \overline{(4 - 5i)} = (3 - 2i)(4 + 5i)$ (taking conjugates)

$$= 22 + 7i \text{ (multiplying)} \qquad [31]$$

The conjugate of a product is the product of the conjugates. This is our next result.

Theorem. For any complex numbers z and w, $\overline{z \cdot w} = \bar{z} \cdot \bar{w}$.

Proof. Let $z = a + bi$ and $w = c + di$. Then

$$\overline{z \cdot w} = \overline{(a + bi)(c + di)}$$

$$= \overline{(ac - bd) + (bc + ad)i}. \quad \text{(multiplying)}$$

Taking the conjugate, we obtain $(ac - bd) - (bc + ad)i$.

Now $\bar{z} \cdot \bar{w} = \overline{(a + bi)} \cdot \overline{(c + di)} = (a - bi)(c - di)$, taking conjugates. By multiplication we obtain $(ac - bd) - (bc + ad)i$, the same result as before. Thus $\overline{z \cdot w} = \bar{z} \cdot \bar{w}$.

Let us now consider conjugates of powers, using the preceding result.

Example. Show that for any complex number z, $\overline{z^2} = \bar{z}^2$.

$$\overline{z^2} = \overline{z \cdot z} \quad \text{(by definition of exponents)}$$

$$= \bar{z} \cdot \bar{z} \quad \text{(by the result proved above)}$$

$$= \bar{z}^2 \quad \text{(by definition of exponents)}$$

[32]

We now state our next result.

Theorem. For any complex number z, $\overline{z^n} = \bar{z}^n$. In other words, the conjugate of a power is the power of the conjugate. We understand that the exponent is a natural number.

The conjugate of a real number $a + 0i$ is $a - 0i$, and both are equal to a. Thus a real number is its own conjugate. We state this as our next result.

Theorem. If z is a real number, then $\bar{z} = z$.

CONJUGATES OF POLYNOMIALS

Given a polynomial in z, where z is a variable for a complex number, we can find its conjugate in terms of $\bar{z}$.

Example. Find a polynomial in $\bar{z}$ that is the conjugate of $3z^2 + 2z - 1$.

We write an expression for the conjugate and then use the properties of conjugates.

$$\overline{3z^2 + 2z - 1}$$

$$= \overline{3z^2} + \overline{2z} - \bar{1} \quad \text{(because the conjugate of a sum is the sum of the conjugates)}$$

$$= \overline{3}\overline{z^2} + \bar{2} \cdot \bar{z} - \bar{1} \quad \text{(because the conjugate of a product is the product of the conjugates)}$$

$$= 3\overline{z^2} + 2\bar{z} - 1 \quad \text{(because the conjugate of a real number is the number itself)}$$

$$= 3\bar{z}^2 + 2\bar{z} - 1 \quad \text{(because the conjugate of a power is the power of the conjugate)}$$

[33, 34]

Exercise Set 11.2

In Exercises 1–8, find the reciprocal and express it in the form $a + bi$.

1. $4 + 3i$ 2. $4 - 3i$ 3. $5 - 2i$ 4. $2 + 5i$

5. i 6. $-i$ 7. $-4i$ 8. $5i$

In Exercises 9–34, simplify.

9. $\dfrac{4 + 3i}{1 - i}$ **10.** $\dfrac{3 + 4i}{2 - i}$ **11.** $\dfrac{2 - 3i}{5 - 4i}$ **12.** $\dfrac{5 - 4i}{2 - 3i}$

13. $\dfrac{\sqrt{2} + i}{\sqrt{2} - i}$ **14.** $\dfrac{\sqrt{3} + i}{\sqrt{3} - i}$ **15.** $\dfrac{3 + 2i}{i}$ **16.** $\dfrac{2 + 3i}{i}$

17. $\dfrac{i}{2 + i}$ **18.** $\dfrac{i}{3 - i}$ **19.** $\dfrac{2}{6 - 5i}$ **20.** $\dfrac{3}{5 - 11i}$

21. $\dfrac{1 - i}{(1 + i)^2}$ **22.** $\dfrac{1 + i}{(1 - i)^2}$ **23.** $\dfrac{3 - 4i}{(2 + i)(3 - 2i)}$ **24.** $\dfrac{4 - 3i}{(2 - i)(3 + 2i)}$

25. $\dfrac{(4 - i)(5 + i)}{(6 - 5i)(7 - 2i)}$ **26.** $\dfrac{(3 + i)(4 - i)}{(4 - 7i)(2 + 6i)}$ **27.** $\dfrac{a + 2bi}{2a - bi}$ **28.** $\dfrac{3x + 2yi}{x - yi}$

29. $\dfrac{1 + i}{1 - i} \cdot \dfrac{2 - i}{1 - i}$ **30.** $\dfrac{1 - i}{1 + i} \cdot \dfrac{2 + i}{1 + i}$ **31.** $\dfrac{3 + 2i}{1 - i} + \dfrac{6 + 2i}{1 - i}$ **32.** $\dfrac{4 - 2i}{1 + i} + \dfrac{2 - 5i}{1 + i}$

33. $\dfrac{2 - 3i}{1 + i} + \dfrac{6 + 2i}{1 - i}$ **34.** $\dfrac{2 - 4i}{1 + i} + \dfrac{5 + 2i}{1 - i}$

In Exercises 35–40, find a polynomial in $\bar{z}$ that is the conjugate.

35. $3z^5 - 4z^2 + 3z - 5$ **36.** $5z^4 - 2z^3 + 5z - 3$ **37.** $7z^4 + 5z^3 - 12z$ **38.** $4z^7 - 3z^5 + 4z$

39. $5z^{10} - 7z^8 + 13z^2 - 4$ **40.** $8z^{12} - 8z^7 + 12z^5 - 8$

▶ **41.** Let $z = a + bi$. Find a general expression for $\dfrac{1}{z}$.

42. Let $z = a + bi$ and $w = c + di$. Find a general expression for $\dfrac{w}{z}$.

11.3 Equations and Complex Numbers

THE QUADRATIC FORMULA

In Chapter 2 we derived the quadratic formula for equations with real number coefficients. A glance at that derivation shows that all of the steps can also be done with complex number coefficients with one exception. We need to know that every nonzero complex number has two square roots that are additive inverses of each other. This is the case, as will be shown later. Thus the quadratic formula holds for equations with complex coefficients.

Theorem. Any equation $ax^2 + bx + c = 0$, where $a \neq 0$ and a, b, and c are complex numbers, has

solutions $\dfrac{-b \pm \sqrt{b^2 - 4ac}}{2a}$.

Example 1. Solve $x^2 + (1 + i)x - 2i = 0$.

We note that $a = 1$, $b = 1 + i$, and $c = -2i$. Thus,

$$x = \frac{-(1 + i) \pm \sqrt{(1 + i)^2 - 4 \cdot 1 \cdot (-2i)}}{2 \cdot 1}$$ (substituting in the formula)

$$= \frac{-1 - i \pm \sqrt{10i}}{2}.$$ (simplifying)

[35]

In Example 1 we have not attempted to evaluate $\sqrt{10i}$. This will be done later. Let us say, however, that $10i$ has two square roots that are additive inverses of each other. This is true of every nonzero complex number. There is no problem of negative numbers not having square roots, because in the system of complex numbers there are no positive or negative numbers. Whenever we speak of positive or negative numbers, we will be referring to the system of real numbers.

QUADRATIC EQUATIONS WITH REAL COEFFICIENTS

Since any real number a is $a + 0i$, we can consider real numbers to be special kinds of complex numbers. If a quadratic equation has real coefficients, the quadratic formula always gives solutions in the system of complex numbers. Recall that in using the formula, we take the square root of $b^2 - 4ac$. If this *discriminant* is negative, the solutions will have nonzero imaginary parts.

Example 2. Solve $x^2 + 2x + 5 = 0$.

We note that $a = 1$, $b = 2$, and $c = 5$. Thus,

$$x = \frac{-2 \pm \sqrt{2^2 - 4 \cdot 1 \cdot 5}}{2 \cdot 1}$$

$$= \frac{-2 \pm \sqrt{-16}}{2} = \frac{-2 \pm 4i}{2}.$$

The solutions are $-1 + 2i$ and $-1 - 2i$.

It is easy to see from Example 2 that when there are nonzero imaginary parts, an equation has two solutions that are conjugates of each other. **[36]**

WRITING EQUATIONS WITH SPECIFIED SOLUTIONS

The principle of zero products for real numbers states that a product is 0 if and only if at least one of the factors is 0. This principle also holds for complex numbers. This will be shown in Section 11.4. Since the principle holds for complex numbers we can write equations having specified solutions.

Example 3. Find an equation having the numbers 1, i, and $-i$ as solutions.

The factors we use will be $x - 1$, $x - i$, and $x + i$. Next we set the product of these factors equal to 0:

$$(x - 1)(x - i)(x + i) = 0.$$

Now we multiply and simplify:

$$(x - 1)(x^2 - i^2) = 0$$
$$(x - 1)(x^2 + 1) = 0$$
$$x^3 - x^2 + x - 1 = 0.$$

Example 4. Find an equation having -1, i, and $1 + i$ as solutions.

$$(x + 1)(x - i)[x - (1 + i)] = 0$$
$$(x^2 + x - ix - i)(x - 1 - i) = 0$$
$$x^3 - 2ix^2 - ix - 2x - 1 + i = 0$$

[37, 38]

SOLVING EQUATIONS

First-degree equations in complex numbers are solved very much like first-degree equations in real numbers.

Example 5. Solve $3ix + 4 - 5i = (1 + i)x + 2i$.

$$3ix - (1 + i)x = 2i - (4 - 5i) \quad \text{(adding } -(1 + i)x \\ \text{and } -(4 - 5i))$$

$$(-1 + 2i)x = -4 + 7i \qquad \text{(simplifying)}$$

$$x = \frac{-4 + 7i}{-1 + 2i} \qquad \text{(dividing)}$$

$$x = \frac{-4 + 7i}{-1 + 2i} \cdot \frac{-1 - 2i}{-1 - 2i}$$

$$= \frac{18 + i}{5} = \frac{18}{5} + \frac{1}{5}i \qquad \textbf{[39]}$$

In Example 1 we used the quadratic formula, but did not evaluate $\sqrt{10i}$. We wish to find complex numbers z for which $z^2 = 10i$. We do this in the following example.

Example 6. Solve $z^2 = 10i$.

Let $z = x + yi$. Then we have $(x + yi)^2 = 10i$, or $x^2 + 2xyi + y^2i^2 = 10i$, or $x^2 - y^2 + 2xyi = 0 + 10i$.

Since the real parts must be equal and the imaginary parts equal, $x^2 - y^2 = 0$ and $2xy = 10$.

Here we have two equations in real numbers. We can find a solution by solving the second equation for y and substituting in the first.

Since

$$y = \frac{5}{x},$$

then

$$x^2 - \left(\frac{5}{x}\right)^2 = 0$$

$$x^2 - \frac{25}{x^2} = 0 \text{ or } x^4 - 25 = 0$$

$$(x^2 + 5)(x^2 - 5) = 0 \qquad \text{(factoring)}$$

$$x^2 + 5 = 0 \text{ or } x^2 - 5 = 0 \qquad \text{(principle of} \\ \text{zero products)}$$

The real solutions are $\sqrt{5}$ and $-\sqrt{5}$.

Now, going back to $2xy = 10$, we see that if $x = \sqrt{5}$, then $y = \sqrt{5}$, and if $x = -\sqrt{5}$, then $y = -\sqrt{5}$. Thus the solutions of our equation (and the square roots of $10i$) are $\sqrt{5} + \sqrt{5}i$ and $-\sqrt{5} - \sqrt{5}i$. **[40]**

Exercise Set 11.3

In Exercises 1–14, find an equation having the specified solutions.

1. $2i, -2i$ **2.** $3i, -3i$ **3.** $1 + i, 1 - i$ **4.** $2 + i, 2 - i$

5. $2 + 3i, 2 - 3i$ **6.** $4 + 3i, 4 - 3i$ **7.** $3, i$ **8.** $5, i$

9. $1, 3i, -3i$ **10.** $1, 2i, -2i$ **11.** $2, 1 + i, i$ **12.** $3, 1 - i, i$

13. $i, 2i, -i$ **14.** $i, -2i, -i$

In Exercises 15–28, solve the equations.

15. $(3 + i)x + i = 5i$ **16.** $(2 + i)x - i = 5 + i$

17. $2ix + 5 - 4i = (2 + 3i)x - 2i$ **18.** $5ix + 3 + 2i = (3 - 2i)x + 3i$

19. $(1 + 2i)x + 3 - 2i = 4 - 5i + 3ix$

20. $(1 - 2i)x + 2 - 3i = 5 - 4i + 2x$

21. $(5 + i)x + 1 - 3i = (2 - 3i)x + 2 - i$

22. $(5 - i)x + 2 - 3i = (3 - 2i)x + 3 - i$

23. $x^2 - 2x + 5 = 0$

24. $x^2 - 4x + 5 = 0$

25. $x^2 - 4x + 13 = 0$

26. $x^2 - 6x + 13 = 0$

27. $x^2 + 3x + 4 = 0$

28. $3x^2 + x + 2 = 0$

In Exercises 29–34, solve using the quadratic formula. You need not evaluate square roots.

29. $x^2 + (1 - i)x + i = 0$

30. $x^2 + (1 + i)x - i = 0$

31. $2x^2 + ix + 1 = 0$

32. $2x^2 - ix + 1 = 0$

33. $3x^2 + (1 + 2i)x + 1 - i = 0$

34. $3x^2 + (1 - 2i)x + 1 + i = 0$

In Exercises 35–38, find the square roots.

35. $4i$ **36.** $-4i$ **37.** $3 + 4i$ **38.** $5 - 12i$

▶ Solve. (*Hint:* Factor first.)

39. $x^3 - 8 = 0$ **40.** $x^3 + 8 = 0$ **41.** $x^3 + 125 = 0$ **42.** $x^3 - 125 = 0$

11.4 Graphical Representation and Polar Notation

The real numbers can be graphed on a line. Complex numbers are graphed on a plane. We graph a complex number $a + bi$ in the same way that we graph an ordered pair of real numbers (a, b). In place of an x-axis we have a *real axis,* and in place of a y-axis we have an *imaginary axis.*

Examples. Graph A: $3 + 2i$, B: $-4 + 5i$, and C: $-5 - 4i$.

Horizontal distances correspond to the real part of a number. Vertical distances correspond to the imaginary part. Graphs of the numbers are shown on the right as vectors. The horizontal component of the vector for $a + bi$ is a and the vertical component is b. Complex numbers are sometimes used in the study of vectors.   **[41]**

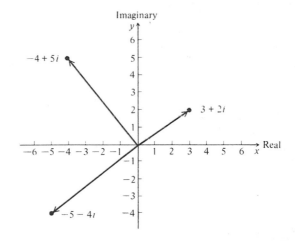

Adding complex numbers is like adding vectors using components. For example, to add $3 + 2i$ and $5 + 4i$ we add the real parts and the imaginary parts to obtain $8 + 6i$. Graphically, then, the sum of two complex numbers looks like a vector sum. It is the diagonal of a parallelogram.

Example. Show graphically $2 + 2i$ and $3 - i$. Show also their sum.

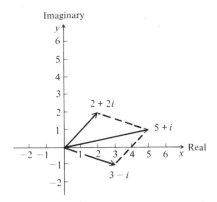

[42]

POLAR NOTATION FOR COMPLEX NUMBERS

In Chapter 10 we studied polar form for vectors, in which we use the length of a vector and the angle that it makes with the x-axis. In a similar way we develop polar notation for complex numbers. From the diagram below we can see that the length of the vector for $a + bi$ is $\sqrt{a^2 + b^2}$. Note that this quantity is a real number. It is called the *absolute value* of $a + bi$, and is denoted $|a + bi|$.

> **Definition.** The *absolute value* of a complex number $a + bi$ is denoted $|a + bi|$ and is defined to be $\sqrt{a^2 + b^2}$.

Example. Find $|3 + 4i|$.

$$|3 + 4i| = \sqrt{3^2 + 4^2} = \sqrt{9 + 16} = 5 \qquad [43]$$

Now let us consider any complex number $a + bi$. Suppose that its absolute value is r. Let us also suppose that the angle that the vector makes with the real axis is θ. As the next diagram shows, we have

$$a = r \cos \theta \qquad \text{and} \qquad b = r \sin \theta.$$

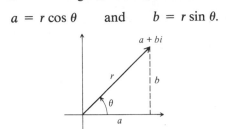

Thus

$$a + bi = r \cos \theta + ir \sin \theta$$
$$= r(\cos \theta + i \sin \theta).$$

This is polar notation for $a + bi$. The angle θ is called the *argument*.

> **Definition. Polar notation for the complex number $a + bi$ is $r(\cos \theta + i \sin \theta)$, where r is the absolute value and θ is the argument. This is sometimes shortened to r cis θ.**

Polar notation for complex numbers is also called *trigonometric notation.*

CHANGE OF NOTATION

To change from polar notation to *binomial*, or *rectangular*, notation $a + bi$, we proceed as in Section 10.6, recalling that $a = r \cos \theta$ and $b = r \sin \theta$.

Example 1. Write binomial, or rectangular, notation for $2(\cos 120° + i \sin 120°)$.

$$a = 2 \cos 120° = -1$$
$$b = 2 \sin 120° = \sqrt{3}$$

Thus $2(\cos 120° + i \sin 120°) = -1 + i\sqrt{3}$.

Example 2. Write binomial notation for $\sqrt{8} \operatorname{cis} \dfrac{7\pi}{4}$.

$$a = \sqrt{8} \cos \frac{7\pi}{4} = \sqrt{8} \cdot \frac{1}{\sqrt{2}} = 2$$

$$b = \sqrt{8} \sin \frac{7\pi}{4} = \sqrt{8} \cdot \frac{-1}{\sqrt{2}} = -2$$

Thus $\sqrt{8} \operatorname{cis} \dfrac{7\pi}{4} = 2 - 2i$.   **[44, 45]**

To change from binomial notation to polar notation, we remember that $r = \sqrt{a^2 + b^2}$ and θ is an angle for which $\sin \theta = b/r$ and $\cos \theta = a/r$.

Example 3. Find polar notation for $1 + i$.

We note that $a = 1$ and $b = 1$. Then

$$r = \sqrt{1^2 + 1^2} = \sqrt{2},$$

$$\sin \theta = \frac{1}{\sqrt{2}} \quad \text{and} \quad \cos \theta = \frac{1}{\sqrt{2}}.$$

Thus $\theta = \dfrac{\pi}{4}$, or 45°, and we have

$$1 + i = \sqrt{2} \operatorname{cis} \frac{\pi}{4} \quad \text{or} \quad 1 + i = \sqrt{2} \operatorname{cis} 45°.$$

Example 4. Find polar notation for $\sqrt{3} - i$.

$$r = \sqrt{(\sqrt{3})^2 + (-1)^2} = 2,$$

$$\sin \theta = -\frac{1}{2} \quad \text{and} \quad \cos \theta = \frac{\sqrt{3}}{2}.$$

Thus $\theta = \dfrac{11\pi}{6}$, or 330°, and we have

$$\sqrt{3} - i = 2 \operatorname{cis} \frac{11\pi}{6} = 2 \operatorname{cis} 330°. \quad \textbf{[46, 47]}$$

In changing to polar notation, note that there are many angles satisfying the given conditions. We ordinarily choose the smallest positive angle.

MULTIPLICATION AND POLAR NOTATION

Multiplication of complex numbers is somewhat easier to do with polar notation than with rectangular notation. We simply multiply the absolute values and add the arguments. Let us state this more formally and then prove it.

> **Theorem.** **For any complex numbers $r_1 \operatorname{cis} \theta_1$ and $r_2 \operatorname{cis} \theta_2$,**
>
> $$(r_1 \operatorname{cis} \theta_1)(r_2 \operatorname{cis} \theta_2) = r_1 \cdot r_2 \operatorname{cis} (\theta_1 + \theta_2).$$

To prove this, let us first multiply $a_1 + b_1 i$ by $a_2 + b_2 i$:

$$(a_1 + b_1 i)(a_2 + b_2 i) = (a_1 a_2 - b_1 b_2) + (a_2 b_1 + a_1 b_2)i.$$

Recall that

$$a_1 = r_1 \cos \theta_1, \qquad b_1 = r_1 \sin \theta_1,$$

and

$$a_2 = r_2 \cos \theta_2, \qquad b_2 = r_2 \sin \theta_2.$$

We substitute these in the product above, to obtain

$$r_1(\cos \theta_1 + i \sin \theta_1) \cdot r_2(\cos \theta_2 + i \sin \theta_2)$$
$$= (r_1 r_2 \cos \theta_1 \cos \theta_2 - r_1 r_2 \sin \theta_1 \sin \theta_2)$$
$$+ (r_1 r_2 \sin \theta_1 \cos \theta_2 + r_1 r_2 \cos \theta_1 \sin \theta_2)i.$$

This simplifies to

$$r_1 r_2(\cos \theta_1 \cos \theta_2 - \sin \theta_1 \sin \theta_2)$$
$$+ r_1 r_2(\sin \theta_1 \cos \theta_2 + \cos \theta_1 \sin \theta_2)i.$$

Now, using identities for sums of angles, we can simplify this to

$$r_1 r_2 \cos (\theta_1 + \theta_2) + r_1 r_2 \sin (\theta_1 + \theta_2)i,$$

or

$$r_1 r_2 \operatorname{cis} (\theta_1 + \theta_2),$$

which was to be shown.

To divide complex numbers we do the reverse of the above. We state this, but will omit the proof.

> **Theorem. For any complex numbers r_1 cis θ_1 and r_2 cis θ_2, $(r_2 \neq 0)$,**
>
> $$\frac{r_1 \text{ cis } \theta_1}{r_2 \text{ cis } \theta_2} = \frac{r_1}{r_2} \text{ cis } (\theta_1 - \theta_2).$$

Example. Find the product of 3 cis 40° and 7 cis 20°.

$$3 \text{ cis } 40° \cdot 7 \text{ cis } 20° = 3 \cdot 7 \text{ cis } (40° + 20°)$$
$$= 21 \text{ cis } 60°$$

Example. Find the product of 2 cis π and 3 cis $\left(-\dfrac{\pi}{2}\right)$.

$$2 \text{ cis } \pi \cdot 3 \text{ cis } \left(-\frac{\pi}{2}\right) = 2 \cdot 3 \text{ cis } \left(\pi - \frac{\pi}{2}\right)$$
$$= 6 \text{ cis } \frac{\pi}{2}.$$

Example. Divide 2 cis π by 4 cis $\dfrac{\pi}{2}$.

$$\frac{2 \text{ cis } \pi}{4 \text{ cis } \dfrac{\pi}{2}} = \frac{2}{4} \text{ cis } \left(\pi - \frac{\pi}{2}\right)$$
$$= \frac{1}{2} \text{ cis } \frac{\pi}{2} \qquad \text{[48–50]}$$

THE PRINCIPLE OF ZERO PRODUCTS

In complex numbers, when we multiply by 0 the result is 0. This is half of the principle of zero products. We have yet to show that the converse is true; that if a product is zero, at least one of the factors must be zero. With polar notation this is easy to do. The number 0 has polar notation 0 cis θ, where θ can be any angle. Now consider a product r_1 cis $\theta_1 \cdot r_2$ cis θ_2, where neither factor is 0. This means that $r_1 \neq 0$ and $r_2 \neq 0$. Since these are nonzero real numbers, their product is not zero, and the product of the complex numbers $r_1 r_2$ cis $(\theta_1 + \theta_2)$ is not zero. Thus the principle of zero products holds in complex numbers.

Exercise Set 11.4

In Exercises 1–8, graph each pair of complex numbers and their sum.

1. $3 + 2i$, $2 - 5i$ **2.** $4 + 3i$, $3 - 4i$ **3.** $-5 + 3i$, $-2 - 3i$ **4.** $-4 + 2i$, $-3 - 4i$

5. $2 - 3i$, $-5 + 4i$ **6.** $3 - 2i$, $-5 + 5i$ **7.** $-2 - 5i$, $5 + 3i$ **8.** $-3 - 4i$, $6 + 3i$

In Exercises 9–22, find rectangular notation.

9. $3(\cos 30° + i \sin 30°)$ **10.** $5(\cos 60° + i \sin 60°)$ **11.** $4(\cos 135° + i \sin 135°)$

12. $6(\cos 150° + i \sin 150°)$ **13.** 10 cis $270°$ **14.** 12 cis $90°$

15. 5 cis $(-45°)$ **16.** 5 cis $(-60°)$ **17.** $\sqrt{8}\left(\cos \dfrac{\pi}{4} + i \sin \dfrac{\pi}{4}\right)$

18. $\sqrt{8}\left(\cos \dfrac{3\pi}{4} + i \sin \dfrac{3\pi}{4}\right)$ **19.** $4\left(\cos \dfrac{\pi}{6} + i \sin \dfrac{\pi}{6}\right)$ **20.** $5\left(\cos \dfrac{\pi}{3} + i \sin \dfrac{\pi}{3}\right)$

21. $\sqrt{8}\,\text{cis}\,\dfrac{5\pi}{4}$ **22.** $\sqrt{8}\,\text{cis}\left(-\dfrac{\pi}{4}\right)$

In Exercises 23–34, find polar notation.

23. $1 - i$ **24.** $-1 - i$ **25.** $\sqrt{3} + i$ **26.** $-\sqrt{3} + i$

27. $10\sqrt{3} - 10i$ **28.** $-10\sqrt{3} + 10i$ **29.** $2i$ **30.** $3i$

31. -5 **32.** -10 **33.** $-4i$ **34.** $-5i$

In Exercises 35–46, convert to polar notation and then multiply or divide.

35. $(1 - i)(2 + 2i)$ **36.** $(\sqrt{3} + i)(1 + i)$ **37.** $(10\sqrt{3} + 10i)(\sqrt{3} - i)$

38. $(1 + i\sqrt{3})(1 + i)$ **39.** $(2\sqrt{3} + 2i)(2i)$ **40.** $(3\sqrt{3} - 3i)(2i)$

41. $\dfrac{1 + i}{1 - i}$ **42.** $\dfrac{1 - i}{1 + i}$ **43.** $\dfrac{-1 + i}{\sqrt{3} + i}$

44. $\dfrac{1 - i}{\sqrt{3} - i}$ **45.** $\dfrac{2\sqrt{3} - 2i}{1 + \sqrt{3}i}$ **46.** $\dfrac{3 - 3\sqrt{3}i}{\sqrt{3} - i}$

▶**47.** Show that for any complex number z, $|z| = |-z|$. (*Hint:* Let $z = a + bi$.)

48. Show that for any complex number z, $|z| = |\bar{z}|$. (*Hint:* Let $z = a + bi$.)

49. Show that for any complex numbers z and w, $|z \cdot w| = |z| \cdot |w|$. (*Hint:* Let $z = r_1 \text{ cis } \theta_1$ and $w = r_2 \text{ cis } \theta_2$.)

50. Show that for any complex number z and any nonzero complex number w, $\left|\dfrac{z}{w}\right| = \dfrac{|z|}{|w|}$. (Use the hint for Exercise 49.)

11.5 DeMoivre's Theorem

An important theorem about powers and roots of complex numbers is named for the French mathematician DeMoivre (1667–1754). Let us consider a number $r \text{ cis } \theta$ and its square:

$$(r \text{ cis } \theta)^2 = (r \text{ cis } \theta)(r \text{ cis } \theta) = r \cdot r \text{ cis }(\theta + \theta)$$
$$= r^2 \text{ cis } 2\theta.$$

Similarly, we see that

$$(r \text{ cis } \theta)^3 = r \cdot r \cdot r \text{ cis }(\theta + \theta + \theta) = r^3 \text{ cis } 3\theta.$$

The generalization of this is DeMoivre's theorem.

> **DeMoivre's Theorem.** For any complex number $r \text{ cis } \theta$ and any natural number n, $(r \text{ cis } \theta)^n = r^n \text{ cis } n\theta$.

Example 1. Find $(1 + i)^9$.

We first find polar notation: $1 + i = \sqrt{2} \text{ cis } 45°$. Then

$$(1 + i)^9 = (\sqrt{2} \text{ cis } 45°)^9$$

$$= \sqrt{2}^9 \text{ cis } 9 \cdot 45°$$

$$= 2^{\frac{9}{2}} \text{ cis } 405°$$

$$= 16\sqrt{2} \text{ cis } 45°. \quad (405° \text{ has the same terminal side as } 45°)$$

[51, 52]

ROOTS OF COMPLEX NUMBERS

As we shall see, every nonzero complex number has two square roots. A number has three cube roots, four fourth roots, and so on. In general a nonzero complex number has n different nth roots. These can be found by the formula that we now state and prove.

> **Theorem. The nth roots of a complex number $r \text{ cis } \theta$ are given by**
>
> $$r^{1/n} \text{ cis } \left(\frac{\theta}{n} + k \cdot \frac{360°}{n}\right),$$
>
> **where $k = 0, 1, 2, \ldots, n - 1$.**

We show that this formula gives us n different roots, using DeMoivre's theorem. We take the expression for the nth roots and raise it to the nth power, to show that we get $r \text{ cis } \theta$:

$$\left[r^{1/n} \text{ cis } \left(\frac{\theta}{n} + k \cdot \frac{360°}{n}\right)\right]^n$$

$$= (r^{1/n})^n \text{ cis } \left(\frac{\theta}{n} \cdot n + k \cdot n \cdot \frac{360°}{n}\right)$$

$$= r \text{ cis } (\theta + k \cdot 360°) = r \text{ cis } \theta.$$

Thus we know that the formula gives us nth roots for any natural number k. Next we show that there are at least n different roots. To see this, consider substituting 0, 1, 2, and so on, for k. When $k = n$ the cycle begins to repeat, but from 0 to $n - 1$ the angles

obtained and their sines and cosines are all different. There cannot be more than n different nth roots. This fact follows from the *fundamental theorem of algebra*, considered in the next chapter.

Example 2. Find the square roots of $2 + 2\sqrt{3}i$.

We first find polar notation: $2 + 2\sqrt{3}i = 4 \text{ cis } 60°$. Then

$$(4 \text{ cis } 60°)^{\frac{1}{2}} = 4^{\frac{1}{2}} \text{ cis } \left(\frac{60°}{2} + k \cdot \frac{360°}{2}\right), \quad k = 0, 1.$$

$$= 2 \text{ cis } \left(30° + k \cdot \frac{360°}{2}\right), \quad k = 0, 1.$$

Thus the roots are $2 \text{ cis } 30°$ and $2 \text{ cis } 210°$, or

$$\sqrt{3} + i \quad \text{and} \quad -\sqrt{3} - i. \quad \textbf{[53]}$$

In Example 2 and in Exercise 53 it should be noted that the two square roots of a number were additive inverses of each other. This is true of the square roots of any complex number. To see this, let us find the square roots of any complex number $r \text{ cis } \theta$.

$$(r \text{ cis } \theta)^{\frac{1}{2}} = r^{\frac{1}{2}} \text{ cis } \left(\frac{\theta}{2} + k \cdot \frac{360°}{2}\right), \quad k = 0, 1.$$

$$= r^{\frac{1}{2}} \text{ cis } \frac{\theta}{2} \quad \text{or} \quad r^{\frac{1}{2}} \text{ cis } \left(\frac{\theta}{2} + 180°\right)$$

Now let us look at these numbers on a graph. They lie on a line, so if one number has binomial notation $a + bi$, the other has binomial notation $-a - bi$. Hence their sum is 0 and they are additive inverses of each other.

Example 3. Find the cube roots of 1. Locate them on a graph.

$$1 = 1 \text{ cis } 0°$$

$$(1 \text{ cis } 0°)^{\frac{1}{3}} = 1^{\frac{1}{3}} \text{ cis} \left(\frac{0°}{3} + k \cdot \frac{360°}{3} \right), \qquad k = 0, 1, 2.$$

The roots are $1 \text{ cis } 0°$, $1 \text{ cis } 120°$, and $1 \text{ cis } 240°$, or

$$1, -\frac{1}{2} + \frac{\sqrt{3}}{2} i, \qquad \text{and} \qquad -\frac{1}{2} - \frac{\sqrt{3}}{2} i.$$

Note in the example that the graphs of the cube roots lie equally spaced about a circle. This is true of the nth roots of any complex number.

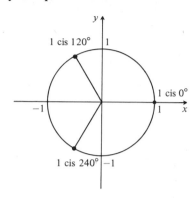

[54]

Exercise Set 11.5

In Exercises 1–6, raise the number to the power and give your answer in polar notation.

1. $\left(2 \text{ cis } \frac{\pi}{3} \right)^3$

2. $\left(3 \text{ cis } \frac{\pi}{2} \right)^4$

3. $\left(2 \text{ cis } \frac{\pi}{6} \right)^6$

4. $\left(2 \text{ cis } \frac{\pi}{5} \right)^5$

5. $(1 + i)^6$

6. $(1 - i)^6$

In Exercises 7–14, raise the number to the power and give your answer in rectangular notation.

7. $(2 \text{ cis } 240°)^4$

8. $(2 \text{ cis } 120°)^4$

9. $(1 + \sqrt{3}i)^4$

10. $(-\sqrt{3} + i)^6$

11. $\left(\frac{1}{\sqrt{2}} + \frac{1}{\sqrt{2}} i \right)^{10}$

12. $\left(\frac{1}{\sqrt{2}} - \frac{1}{\sqrt{2}} i \right)^{12}$

13. $\left(\frac{\sqrt{3}}{2} + \frac{1}{2} i \right)^{12}$

14. $\left(\frac{\sqrt{3}}{2} - \frac{1}{2} i \right)^{14}$

15. Find the square roots of $-1 + \sqrt{3}i$.

16. Find the square roots of $-\sqrt{3} - i$.

17. Find the cube roots of i.

18. Find the cube roots of $-i$.

19. Find the fourth roots of 16.

20. Find the fourth roots of -16.

21. Find the cube roots of 68.4321.

22. Find the cube roots of 456.86.

Chapter 11 Test, or Review

Simplify.

1. $(2 - 2i)(3 + 4i)$

2. $(3 - 5i) - (2 - i)$

3. $(6 + 2i) + (-4 - 3i)$

4. $\dfrac{2 - 3i}{1 - 3i}$

5. Solve for x and y: $4x + 2i = 8 - (2 + y)i$.

6. Find a polynomial in $\bar{z}$ that is the conjugate: $3z^3 + z - 7$.

7. Find an equation having the solutions $1 - 2i$, $1 + 2i$.

Solve.

8. $5x^2 - 4x + 1 = 0$

9. $x^2 + 3ix - 1 = 0$

10. Find the square roots of $4i$.

11. Graph the pair of complex numbers $-3 - 2i$, $4 + 7i$, and their sum.

12. Find rectangular notation for $2(\cos 135° + i \sin 135°)$.

13. Find polar notation for $1 + i$.

14. Find the product of $7 \operatorname{cis} 18°$ and $10 \operatorname{cis} 32°$.

15. Find the cube roots of $1 + i$.

CHAPTER 12

Polynomials, Polynomial Functions, and Rational Functions

12.1 Polynomials and Polynomial Functions

We have considered polynomials before. Now we give a formal definition.

> **Definition.** A *polynomial* is any expression of the type
>
> $$a_n x^n + a_{n-1} x^{n-1} + \cdots + a_2 x^2 + a_1 x + a_0,$$
>
> where n is a nonnegative integer and $a_0, \ldots, a_n$ are numbers.

The numbers $a_0, \ldots, a_n$ are called *coefficients*. They are complex numbers, but may in certain cases be restricted to real numbers, or rational numbers, or integers. The coefficient of the term of highest degree, a_n, is called the *leading coefficient*.

Some or all of the coefficients of a polynomial may be 0. If all of them are, we simply write 0 and refer to it as the *zero polynomial*. The *degree* of a polynomial is the number n, but the 0 polynomial is not given any degree. A polynomial consisting only of a nonzero constant has degree 0.

Examples.

Polynomial	Degree
$5x^3 - 3x^2 + i$	3
$-4x + \sqrt{2}$	1
25	0
0	No degree

[1–5]

ROOTS OF POLYNOMIALS

When a number is substituted for the variable in a polynomial, the result is some unique number. Thus every polynomial defines a function. We often refer to polynomials, therefore, using function notation $P(x)$. If a number a makes a polynomial 0, then a is called a *root*, or a *zero*, of the polynomial.

Examples. $P(x) = x^3 + 2x^2 - 5x - 6.$

a) Is 3 a root of $P(x)$?

   We substitute 3 into the polynomial:

   $$P(3) = 3^3 + 2(3)^2 - 5 \cdot 3 - 6 = 24.$$

   Since $P(3) \neq 0$, 3 is not a root.

b) Is -1 a root of $P(x)$?

   $$P(-1) = (-1)^3 + 2(-1)^2 - 5(-1) - 6 = 0.$$

   Since $P(-1) = 0$, -1 is a root of the polynomial.

   [6–8]

DIVISION OF POLYNOMIALS AND FACTORS

When we divide one polynomial by another we obtain a quotient and a remainder. If the remainder is 0, then the divisor is a *factor* of the dividend.

Example 1. Divide, to find whether $x^2 + 9$ is a factor of $x^4 - 81$.

$$
\begin{array}{r}
x^2 - 9 \\
x^2 + 9 \overline{)x^4 - 81} \\
\underline{x^4 + 9x^2 } \\
-9x^2 - 81 \\
\underline{-9x^2 - 81} \\
0
\end{array}
$$

(Note how spaces have been left for missing terms in the dividend.)

Since the remainder is 0, we know that $x^2 + 9$ is a factor.

Example 2. Divide, to find whether $x^2 + 3x - 1$ is a factor of $x^4 - 81$.

$$
\begin{array}{r}
x^2 - 3x + 10 \\
x^2 + 3x - 1 \overline{)x^4 - 81} \\
\underline{x^4 + 3x^3 - x^2 } \\
-3x^3 + x^2 \\
\underline{-3x^3 - 9x^2 + 3x } \\
10x^2 - 3x - 81 \\
\underline{10x^2 + 30x - 10} \\
-33x - 71
\end{array}
$$

Since the remainder is not 0, we know that $x^2 + 3x - 1$ is not a factor of $x^4 - 81$.   [9, 10]

In general, when we divide a <u>polynomial $P(x)$</u> by a <u>divisor $d(x)$</u> we obtain some <u>polynomial $Q(x)$</u> for a quotient and some polynomial <u>$R(x)$ for a remainder</u>. The remainder must either be 0 or have degree less than that of $d(x)$. To check a division we multiply the quotient by the divisor and add the remainder, to see if we get the dividend. Thus these polynomials are related as follows:

$$P(x) = d(x) \cdot Q(x) + R(x).$$

Example 3. If $P(x) = x^4 - 81$, $d(x) = x^2 + 9$, then $Q(x) = x^2 - 9$ and $R(x) = 0$, and

$$\underbrace{x^4 - 81}_{P(x)} = \underbrace{(x^2 + 9)}_{d(x)} \ \underbrace{(x^2 - 9)}_{Q(x)} + \underbrace{0}_{R(x)} \ .$$

Example 4. If $P(x) = x^4 - 81$, $d(x) = x^2 + 3x - 1$, then $Q(x) = x^2 - 3x + 10$ and $R(x) = -33x - 71$, and

$$\underbrace{x^4 - 81}_{P(x)} = \underbrace{(x^2 + 3x - 1)}_{d(x)} \cdot \underbrace{(x^2 - 3x + 10)}_{Q(x)} + \underbrace{(-33x - 71)}_{R(x)}$$

[11]

Exercise Set 12.1

Determine the degree of each polynomial.

1. $x^4 - 3x^2 + 1$

2. $2x^5 - x^4 + \dfrac{1}{4}x - 7$

3. $-2x + 5$

4. $3x - \sqrt{\pi}$

5. $2x^2 - 3x + 4$

6. $\dfrac{1}{4}x^2 - 7$

7. $0x + 7$

8. $0x - 4$

9. $0x + 0$

10. $0x^2 + 0$

11. 0

12. $9 - 9$

13. Determinine whether 2, 3, and -1 are roots of $P(x) = x^3 + 6x^2 - x - 30$.

14. Determine whether 2, 3, and -1 are roots of $P(x) = 2x^3 - 3x^2 + x - 1$.

15. For $P(x)$ of Exercise 13, which of the following are factors of $P(x)$?

a) $x - 2$ b) $x - 3$ c) $x + 1$

16. For $P(x)$ of Exercise 14, which of the following are factors of $P(x)$?

a) $x - 2$ b) $x - 3$ c) $x + 1$

In each of the following, a polynomial $P(x)$ and a divisor $d(x)$ are given. Find the quotient $Q(x)$ and the remainder $R(x)$ when $P(x)$ is divided by $d(x)$ and express $P(x)$ in the form $d(x) \cdot Q(x) + R(x)$.

17. $P(x) = x^3 + 6x^2 - x - 30$,
    $d(x) = x - 2$

18. $P(x) = 2x^3 - 3x^2 + x - 1$,
    $d(x) = x - 2$

19. $P(x)$ as in Exercise 17,
    $d(x) = x - 3$

20. $P(x)$ as in Exercise 18,
    $d(x) = x - 3$

21. $P(x) = x^3 - 8$,
   $d(x) = x + 2$

22. $P(x) = x^3 + 27$,
   $d(x) = x + 1$

23. $P(x) = x^4 + 9x^2 + 20$,
   $d(x) = x^2 + 4$

24. $P(x) = x^4 + x^2 + 2$,
   $d(x) = x^2 + x + 1$

25. For $P(x) = x^5 - 64$,
   a) find $P(2)$;
   b) find the remainder when $P(x)$ is divided by $x - 2$, and compare your answer to (a);
   c) find $P(-1)$;
   d) find the remainder when $P(x)$ is divided by $x + 1$, and compare your answer to (c).

26. For $P(x) = x^3 + x^2$,
   a) find $P(-1)$;
   b) find the remainder when $P(x)$ is divided by $x + 1$, and compare your answer to (a);
   c) find $P(2)$;
   d) find the remainder when $P(x)$ is divided by $x - 2$, and compare your answer to (c).

▶ **27.** For $P(x) = 2x^2 - ix + 1$,
   a) find $P(-i)$;
   b) find the remainder when $P(x)$ is divided by $x + i$.

28. For $P(x) = 2x^2 + ix - 1$,
   a) find $P(i)$;
   b) find the remainder when $P(x)$ is divided by $x - i$.

12.2 The Remainder and Factor Theorems

Some of the exercises in the previous exercise set illustrate the following theorem.

The Remainder Theorem. If a number r is substituted for x in the polynomial $P(x)$, then the result $P(r)$ is the remainder that would be obtained by dividing $P(x)$ by $x - r$.

Proof. The equation $P(x) = d(x) \cdot Q(x) + R(x)$ is the basis of this proof. If we divide $P(x)$ by $x - r$, we obtain a quotient $Q(x)$ and a remainder $R(x)$ related as follows:

$$P(x) = (x - r) \cdot Q(x) + R(x).$$

The remainder $R(x)$ must either be 0 or have degree less than $x - r$. Thus $R(x)$ must be a constant. Let us call this constant R. In the above expression we get a true sentence whenever we replace x by any number.

Let us replace x by r. We get

$$P(r) = (r - r) \cdot Q(r) + R$$
$$P(r) = \qquad 0 \cdot Q(r) + R$$
$$P(r) = R.$$

This tells us that the function value $P(r)$ is the remainder obtained when we divide $P(x)$ by $x - r$.

Example 1. If $P(x) = x^3 + 6x^2 - x - 30$, what is the remainder when $P(x)$ is divided by $x + 1$ [or $x - (-1)$]?

$$P(-1) = (-1)^3 + 6(-1)^2 - (-1) - 30$$
$$= -1 + 6 + 1 - 30 = -24$$

Thus when $P(x)$ is divided by $x + 1$, the remainder is -24.

Example 2. If $P(x)$, in Example 1, is divided by $x - 2$, what is the remainder?

$$P(2) = 2^3 + 6 \cdot 2^2 - 2 - 30 = 8 + 24 - 2 - 30 = 0$$

Thus when $P(x)$ is divided by $x - 2$, the remainder is 0. Note that this also tells us that $x - 2$ is a factor of $x^3 + 6x^2 - x - 30$. **[12–14]**

The Factor Theorem. For a polynomial $P(x)$, if $P(r) = 0$, then the polynomial $x - r$ is a factor of $P(x)$.

Proof. From the remainder theorem we have

$$P(x) = (x - r) \cdot Q(x) + P(r).$$

Then if $P(r) = 0$, we have

$$P(x) = (x - r) \cdot Q(x),$$

so $x - r$ is a factor of $P(x)$.

The factor theorem is very helpful in the process of factoring polynomials.

Example 3. Let $P(x) = x^3 + 2x^2 - 5x - 6$.

a) Decide whether $x + 1$ is a factor of $P(x)$.

We think of $x + 1$ as $x - (-1)$. Thus we find $P(-1)$:

$$P(-1) = (-1)^3 + 2(-1)^2 - 5(-1) - 6 = 0.$$

Since $P(-1) = 0$, we know that $x + 1$ is a factor of $P(x)$, by the remainder theorem.

b) Find another factor of $P(x)$.

We divide $P(x)$ by $x + 1$, obtaining for a quotient $x^2 + x - 6$.

c) Find a complete factorization of $P(x)$.

In part (b) we have determined that $P(x) = (x + 1)(x^2 + x - 6)$. The second factor can be factored further giving the complete factorization:

$$(x + 1)(x + 3)(x - 2). \qquad \textbf{[15–17]}$$

Exercise Set 12.2

In each of the following, find the remainder when $P(x)$ is divided by the binomial. Use the remainder theorem.

1. $P(x) = x^3 - 2x^2 + 5x - 4, \ x - 2$

2. $P(x) = x^3 - 2x^2 + 5x - 4, \ x + 2$

3. $P(x) = x^5 - 3x^2 + 2x - 1, \ x - 1$

4. $P(x) = x^5 - 3x^2 + 2x - 1, \ x + 1$

5. $P(x) = x^3 - 2x^2 + 5x - 4, \ x + 1$

6. $P(x) = x^3 - 2x^2 + 5x - 4, \ x - 1$

7. $P(x) = x^3 + 8, \ x + 2$

8. $P(x) = x^4 - 65, \ x - 4$

9. $P(x) = x^2 - 8x + 4, \ x - 3i$

10. $P(x) = x^2 + 8x - 4, \ x - 2i$

11. $P(x) = x^2 - 2x + 2, \ x - (1 + i)$

12. $P(x) = x^2 - 2x + 5, \ x - (1 + 2i)$

In each of the following, determine whether the expression of the type $x - r$ is a factor of the polynomial $P(x)$. Use the factor theorem.

13. $P(x) = x^3 - 3x^2 - 4x - 12, \ x + 2$

14. $P(x) = x^3 - 4x^2 + 3x + 8, \ x + 1$

15. $P(x) = 2x^4 + x^3 + x - \dfrac{3}{4}, \ x - \dfrac{1}{2}$

16. $P(x) = 4x^3 - 4x^2 - 11x + 6, \ x - \dfrac{1}{2}$

17. $P(x) = 2x^2 + 2x + 1, \, x - \left(-\dfrac{1}{2} - \dfrac{1}{2}i\right)$

18. $P(x) = 9x^2 + 6x + 2, \, x - \left(\dfrac{1}{3} - \dfrac{1}{3}i\right)$

19. $P(x) = x^5 - 1, \, x - 1$

20. $P(x) = x^5 + 1, \, x + 1$

21. a) Let $P(x) = x^3 + 2x^2 - x - 2$. Determine whether $x - 1$ is a factor of $P(x)$.

   b) Find another factor of $P(x)$.

   c) Find a complete factorization of $P(x)$.

22. a) Let $P(x) = x^3 + 4x^2 - x - 4$. Determine whether $x + 1$ is a factor of $P(x)$.

   b) Find another factor of $P(x)$.

   c) Find a complete factorization of $P(x)$.

23. Which, if any, of the binomials $x - 3$, $x + 4$, $x + 1$, $x - 1$, $x + 2$ are factors of $x^4 + x^3 - 13x^2 - x + 12$?

24. Which, if any, of the binomials $x - 3$, $x - 2$, $x + 3$, $x + 2$, $x - 1$ are factors of $x^3 - 2x^2 + 1$?

▶ Find k so that:

25. $x - 1$ is a factor of $x^3 - 3x^2 + kx - 1$.

26. $x + 2$ is a factor of $x^3 - kx^2 + 3x + 7k$.

Use the factor theorem to prove that:

27. $x + a$ is a factor of $x^{2n} - a^{2n}$, for any natural number n.

28. $x + a$ is a factor of $x^{2n+1} + a^{2n+1}$, for any natural number n.

29. $x - a$ is a factor of $x^n - a^n$, for any natural number n.

30. $x - a$ is a factor of $x^{2n} - a^{2n}$, for any natural number n.

12.3 Synthetic Division

In dividing polynomials there is much writing duplicated. To streamline division, we can arrange the work so that duplicate and unnecessary writing is avoided. Consider the procedures outlined below.

A.

$$
\begin{array}{r}
4x^2 + 5x + 11 \\
x - 2\overline{\smash{)}4x^3 - 3x^2 + x + 7} \\
\underline{4x^3 - 8x^2} \\
5x^2 + x \\
\underline{5x^2 - 10x} \\
11x + 7 \\
\underline{11x - 22} \\
29
\end{array}
$$

remainder

B.

$$
\begin{array}{r}
\boxed{4} \quad \boxed{5} \quad \boxed{11} \\
1 - 2\overline{\smash{)}4 - 3 + 1 + 7} \\
\underline{\boxed{4} - 8} \\
5 + 1 \\
\underline{\boxed{5} - 10} \\
11 + 7 \\
\underline{\boxed{11} - 22} \\
29
\end{array}
$$

remainder

In A we performed a division. In B we performed the same division, but we wrote only the coefficients. Should there have been a missing term, we would have written a 0 for its coefficient. Note also that the shaded numerals are duplicated. There would be no loss of understanding if we did not write them twice. Note also that when we subtract we add an additive inverse. We can accomplish this by using the additive inverse of -2, and then adding instead of subtracting.

C. Synthetic Division

$$\begin{array}{r} 2\,\lfloor\,4 - 3 + 1\ \ + 7 \\ +\ 8 + 10\ \ + 22 \\ \hline 4 + 5 + 11\,\lfloor\,+29 \end{array}$$

In C we "bring down" the first coefficient (4), then multiply it by the divisor (2), and write the result under the next coefficient (-3). Then we add, multiply the sum (5) by the divisor (2), and write the result under the next coefficient (1), and add, and keep repeating the process. The last term (29) is the remainder. The other terms are coefficients of the quotient. If the remainder is 0, then the quotient is a factor of the dividend.

Example 1. Use synthetic division to find the quotient and remainder:

$$(2x^3 + 7x^2 - 5) \div (x + 3).$$

First note that $x + 3 = x - (-3)$. Then

$$\begin{array}{r} -3\,\lfloor\,2 + 7 + 0\ \ -5 \\ -\ 6 - 3\ \ +9 \\ \hline 2 + 1 - 3\,\lfloor\,+4 \end{array}$$

The quotient is $2x^2 + x - 3$. The remainder is 4.

[18–20]

Example 2. Use synthetic division to find the quotient and remainder:

$$(x^5 + y^5) \div (x + y).$$

$$\begin{array}{r} -y\,\lfloor\,1 + 0 + 0\ \ + 0\ \ + 0\ \ \ + y^5 \\ -\ y + y^2 - y^3 + y^4\ \ - y^5 \\ \hline 1 - y + y^2 - y^3 + y^4\ \ \lfloor\ \ 0 \end{array}$$

The quotient is $x^4 - yx^3 + y^2x^2 - y^3x + y^4$. The remainder is 0.

[21]

We can also use synthetic division to find function values, especially when large powers are involved.

Example 3. $P(x) = 2x^5 - 3x^4 + x^3 - 2x^2 + x - 8$. Find $P(10)$.

Recall that $P(10)$ is the remainder when $P(x)$ is divided by $x - 10$.

$$\begin{array}{r} 10\,\lfloor\,2\ \ -3\ \ +1\ \ \ -2\ \ \ \ +1\ \ \ \ \ \ -8 \\ 20\ \ \ 170\ \ 1710\ \ 17{,}080\ \ 170{,}810 \\ \hline 2\ \ 17\ \ 171\ \ 1708\ \ 17{,}081\ \ \lfloor\ 170{,}802 \end{array}$$

Thus $P(10) = 170{,}802$. Compare this procedure to substituting 10 for x in the polynomial!

[22]

We can use synthetic division to determine whether a number is a root of a polynomial.

Example 4. Let $P(x) = x^3 + 8x^2 + 8x - 32$. Determine whether -4 is a root of $P(x)$. We must decide if $P(-4) = 0$. We find $P(-4)$ as the remainder, using synthetic division.

$$\begin{array}{r} -4\,\lfloor\,1 + 8 + \ \ 8\ \ \ -32 \\ -\ 4 - 16\ \ +32 \\ \hline 1 + 4 - \ \ 8\,\lfloor\ \ \ \ 0 \end{array}$$

Since $P(-4) = 0$, -4 is a root of $P(x)$.

[23]

Exercise Set 12.3

Use synthetic division to find the quotient and remainder.

1. $(x^3 - 7x^2 - 13x + 3) \div (x + 2)$

2. $(x^3 - 7x^2 + 13x + 3) \div (x - 2)$

3. $(2x^4 + 7x^3 + x - 12) \div (x + 3)$

4. $(2x^4 - 3x^2 + x - 7) \div (x + 4)$

5. $(x^3 - 2x^2 - 8) \div (x + 2)$

6. $(x^3 - 3x + 10) \div (x - 2)$

7. $(x^3 + 27) \div (x + 3)$

8. $(x^3 - 27) \div (x - 3)$

9. $(x^4 - 1) \div (x - 1)$

10. $(x^5 + 32) \div (x + 2)$

11. $(2x^4 + 3x^2 - 1) \div \left(x - \dfrac{1}{2}\right)$

12. $(3x^4 - 2x^2 + 2) \div \left(x - \dfrac{1}{4}\right)$

13. $(x^4 - y^4) \div (x - y)$

14. $(x^6 + y^6) \div (x + y)$

15. $(x^3 - 2ix^2 + ix + 5) \div (x - i)$

16. $(x^3 + 3ix^2 - 4ix - 2) \div (x + i)$

Use synthetic division to find the function values.

17. $P(x) = x^3 - 6x^2 + 11x - 6$; find $P(1)$, $P(-2)$, $P(3)$.

18. $P(x) = x^3 + 7x^2 - 12x - 3$; find $P(-3)$, $P(-2)$, $P(1)$.

19. $P(x) = 2x^5 - 3x^4 + 2x^3 - x + 8$; find $P(20)$, $P(-3)$.

20. $P(x) = x^5 - 10x^4 + 20x^3 - 5x - 100$; find $P(-10)$, $P(5)$.

Using synthetic division, determine whether the numbers are roots of the polynomials.

21. $-3, 2$; $P(x) = 3x^3 + 5x^2 - 6x + 18$

22. $-4, 2$; $P(x) = 3x^3 + 11x^2 - 2x + 8$

23. $-3, \dfrac{1}{2}$; $P(x) = x^3 - \dfrac{7}{2}x^2 + x - \dfrac{3}{2}$

24. $-6, \dfrac{1}{4}$; $P(x) = x^3 - \dfrac{7}{2}x^2 - 13x + 3$

25. $i, -i, -2$; $P(x) = x^3 + 2x^2 + x + 2$

26. $i, -i, 4$; $P(x) = x^3 - 4x^2 + x - 4$

27. Given that $f(x) = 2.13x^5 - 42.1x^3 + 17.5x^2 + 0.953x - 1.98$, find $f(3.21)$

a) by synthetic division;

b) by substitution.

28. Given that $f(x) = 0.673x^4 - 17.3x^2 + 923x - 1230$, find $f(-16.3)$

a) by synthetic division;

b) by substitution.

29. (*Nondecimal notation*). Ordinary notation for numbers is *decimal* (base ten). For example,

4325 means $4 \times 10^3 + 3 \times 10^2 + 2 \times 10 + 5$.

When the base is a number other than ten, the notation is called *nondecimal* and is defined in a similar way. For example,

4312_5 means $4 \times 5^3 + 3 \times 5^2 + 1 \times 5 + 2$.

Synthetic division can be used to convert from a nondecimal base to base ten. For example to convert 31214_5 to base ten we divide as follows.

$$
\begin{array}{r|rrrrr}
5 & 3 & 1 & 2 & 1 & 4 \\
  &   & 15 & 80 & 410 & 2055 \\
\hline
  & 3 & 16 & 82 & 411 & 2059 \\
\end{array}
$$

Decimal notation for this number is 2059.

a) Convert 4352_6 to decimal notation.

b) Prove that in general the procedure gives correct results.

12.4 Theorems about Roots

THE FUNDAMENTAL THEOREM OF ALGEBRA

A linear, or first-degree, polynomial $ax + b$ (where $a \neq 0$, of course) has just one root, $-b/a$. From Chapter 11 we know that any quadratic polynomial, with complex numbers for coefficients, has at least one, and at most two roots. The following theorem is a generalization. A proof is beyond this text.

> **The Fundamental Theorem of Algebra. Every polynomial of degree greater than 1, with complex coefficients, has at least one root in the system of complex numbers.**

This is a very powerful theorem. Note that while it guarantees that a root exists, it does not tell how to find it. We now develop some theory that can help in finding roots. First, we prove a corollary of the Fundamental Theorem of Algebra.

> **Theorem. Every polynomial of degree n, where $n > 0$, having complex coefficients, can be factored into n linear factors.**

Proof. Let us consider any polynomial of degree n, say $P(x)$. By the Fundamental Theorem, it has a root r_1. By the factor theorem, $x - r_1$ is a factor of $P(x)$. Thus we know that

$$P(x) = (x - r_1) \cdot Q_1(x),$$

where $Q_1(x)$ is the quotient that would be obtained upon dividing $P(x)$ by $x - r_1$. Let the leading coefficient of $P(x)$ be a_n. By considering the actual division process we see that the leading coefficient of $Q_1(x)$ is also a_n and that the degree of $Q_1(x)$ is $n - 1$. Now if the degree of $Q_1(x)$ is greater than 1, then it has a root r_2, and we have

$$Q_1(x) = (x - r_2) \cdot Q_2(x),$$

where the degree of $Q_2(x)$ is $n - 2$ and the leading coefficient is a_n. Thus we have

$$P(x) = (x - r_1)(x - r_2) \cdot Q_2(x).$$

This process can be continued until a quotient $Q_n(x)$ is obtained having degree 0. The leading coefficient will be a_n, so $Q_n(x)$ is actually the constant a_n. We now have the following:

$$P(x) = a_n(x - r_1)(x - r_2)(x - r_3) \cdots (x - r_n).$$

This completes the proof. We have actually shown a little more than what the theorem states. We see that $P(x)$ has been factored with one constant factor a_n and n linear factors having leading coefficient 1.

To find the roots of a polynomial, we can attempt to factor it.

Examples

a) $x^4 + x^3 - 13x^2 - x + 12$ can be factored as

$$(x - 3)(x + 4)(x + 1)(x - 1),$$

so the roots are 3, -4, -1, and 1.

b) $3x^4 - 15x^3 + 18x^2 + 12x - 24$ can be factored as

$$3(x - 2)(x - 2)(x - 2)(x + 1),$$

so the roots are 2 and -1.

In Example (b) the factor $x - 2$ occurs three times. In a case like this we sometimes say that the root we obtain, 2, has a *multiplicity* of three.

From the preceding theorem and the above examples, we have the following theorem.

> **Theorem. Every polynomial of degree n, where $n > 0$, has at least one root and at most n roots.**

[24–28]

Given the roots of a polynomial, we can find the polynomial.

Example 1. Find a polynomial of degree three, having the roots -2, 1, and $3i$.

Such a polynomial has factors $x + 2$, $x - 1$, and $x - 3i$, so we have

$$P(x) = a_n(x + 2)(x - 1)(x - 3i).$$

The number a_n can be any nonzero number. The simplest polynomial will be obtained if we let it be 1. If we then multiply the factors we obtain

$$P(x) = x^3 + (1 - 3i)x^2 + (-2 - 3i)x + 6i.$$

Example 2. Find a polynomial of degree 5 with -1 as a root of multiplicity 3, 4 as a root of multiplicity 1, and 0 as a root of multiplicity 1.

Proceeding as in Example 1, letting $a_n = 1$, we obtain

$$(x + 1)^3(x - 4)(x - 0),$$

or

$$x^5 - x^4 - 9x^3 - 11x^2 - 4x. \qquad \textbf{[29–32]}$$

ROOTS OF POLYNOMIALS WITH REAL COEFFICIENTS

Consider the quadratic equation $x^2 - 2x + 2 = 0$, with real coefficients. Its roots are $1 + i$, and $1 - i$. Note that they are complex conjugates. This generalizes to any polynomial with real coefficients.

> **Theorem.** If a complex number z is a root of a polynomial $P(x)$ of degree greater than or equal to 1 with real coefficients, then its conjugate $\bar{z}$ is also a root. (Complex roots occur in conjugate pairs.)

Proof. Let

$$P(x) = a_n x^n + a_{n-1} x^{n-1} + \cdots + a_1 x + a_0,$$

where the coefficients are real numbers. Suppose z is a complex root of $P(x)$. Then $P(z) = 0$, or

$$a_n z^n + a_{n-1} z^{n-1} + \cdots + a_1 z + a_0 = 0.$$

Now let us find the conjugate of each side of the equation. First note that $\bar{0} = 0$, since 0 is a real number. Then we have the following.

$$0 = \bar{0} = \overline{a_n z^n + a_{n-1} z^{n-1} + \cdots + a_1 z + a_0}$$

$$= \overline{a_n z^n} + \overline{a_{n-1} z^{n-1}} + \cdots + \overline{a_1 z} + \overline{a_0}$$

(The conjugate of a sum is the sum of the conjugates.)

$$= \overline{a_n} \cdot \overline{z^n} + \overline{a_{n-1}} \cdot \overline{z^{n-1}} + \cdots + \overline{a_1} \cdot \overline{z} + \overline{a_0}$$

(The conjugate of a product is the product of the conjugates.)

$$= a_n \overline{z^n} + a_{n-1} \overline{z^{n-1}} + \cdots + a_1 \bar{z} + a_0$$

(Every real number is its own conjugate: $\bar{a}_i = a_i$.)

$$= a_n \bar{z}^n + a_{n-1} \bar{z}^{n-1} + \cdots + a_1 \bar{z} + a_0.$$

(The conjugate of a power is the power of the conjugate.)

Thus $P(\bar{z}) = 0$, so $\bar{z}$ is a root of the polynomial.

For the above theorem, it is essential that the coefficients be real numbers. This can be seen by considering Example 1. In that polynomial the root $3i$ occurs but its conjugate does not. This can happen because some of the coefficients of the polynomial are not real.

RATIONAL COEFFICIENTS

When a polynomial has rational numbers for coefficients, certain irrational roots also occur in pairs, as described in the following theorem.

> **Theorem.** Suppose $P(x)$ is a polynomial with rational coefficients and of degree greater than 0. Then if either of the following is a root, so is the other: $a + c\sqrt{b}, \ a - c\sqrt{b}$.

This theorem can be proved in a manner analogous to the one above, but we shall not do it here. The theorem can be used to help in finding roots.

Example 3. Suppose a polynomial of degree 6 with rational coefficients has $-2 + 5i$, $-2i$, and $1 - \sqrt{3}$ as some of its roots. Find the other roots.

The other roots are $-2 - 5i$, $2i$, and $1 + \sqrt{3}$. There are no other roots since the degree is 6.

Example 4. Find a polynomial of lowest degree with rational coefficients that has $1 - \sqrt{2}$ and $1 + 2i$ as some of its roots.

The polynomial must also have the roots $1 + \sqrt{2}$ and $1 - 2i$. Thus the polynomial is

$$[x - (1 - \sqrt{2})][x - (1 + \sqrt{2})]$$
$$\times [x - (1 + 2i)][x - (1 - 2i)],$$

or

$$(x^2 - 2x - 1)(x^2 - 2x + 5),$$

or

$$x^4 - 4x^3 + 8x^2 - 8x - 5. \qquad \textbf{[33–35]}$$

Example 5. Let $P(x) = x^4 - 5x^3 + 10x^2 - 20x + 24$. Find the other roots of $P(x)$, given that $2i$ is a root.

Since $2i$ is a root, we know that $-2i$ is also a root. Thus

$$P(x) = (x - 2i)(x + 2i) \cdot Q(x)$$

for some $Q(x)$. Since $(x - 2i)(x + 2i) = x^2 + 4$, we know that

$$P(x) = (x^2 + 4) \cdot Q(x).$$

We find, using division, that $Q(x) = x^2 - 5x + 6$, and since we can factor $x^2 - 5x + 6$, we get

$$P(x) = (x^2 + 4)(x - 2)(x - 3).$$

Thus the other roots are $-2i$, 2, and 3. **[36]**

Exercise Set 12.4

Find the roots of each polynomial and state the multiplicity of each.

1. $(x + 3)^2(x - 1)$ **2.** $-4(x + 2)(x - \pi)^5$ **3.** $-8(x - 3)^2(x + 4)^3 x^4$

4. $x^3(x - 1)^2(x + 4)$ **5.** $(x^2 - 5x + 6)^2$ **6.** $(x^2 - x - 2)^2$

Find a polynomial of degree 3 with the given numbers as roots.

7. $-2, 3, 5$ **8.** $3, 2, -1$ **9.** $2, i, -i$

10. $-3, 2i, -2i$ **11.** $2 + i, 2 - i, 3$ **12.** $1 + 4i, 1 - 4i, -1$

13. $\sqrt{2}, -\sqrt{2}, \sqrt{3}$. Are the coefficients rational?   **14.** $\sqrt{3}, -\sqrt{3}, \sqrt{2}$. Are the coefficients rational?

15. Find a polynomial of degree 4 with 0 as a root of multiplicity 2 and 5 as a root of multiplicity 2.

16. Find a polynomial of degree 4 with 0 as a root of multiplicity 4.

17. Find a polynomial of degree 4 with -2 as a root of multiplicity 1, 3 as a root of multiplicity 2, and -1 as a root of multiplicity 1.

18. Find a polynomial of degree 5 with 4 as a root of multiplicity 3 and -2 as a root of multiplicity 2.

Suppose a polynomial of degree 5 with rational coefficients has the given roots. Find the other roots.

19. $6, -3 + 4i, 4 - \sqrt{5}$ **20.** $8, 6 - 7i, \frac{1}{2} + \sqrt{11}$ **21.** $-2, 3, 4, 1 - i$ **22.** $3, 4, -5, 7 + i$

Find a polynomial of lowest degree with rational coefficients that has the given numbers as some of its roots.

23. $1 + i, 2$ **24.** $2 - i, -1$ **25.** $3i, -2$ **26.** $-4i, 5$

27. $2 - \sqrt{3}, 1 + i$ **28.** $3 + \sqrt{2}, 2 - i$ **29.** $\sqrt{5}, -3i$ **30.** $-\sqrt{2}, 4i$

Given that the polynomial has the given root, find the other roots.

31. $x^4 - 5x^3 + 7x^2 - 5x + 6; \; -i$ **32.** $x^3 - 4x^2 + x - 4; \; -i$

33. $x^4 - 16; \; 2i$ **34.** $x^4 - 1; \; i$

35. $x^3 - x^2 - 7x + 15; \; -3$ **36.** $x^3 - 6x^2 + 13x - 20; \; 4$

37. $x^3 - 8; \; 2$ **38.** $x^3 + 8; \; -2$

---

39. Prove that every polynomial of degree 3 with real coefficients has at least one real root.

40. Prove that every polynomial of degree 5 with real coefficients has at least one real root.

41. Comment on the number of roots the following polynomial has.
$$x^5 - x^2 + 1$$

42. Prove that a polynomial of degree n cannot have more than $n/2$ roots of multiplicity 2.

12.5 Rational Roots

INTEGER COEFFICIENTS

It is not always easy to find the roots of a polynomial. However, if a polynomial has integer coefficients, there is a procedure that will yield all of the rational roots.

> **Rational Roots Theorem. Let**
> $$P(x) = a_n x^n + a_{n-1} x^{n-1} + \cdots + a_1 x + a_0,$$
> **where all the coefficients are integers. Consider a rational number denoted by c/d, where c and d are relatively prime (having no common factor besides 1 and -1). If c/d is a root of $P(x)$, then c is a factor of a_0 and d is a factor of a_n.**

Proof. Since c/d is a root of $P(x)$, we know that

$$a_n \left(\frac{c}{d}\right)^n + a_{n-1}\left(\frac{c}{d}\right)^{n-1} + \cdots + a_1\left(\frac{c}{d}\right) + a_0 = 0. \tag{1}$$

We multiply by d^n and get the equation

$$a_n c^n + a_{n-1} c^{n-1} d + \cdots + a_1 c d^{n-1} + a_0 d^n = 0. \tag{2}$$

Then we have

$$a_n c^n = (-a_{n-1} c^{n-1} - \cdots - a_1 c d^{n-2} - a_0 d^{n-1})d.$$

Note that d is a factor of $a_n c^n$. Now d is not a factor of c because c and d are relatively prime. Thus d is not a factor of c^n. So d is a factor of a_n.

In a similar way we can show from equation (2) that

$$a_0 d^n = (-a_n c^{n-1} - a_{n-1} c^{n-2} d - \cdots - a_1 d^{n-1})c.$$

Thus c is a factor of $a_0 d^n$. Again, c is not a factor of d^n, so it must be a factor of a_0.

Example 1. Let $P(x) = 3x^4 - 11x^3 + 10x - 4$. Find the rational roots of $P(x)$. If possible, find the other roots.

By the rational roots theorem if c/d is a root of $P(x)$, then c must be a factor of -4 and d must be a factor of 3. Thus the possibilities for c and d are

$$c: \quad 1, -1, 4, -4, 2, -2; \qquad d: \quad 1, -1, 3, -3.$$

Then the resulting possibilities for c/d are

$$\frac{c}{d}: \quad 1, -1, 4, -4, \frac{1}{3}, -\frac{1}{3}, \frac{4}{3}, -\frac{4}{3}, \frac{2}{3}, -\frac{2}{3}, 2, -2.$$

Of these 12 possibilities, we know that at most 4 of them could be roots because $P(x)$ is of degree 4. To find which are roots we could use substitution, but synthetic division is usually more efficient.

We try 1:

```
1│ 3  -11    0   10   -4
        3   -8   -8    2
   ─────────────────────
   3  - 8   -8    2 │-2
```

We try -1:

```
-1│ 3  -11    0   10   -4
         - 3   14  -14    4
    ─────────────────────
    3  -14   14  - 4 │  0
```

Thus $P(1) = -2$, so 1 is not a root; and $P(-1) = 0$, so -1 is a root. Using the results of the second synthetic division, we can express $P(x)$ as follows:

$$P(x) = (x + 1)(3x^3 - 14x^2 + 14x - 4).$$

We now use $3x^3 - 14x^2 + 14x - 4$ and check the other possible roots.

We try $\frac{2}{3}$:

```
2/3│ 3  -14   14   -4
          2   -8    4
    ───────────────────
    3  -12    6 │  0.
```

Thus $P(\frac{2}{3}) = 0$, so $\frac{2}{3}$ is a root. Again using the results of the synthetic division, we can express $P(x)$ as follows:

$$P(x) = (x + 1)\left(x - \frac{2}{3}\right)(3x^2 - 12x + 6).$$

Since the factor $3x^2 - 12x + 6$ is quadratic, we can use the quadratic formula to find that the other roots are $2 + \sqrt{2}$ and $2 - \sqrt{2}$. These are irrational numbers. Thus the rational roots are -1 and $\frac{2}{3}$.   **[37]**

Example 2. Let $P(x) = x^3 + 6x^2 + x + 6$. Find the rational roots of $P(x)$. If possible, find the other roots.

By the rational roots theorem if c/d is a root of $P(x)$, then c must be a factor of 6 and d must be a factor of 1. Thus the possibilities for c and d are

$$c: \quad 1, -1, 2, -2, 3, -3, 6, -6; \qquad d: \quad 1, -1.$$

Then the resulting possibilities for c/d are

$$\frac{c}{d}: \quad 1, -1, 2, -2, 3, -3, 6, -6.$$

Note that these are the same as the possibilities for c. If the leading coefficient is 1, we need only check the factors of the last coefficient as possibilities for rational roots.

There is another aid in eliminating possibilities for rational roots. Note that all coefficients of $P(x)$ are positive. Thus when any positive number is substituted in $P(x)$, we get a positive value, never 0. Therefore no positive number can be a root. Thus the only possibilities for roots are

$$-1, -2, -3, -6.$$

We try -6:

```
-6│ 1    6    1    6
         -6    0   -6
    ───────────────────
    1    0    1 │  0.
```

Thus $P(-6) = 0$, so -6 is a root. We can then factor $P(x)$ as

$$P(x) = (x + 6)(x^2 + 1).$$

Now $x^2 + 1$ has the complex roots i and $-i$. Thus the only rational root of $P(x)$ is -6.   [38]

Example 3. Find the rational roots of $x^4 + 2x^3 + 2x^2 - 4x - 8$.

Since the leading coefficient is 1, the only possibilities for rational roots are the factors of the last coefficient -8:
$$1, -1, 2, -2, 4, -4, 8, -8.$$

But, using substitution or synthetic division, we find that none of the possibilities is a root. We leave it to the student to verify this. Thus there are no rational roots.

The polynomial of Example 3 has no rational roots. We can approximate the irrational roots of such a polynomial by graphing it and determining the x-intercepts.   [39, 40]

RATIONAL COEFFICIENTS

Suppose some (or all) of the coefficients of a polynomial are rational, but not integers. After multiplying on both sides by the LCM of the denominators, we can then find the rational roots.

Example 4. Let $P(x) = \frac{1}{12}x^3 - \frac{1}{12}x^2 - \frac{2}{3}x + 1$. Find the rational roots of $P(x)$.

The LCM of the denominators is 12. When we multiply on both sides by 12, we get
$$12P(x) = x^3 - x^2 - 8x + 12.$$

This equation is equivalent to the first, and all coefficients on the right are integers. Thus any root of $12P(x)$ is a root of $P(x)$. We leave it to the student to verify that 2 and -3 are the rational roots, in fact the only roots, of $P(x)$.   [41]

Exercise Set 12.5

Find the rational roots, if they exist, of each polynomial. If possible, find the other roots.

1. $x^3 + 3x^2 - 2x - 6$ **2.** $x^3 - x^2 - 3x + 3$ **3.** $5x^4 - 4x^3 + 19x^2 - 16x - 4$

4. $3x^4 - 4x^3 + x^2 + 6x - 2$ **5.** $x^4 - 3x^3 - 20x^2 - 24x - 8$ **6.** $x^4 + 5x^3 - 27x^2 + 31x - 10$

7. $x^3 + 3x^2 - x - 3$ **8.** $x^3 + 5x^2 - x - 5$ **9.** $x^3 + 8$

10. $x^3 - 8$ **11.** $\frac{1}{3}x^3 - \frac{1}{2}x^2 - \frac{1}{6}x + \frac{1}{6}$ **12.** $\frac{2}{3}x^3 - \frac{1}{2}x^2 + \frac{2}{3}x - \frac{1}{2}$

Find only the rational roots of the following polynomials.

13. $x^4 + 32$ **14.** $x^6 + 8$

15. $x^3 - x^2 - 4x + 3$ **16.** $2x^3 + 3x^2 + 2x + 3$

17. $x^4 + 2x^3 + 2x^2 - 4x - 8$ **18.** $x^4 + 6x^3 + 17x^2 + 36x + 66$

19. $x^5 - 5x^4 + 5x^3 + 15x^2 - 36x + 20$ **20.** $x^5 - 3x^4 - 3x^3 + 9x^2 - 4x + 12$

21. The volume of a cube is 64 cm^3. Find the length of a side. [*Hint:* Solve $x^3 - 64 = 0$.]

22. The volume of a cube is 125 cm^3. Find the length of a side.

23. An open box of volume 48 cm^3 can be made from a piece of tin 10 cm on a side by cutting a square from each corner and folding up the edges. What is the length of a side of the squares?

24. An open box of volume 500 cm^3 can be made from a piece of tin 20 cm on a side by cutting a square from each corner and folding up the edges. What is the length of a side of the squares?

25. Prove that if n is an even positive integer and b is positive, then $x^n + b$ has no rational root.

26. Prove that if n is an even positive integer, then $-3x^n - 8$ has no rational root.

12.6 Graphs of Polynomial Functions

We have studied constant functions and linear functions. Their graphs are, of course, straight lines. Graphs of quadratic functions are parabolas. We now consider polynomials of higher degree. First, we describe some general principles to be kept in mind while graphing. We consider only polynomials with real coefficients.

1. Every polynomial function with real number coefficients is a continuous function, whose domain is the set of all real numbers. Remember that the graph of any function must pass the vertical line test. Therefore no graph of a function, including a polynomial function, can look like this.

2. A polynomial of degree n cannot have more than n real roots. This means that the graph cannot cross the x-axis more than n times, and this tells us something about how the curve "wiggles." Third-degree, or *cubic*, functions have graphs like these.

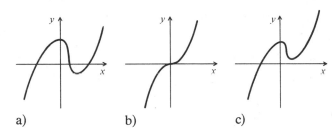

a)   b)   c)

In (a) the graph crosses the axis three times, so there are three real roots. In (b) and (c) there is only one x-intercept, so there is only one real root in each case. The graph of a cubic cannot look like this, because there would be a possibility that it might cross the x-axis more than three times.

Graphs of fourth-degree, or *quartic*, polynomials look like these.

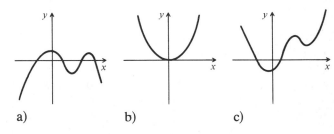

a)   b)   c)

In (a) there are four real roots, in (b) there is one, and in (c) there are two.

Multiple roots occur at points like these.

When a graph looks like this, missing the x-axis at one of its opportunities, a pair of complex roots occurs. There is no easy way to find them from the graph.

3. The leading term of a polynomial tells a lot about how the graph looks for values of x with large absolute value. This is so because for such values of x the contributions of the other terms are relatively minor. First, let us suppose that the coefficient is positive. Then for large positive values of x, the function value will be positive and increasing. Thus we know that as we move far to the right the graph looks like (a) below.

a)   b)   c)

If the exponent of the leading term is even, the same thing happens as we move far to the left, as in (b) above. If the exponent is odd, then the function values are negative and they decrease as we move far to the left, as in (c) above. If the leading coefficient is negative, the above graphs will of course be reflected across the x-axis.

To graph polynomials, keep in mind the principles studied in Chapter 3, as well as those stated above. Then make tables of values, plot points and connect them appropriately.

Example 1. Graph $P(x) = x^3 + 3x^2 - 2x - 6$.

a) We will try to find some roots of $P(x)$. We try to find rational roots first. The possibilities are ± 1, ± 2, ± 3, and ± 6. Using substitution or synthetic division, we find that $P(-3) = 0$, so -3 is a rational root, and -3 is the only rational root. Then factoring $P(x)$, we have

$$P(x) = (x + 3)(x^2 - 2)$$
$$= (x + 3)(x - \sqrt{2})(x + \sqrt{2}).$$

Thus the roots are 3, $\sqrt{2}$, and $-\sqrt{2}$.

b) Starting with the results of (a), we make a table of function values, using substitution or synthetic division, plot the resulting points, and connect them.

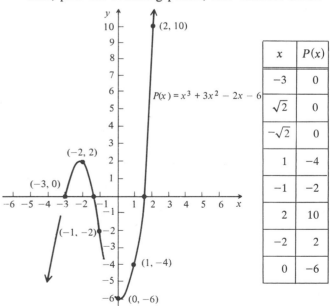

x	$P(x)$
-3	0
$\sqrt{2}$	0
$-\sqrt{2}$	0
1	-4
-1	-2
2	10
-2	2
0	-6

[42]

APPROXIMATING ROOTS

When irrational roots occur they are usually approximated using graphical or numerical methods. These methods are based on the following geometric idea.

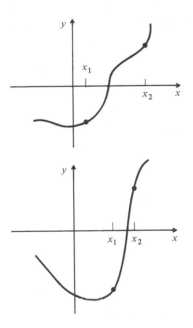

Since all polynomial functions are continuous, given a point above the x-axis and one below, the curve must cross the x-axis somewhere between the two x-values. Thus there is a zero between x_1 and x_2.

The closer together the two x-values, the more nearly the graph of the function approximates a straight line between those points.

For a first approximation to an irrational root, we can simply graph the polynomial and read off the approximation from the graph. This is done in Example 1 below. For better approximations, we can approximate the function by straight lines in smaller and smaller intervals, as in Example 2 on the right.

Example 1. Graph $P(x) = x^3 - 3x + 1$. Use the graph to approximate irrational roots.

a) We first try to find the rational roots. The possibilities are 1 and -1. But $P(1) = -1$ and $P(-1) = 3$. Thus there are no rational roots. Hence there is no convenient way to factor and find any other roots of $P(x)$. We make a table of function values using substitution or synthetic division, plot the resulting points, and connect them.

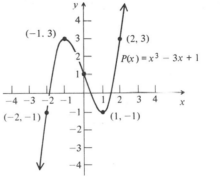

x	$P(x)$
0	1
1	-1
-1	3
2	3
-2	-1

b) Using the graph we locate the x-intercepts. They are approximately -1.8, 0.3, and 1.6, and they approximate the irrational roots.   **[43]**

Example 2. (Optional, calculator highly desirable). In the polynomial of Example 1, approximate the irrational root between 0 and 1 to hundredths. We

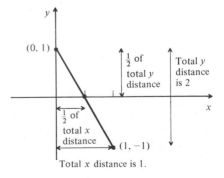

choose two known points, one with a positive function value and one with a negative value. We approximate the curve with a straight line between these two points. Using a process very similar to interpolation, we find that this line crosses the x-axis at $x = 0.5$. We check function values in the vicinity of $x = 0.5$.

x	0.3	0.4	0.5
$P(x)$	0.127	−0.136	−0.375

Since $P(0.3)$ is positive and $P(0.4)$ is negative, we know that the root is between 0.3 and 0.4. We now have the tenths digit.

We now repeat the above process, approximating the graph with a straight line again. This line, we find, crosses the x-axis where $x = 0.348$. Therefore we check function values in this vicinity.

x	0.34	0.35
$P(x)$	0.0193	−0.007

Since $P(0.34)$ is positive and $P(0.35)$ is negative, we know that the root is between 0.34 and 0.35. Thus the hundredths digit is 4. The process can be continued to get whatever degree of approximation is desired.

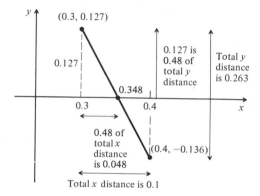

Exercise Set 12.6

Graph.

1. $P(x) = x^3 - 3x^2 - 2x - 6$

2. $P(x) = x^3 + 4x^2 - 3x - 12$

3. $P(x) = x^4 + x^3 - 7x^2 - x + 6$

4. $P(x) = x^4 + 5x^3 + 5x^2 - 5x^2 - 6$

5. $P(x) = x^5 - 2x^4 - x^3 + 2x^2$

6. $P(x) = x^5 + 4x^4 - 5x^3 - 14x^2 - 8x$

For each of the following (a) graph, and (b) use the graph to approximate irrational roots.

7. $P(x) = x^3 - 3x - 2$

8. $P(x) = x^3 - 3x^2 + 3$

9. $P(x) = x^3 - 3x - 4$

10. $P(x) = x^3 - 3x^2 + 5$

11. $P(x) = x^4 + x^2 + 1$

12. $P(x) = x^4 + 2x^2 + 2$

13. $P(x) = x^4 - 6x^2 + 8$

14. $P(x) = x^4 - 4x^2 + 2$

15. $P(x) = x^4 - 6x^2 + 10$

16. $P(x) = x^4 - 4x^2 + 5$

17. The volume of a cube is 75 cm³. Find the length of a side. [*Hint:* Graph $P(x) = x^3 - 75$.]

18. The volume of a cube is 43 cm³. Find the length of a side.

 In each of the following, graph and then approximate the irrational roots, to tenths and hundredths.

19. $P(x) = x^3 - 2x^2 - x + 4$

20. $P(x) = x^3 - 4x^2 + x + 3$

12.7 Rational Functions

A *rational function* is a function definable as the quotient of two polynomials. Here are some examples:

$$y = \frac{x^2 + 3x - 5}{x + 4}, \quad y = \frac{5}{x^2 + 3}, \quad y = \frac{3x^5 - 5x + 2}{4}.$$

> **Definition. A *rational function* is a function that can be defined as $y = P(x)/Q(x)$, where $P(x)$ and $Q(x)$ are polynomials, with $Q(x)$ not the zero polynomial.**

Note that polynomial functions are themselves special kinds of rational functions, since $Q(x)$ can be the polynomial 1. Here we are interested in rational functions in which the denominator is not a constant. We begin with the simplest such function.

Example 1. Graph the function $y = 1/x$.

a) Note that the domain of this function consists of all real numbers except 0.

b) Note that, for nonzero x or y, the above equation is equivalent to $xy = 1$. Now it is easy to see that the graph is symmetric with respect to the line $y = x$ (because interchanging x and y produces an equivalent equation.)

c) The graph is also symmetric with respect to the origin (because replacing x with $-x$ and y with $-y$ produces an equivalent equation).

d) Now we find some values, keeping in mind the two symmetries.

x	1	2	3	4	5
y	1	$\frac{1}{2}$	$\frac{1}{3}$	$\frac{1}{4}$	$\frac{1}{5}$

e) We plot these points. We use one symmetry to get other points in the first quadrant. We use the other symmetry to get the points in the third quadrant.

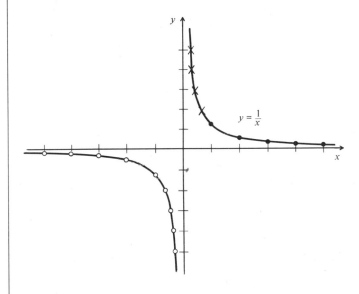

The points indicated by ● are obtained from the table. Those marked × are obtained by reflection across the line $y = x$. Following this, the points marked ○ are obtained by reflection across the origin.

ASYMPTOTES

Note that this curve does not touch either axis, but comes very close. As $|x|$ becomes very large the curve comes very near to the x-axis. In fact, we can find points as close to the x-axis as we please by choosing x large enough. We say that the curve approaches the x-axis *asymptotically*, and we say that the x-axis is an *asymptote* to the curve. The y-axis is also an asymptote to this curve.

Using the ideas of transformations we can easily graph certain variations of the above function.

Example 2. $y = -1/x$ is a reflection across the x-axis (or the y-axis; the result is the same).

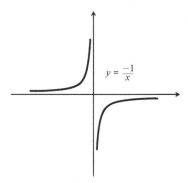

Example 3. $y = 1/(x - 2)$ is a translation 2 units to the right.

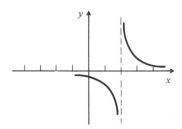

[45–48]

Example 4. Graph the function $y = 1/x^2$.

a) Note that this function is defined for all x except 0. Therefore the line $x = 0$ is an asymptote.

b) Note that as $|x|$ gets very large, y approaches 0. Therefore the x-axis is also an asymptote.

c) Note that this function is even. Therefore it is symmetric with respect to the y-axis.

d) Note that all function values are positive. Therefore the entire graph is above the x-axis.

e) With this much information, we can already sketch a rough graph of the function. However, a table of values will help.

x	1	2	3	4	$\frac{1}{2}$	$\frac{1}{3}$
y	1	$\frac{1}{4}$	$\frac{1}{9}$	$\frac{1}{16}$	4	9

The graph is as follows. Points marked ● are obtained from the table. Points marked × are obtained by reflection across the y-axis.

[49–51]

OCCURRENCE OF ASYMPTOTES

It is important in graphing rational functions to determine where the asymptotes, if any, occur. Vertical asymptotes are easy to locate when a denominator is factored. The x-values that make a denominator 0 are those of the vertical asymptotes.

Examples

a) The vertical asymptotes of $y = \dfrac{3x - 2}{x(x - 5)(x + 3)}$

are the lines $x = 0$, $x = 5$, and $x = -3$.

b) The vertical asymptotes of $y = \dfrac{x - 2}{x^3 - x}$ can be

determined by factoring the denominator:

$$x^3 - x = x(x + 1)(x - 1).$$

The asymptotes are $x = 0$, $x = -1$, and $x = 1$.

[52]

Horizontal asymptotes occur when the degree of the numerator is the same as or less than that of the denominator. Let us first consider a function for which the degree of the numerator is smaller than that of the denominator:

$$y = \frac{2x + 3}{x^3 - 2x^2 + 4}.$$

We shall multiply by $\dfrac{1/x^3}{1/x^3}$, to obtain

$$y = \frac{\dfrac{2}{x^2} + \dfrac{3}{x^3}}{1 - \dfrac{2}{x} + \dfrac{4}{x^3}}.$$

Let us now consider what happens to the function values as $|x|$ becomes very large. Each expression with x in its denominator takes on smaller and smaller values, approaching 0. Thus the numerator approaches 0 and the denominator approaches 1; hence the entire expression takes on values closer and closer to 0. Therefore, the x-axis is an asymptote. Whenever the degree of a numerator is less than that of the denominator, the x-axis will be an asymptote.   **[53]**

Next, we consider a function for which the numerator and denominator have the same degree:

$$y = \frac{3x^2 + 2x - 4}{2x^2 - x + 1} = \frac{3x^2 + 2x - 4}{2x^2 - x + 1} \cdot \frac{\dfrac{1}{x^2}}{\dfrac{1}{x^2}}$$

$$= \frac{3 + \dfrac{2}{x} - \dfrac{4}{x^2}}{2 - \dfrac{1}{x} + \dfrac{1}{x^2}}.$$

As $|x|$ gets very large the numerator approaches 3 and the denominator approaches 2. Therefore the function values get very close to $\frac{3}{2}$, and thus the line $y = \frac{3}{2}$ is an asymptote. From this example, we can see that the asymptote in such cases can be determined by dividing the leading coefficients of the two polynomials.

Examples

a) For $y = \dfrac{5x^3 - x^2 + 7}{3x^3 + x - 10}$, the line $y = \frac{5}{3}$ is an asymptote.

b) For $y = \dfrac{-7x^4 - 10x^2 + 1}{11x^4 + x - 2}$, the line $y = -\frac{7}{11}$ is an asymptote.   **[54, 55]**

There are asymptotes that are neither vertical nor horizontal. They are called *oblique*, and they occur when the degree of the numerator is greater than that of the denominator by 1. To find the asymptote we divide the numerator by the denominator. Consider

$$y = \frac{2x^2 - 3x - 1}{x - 2}.$$

When we divide the numerator by the denominator we obtain a quotient of $2x + 1$ and a remainder of 1. Thus,

$$y = 2x + 1 + \frac{1}{x - 2}.$$

Now we can see that when $|x|$ becomes very large, $1/(x - 2)$ approaches 0, and the y-values thus approach $2x + 1$. This means that the graph comes closer and closer to the straight line $y = 2x + 1$.

Example. Find and draw the asymptotes of the function $y = \dfrac{2x^2 - 11x - 10}{x - 4}$.

a) We first note that $x = 4$ is a vertical asymptote.

b) We divide, to obtain $y = 2x - 3 - \dfrac{22}{x - 4}$.

Thus the line $y = 2x - 3$ is an asymptote.

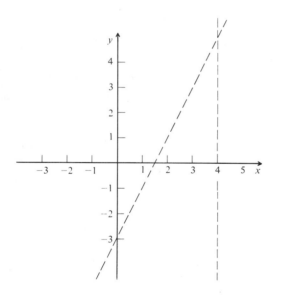

[56, 57]

ZEROS

Zeros of a rational function occur when the numerator is 0 but the denominator is not 0. The zeros of a function occur at points where the graph crosses the x-axis. Therefore knowing the zeros helps in making a graph. If the numerator can be factored, the zeros are easy to determine.

Example. Find the zeros of the function $y = \dfrac{x^3 - x^2 - 6x}{x^2 - 3x + 2}$.

We factor numerator and denominator:

$$y = \frac{x(x + 2)(x - 3)}{(x - 1)(x - 2)}.$$

The values making the numerator zero are 0, -2, and 3. Since none of these make the denominator zero, they are the zeros of the function.   **[58, 59]**

The following is an outline of a procedure to be followed in graphing rational functions.

> **To Graph a Rational Function.**
> 1. **Determine any symmetries.**
> 2. **Determine any horizontal or oblique asymptotes and sketch them.**
> 3. **Factor the denominator and the numerator.**
>   a) **Determine any vertical asymptotes and sketch them.**
>   b) **Determine the zeros if possible, and plot them.**
> 4. **In each interval between zeros and asymptotes, find at least one function value and plot a point.**
> 5. **Sketch the curve.**

Example 1. Graph $y = \dfrac{1}{x^2 + 1}$.

We follow the outline above.

1. The function is even, so the graph is symmetric with respect to the y-axis.

2. The degree of the denominator is greater than that of the numerator. Thus the x-axis is an asymptote.

3. The denominator is not factorable. Neither is the numerator. Therefore there are no vertical asymptotes and there are no zeros.

4. We tabulate some values:

x	0	1	2	3
y	1	$\frac{1}{2}$	$\frac{1}{5}$	$\frac{1}{10}$

5. We sketch the graph, keeping in mind all of the above data. An additional fact worth noting is that this function never has negative values. This is so because the numerator is a positive constant and the denominator never takes on negative values.

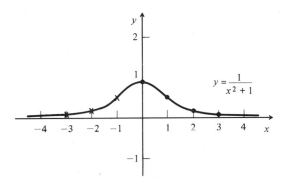

Example 2. Graph $y = \dfrac{x^2 - 4}{x - 1}$.

1. There are no apparent symmetries.

2. Since the degree of the numerator is one greater than that of the denominator, there is an oblique asymptote. We find it by dividing:

$$y = x + 1 - \frac{3}{x - 1}.$$

The asymptote is the line $y = x + 1$.

3. We factor the numerator:

$$y = \frac{(x + 2)(x - 2)}{x - 1}.$$

This function has zeros at 2 and -2 and a vertical asymptote at $x = 1$.

4. We tabulate some values. We want at least one value for $x < -2$, one for $x > 2$, and one for x between -2 and 1.

x	0	$\frac{1}{2}$	-3	-5	1.5	3	5	10
y	4	5	-1.25	-3.5	-3.5	2.5	5.25	10.7

5. We sketch the asymptotes and plot the points. Then we sketch the graph. We must be sure that the curve approaches the asymptotes properly, and that it does not cross the x-axis except at zeros.

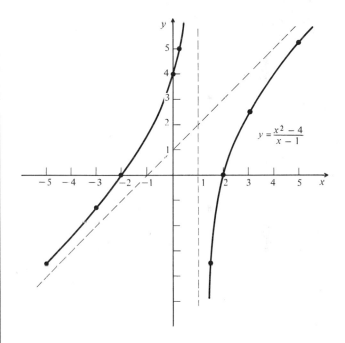

Example 3. Graph $y = \dfrac{2x^2 + 1}{4x^2 - 4}$.

1. This is an even function, so the graph is symmetric with respect to the y-axis.

2. There is a horizontal asymptote at $y = \frac{1}{2}$.

3. We factor the denominator; the numerator cannot be factored:

$$y = \frac{2x^2 + 1}{4(x + 1)(x - 1)}.$$

There are vertical asymptotes at $x = -1$ and $x = 1$. This function has no zeros.

4. We make a table of values.

x	0	$\frac{1}{2}$	2
y	$-\frac{1}{4}$	$-\frac{1}{2}$	$\frac{3}{4}$

5. We draw in the asymptotes, plot the points, and then draw the curve.

$y = \frac{2x^2 + 1}{4x^2 - 4}$

[60]

Exercise Set 12.7

Graph these functions.

1. $y = \dfrac{1}{x - 3}$

2. $y = \dfrac{1}{x - 5}$

3. $y = \dfrac{-2}{x - 5}$

4. $y = \dfrac{-3}{x - 3}$

5. $y = \dfrac{2x + 1}{x}$

6. $y = \dfrac{3x - 1}{x}$

7. $y = \dfrac{1}{(x - 2)^2}$

8. $y = \dfrac{-2}{(x - 3)^2}$

9. $y = \dfrac{2}{x^2}$

10. $y = \dfrac{1}{3x^2}$

11. $y = \dfrac{1}{x^2 + 3}$

12. $y = \dfrac{-1}{x^2 + 2}$

13. $y = \dfrac{x - 1}{x + 2}$

14. $y = \dfrac{x - 2}{x + 1}$

15. $y = \dfrac{3x}{x^2 + 5x + 4}$

16. $y = \dfrac{x + 3}{2x^2 - 5x - 3}$

17. $y = \dfrac{x^2 - 4}{x - 1}$

18. $y = \dfrac{x^2 - 9}{x + 1}$

19. $y = \dfrac{x^2 + x - 2}{2x^2 + 1}$

20. $y = \dfrac{x^2 - 2x - 3}{3x^2 + 2}$

21. $y = \dfrac{x - 1}{x^2 - 2x - 3}$

22. $y = \dfrac{x + 2}{x^2 + 2x - 15}$

23. $y = \dfrac{x + 2}{(x - 1)^3}$

24. $y = \dfrac{x - 3}{(x + 1)^3}$

25. $y = \dfrac{x^3 + 1}{x}$ $\qquad\qquad$ **26.** $y = \dfrac{x^3 - 1}{x}$ $\qquad\qquad$ **27.** $y = \dfrac{x^3 + 2x^2 - 15x}{x^2 - 5x - 14}$ $\quad$ **28.** $y = \dfrac{x^3 + 2x^2 - 3x}{x^2 - 25}$

Chapter 12 Test, or Review

1. Find the remainder when $x^4 + 3x^3 + 3x^2 + 3x + 2$ is divided by $x + 2$.

2. Use synthetic division to find the quotient and remainder.

$$(2x^4 - 6x^3 + 7x^2 - 5x + 1) \div (x + 2)$$

3. Find a polynomial of degree 3 with roots 0, 1, and 2.

4. Find a polynomial of lowest degree having roots 1 and -1, and having 2 as a root of multiplicity 2 and -3 as a root of multiplicity 3.

5. Find a complete factorization of $x^3 - 1$.

6. Find all the roots of $x^3 - 7x^2 + 16x - 12$.

7. Use synthetic division to find $P(3)$.

$$P(x) = 2x^4 - 3x^3 + x^2 - 3x + 7$$

8. What is the degree of $x^5 - 3x^2 + 2x - 1$?

9. Determine whether $x + 1$ is a factor of $x^3 + 6x^2 + x + 30$.

10. A polynomial of degree 4 with rational coefficients has roots $-8 - 7i$ and $10 + \sqrt{5}$. Find the other roots.

11. Graph $P(x) = x^3 - 3x^2 + 3$. Use the graph to approximate the irrational roots.

12. Graph $y = \dfrac{x^2 + x - 6}{x^2 - x - 20}$.

Equations of Second Degree and Their Graphs

13.1 Conic Sections

CONES

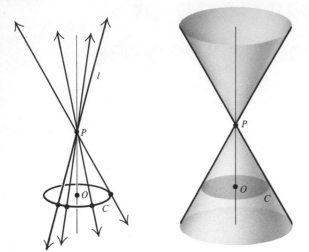

Suppose C is a circle with center O and P is a point not in the same plane as C such that line $\overleftrightarrow{OP}$ is perpendicular to the plane of the circle C. The set of points on all lines through P and a point of the circle form a *right circular cone* (or *conical surface*). Any line contained in the surface is called a *surface element*. Note that there are two parts or *nappes* of a cone. Point P is called the *vertex* and line $\overleftrightarrow{OP}$ is called the *axis*.

CONIC SECTIONS

The intersection of any plane with a cone is a *conic section*. On the following page we give some drawings of conic sections. Most of them will not be defined until we study them in more detail in later sections.

INTERSECTING LINES

Our main objectives in this chapter are to define the most common conic sections and to find their equations. We will then solve systems of these equations graphically and algebraically. The conic section shown in (b) of the figure on the following page has an equation like the following.

Example 1. Graph $3x^2 + 2xy - y^2 = 0$.

We first factor:
$$(3x - y)(x + y) = 0$$
$$3x - y = 0 \quad \text{or} \quad x + y = 0$$
$$y = 3x \quad \text{or} \quad y = -x.$$

The graphs of the two equations found by factoring are straight lines. Thus the graph $3x^2 + 2xy - y^2 = 0$ is the union of the two lines through the origin.

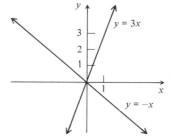

Generally, a second-degree equation that has 0 on one side and a factorable expression on the other has a graph that is the union of two lines. A special case of this is the equation $xy = 0$ in which the lines are the x-axis and y-axis. **[1, 2]**

SINGLE POINTS

When a plane intersects only the vertex of a cone, the result is a single point. See (c) of the previous figure. The following is an equation for such a conic section.

Example 2. Graph $x^2 + 4y^2 = 0$.

The expression $x^2 + 4y^2$ is not factorable in the real number system. The only real number solution of the equation is $(0, 0)$.

[3, 4]

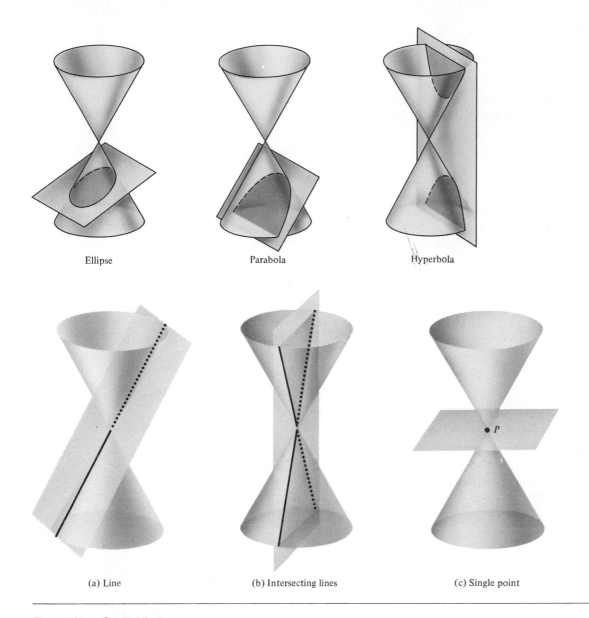

Ellipse   Parabola   Hyperbola

(a) Line   (b) Intersecting lines   (c) Single point

Exercise Set 13.1

Graph.

1. $x^2 - y^2 = 0$ **2.** $y^2 - x^2 = 0$ **3.** $x^2 - 9y^2 = 0$ **4.** $x^2 - 16y^2 = 0$

5. $3x^2 + xy - 2y^2 = 0$ **6.** $x^2 - xy - 2y^2 = 0$ **7.** $2x^2 + y^2 = 0$ **8.** $8x^2 + y^2 = 0$

13.2 The Circle

From geometry we know the following.

> **Definition. A** *circle* **is the locus or set of all points in a plane that are at a fixed distance from a fixed point in that plane.**

As a conic section:

> **A** *circle* **is formed by the intersection of a right circular cone by a plane perpendicular to the axis of the cone (and hence parallel to its circular base).**

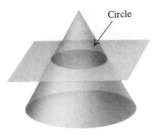

Circle

We first obtain an equation for a circle centered at the origin. We let r represent the radius. The center is $(0, 0)$. Then for any point (x, y) on the circle, we know from the distance formula that

$$r = \sqrt{(x - 0)^2 + (y - 0)^2},$$

$$r = \sqrt{x^2 + y^2}, \quad \text{or} \quad x^2 + y^2 = r^2.$$

Points satisfying this equation are on the circle, and points not satisfying this equation are not on the circle. Note that a circle centered at the origin is symmetric with respect to the y-axis, the x-axis, and the origin. This is because replacing x by $-x$ or y by $-y$, or both, yields an equivalent equation.

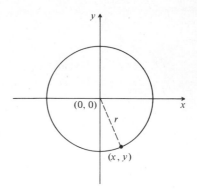

When a circle is translated so its center is (h, k), then its equation is found by replacing x by $x - h$ and y by $y - k$.

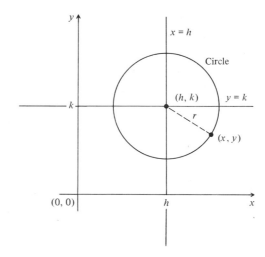

> **Theorem. The equation in standard form of a circle with center** (h, k) **and radius** r **is**
> $$(x - h)^2 + (y - k)^2 = r^2.$$

Example 1. Find the center and radius of $(x - 2)^2 + (y + 3)^2 = 16$. Then graph the circle.

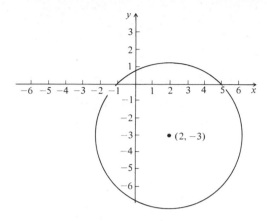

We may first rewrite the equation as $(x - 2)^2 + [y - (-3)]^2 = 4^2$.

Then the *center* is $(2, -3)$ and the *radius* is 4. The graph is then easy to draw, as shown, using a compass.
[5–7]

Completing the square allows us to find the standard form for the equation of a circle.

Example 2. Find the center and radius of the circle

$$x^2 + y^2 + 8x - 2y + 15 = 0.$$

We complete the square twice to get the standard form.

$$(x^2 + 8x + \quad) + (y^2 - 2y + \quad) = -15$$
$$(x^2 + 8x + 16) + (y^2 - 2y + 1) = -15 + 16 + 1$$
$$(x + 4)^2 + (y - 1)^2 = 2$$
$$[x - (-4)]^2 + (y - 1)^2 = (\sqrt{2})^2 \qquad \textbf{[8]}$$

The *center* is $(-4, 1)$ and the *radius* is $\sqrt{2}$.

Example 3. Find an equation of a circle with center $(-2, -3)$ that passes through the point $(1, 1)$.

Since $(-2, -3)$ is the center, we have

$$(x + 2)^2 + (y + 3)^2 = r^2.$$

The circle passes through $(1, 1)$. We find r by substituting in the above equation:

$$(1 + 2)^2 + (1 + 3)^2 = r^2$$
$$9 + 16 = r^2$$
$$25 = r^2$$
$$5 = r.$$

Then $(x + 2)^2 + (y + 3)^2 = 25$ is an equation of the circle.
[9]

Exercise Set 13.2

Find an equation of a circle with center and radius as given.

1. Center: $(0, 0)$
   Radius: 7

2. Center: $(0, 0)$
   Radius: π

3. Center: $(-2, 7)$
   Radius: $\sqrt{5}$

4. Center: $(5, 6)$
   Radius: $2\sqrt{3}$

Find the center and radius of each circle. Then graph the circle.

5. $(x + 1)^2 + (y + 3)^2 = 4$

6. $(x - 2)^2 + (y + 3)^2 = 1$

Find the center and radius of each circle.

7. $(x - 8)^2 + (y + 3)^2 = 40$

8. $(x + 5)^2 + (y - 1)^2 = 75$

9. $x^2 + y^2 = 2$

10. $x^2 + y^2 = 3$

11. $(x - 5)^2 + y^2 = \dfrac{1}{4}$

12. $x^2 + (y - 1)^2 = \dfrac{1}{25}$

13. $x^2 + y^2 + 8x - 6y - 15 = 0$

14. $x^2 + y^2 + 6x - 4y - 15 = 0$

15. $x^2 + y^2 + 25x + 10y + 12 = 0$

16. $x^2 + y^2 + 6x + 4y + 12 = 0$

17. $x^2 + y^2 - 4x = 0$

18. $x^2 + y^2 + 10y - 75 = 0$

19. $9x^2 + 9y^2 = 1$

20. $16x^2 + 16y^2 = 1$

Find an equation of a circle satisfying the given conditions.

21. Center $(0, 0)$, passing through $(-3, 4)$

22. Center $(0, 0)$, passing through $\left(\dfrac{\sqrt{3}}{2}, \dfrac{1}{2}\right)$

23. Center $(3, -2)$, passing through $(11, -2)$

24. Center $(2, -4)$, passing through $(0, 1)$.

25. Center $(2, 4)$ and tangent (touching at one point) to the x-axis.

26. Center $(-3, -2)$ and tangent to the y-axis.

▦ Find the center and radius of each circle.

27. $x^2 + y^2 + 8.246x - 6.348y - 74.35 = 0$

28. $x^2 + y^2 + 25.074x + 10.004y + 12.054 = 0$

▶ Recall from Chapter 3 that the *midpoint* of the line segment with endpoints (x_1, y_1) and (x_2, y_2) is $\left(\dfrac{x_1 + x_2}{2}, \dfrac{y_1 + y_2}{2}\right)$.

Find an equation of a circle such that:

29. The endpoints of a diameter are $(5, -3)$ and $(-3, 7)$.

30. The endpoints of a diameter are $(7, 3)$ and $(-1, -3)$.

31. a) Graph $x^2 + y^2 = 4$. Is this relation a function?

    b) Solve $x^2 + y^2 = 4$ for y.

    c) Graph $y = \sqrt{4 - x^2}$ and decide whether it is a function. Find the domain and range.

    d) Graph $y = -\sqrt{4 - x^2}$ and decide whether it is a function. Find the domain and range.

32. a) Graph $x^2 + y^2 = 1$. Is this relation a function?

    b) Solve $x^2 + y^2 = 1$ for y.

    c) Graph $y = \sqrt{1 - x^2}$ and decide whether it is a function. Find the domain and range.

    d) Graph $y = -\sqrt{1 - x^2}$ and decide whether it is a function. Find the domain and range.

33. Show that the following equation is an equation of a circle with center (h, k) and radius r.

$$\begin{vmatrix} x - h & -(y - k) \\ y - k & x - h \end{vmatrix} = r^2$$

Decide whether each of the following points lies on the *unit circle* $x^2 + y^2 = 1$.

34. $(1, 0)$

35. $(0, -1)$

36. $\left(\dfrac{\sqrt{3}}{2}, -\dfrac{1}{2}\right)$

37. $\left(\dfrac{\sqrt{2}}{2}, -\dfrac{\sqrt{2}}{2}\right)$

38. $\left(\dfrac{\sqrt{2}}{2}, \dfrac{\sqrt{2}}{2}\right)$

39. $\left(\dfrac{1}{2}, \dfrac{\sqrt{3}}{2}\right)$

40. $(\sqrt{2} + \sqrt{3}, 0)$

41. $\left(\dfrac{\pi}{4}, \dfrac{4}{\pi}\right)$

42. $(\cos\theta, \sin\theta)$

43. $(\sin\phi, \cos\phi)$

44. $(\tan\theta, \sec\theta)$

45. $(\sec\theta, \tan\theta)$

46. Prove that $\angle ABC$ is a right angle. Assume point B is on the circle whose radius is a and whose center is at the origin. (*Hint:* Use slopes and an equation of the circle.)

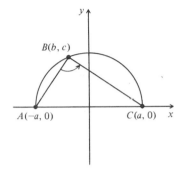

13.3 The Ellipse

As a conic section (see the figure on the right):

> An *ellipse* is formed when a plane intersecting a right circular cone is not perpendicular to the axis of the cone, and intersects all elements of the conical surface (hence is not parallel to a surface element).

The precise definition of an ellipse is as follows.

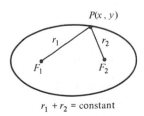

$r_1 + r_2 = \text{constant}$

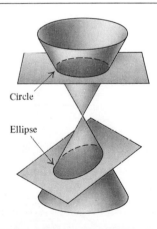

Circle

Ellipse

> **Definition.** An *ellipse* is the locus, or set of all points $P(x, y)$ in a plane such that the sum of the distances from P to two fixed points F_1 and F_2 is constant. Each fixed point is called a *focus* (plural *foci*) of the ellipse.

There is a clever way to make a drawing of an ellipse. Stick two tacks in a piece of cardboard. These will be the foci F_1 and F_2. Attach a piece of string to the tacks. The length of the string will be the constant sum of the distances from the foci to points on the ellipse. Take a pencil and pull the string tight. Now swing the pencil around, keeping the string tight.

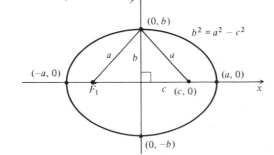

[10, 11]

Now let us find equations for ellipses. We first consider an equation of an ellipse whose center is at the origin and whose foci lie on one of the coordinate axes.

Figure 1

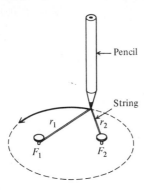

Figure 2

Suppose we have an ellipse like the one in Figure 1, with foci $F_1(-c, 0)$ and $F_2(c, 0)$. If $P(x, y)$ is a point on the ellipse, then $F_1P + F_2P$ is the given constant distance. We will call it $2a$:

$$F_1P + F_2P = 2a.$$

By the distance formula,

$$\sqrt{(x + c)^2 + y^2} + \sqrt{(x - c)^2 + y^2} = 2a,$$

or

$$\sqrt{(x + c)^2 + y^2} = 2a - \sqrt{(x - c)^2 + y^2}.$$

Squaring, we get

$$x^2 + 2cx + c^2 + y^2$$
$$= 4a^2 - 4a\sqrt{(x - c)^2 + y^2} + x^2 - 2cx + c^2 + y^2,$$

or

$$-4a^2 + 4cx = -4a\sqrt{(x - c)^2 + y^2},$$
$$-a^2 + cx = -a\sqrt{(x - c)^2 + y^2}.$$

Squaring again, we get

$$a^4 - 2a^2cx + c^2x^2 = a^2x^2 - 2cxa^2 + a^2c^2 + a^2y^2,$$

or

$$x^2(a^2 - c^2) + a^2y^2 = a^2(a^2 - c^2).$$

It follows from Figure 2 when P is at $(0, b)$, that $b^2 = a^2 - c^2$.

Substituting b^2 for $a^2 - c^2$ in the last equation, we have the equation of the ellipse $b^2x^2 + a^2y^2 = a^2b^2$, or the following.

$$\frac{x^2}{a^2} + \frac{y^2}{b^2} = 1 \qquad \textbf{Standard form of an equation of an ellipse.}$$

We have proved that if a point is on the ellipse, then its coordinates satisfy this equation. We also need to know the converse, that is, if the coordinates of a point satisfy this equation, then the point is on the ellipse. The proof of the latter will be omitted here. In the above, the longer axis of symmetry $\overline{A'A}$ is called the *major axis*. The shorter axis of symmetry $\overline{B'B}$ is called the *minor axis*. The intersection of these axes is called the *center*. The points A, A', B, and B' are called *vertices*. If the center of an ellipse is at the origin, the vertices are also the intercepts.

ELLIPSES AS STRETCHED CIRCLES

Let us consider a unit circle centered at the origin:

$$x^2 + y^2 = 1.$$

If we replace x by x/a and y by y/b we get an equation of an ellipse:

$$\left(\frac{x}{a}\right)^2 + \left(\frac{y}{b}\right)^2 = 1 \quad \text{or} \quad \frac{x^2}{a^2} + \frac{y^2}{b^2} = 1.$$

It follows that an ellipse is a circle transformed by a stretch or shrink in the x-direction and also in the y-direction. If $a = 2$, for example, the unit circle is stretched in the x-direction by a factor of 2. In any case, the x-intercepts become a and $-a$ and the y-intercepts become b and $-b$.

Example 1. For the ellipse $x^2 + 16y^2 = 16$, find the vertices and the foci. Then graph the ellipse.

a) We first multiply by $\frac{1}{16}$:

$$\frac{x^2}{16} + \frac{y^2}{1} = 1, \quad \text{or} \quad \frac{x^2}{4^2} + \frac{y^2}{1^2} = 1.$$

Thus $a = 4$ and $b = 1$. Then two of the vertices are $(-4, 0)$ and $(4, 0)$. These are also x-intercepts. The other vertices are $(0, 1)$ and $(0, -1)$. These are also y-intercepts. Since $c^2 = a^2 - b^2$, we have $c^2 = 16 - 1$, so $c = \sqrt{15}$ and the foci are $(-\sqrt{15}, 0)$ and $(\sqrt{15}, 0)$.

b) The graph is as follows.

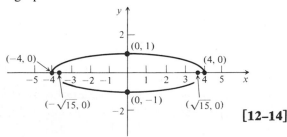

[12–14]

Example 2. Graph this ellipse and its foci: $9x^2 + 2y^2 = 18$.

a) We first multiply by $\frac{1}{18}$:

$$\frac{x^2}{2} + \frac{y^2}{9} = 1 \quad \text{or} \quad \frac{x^2}{(\sqrt{2})^2} + \frac{y^2}{3^2} = 1.$$

Thus $a = \sqrt{2}$ and $b = 3$.

b) Since $b > a$ the foci are on the y-axis and the major axis lies along the y-axis. To find c in this case we proceed as follows:

$$c^2 = b^2 - a^2 = 9 - 2 = 7$$
$$c = \sqrt{7}.$$

c) The graph is as follows.

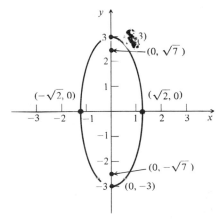

[15–17]

If the center of an ellipse is not at the origin, but at some point (h, k), then the standard equation is as follows.

$$\frac{(x - h)^2}{a^2} + \frac{(y - k)^2}{b^2} = 1 \qquad \textbf{Ellipse, center at } (h, k)$$

Example 3. For the ellipse

$$16x^2 + 4y^2 + 96x - 8y + 84 = 0,$$

find the center, vertices, foci. Then graph the ellipse.

a) We first complete the square to get standard form:

$$16(x^2 + 6x + \quad) + 4(y^2 - 2y + \quad) = -84$$
$$16(x^2 + 6x + 9) + 4(y^2 - 2y + 1) = -84 + 144 + 4$$
$$16(x + 3)^2 + 4(y - 1)^2 = 64$$
$$\frac{(x + 3)^2}{2^2} + \frac{(y - 1)^2}{4^2} = 1.$$

Thus the center is $(-3, 1)$, $a = 2$, and $b = 4$.

b) The vertices of $x^2/2^2 + y^2/4^2 = 1$ are $(2, 0)$, $(-2, 0)$, $(0, 4)$, and $(0, -4)$; and since $c^2 = 16 - 4 = 12$, $c = 2\sqrt{3}$, and its foci are $(0, 2\sqrt{3})$ and $(0, -2\sqrt{3})$.

c) Then the vertices and foci of the translated ellipse are found by translation in the same way in which the center has been translated. Thus the vertices are

$$(-3 + 2, 1), \ (-3 - 2, 1), \ (-3, 1 + 4), \ (-3, 1 - 4),$$

or

$$(-1, 1), \ (-5, 1), \ (-3, 5), \ (-3, -3).$$

The foci are $(-3, 1 + 2\sqrt{3})$ and $(-3, 1 - 2\sqrt{3})$.

d) The graph is as follows.

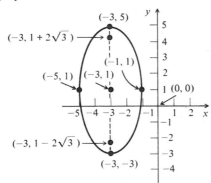

[18, 19]

Ellipses have many applications in space mathematics. Satellites travel in elliptical orbits. Planets travel around the sun in elliptical orbits with the sun being one of the foci.*

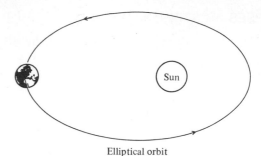

Elliptical orbit

On a pool table in the shape of an ellipse, any ball shot through one focus would bounce off the side and pass through the other focus.

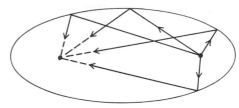

Elliptical pool table

---

* Historical Note. It is interesting that the Greeks studied the mathematical properties of ellipses and other conic sections over a thousand years before Johann Kepler discovered (ca. 1600 A.D.) that planets have elliptical orbits. It was fortunate for Kepler and the advancement of science that the Greeks had studied conic sections just because they thought they were interesting mathematically.

Exercise Set 13.3

For each ellipse find the center, the vertices, and the foci, and draw a graph.

1. $\dfrac{x^2}{4} + \dfrac{y^2}{1} = 1$ **2.** $\dfrac{x^2}{1} + \dfrac{y^2}{4} = 1$ **3.** $\dfrac{(x - 1)^2}{4} + \dfrac{(y - 2)^2}{1} = 1$ **4.** $\dfrac{(x - 1)^2}{1} + \dfrac{(y - 2)^2}{4} = 1$

5. $\dfrac{(x+3)^2}{25} + \dfrac{(y-2)^2}{16} = 1$

6. $\dfrac{(x-2)^2}{25} + \dfrac{(y+3)^2}{16} = 1$

7. $16x^2 + 9y^2 = 144$

8. $9x^2 + 16y^2 = 144$

9. $3(x+2)^2 + 4(y-1)^2 = 192$

10. $4(x-5)^2 + 3(y-5)^2 = 192$

11. $2x^2 + 3y^2 = 6$

12. $5x^2 + 7y^2 = 35$

13. $4x^2 + 9y^2 = 1$

14. $25x^2 + 16y^2 = 1$

15. $4x^2 + 9y^2 - 16x + 18y - 11 = 0$

16. $x^2 + 2y^2 - 10x + 8y + 29 = 0$

17. $4x^2 + y^2 - 8x - 2y + 1 = 0$

18. $9x^2 + 4y^2 + 54x - 8y + 49 = 0$

For each ellipse find the center and vertices.

19. $4x^2 + 9y^2 - 16.025x + 18.0927y - 11.346 = 0$

20. $9x^2 + 4y^2 + 54.063x - 8.016y + 49.872 = 0$

▶ Find an equation of the ellipse with the following vertices. (*Hint:* Graph the vertices.)

21. $(2,0), (-2,0), (0,3), (0,-3)$

22. $(1,0), (-1,0), (0,4), (0,-4)$

23. $(1,1), (5,1), (3,6), (3,-4)$

24. $(-1,-1), (-1,5), (-3,2), (1,2)$

Find an equation of an ellipse satisfying the given conditions.

25. Center at $(-2,3)$ with major axis of length 4 and parallel to the y-axis, minor axis of length 1.

26. Center at $(1,7)$ with major axis of length 5 and parallel to the x-axis, minor axis of length 2.

27. Vertices $(3,0)$ and $(-3,0)$ and containing the point $\left(2, \dfrac{22}{3}\right)$.

28. Vertices $(0,4)$ and $(0,\ 4)$ and containing the point $(-1, 2\sqrt{3})$.

29. a) Graph $9x^2 + y^2 = 9$. Is this relation a function?

b) Solve $9x^2 + y^2 = 9$ for y.

c) Graph $y = 3\sqrt{1-x^2}$ and decide whether it is a function. Find the domain and range.

d) Graph $y = -3\sqrt{1-x^2}$ and decide whether it is a function. Find the domain and range.

30. a) Graph $16x^2 + y^2 = 16$. Is this relation a function?

b) Solve $16x^2 + y^2 = 16$ for y.

c) Graph $y = 4\sqrt{1-x^2}$ and decide whether it is a function. Find the domain and range.

d) Graph $y = -4\sqrt{1-x^2}$ and decide whether it is a function. Find the domain and range.

31. Describe the graph of $\dfrac{x^2}{a^2} + \dfrac{y^2}{b^2} = 1$ when $a^2 = b^2$.

33. The unit square on the left is transformed to the rectangle on the right by a stretch or shrink in the x-direction and a stretch or shrink in the y-direction.

a) Use the above result to develop a formula for the area of the ellipse $\dfrac{x^2}{a^2} + \dfrac{y^2}{b^2} = 1$. (*Hint:* The area of the circle $x^2 + y^2 = r^2$ is $\pi \cdot r \cdot r$.

b) Use the result of (a) to find the area of the ellipse $\dfrac{x^2}{16} + \dfrac{y^2}{25} = 1$.

c) Use the result of (a) to find the area of the ellipse $\dfrac{x^2}{4} + \dfrac{y^2}{3} = 1$.

32. Show that the equation

$$\begin{vmatrix} \dfrac{x-h}{a} & -\dfrac{y-k}{b} \\[2ex] \dfrac{y-k}{b} & \dfrac{x-h}{a} \end{vmatrix} = 1, \quad a > b$$

is an equation of an ellipse with center (h, k).

13.4 The Hyperbola

As a conic section:

Hyperbola

A hyperbola is formed by the intersection of both nappes of a conical surface by a plane parallel to the axis of the cone.

Note that a hyperbola has two parts, called *branches*. The precise definition of a hyperbola is as follows.

Definition. A *hyperbola* is a locus, or set of all points $P(x, y)$ in a plane such that the absolute value of the difference of the distances from P to two fixed points F_1 and F_2 is constant. The fixed points F_1 and F_2 are called *foci*. The midpoint of the segment F_1F_2 is called the *center*.

Now let us find equations for hyperbolas. We first consider an equation of a hyperbola whose center is at the origin and whose foci lie on one of the coordinate axes.

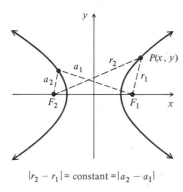

$$|r_2 - r_1| = \text{constant} = |a_2 - a_1|$$

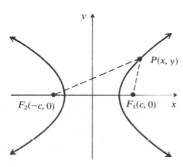

Suppose we have a hyperbola as shown with foci $F_1(c, 0)$ and $F_2(-c, 0)$ on the x-axis. We consider a point $P(x, y)$ in the first quadrant. The proof for the other quadrants is similar to the proof that follows.

We know that $PF_2 > PF_1$, so $PF_2 - PF_1 > 0$ and $|PF_2 - PF_1| = PF_2 - PF_1$. Let the constant difference be $2a$. Then

$$|PF_2 - PF_1| = PF_2 - PF_1 = 2a.$$

In the triangle F_2PF_1, $PF_2 - PF_1 < F_1F_2$, or $2a < 2c$; therefore $a < c$.

Using the distance formula, we have

$$\sqrt{(x + c)^2 + y^2} - \sqrt{(x - c)^2 + y^2} = 2a,$$

or

$$\sqrt{(x + c)^2 + y^2} = 2a + \sqrt{(x - c)^2 + y^2}.$$

Squaring, we get

$$x^2 + 2xc + c^2 + y^2$$

$$= 4a^2 + 4a\sqrt{(x - c)^2 + y^2} + x^2 - 2xc + c^2 + y^2,$$

which simplifies to

$$4cx - 4a^2 = 4a\sqrt{(x - c)^2 + y^2},$$

or

$$cx - a^2 = a\sqrt{(x - c)^2 + y^2}.$$

Squaring again, we get

$$c^2x^2 - 2a^2cx + a^4 = a^2x^2 - 2a^2cx + a^2c^2 + a^2y^2,$$

or

$$x^2(c^2 - a^2) - a^2y^2 = a^2(c^2 - a^2).$$

Since $c > a$, $c^2 > a^2$, so $c^2 - a^2$ is positive. We represent $c^2 - a^2$ by b^2. The previous equation then becomes

$$x^2b^2 - a^2y^2 = a^2b^2,$$

or the following.

$$\frac{x^2}{a^2} - \frac{y^2}{b^2} = 1$$ **Standard equation of a hyperbola, foci on x-axis**

We have shown that if a point is on the hyperbola it satisfies this equation. We also need to know the converse: If a point satisfies the equation, then it is on the hyperbola. We omit the proof.

The following figure is a hyperbola.

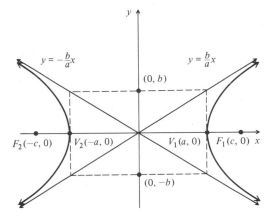

Points V_1 $(a, 0)$ and V_2 $(-a, 0)$ are called the *vertices*, and the line segment $\overline{V_1 V_2}$ is called the *transverse axis*. The line segment from $(0, b)$ to $(0, -b)$ is called the *conjugate axis*. Note that when we replace either or both of x by $-x$ and/or y by $-y$, we get an equivalent equation. Thus the hyperbola is symmetric with respect to the origin, and the x- and y-axes are lines of symmetry.

The lines $y = (b/a)x$ and $y = -(b/a)x$ are *asymptotes*. They have slopes b/a and $-b/a$.

Example 1. For the hyperbola $9x^2 - 16y^2 = 144$, find the vertices, the foci, and the asymptotes. Then graph the hyperbola.

a) We first multiply by $\frac{1}{144}$ to find the standard form:

$$\frac{x^2}{16} - \frac{y^2}{9} = 1.$$

Thus $a = 4$ and $b = 3$. The vertices are $(4, 0)$ and $(-4, 0)$. Since $b^2 = c^2 - a^2$, $c = \sqrt{a^2 + b^2} = \sqrt{4^2 + 3^2} = 5$. Thus the foci are $(5, 0)$ and $(-5, 0)$. The asymptotes are $y = \frac{3}{4}x$ and $y = -\frac{3}{4}x$.

b) To graph the hyperbola it is helpful to first graph the asymptotes. An easy way to do this is to draw the rectangle shown in the figure. Then draw the branches of the hyperbola outward from the vertices toward the asymptotes.

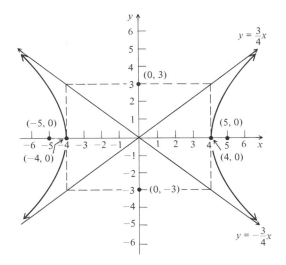

Why are $y = (b/a)x$ and $y = -(b/a)x$ asymptotes? To answer this we solve $x^2/16 - y^2/9 = 1$ for y^2:

$$-16y^2 = 144 - 9x^2$$

$$16y^2 = 9x^2 - 144$$

$$y^2 = \tfrac{1}{16}(9x^2 - 144)$$

$$y^2 = \frac{9x^2 - 144}{16}.$$

From this last equation, we see that as $|x|$ gets larger the term -144 is very small compared to $9x^2$, so y^2 gets close to $9x^2/16$. That is, when $|x|$ is large,

$$y^2 \approx \frac{9x^2}{16},$$

so

$$y \approx |\tfrac{3}{4}x|$$

or

$$y \approx \pm\tfrac{3}{4}x.$$

Thus the lines $y = \tfrac{3}{4}x$ and $y = -\tfrac{3}{4}x$ are asymptotes.

[20, 21]

The foci of a hyperbola can be on the y-axis. In this case, the equation is as follows.

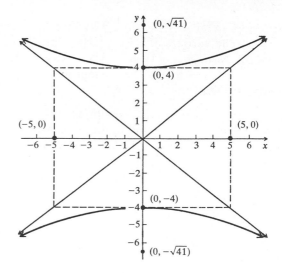

$$\frac{y^2}{b^2} - \frac{x^2}{a^2} = 1 \qquad \text{Standard equation of a hyperbola, foci on y-axis}$$

In this case the slopes of the asymptotes are still $\pm b/a$ and it is still true that $c^2 = a^2 + b^2$. There are now y-intercepts and they are $\pm b$.

Example 2. For the hyperbola $25y^2 - 16x^2 = 400$, find the vertices, the foci, and the asymptotes. Then draw a graph.

a) We first multiply by $\tfrac{1}{400}$ to find the standard form:

$$\frac{y^2}{16} - \frac{x^2}{25} = 1.$$

Thus $a = 5$ and $b = 4$. The vertices are $(0, 4)$ and $(0, -4)$. Since $c = \sqrt{4^2 + 5^2} = \sqrt{41}$, the foci are $(0, \sqrt{41})$ and $(0, -\sqrt{41})$. The asymptotes are $y = \tfrac{4}{5}x$ and $y = -\tfrac{4}{5}x$.

b) The graph is shown at top right.   **[22, 23]**

If the center of a hyperbola is not at the origin, but at some point (h, k), then the standard equation is one of these

$$\frac{(x - h)^2}{a^2} - \frac{(y - k)^2}{b^2} = 1 \qquad \text{Hyperbola, transverse axis parallel to x-axis.}$$

$$\frac{(y - k)^2}{b^2} - \frac{(x - h)^2}{a^2} = 1 \qquad \text{Hyperbola, transverse axis parallel to y-axis.}$$

Example 3. For the hyperbola

$$4x^2 - y^2 + 24x + 4y + 28 = 0,$$

find the center, the vertices, the foci, and the asymptotes. Then graph the hyperbola.

a) We complete the square to find standard form:

$$4(x^2 + 6x +\quad) - (y^2 - 4y +\quad) = -28$$
$$4(x^2 + 6x + 9) - (y^2 - 4y + 4) = -28 + 36 - 4$$
$$4(x + 3)^2 - (y - 2)^2 = 4$$
$$\frac{(x + 3)^2}{1} - \frac{(y - 2)^2}{4} = 1.$$

The center is $(-3, 2)$.

b) Consider $x^2/1 - y^2/4 = 1$. We have $a = 1$ and $b = 2$. The vertices of this hyperbola are $(1, 0)$ and $(-1, 0)$. Also, $c = \sqrt{1^2 + 2^2} = \sqrt{5}$, so the foci are $(\sqrt{5}, 0)$ and $(-\sqrt{5}, 0)$. The asymptotes are $y = 2x$ and $y = -2x$.

c) The vertices, foci, and asymptotes of the translated hyperbola are found in the same way in which the center has been translated. The vertices are $(-3 + 1, 2)$, $(-3 - 1, 2)$, or $(-2, 2)$, $(-4, 2)$. The foci are $(-3 + \sqrt{5}, 2)$ and $(-3 - \sqrt{5}, 2)$. The asymptotes are

$$y - 2 = 2(x + 3) \quad \text{and} \quad y - 2 = -2(x + 3).$$

d) The graph is as follows.

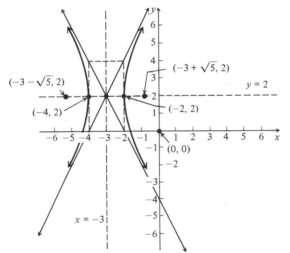

[24, 25]

Another type of equation whose graph is a hyperbola is the following.

$$xy = c, \quad \text{or} \quad y = \frac{c}{x}, \quad \text{where } c \neq 0.$$

If c is positive, the branches of the hyperbola lie in the first and third quadrants. If c is negative, the branches

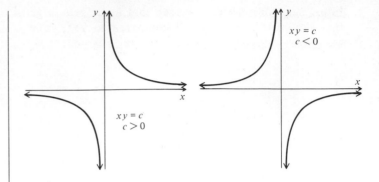

lie in the second and fourth quadrants. In either case the asymptotes are the x-axis and the y-axis.

[26, 27]

Hyperbolas also have many applications. A jet breaking the sound barrier creates a sonic boom whose wave front has the shape of a cone. This cone intersects the ground in one branch of the hyperbola.

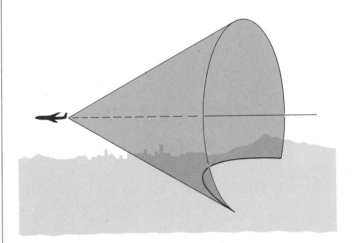

Some comets travel in hyperbolic orbits. A cross section of an amphitheater may be half of one branch of a hyperbola.

Exercise Set 13.4

For each hyperbola find the center, the vertices, the foci, and the asymptotes, and graph the hyperbola.

1. $\dfrac{x^2}{9} - \dfrac{y^2}{1} = 1$

2. $\dfrac{x^2}{1} - \dfrac{y^2}{9} = 1$

3. $\dfrac{(x-2)^2}{9} - \dfrac{(y+5)^2}{1} = 1$

4. $\dfrac{(x-2)^2}{1} - \dfrac{(y+5)^2}{9} = 1$

5. $\dfrac{(y+3)^2}{4} - \dfrac{(x+1)^2}{16} = 1$

6. $\dfrac{(y+3)^2}{25} - \dfrac{(x+1)^2}{16} = 1$

7. $x^2 - 4y^2 = 4$

8. $4x^2 - y^2 = 4$

9. $4y^2 - x^2 = 4$

10. $y^2 - 4x^2 = 4$

11. $x^2 - y^2 = 2$

12. $x^2 - y^2 = 3$

13. $x^2 - y^2 = \dfrac{1}{4}$

14. $x^2 - y^2 = \dfrac{1}{9}$

15. $x^2 - y^2 - 2x - 4y - 4 = 0$

16. $4x^2 - y^2 + 8x - 4y - 4 = 0$

17. $36x^2 - y^2 - 24x + 6y - 41 = 0$

18. $9x^2 - 4y^2 + 54x + 8y + 45 = 0$

Graph.

19. $xy = 1$ **20.** $xy = -4$ **21.** $xy = -8$ **22.** $xy = 3$

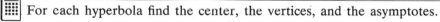

For each hyperbola find the center, the vertices, and the asymptotes.

23. $x^2 - y^2 - 2.046x - 4.088y - 4.228 = 0$

24. $x^2 - y^2 + 8.888x - 4.626y - 4.638 = 0$

▶ Find an equation of a hyperbola having:

25. Vertices at $(1, 0)$ and $(-1, 0)$; and foci at $(2, 0)$ and $(-2, 0)$.

26. Vertices at $(0, 1)$ and $(0, -1)$; and foci at $(0, 2)$ and $(0, -2)$.

27. Asymptotes $y = \dfrac{3}{2}x$ and $y = -\dfrac{3}{2}x$ and one vertex $(2, 0)$.

28. Asymptotes $y = \dfrac{3}{4}x$ and $y = -\dfrac{3}{4}x$ and one vertex $(4, 0)$.

29. a) Graph $x^2 - 4y^2 = 4$. Is this relation a function?

b) Solve $x^2 - 4y^2 = 4$ for y.

c) Graph $y = \frac{1}{2}\sqrt{x^2 - 4}$ and decide whether it is a function. Find the domain and range.

d) Graph $y = -\frac{1}{2}\sqrt{x^2 - 4}$ and decide whether it is a function. Find the domain and range.

30. a) Graph $x^2 - 16y^2 = 16$. Is this relation a function?

b) Solve $x^2 - 16y^2 = 16$ for y.

c) Graph $y = \frac{1}{4}\sqrt{x^2 - 16}$ and decide whether it is a function. Find the domain and range.

d) Graph $y = -\frac{1}{4}\sqrt{x^2 - 16}$ and decide whether it is a function. Find the domain and range.

31. Show that the equation

$$\begin{vmatrix} \dfrac{x-h}{a} & \dfrac{y-k}{b} \\[2mm] \dfrac{y-k}{b} & \dfrac{x-h}{a} \end{vmatrix} = 1$$

is an equation of a hyperbola with center (h, k).

13.5 The Parabola

As a conic section:

> A *parabola* is formed when a conical surface is cut by a plane that is parallel to a surface element.

Thus a parabola intersects only one nappe of the cone.

The precise definition of a parabola is as follows.

> **Definition.** A *parabola* is a locus, or set of all points P in a plane, equidistant from a fixed line L, called the *directrix*, and a fixed point F, called the *focus*.

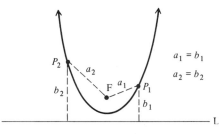

Now let us find equations for parabolas. Consider this figure.

Parabola   Hyperbola

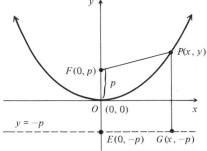

Let us consider a parabola with focus $F(0, p)$ on the y-axis, $p > 0$. The directrix has equation $y = -p$ since $FO = OE$. The fixed distance is p. Thus the origin is a point of the parabola (also called the *vertex* in this case). Let $P(x, y)$ be any point of the parabola and consider $\overline{PG}$ perpendicular to the line $y = -p$. The coordinates of G are $(x, -p)$. By definition of a parabola,

$$PF = PG.$$

Then using the distance formula, we have

$$\sqrt{(x - 0)^2 + (y - p)^2} = \sqrt{(x - x)^2 + (y + p)^2}.$$

Squaring, we get

$$x^2 + y^2 - 2py + p^2 = y^2 + 2py + p^2$$
$$x^2 = 4py.$$

Thus

$$x^2 = 4py$$

Standard equation of a parabola with focus at $(0, p)$ and directrix $y = -p$. The vertex is $(0, 0)$ and the y-axis is the only line of symmetry.

We have shown that if $p(x, y)$ is on the parabola, then its coordinates satisfy this equation. The converse is also true, but we omit the proof.

Note that if $p > 0$, as above, the graph opens upward. If $p < 0$, the graph opens downward and the focus and directrix exchange sides of the x-axis.

The inverse of the above parabola is described as follows.

$$y^2 = 4px$$

Standard equation of a parabola with focus at $(p, 0)$ and directrix $x = -p$. The vertex is $(0, 0)$ and the x-axis is the only line of symmetry.

Example 1. For the parabola $y = x^2$, find the vertex, the focus, and the directrix, and draw a graph.

We first write $x^2 = 4py$:

$$x^2 = 4\left(\frac{1}{4}\right)y.$$

Vertex: $(0, 0)$

Focus: $\left(0, \frac{1}{4}\right)$

Directrix: $y = -\frac{1}{4}$

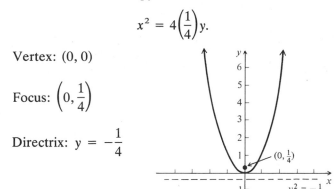

Example 2. For the parabola $y^2 = -12x$, find the vertex, the focus, and the directrix, and draw a graph.

We first write $y^2 = 4px$:

$$y^2 = 4(-3)x.$$

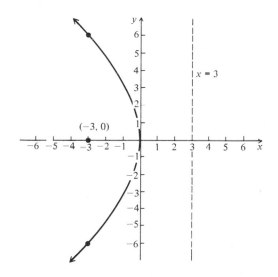

Vertex: $(0, 0)$

Focus: $(-3, 0)$

Directrix: $x = -(-3) = 3$ **[28–30]**

Example 3. Find an equation of a parabola with focus $(5, 0)$ and directrix $x = -5$.

The focus is on the x-axis and $x = -5$ is the directrix, so the line of symmetry is the x-axis. Thus the equation is of the type

$$y^2 = 4px.$$

Since $p = 5$, the equation is $y^2 = 20x$.

Example 4. Find an equation of a parabola with focus $(0, -7)$ and directrix $y = 7$.

The focus is on the y-axis and $y = 7$ is the directrix, so the line of symmetry is the y-axis. Thus the equation is of the type

$$x^2 = 4py.$$

Since $p = -7$, we obtain $x^2 = -28y$.   **[31–34]**

If a parabola is translated so that its vertex is (h, k) and its axis of symmetry is parallel to the y-axis, it has an equation

$$(x - h)^2 = 4p(y - k),$$

where the vertex is (h, k), the focus is $(h, k + p)$, and the directrix is $y = k - p$.

If a parabola is translated so that its vertex is (h, k) and its axis of symmetry is parallel to the x-axis, it has an equation

$$(y - k)^2 = 4p(x - h),$$

where the vertex is (h, k), the focus is $(h + p, k)$, and the directrix is $x = h - p$.

Example 5. For the parabola

$$x^2 + 6x + 4y + 5 = 0,$$

find the vertex, the focus, and the directrix, and graph the parabola.

We complete the square:

$$x^2 + 6x \qquad = -4y - 5$$
$$x^2 + 6x + 9 = -4y - 5 + 9$$
$$(x + 3)^2 = -4y + 4 = 4(-1)(y - 1).$$

Vertex: $(-3, 1)$

Focus: $(-3, 1 + (-1))$
  or $(-3, 0)$

Directrix: $y = 2$

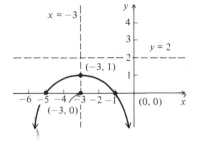

Example 6. For the parabola

$$y^2 + 6y - 8x - 31 = 0,$$

find the vertex, the focus, and the directrix, and draw a graph.

We complete the square:

$$y^2 + 6y \qquad = 8x + 31$$
$$y^2 + 6y + 9 = 8x + 31 + 9$$
$$(y + 3)^2 = 8x + 40 = 8(x + 5) = 4(2)(x + 5).$$

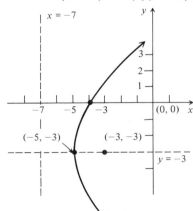

Vertex: $(-5, -3)$

Focus: $(-5 + 2, -3)$ or $(-3, -3)$

Directrix: $x = -5 - 2 = -7$ **[35, 36]**

Parabolas have many applications. Cross sections of headlights are parabolas. The bulb is located at the focus. All light from this point is reflected outward, parallel to the axis of symmetry.

Radar and radio antennas may have cross sections that are parabolas. Incoming radio waves are reflected and concentrated at the focus. Cables hung between structures to form suspension bridges form parabolas. When a cable supports only its own weight it does not form a parabola, but rather a curve called a *catenary*.

Exercise Set 13.5

For each parabola find the vertex, the focus, and the directrix, and graph the parabola.

1. $x^2 = 8y$ **2.** $x^2 = 16y$ **3.** $y^2 = -6x$ **4.** $y^2 = -2x$

5. $x^2 - 4y = 0$ **6.** $y^2 + 4x = 0$ **7.** $y = 2x^2$ **8.** $y = \frac{1}{2}x^2$

9. $(x + 2)^2 = -6(y - 1)$ **10.** $(y - 3)^2 = -20(x + 2)$ **11.** $x^2 + 2x + 2y + 7 = 0$

12. $y^2 + 6y - x + 16 = 0$ **13.** $x^2 - y - 2 = 0$ **14.** $x^2 - 4x - 2y = 0$

15. $y = x^2 + 4x + 3$ **16.** $y = x^2 + 6x + 10$ **17.** $4y^2 - 4y - 4x + 24 = 0$

18. $4y^2 + 4y - 4x - 16 = 0$

Find an equation of a parabola satisfying the given conditions.

19. Focus $(4, 0)$, directrix $x = -4$

20. Focus $\left(0, \frac{1}{4}\right)$, directrix $y = -\frac{1}{4}$

21. Focus $(-\sqrt{2}, 0)$, directrix $x = \sqrt{2}$

22. Focus $(0, -\pi)$, directrix $y = \pi$

23. Focus $(3, 2)$, directrix $x = -4$

24. Focus $(-2, 3)$, directrix $y = -3$

25. Graph each of the following, using the same set of axes.

$$x^2 - y^2 = 0, \quad x^2 - y^2 = 1,$$
$$x^2 + y^2 = 1, \quad y = x^2.$$

26. Graph each of the following using the same set of axes.

$$x^2 - 4y^2 = 0, \quad x^2 - 4y^2 = 1,$$
$$x^2 + 4y^2 = 1, \quad x = 4y^2.$$

For each parabola find the vertex, the focus, and the directrix.

27. $x^2 = 8056.25y$

28. $y^2 = -7645.88x$

Find equations of the following parabolas.

29. Line of symmetry parallel to the y-axis, vertex $(-1, 2)$, and passing through $(-3, 1)$.

30. Line of symmetry parallel to the x-axis, vertex $(2, 1)$, and passing through $(4, \frac{1}{3})$.

31. a) Graph $(y - 3)^2 = -20(x + 1)$. Is this relation a function?

b) In general, is $(y - k)^2 = 4p(x - h)$ a function?

32. a) Graph $(x - 2)^2 = 8(y + 1)$. Is this relation a function?

b) In general, is $(x - h)^2 = 4p(y - k)$ a function?

33. Show that the equation

$$\begin{vmatrix} y - k & x - h \\ 4p & y - k \end{vmatrix} = 0$$

is an equation of a parabola with vertex (h, k).

34. Show that the equation

$$\begin{vmatrix} x - h & y - k \\ 4p & x - h \end{vmatrix} = 0$$

is an equation of a parabola with vertex (h, k).

13.6 Systems of First-Degree and Second-Degree Equations

When we studied systems of linear equations, we solved them both graphically and algebraically. Here we study systems in which one equation is of first degree and one is of second degree. We will use graphical and then algebraic methods of solving.

We consider a system of equations, an equation of a circle and an equation of a line. Let us think about the possible ways in which a circle and a line can intersect. The three possibilities are shown in this figure. For L_1 there is no point of intersection, hence the system of equations has no real solution. For L_2 there is one point of intersection, hence one real solution. For L_3 there are two points of intersection, hence two real solutions.

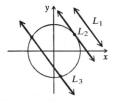

Example 1. Solve this system graphically:

$$x^2 + y^2 = 25$$
$$3x - 4y = 0.$$

We graph the two equations, using the same axes. The points of intersection have coordinates that must satisfy both equations. The solutions seem to be $(4, 3)$ and $(-4, -3)$. We check.

Check: For $(-4, -3)$. You should do the check for $(4, 3)$.

$x^2 + y^2 = 25$		$3x - 4y = 0$	
$(-4)^2 + (-3)^2$	25	$3(-4) - 4(-3)$	0
$16 + 9$		$-12 + 12$	
25			0

[37–39]

Remember that we used the *addition* and *substitution* methods to solve systems of linear equations. In solving systems where one equation is of first degree and one is of second degree, it is preferable to use the <u>*substitution*</u> method.

Example 2. Solve this system algebraically:

$$x^2 + y^2 = 25 \qquad (1)$$
$$3x - 4y = 0. \qquad (2)$$

First solve the linear equation (2) for x:

$$x = \frac{4}{3}y.$$

Then substitute $\frac{4}{3}y$ for x in equation (1) and solve for y:

$$\left(\boxed{\frac{4}{3}y}\right)^2 + y^2 = 25$$

$$\frac{16}{9}y^2 + y^2 = 25$$

$$\frac{16}{9}y^2 + \frac{9}{9}y^2 = 25$$

$$\frac{25}{9}y^2 = 25$$

$$\frac{9}{25} \cdot \frac{25}{9}y^2 = \frac{9}{25} \cdot 25$$

$$y^2 = 9$$

$$y = \pm 3.$$

Now substitute these numbers into the linear equation and solve for x:

$$x = \frac{4}{3}(3), \quad \text{or} \quad 4$$

$$x = \frac{4}{3}(-3), \quad \text{or} \quad -4.$$

The pairs $(4, 3)$ and $(-4, -3)$ check and are solutions.

$$[40\text{–}42]$$

Sometimes an equation may not take on a familiar form like those studied previously in this chapter. We can still rely on the substitution method for solution.

Example 3. Solve the system

$$y + 3 = 2x \qquad (1)$$
$$x^2 + 2xy = -1 \qquad (2)$$

First solve the linear equation (1) for y:

$$y = 2x - 3.$$

Then substitute $2x - 3$ for y in equation (2) and solve for x:

$$x^2 + 2x(\boxed{2x - 3}) = -1$$

$$x^2 + 4x^2 - 6x = -1$$

$$5x^2 - 6x + 1 = 0$$

$$(5x - 1)(x - 1) = 0$$

$$5x - 1 = 0 \quad \text{or} \quad x - 1 = 0$$

$$x = \frac{1}{5} \quad \text{or} \quad x = 1.$$

Now substitute these numbers into the linear equation and solve for y:

$$y = 2\left(\boxed{\frac{1}{5}}\right) - 3, \quad \text{or} \quad -\frac{13}{5}$$

$$y = 2(\boxed{1}) - 3, \quad \text{or} \quad -1.$$

The pairs $\left(\frac{1}{5}, -\frac{13}{5}\right)$ and $(1, -1)$ check and are solutions.

$$[43]$$

APPLIED PROBLEMS

Example. The perimeter of a rectangular field is 204 m and the area is 2565 m^2. Find the dimensions of the field.

We first translate the conditions of the problem to equations, using w for the width and l for the length:

Perimeter: $2w + 2l = 204$

Area: $lw = 2565$

Now we *solve* the system

$$2w + 2l = 204$$
$$lw = 2565$$

and get the solution $(45, 57)$. Now check in the original problem: The perimeter is $2 \cdot 45 + 2 \cdot 57$, or 204. The area is $45 \cdot 57$, or 2565. The numbers check, so the answer is $l = 57$ m, $w = 45$ m.   **[44, 45]**

Exercise Set 13.6

Solve each system graphically. Then solve algebraically.

1. $x^2 + y^2 = 25$
$y - x = 1$

2. $x^2 + y^2 = 100$
$y - x = 2$

3. $y^2 - x^2 = 9$
$2x - 3 = y$

4. $x + y = -6$
$xy = -7$

5. $4x^2 + 9y^2 = 36$
$3y + 2x = 6$

6. $9x^2 + 4y^2 = 36$
$3x + 2y = 6$

7. $y^2 = x + 3$
$2y = x + 4$

8. $y = x^2$
$3x = y + 2$

Solve.

9. $x^2 + 4y^2 = 25$
$x + 2y = 7$

10. $y^2 - x^2 = 16$
$2x - y = 1$

11. $x^2 - xy + 3y^2 = 27$
$x - y = 2$

12. $2y^2 + xy + x^2 = 7$
$x - 2y = 5$

13. $3x + y = 7$
$4x^2 + 5y = 56$

14. $2y^2 + xy = 5$
$4y + x = 7$

Applied problems

15. The sum of two numbers is 14 and the sum of their squares is 106. What are the numbers?

16. The sum of two number is 15 and the difference of their squares is also 15. What are the numbers?

17. A rectangle has perimeter 28 cm and the length of a diagonal is 10 cm. What are its dimensions?

18. A rectangle has perimeter 6 m and the length of a diagonal $\sqrt{5}$ m. What are its dimensions?

19. A rectangle has area 20 in.^{2} and perimeter 18 in. Find its dimensions.

20. A rectangle has area 2 yd^2 and perimeter 6 yd. Find its dimensions.

Solve.

21. $x^2 + y^2 = 19{,}380{,}510.36$
$27{,}942.25x - 6.125y = 0$

22. $2x + 2y = 1660$
$xy = 35{,}325$

---

23. Given the area A and the perimeter P of a rectangle, show that the length L and the width W are given by the formulas

$$L = \frac{1}{4}(P + \sqrt{P^2 - 16A}),$$

$$W = \frac{1}{4}(P - \sqrt{P^2 - 16A}).$$

25. Find an equation of a circle that passes through the points $(2, 4)$ and $(3, 3)$ and whose center is on the line $3x - y = 3$.

24. Show that a hyperbola cannot intersect its asymptotes. That is, solve the system

$$\frac{x^2}{a^2} - \frac{y^2}{b^2} = 1$$

$$y = \frac{b}{a}x \left(\text{or, } y = -\frac{b}{a}x \right).$$

26. Find an equation of a circle that passes through the points $(7, 3)$ and $(5, 5)$ and whose center is on the line $y - 4x = 1$.

13.7 Systems of Second-Degree Equations

We now consider systems of two second-degree equations. The following shows ways in which a circle and a hyperbola can intersect.

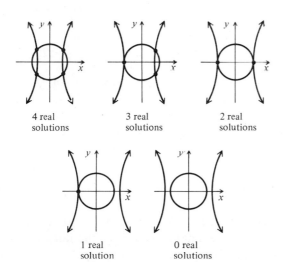

4 real
solutions

3 real
solutions

2 real
solutions

1 real
solution

0 real
solutions

Example 1. Solve this system graphically:

$$x^2 + y^2 = 25$$

$$\frac{x^2}{25} - \frac{y^2}{25} = 1.$$

We graph the two equations using the same axes. The points of intersection have coordinates that must satisfy both equations. thc solutions seem to be $(5, 0)$ and $(-5, 0)$.

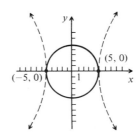

Check: Since $(5)^2 = 25$ and $(-5)^2 = 25$, we can do both checks at once.

$$x^2 + y^2 = 25$$

$(\pm 5)^2 + 0^2$	25
$25 + 0$	
25	

$$\frac{x^2}{25} - \frac{y^2}{25} = 1$$

$\dfrac{(\pm 5)^2}{25} - \dfrac{0^2}{25}$	1
$\dfrac{25}{25} - 0$	
1	**[46–48]**

To solve systems of two second-degree equations we can use either the substitution or the addition method.

Example 2. Solve this system:

$$2x^2 + 5y^2 = 22 \tag{1}$$
$$3x^2 - y^2 = -1. \tag{2}$$

Here we use the addition method.

$$2x^2 + 5y^2 = 22$$

From the second equation, we get

$$\underline{15x^2 - 5y^2 = -5} \qquad \text{(multiply by 5)}$$
$$17x^2 = 17 \qquad \text{(adding)}$$
$$x^2 = 1$$
$$x = \pm 1.$$

If $x = 1$, $x^2 = 1$, and if $x = -1$, $x^2 = 1$, so substituting 1 or -1 for x in equation (2) we have

$$3 \cdot \boxed{1} - y^2 = -1$$
$$y^2 = 4$$
$$y = \pm 2.$$

Thus, if $x = 1$, $y = 2$ or $y = -2$, and if $x = -1$, $y = 2$ or $y = -2$.

The possible solutions are $(1, 2)$, $(1, -2)$, $(-1, 2)$, and $(-1, -2)$.

Check: Since $(2)^2 = 4$, $(-2)^2 = 4$, $(1)^2 = 1$, and $(-1)^2 = 1$, we can check all four pairs at one time.

$$2x^2 + 5y^2 = 22$$

$2(\pm 1)^2 + 5(\pm 2)^2$	22
$2 + 20$	
22	

$$3x^2 - y^2 = -1$$

$3(\pm 1)^2 - (\pm 2)^2$	-1
$3 - 4$	
-1	**[49]**

Example 3. Solve the system

$$x^2 + 4y^2 = 20 \tag{1}$$
$$xy = 4. \tag{2}$$

Here we use the substitution method. First solve equation (2) for y:

$$y = \frac{4}{x}.$$

Then substitute $4/x$ for y in equation (1) and solve for x:

$$x^2 + 4\left(\frac{4}{x}\right)^2 = 20$$
$$x^2 + \frac{64}{x^2} = 20$$
$$x^4 + 64 = 20x^2 \qquad \text{(multiplying by } x^2\text{)}$$
$$x^4 - 20x^2 + 64 = 0 \qquad \text{(quadratic in form)}$$
$$u^2 - 20u + 64 = 0 \qquad \text{(letting } u = x^2\text{)}$$
$$(u - 16)(u - 4) = 0.$$

Then $x = 4$ or $x = -4$ or $x = 2$ or $x = -2$.

Since $y = 4/x$, if $x = 4$, $y = 1$; if $x = -4$, $y = -1$; if $x = 2$, $y = 2$; if $x = -2$, $y = -2$.

The solutions are $(4, 1)$, $(-4, -1)$, $(2, 2)$, and $(-2, -2)$.

[50]

AN APPLIED PROBLEM

Example. The area of a rectangle is 300 yd^2 and the length of a diagonal is 25 yd. Find the dimensions.

First make a drawing.

We use l for the length and w for the width and translate to equations.

From the Pythagorean theorem: $l^2 + w^2 = 25^2$

Area: $\quad lw = 300$

Now we *solve* the system

$$l^2 + w^2 = 625$$
$$lw = 300$$

and get the solutions $(15, 20)$ and $(-15, -20)$. Now check in the original problem: $15^2 + 20^2 = 25^2$ and $15 \cdot 20 = 300$, so $(15, 20)$ is a solution of the problem. Lengths of sides cannot be negative so $(-15, -20)$ is not. The answer is $l = 20$ yd and $w = 15$ yd.   **[51]**

Exercise Set 13.7

Solve each system graphically. Then solve algebraically.

1. $x^2 + y^2 = 25$
$\quad y^2 = x + 5$

2. $y = x^2$
$\quad x = y^2$

3. $x^2 + y^2 = 9$
$\quad x^2 - y^2 = 9$

4. $y^2 - 4x^2 = 4$
$\quad 4x^2 + y^2 = 4$

5. $x^2 + y^2 = 25$
$\quad xy = 12$

6. $x^2 - y^2 = 16$
$\quad x + y^2 = 4$

7. $x^2 + y^2 = 4$
$\quad 16x^2 + 9y^2 = 144$

8. $x^2 + y^2 = 25$
$\quad 25x^2 + 16y^2 = 400$

Solve.

9. $x^2 + y^2 = 16$
$\quad y^2 - 2x^2 = 10$

10. $x^2 + y^2 = 14$
$\quad x^2 - y^2 = 4$

11. $x^2 + y^2 = 5$
$\quad xy = 2$

12. $x^2 + y^2 = 20$
$\quad xy = 8$

13. $x^2 + y^2 = 13$
$\quad xy = 6$

14. $x^2 + 4y^2 = 20$
$\quad xy = 4$

15. $x^2 + y^2 + 6y + 5 = 0$
$\quad x^2 + y^2 - 2x - 8 = 0$

16. $2xy + 3y^2 = 7$
$\quad 3xy - 2y^2 = 4$

Applied problems

17. Find two numbers whose product is 156 if the sum of their squares is 313.

18. Find two numbers whose product is 60 if the sum of their squares is 136.

19. The area of a rectangle is $\sqrt{3}$ m^2 and the length of a diagonal is 2 m. Find the dimensions.

20. The area of a rectangle is $\sqrt{2}$ m^2 and the length of a diagonal is $\sqrt{3}$ m. Find the dimensions.

21. A garden contains two square peanut beds. Find the length of each bed if the sum of their areas is 832 ft^2, and the difference of their areas is 320 ft^2.

22. A certain amount of money saved for 1 yr at a certain interest rate yielded $7.50. If the principal has been $25 more and the interest rate 1% less, the interest would have been the same. Find the principal and the rate.

Solve.

23. $18.465x^2 + 788.723y^2 = 6408$
$106.535x^2 - 788.723y^2 = 2692$

24. $0.319x^2 + 2688.7y^2 = 56,548$
$0.306x^2 - 2688.7y^2 = 43,452$

25. Find an equation of the circle that passes through the points $(4, 6)$, $(-6, 2)$, and $(1, -3)$.

26. Find an equation of the circle that passes through the points $(2, 3)$, $(4, 5)$, and $(0, -3)$.

Chapter 13 Test, or Review

1. Graph $2x^2 - 3xy - 2y^2 = 0$.

2. Find an equation of the circle with center $(-2, 6)$ and radius $\sqrt{13}$.

3. Find the center and radius of the circle

$$2x^2 + 2y^2 - 3x - 5y + 3 = 0.$$

4. Find an equation of the parabola with directrix $Y = \frac{3}{2}$ and focus $(0, -\frac{3}{2})$.

5. Find the focus, vertex, and directrix of the parabola $y^2 = -12x$.

6. Find the center, vertices, and foci of the ellipse

$$16x^2 + 25y^2 - 64x + 50y - 311 = 0.$$

Then graph the ellipse.

7. Find the center, vertices, foci, and asymptotes of the hyperbola

$$x^2 - 2y^2 + 4x + y - \frac{1}{8} = 0.$$

8. Solve.

$x^2 - 16y = 0$
$x^2 - y^2 = 64$

9. Solve.

$4x^2 + 4y^2 = 65$
$6x^2 - 4y^2 = 25$

10. The sum of two numbers is 11 and the sum of their squares is 65. Find the numbers.

11. The sides of a triangle are 8, 10, and 14. Find the altitude to the longest side.

Sequences, Series, and Mathematical Induction

14.1 Sequences and Series

SEQUENCES

A *sequence* is an ordered set of numbers. Here is an example:

$$3, 5, 7, 9, \ldots.$$

Each number is called a *term* of the sequence. The first term is 3, the second term is 5, the third term is 7, and so on. We can also think of a sequence as a function a whose domain is a set of consecutive natural numbers. The first term is 3, so $a(1) = 3$; the second term is 5, so $a(2) = 5$; the third term is 7, so $a(3) = 7$; the fourth term is 9, so $a(4) = 9$; and so on.

Some sequences have a rule or formula for finding the nth term. The above sequence could be described

$$3, 5, 7, 9, \ldots, 2n + 1, \ldots$$

where the nth term is $2n + 1$. We also say that $a(n) = 2n + 1$, or $a_n = 2n + 1$.

We can find the terms of the sequence by consecutively substituting the numbers $1, 2, 3, \ldots, n$, and so on. Thus

$$a(\boxed{1}) = 2 \cdot \boxed{1} + 1, \quad \text{or} \quad 3$$
$$a(\boxed{2}) = 2 \cdot \boxed{2} + 1, \quad \text{or} \quad 5$$
$$a(\boxed{3}) = 2 \cdot \boxed{3} + 1, \quad \text{or} \quad 7$$
$$\vdots \qquad\qquad \vdots \qquad\quad \vdots$$

We also call the nth term the *general term*.

Example 1. A sequence is given by $a(n) = 5 + 2/n$.

a) Find the first four terms of the sequence

$$5 + \frac{2}{\boxed{1}}, 5 + \frac{2}{\boxed{2}}, 5 + \frac{2}{\boxed{3}}, 5 + \frac{2}{\boxed{4}},$$

or

$$7, 6, 5\frac{2}{3}, 5\frac{1}{2}.$$

b) Find the 44th term:

$$5 + \frac{2}{\boxed{44}}, \quad \text{or} \quad 5\frac{1}{22}. \qquad \textbf{[1–3]}$$

We may know the first few terms of a sequence, but not know the nth term or general term. This can happen in practical problems. In such cases we can make a guess by looking for a pattern.

Examples. For each sequence try to find a rule for finding the general term, or nth term.

Sequence	General term
$1, 4, 9, 16, 25, \ldots$	$a(n) = n^2$
$\sqrt{1}, \sqrt{2}, \sqrt{3}, \sqrt{4}, \ldots$	$a(n) = \sqrt{n}$
$1, 3, 5, 7, 9, 11, \ldots$	$a(n) = 2n - 1$
$-1, 2, -4, 8, -16, \ldots$	$a(n) = (-1)^n 2^{n-1}$
$x, x^2, x^3, x^4, \ldots$	$a(n) = x^n$

Rules found in this manner are not unique. For example, consider the sequence

$$2, 4, 6, \cdots.$$

We might guess that the general term is $2n$. Then the 4th term would be 8. But, the sequence whose general term is

$$2n + (1 - n)(2 - n)(3 - n)$$

has 2, 4, 6 as its first three terms. However its 4th term is

$$a(\boxed{4}) = 2 \cdot \boxed{4} + (1 - \boxed{4})(2 - \boxed{4})(3 - \boxed{4}), \quad \text{or} \quad 2.$$
$$\textbf{[4–8]}$$

A sequence that ends is called *finite*.

A sequence that is unending is called *infinite*. We often use dots to indicate an infinite sequence, as follows:

$$2, 4, 6, 8, 10, \ldots$$
$$\sqrt{2}, \sqrt{3}, \sqrt{4}, \ldots. \qquad \textbf{[9–11]}$$

It is customary to use a_n as well as $a(n)$ for the general term of a sequence.

Example. Find first four terms of the sequence whose general term is given by

$$a_n = \frac{(-1)^n}{n+1}.$$

$$a_1 = \frac{(-1)^1}{1+1} = -\frac{1}{2} \qquad a_3 = \frac{(-1)^3}{3+1} = -\frac{1}{4}$$

$$a_2 = \frac{(-1)^2}{2+1} = \frac{1}{3} \qquad a_4 = \frac{(-1)^4}{4+1} = \frac{1}{5} \qquad \textbf{[12]}$$

An infinite sequence may be defined by what is called a *recursive definition*. Such a definition lists the first term and tells how to get the $(k+1)$st term from the kth term.

Example. Find the first five terms of the sequence defined by

$$a_1 = 5,$$
$$a_{k+1} = 2a_k - 3, \qquad \text{for } k \geq 1.$$

$$a_1 = 5,$$
$$a_2 = 2a_1 - 3 = 2 \cdot 5 - 3 = 7,$$
$$a_3 = 2a_2 - 3 = 2 \cdot 7 - 3 = 11,$$
$$a_4 = 2a_3 - 3 = 2 \cdot 11 - 3 = 19,$$
$$a_5 = 2a_4 - 3 = 2 \cdot 19 - 3 = 35. \qquad \textbf{[13]}$$

SERIES

With any sequence there is an associated *series*, which is the sum of the terms of the sequence. For example, associated with the sequence

$$3, 5, 7, 9, \ldots, 2n+1$$

is the series

$$S_n = 3 + 5 + 7 + 9 + \cdots + (2n+1).$$

In other words, S_n represents the sum of the first n terms of the sequence.   **[14, 15]**

The Greek letter $\sum$ (sigma) is used to signify a sum. The statement above can be abbreviated as follows:

$$S_n = \sum_{k=1}^{n} (2k+1).$$

The right side is read "the sum as k goes from 1 to n of $(2k+1)$."

Example. Rewrite without using $\sum$:

$$\sum_{k=1}^{4} (2^k + k).$$

To find the terms we replace k by each of the numbers 1 through 4.

For $k = 1$: $2^1 + 1 = 3$; for $k = 2$: $2^2 + 2 = 6$;

for $k = 3$: $2^3 + 3 = 11$; for $k = 4$: $2^4 + 4 = 20$

Then $\sum_{k=1}^{4} (2^k + k) = 3 + 6 + 11 + 20$.

Sigma notation may not always start at 1.

Examples

a) $\sum_{k=0}^{3} \pi^k = \pi^0 + \pi^1 + \pi^2 + \pi^3$

b) $\sum_{k=10}^{12} \log k = \log 10 + \log 11 + \log 12$ **[16]**

To find sigma notation we look for a formula for the nth term.

Examples. Find sigma notation for each series.

Series	Sigma notation
$1 + 4 + 9 + 16 + 25$	$\displaystyle\sum_{k=1}^{5} k^2$
$x^1 + x^2 + x^3 + x^4 + x^5 + x^6 + x^7$	$\displaystyle\sum_{k=1}^{7} x^k$
$\sqrt{1} + \sqrt{2} + \sqrt{3} + \cdots + \sqrt{n}$	$\displaystyle\sum_{k=1}^{n} \sqrt{k}$
$7 + 11 + 15 + 19 + 23 + 27$	$\displaystyle\sum_{k=1}^{6} (4k + 3)$
$-1 + 3 + (-5) + 7$	$\displaystyle\sum_{k=1}^{4} (-1)^k(2k - 1)$

Let us verify that the last rule works.

$$(-1)^{\boxed{1}}(2 \cdot \boxed{1} - 1) = (-1)(1) = -1,$$

$$(-1)^{\boxed{2}}(2 \cdot \boxed{2} - 1) = 1 \cdot (3) = 3,$$

$$(-1)^{\boxed{3}}(2 \cdot \boxed{3} - 1) = (-1)(5) = -5,$$

$$(-1)^{\boxed{4}}(2 \cdot \boxed{4} - 1) = 1 \cdot (7) = 7. \qquad \textbf{[17–20]}$$

Associated with an infinite sequence is an *infinite series*. For example, associated with the sequence

$$1, 4, 9, 16, \ldots$$

is the series

$$1 + 4 + 9 + 16 + \cdots.$$

For such a series we use the sigma notation

$$\sum_{k=1}^{\infty} k^2. \qquad \text{(read "the sum as } k \text{ goes from 1 to infinity")}$$

Example 1. Rewrite without using Σ.

$$\sum_{k=1}^{\infty} (3k + 4) = 7 + 10 + 13 + 16 + \cdots$$

Example 2. Find sigma notation for this series.

$$1 + 3 + 5 + 7 + \cdots = \sum_{k=1}^{\infty} (2k - 1)$$

$$\textbf{[21, 22]}$$

Exercise Set 14.1

In each of the following the nth term of a sequence is given. In each case find the first four terms, the 10th term, and the 15th term.

1. $a_n = 3n + 1$ **2.** $a_n = 3n - 1$ **3.** $a_n = \dfrac{1}{n}$ **4.** $a_n = \dfrac{(-1)^n}{n}$

5. $a_n = \dfrac{n}{n + 1}$ **6.** $a_n = n^2 + 1$ **7.** $a_n = n^2 - 2n + 1$ **8.** $a_n = \dfrac{n^2 - 1}{n^2 + 1}$

9. $a_n = n + \dfrac{1}{n}$ **10.** $a_n = n + \dfrac{(-1)^n}{n}$ **11.** $a_n = 2^n$ **12.** $a_n = (-\tfrac{1}{2})^{n-1}$

For each of the following sequences find a rule for finding the general term or nth term. Answers may vary.

13. $1, 3, 5, 7, 9, \ldots$ **14.** $3, 9, 27, 81, 243, \ldots$

15. $\dfrac{2}{3}, \dfrac{3}{4}, \dfrac{4}{5}, \dfrac{5}{6}, \dfrac{6}{7}, \ldots$

16. $\sqrt{2}, \sqrt{4}, \sqrt{6}, \sqrt{8}, \sqrt{10}, \ldots$

17. $\sqrt{3}, 3, 3\sqrt{3}, 9, 9\sqrt{3}, \ldots$

18. $1 \cdot 2, 2 \cdot 3, 3 \cdot 4, 4 \cdot 5, \ldots$

19. $-1, -4, -7, -10, -13, \ldots$

20. $\dfrac{1}{10}, \dfrac{2}{100}, \dfrac{3}{1000}, \ldots$

Which of the following sequences are finite?

21. $1, 3, 6, 10, 15, \ldots$

22. $2, 4, 6, 8, 10, 12, 14, 16$

23. $5, 10, 15, 20, 25$

24. $-\dfrac{1}{2}, -\dfrac{1}{3}, -\dfrac{1}{4}, -\dfrac{1}{5}, \ldots$

Find the first four terms of each recursively defined sequence.

25. $a_1 = 4, a_{k+1} = 1 + \dfrac{1}{a_k}$

26. $a_1 = 16, a_{k+1} - \sqrt{a_k}$

27. $a_1 = 64, a_{k+1} = \sqrt{a_k}$

28. $a_1 = \pi, a_{k+1} = \sin a_k$

For each sequence find its associated series.

29. $1, 2, 3, 4, 5, 6, 7$

30. $1, -3, 5, -7, 9, -11$

31. $2, 4, 6, 8, \ldots, 2n$

32. $1, \dfrac{1}{4}, \dfrac{1}{9}, \dfrac{1}{16}, \dfrac{1}{25}$

Rewrite without using Σ.

33. $\displaystyle\sum_{k=1}^{5} \dfrac{1}{2k}$

34. $\displaystyle\sum_{k=1}^{6} \dfrac{1}{2k+1}$

35. $\displaystyle\sum_{k=0}^{5} 2^k$

36. $\displaystyle\sum_{k=4}^{7} \sqrt{2k-1}$

37. $\displaystyle\sum_{k=7}^{10} \log k$

38. $\displaystyle\sum_{k=0}^{4} \pi k$

Find sigma notation for each series.

39. $\dfrac{1}{2} + \dfrac{2}{3} + \dfrac{3}{4} + \dfrac{4}{5} + \dfrac{5}{6} + \dfrac{6}{7}$

40. $3 + 6 + 9 + 12 + 15$

41. $-2 + 4 - 8 + 16 - 32 + 64$

42. $\dfrac{1}{1^2} + \dfrac{1}{2^2} + \dfrac{1}{3^2} + \dfrac{1}{4^2}$

43. $1 + 4 + 9 + 16 + \cdots$

44. $\dfrac{1}{3} + \dfrac{1}{9} + \dfrac{1}{27} + \dfrac{1}{81} + \cdots$

45. $-1 - 2 - 3 - 4 - 5 - \cdots$

46. $1 + \dfrac{1}{\sqrt{2}} + \dfrac{1}{\sqrt{3}} + \dfrac{1}{2} + \cdots$

47. $\dfrac{1}{2} + \dfrac{2}{4} + \dfrac{3}{8} + \dfrac{4}{16} + \cdots$

48. $\dfrac{2}{3} + \dfrac{3}{4} + \dfrac{4}{5} + \dfrac{5}{6} + \cdots$

Rewrite without using $\sum$.

49. $\displaystyle\sum_{k=1}^{\infty} \dfrac{1}{k}$

50. $\displaystyle\sum_{k=1}^{\infty} \dfrac{k+1}{4k}$

51. $\displaystyle\sum_{k=1}^{\infty} (-3)^k$

52. $\displaystyle\sum_{k=1}^{\infty} \dfrac{2k-1}{2k+1}$

53. $\displaystyle\sum_{k=1}^{\infty} \dfrac{k^2+1}{k+5}$

54. $\displaystyle\sum_{k=1}^{\infty} \dfrac{(-1)^k}{2k}$

14.2 Arithmetic Sequences and Series

ARITHMETIC SEQUENCES

Consider this sequence:

$$2, 5, 8, 11, 14, \ldots.$$

Note that the number 3 can be added to each term to obtain the next term. Sequences in which a certain number can be added to any term to get the next term are called *arithmetic sequences* (or arithmetic *progressions*). We will use the following notation with arithmetic sequences.

a_1 is the first term.
a_n is the nth term.
n is the number of terms from a_1 up to and including a_n.
d is the number we add to one term to get the next.

The number d is also referred to as the *common difference* because if we subtract any term from the one that follows it, we get d. Recursively,

$$a_{k+1} - a_k = d, \; k \geqslant 1.$$

Examples. The following are arithmetic sequences. Identify the first term and the common difference.

Sequence	First term	Common difference
$2, 5, 8, 11, 14, \ldots$	2	3
$4, 9, 14, 19, 24, \ldots$	4	5
$34, 27, 20, 13, 6, -1, -8, -15, \ldots$	34	-7
$2, 1, 0, -1, -2, -3, \ldots$	2	-1
$2, 2\frac{1}{2}, 3, 3\frac{1}{2}, 4, 4\frac{1}{2}, \ldots$	2	$\frac{1}{2}$

[23–28]

Note the following:

First term: a_1

Second term: $a_2 = a_1 + d$

Third term: $a_3 = (a_1 + d) + d = a_1 + 2d$

Fourth term: $a_4 = [(a_1 + d) + d] + d = a_1 + 3d$

and so on. Generalizing, we obtain the following.

> **Theorem. The nth term of an arithmetic sequence is given by**
> $$a_n = a_1 + (n - 1)d.$$

Example 1. Find the 14th term of the arithmetic sequence 4, 7, 10, 13, ... First note that $a_1 = 4$, $d = 3$, and $n = 14$. Then using the formula

$$a_n = a_1 + (n - 1)d,$$

we have

$$a_{14} = 4 + (14 - 1)3$$
$$= 4 + 39$$
$$a_{14} = 43.$$

We could check this by writing out 14 terms of the sequence.

Example 2. In the sequence of Example 1, what term is 301? That is, what is n if $a_n = 301$?

$$a_n = a_1 + (n - 1)d$$
$$301 = 4 + (n - 1)3$$
$$301 = 4 + 3n - 3$$
$$300 = 3n$$
$$100 = n$$

Thus the 100th term is 301.

In a similar manner we can find a_1 if we know n, a_n, and d. Also, we can find d if we know a_1, n, and a_n. **[29–32]**

Given two terms and their places in a sequence, we can find a_1 and d and then construct the sequence.

Example. The 3rd term of an arithmetic sequence is 8 and the 16th term is 47. Find a_1 and d. Construct the sequence.

Using the formula $a_n = a_1 + (n - 1)d$, where $a_3 = 8$, we have

$$\boxed{8} = a_1 + (\boxed{3} - 1)d$$

or

$$8 = a_1 + 2d.$$

Using the formula $a_n = a_1 + (n - 1)d$, where $a_{16} = 47$, we have

$$\boxed{47} = a_1 + (\boxed{16} - 1)d$$

or

$$47 = a_1 + 15d.$$

Now we solve the system

$$a_1 + 15d = 47$$
$$a_1 + \ \ 2d = 8.$$

$$\begin{aligned} a_1 + 15d &= 47 \\ -a_1 - \ \ 2d &= -8 \qquad \text{(multiplying by } -1\text{)} \\ \hline 13d &= 39 \qquad \text{(adding)} \\ d &= 3 \\ a_1 + 2 \cdot \boxed{3} &= 8 \\ a_1 &= 2 \end{aligned}$$

Thus a_1 is 2, d is 3, and the sequence is 2, 5, 8, 11, 14, ... **[33]**

ARITHMETIC SERIES

An *arithmetic series* is the series associated with an arithmetic sequence. We can denote an arithmetic sequence as

$$a_1, (a_1 + d), (a_1 + 2d), \ldots, (a_n - 2d), (a_n - d), a_n.$$

Then the associated series S_n, or the sum of the first n terms, is

$$S_n = a_1 + (a_1 + d) + (a_1 + 2d) + \cdots$$
$$+ (a_n - 2d) + (a_n - d) + a_n.$$

Reversing the right side, we get

$$S_n = a_n + (a_n - d) + (a_n - 2d) + \cdots$$
$$+ (a_1 + 2d) + (a_1 + d) + a_1.$$

Now we add:

$$2S_n = [a_1 + a_n] + [(a_1 + d) + (a_n - d)]$$
$$+ [(a_1 + 2d) + (a_n - 2d)] + \cdots$$
$$+ [(a_n - d) + (a_1 + d)] + [a_1 + a_n].$$

This simplifies to

$$2S_n = (a_1 + a_n) + (a_1 + a_n)$$
$$+ (a_1 + a_n) + \cdots + (a_1 + a_n).$$

Since there are **n** binomials $(a_1 + a_n)$, it follows that $2S_n = \mathbf{n} \cdot (a_1 + a_n)$. Thus we have the following.

> **Theorem.** The sum of the first n terms of an arithmetic series is given by
> $$S_n = \frac{n}{2}(a_1 + a_n).$$

This formula is useful when we know a_1 and a_n, the first and last terms, but it often happens that a_n is not known. We thus need a formula in terms of a_1, n, and d.

Substituting $a_1 + (n - 1)d$ for a_n in the formula $S_n = \frac{n}{2}(a_1 + a_n)$ we get

$$S_n = \frac{n}{2}(a_1 + [a_1 + (n - 1)d]).$$

Thus we have the following.

> **Theorem.** The sum of the first n terms of an arithmetic series is given by
> $$S_n = \frac{n}{2}[2a_1 + (n - 1)d].$$

Example 1. Find the sum of the first 100 natural numbers.

The series is $1 + 2 + 3 + \cdots + 99 + 100$. So $a_1 = 1$, $a_n = 100$, and $n = 100$.

Then substituting in the formula $S_n = \frac{n}{2}(a_1 + a_n)$, we get

$$S_{100} = \frac{100}{2}(1 + 100)$$
$$= 50(101), \text{ or } 5050. \qquad [34]$$

Example 2. Find the sum of the first 14 terms of the arithmetic sequence $2, 5, 8, 11, 14, 17, \ldots$.

Note that $a_1 = 2$, $d = 3$, and $n = 14$. Using the formula

$$S_n = \frac{n}{2}(2a_1 + (n - 1)d],$$

we have

$$S_{14} = \frac{14}{2} \cdot [2 \cdot 2 + -14 - 1)3]$$
$$= 7 \cdot [4 + 13 \cdot 3]$$
$$= 7 \cdot 43$$
$$S_{14} = 301. \qquad [35]$$

Example 3. Find the sum of the series $\sum_{k=1}^{13} (4k + 5)$.

First find a few terms:

$$9 + 13 + 17 + \cdots.$$

We see that this is an arithmetic series with $a_1 = 9$, $d = 4$, and $n = 13$. Using the formula

$$S_n = \frac{n}{2}[2a_1 + (n - 1)d],$$

we have

$$S_{13} = \frac{13}{2}[2 \cdot 9 + (13 - 1)4]$$
$$= \frac{13}{2}[18 + 12 \cdot 4]$$
$$= \frac{13}{2} \cdot 66$$
$$S_{13} = 429. \qquad [36]$$

Example 4. Find the sum of all numbers divisible by five whose numerals have two digits.

The first number of this type is 10, the last is 95, and the common difference is 5. Thus $a_1 = 10$, $a_n = 95$, and $d = 5$. We still need to know what the number of terms, n, is. We use the equation

$$a_n = a_1 + (n - 1)d$$

and solve for n:

$$95 = 10 + (n - 1)5$$
$$95 = 10 + 5n - 5$$
$$90 = 5n$$
$$18 = n.$$

Then using the formula

$$S_n = \frac{n}{2}(a_1 + a_n),$$

we have

$$S_{18} = \frac{18}{2}(10 + 95)$$
$$= 9(105)$$
$$S_{18} = 945.$$ [37]

Example 5. A man saves money in an arithmetic sequence. He saves \$500 one year, \$600 the next, \$700 the next, and so on, for 10 years. How much does he save?

We have the arithmetic series

$$500 + 600 + 700 + \cdots$$

(In this case the dots indicate that the pattern continues, even though this is not an infinite series.)

Thus $a_1 = 500$, $n = 10$, and $d = 100$. Using the formula

$$S_n = \frac{n}{2}[2a_1 + (n - 1)d],$$

we have

$$S_{10} = \frac{10}{2}[2 \cdot 500 + (10 - 1)100]$$
$$S_{10} = 9500.$$

He saved \$9500. [38]

Exercise Set 14.2

For each of the following arithmetic sequences find the first term and the common difference.

1. $2, 7, 12, 17, \ldots$

2. $1.06, 1.12, 1.18, 1.24, \ldots$

3. $7, 3, -1, -5, \ldots$

4. $-9, -6, -3, 0, \ldots$

5. $\frac{3}{2}, \frac{9}{4}, 3, \frac{15}{4}, \ldots$

6. $3x + 2y, 4x + y, 5x, 6x - y, \ldots$

7. Find the 12th term of the arithmetic sequence $2, 6, 10, \ldots$

8. Find the 11th term of the arithmetic sequence $0.07, 0.12, 0.17, \ldots$

9. Find the 17th term of the arithmetic sequence $7, 4, 1, \ldots$

10. Find the 14th term of the arithmetic sequence 3, $\frac{7}{3}, \frac{5}{3}, \ldots$

11. In the sequences of Exercise 7, what term is 106?

12. In the sequence of Exercise 8, what term is 1.67?

13. In the sequence of Exercise 9, what term is -296?

14. In the sequence of Exercise 10, what term is -27?

15. If $a_1 = 5$ and $d = 6$, find a_{17}.

16. If $a_1 = 14$ and $d = -3$, what is a_{20}?

17. If $d = 4$ and $a_8 = 33$, find a_1.

18. If $a_1 = 8$ and $a_{11} = 26$, what is d?

19. If $a_1 = 5$, $d = -3$ and $a_n = -76$, find n.

20. If $a_1 = 25$, $d = -14$, and $a_n = -507$, what is n?

21. In an arithmetic sequence $a_{17} = -40$ and $a_{28} = -73$. Find a_1 and d. Find the first 5 terms of the sequence.

22. In an arithmetic sequence $a_{17} = \dfrac{25}{3}$ and $a_{32} = \dfrac{95}{6}$. Find a_1 and d. Find the first 5 terms of the sequence.

23. A bomb drops from a plane and falls 16 ft the first sec, 48 ft the second sec, and so on, forming an arithmetic sequence. How many feet will the bomb fall during the 20th sec?

24. Smalltown, whose population was 18,395 ten years ago, has lost 270 inhabitants each year since then. What is the present population of Smalltown?

25. Find the sum of the first 20 terms of the sequence $5, 8, 11, 14, \ldots$

26. Find the sum of the first 14 terms of the sequence $11, 7, 3, \ldots$

27. Find the sum of the first 15 terms of the sequence $5, \dfrac{55}{7}, \dfrac{75}{7}, \dfrac{95}{7}, \ldots$

28. Find the sum of the first 16 terms of the sequence $\dfrac{3}{4}, \dfrac{5}{4}, \dfrac{7}{4}, \ldots$

29. Find the sum of the even numbers from 2 to 100, inclusive.

30. Find the sum of the odd numbers from 1 to 99, inclusive.

31. Find the sum of the multiples of 3 from 3 to 99, inclusive.

32. Find the sum of the multiples of 7, from 7 to 98 inclusive.

33. An arithmetic sequence has $a_1 = 2$, $d = 5$, and $n = 20$. What is S_n?

34. An arithmetic sequence has $a_1 = 7$, $d = -3$, and $n = 32$. What is S_n?

35. Find the sum of the series $\sum_{k=1}^{12} (6k - 3)$.

36. Find the sum of the series $\sum_{k=1}^{16} (7k - 16)$.

37. Find the sum of the natural numbers between 9 and 401 that are divisible by 5.

38. Find the sum of the natural numbers between 14 and 523 that are divisible by 4.

39. How many poles will be in a pile of telephone poles if there are 30 in the first layer, 29 in the second, and so on until there is one in the last layer?

40. If a student saved 10¢ on October 1, 20¢ on October 2, 30¢ on October, etc., how much would he save during October? (October has 31 days.)

41. Find the first 10 terms of the arithmetic sequence where $a_1 = 524.011$ and $d = 0.6499$.

42. Find the first 10 terms of the arithmetic sequence where $a_1 = 684.012$ and $d = 0.7398$.

▶ **43.** Prove that the sum of the first n consecutive odd natural numbers starting with 1 is n^2.

44. Prove that the sum of the first n even natural numbers is $n(n + 1)$.

14.3 Geometric Sequences and Series

GEOMETRIC SEQUENCES

Consider the sequence

$$3, 6, 12, 24, 48, 96, \ldots$$

If we multiply each term by 2 we get the next term. Sequences in which each term can be multiplied by a certain number to get the next term are called *geometric*. We usually denote this number r. We refer to it as the *common ratio* because we can get r by dividing any term by the preceding term:

$$\frac{a_{k+1}}{a_k} = r.$$

Examples. Each of the following are geometric sequences. Identify the common ratio.

Sequence	Common ratio
$3, 6, 12, 24, \ldots$	2
$3, -6, 12, -24, \ldots$	-2
$1, \dfrac{1}{2}, \dfrac{1}{4}, \dfrac{1}{8}, \ldots$	$\dfrac{1}{2}$

[39–41]

If we let a_1 be the first term and r be the common ratio, then $a_1 r$ is the second term, $a_1 r^2$ is the third term, and so on. Generalizing, we have the following.

Theorem. In a geometric sequence, the nth term is given by

$$a_n = a_1 r^{n-1}.$$

Note that the exponent is one less than the number of the term.

Example 1. Find the 6th term of the geometric sequence $4, 20, 100, \ldots$

Note that $a_1 = 4$, $n = 6$, and $r = \frac{20}{4}$, or 5. Then using the formula

$$a_n = a_1 r^{n-1},$$

we have

$$a_6 = 4 \cdot 5^{6-1}$$

$$= 4 \cdot 5^5$$

$$= 4 \cdot 3125, \text{ or } 12{,}500. \qquad \textbf{[42]}$$

Example 2. Find the 11th term of the geometric sequence $64, -32, 16, -8, \ldots$

Note that $a_1 = 64$, $n = 11$, and $r = \dfrac{-32}{64}$, or $-\dfrac{1}{2}$.

Then using the formula

$$a_n = a_1 r^{n-1},$$

we have

$$a_{11} = 64 \cdot \left(-\frac{1}{2}\right)^{11-1}$$

$$= 64 \cdot \left(-\frac{1}{2}\right)^{10}$$

$$= 2^6 \cdot \frac{1}{2^{10}}$$

$$= 2^{-4}, \text{ or } \frac{1}{16}. \qquad \textbf{[43]}$$

Example 3. A college student borrows $600 at 7% interest compounded annually. He pays off the loan at the end of 3 yr. How much does he pay?

For any principal P, at 7% interest, he will owe $P + 0.07P$ at the end of 1 yr, or $1.07P$. Then $1.07P$ is the principal for the second year. So at the end of the second year he owes $1.07(1.07P)$. Then the principal at the beginning of consecutive years is

$$P, 1.07P, 1.07(1.07P), \ldots$$

This is a geometric sequence with $a_1 = 600$, $n = 4$, $r = 1.07$. Then using the formula

$$a_n = a_1 r^{n-1}.$$

we have

$$a_4 = 600 \cdot (1.07)^{4-1}$$

$$= 600 \cdot (1.07)^3$$

$$= 600 \cdot 1.225043$$

$$a_4 = \$735.03.$$

Note that in the form

$$a_4 = 600 \cdot (1.07)^3$$

the equation fits the compound interest formula

$$A = P(1 + i)^t$$

developed on p. 44 of Chapter 2. Look back at that development. Note that the numbers A_1, A_2, A_3, and so on, form a geometric sequence where

$$A_1 = P, \qquad A_1 = P(1 + i), \qquad r = 1 + i,$$

and

$$n - 1 = t.$$

Note that "after t years" and "at the beginning of the nth year" have the same meaning.   **[44]**

GEOMETRIC SERIES

A *geometric series* is the series associated with a geometric sequence. We can denote a geometric sequence

$$a_1, a_1 r, a_1 r^2, a_1 r^3, \ldots, a_1 r^{n-1}.$$

Then the associated series S_n, or the sum of the first n terms, is

$$S_n = a_1 + a_1 r + a_1 r^2 + \cdots + a_1 r^{n-2} + a_1 r^{n-1}.$$

We want to derive a formula that allows us to find this sum without a great amount of adding. If we multiply both sides of the preceding equation by $-r$, we have

$$-rS_n = -a_1 r - a_1 r^2 - \cdots - a_1 r^{n-1} - a_1 r^n.$$

When we add S_n and $-rS_n$, we get

$$S_n - rS_n = a_1 - a_1 r^n$$

$$S_n(1 - r) = a_1 - a_1 r^n.$$

Thus we have the following.

Theorem. The sum of the first n terms of a geometric series, when $r \neq 1$, is given by

$$S_n = \frac{a_1 - a_1 r^n}{1 - r}. \qquad \textbf{(1)}$$

We know that $a_n = a_1 r^{n-1}$ so $r \cdot a_n = a_1 r^n$. Substituting $r a_n$ for $a_1 r^n$ in the above formula, we have the following.

> **Theorem.** The sum of the first n terms of a geometric series, when $r \neq 1$, is given by
>
> $$S_n = \frac{a_1 - ra_n}{1 - r}. \qquad (2)$$

We will probably use formula (1) most often.

Example 1. Find the sum of the first 6 terms of the geometric sequence 3, 6, 12, 24, ...

Note that $a_1 = 3$, $n = 6$, and $r = \frac{6}{3}$, or 2. Then using the formula

$$S_n = \frac{a_1 - a_1 r^n}{1 - r},$$

we have

$$S_6 = \frac{3 - 3 \cdot 2^6}{1 - 2} = \frac{3 - 192}{-1}, \qquad \text{or} \qquad 189.$$

[45, 46]

Example 2. Find the sum of the series

$$\sum_{k=1}^{5} \left(\frac{1}{2}\right)^{k+1}.$$

First find a few terms

$$\left(\frac{1}{2}\right)^2 + \left(\frac{1}{2}\right)^3 + \left(\frac{1}{2}\right)^4 + \cdots$$

We see that this is a geometric series with $a_1 = \frac{1}{4}$, $n = 5$, and $r = \frac{1}{2}$. Then using the formula

$$S_n = \frac{a_1 - a_1 r^n}{1 - r},$$

we have

$$S_5 = \frac{\dfrac{1}{4} - \dfrac{1}{4} \cdot \left(\dfrac{1}{2}\right)^5}{1 - \dfrac{1}{2}}$$

$$= \frac{\dfrac{1}{4} - \dfrac{1}{4} \cdot \dfrac{1}{32}}{\dfrac{1}{2}} = \frac{\dfrac{1}{4}\left(1 - \dfrac{1}{32}\right)}{\dfrac{1}{2}}$$

$$= \frac{1}{4} \cdot \frac{31}{32} \cdot 2, \qquad \text{or} \qquad \frac{31}{64}. \qquad \textbf{[47]}$$

Example 3. Suppose someone offered you a job for a 30-day month under the following conditions. You would be paid \$0.01 of the first day, \$0.02 for the second, \$0.04 for the third, and so on, doubling your previous day's salary. How much would you earn? (Would you take the job? Make a decision before reading further.)

We have the geometric series

$$0.01 + (0.01)2 + (0.01)2^2 + \cdots + (0.01)2^{30},$$

where $a_1 = 0.01$, $n = 30$, $r = 2$.

Then using the formula

$$S_n = \frac{a_1 - a_1 r^n}{1 - r},$$

$$S_{30} = \frac{0.01 - (0.01)2^{30}}{1 - 2}$$

$$\approx \frac{0.01(1 - 1{,}070{,}000{,}000)}{-1} \qquad \text{(using logarithms or calculator to approximate } 2^{30}\text{)}$$

$$\approx 0.01(1{,}070{,}000{,}000)$$

$$= \$10{,}700{,}000.$$

Now would you take the job? **[48]**

Exercise Set 14.3

For each of the following geometric sequences find the common ratio.

1. $4, 8, 16, 32, \ldots$

2. $2, 1, \dfrac{1}{2}, \dfrac{1}{4}, \dfrac{1}{8}, \ldots$

3. $12, -4, \dfrac{4}{3}, -\dfrac{4}{9}, \ldots$

4. $5, 15, 45, 135, \ldots$

5. $1, -1, 1, -1, 1, \ldots$

6. $-5, -0.5, -0.05, -0.005, \ldots$

7. $\dfrac{1}{x}, \dfrac{1}{x^2}, \dfrac{1}{x^3}, \ldots$

8. $5, \dfrac{5m}{2}, \dfrac{5m^2}{4}, \dfrac{5m^3}{8}, \ldots$

9. Find the 6th term of the geometric sequence $1, 3, 9, \ldots$

10. Find the 10th term of the geometric sequence $\frac{8}{243}, \frac{4}{81}, \frac{2}{27}, \ldots$

11. Find the 5th term of the geometric sequence $2, -10, 50, \ldots$

12. Find the 9th term of the geometric sequence $2, 2\sqrt{3}, 6, \ldots$

13. A college student borrows \$800 at 8% interest compounded annually. She pays off the loan in full at the end of 2 yr. How much does she pay?

14. A college student borrows \$1000 at 8% interest compounded annually. He pays off the loan in full at the end of 4 yr. How much does he pay?

15. A ping-pong ball is dropped from a height of 16 ft and always rebounds $\frac{1}{4}$ of the distance of the previous fall. What distance does it rebound the 6th time?

16. A super ball is dropped from the top of the Washington Monument (556 ft high) and always rebounds $\frac{3}{4}$ of the distance of the previous fall. What distance does it rebound the 5th time?

17. Gaintown has a population of 100,000 now and the population is increasing 10% every year. What will be the population in 5 yr?

18. In Exercise 17 if the population of Gaintown had been increasing 20% every year, what would its population be in 5 yr?

19. Find the sum of the first 7 terms of the geometric sequence $6, 12, 24, \ldots$

20. Find the sum of the first 6 terms of the geometric sequence $16, -8, 4, \ldots$

21. Find the sum of the first 8 terms of the geometric sequence $5, 10, 20, \ldots$

22. Find the sum of the first 6 terms of the geometric sequence $24, 12, 6, \ldots$

23. Find the sum of the first 7 terms of the geometric sequence $\frac{1}{18}, -\frac{1}{6}, \frac{1}{2}, \ldots$

24. Find the sum of the first 5 terms of the geometric sequence $6, 0.6, 0.06, \ldots$

25. Find the sum of the geometric sequence $-8, 4, -2, \ldots, -\frac{1}{32}$.

26. Find the sum of the first 10 terms of the geometric sequence $1, x^2, x^4, x^6, \ldots$

27. Find the sum of the geometric series

$$\sum_{k=1}^{6} \left(\frac{1}{2}\right)^{k-1}.$$

28. Find the sum of the geometric series

$$\sum_{k=1}^{10} 2^{k}.$$

29. A piece of paper is 0.01 in. thick. It is folded in such a way that its thickness is doubled each time for 20 times. How thick is the result?

30. A super ball dropped from the top of the Washington Monument (556 ft high) always rebounds $\frac{3}{4}$ of the distance of the previous fall. How far up and down has it traveled when it hits the ground for the sixth time?

31. (*An annuity*). A person decides to save money in a savings account for retirement. At the beginning of each year $1000 is invested at 8% compounded annually. How much is in the retirement fund at the end of 40 years?

32. (*Yearly annuity payment*). A person wants to have $388,585 accumulated in a retirement fund over a period of 40 years. How much would he have to deposit at the beginning of each year for 40 years at 8% compounded annually?

14.4 Infinite Geometric Series

Let us consider infinite geometric series. Look at the series

$$3 + 6 + 12 + 24 + \cdots.$$

Note that the terms get larger and larger in absolute value. We cannot find a sum. Look at the series

$$\frac{1}{2} + \frac{1}{4} + \frac{1}{8} + \frac{1}{16} + \cdots + \left(\frac{1}{2}\right)^{n} + \cdots.$$

Note that the absolute values of the terms decrease. Note also some finite sums.

$$S_1 = \frac{1}{2} \qquad S_4 = \frac{15}{16}$$

$$S_2 = \frac{3}{4} \qquad S_5 = \frac{31}{32}$$

$$S_3 = \frac{7}{8}$$

They never exceed 1, but they get closer and closer to 1. In this sense we say that the series has a "sum."

This is different from the usual sum; an infinite series has a sum if S_n gets closer and closer to some real number as n gets larger and larger. In calculus it will be proved that any infinite geometric series for which $|r| < 1$ has a sum. No other infinite geometric series have sums.

Examples. Decide which infinite geometric series have sums.

Series

$$1 - \frac{1}{2} + \frac{1}{4} - \frac{1}{8} + \frac{1}{16} - \cdots$$

$$r = -\frac{1}{2}, |r| < 1. \qquad \text{Series has a sum.}$$

Check this by computing some finite sums using a calculator.

$$1 + 5 + 25 + 125 + \cdots$$

$$r = 5, |r| \not< 1. \qquad \text{Series does not have a sum.}$$

$1 + (-1) + 1 + (-1) + \cdots$

$r = -1, |r| \not< 1.$

Series does not have a sum.

[49–51]

Let us try to find a formula for the sum of an infinite geometric series. We start with the formula for the sum of a finite series,

$$S_n = \frac{a_1 - a_1 r^n}{1 - r}.$$

When $|r| < 1$, it follows that the absolute values of r^n and $a_1 r^n$ get smaller and smaller as n gets larger. Then $a_1 r^n$ gets closer and closer to 0 as n gets larger. Thus we have the following.

Theorem. The sum of an infinite geometric series, with $|r| < 1$, is given by

$$S_\infty = \frac{a_1}{1 - r}.$$

Example 1. Find the sum of the infinite geometric series

$$5 + \frac{5}{2} + \frac{5}{4} + \frac{5}{8} + \cdots$$

Note that $a_1 = 5$ and $r = \frac{1}{2}$. Then using the formula

$$S_\infty = \frac{a_1}{1 - r},$$

we have

$$S_\infty = \frac{5}{1 - \frac{1}{2}}$$

$$S_\infty = 10. \qquad [52, 53]$$

REPEATING DECIMALS

Repeating decimal notation always represents a geometric series. In $0.66666666\ldots$ or $0.6\overline{6}$,* for example, we have an infinite geometric series whose terms are

0.6

0.06

0.006

0.0006, and so on.

Thus $a_1 = 0.6$ and $r = 0.1$. So $|r| < 1$ and we can use the formula

$$S_\infty = \frac{a_1}{1 - r}$$

$$= \frac{0.6}{1 - 0.1}$$

$$= \frac{0.6}{0.9}$$

$$S_\infty = \frac{2}{3}.$$

Example 1. Find fractional notation for $0.27\overline{27}$.

Note that $a_1 = 0.27$ and $r = 0.01$ so

$$S_\infty = \frac{a_1}{1 - r}$$

$$= \frac{0.27}{1 - 0.01}$$

$$= \frac{0.27}{0.99}$$

$$= \frac{3}{11}.$$

Thus $0.27\overline{27} = \frac{3}{11}$. This can be checked by doing the division $3 \div 11$.

---

* The bar indicates the repeating cycle.

Example 2. Find fractional notation for $0.58\overline{8}$.

Note that $0.58\overline{8} = 0.5 + 0.08\overline{8}$, and that $0.08\overline{8}$ is a geometric series. We first find fractional notation for $0.08\overline{8}$. Note that $a_1 = 0.08$ and $r = 0.1$. Then

$$S_\infty = \frac{a_1}{1 - r}$$

$$S_\infty = \frac{0.08}{1 - 0.1}$$

$$= \frac{0.08}{0.9}$$

$$= \frac{8}{90}.$$

Then $0.58\overline{8} = \frac{5}{10} + \frac{8}{90} = \frac{45}{90} + \frac{8}{90} = \frac{53}{90}.$ **[54, 55]**

Exercise Set 14.4

In each geometric series find r and decide which series have sums.

1. $5 + 10 + 20 + 40 + \cdots$

2. $16 + 8 + 4 + 2 + \cdots$

3. $6 + 2 + \dfrac{2}{3} + \dfrac{2}{9} + \cdots$

4. $2 - 4 + 8 - 16 + 32 - \cdots$

5. $1 + 0.1 + 0.01 + 0.001 + \cdots$

6. $-\dfrac{5}{3} - \dfrac{10}{9} - \dfrac{20}{27} - \dfrac{40}{81} - \cdots$

7. $1 - \dfrac{1}{5} + \dfrac{1}{25} - \dfrac{1}{125} + \cdots$

8. $6 + \dfrac{42}{5} + \dfrac{294}{25} + \cdots$

Find the sum of each geometric series.

9. $4 + 2 + 1 + \cdots$

10. $7 + 3 + \dfrac{9}{7} + \cdots$

11. $25 + 20 + 16 + \cdots$

12. $12 + 9 + \dfrac{27}{4} + \cdots$

13. $1 + \dfrac{1}{2} + \dfrac{1}{4} + \cdots$

14. $\dfrac{8}{3} + \dfrac{4}{3} + \dfrac{2}{3} + \cdots$

15. $16 + 1.6 + 0.16 + \cdots$

16. $4 + 2.4 + 1.44 + \cdots$

Find fractional notation for these numbers.

17. $0.777\overline{7}$

18. $0.533\overline{3}$

19. $0.2121\overline{21}$

20. $0.6444\overline{4}$

21. $5.15\overline{15}15$

22. $0.4125\overline{125}$

23. The infinite series

$$2 + \frac{1}{2} + \frac{1}{2 \cdot 3} + \frac{1}{2 \cdot 3 \cdot 4} + \frac{1}{2 \cdot 3 \cdot 4 \cdot 5}$$
$$+ \frac{1}{2 \cdot 3 \cdot 4 \cdot 5 \cdot 6} + \cdots$$

is not geometric, but does have a sum. Use a calculator to find S_1, S_2, S_3, S_4, S_5, and S_6. Make a conjecture about the value of S_∞.

24. The infinite series

$$\frac{1}{1 \cdot 3} + \frac{1}{3 \cdot 5} + \frac{1}{5 \cdot 7} + \frac{1}{7 \cdot 9} + \frac{1}{9 \cdot 11} + \frac{1}{11 \cdot 13}$$
$$+ \cdots$$

is not geometric, but does have a sum. Use a calculator to find S_1, S_2, S_3, S_4, S_5, and S_6. Make a conjecture about the value of S_∞.

25. How far up and down will a ball travel before stopping if it is dropped from a height of 12 ft, and each rebound is $\frac{1}{3}$ of the previous distance? (*Hint:* Use an infinite geometric series.)

26. The sides of a square are each 16 in. long. A second square is inscribed by joining the midpoints of the sides, successively. In the second square we repeat the process, inscribing a third square. If this process is continued indefinitely, what is the sum of the perimeters of all of the squares? (*Hint:* Use an infinite geometric series.)

14.5 Mathematical Induction

In this section we consider a method of proof known as *mathematical induction*.   **[56, 57]**

In situations where we use mathematical induction there is an infinite set of statements, S_n, one for each natural number n. For example, consider

$$S_n: 1 + 3 + 5 + \cdots + (2n - 1) = n^2.$$

We get an infinite set of statements by replacing n by each of the natural numbers as follows:

$$S_1: 1 = 1^2,$$
$$S_2: 1 + 3 = 2^2,$$
$$S_3: 1 + 3 + 5 = 3^2,$$
$$S_4: 1 + 3 + 5 + 7 = 4^2. \quad \text{and so on.}$$

We cannot prove the statement S_n *for all natural numbers n* just by checking a few cases, but we can do so using a method called *mathematical induction*. Be-fore learning this method of proof we need some background.

A statement of the type "*If P, then Q*," or "*P implies Q*," is often abbreviated $P \rightarrow Q$. A proof of $P \rightarrow Q$ does not establish that P is true or that Q is true. All that *has* been established is that *if P* is true, *then Q* must be true. It can happen that both P and Q might be false. We do know, though, that if $P \rightarrow Q$ is true and also that P is true, then we can conclude that Q is true. To illustrate this, we can prove that

$$if\ x + 2 = x + 10, \quad then \quad x + 3 = x + 11.$$

To do this we can take $x + 2 = x + 10$ as hypothesis and deduce $x + 3 = x + 11$, by adding 1. Note that both $x + 2 = x + 10$ and $x + 3 = x + 11$ are *false* for every number even though

$$x + 2 = x + 10 \rightarrow x + 3 = x + 11$$

is true.

In a similar manner we can prove that $3x = x \rightarrow 3x + 2 = x + 2$. Now $3x = x$ is true when $x = 0$. It follows that $3x + 2 = x + 2$ is true when $x = 0$.

Now suppose we want to prove a statement of this type:

For every natural number n, S_n is true.

Another way to express this is to say that we want to establish all of the following:

$$S_1, S_2, S_3, S_4, \ldots$$

The following principle can be used for such a proof.

> **Principle of mathematical induction. We can prove:**
>
> **A statement S_n is true for every natural number n by showing:**
>
> **1. Basis step: S_1 is true.**
> **2. Induction step: For all natural numbers k, $S_k \rightarrow S_{k+1}$.**

To see this more clearly suppose both parts of the proof are completed. We have the following endless sequence of statements.

S_1 *Basis step*

$S_1 \rightarrow S_2$
$S_2 \rightarrow S_3$
$S_3 \rightarrow S_4$
.
.   *Induction step*
.   For all natural numbers k,
. $S_k \rightarrow S_{k+1}$
$S_k \rightarrow S_{k+1}$
.
.
.

The process then becomes similar to knocking over a row of dominoes:

S_1	S_2	S_3
$S_1 \rightarrow S_2$	$S_2 \rightarrow S_3$	$S_3 \rightarrow S_4$
$S_1, \quad \therefore S_2,$	$\therefore S_3,$	$\therefore S_4,$

and so on.

The induction step lines up the dominoes. The basis step knocks over the first one, which knocks over the second, and so on.   **[58, 59]**

Let us now do a proof by mathematical induction. It is quite helpful to first write out S_n, S_1, S_k, and S_{k+1}. This aids in identifying what is to be assumed and what is to be deduced.

Example 1. Prove: For every natural number n,

$$1 + 3 + 5 + 7 + \cdots + (2n - 1) = n^2.$$

We first list S_n, S_1, S_k, and S_{k+1}:

S_n: $1 + 3 + 5 + 7 + \cdots + (2n - 1) = n^2$

S_1: $1 = 1^2$

S_k: $1 + 3 + 5 + \cdots + (2k - 1) = k^2$

S_{k+1}: $1 + 3 + 5 + \cdots + (2k - 1)$
$$\qquad\qquad + [2(k + 1) - 1] = (k + 1)^2.$$

1. *Basis step:* S_1 is clearly true.
2. *Induction step:*

   a) Assume S_k: $1 + 3 + 5 + \cdots + (2k - 1) = k^2$.

   b) Deduce S_{k+1}: $1 + 3 + 5 + \cdots + (2k - 1) + [2(k + 1) - 1] = (k + 1)^2$.

By adding one term to the left side of S_k, we can get the left side of S_{k+1}. We shall add that term on both sides of S_k. Then we have

$$1 + 3 + \cdots + (2k - 1) + [2(k + 1) - 1]$$
$$= k^2 + [2(k + 1) - 1]$$
$$= k^2 + 2k + 1$$
$$= (k + 1)^2.$$

We have deduced S_{k+1}.

Thus we have shown that $S_k \rightarrow S_{k+1}$, for all k, and the proof is complete. **[60]**

Example 2. Prove: For every natural number n,

$$1^2 + 2^2 + 3^2 + \cdots + n^2 = \frac{n(n + 1)(2n + 1)}{6}.$$

We first list S_n, S_1, S_k, S_{k+1}:

S_n: $1^2 + 2^2 + 3^2 + \cdots + n^2 = \dfrac{n(n + 1)(2n + 1)}{6}$

S_1: $1^2 = \dfrac{1(1 + 1)(2 \cdot 1 + 1)}{6}$

S_k: $1^2 + 2^2 + 3^2 + \cdots + k^2 = \dfrac{k(k + 1)(2k + 1)}{6}$

S_{k+1}: $1^2 + 2^2 + 3^2 + \cdots + k^2 + (k + 1)^2$

$$= \frac{(k + 1)[(k + 1) + 1][2(k + 1) + 1]}{6}$$

$$= \frac{(k + 1)(k + 2)(2k + 3)}{6}.$$

1. *Basis step:* $1^2 = 1$ and $\dfrac{1(1 + 1)(2 \cdot 1 + 1)}{6} = 1$.

   S_1 is true.

2. *Induction step:*
   a) Assume S_k:

   $$1^2 + 2^2 + 3^2 + \cdots + k^2 = \frac{k(k + 1)(2k + 1)}{6}.$$

   b) Deduce S_{k+1}:

   $$1^2 + 2^2 + 3^2 + \cdots + k^2 + (k + 1)^2$$
   $$= \frac{(k + 1)(k + 2)(2k + 3)}{6}.$$

We add $(k + 1)^2$ on both sides of S_k.

$\underbrace{1^2 + 2^2 + 3^2 + \cdots + k^2}_{} + (k + 1)^2$

$= \dfrac{k(k + 1)(2k + 1)}{6} + (k + 1)^2$

$= (k + 1) \cdot \left[\dfrac{k(2k + 1)}{6} + \dfrac{6(k + 1)}{6} \right]$ (factoring; distributive law)

$= (k + 1) \cdot \left[\dfrac{(2k^2 + k)}{6} + \dfrac{6(k + 1)}{6} \right]$

$= (k + 1) \cdot \dfrac{2k^2 + 7k + 6}{6}$

$= \dfrac{(k + 1)(k + 2)(2k + 3)}{6}$

We have shown that $S_k \rightarrow S_{k+1}$, for all k, and the proof is complete. **[61]**

We can use mathematical induction to prove other types of statements.

Example 3. Prove: For every natural number n, $n < 2^n$.

We first list S_n, S_1, S_k, and S_{k+1}:

$$S_n: n < 2^n$$
$$S_1: 1 < 2^1$$
$$S_k: k < 2^k$$
$$S_{k+1}: k + 1 < 2^{k+1}.$$

1. *Basis step:* Since $2^1 = 2$ and $1 < 2$, S_1 is true.

2. *Induction step:*

   a) Assume S_k: $k < 2^k$.

   b) Deduce S_{k+1}: $k + 1 < 2^{k+1}$.

Look at S_{k+1}. Try to discover a way of deducing it from S_k.

Now

$$k < 2^k \qquad \text{(by } S_k)$$
$$2k < 2 \cdot 2^k \qquad \text{(multiplying by 2)}$$
$$2k < 2^{k+1}. \qquad \text{(adding exponents)}$$

Since k is a natural number

$$1 \le k$$

so

$$k + 1 \le k + k = 2k. \qquad \text{(adding } k)$$

Thus $k + 1 \le 2k < 2^{k+1}$, so $k + 1 < 2^{k+1}$, and the proof is complete. **[62]**

Example 4. Prove: If x is a number such that $0 < x < 1$, then for every natural number n, $0 < x^n < 1$.

Proof. Let x be a number such that $0 < x < 1$. Then list S_n, S_1, S_k, and S_{k+1}:

$$S_n: 0 < x^n < 1 \qquad S_k: 0 < x^k < 1$$
$$S_1: 0 < x < 1 \qquad S_{k+1}: 0 < x^{k+1} < 1.$$

1. *Basis step:* $0 < x < 1$ by assumption, so S_1 is true.
2. *Induction step:*

a) Assume S_k: $0 < x^k < 1$

b) Deduce S_{k+1}: $0 < x^{k+1} < 1$

Now

$$0 < x^k < 1 \qquad \text{(by } S_k)$$
$$x \cdot 0 < x \cdot x^k < x \cdot 1 \qquad \text{(multiplying by } x)$$
$$0 < x^{k+1} < x \qquad \text{(simplifying)}$$
$$0 < x^{k+1} < 1 \qquad \text{(since } 0 < x < 1)$$

Thus we have proved $S_k \to S_{k+1}$ for all k, and the proof is complete. **[63]**

In mathematical induction we may begin at some integer other than 1 with our basis step. If we begin at an integer a, we establish that S_n is true for all integers from a upward.

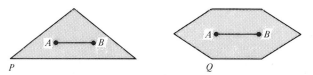

We can prove:

A statement S_n is true for every n greater than or equal to an integer a,

by showing:

1. **Basis step:** S_a is true.
2. **Induction step:** For all integers $k \ge a$, $S_k \to S_{k+1}$.

For example, if we show S_2 is true and "for every integer $k \ge 2$, $S_k \to S_{k+1}$," we know that S_n is true for all $n \ge 2$.

Definition. A *convex polygon* is a polygon P for which, given any two points A and B in the interior of P, the segment $\overline{AB}$ is in the interior of P.

[64]

P and Q are convex polygons

R is *not* a convex polygon

Example 5. Prove: For every natural number $n \ge 3$, the sum of the interior angles of a convex n-gon (polygon of n sides) is $(n - 2) \cdot 180°$.

Note that our induction begins at $n = 3$.

S_n: The sum of the interior angles of a convex n-gon is $(n - 2) \cdot 180°$.

S_3: The sum of the interior angles of a convex 3-gon (triangle) is $(3 - 2) \cdot 180°$.

S_k: The sum of the interior angles of a convex k-gon is $(k - 2) \cdot 180°$.

S_{k+1}: The sum of the interior angles of a convex $(k + 1)$-gon is
$[(k + 1) - 2] \cdot 180°$, or $(k - 1) \cdot 180°$.

1. *Basis step:* From geometry we know that the sum of the interior angles of a triangle is $180°$, or $(3 - 2) \cdot 180°$.

2. *Induction step:* Assume S_k. Deduce S_{k+1}.

Suppose we have the $(k + 1)$-sided convex polygon $A_1 A_2 \ldots A_k A_{k+1}$ as shown below. If we draw the segment $\overline{A_1 A_k}$, we form polygon $A_1 A_2 \ldots A_k$ with k

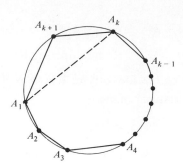

sides. Thus, by S_k, the sum of the interior angles of $A_1 A_2 \ldots A_k$ is $(k - 2) \cdot 180°$. If we add to this the sum of the interior angles of triangle $A_1 A_k A_{k+1}$, which is $180°$, we get the sum of the interior angles of the $(k + 1)$-sided polygon, which is

$$(k - 2) \cdot 180° + 180°$$
$$= [(k - 2) + 1] \cdot 180°, \quad \text{or} \quad (k - 1) \cdot 180°.$$

Thus $S_k \rightarrow S_{k+1}$ for all $k \geq 3$ and the proof is complete. **[65]**

Exercise Set 14.5

Use mathematical induction. In Exercises 1–19, prove: For every natural number n,

1. $1 + 2 + 3 + \cdots + n = \dfrac{n(n + 1)}{2}$

2. $4 + 8 + 12 + \cdots + 4n = 2n(n + 1)$

3. $1 + 5 + 9 + \cdots + (4n - 3) = n(2n - 1)$

4. $3 + 6 + 9 + \cdots + 3n = \dfrac{3n(n + 1)}{2}$

5. $\dfrac{1}{1 \cdot 2} + \dfrac{1}{2 \cdot 3} + \cdots + \dfrac{1}{n(n + 1)} = \dfrac{n}{n + 1}$

6. $2 + 4 + 8 + \cdots + 2^n = 2(2^n - 1)$

7. $n < n + 1$ **8.** $n < n + 2$

9. $2 \leq 2^n$ **10.** $3 \leq 3^n$

11. $2^n < 2^{n+1}$ **12.** $3^n < 3^{n+1}$

13. $2n \leq 2^n$ **14.** $3n \leq 3^n$

15. $\left(1 + \dfrac{1}{1}\right)\left(1 + \dfrac{1}{2}\right)\left(1 + \dfrac{1}{3}\right) \cdots \left(1 + \dfrac{1}{n}\right) = n + 1$

16. $a_1 + (a_1 + d) + (a_2 + d) + (a_1 + 2d) + \cdots + [a_1 + (n - 1)d] = \dfrac{n}{2}[2a_1 + (n - 1)d]$

(This is a formula for the sum of the first n terms of an *arithmetic* sequence.)

17. $a_1 + a_1r + a_1r^2 + \cdots + a_1r^{n-1} = \dfrac{a_1 - a_1r^n}{1 - r}$ (This is a formula for the sum of the first n terms of a *geometric* sequence.)

18. $\cos n\pi = (-1)^n$
[*Hint:* Use the identity for $\cos(\alpha + \beta)$.]

19. *DeMoivre's theorem.* For any angle θ and any nonnegative number r, and $i^2 = -1$,

$$[r(\cos\theta + i\sin\theta)]^n = r^n(\cos n\theta + i\sin n\theta).$$

20. For every natural number $n \geqslant 2$,

$$\left(1 - \frac{1}{2^2}\right)\left(1 - \frac{1}{3^2}\right)\cdots\left(1 - \frac{1}{n^2}\right) = \frac{n+1}{2n}.$$

21. For every natural number $n \geqslant 2$,

$$\cos x \cdot \cos 2x \cdot \cos 4x \cdots \cos 2^{n-1} x = \frac{\sin 2^n x}{2^n \sin x}.$$

▶ **22.** For every natural number $n \geqslant 2$,

$$\frac{1}{\sqrt{1}} + \frac{1}{\sqrt{2}} + \frac{1}{\sqrt{3}} + \cdots + \frac{1}{\sqrt{n}} > \sqrt{n}.$$

23. *Bernoulli's inequality:* For any real number $a > 1$ and any natural number $n \geqslant 2$,

$$(1 + a)^n > 1 + na.$$

24. Consider the statement: For every natural number n, $n = n + 1$.

a) Can you prove the basis step? If so, do it.

b) Can you prove the induction step? If so, do it.

c) Is the statement true?

25. Find the error in this proof.

Statement. Everyone is of the same sex.

Proof. Let S_n be the statement: If A is a set of n people, then all the people are of the same sex.

Clearly, S_1 is true. Assume S_k. Let A be a set of $k + 1$ people. Then A is the union of two overlapping sets B and C each containing k people. (Consider the illustration for $k = 5$.) By S_k all the people in B are of the same sex. Since B and C overlap, all the people in A are of the same sex, and $S_k \to S_{k+1}$.

26. *The Tower of Hanoi problem.* There are three pegs on a board. On one peg are n disks, each smaller than the one on which it rests. The problem is to move this pile of disks to another peg. The final order must be the same, but you can move only one disk at a time and you can never place a larger disk on a smaller one.

a) What is the *least* number of moves it takes to move 3 disks?

b) What is the *least* number of moves it takes to move 4 disks?

c) What is the *least* number of moves it takes to move 2 disks?

d) What is the *least* number of moves it takes to move 1 disk?

e) Conjecture a formula for the *least* number of moves it takes to move n disks. Prove it by mathematical induction.

Chapter 14 Test, or Review

1. Find the 10th term in the arithmetic sequence $\dfrac{3}{4}, \dfrac{13}{12}, \dfrac{17}{12}, \dots$

2. Find the sum of the first 30 positive integers.

3. The first term of an arithmetic sequence is 5. The 17th term is 53. Find the 3rd term.

4. For a geometric sequence, $r = \dfrac{1}{2}$, $n = 5$, $S_n = \dfrac{31}{2}$. Find a_1 and a_n.

5. Write the first 3 terms of the infinite geometric sequence with $r = 0.01$ and $S = \dfrac{3}{11}$.

6. Find fractional notation for $2.\overline{13}$.

7. You receive 10¢ on the first day of the year, 12¢ on the 2nd day, 14¢ on the 3rd day, and so on. How much will you receive on the 365th day? What is the sum of all these 365 gifts?

8. The present population of a city is 30,000. Its population is supposed to double every 10 yr. What will its population be at the end of 80 yr?

9. Use mathematical induction. Prove: For all natural numbers n

$$1 + 4 + 7 + \cdots + (3n - 2) = \frac{n(3n - 1)}{2}.$$

Combinatorial Algebra and Probability

15.1 Combinatorial Algebra: Permutations

Here we will develop procedures for determining the number of ways in which a set of objects can be arranged or combined, certain objects can be chosen, or a succession of events may occur. The following example leads up to *The Fundamental Counting Principle*.

Example 1. How many 3-letter code symbols can be formed with the letters A, B, and C *without* repetition?

Consider such a symbol: ☐☐☐

We can select any of the 3 letters for the first letter in the symbol. Once this letter has been selected, the second is selected from the remaining 2 letters. Then the third is already determined since there is only 1 choice left. Thus the symbols are

ABC,   ACB,   BAC,

BCA,   CAB,   CBA.

We have $3 \cdot 2 \cdot 1$ or 6 possibilities.

In the preceding example, a selection was made. Such a happening is called an *event*. The acts together form *compound events*. The following principle concerns compound events.

Fundamental Counting Principle. Given a compound event in which the first event may occur independently in n_1 ways, the second may occur independently in n_2 ways, and so on, and the kth event may occur independently in n_k ways, then the total number of ways the compound event may occur is

$$n_1 \cdot n_2 \cdot n_3 \cdots n_k.$$

Example 2. How many 3-letter code symbols can be formed with the letters A, B, and C *with* repetition?

There are 3 choices for the first letter, and since we allow repetition, 3 choices for the second, and 3 for the third. Thus by the Fundamental Counting Principle there are $3 \cdot 3 \cdot 3$, or 27, choices.   **[1–3]**

PERMUTATIONS

A *permutation* of a set of n objects is an ordered arrangement, without repetition, of the objects. Consider, for example, a set of 4 objects

$$\{A, B, C, D\}.$$

To find the number of ordered arrangements of the set we select a first one; there are 4 choices. Then we select a second one; there are 3 choices. Then we select a third one; there are 2 choices. Finally there is 1 choice for the last selection. Thus by the Fundamental Counting Principle, there are $4 \cdot 3 \cdot 2 \cdot 1$, or 24 permutations of a set of 4 objects.   **[4]**

We can generalize this to a set of n objects. We have n choices for the first selection, $n - 1$ for the second, $n - 2$ for the third, and so on. For the nth selection there is only one choice.

Theorem. The total number of permutations of a set of n objects, denoted $_nP_n$, is given by

$$_nP_n = \underbrace{n(n - 1)(n - 2)\ldots 3 \cdot 2 \cdot 1.}_{n \text{ factors}}$$

Example 3. Find $_4P_4$ and $_7P_7$.

a) $_4P_4 = 4 \cdot 3 \cdot 2 \cdot 1 = 24$

b) $_7P_7 = 7 \cdot 6 \cdot 5 \cdot 4 \cdot 3 \cdot 2 \cdot 1 = 5040$ **[5–10]**

FACTORIAL NOTATION

Products of successive natural numbers, such as $7 \cdot 6 \cdot 5 \cdot 4 \cdot 3 \cdot 2 \cdot 1$ and $9 \cdot 8 \cdot 7 \cdot 6 \cdot 5 \cdot 4 \cdot 3 \cdot 2 \cdot 1$, are used so often that it is convenient to adopt a notation for them.

For the product $7 \cdot 6 \cdot 5 \cdot 4 \cdot 3 \cdot 2 \cdot 1$ we write 7!, read "7-factorial."

In general,

$$n! = n(n - 1)(n - 2)\ldots 3 \cdot 2 \cdot 1.$$

Here are some examples.

$$
\begin{aligned}
7! &= 7 \cdot 6 \cdot 5 \cdot 4 \cdot 3 \cdot 2 \cdot 1 = 5040 \\
6! &= 6 \cdot 5 \cdot 4 \cdot 3 \cdot 2 \cdot 1 = 720 \\
5! &= 5 \cdot 4 \cdot 3 \cdot 2 \cdot 1 = 120 \\
4! &= 4 \cdot 3 \cdot 2 \cdot 1 = 24 \\
3! &= 3 \cdot 2 \cdot 1 = 6 \\
2! &= 2 \cdot 1 = 2 \\
1! &= 1 = 1 \quad \textbf{[11, 12]}
\end{aligned}
$$

We also define 0! to be 1. We do this so that the binomial theorem (studied in Section 15.3) can be stated concisely, using factorial notation. This also allows for consistency in other formulas involving factorial notation.

We can now restate the formula for the total number of permutations of n objects as follows.

$$_nP_n = n!$$

[13]

Note how we can manipulate with factorial notation:

$$8! = 8 \cdot 7 \cdot 6 \cdot 5 \cdot 4 \cdot 3 \cdot 2 \cdot 1$$
$$= 8 \cdot (7 \cdot 6 \cdot 5 \cdot 4 \cdot 3 \cdot 2 \cdot 1) = 8 \cdot 7!,$$

$$7! = 7 \cdot 6 \cdot 5 \cdot 4 \cdot 3 \cdot 2 \cdot 1$$
$$= 7 \cdot (6 \cdot 5 \cdot 4 \cdot 3 \cdot 2 \cdot 1) = 7 \cdot 6!.$$

In general,

$$n! = n(n - 1)!$$

[14]

Note also that

$$
\begin{aligned}
8! &= 8 \cdot 7! \\
&= 8 \cdot 7 \cdot 6! \\
&= 8 \cdot 7 \cdot 6 \cdot 5!.
\end{aligned}
$$

In general, for any $r \leqslant n$,

$$n! = \underbrace{\underbrace{n(n - 1)(n - 2) \cdots [n - (r - 1)]}_{r \text{ factors}} \underbrace{(n - r)!}_{\substack{n - r \\ \text{factors}}}}_{n \text{ factors}},$$

PERMUTATIONS OF n OBJECTS TAKEN r AT A TIME

Now let us consider the set $\{a, b, c, d, e, f\}$. There are 6 objects. Let us consider the number of ways in which we can arrange a 3-object subset of the given set. There are 6 choices for the first selection. Having made that selection, we have 5 choices for the second and then 4 for the third. Thus there are $6 \cdot 5 \cdot 4$ permutations of a set of 6 objects taken 3 at a time. We denote this $_6P_3 = 6 \cdot 5 \cdot 4$, or 120.

Let us again generalize this result. How many permutations are there of a set of n objects taken r at a time? There are n choices for the first selection, $n - 1$ for the second, $n - 2$ for the third, and so on. We do this r times and get the following.

Theorem. The total number of permutations of a set of n objects taken r at a time, denoted $_nP_r$ is given by

$$_nP_r = \underbrace{n(n - 1)(n - 2) \cdots [n - (r - 1)]}_{r \text{ factors}}.$$

We can find another useful symbol for $_nP_r$ by multiplying by 1, using the symbol $\dfrac{(n - r)!}{(n - r)!}$.

$$_nP_r = n(n-1)(n-2)\cdots[n-(r-1)]\cdot\frac{(n-r)!}{(n-r)!}$$

$$= \frac{n(n-1)(n-2)\cdots[n-(r-1)]\cdot(n-r)!}{(n-r)!}$$

Now

$$n(n-1)(n-2)\cdots[n-(r-1)](n-r)! = n!,$$

so

$$_nP_r = \frac{n!}{(n-r)!}.$$

Therefore,

> **The total number of permutations of a set of n objects taken r at a time is given by**
>
> $$_nP_r = n(n-1)(n-2)\ldots[n-(r-1)] \qquad (1)$$
>
> **or**
>
> $$_nP_r = \frac{n!}{(n-r)!} \qquad (2)$$

Formula (1) is the easiest to use in computations, but we will make use of formula (2) in Section 15.2.

Example 4. Compute $_6P_4$ using both formulas.
Using formula (1) we have

————This number tells where to start.

$$_6P_4 = \underbrace{6\cdot5\cdot4\cdot3}_{} = 360.$$

————This number tells how many factors.

Using formula (2) we have

$$_6P_4 = \frac{6!}{(6-4)!} = \frac{6!}{2!} = \frac{6\cdot5\cdot4\cdot3\cdot2\cdot1}{2\cdot1}$$

$$= 6\cdot5\cdot4\cdot3 = 360. \qquad [15,16]$$

Example 5. How many ways can letters of the set $\{A, B, C, D, E, F, G\}$ be arranged to form code words of (a) 7 letters? (b) 5 letters? (c) 4 letters? (d) 2 letters?

a) $_7P_7 = 7\cdot6\cdot5\cdot4\cdot3\cdot2\cdot1 = 5040$

b) $_7P_5 = 7\cdot6\cdot5\cdot4\cdot3 \qquad = 2520$

c) $_7P_4 = 7\cdot6\cdot5\cdot4 \qquad\quad = 840$

d) $_7P_2 = 7\cdot6 \qquad\qquad\quad = 42$

Example 6. A baseball manager arranges his batting order as follows: The 4 infielders will bat first, then the outfielders, catcher, and pitcher will follow, not necessarily in that order. How many batting orders are possible?

The infielders can bat in 4! different ways; the rest in 5! different ways. Then by the Fundamental Counting Principle we have $_4P_4 \cdot _5P_5 = 4! \cdot 5!$, or 2880, possible batting orders. **[17–19]**

PERMUTATIONS OF SETS WITH NONDISTINGUISHABLE OBJECTS

Sometimes parts of sets are indistinguishable. Suppose, for example, we have 4 red marbles and 3 black marbles,

Ⓡ Ⓡ Ⓡ Ⓡ Ⓑ Ⓑ Ⓑ

and we want to find the number P of permutations of the marbles. We want to consider the red marbles indistinguishable and the black marbles indistinguishable. But for the moment let us assume that they are distinguishable (different). To do this we can replace the 4 R's by R_1, R_2, R_3, R_4. Thus from the P arrangements we form 4! permutations of $R_1, R_2, R_3,$ and R_4. This will yield $4! \cdot P$ permutations when we include all of $R_1, R_2, R_3, R_4, B, B, B$. Now let us replace the 3 B's by B_1, B_2, B_3. There are 3! arrangements of these, so from each of the $4! \cdot P$ permutations we can form 3! permutations of $R_1, R_2, R_3, R_4, B_1, B_2, B_3$. This would yield all 7! permutations of the 7-object set if all objects were considered distinguishable. Thus

$$3! \cdot 4! \cdot P = 7!, \quad \text{so} \quad P = \frac{7!}{4! \cdot 3!}, \quad \text{or} \quad 35.$$

This can be generalized as follows.

> **Theorem. Given a set of n objects in which n_1 are of one kind, n_2 are of a second kind, . . . , n_k are of the kth kind, then the number of distinguishable permutations is**
> $$\frac{n!}{n_1! \cdot n_2! \cdot n_3! \cdots n_k!}.$$

Example 7. How many distinguishable ways can the letters of the word CINCINNATI be arranged?

Note: There are 2C's, 3I's, 3N's, 1A, and 1T, for a total of 10.

Thus
$$P = \frac{10!}{2! \cdot 3! \cdot 3! \cdot 1! \cdot 1!}, \quad \text{or} \quad 50,400.$$
[20–22]

CIRCULAR ARRANGEMENTS

Suppose we arrange the 4 letters A, B, C, and D in a circular arrangement.

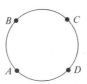

Note that the arrangements ABCD, BCDA, CDAB,

and DABC are not distinguishable. For each circular arrangement there would be 4 distinguishable arrangements on a line. Thus if there are P circular arrangements, these would yield $4 \cdot P$ arrangements on a line which we know is 4!. Thus $4 \cdot P = 4!$, so $P = 4!/4$, or 3!. To generalize:

> **Theorem. The number of distinct circular arrangements of n objects is $(n - 1)!$.**

Example 8. How many ways can 9 different foods be arranged around a lazy Susan?

$$(9 - 1)! = 8! = 8 \cdot 7 \cdot 6 \cdot 5 \cdot 4 \cdot 3 \cdot 2 \cdot 1 = 40,320$$
[23, 24]

REPEATED USE OF THE SAME OBJECT

Example 9. How many 5-letter code symbols can be formed with the letters A, B, C, and D if we allow repeated use of the same letter?

We have five spaces: ☐☐☐☐☐

We can select the first in 4 ways, the second in 4 ways, and so on. Thus there are 4^5, or 1024, arrangements. Generalizing we have the following.

> **Theorem. The number of distinct arrangements of n objects taken r at a time, with repetition, is n^r.**

[25]

Exercise Set 15.1

Compute.

1. $_4P_3$
2. $_7P_5$
3. $_{10}P_7$
4. $_{10}P_3$

Table 5 at the back of the book can help with many of these problems.

5. How many 5-digit numbers can be named using the digits 5, 6, 7, 8, and 9 without repetition? with repetition?

6. How many 4-digit numbers can be named using the digits 2, 3, 4, and 5 without repetition? with repetition?

7. How many ways can 5 students be arranged in a straight line? in a circle?

8. How many ways can 7 athletes be arranged in a straight line? in a circle?

9. How many distinguishable ways can the letters of the word PEACE be arranged?

10. How many distinguishable ways can the letters of the word GROOVY be arranged?

11. How many 7-digit phone numbers can be formed with the digits 0, 1, 2, 3, 4, 5, 6, 7, 8, and 9, assuming that no digit is used more than once and the first digit is not 0?

12. A program is planned and is to have 5 rock numbers and 4 speeches. In how many ways can this be done if a rock number and a speech are to alternate and the rock numbers come first?

13. Suppose the expression $a^2b^3c^4$ is expressed without exponents. In how many ways can this be done?

14. Suppose the expression a^3bc^2 is rewritten without exponents. In how many ways can this be done?

15. In how many ways could King Arthur and his 12 knights sit at his Round Table?

16. How many ways can 4 people be seated at a bridge table?

17. A penny, nickel, dime, quarter, and half dollar (if you have one) are arranged in a straight line. (a) Considering just the coins, in how many ways can they be lined up? (b) Considering the coins and heads and tails, in how many ways can they be lined up?

18. A penny, nickel, dime, and quarter are arranged in a straight line. (a) Considering just the coins, in how many ways can they be lined up? (b) Considering the coins and heads and tails, in how many ways can they be lined up?

19. Compute $_{52}P_4$.

20. Compute $_{50}P_5$.

21. A professor is going to grade his 24 students on a curve. He will give 3 A's, 5 B's, 9 C's, 4 D's, and 3 F's. In how many ways can he do this?

22. A professor is planning to grade his 20 students on a curve. He will give 2 A's, 5 B's, 8 C's, 3 D's, and 2 F's. In how many ways can he do this?

▶ Solve for n.

23. $_nP_5 = 7 \cdot _nP_4$ 24. $_nP_4 = 8 \cdot _{n-1}P_3$ 25. $_nP_5 = 9 \cdot _{n-1}P_4$ 26. $_nP_4 = 8 \cdot _nP_3$

15.2 Combinatorial Algebra: Combinations

Sometimes when we make selections from a set, we are not concerned with order. Such selections are called *combinations*.

Example 1. How many combinations taken 3 at a time are there of the set $\{A, B, C, D\}$?

Combinations $\{A, B, C\}$ and $\{A, C, D\}$, and $\{B, C, D\}$ and $\{A, B, D\}$.

Note that the set $\{A, B, C\}$ is the same as the set $\{B, A, C\}$ since they contain the same objects. Thus a combination is a subset of the given set.

Definition. A *combination* of *r* objects of a set is a subset containing *r* objects.

[26]

> **Definition.** The number of combinations taken r at a time from a set of n objects, denoted $_nC_r$, is the number of subsets of exactly r objects.

We want to find a general formula for $_nC_r$. Some general results can be derived without a formula. First, $_nC_n = 1$, because a set of n objects has only one subset of n objects, the set itself. Second, $_nC_1 = n$, since there are exactly n subsets of 1 object each. Finally, $_nC_0 = 1$, since there is only 1 subset with 0 objects, the empty set.

Now let us derive a general formula for $_nC_r$, for any $r \leq n$. Let us consider Example 1 again. We shall compare the number of combinations of 4 objects taken 3 at a time, with the number of permutations of 4 objects taken 3 at a time.

Combinations	Permutations
$\{A, B, C\} \rightarrow$	ABC ACB BAC BCA CAB CBA
$\{A, C, D\} \rightarrow$	ACD ADC CAD CDA DAC DCA
$\{B, C, D\} \rightarrow$	BCD BDC CBD CDB DBC DCB
$\{A, B, D\} \rightarrow$	ABD ADB BAD BDA DAB DBA

Note that each combination of 3 objects yields 3!, or 6, permutations as shown. Thus,

$$3! \cdot {}_4C_3 = {}_4P_3.$$

To find a formula for $_nC_r$, consider a combination of r objects:

$$\{A_1, A_2, A_3, \ldots, A_r\}.$$

There are $r!$ permutations of this set and each permutation of n objects taken r at a time will arise in this manner. Thus the number of combinations taken r at a time multiplied by $r!$ will yield the number of permutations taken r at a time:

$$r! \cdot {}_nC_r = {}_nP_r$$

so

$$_nC_r = \frac{1}{r!} \cdot {}_nP_r.$$

Since we already have a formula for $_nP_r$, we can use it to obtain one for $_nC_r$:

$$_nC_r = \frac{_nP_r}{r!} = \frac{n(n-1)(n-2) \cdots [n - (r-1)]}{r(r-1)(r-2) \cdots 3 \cdot 2 \cdot 1}. \quad (1)$$

This expression for $_nC_r$ is the quotient of two expressions, each of which has r factors. This formula is easiest to use in practice.

An alternate formula can be found by substituting $n!/(n-r)!$ for $_nP_r$:

$$_nC_r = \frac{1}{r!} \cdot {}_nP_r = \frac{1}{r!} \cdot \frac{n!}{(n-r)!} = \frac{n!}{r!\,(n-r)!}.$$

The notation $\begin{pmatrix} n \\ r \end{pmatrix}$ is also used for $_nC_r$. We will use this in Section 15.3. In summary, we have the following.

> **The number of combinations taken r at a time of a set of n objects is given by**
>
> $$_nC_r = \begin{pmatrix} n \\ r \end{pmatrix} = \frac{n(n-1)(n-2) \cdots [n - (r-1)]}{r(r-1)(r-2) \cdots 3 \cdot 2 \cdot 1}$$
>
> or $\qquad\qquad\qquad\qquad\qquad\qquad\qquad\qquad$ (1)
>
> $$_nC_r = \begin{pmatrix} n \\ r \end{pmatrix} = \frac{n!}{r!\,(n-r)!}. \qquad\qquad (2)$$

Example 2. Compute $\begin{pmatrix} 7 \\ 4 \end{pmatrix}$ using formulas (1) and (2).

Using formula (1) we have

This number tells where to start

$$\begin{pmatrix} 7 \\ 4 \end{pmatrix} = \frac{7 \cdot 6 \cdot 5 \cdot 4}{4 \cdot 3 \cdot 2 \cdot 1} = 7 \cdot 5 \cdot 4 = 140.$$

This number tells how many factors are in the numerator and denominator and where to start the denominator.

Using formula (2) we have

$$\binom{7}{4} = \frac{7!}{4! \, 3!} = \frac{7 \cdot 6 \cdot 5 \cdot 4 \cdot 3 \cdot 2 \cdot 1}{4 \cdot 3 \cdot 2 \cdot 1 \cdot 3 \cdot 2 \cdot 1}$$

$$= \frac{7 \cdot 6 \cdot 5 \cdot 4}{4 \cdot 3 \cdot 2 \cdot 1} = 7 \cdot 5 = 35.$$

[27, 28]

Note that

$$\binom{7}{4} = \frac{7 \cdot 6 \cdot 5 \cdot 4}{4 \cdot 3 \cdot 2 \cdot 1} = 35$$

and

$$\binom{7}{3} = \frac{7 \cdot 6 \cdot 5}{3 \cdot 2 \cdot 1} = 35.$$

In general,

$$\binom{n}{r} = \binom{n}{n-r}. \qquad (3)$$

This result can ease some calculations. [29]

Example 3. How many committees can be formed from a set of 5 governors and 7 senators if each committee contains 3 governors and 4 senators?

The 3 governors can be selected in $_5C_3$ ways and the 4 senators can be selected in $_7C_4$ ways. Using the Fundamental Counting Principle, it follows that the number of committees will be

$$_5C_3 \cdot _7C_4 = 10 \cdot 35 = 350.$$

Example 4. Find an expression for the total number of subsets of a set of n objects (including the empty set).

There are $\binom{n}{0}$ subsets with 0 objects, $\binom{n}{1}$ subsets with 1 object, $\binom{n}{2}$ subsets with 2 objects, and so on, up to $\binom{n}{n}$ subsets of n objects. Thus the total number of subsets is

$$\binom{n}{0} + \binom{n}{1} + \binom{n}{2} + \cdots + \binom{n}{n}. \qquad \text{[30, 31]}$$

Exercise Set 15.2

Compute.

1. $_9C_5$

2. $_{14}C_2$

3. $\binom{50}{2}$

4. $\binom{40}{3}$

5. $_nC_3$

6. $_nC_2$

Table 5 at the end of the book can be of help with these problems.

7. There are 23 students in a fraternity. How many sets of 4 officers can be selected?

8. How many basketball games can be played in a 9-team league if each team plays all other teams twice?

9. On a test a student is to select 6 out of 10 questions. In how many ways can he do this?

10. On a test a student is to select 7 out of 11 questions. In how many ways can she do this?

11. How many lines are determined by 8 points, no three of which are collinear? How many triangles are determined by the same points if no four are coplanar?

12. How many lines are determined by 7 points, no three of which are collinear? How many triangles are determined by the same points if no four are coplanar?

13. Of the first 10 questions on a test, a student must answer 7. On the second 5 questions, she must answer 3. In how many ways can this be done?

14. Of the first 8 questions on a test, a student must answer 6. On the second 4 questions, he must answer 3. In how many ways can this be done?

15. Suppose the Senate of the United States consisted of 58 Democrats and 42 Republicans. How many committees consisting of 6 Democrats and 4 Republicans could be formed? You do not need to simplify the expression.

16. Suppose the Senate of the United States consisted of 63 Republicans and 37 Democrats. How many committees consisting of 8 Republicans and 12 Democrats could be formed? You need not simplify the expression.

17. How many 5-card poker hands consisting of 3 aces and 2 cards that are not aces are possible with a 52-card deck? See p. 426 for a description of a 52-card deck.

18. How many 5-card poker hands consisting of 2 kings and 3 cards that are not kings are possible with a 52-card deck?

---

19. How many 5-card poker hands are possible with a 52-card deck?

20. How many 13-card bridge hands are possible with a 52-card deck?

---

21. How many line segments are determined by the 5 vertices of a pentagon? Of these, how many are diagonals?

22. How many line segments are determined by the 6 vertices of a hexagon? Of these, how many are diagonals?

23. How many line segments are determined by the n vertices of an n-gon? Of these, how many are diagonals? Use mathematical induction to prove the result for the diagonals.

24. Prove. For any natural numbers n and $r \le n$,

$$\binom{n}{r-1} + \binom{n}{r} = \binom{n+1}{r}.$$

Solve for n.

25. $\binom{n+1}{3} = 2 \cdot \binom{n}{2}$

26. $\binom{n}{n-2} = 6$

27. $\binom{n+2}{4} = 6 \cdot \binom{n}{2}$

28. $\binom{n}{3} = 2 \cdot \binom{n-1}{2}$

15.3 Binomial Series

Consider the following expanded powers of $(a + b)^n$, where $a + b$ is any binomial. Look for patterns.

$$(a + b)^0 = \qquad\qquad 1$$
$$(a + b)^1 = \qquad\qquad a + b$$
$$(a + b)^2 = \qquad\quad a^2 + 2ab + b^2$$
$$(a + b)^3 = \qquad a^3 + 3a^2b + 3ab^2 + b^3$$
$$(a + b)^4 = \quad a^4 + 4a^3b + 6a^2b^2 + 4ab^3 + b^4$$
$$(a + b)^5 = a^5 + 5a^4b + 10a^3b^2 + 10a^2b^3 + 5ab^4 + b^5$$

Note that each expansion is a polynomial that is also a series, though not arithmetic or geometric. There are some patterns to be noted for $(a + b)^n$, where n is a natural number.

1. In each term, the sum of the exponents is n.
2. The exponents of a start with n and decrease. The last term has no factor of a. The first term has no factor of b. The exponents of b start in the second term with 1 and increase to n.
3. There is one more term than the degree of the polynomial. The expansion of $(a + b)^n$ has $n + 1$ terms.
4. If a and b are positive, all the terms are positive. If b is negative, its odd powers are negative, so the terms alternate in sign.
5. All that remains is finding a way to determine the coefficients.

If we write just the coefficients of the expansions as follows

$$
\begin{array}{ccccccccccc}
&&&&& 1 \\
&&&& 1 && 1 \\
&&& 1 && 2 && 1 \\
&& 1 && 3 && 3 && 1 \\
& 1 && 4 && 6 && 4 && 1 \\
1 && 5 && 10 && 10 && 5 && 1 \\
\cdot && \cdot && \cdot && \cdot && \cdot && \cdot
\end{array}
$$

we obtain what is known as *Pascal's* (1623–1662) *Triangle*. Look for patterns in the triangle and then extend it another row. Use the resulting coefficients to find the expansion of $(a + b)^6$. We obtain

$$(a + b)^6 = a^6 + 6a^5b + 15a^4b^2 + 20a^3b^3$$
$$+ 15a^2b^4 + 6ab^5 + b^6.$$

Perhaps you have discovered that a coefficient is found by adding the two above it:

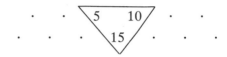

For higher powers, we develop a more efficient method. Consider

$$(a + b)^2 = (a + b)(a + b) = a^2 + 2ab + b^2.$$

We can think of finding this expansion as follows. We want all possible products of a and b. We get them by selecting factors from the $(a + b)$'s. This amounts to finding the *combinations* that follow.

Term	Way term obtained	Coefficient (the number of ways term obtained)
a^2	a from 2 of the factors b from 0 of the factors	$\binom{2}{0} = \binom{2}{2} = 1$
ab	a from 1 of the factors b from 1 of the factors	$\binom{2}{1} = \qquad 2$
b^2	a from 0 of the factors b from 2 of the factors	$\binom{2}{2} = \binom{2}{0} = 1$

Now consider

$$(a + b)^5 = (a + b)(a + b)(a + b)(a + b)(a + b).$$

Term	Way term obtained	Coefficient (the number of ways term obtained)
a^5	a from 5 of the factors b from 0 of the factors	$\binom{5}{0} = \binom{5}{5} = 1$
a^4b	a from 4 of the factors b from 1 of the factors	$\binom{5}{1} = \binom{5}{5} = 5$
a^3b^2	a from 3 of the factors b from 2 of the factors	$\binom{5}{2} = \binom{5}{3} = 10$
a^2b^3	a from 2 of the factors b from 3 of the factors	$\binom{5}{3} = \binom{5}{2} = 10$
ab^4	a from 1 of the factors b from 4 of the factors	$\binom{5}{4} = \binom{5}{1} = 5$
b^5	a from 0 of the factors b from 5 of the factors	$\binom{5}{5} = \binom{5}{0} = 5$

We can generalize as follows:

The Binomial Theorem*. For any natural number n, and any numbers a and b,

$$(a + b)^n = \binom{n}{0}a^n + \binom{n}{1}a^{n-1}b$$
$$+ \binom{n}{2}a^{n-2}b^2 + \cdots + \binom{n}{n}b^n$$
$$= \sum_{r=0}^{n} \binom{n}{r}a^{n-r}b^r.$$

The expression $\binom{n}{r}$ is also called a *binomial coefficient* as a result of this theorem. Look at the theorem. We see that the $(r + 1)$st term is $\binom{n}{r}a^{n-r}b^r$.

That is, the 1st term is $\binom{n}{0}a^{n-0}b^0$, the 2nd term is

---
* Isaac Newton proved the binomial theorem around 1676.

$\binom{n}{1}a^{n-1}b^1$, the 3rd term is $\binom{n}{2}a^{n-2}b^2$, the 8th term is $\binom{n}{7}a^{n-7}b^7$, and so on.

Example 1. Find the 7th term of $(4x - y^2)^9$.

We let $r = 6$, $n = 9$, $a = 4x$, and $b = -y^2$ in the formula $\binom{n}{r}a^{n-r}b^r$. Then

$$\binom{9}{6}(4x)^3(-y^2)^6 = \frac{9!}{6!\,3!}(4x)^3(-y^2)^6$$
$$= \frac{9 \cdot 8 \cdot 7 \cdot 6!}{3! \cdot 6!}64x^3y^{12}$$
$$= 5376x^3y^{12}. \qquad \textbf{[32–35]}$$

Example 2. Expand $(x^2 - 2y)^5$.

Note that $a = x^2$, $b = -2y$, and $n = 5$. Then using the binomial theorem we have

$$(x^2 - 2y)^5 = \binom{5}{0}(x^2)^5 + \binom{5}{1}(x^2)^4(-2y)$$
$$+ \binom{5}{2}(x^2)^3(-2y)^2 + \binom{5}{3}(x^2)^2(-2y)^3$$
$$+ \binom{5}{4}x^2(-2y)^4 + \binom{5}{5}(-2y)^5$$
$$= \frac{5!}{0!\,5!}x^{10} + \frac{5!}{1!\,4!}x^8(-2y)$$
$$+ \frac{5!}{2!\,3!}x^6(-2y)^2 + \frac{5!}{3!\,2!}x^4(-2y)^3$$
$$+ \frac{5!}{4!\,1!}x^2(-2y)^4 + \frac{5!}{5!\,1!}(-2y)^5$$
$$= x^{10} - 10x^8y + 40x^6y^2 - 80x^4y^3$$
$$+ 80x^2y^4 - 32y^5.$$

Example 3. Expand $\left(\dfrac{2}{x} + 3\sqrt{x}\right)^4$.

Note that $a = 2/x$, $b = 3\sqrt{x}$, and $n = 4$. Then using the binomial theorem, we have

$$\left(\frac{2}{x} + 3\sqrt{x}\right)^4 = \binom{4}{0} \cdot \left(\frac{2}{x}\right)^4 + \binom{4}{1} \cdot \left(\frac{2}{x}\right)^3 (3\sqrt{x})$$

$$+ \binom{4}{2} \cdot \left(\frac{2}{x}\right)^2 (3\sqrt{x})^2$$

$$+ \binom{4}{3}\left(\frac{2}{x}\right)(3\sqrt{x})^3 + \binom{4}{4}(3\sqrt{x})^4$$

$$= \frac{4!}{0!\,4!} \cdot \frac{16}{x^4} + \frac{4!}{1!\,3!} \cdot \frac{8}{x^3} 3\sqrt{x}$$

$$+ \frac{4!}{2!\,2!} \cdot \frac{4}{x^2} \cdot 9x$$

$$+ \frac{4!}{3!\,1!} \cdot \frac{2}{x} \cdot 27x^{\frac{3}{2}} + \frac{4!}{4!\,0!} \cdot 81x^2$$

$$= \frac{16}{x^4} + \frac{96}{x^{5/2}} + \frac{216}{x} + 216\sqrt{x} + 81x^2.$$

[36–38]

Example 4. Use four terms of a binomial series to approximate $(1.02)^8$.

First note that $1.02 = 1 + 0.02$. We write the first four terms.

$$(1 + 0.02)^8 \approx \binom{8}{0}1^8 + \binom{8}{1}1^7(0.02) + \binom{8}{2}1^6(0.02)^2$$

$$+ \binom{8}{3}1^5(0.02)^3$$

$$\approx 1 + 0.16 + 0.0112 + 0.000448$$

$$\approx 1.171648$$

$$\approx 1.172. \qquad \textbf{[39]}$$

Example 5. Use $(1 + 1)^n$ for 2^n to find a binomial expansion for 2^n.

$$2^n = (1 + 1)^n = \binom{n}{0} + \binom{n}{1} + \binom{n}{2} + \cdots + \binom{n}{n}$$

Earlier we proved that the right side is an expression for the number of subsets of a set of n objects. Thus:

> **Theorem. A set with n objects has 2^n subsets.**

Example 6. How many subsets are in

a) A set of 15 objects?
   Answer: 2^{15}

b) The set of letters of the alphabet?
   Answer: 2^{26} **[40–42]**

Exercise Set 15.3

Find the indicated term of the binomial expansion.

1. 3rd, $(a + b)^6$

2. 6th, $(x + y)^7$

3. 12th, $(a - 2)^{14}$

4. 11th, $(x - 3)^{12}$

5. 5th, $(2x^3 - \sqrt{y})^8$

6. 4th, $\left(\frac{1}{b^2} + \frac{b}{3}\right)^7$

7. Middle, $(2u - 3v^2)^{10}$

8. Middle two, $(\sqrt{x} + \sqrt{3})^5$

Expand.

9. $(m + n)^5$

10. $(a - b)^4$

11. $(x^2 - 3y)^5$

12. $(3c - d)^6$

13. $(x^{-2} + x^2)^4$

14. $\left(\dfrac{1}{\sqrt{x}} - \sqrt{x}\right)^6$

Compute, using the binomial theorem.

15. $(\sqrt{2} + 1)^6 - (\sqrt{2} - 1)^6$

16. $(1 - \sqrt{2})^4 + (1 + \sqrt{2})^4$

17. $(\sqrt{2} - i)^4$, where $i^2 = -1$

18. $(1 + i)^6$, where $i^2 = -1$

In Exercises 19–22, use four terms of a binomial series to approximate. Round to thousandths.

19. Find $(1.01)^7$.

20. Find $(1.02)^6$.

21. Find $(0.99)^5$. Use $(1 - 0.01)^5$.

22. Find $(1.99)^4$. Use $(2 - 0.01)^4$.

23. Use $(1 - 1)^n$ to find a binomial expansion of 0^n.

24. Use $(1 + 3)^n$ to find a binomial expansion of 4^n.

▶ In calculus it is proved that the binomial theorem can be extended as follows:

$$(1 + a)^x = 1 + xa + \frac{x(x - 1)}{2!}a^2 + \frac{x(x - 1)(x - 2)}{3!}a^3 + \cdots,$$

where $|a| < 1$ and x is any real number. This is an infinite series unless x is a natural number. Use this to approximate each of the following.

25. $\sqrt{1.03} = (1 + 0.03)^{\frac{1}{2}}$

26. $\sqrt[4]{1.08} = (1 + 0.08)^{\frac{1}{4}}$

27. Use mathematical induction and the property $\begin{pmatrix} k \\ r - 1 \end{pmatrix} + \begin{pmatrix} k \\ r \end{pmatrix} = \begin{pmatrix} k + 1 \\ r \end{pmatrix}$ to prove the binomial theorem.

15.4 Probability

WHAT IS PROBABILITY?

When a coin is tossed, the chances are 1 out of 2 that it will fall heads. We say that the *probability* that a coin will fall heads is $\frac{1}{2}$ or 0.50. In practice, this may not work. For example, we might toss a penny 100 times, and if it fell heads 47 times, we might conclude that the

probability of getting a head is $\dfrac{47}{100}$, or 0.47.

We might toss the penny 100 times and if it fell heads 54 times, we might conclude that the

probability of getting a head is $\frac{54}{100}$, or 0.54.

We call 0.47 and 0.54 *experimental probabilities*. But when we reason that we should get a head one out of 2 times, and the probability is 0.50, we call this *theoretical probability*. **[43]**

You might ask, "What is the *true* probability?" In fact, there is none. Experimentally we can determine probabilities within certain limits. These may or may not agree with what we reason theoretically. Henceforth we will consider only theoretical probability and omit the word "theoretical."

The probability that an event E can occur will be denoted $P(E)$. For example, the event that a coin falls heads may be denoted by H. The probability that the event will occur may then be denoted by $P(H)$. We can calculate theoretical probabilities in certain situations when outcomes are equally likely. For example, to calculate the probability that a penny comes up heads when tossed, we note that there are exactly two ways it can fall, and the chances that it can fall either way seem equally likely. That is, the probability is 1

out of 2, or $\frac{1}{2}$. This example illustrates the principle to calculate probabilities without experiment, as follows.

Principle P. If an event E can occur in *m* ways out of *n* equally likely possible outcomes, then

$$P(E) = \frac{m}{n}.$$

We will consider many examples involving a standard 52-card deck. Such a deck is shown below.

Example 1. What is the probability of drawing an ace from a well-shuffled deck of 52 cards?

Since there are 52 equally likely outcomes (cards in the deck) and there are 4 ways to obtain an ace, we have

$$P(\text{drawing an ace}) = \frac{4}{52}, \quad \text{or} \quad \frac{1}{13}.$$

Example 2. Suppose we select, without looking, one marble from a bag containing 3 red marbles and 4 green marbles. What is the probability of selecting a red marble?

A DECK OF 52 CARDS														
Black	Spades:	A	K	Q	J	10	9	8	7	6	5	4	3	2
		|	|	|	|									
		(ace)	(king)	(queen)	(jack)									
	Clubs:	A	K	Q	J	10	9	8	7	6	5	4	3	2
Red	Hearts:	A	K	Q	J	10	9	8	7	6	5	4	3	2
	Diamonds:	A	K	Q	J	10	9	8	7	6	5	4	3	2

There are 7 equally likely ways of selecting any marble, and since the number of ways for success (the marble is red) is 3,

$$P(\text{selecting a red marble}) = \frac{3}{7}. \qquad [44, 45]$$

We can use Principle P only when outcomes are equally likely. We could reason that the probability that a thumbtack will land point up is $\frac{1}{2}$ because there are just two ways for it to land. But these are not equally likely. If the point of the tack is very long, like a nail, it would almost always land on its side. If the point is short, so that it looks like a coin, it should land point up about half the time. The following are some results that follow from Principle P.

> **Theorem. If an event E cannot occur, then $P(E) = 0$.**

For example in coin tossing, the event that a coin would land on its edge has probability 0.

> **Theorem. If an event E is certain to occur (every trial is a success), then $P(E) = 1$.**

For example in coin tossing, the event that a coin falls either heads or tails has probability 1.

In general,

> **Theorem. The probability that an event E will occur is a number from 0 to 1.**
>
> $$0 \leqslant P(E) \leqslant 1.$$

$$[46, 47]$$

Example 3. Suppose 2 cards are drawn from a well-shuffled deck of 52 cards. What is the probability that both of them are spades?

The number n of ways of drawing 2 cards from a deck of 52 is $_{52}C_2$. Now 13 of the 52 cards are spades, so the number m of ways of drawing 2 spades is $_{13}C_2$. Thus,

$$P(\text{getting 2 spades}) = \frac{m}{n} = \frac{_{13}C_2}{_{52}C_2} = \frac{78}{1326} = \frac{1}{17}.$$

Example 4. Suppose 2 people are selected at random from a group that consists of 6 men and 4 women. What is the probability that both of them are women?

The number of ways of selecting 2 people from a group of 10 is $_{10}C_2$. The number of ways of selecting 2 women from a group of 4 is $_4C_2$. Thus the probability of selecting 2 women from the group of 10 is P, where

$$P = \frac{_4C_2}{_{10}C_2} = \frac{6}{45} = \frac{2}{15}.$$

Example 5. Suppose 3 people are selected at random from a group that consists of 6 men and 4 women. What is the probability that 1 man and 2 women are selected?

The number of ways of selecting 3 people out of a group of 10 is $_{10}C_3$. One man can be selected in $_6C_1$ ways, and 2 women can be selected in $_4C_2$ ways. By the Fundamental Counting Principle the number of ways of selecting 1 man and 2 women is $_6C_1 \cdot _4C_2$. Thus the probability is

$$\frac{_6C_1 \cdot _4C_2}{_{10}C_3}, \qquad \text{or} \qquad \frac{3}{10}. \qquad [48\text{--}50]$$

A die (plural, dice) is a cube with six faces, each of which contains dots as shown.

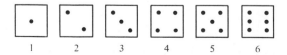

Example 6. What is the probability of getting a total of 8 on a roll of a pair of dice? (Assume the dice are different, say one red and one green.)

On each die there are 6 possible outcomes. The outcomes are paired so there are $6 \cdot 6$, or 36, possible ways in which the two can fall.

Red die

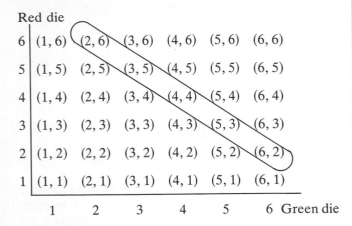

The pairs that total 8 are as shown. Thus there are 5 possible ways of getting a total of 8, so the probability is $\frac{5}{36}$.   **[51]**

ORIGIN AND USE OF PROBABILITY

A desire to calculate odds in games of chance gave rise to the theory of probability. Today the theory of probability and its closely related field, mathematical statistics, have many applications, most of them not related to games of chance. Opinion polls, with such uses as predicting elections, are a familiar example. Quality control, in which a prediction about the percentage of faulty items manufactured is made without testing them all, is an important application, among many, in business. Still other applications are in the areas of genetics, medicine, and the kinetic theory of gases.

Exercise Set 15.4

Suppose we draw a card from a well-shuffled deck of 52 cards.

1. How many equally likely outcomes are there?

2. What is the probability of drawing a queen?

3. What is the probability of drawing a heart?

4. What is the probability of drawing a club?

5. What is the probability of drawing a 4?

6. What is the probability of drawing a red card?

7. What is the probability of drawing a black card?

8. What is the probability of drawing an ace or a deuce?

9. What is the probability of drawing a 9 or a king?

Suppose we select, without looking, one marble from a bag containing 4 red marbles and 10 green marbles.

10. What is the probability of selecting a red marble?

11. What is the probability of selecting a green marble?

12. What is the probability of selecting a purple marble?

13. What is the probability of selecting a white marble?

Suppose 4 cards are drawn from a well-shuffled deck of 52 cards.

14. What is the probability that all 4 are spades?

15. What is the probability that all 4 are hearts?

16. If 4 marbles are drawn at random all at once from a bag containing 8 white marbles and 6 black marbles, what is the probability that 2 will be white and 2 will be black?

17. From a group of 8 men and 7 women, a committee of 4 is chosen. What is the probability that 2 men and 2 women will be chosen?

18. What is the probability of getting a total of 6 on a roll of a pair of dice?

19. What is the probability of getting a total of 3 on a roll of a pair of dice?

20. What is the probability of getting snake eyes (a total of 2) on a roll of a pair of dice?

21. What is the probability of getting box-cars (a total of 12) on a roll of a pair of dice?

22. From a bag containing 5 nickels, 8 dimes, and 7 quarters, 5 coins are drawn at random all at once. What is the probability of getting 2 nickels, 2 dimes, and 1 quarter?

23. From a bag containing 6 nickels, 10 dimes, and 4 quarters, 6 coins are drawn at random all at once. What is the probability of getting 3 nickels, 2 dimes, and 1 quarter?

Roulette.   A roulette wheel contains slots numbered 00, 0, 1, 2, 3, . . . , 35, 36. Eighteen of the slots numbered 1 through 36 are colored red and eighteen are colored black. The 00 and 0 slots are uncolored. The wheel is spun, and a ball is rolled around the rim until it falls into a slot. What is the probability that the ball falls in

24. a black slot?

25. a red slot?

26. a red or black slot?

27. the 00 slot?

28. the 0 slot?

29. either the 00 or 0 slot? (Here the house always wins.)

30. an odd-numbered slot?

Five-card poker hands and probabilities. In part (a) of each problem, give a reasoned expression as well as the answer. Read all the problems before beginning.

31. How many 5-card poker hands can be dealt from a standard 52-card deck?

32. A *royal flush* consists of a 5-card hand with A-K-Q-J-10 of the same suit.

a) How many royal flushes are there?

b) What is the probability of getting a royal flush?

33. A *straight flush* consists of five cards in sequence in the same suit, but excludes royal flushes.

a) How many straight flushes are there?

b) What is the probability of getting a straight flush?

34. *Four of a kind* is a 5-card hand in which 4 of the cards are of the same denomination, such as J-J-J-J-6, 7-7-7-7-A, or 2-2-2-2-5.

a) How many are there?

b) What is the probability of getting four of a kind?

35. A *full house* consists of a pair and three of a kind, such as Q-Q-Q-4-4.

a) How many are there?

b) What is the probability of getting a full house?

37. *Three of a kind* consists of a 5-card hand in which 3 of the cards are the same denomination, such as Q-Q-Q-10-7.

a) How many are there?

b) What is the probability of getting three of a kind?

39. *Two pairs* is a hand such as Q-Q-3-3-A.

a) How many are there?

b) What is the probability of getting two pairs?

36. A *pair* is a 5-card hand in which just 2 of the cards are the same denomination, such as Q-Q-8-A-3.

a) How many are there?

b) What is the probability of getting a pair?

38. A *flush* is a 5-card hand in which all the cards are the same suit, but not all in sequence (not a straight flush or royal flush).

a) How many are there?

b) What is the probability of getting a flush?

40. A *straight* is any five cards in sequence, but not in the same suit. For example, 4 of spades, 5 of spades, 6 of diamonds, 7 of hearts, and 8 of clubs.

a) How many are there?

b) What is the probability of getting a straight?

15.5 Compound Events

In this section, some theorems will be established that allow the calculation of the probability of certain compound events, provided the probabilities of the events comprising them are known.

COMPLEMENTARY EVENTS

The nonoccurrence of an event is also an event. For example, obtaining a head on tossing a coin is an event, and *not* obtaining a head is also an event. If A is a symbol for an event, the nonoccurrence of A can be symbolized $\bar{A}$ (read "not A"). Pairs of events like this are called *complementary events*.

> **Theorem 1. The probability that an event A will not occur, $P(\bar{A})$, is $1 - P(A)$.**

Proof. By Principle P, $P(A)$ is the ratio of the number m of times that A can occur to the total number n of possible outcomes. Then $P(A) = m/n$.

The number of times A cannot occur is then $n - m$, and therefore

$$P(\bar{A}) = \frac{n - m}{n} = \frac{n}{n} - \frac{m}{n} = 1 - P(A).$$

This theorem can be visualized in the following figure showing the sets of outcomes (outcome sets) for A and $\bar{A}$.

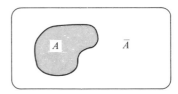

The outcome sets for A and $\bar{A}$ are known as *complements* of each other.

Example 1. Suppose $P(A) = \dfrac{5}{17}$. Find $P(\bar{A})$.

$$P(\bar{A}) = 1 - P(A) = 1 - \frac{5}{17} = \frac{12}{17}$$

Example 2. Find the probability that when 1 card is drawn from a well-shuffled deck of 52, it is not an ace.

Let A = event of getting an ace. Then $\bar{A}$ = event of not getting an ace. Now $P(A) = \frac{4}{52}$, or $\frac{1}{13}$, so $P(\bar{A}) = 1 - \frac{1}{13}$ or $\frac{12}{13}$.   **[52, 53]**

DISJUNCTIONS OF EVENTS

A disjunction is an event described by a disjunction of sentences. For example, if A is the event of obtaining two heads on tossing two coins and B is the event of obtaining two tails, the event $(A$ or $B)$ is the event of obtaining two heads *or* two tails. Similarly, a conjunction of events is an event described by a conjunction of sentences. The event $(A$ and $B)$ is the event that both A and B occur.

If we know the probabilities of two or more events, we can calculate the probability of their disjunction, using the next theorems. Theorem 2 is more general and Theorem 3, a special case of Theorem 2, is more useful.

> **Theorem 2. For any events A and B,**
>
> $$P(A \text{ or } B) = P(A) + P(B) - P(A \text{ and } B).$$

Proof. Using Principle P, suppose A can occur s times out of n possible outcomes and that B can occur t times. Suppose, moreover, that A and B can occur together v times. Then the total number of times $(A$ or $B)$ occurs is $s + t - v$. Then

$$P(A \text{ or } B) = \frac{s + t - v}{n} = \frac{s}{n} + \frac{t}{n} - \frac{v}{n}$$

$$= P(A) + P(B) - P(A \text{ and } B)$$

since $P(A) = \dfrac{s}{n}$, $P(B) = \dfrac{t}{n}$, and $P(A \text{ and } B) = \dfrac{v}{n}$.

This theorem can be visualized using outcome sets as in this figure.

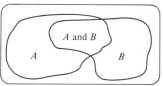

The number of outcomes favorable to $(A$ or $B)$ is not quite the sum of those favorable to A and those favorable to B, because the number of outcomes favorable to $(A$ and $B)$ is counted twice in the sum. Thus if we subtract the number of outcomes favorable to $(A$ and $B)$ from the sum, we will have the number of outcomes favorable to $(A$ or $B)$.   **[54]**

A special case of Theorem 2 can be used when events are *mutually exclusive*, meaning that they cannot both happen at the same time. If A is "obtaining two heads on tossing two coins" and B is "obtaining two tails," then A and B are mutually exclusive events, because they cannot both happen at once. The probability of their conjunction is 0. This leads to the next theorem.

> **Theorem 3. If A and B are mutually exclusive events, then**
>
> $$P(A \text{ or } B) = P(A) + P(B).$$

Proof. By Theorem 2,

$$P(A \text{ or } B) = P(A) + P(B) - P(A \text{ or } B),$$

and since A and B are mutually exclusive, $P(A$ and $B) = 0$. It follows that

$$P(A \text{ or } B) = P(A) + P(B).$$

This theorem can be visualized in this figure.

The set of outcomes for A and the set for B have an empty intersection. Thus the sum of the outcomes favorable to A and the outcomes favorable to B is the number of outcomes favorable to (A or B).

Example 1. If A and B are mutually exclusive and $P(A) = 0.26$ and $P(B) = 0.37$, what is $P(A \text{ or } B)$?

$$P(A \text{ or } B) = P(A) + P(B) = 0.26 + 0.37 = 0.63$$

[55, 56]

Theorem 3 extends to disjunctions of 3 or more events.

Example 2. A card is drawn from a deck of 52 cards. What is the probability that it is a king, a red ace, or the jack of spades?

The 3 events are mutually exclusive, hence Theorem 3 may be used.

$$P(K) = \text{probability of getting a king} = \frac{4}{52}$$

$$P(\text{red A}) = \text{probability of getting a red ace} = \frac{2}{52}$$

$$P(J) = \text{probability of getting the jack of spades} = \frac{1}{52}$$

Thus

$$P(K \text{ or Red A or J}) = P(K) + P(\text{Red A}) + P(J)$$

$$= \frac{4}{52} + \frac{2}{52} + \frac{1}{52} = \frac{7}{52}.$$

[57, 58]

CONJUNCTIONS OF EVENTS

A conjunction of events is described by a conjunction of sentences.

Probabilities of conjunctions of events can be calculated in certain cases. Some examples will lead us to the next theorems.

Example 1. The probability, $P(H)$, of obtaining a head on tossing a coin is $\frac{1}{2}$. What is the probability of obtaining two heads when two coins are tossed?

From the outcome set $\{(H, H), (H, T), (T, H), (T, T)\}$ we see that $P(H, H)$ is $\frac{1}{4}$. This is also the product of $P(H)$ and $P(H)$.

Example 2. What is the probability that when a red die and a green die are rolled, a 1 is obtained on the red die and an even number on the green die?

From the outcome set in Example 6 of Section 15.4, we see that a 1 on the red die is obtained in 6 out of 36 cases, so

$$P(1 \text{ on red}) = \frac{1}{6}.$$

An even number is obtained on the green die in 18 out of 36 cases, hence,

$$P(\text{even on green}) = \frac{1}{2}.$$

There are 3 cases in which (1 on red and even on green) occurs. Hence

$$P(1 \text{ on red and even on green}) = \frac{3}{36} = \frac{1}{12}.$$

Note again in this example that the probability of the conjunction is also the product of the individual probabilities. [59, 60]

Example 3. A bag contains 3 red, 3 white, and 3 blue marbles. A marble is drawn and replaced, and a second marble is drawn. What is the probability, P (first red and second blue), that the first one is red and the second blue?

This is the outcome set.

		Second marble		
		R	W	B
First marble	R	(R, R)	(R, W)	(R, B)
	W	(W, R)	(W, W)	(W, B)
	B	(B, R)	(B, W)	(B, B)

We see that P(1st red $= \frac{1}{3}$) and that P(2nd blue) $= \frac{1}{3}$. Also, P(1st red and 2nd blue), or P(R, B), is $\frac{1}{9}$, and the probability of the conjunction is the product of the individual probabilities.

Example 4. Suppose from the bag of marbles of Example 3 one marble is drawn but not replaced, and then a second marble is drawn. What is the probability that the first one is red and the second is blue?

This time, P(1st red) $= \frac{1}{3}$, as before, but P(2nd blue) is different. Given that the first one drawn was red, there remain 3 blue marbles out of 8, rather than 3 out of 9, since the first one was not replaced. Hence the probability that the second marble is blue is $\frac{3}{8}$ if the first one drawn was red. The probability, P(2nd blue | 1st red), that *if* the first one drawn was red, the second will be blue is $\frac{3}{8}$. Thus

$$P(\text{1st red and 2nd blue}) = \frac{3}{8} \cdot \frac{1}{3}$$

$$= P(\text{2nd blue} \mid \text{1st red}) \cdot P(\text{1st red}) = \frac{1}{8}. \quad \textbf{[61, 62]}$$

In each of the preceding examples the probability of a conjunction was obtainable as a product of probabilities. In the first three examples the probability of an individual event did not depend on the outcome of the other individual event. In other words, the events were *independent*. In Example 4, however, the probability of one event did depend on whether the other one happened or not. This is an example of *conditional probability*. Note that when events are dependent, as in Example 4, the conditional probability cannot be calculated by using an ordinary outcome set. The following theorems summarize these results.

Theorem 4 (Dependent events). If the probability of an event A depends on the occurrence of an event B, then

$$P(A \text{ and } B) = P(A \mid B) \cdot P(B),$$

where $P(A \mid B) =$ the probability that *if* B has occurred, then A occurs.

Theorem 5 (Independent events). If A and B are independent events,

$$P(A \text{ and } B) = P(A) \cdot P(B).$$

This theorem is easily extended to conjunctions of three or more independent events.   **[63, 64]**

In calculating probabilities of conjunctions it is helpful to consider that one event occurs first and the other second.

Example 5. Suppose a bag contains 7 red, 5 white, and 8 blue marbles. What is the probability of drawing a white marble and a blue marble, in two draws, given that the first marble is replaced before the second one is drawn?

The probability P(W and B), where W means white and B means blue, is sought. The event (W and B) can occur in two mutually exclusive ways: (W on 1st and B on 2nd) or (B on 1st and W on 2nd). Thus

$$P(\text{W and B}) = P(\text{W on 1st and B on 2nd})$$
$$+ P(\text{B on 1st and W on 2nd})$$
$$= P(\text{W on 1st}) \cdot P(\text{B on 2nd})$$
$$+ P(\text{B on 1st}) \cdot P(\text{W on 2nd})$$
$$= \frac{5}{20} \cdot \frac{8}{20} + \frac{8}{20} \cdot \frac{5}{20} = \frac{1}{5}. \quad \textbf{[65]}$$

Exercise Set 15.5

In Exercises 1–6, $P(A)$ is given. Find $P(\bar{A})$.

1. $P(A) = \dfrac{21}{23}$

2. $P(A) = \dfrac{2}{47}$

3. $P(A) = 0.012$

4. $P(A) = 0.69$

5. $P(A) = 1$

6. $P(A) = 0$

In Exercises 7–10, $P(A)$ and $P(B)$ are given. Assuming A and B are mutually exclusive, find $P(A \text{ or } B)$.

7. $P(A) = \dfrac{3}{8}$, $P(B) = \dfrac{2}{7}$

8. $P(A) = 0.083$, $P(B) = 0.216$

9. $P(A) = 0.101$, $P(B) = 0.898$

10. $P(A) = \dfrac{2}{10}$, $P(B) = \dfrac{4}{5}$

In Exercises 11–14, $P(A)$ and $P(B)$ are given. Assuming A and B are independent, find $P(A \text{ and } B)$.

11. $P(A) = 0.34$, $P(B) = 0.15$

12. $P(A) = \dfrac{3}{8}$, $P(B) = \dfrac{4}{7}$

13. $P(A) = \dfrac{11}{12}$, $P(B) = \dfrac{5}{12}$

14. $P(A) = 0.02$, $P(B) = 0.43$

15. When a card is drawn from a deck of playing cards, what is the probability that it is
a) a face card?
b) not a face card?
c) a club?
d) not a club?

16. When a die is rolled, what is the probability that it is
a) a 4?
b) not a 4?
c) an even number?
d) not an even number?

17. A card is drawn from a deck of 52 cards. What is the probability that it is a jack, queen, or king?

18. A card is drawn from a deck of 52 cards. What is the probability that it is a red 8, red 9, or red 10?

19. A bag contains 3 red marbles, 5 blue marbles, and 2 yellow marbles. Two marbles are drawn; the first marble is replaced before the second is drawn; what is the probability that
a) 1 will be red and 1 blue?
b) 1 will be red and 1 yellow?
c) 1 blue and 1 yellow?
d) they will be different colors?
e) they will be the same color?

20. A bag contains 4 red marbles, 5 blue marbles, and 2 yellow marbles. Two marbles are drawn; the first replaced before the second is drawn, what is the probability that
a) 1 will be red and 1 blue?
b) 1 will be red and 1 yellow?
c) 1 will be blue and 1 yellow?
d) they will be different colors?
e) they will be the same color?

21. A bag contains 3 blue and 5 yellow marbles. If 3 marbles are drawn at once, what is the probability that at least 2 are yellow?

22. In Exercise 21, what is the probability that at least 1 is yellow?

23. Suppose your probability of passing a test on this chapter is $\frac{3}{4}$, and the probability of your passing a chemistry test the same day is $\frac{5}{8}$. Assuming the events to be independent, what is the probability that you

a) pass both tests?

b) pass one test but not the other?

c) fail both tests?

24. For any event A, find $P(A) + P(\bar{A})$.

25. Suppose $P(A) = p$, $P(B) = q$, and $\bar{A}$ and B are independent. Find $P(\bar{A}$ and $B)$.

26. A bag contains 4 red marbles, 4 white marbles, and 4 blue marbles. Three marbles are drawn at random, without replacement. What is the probability that

a) they are all red?

b) they are all of the same color?

c) they are all of different colors?

27. Three cards are drawn at random from a deck of 52 cards, without replacement. What is the probability that

a) they are all spades?

b) they are all of the same suit?

c) they are all red?

d) they are all the same color?

e) they are all face cards?

f) they are all aces?

28. Suppose the probability that man A passes a course is $\frac{1}{4}$ and that of man B is $\frac{1}{5}$. Assuming events to be independent, what is the probability that

a) both A and B pass?

b) A passes and B fails?

c) A fails and B passes?

d) A fails and B fails?

Chapter 15 Test, or Review

1. If 9 different signal flags are available, how many different displays are possible using 4 flags in a row?

2. The Greek alphabet contains 24 letters. How many fraternity names can be formed using 3 different letters?

3. Solve for n: $\binom{n}{n-1} = 36$.

4. A bag contains 4 white balls, 3 blue balls, and 7 red balls. A ball is drawn at random. What is the probability that it is red?

5. What is the probability of obtaining a total of 10 on a roll of a pair of dice? on a roll of one die?

6. Find the 12th term of $(a + x)^{18}$. Do *not* multiply out the factorials in the binomial coefficient.

7. Expand: $(m + n)^7$.

8. Approximate $(1.03)^5$ using four terms of a binomial series.

9. In how many distinguishable ways can the letters of the word TENNESSEE be arranged?

10. In how many different ways can 7 people be seated at a round table?

11. Suppose $P(A) = \frac{5}{8}$ and $P(B) = \frac{2}{3}$. Assuming A and $\bar{B}$ to be independent, find $P(A$ and $\bar{B})$.

TABLE 1. Powers, Roots, and Reciprocals

n	n^2	n^3	$\sqrt{n}$	$\sqrt[3]{n}$	$\sqrt{10n}$	$\dfrac{1}{n}$	n	n^2	n^3	$\sqrt{n}$	$\sqrt[3]{n}$	$\sqrt{10n}$	$\dfrac{1}{n}$
1	1	1	1.000	1.000	3.162	1.0000	51	2,601	132,651	7.141	3.708	22.583	.0196
2	4	8	1.414	1.260	4.472	.5000	52	2,704	140,608	7.211	3.733	22.804	.0192
3	9	27	1.732	1.442	5.477	.3333	53	2,809	148,877	7.280	3.756	23.022	.0189
4	16	64	2.000	1.587	6.325	.2500	54	2,916	157,464	7.348	3.780	23.238	.0185
5	25	125	2.236	1.710	7.071	.2000	55	3,025	166,375	7.416	3.803	23.452	.0182
6	36	216	2.449	1.817	7.746	.1667	56	3,136	175,616	7.483	3.826	23.664	.0179
7	49	343	2.646	1.913	8.367	.1429	57	3,249	185,193	7.550	3.849	23.875	.0175
8	64	512	2.828	2.000	8.944	.1250	58	3,364	195,112	7.616	3.871	24.083	.0172
9	81	729	3.000	2.080	9.487	.1111	59	3,481	205,379	7.681	3.893	24.290	.0169
10	100	1,000	3.162	2.154	10.000	.1000	60	3,600	216,000	7.746	3.915	24.495	.0167
11	121	1,331	3.317	2.224	10.488	.0909	61	3,721	226,981	7.810	3.936	24.698	.0164
12	144	1,728	3.464	2.289	10.954	.0833	62	3,844	238,328	7.874	3.958	24.900	.0161
13	169	2,197	3.606	2.351	11.402	.0769	63	3,969	250,047	7.937	3.979	25.100	.0159
14	196	2,744	3.742	2.410	11.832	.0714	64	4,096	262,144	8.000	4.000	25.298	.0156
15	225	3,375	3.873	2.466	12.247	.0667	65	4,225	274,625	8.062	4.021	25.495	.0154
16	256	4,096	4.000	2.520	12.648	.0625	66	4,356	287,496	8.124	4.041	25.690	.0152
17	289	4,913	4.123	2.571	13.038	.0588	67	4,489	300,763	8.185	4.062	25.884	.0149
18	324	5,832	4.243	2.621	13.416	.0556	68	4,624	314,432	8.246	4.082	26.077	.0147
19	361	6,859	4.359	2.668	13.784	.0526	69	4,761	328,509	8.307	4.102	26.268	.0145
20	400	8,000	4.472	2.714	14.142	.0500	70	4,900	343,000	8.367	4.121	26.458	.0143
21	441	9,261	4.583	2.759	14.491	.0476	71	5,041	357,911	8.426	4.141	26.646	.0141
22	484	10,648	4.690	2.802	14.832	.0455	72	5,184	373,248	8.485	4.160	26.833	.0139
23	529	12,167	4.796	2.844	15.166	.0435	73	5,329	389,017	8.544	4.179	27.019	.0137
24	576	13,824	4.899	2.884	15.492	.0417	74	5,476	405,224	8.602	4.198	27.203	.0135
25	625	15,625	5.000	2.924	15.811	.0400	75	5,625	421,875	8.660	4.217	27.386	.0133
26	676	17,576	5.099	2.962	16.125	.0385	76	5,776	438,976	8.718	4.236	27.568	.0132
27	729	19,683	5.196	3.000	16.432	.0370	77	5,929	456,533	8.775	4.254	27.749	.0130
28	784	21,952	5.292	3.037	16.733	.0357	78	6,084	474,552	8.832	4.273	27.928	.0128
29	841	24,389	5.385	3.072	17.029	.0345	79	6,241	493,039	8.888	4.291	28.107	.0127
30	900	27,000	5.477	3.107	17.321	.0333	80	6,400	512,000	8.944	4.309	28.284	.0125
31	961	29,791	5.568	3.141	17.607	.0323	81	6,561	531,441	9.000	4.327	28.460	.0123
32	1,024	32,768	5.657	3.175	17.889	.0312	82	6,724	551,368	9.055	4.344	28.636	.0122
33	1,089	35,937	5.745	3.208	18.166	.0303	83	6,889	571,787	9.110	4.362	28.810	.0120
34	1,156	39,304	5.831	3.240	18.439	.0294	84	7,056	592,704	9.165	4.380	28.983	.0119
35	1,225	42,875	5.916	3.271	18.708	.0286	85	7,225	614,125	9.220	4.397	29.155	.0118
36	1,296	46,656	6.000	3.302	18.974	.0278	86	7,396	636,056	9.274	4.414	29.326	.0116
37	1,369	50,653	6.083	3.332	19.235	.0270	87	7,569	658,503	9.327	4.431	29.496	.0115
38	1,444	54,872	6.164	3.362	19.494	.0263	88	7,744	681,472	9.381	4.448	29.665	.0114
39	1,521	59,319	6.245	3.391	19.748	.0256	89	7,921	704,969	9.434	4.465	29.833	.0112
40	1,600	64,000	6.325	3.420	20.000	.0250	90	8,100	729,000	9.487	4.481	30.000	.0111
41	1,681	68,921	6.403	3.448	20.248	.0244	91	8,281	753,571	9.539	4.498	30.166	.0110
42	1,764	74,088	6.481	3.476	20.494	.0238	92	8,464	778,688	9.592	4.514	30.332	.0109
43	1,849	79,507	6.557	3.503	20.736	.0233	93	8,649	804,357	9.644	4.531	30.496	.0108
44	1,936	85,184	6.633	3.530	20.976	.0227	94	8,836	830,584	9.695	4.547	30.659	.0106
45	2,025	91,125	6.708	3.557	21.213	.0222	95	9,025	857,375	9.747	4.563	30.822	.0105
46	2,116	97,336	6.782	3.583	21.448	.0217	96	9,216	884,736	9.798	4.579	30.984	.0104
47	2,209	103,823	6.856	3.609	21.679	.0213	97	9,409	912,673	9.849	4.595	31.145	.0103
48	2,304	110,592	6.928	3.634	21.909	.0208	98	9,604	941,192	9.899	4.610	31.305	.0102
49	2,401	117,649	7.000	3.659	22.136	.0204	99	9,801	970,299	9.950	4.626	31.464	.0101
50	2,500	125,000	7.071	3.684	22.361	.0200	100	10,000	1,000,000	10.000	4.642	31.623	.0100

TABLE 2. Common Logarithms

x	0	1	2	3	4	5	6	7	8	9
1.0	.0000	.0043	.0086	.0128	.0170	.0212	.0253	.0294	.0334	.0374
1.1	.0414	.0453	.0492	.0531	.0569	.0607	.0645	.0682	.0719	.0755
1.2	.0792	.0828	.0864	.0899	.0934	.0969	.1004	.1038	.1072	.1106
1.3	.1139	.1173	.1206	.1239	.1271	.1303	.1335	.1367	.1399	.1430
1.4	.1461	.1492	.1523	.1553	.1584	.1614	.1644	.1673	.1703	.1732
1.5	.1761	.1790	.1818	.1847	.1875	.1903	.1931	.1959	.1987	.2014
1.6	.2041	.2068	.2095	.2122	.2148	.2175	.2201	.2227	.2253	.2279
1.7	.2304	.2330	.2355	.2380	.2405	.2430	.2455	.2480	.2504	.2529
1.8	.2553	.2577	.2601	.2625	.2648	.2672	.2695	.2718	.2742	.2765
1.9	.2788	.2810	.2833	.2856	.2878	.2900	.2923	.2945	.2967	.2989
2.0	.3010	.3032	.3054	.3075	.3096	.3118	.3139	.3160	.3181	.3201
2.1	.3222	.3243	.3263	.3284	.3304	.3324	.3345	.3365	.3385	.3404
2.2	.3424	.3444	.3464	.3483	.3502	.3522	.3541	.3560	.3579	.3598
2.3	.3617	.3636	.3655	.3674	.3692	.3711	.3729	.3747	.3766	.3784
2.4	.3802	.3820	.3838	.3856	.3874	.3892	.3909	.3927	.3945	.3962
2.5	.3979	.3997	.4014	.4031	.4048	.4065	.4082	.4099	.4116	.4133
2.6	.4150	.4166	.4183	.4200	.4216	.4232	.4249	.4265	.4281	.4298
2.7	.4314	.4330	.4346	.4362	.4378	.4393	.4409	.4425	.4440	.4456
2.8	.4472	.4487	.4502	.4518	.4533	.4548	.4564	.4579	.4594	.4609
2.9	.4624	.4639	.4654	.4669	.4683	.4698	.4713	.4728	.4742	.4757
3.0	.4771	.4786	.4800	.4814	.4829	.4843	.4857	.4871	.4886	.4900
3.1	.4914	.4928	.4942	.4955	.4969	.4983	.4997	.5011	.5024	.5038
3.2	.5051	.5065	.5079	.5092	.5105	.5119	.5132	.5145	.5159	.5172
3.3	.5185	.5198	.5211	.5224	.5237	.5250	.5263	.5276	.5289	.5307
3.4	.5315	.5328	.5340	.5353	.5366	.5378	.5391	.5403	.5416	.5428
3.5	.5441	.5453	.5465	.5478	.5490	.5502	.5514	.5527	.5539	.5551
3.6	.5563	.5575	.5587	.5599	.5611	.5623	.5635	.5647	.5658	.5670
3.7	.5682	.5694	.5705	.5717	.5729	.5740	.5752	.5763	.5775	.5786
3.8	.5798	.5809	.5821	.5832	.5843	.5855	.5866	.5877	.5888	.5899
3.9	.5911	.5922	.5933	.5944	.5955	.5966	.5977	.5988	.5999	.6010
4.0	.6021	.6031	.6042	.6053	.6064	.6075	.6085	.6096	.6107	.6117
4.1	.6128	.6138	.6149	.6160	.6170	.6180	.6191	.6201	.6212	.6222
4.2	.6232	.6243	.6253	.6263	.6274	.6284	.6294	.6304	.6314	.6325
4.3	.6335	.6345	.6355	.6365	.6375	.6385	.6395	.6405	.6415	.6425
4.4	.6435	.6444	.6454	.6464	.6474	.6484	.6493	.6503	.6513	.6522
4.5	.6532	.6542	.6551	.6561	.6571	.6580	.6590	.6599	.6609	.6618
4.6	.6628	.6637	.6646	.6656	.6665	.6675	.6684	.6693	.6702	.6712
4.7	.6721	.6730	.6739	.6749	.6758	.6767	.6776	.6785	.6794	.6803
4.8	.6812	.6821	.6830	.6839	.6848	.6857	.6866	.6875	.6884	.6893
4.9	.6902	.6911	.6920	.6928	.6937	.6946	.6955	.6964	.6972	.6981
5.0	.6990	.6998	.7007	.7016	.7024	.7033	.7042	.7050	.7059	.7067
5.1	.7076	.7084	.7093	.7101	.7110	.7118	.7126	.7135	.7143	.7152
5.2	.7160	.7168	.7177	.7185	.7193	.7202	.7210	.7218	.7226	.7235
5.3	.7243	.7251	.7259	.7267	.7275	.7284	.7292	.7300	.7308	.7316
5.4	.7324	.7332	.7340	.7348	.7356	.7364	.7372	.7380	.7388	.7396
x	0	1	2	3	4	5	6	7	8	9

TABLE 2 (continued)

x	0	1	2	3	4	5	6	7	8	9
5.5	.7404	.7412	.7419	.7427	.7435	.7443	.7451	.7459	.7466	.7474
5.6	.7482	.7490	.7497	.7505	.7513	.7520	.7528	.7536	.7543	.7551
5.7	.7559	.7566	.7574	.7582	.7589	.7597	.7604	.7612	.7619	.7627
5.8	.7634	.7642	.7649	.7657	.7664	.7672	.7679	.7686	.7694	.7701
5.9	.7709	.7716	.7723	.7731	.7738	.7745	.7752	.7760	.7767	.7774
6.0	.7782	.7789	.7796	.7803	.7810	.7818	.7825	.7832	.7839	.7846
6.1	.7853	.7860	.7868	.7875	.7882	.7889	.7896	.7903	.7910	.7917
6.2	.7924	.7931	.7938	.7945	.7952	.7959	.7966	.7973	.7980	.7987
6.3	.7993	.8000	.8007	.8014	.8021	.8028	.8035	.8041	.8048	.8055
6.4	.8062	.8069	.8075	.8082	.8089	.8096	.8102	.8109	.8116	.8122
6.5	.8129	.8136	.8142	.8149	.8156	.8162	.8169	.8176	.8182	.8189
6.6	.8195	.8202	.8209	.8215	.8222	.8228	.8235	.8241	.8248	.8254
6.7	.8261	.8267	.8274	.8280	.8287	.8293	.8299	.8306	.8312	.8319
6.8	.8325	.8331	.8338	.8344	.8351	.8357	.8363	.8370	.8376	.8382
6.9	.8388	.8395	.8401	.8407	.8414	.8420	.8426	.8432	.8439	.8445
7.0	.8451	.8457	.8463	.8470	.8476	.8482	.8488	.8494	.8500	.8506
7.1	.8513	.8519	.8525	.8531	.8537	.8543	.8549	.8555	.8561	.8567
7.2	.8573	.8579	.8585	.8591	.8597	.8603	.8609	.8615	.8621	.8627
7.3	.8633	.8639	.8645	.8651	.8657	.8663	.8669	.8675	.8681	.8686
7.4	.8692	.8698	.8704	.8710	.8716	.8722	.8727	.8733	.8739	.8745
7.5	.8751	.8756	.8762	.8768	.8774	.8779	.8785	.8791	.8797	.8802
7.6	.8808	.8814	.8820	.8825	.8831	.8837	.8842	.8848	.8854	.8859
7.7	.8865	.8871	.8876	.8882	.8887	.8893	.8899	.8904	.8910	.8915
7.8	.8921	.8927	.8932	.8938	.8943	.8949	.8954	.8960	.8965	.8971
7.9	.8976	.8982	.8987	.8993	.8998	.9004	.9009	.9015	.9020	.9025
8.0	.9031	.9036	.9042	.9047	.9053	.9058	.9063	.9069	.9074	.9079
8.1	.9085	.9090	.9096	.9101	.9106	.9112	.9117	.9122	.9128	.9133
8.2	.9138	.9143	.9149	.9154	.9159	.9165	.9170	.9175	.9180	.9186
8.3	.9191	.9196	.9201	.9206	.9212	.9217	.9222	.9227	.9232	.9238
8.4	.9243	.9248	.9253	.9258	.9263	.9269	.9274	.9279	.9284	.9289
8.5	.9294	.9299	.9304	.9309	.9315	.9320	.9325	.9330	.9335	.9340
8.6	.9345	.9350	.9555	.9360	.9365	.9370	.9375	.9380	.9385	.9390
8.7	.9395	.9400	.9405	.9410	.9415	.9420	.9425	.9430	.9435	.9440
8.8	.9445	.9450	.9455	.9460	.9465	.9469	.9474	.9479	.9484	.9489
8.9	.9494	.9499	.9504	.9509	.9513	.9518	.9523	.9528	.9533	.9538
9.0	.9542	.9547	.9552	.9557	.9562	.9566	.9571	.9576	.9581	.9586
9.1	.9590	.9595	.9600	.9605	.9609	.9614	.9619	.9624	.9628	.9633
9.2	.9638	.9643	.9647	.9652	.9657	.9661	.9666	.9671	.9675	.9680
9.3	.9685	.9689	.9694	.9699	.9703	.9708	.9713	.9717	.9722	.9727
9.4	.9731	.9736	.9741	.9745	.9750	.9754	.9759	.9763	.9768	.9773
9.5	.9777	.9782	.9786	.9791	.9795	.9800	.9805	.9809	.9814	.9818
9.6	.9823	.9827	.9832	.9836	.9841	.9845	.9850	.9854	.9859	.9863
9.7	.9868	.9872	.9877	.9881	.9886	.9890	.9894	.9899	.9903	.9908
9.8	.9912	.9917	.9921	.9926	.9930	.9934	.9939	.9943	.9948	.9952
9.9	.9956	.9961	.9965	.9969	.9974	.9978	.9983	.9987	.9991	.9996
x	0	1	2	3	4	5	6	7	8	9

TABLE 3. Values of Trigonometric Functions

Degrees	Radians	Sin	Cos	Tan	Cot	Sec	Csc		
0° 00′	.0000	.0000	1.0000	.0000	——	1.000	——	1.5708	**90° 00′**
10	029	029	000	029	343.8	000	343.8	679	50
20	058	058	000	058	171.9	000	171.9	650	40
30	.0087	.0087	1.0000	.0087	114.6	1.000	114.6	1.5621	30
40	116	116	.9999	116	85.94	000	85.95	592	20
50	145	145	999	145	68.75	000	68.76	563	10
1° 00′	.0175	.0175	.9998	.0175	57.29	1.000	57.30	1.5533	**89° 00′**
10	204	204	998	204	49.10	000	49.11	504	50
20	233	233	997	233	42.96	000	42.98	475	40
30	.0262	.0262	.9997	.0262	38.19	1.000	38.20	1.5446	30
40	291	291	996	291	34.37	000	34.38	417	20
50	320	320	995	320	31.24	001	31.26	388	10
2° 00′	.0349	.0349	.9994	.0349	28.64	1.001	28.65	1.5359	**88° 00′**
10	378	378	993	378	26.43	001	26.45	330	50
20	407	407	992	407	24.54	001	24.56	301	40
30	.0436	.0436	.9990	.0437	22.90	1.001	22.93	1.5272	30
40	465	465	989	466	21.47	001	21.49	243	20
50	495	494	988	495	20.21	001	20.23	213	10
3° 00′	.0524	.0523	.9986	.0524	19.08	1.001	19.11	1.5184	**87° 00′**
10	553	552	985	553	18.07	002	18.10	155	50
20	582	581	983	582	17.17	002	17.20	126	40
30	.0611	.0610	.9981	.0612	16.35	1.002	16.38	1.5097	30
40	640	640	980	641	15.60	002	15.64	068	20
50	669	669	978	670	14.92	002	14.96	039	10
4° 00′	.0698	.0698	.9976	.0699	14.30	1.002	14.34	1.5010	**86° 00′**
10	727	727	974	729	13.73	003	13.76	981	50
20	756	756	971	758	13.20	003	13.23	952	40
30	.0785	.0785	.9969	.0787	12.71	1.003	12.75	1.4923	30
40	814	814	967	816	12.25	003	12.29	893	20
50	844	843	964	846	11.83	004	11.87	864	10
5° 00′	.0873	.0872	.9962	.0875	11.43	1.004	11.47	1.4835	**85° 00′**
10	902	901	959	904	11.06	004	11.10	806	50
20	931	929	957	934	10.71	004	10.76	777	40
30	.0960	.0958	.9954	.0963	10.39	1.005	10.43	1.4748	30
40	989	987	951	992	10.08	005	10.13	719	20
50	.1018	.1016	948	.1022	9.788	005	9.839	690	10
6° 00′	.1047	.1045	.9945	.1051	9.514	1.006	9.567	1.4661	**84° 00′**
10	076	074	942	080	9.255	006	9.309	632	50
20	105	103	939	110	9.010	006	9.065	603	40
30	.1134	.1132	.9936	.1139	8.777	1.006	8.834	1.4573	30
40	164	161	932	169	8.556	007	8.614	544	20
50	193	190	929	198	8.345	007	8.405	515	10
7° 00′	.1222	.1219	.9925	.1228	8.144	1.008	8.206	1.4486	**83° 00′**
10	251	248	922	257	7.953	008	8.016	457	50
20	280	276	918	287	7.770	008	7.834	428	40
30	.1309	.1305	.9914	.1317	7.596	1.009	7.661	1.4399	30
40	338	334	911	346	7.429	009	7.496	370	20
50	367	363	907	376	7.269	009	7.337	341	10
8° 00′	.1396	.1392	.9903	.1405	7.115	1.010	7.185	1.4312	**82° 00′**
10	425	421	899	435	6.968	010	7.040	283	50
20	454	449	894	465	6.827	011	6.900	254	40
30	.1484	.1478	.9890	.1495	6.691	1.011	6.765	1.4224	30
40	513	507	886	524	6.561	012	6.636	195	20
50	542	536	881	554	6.435	012	6.512	166	10
9° 00′	.1571	.1564	.9877	.1584	6.314	1.012	6.392	1.4137	**81° 00′**
		Cos	Sin	Cot	Tan	Csc	Sec	Radians	Degrees

440

TABLE 3 (continued)

Degrees	Radians	Sin	Cos	Tan	Cot	Sec	Csc		
9° 00'	.1571	.1564	.9877	.1584	6.314	1.012	6.392	1.4137	**81° 00'**
10	600	593	872	614	197	013	277	108	50
20	629	622	868	644	084	013	166	079	40
30	.1658	.1650	.9863	.1673	5.976	1.014	6.059	1.4050	30
40	687	679	858	703	871	014	5.955	1.4021	20
50	716	708	853	733	769	015	855	992	10
10° 00'	.1745	.1736	.9848	.1763	5.671	1.015	5.759	1.3963	**80° 00'**
10	774	765	843	793	576	016	665	934	50
20	804	794	838	823	485	016	575	904	40
30	.1833	.1822	.9833	.1853	5.396	1.017	5.487	1.3875	30
40	862	851	827	883	309	018	403	846	20
50	891	880	822	914	226	018	320	817	10
11° 00'	.1920	.1908	.9816	.1944	5.145	1.019	5.241	1.3788	**79° 00'**
10	949	937	811	974	066	019	164	759	50
20	978	965	805	.2004	4.989	020	089	730	40
30	.2007	.1994	.9799	.2035	4.915	1.020	5.016	1.3701	30
40	036	.2022	793	065	843	021	4.945	672	20
50	065	051	787	095	773	022	876	643	10
12° 00'	.2094	.2079	.9781	.2126	4.705	1.022	4.810	1.3614	**78° 00'**
10	123	108	775	156	638	023	745	584	50
20	153	136	769	186	574	024	682	555	40
30	.2182	.2164	.9763	.2217	4.511	1.024	4.620	1.3526	30
40	211	193	757	247	449	025	560	497	20
50	240	221	750	278	390	026	502	468	10
13° 00'	.2269	.2250	.9744	.2309	4.331	1.026	4.445	1.3439	**77° 00'**
10	298	278	737	339	275	027	390	410	50
20	327	306	730	370	219	028	336	381	40
30	.2356	.2334	.9724	.2401	4.165	1.028	4.284	1.3352	30
40	385	363	717	432	113	029	232	323	20
50	414	391	710	462	061	030	182	294	10
14° 00'	.2443	.2419	.9703	.2493	4.011	1.031	4.134	1.3265	**76° 00'**
10	473	447	696	524	3.962	031	086	235	50
20	502	476	689	555	914	032	039	206	40
30	.2531	.2504	.9681	.2586	3.867	1.033	3.994	1.3177	30
40	560	532	674	617	821	034	950	148	20
50	589	560	667	648	776	034	906	119	10
15° 00'	.2618	.2588	.9659	.2679	3.732	1.035	3.864	1.3090	**75° 00'**
10	647	616	652	711	689	036	822	061	50
20	676	644	644	742	647	037	782	032	40
30	.2705	.2672	.9636	.2773	3.606	1.038	3.742	1.3003	30
40	734	700	628	805	566	039	703	974	20
50	763	728	621	836	526	039	665	945	10
16° 00'	.2793	.2756	.9613	.2867	3.487	1.040	3.628	1.2915	**74° 00'**
10	822	784	605	899	450	041	592	886	50
20	851	812	596	931	412	042	556	857	40
30	.2880	.2840	.9588	.2962	3.376	1.043	3.521	1.2828	30
40	909	868	580	994	340	044	487	799	20
50	938	896	572	.3026	305	045	453	770	10
17° 00'	.2967	.2924	.9563	.3057	3.271	1.046	3.420	1.2741	**73° 00'**
10	996	952	555	089	237	047	388	712	50
20	.3025	979	546	121	204	048	356	683	40
30	.3054	.3007	.9537	.3153	3.172	1.049	3.326	1.2654	30
40	083	035	528	185	140	049	295	625	20
50	113	062	520	217	108	050	265	595	10
18° 00'	.3142	.3090	.9511	.3249	3.078	1.051	3.236	1.2566	**72° 00'**
		Cos	Sin	Cot	Tan	Csc	Sec	Radians	Degrees

(Continued)

TABLE 3 (continued)

Degrees	Radians	Sin	Cos	Tan	Cot	Sec	Csc		
18° 00′	.3142	.3090	.9511	.3249	3.078	1.051	3.236	1.2566	**72° 00′**
10	171	118	502	281	047	052	207	537	50
20	200	145	492	314	018	053	179	508	40
30	.3229	.3173	.9483	.3346	2.989	1.054	3.152	1.2479	30
40	258	201	474	378	960	056	124	450	20
50	287	228	465	411	932	057	098	421	10
19° 00′	.3316	.3256	.9455	.3443	2.904	1.058	3.072	1.2392	**71° 00′**
10	345	283	446	476	877	059	046	363	50
20	374	311	436	508	850	060	021	334	40
30	.3403	.3338	.9426	.3541	2.824	1.061	2.996	1.2305	30
40	432	365	417	574	798	062	971	275	20
50	462	393	407	607	773	063	947	246	10
20° 00′	.3491	.3420	.9397	.3640	2.747	1.064	2.924	1.2217	**70° 00′**
10	520	448	387	673	723	065	901	188	50
20	549	475	377	706	699	066	878	159	40
30	.3578	.3502	.9367	.3739	2.675	1.068	2.855	1.2130	30
40	607	529	356	772	651	069	833	101	20
50	636	557	346	805	628	070	812	072	10
21° 00′	.3665	.3584	.9336	.3839	2.605	1.071	2.790	1.2043	**69° 00′**
10	694	611	325	872	583	072	769	1.2014	50
20	723	638	315	906	560	074	749	985	40
30	.3752	.3665	.9304	.3939	2.539	1.075	2.729	1.1956	30
40	782	692	293	973	517	076	709	926	20
50	811	719	283	.4006	496	077	689	897	10
22° 00′	.3840	.3746	.9272	.4040	2.475	1.079	2.669	1.1868	**68° 00′**
10	869	773	261	074	455	080	650	839	50
20	898	800	250	108	434	081	632	810	40
30	.3927	.3827	.9239	.4142	2.414	1.082	2.613	1.1781	30
40	956	854	228	176	394	084	595	752	20
50	985	881	216	210	375	085	577	723	10
23° 00′	.4014	.3907	.9205	.4245	2.356	1.086	2.559	1.1694	**67° 00′**
10	043	934	194	279	337	088	542	665	50
20	072	961	182	314	318	089	525	636	40
30	.4102	.3987	.9171	.4348	2.300	1.090	2.508	1.1606	30
40	131	.4014	159	383	282	092	491	577	20
50	160	041	147	417	264	093	475	548	10
24° 00′	.4189	.4067	.9135	.4452	2.246	1.095	2.459	1.1519	**66° 00′**
10	218	094	124	487	229	096	443	490	50
20	247	120	112	522	211	097	427	461	40
30	.4276	.4147	.9100	.4557	2.194	1.099	2.411	1.1432	30
40	305	173	088	592	177	100	396	403	20
50	334	200	075	628	161	102	381	374	10
25° 00′	.4363	.4226	.9063	.4663	2.145	1.103	2.366	1.1345	**65° 00′**
10	392	253	051	699	128	105	352	316	50
20	422	279	038	734	112	106	337	286	40
30	.4451	.4305	.9026	.4770	2.097	1.108	2.323	1.1257	30
40	480	331	013	806	081	109	309	228	20
50	509	358	001	841	066	111	295	199	10
26° 00′	.4538	.4384	.8988	.4877	2.050	1.113	2.281	1.1170	**64° 00′**
10	567	410	975	913	035	114	268	141	50
20	596	436	962	950	020	116	254	112	40
30	.4625	.4462	.8949	.4986	2.006	1.117	2.241	1.1083	30
40	654	488	936	.5022	1.991	119	228	054	20
50	683	514	923	059	977	121	215	1.1025	10
27° 00′	.4712	.4540	.8910	.5095	1.963	1.122	2.203	1.0996	**63° 00′**
		Cos	Sin	Cot	Tan	Csc	Sec	Radians	Degrees

442

TABLE 3 (continued)

Degrees	Radians	Sin	Cos	Tan	Cot	Sec	Csc		
27° 00'	.4712	.4540	.8910	.5095	1.963	1.122	2.203	1.0996	**63° 00'**
10	741	566	897	132	949	124	190	966	50
20	771	592	884	169	935	126	178	937	40
30	.4800	.4617	.8870	.5206	1.921	1.127	2.166	1.0908	30
40	829	643	857	243	907	129	154	879	20
50	858	669	843	280	894	131	142	850	10
28° 00'	.4887	.4695	.8829	.5317	1.881	1.133	2.130	1.0821	**62° 00'**
10	916	720	816	354	868	134	118	792	50
20	945	746	802	392	855	136	107	763	40
30	.4974	.4772	.8788	.5430	1.842	1.138	2.096	1.0734	30
40	.5003	797	774	467	829	140	085	705	20
50	032	823	760	505	816	142	074	676	10
29° 00'	.5061	.4848	.8746	.5543	1.804	1.143	2.063	1.0647	**61° 00'**
10	091	874	732	581	792	145	052	617	50
20	120	899	718	619	780	147	041	588	40
30	.5149	.4924	.8704	.5658	1.767	1.149	2.031	1.0559	30
40	178	950	689	696	756	151	020	530	20
50	207	975	675	735	744	153	010	501	10
30° 00'	.5236	.5000	.8660	.5774	1.732	1.155	2.000	1.0472	**60° 00'**
10	265	025	646	812	720	157	1.990	443	50
20	294	050	631	851	709	159	980	414	40
30	.5323	.5075	.8616	.5890	1.698	1.161	1.970	1.0385	30
40	352	100	601	930	686	163	961	356	20
50	381	125	587	969	675	165	951	327	10
31° 00'	.5411	.5150	.8572	.6009	1.664	1.167	1.942	1.0297	**59° 00'**
10	440	175	557	048	653	169	932	268	50
20	469	200	542	088	643	171	923	239	40
30	.5498	.5225	.8526	.6128	1.632	1.173	1.914	1.0210	30
40	527	250	511	168	621	175	905	181	20
50	556	275	496	208	611	177	896	152	10
32° 00'	.5585	.5299	.8480	.6249	1.600	1.179	1.887	1.0123	**58° 00'**
10	614	324	465	289	590	181	878	094	50
20	643	348	450	330	580	184	870	065	40
30	.5672	.5373	.8434	.6371	1.570	1.186	1.861	1.0036	30
40	701	398	418	412	560	188	853	1.0007	20
50	730	422	403	453	550	190	844	977	10
33° 00'	.5760	.5446	.8387	.6494	1.540	1.192	1.836	.9948	**57° 00'**
10	789	471	371	536	530	195	828	919	50
20	818	495	355	577	520	197	820	890	40
30	.5847	.5519	.8339	.6619	1.511	1.199	1.812	.9861	30
40	876	544	323	661	501	202	804	832	20
50	905	568	307	703	1.492	204	796	803	10
34° 00'	.5934	.5592	.8290	.6745	1.483	1.206	1.788	.9774	**56° 00'**
10	963	616	274	787	473	209	781	745	50
20	992	640	258	830	464	211	773	716	40
30	.6021	.5664	.8241	.6873	1.455	1.213	1.766	.9687	30
40	050	688	225	916	446	216	758	657	20
50	080	712	208	959	437	218	751	628	10
35° 00'	.6109	.5736	.8192	.7002	1.428	1.221	1.743	.9599	**55° 00'**
10	138	760	175	046	419	223	736	570	50
20	167	783	158	089	411	226	729	541	40
30	.6196	.5807	.8141	.7133	1.402	1.228	1.722	.9512	30
40	225	831	124	177	393	231	715	483	20
50	254	854	107	221	385	233	708	454	10
36° 00'	.6283	.5878	.8090	.7265	1.376	1.236	1.701	.9425	**54° 00'**
		Cos	Sin	Cot	Tan	Csc	Sec	Radians	Degrees

(Continued)

443

TABLE 3 (continued)

Degrees	Radians	Sin	Cos	Tan	Cot	Sec	Csc		
36° 00'	.6283	.5878	.8090	.7265	1.376	1.236	1.701	.9425	**54° 00'**
10	312	901	073	310	368	239	695	396	50
20	341	925	056	355	360	241	688	367	40
30	.6370	.5948	.8039	.7400	1.351	1.244	1.681	.9338	30
40	400	972	021	445	343	247	675	308	20
50	429	995	004	490	335	249	668	279	10
37° 00'	.6458	.6018	.7986	.7536	1.327	1.252	1.662	.9250	**53° 00'**
10	487	041	969	581	319	255	655	221	50
20	516	065	951	627	311	258	649	192	40
30	.6545	.6088	.7934	.7673	1.303	1.260	1.643	.9163	30
40	574	111	916	720	295	263	636	134	20
50	603	134	898	766	288	266	630	105	10
38° 00'	.6632	.6157	.7880	.7813	1.280	1.269	1.624	.9076	**52° 00'**
10	661	180	862	860	272	272	618	047	50
20	690	202	844	907	265	275	612	.9018	40
30	.6720	.6225	.7826	.7954	1.257	1.278	1.606	.8988	30
40	749	248	808	.8002	250	281	601	959	20
50	778	271	790	050	242	284	595	930	10
39° 00'	.6807	.6293	.7771	.8098	1.235	1.287	1.589	.8901	**51° 00'**
10	836	316	753	146	228	290	583	872	50
20	865	338	735	195	220	293	578	843	40
30	.6894	.6361	.7716	.8243	1.213	1.296	1.572	.8814	30
40	923	383	698	292	206	299	567	785	20
50	952	406	679	342	199	302	561	756	10
40° 00'	.6981	.6428	.7660	.8391	1.192	1.305	1.556	.8727	**50° 00'**
10	.7010	450	642	441	185	309	550	698	50
20	039	472	623	491	178	312	545	668	40
30	.7069	.6494	.7604	.8541	1.171	1.315	1.540	.8639	30
40	098	517	585	591	164	318	535	610	20
50	127	539	566	642	157	322	529	581	10
41° 00'	.7156	.6561	.7547	.8693	1.150	1.325	1.524	.8552	**49° 00'**
10	185	583	528	744	144	328	519	523	50
20	214	604	509	796	137	332	514	494	40
30	.7243	.6626	.7490	.8847	1.130	1.335	1.509	.8465	30
40	272	648	470	899	124	339	504	436	20
50	301	670	451	952	117	342	499	407	10
42° 00'	.7330	.6691	.7431	.9004	1.111	1.346	1.494	.8378	**48° 00'**
10	359	713	412	057	104	349	490	348	50
20	389	734	392	110	098	353	485	319	40
30	.7418	.6756	.7373	.9163	1.091	1.356	1.480	.8290	30
40	447	777	353	217	085	360	476	261	20
50	476	799	333	271	079	364	471	232	10
43° 00'	.7505	.6820	.7314	.9325	1.072	1.367	1.466	.8203	**47° 00'**
10	534	841	294	380	066	371	462	174	50
20	563	862	274	435	060	375	457	145	40
30	.7592	.6884	.7254	.9490	1.054	1.379	1.453	.8116	30
40	621	905	234	545	048	382	448	087	20
50	650	926	214	601	042	386	444	058	10
44° 00'	.7679	.6947	.7193	.9657	1.036	1.390	1.440	.8029	**46° 00'**
10	709	967	173	713	030	394	435	999	50
20	738	988	153	770	024	398	431	970	40
30	.7767	.7009	.7133	.9827	1.018	1.402	1.427	.7941	30
40	796	030	112	884	012	406	423	912	20
50	825	050	092	942	006	410	418	883	10
45° 00'	.7854	.7071	.7071	1.000	1.000	1.414	1.414	.7854	**45° 00'**
		Cos	Sin	Cot	Tan	Csc	Sec	Radians	Degrees

TABLE 4. Exponential Functions

x	e^x	e^{-x}	x	e^x	e^{-x}	x	e^x	e^{-x}
0.00	1.0000	1.0000	0.55	1.7333	0.5769	3.6	36.598	0.0273
0.01	1.0101	0.9900	0.60	1.8221	0.5488	3.7	40.447	0.0247
0.02	1.0202	0.9802	0.65	1.9155	0.5220	3.8	44.701	0.0224
0.03	1.0305	0.9704	0.70	2.0138	0.4966	3.9	49.402	0.0202
0.04	1.0408	0.9608	0.75	2.1170	0.4724	4.0	54.598	0.0183
0.05	1.0513	0.9512	0.80	2.2255	0.4493	4.1	60.340	0.0166
0.06	1.0618	0.9418	0.85	2.3396	0.4274	4.2	66.686	0.0150
0.07	1.0725	0.9324	0.90	2.4596	0.4066	4.3	73.700	0.0136
0.08	1.0833	0.9231	0.95	2.5857	0.3867	4.4	81.451	0.0123
0.09	1.0942	0.9139	1.0	2.7183	0.3679	4.5	90.017	0.0111
0.10	1.1052	0.9048	1.1	3.0042	0.3329	4.6	99.484	0.0101
0.11	1.1163	0.8958	1.2	3.3201	0.3012	4.7	109.95	0.0091
0.12	1.1275	0.8869	1.3	3.6693	0.2725	4.8	121.51	0.0082
0.13	1.1388	0.8781	1.4	4.0552	0.2466	4.9	134.29	0.0074
0.14	1.1503	0.8694	1.5	4.4817	0.2231	5	148.41	0.0067
0.15	1.1618	0.8607	1.6	4.9530	0.2019	6	403.43	0.0025
0.16	1.1735	0.8521	1.7	5.4739	0.1827	7	1096.6	0.0009
0.17	1.1853	0.8437	1.8	6.0496	0.1653	8	2981.0	0.0003
0.18	1.1972	0.8353	1.9	6.6859	0.1496	9	8103.1	0.0001
0.19	1.2092	0.8270	2.0	7.3891	0.1353	10	22026	0.00005
0.20	1.2214	0.8187	2.1	8.1662	0.1225	11	59874	0.00002
0.21	1.2337	0.8106	2.2	9.0250	0.1108	12	162,754	0.000006
0.22	1.2461	0.8025	2.3	9.9742	0.1003	13	442,413	0.000002
0.23	1.2586	0.7945	2.4	11.023	0.0907	14	1,202,604	0.0000008
0.24	1.2712	0.7866	2.5	12.182	0.0821	15	3,269,017	0.0000003
0.25	1.2840	0.7788	2.6	13.464	0.0743			
0.26	1.2969	0.7711	2.7	14.880	0.0672			
0.27	1.3100	0.7634	2.8	16.445	0.0608			
0.28	1.3231	0.7558	2.9	18.174	0.0550			
0.29	1.3364	0.7483	3.0	20.086	0.0498			
0.30	1.3499	0.7408	3.1	22.198	0.0450			
0.35	1.4191	0.7047	3.2	24.533	0.0408			
0.40	1.4918	0.6703	3.3	27.113	0.0369			
0.45	1.5683	0.6376	3.4	29.964	0.0334			
0.50	1.6487	0.6065	3.5	33.115	0.0302			

TABLE 5. Factorials and Large Powers of 2

n	n!	2^n
0	1	1
1	1	2
2	2	4
3	6	8
4	24	16
5	120	32
6	720	64
7	5040	128
8	40,320	256
9	362,880	512
10	3,628,800	1024
11	39,916,800	2048
12	479,001,600	4096
13	6,227,020,800	8192
14	87,178,291,200	16,384
15	1,307,674,368,000	32,768
16	20,922,789,888,000	65,536
17	355,687,428,096,000	131,072
18	6,402,373,705,728,000	262,144
19	121,645,100,408,832,000	524,288
20	2,432,902,008,176,640,000	1,048,576

TABLE 6. Tables of Measures

LENGTH

1 *kilo*meter (km) = 1000 meters (m)
1 *hecto*meter (hm) = 100 meters
1 *deka*meter (dam) =   10 meters
1 *deci*meter (dm) =   0.1 meter
1 *centi*meter (cm) = 0.01 meter
1 *milli*meter (mm) = 0.001 meter

MASS OR WEIGHT

1 *kilo*gram (kg)   = 1000 grams (g)
1 *hecto*gram (hg) =   100 grams
1 *deka*gram (dag) =   10 grams
1 *deci*gram (dg) =   0.1 gram
1 *centi*gram (dg) = 0.01 gram
1 metric ton (MT or t) = 1000 kilograms

AREA

1 *hect*are (ha) = 100 are (a), or 10,000 sq m (m^2)
1 are (a)   = 100 sq m (m^2)
1 *cent*are (ca) = 0.01 are, or 1 m^2
The word "are" is pronounced "AIR."

VOLUME

1000 cubic centimeters (cc or cm^3) = 1 liter (ℓ)
1 cubic centimeter (cc) = 1 milliliter (mℓ)
1 mℓ of water weighs 1 g
1 stere = 1 cubic meter

Metric-American Conversions (Approximate)

LENGTH

1 m = 39.37 in = 3.3 ft
1 in. = 2.54 cm
1 km = 0.62 mi
1 mi = 1.6 km
1 cm = 3/8 in.

MASS OR WEIGHT

1 kg = 2.2 lb
1 MT = 1.1 tons
1 lb = 454 g
1 oz = 28 g

AREA

1 hectare = 2.47 acres
1 are = 120 sq yd

VOLUME

1 liter = 1.057 qt = 2.1 pt
1 cup = 240 mℓ
1 ounce (liquid) = 30 mℓ
1 gallon = 3.78 liters
1 tablespoon = 15 mℓ
1 teaspoon = 5 mℓ

Answers

Exercise Set 1.1, p. 3

1. -8, $^-8$ **3.** $\frac{10}{3}$, $-(-\frac{10}{3})$ **5.** $-3x$, ^-3x **7.** $-(a+b)$, $^-(a+b)$ **9.** 12 **11.** 47 **13.** $\frac{1}{3}$ **15.** $-\frac{3}{2}$ **17.** -10.3
19. -110 **21.** $-\frac{4}{5}$ **23** -226 **25.** -4 **27.** $\frac{39}{10}$ **29.** -24 **31.** -1 **33.** -30 **35.** $-\frac{204}{35}$ **37.** -56.8 **39.** $\frac{20}{3}$ **41.** -42
43. $-\frac{833}{5}$ **45.** 5 **47.** -6 **49.** -5 **51.** $-\frac{1}{5}$ **53.** -4 **55.** 18 **57.** $\frac{7}{3}$ **59.** -20 **61.** -13.72 **63.** -10.43 **65.** -0.234312
67. 50.882 **69.** -3.051 **71.** 21266.506 **73.** 0.733

Exercise Set 1.2, p. 7

1. 2^{-1} **3.** 1 **5.** 4^3 **7.** $6x^5$ **9.** $15a^{-1}b^5$ **11.** $72x^5$ **13.** $-18x^7yz$ **15.** b^3 **17.** x^3y^{-3} **19.** 1 **21.** $3ab^2$ **23.** $\frac{4}{7}xyz^{-5}$
25. $8a^3b^6$ **27.** $16x^{12}$ **29.** $-16x^{12}$ **31.** $36a^4b^6c^2$ **33.** $\frac{1}{25}c^2d^4$ **35.** 1 **37.** 32 **39.** $\frac{27}{4}a^8b^{-10}c^{18}$ **41.** $\frac{3}{4}xy$ **43.** 5.8×10^7
45. 3.65×10^5 **47.** 2.7×10^{-6} **49.** 2.7×10^{-2} **51.** 5.0×10^{-2} **53.** 0.0005 **55.** 7,800,000 **57.** 0.000000854

Exercise Set 1.3, p. 9

1. $3x^2y - 5xy^2 + 7xy + 2$ **3.** $-10pq^2 - 5p^2q + 7pq - 4p + 2q + 3$ **5.** $3x + 2y - 2z - 3$ **7.** $5x\sqrt{y} - 4y\sqrt{x} - \frac{2}{5}$

9. $-5x^3 + 7x^2 - 3x + 6$ **11.** $-2x^2 + 6x - 2$ **13.** $6a - 5b - 2c + 4d$ **15.** $x^4 - 3x^3 - 4x^2 + 9x - 3$

17. $9x\sqrt{y} - 3y\sqrt{x} + 9.1$ **19.** $-1.047p^2q - 2.479pq^2 + 8.879pq - 104.144$ **21.** $-37.048p^2\sqrt{q} + 0.063\sqrt[3]{pq} + 0.2098\sqrt{p}$

23. $8.1172xy^{-2} - 2.1057xy - 2.9958\sqrt{xy} - 1.101$

Exercise Set 1.4, p. 11

1. $6x^3 + 4x^2 + 32x - 64$ **3.** $4a^3b^2 - 10a^2b^2 + 3ab^3 + 4ab^2 - 6b^3 + 4a^2b - 2ab + 3b^2$ **5.** $6y^2 + 5y - 6$ **7.** $4x^2 + 8xy + 3y^2$ **9.** $12x^3 + x^2y - \frac{3}{2}xy - \frac{1}{8}y^2$ **11.** $2x^3 - 2\sqrt{2}x^2y - \sqrt{2}xy^2 + 2y^3$ **13.** $4x^2 + 12xy + 9y^2$ **15.** $4x^4 - 12x^2y + 9y^2$ **17.** $4x^6 + 12x^3y^2 + 9y^4$ **19.** $\frac{1}{4}x^4 - \frac{3}{5}x^2y + \frac{9}{25}y^2$ **21.** $0.25x^2 + 0.70xy^2 + 0.49y^4$ **23.** $9x^2 - 4y^2$ **25.** $x^4 - y^2z^2$ **27.** $9x^4 - 2$ **29.** $4x^2 + 12xy + 9y^2 - 16$ **31.** $x^4 + 6x^2y + 9y^2 - y^4$ **33.** $x^4 - 1$ **35.** $16x^4 - y^4$ **37.** $0.002601x^2 + 0.00408xy + 0.0016y^2$ **39.** $2462.0358x^2 - 945.0214x - 38.908$ **41.** $0.006798x^2 + 0.91882xy + 2.941952y^2$

Exercise Set 1.5, p. 14

1. $3ab(6a - 5b)$ **3.** $(a + c)(b - 2)$ **5.** $(x + 6)(x + 3)$ **7.** $(3x - 5)(3x + 5)$ **9.** $4x(y^2 - z)(y^2 + z)$ **11.** $(y - 3)^2$ **13.** $(1 - 4x)^2$ **15.** $(2x - \sqrt{5})(2x + \sqrt{5})$ **17.** $(xy - 7)^2$ **19.** $4a(x + 7)(x - 2)$ **21.** $(a + b + c)(a + b - c)$ **23.** $(x + y - a - b)(x + y + a + b)$ **25.** $5(y^2 + 4x^2)(y - 2x)(y + 2x)$ **27.** $(x + 2)(x^2 - 2x + 4)$ **29.** $3(x - \frac{1}{2})(x^2 + \frac{1}{2}x + \frac{1}{4})$ **31.** $(x + 0.1)(x^2 - 0.1x + 0.01)$ **33.** $3(z - 2)(z^2 + 2z + 4)$ **35.** $(x + 4.19524)(x - 4.19524)$ **37.** $37(x + 0.626y)(x - 0.626y)$

Exercise Set 1.6, p. 17

1. 12 **3.** -6 **5.** 8 **7.** $\frac{4}{5}$ **9.** 2 **11.** $-\frac{3}{2}$ **13.** -2 **15.** $\frac{3}{2}, \frac{2}{3}$ **17.** $0, 1, -2$ **19.** $\frac{2}{3}, -1$ **21.** $4, 1$ **23.** $x > 3$ **25.** $x \geqslant \frac{-5}{12}$ **27.** 0.7892 **29.** -0.7848

Exercise Set 1.7, p. 21

1. $0, 1$ **3.** $0, 3, -2$ **5.** $\frac{x - 2}{x + 3}; -3$ **7.** $\frac{1}{x - y}$ **9.** $\frac{(x + 5)(2x + 3)}{7x}$ **11.** $\frac{a + 2}{a - 5}$ **13.** $m + n$ **15.** $\frac{3(x - 4)}{2(x + 4)}$ **17.** $\frac{1}{x + y}$ **19.** $\frac{x - y - z}{x + y + z}$ **21.** 1 **23.** $\frac{y - 2}{y - 1}$ **25.** $\frac{x + y}{2x - 3y}$ **27.** $\frac{3x - 4}{x^2 - 4}$ **29.** $\frac{3y - 10}{(y - 5)(y + 4)}$ **31.** $\frac{4x - 8y}{x^2 - y^2}$ **33.** $\frac{3x - 4}{(x - 2)(x - 1)}$ **35.** $\frac{5a^2 + 10ab - 4b^2}{(a - b)(a + b)}$ **37.** $\frac{11x^2 - 18x + 8}{(x + 2)(x - 2)^2}$ **39.** 0 **41.** $\frac{x + y}{x}$ **43.** $\frac{x^2 - 1}{x^2 + 1}$ **45.** $\frac{c^2 - 2c + 4}{c}$ **47.** $\frac{xy}{x - y}$ **49.** $x - y$ **51.** $\frac{x^2 - y^2}{xy}$ **53.** $\frac{1 + a}{1 - a}$ **55.** $\frac{b + a}{b - a}$

Exercise Set 1.8, p. 26

1. $x < 3$ **3.** $x > \frac{3}{4}$ **5.** 11 **7.** $4|x|$ **9.** $|b + 1|$ **11.** $-3x$ **13.** $|x - 2|$ **15.** 2 **17.** $6\sqrt{5}$ **19.** $3\sqrt[3]{2}$ **21.** $\frac{8|c|\sqrt{2}}{d^2}$ **23.** $3\sqrt{2}$ **25.** $2x^2y\sqrt{6}$ **27.** $3x\sqrt[3]{4y}$ **29.** $2(x + 4)\sqrt[3]{(x + 4)^2}$ **31.** $\sqrt{7b}$ **33.** 2 **35.** $\frac{1}{2x}$ **37.** $\sqrt{a + b}$ **39.** $\frac{3a}{2\sqrt{2b}}$ **41.** $\frac{y}{z}\sqrt[3]{\frac{4x^2}{25z}}$ **43.** $8x^2\sqrt[3]{2}$ **45.** $ab^2x^2y\sqrt{a}$ **47.** $10.124x^2y$ **49.** $\frac{0.5933a}{\sqrt{b}}$ **51.** All positive n

53. x, y both positive; both negative; one or both 0.

Exercise Set 1.9, p. 29

1. $-12\sqrt{5} - 2\sqrt{2}$ **3.** $19\sqrt[3]{x^2} - 3x$ **5.** $4y\sqrt{3} - 2y\sqrt{6}$ **7.** 1   **9.** $3m^2y - 5m\sqrt{xy} - 2x$ **11.** x **13.** $\dfrac{3(3 - \sqrt{5})}{2}$ **15.** $\dfrac{2\sqrt[3]{6}}{3}$

17. $\dfrac{8x - 20\sqrt{xy} - 6x\sqrt{y} + 15y\sqrt{x}}{4x - 25y}$ **19.** $\dfrac{2 - 5a}{6(\sqrt{2} - \sqrt{5a})}$ **21.** $\dfrac{x}{x + 2 - 2\sqrt{x + 1}}$ **23.** $\dfrac{a}{3(\sqrt{a + 3} + \sqrt{3})}$

Exercise Set 1.10, p. 31

1. $\sqrt[4]{x^3}$ **3.** $(\sqrt[4]{16})^3$ or $\sqrt[4]{(2^4)^3}$ or 8   **5.** $\dfrac{x}{y}\sqrt[4]{xy}$ **7.** $\sqrt{a^3b^{-1}}$ or $\dfrac{a}{b}\sqrt{ab}$ **9.** $20^{\frac{2}{3}}$ **11.** $13^{\frac{3}{4}}$ **13.** $11^{\frac{1}{6}}$ **13.** $5^{\frac{5}{6}}$ **17.** 4   **19.** $2y^2$

21. $(a^2 + b^2)^{\frac{1}{3}}$ **23.** $3ab^3$ **25.** $\dfrac{m^2n^4}{2}$ **27.** $8a^{\frac{4}{3}}$ or $8a^2$ **29.** $\dfrac{x^{-3}}{3^{-1}b^2}$ or $\dfrac{3}{x^3b^2}$ **31.** $xy^{\frac{1}{3}}$ or $x\sqrt[3]{y}$ **33.** $\sqrt[6]{288}$ **35.** $\sqrt[12]{x^{11}y^7}$

37. $a\sqrt[6]{a^5}$ **39.** $(a + x)^{\frac{1}{12}}\sqrt[12]{(a + x)^{11}}$ **41.** 24.685   **43.** 43.138   **45.** 32.942

Exercise Set 1.11, p. 33

1. 12 yd   **3.** 48 hr   **5.** 3 g   **7.** 8 m   **9.** 12 ft³   **11.** $\dfrac{7}{10}\dfrac{\text{kg}^2}{\text{m}^2}$ **13.** $720 \dfrac{\text{lb-mi}^2}{\text{hr}^2\text{-ft}}$ **15.** $\dfrac{15}{2}\dfrac{\text{cm}^5\text{-kg}}{\text{sec}^3}$ **17.** 6 ft   **19.** 172,800 sec

21. 600 g/cm   **23.** 2,160,000 cm²   **25.** 150 ¢/hr   **27.** 5,865,696,000,000 mi/yr   **29.** 1631.3 m/min   **31.** 1638.4 km²

Chapter 1 Test, or Review, p. 34

1. 14   **3.** 63   **5.** 24   **7.** 0.000321   **9.** 2×10^{-5} **11.** $\frac{2}{3}x^3yz^{-7}$ **13.** -2 **15.** 2   **17.** $\sqrt[5]{a^3}$ **19.** 6, -3 **21.** -2, 1

23. $\dfrac{2a}{a^2 - 1}$ **25.** 166.7 m/min

Exercise Set 2.1, p. 40

1. Yes   **3.** No   **5.** $\{0, 3\}$ **7.** $\{0, 2, -\frac{1}{3}\}$ **9.** $\{\frac{4}{5}, -\frac{2}{3}, 1\}$ **11.** $\{\frac{1}{2}, 0, -3\}$ **13.** $\{-2, 1, -1\}$ **15.** $\{-2\}$ **17.** $\{6\}$ **19.** ϕ **21.** ϕ

23. $\{8, -5\}$ **25.** $\{\frac{5}{3}\}$ **27.** $\{0, 2.1522\}$ **29.** -2.9553 **31.** 0.9191   **33.** $\{2.8454, -0.0055842, 5.3593\}$

Exercise Set 2.2, p. 47

1. $w = \dfrac{P - 2l}{2}$ **3.** $I = \dfrac{E}{R}$ **5.** $T_1 = \dfrac{T_2P_1V_1}{P_2V_2}$ **7.** $v_1 = \dfrac{H}{Sm} + v_2$ **9.** $p = \dfrac{Fm}{m - F}$ **11.** $x = \dfrac{5 + ab}{a - b}$ **13.** $x = -\dfrac{a}{9}$ **15.** 44%

17. 6%   **19.** $8000, $8480   **21.** $650   **23.** 26°, 130°, 24°   **25.** 68 m, 93 m   **27.** 91%   **29.** 2 cm   **31.** 810,000

33. 32 mph   **35.** 12 km/h   **37.** $1\frac{34}{71}$ hr   **39.** 2.97 hr, 6.12 hr   **41.** (a) $1080; (b) $1081.60; (c) $1082.43; (d) $1083.28

43. 60 km

Exercise Set 2.3, p. 53

1. $\pm\sqrt{7}$ **3.** $\pm\dfrac{\sqrt{5}}{3}$ **5.** $\pm\sqrt{\dfrac{b}{a}}$. **7.** $7 \pm \sqrt{5}$ **9.** $h \pm \sqrt{a}$ **11.** $-3 \pm \sqrt{5}$ **13.** $\{3, -10\}$ **15.** $\dfrac{2 \pm \sqrt{14}}{5}$ **17.** $-5, \frac{3}{2}$ **19.** $1, -5$

21. $2, -\frac{1}{2}$ **23.** $-1, -\frac{5}{3}$ **25.** $6 \pm \sqrt{33}$ **27.** $2, -\frac{3}{2}$ **29.** $\dfrac{-3 \pm \sqrt{41}}{2}$ **31.** $\frac{3}{2}, \frac{2}{3}$ **33.** $-0.1 \pm \sqrt{.31}$ **35.** $\dfrac{-1 \pm \sqrt{1 + 4\sqrt{2}}}{2}$

37. $\dfrac{-\sqrt{5} \pm \sqrt{5 + 4\sqrt{3}}}{2}$ **39.** $\dfrac{\sqrt{6} \pm \sqrt{6 + 8\sqrt{10}}}{4}$ **41.** $-2, \frac{3}{4}$ **43.** $\dfrac{1 \pm \sqrt{113}}{2}$ **45.** $3 \pm \sqrt{5}$ **47.** No real solution **49.** Two real

solutions **51.** $x^2 - 16 = 0$ **53.** $x^2 + 10x + 25 = 0$ **55.** $x^2 + \frac{3}{4}x + \frac{1}{8} = 0$ **57.** $x^2 - \left(\dfrac{k}{3} + \dfrac{m}{4}\right)x + \dfrac{km}{12} = 0$ or

$12x^2 - (4k + 3m)x + km = 0$ **59.** $x^2 - \sqrt{3}x - 6 = 0$ **61.** $1.175, -.4254$ **63.** $1.869, -0.3251$

65. $x = \dfrac{-y \pm \sqrt{108 - 47y^2}}{6}$ **67.** $\frac{1}{2}$

Exercise Set 2.4, p. 56

1. $d = \sqrt{\dfrac{kM_1M_2}{F}}$ **3.** $t = \sqrt{\dfrac{2S}{a}}$ **5.** $t = \dfrac{-v_0 \pm \sqrt{v_0^2 - 64s}}{-32}$ **7.** $s = \dfrac{-R + \sqrt{R^2 + 4cL}}{2L}$ **9.** $2, -\dfrac{3}{k}$ **11.** $\dfrac{1}{m + n}, \dfrac{-2}{m + n}$

13. $1, \dfrac{1}{1 - k}$ **15.** (a) $4y, -y$; (b) $-x, \dfrac{x}{4}$ **17.** 2 ft **19.** 4.685 cm **21.** A: 15 mph; B: 20 mph **23.** (a) 3.91 sec; (b) 1.906

sec; (c) 79.6 m **25.** 7 **27.** 12 **29.** 3.237 cm **31.** 3 cm $\times$ 4 cm

Exercise Set 2.5, p. 59

1. $\frac{5}{3}$ **3.** $\pm\sqrt{2}$ **5.** $\emptyset$ **7.** 4 **9.** $\emptyset$ **11.** -6 **13.** $3, -1$ **15.** $\frac{80}{9}$ **17.** $5 \pm 2\sqrt{2}$ **19.** $-\frac{8}{9}$ **21.** $m = \dfrac{gT^2}{4\pi^2}$; $g = \dfrac{4m\pi^2}{T^2}$

23. 66.446 -1.0827

Exercise Set 2.6, p. 62

1. $1, 81$ **3.** $\pm\sqrt{5}$ **5.** $-27, 8$ **7.** 16 **9.** $7, 5, -1, 1$ **11.** $1, 4, \dfrac{5 \pm \sqrt{37}}{2}$ **13.** $\pm\sqrt{2 + \sqrt{6}}$ **15.** $-\frac{1}{2}, \frac{1}{3}$ **17.** $-1, 2$

19. $-1 \pm \sqrt{3}\ \dfrac{9 \pm \sqrt{89}}{2}$ **21.** $\frac{100}{99}$ **23.** $-\frac{6}{7}$ **25.** 132.66 ft **27.** 2.0486

Exercise Set 2.7, p. 66

1. $y = \frac{3}{2}x$ **3.** $y = \dfrac{0.0015}{x^2}$ **5.** $y = \dfrac{xz}{w}$ **7.** $y = \dfrac{5}{4}\dfrac{xz}{w^2}$ **9.** y is doubled **11.** y is multiplied by $\dfrac{1}{n^2}$ **13.** 532,500 tons

15. L is multiplied by 16 **17.** 68.56 m **19.** If u varies inversely as v, then $u = \dfrac{k}{v}$. Then $\dfrac{1}{u} = \dfrac{v}{k} = \left(\dfrac{1}{k}\right)v$.

Chapter 2 Test, or Review, p. 67

1. -1 **3.** $\frac{4}{3}, -2$ **5.** $19, 20, 22$ **7.** 4.5 **9.** Two real number solutions **11.** $2x^2 + 7x + 3 = 0$ **13.** $250\,\text{km/hr}, 600\,\text{km/hr}$
15. $0, 3$ **17.** $s = 16t^2, 7\frac{1}{2}\,\text{sec}$

Exercise Set 3.1, p. 72

1. $(-1, 0)$, $(-1, 1)$, $(-1, 2)$, $(0, 1)$, $(0, 2)$, $(1, 2)$ **3.** $(-1, -1)$, $(-1, 0)$, $(-1, 1)$, $(-1, 2)$, $(0, 0)$, $(0, 1)$, $(0, 2)$, $(1, 1)$, $(1, 2)$, $(2, 2)$
5. $(-1, -1)$, $(0, 0)$, $(1, 1)$, $(2, 2)$ **7.** $(0, a)$, $(0, b)$, $(0, c)$, $(2, a)$, $(2, b)$, $(2, c)$, $(4, a)$, $(4, b)$, $(4, c)$, $(5, a)$, $(5, b)$, $(5, c)$
9. Domain $\{0, 1\}$, range $\{0, 1, 2\}$ **11.** Horizontal line through $(0, 2)$ **13.** Line through $(0, 1)$ and $(-1, 0)$ **15.** Line through
$(0, 0)$ and $(1, 2)$

17.

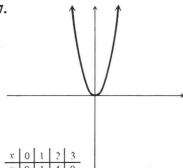

x	0	1	2	3
y	0	1	4	9

19. Domain $\{x \mid 2 \leqslant x \leqslant 6\}$, range $\{y \mid 1 \leqslant y \leqslant 5\}$

Exercise Set 3.2, p. 76

1.

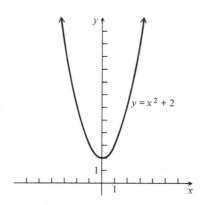

$y = x^2 + 2$

3.

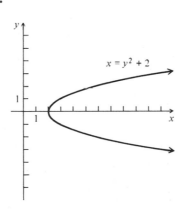

$x = y^2 + 2$

5.

$xy = 10$

7.

9.

11.

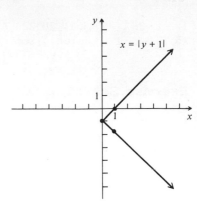

13. a, b, d, h **15.** Line through $(0, -8)$ and $(3, 0)$ **17.** Line through $(0, 3)$ and $(-4, 0)$ **19.** Horizontal line through $(0, -2)$ **21.** Vertical line through $(3, 0)$ **23.** Same graphs

25.

27.

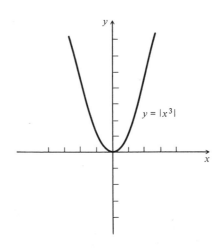

Exercise Set 3.3, p. 82

1. $(3, 7)$ **3.** $(4, 3)$ **5.** $(3, 6)$ **7.** x-axis, no; y-axis, yes; origin, no **9.** x-axis, no; y-axis, yes; origin, no **11.** x-axis, yes; y-axis, yes; origin, yes **13.** All yes **15.** All no **17.** All no **19.** Yes **21.** Yes **23.** Yes **25.** Yes **27.** No **29.** No **31.** No **33.** Yes **35.** Yes **37.** Yes **39.** No **41.** Yes **43.** $x = 4y - 5$ **45.** $y^2 - 3x^2 = 3$ **47.** $x = 3y^2 + 2$ **49.** $yx = 7$

51.

53.

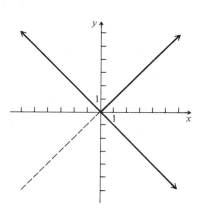

Exercise Set 3.4, p. 88

1. b, c, d **3.** a, c **5.** $0, -2.8, 3.2, 2.2$ **7.** (a) 0; (b) 1; (c) 57; (d) $5t^2 + 4t$; (e) $5t^2 - 6t + 1$; (f) $10a + 5h + 4$

9. (a) 5; (b) -2; (c) -4; (d) $4|y| + 6y$; (e) $2|a + h| + 3a + 3h$; (f) $\dfrac{2|a + h| + 3h - 2|a|}{h}$ **11.** $f^{-1}(x) = \dfrac{x - 5}{2}$

13. $f^{-1}(x) = x^2 - 1$ **15.** $3; -125$ **17.** $12{,}053; -17{,}243$ **19.** $f \circ g(x) = 12x^2 - 12x + 5$; $g \circ f(x) = 6x^2 + 3$

21. $f \circ g(x) = \dfrac{16}{x^2} - 1$; $g \circ f(x) = \dfrac{2}{4x^2 - 1}$ **23.** $f \circ g(x) = x^4 - 2x^2 + 2$; $g \circ f(x) = x^4 + 2x^2$

25. (a) 3.14977; (b) 55.73147; (c) 3178.20675; (d) 1116.70323

Exercise Set 3.5, p. 95

1. *and* **3.**

5. *and* **7.**

9.

11.

$y = -4|x|$

13.

$y = \frac{1}{4}|x|$

15.

$y = -\frac{1}{4}|x|$

17.

$y = |2x|$

19.

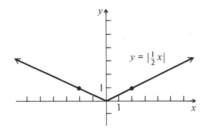

$y = |\frac{1}{2}x|$

21. *and* **23.**

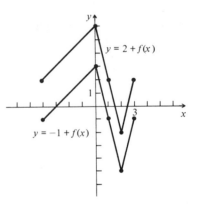

$y = 2 + f(x)$

$y = -1 + f(x)$

25.

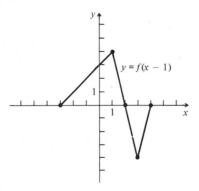

$y = f(x - 1)$

27.

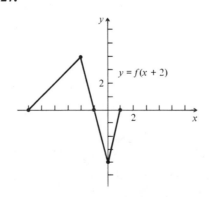

$y = f(x + 2)$

29.

$y = 2f(x)$

31.

33.

35.

37.

39.

41.

43.

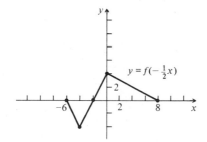

45. $x' = 2x + 1$; -1 **47.** Suppose x goes to x. Then $x = ax + b$. Solving this equation gives $x = \dfrac{b}{1-a}$. Therefore if there is a fixed point it is $\dfrac{b}{1-a}$. We check by substituting to see if it is, and find that such is the case.

Exercise Set 3.6, p. 101

1. Even: (a), (b); neither: (c), (d)   **3.** Even: (b), (c); odd: (d), (e), (f); neither: (a)   **5.** b, c **7.** 4   **9.** (a) yes; (b) yes; (c) no; (d) yes; (e) yes   **11.** Where $x = -3$ and $x = 2$ **13.** (a) $(-2, 2)$; (b) $(-5, -1]$; (c) $[c, d]$; (d) $[-5, 1)$ **15.** (a) $(-2, 4)$; (b) $(-\frac{1}{4}, \frac{1}{4}]$; (c) $[7, 10\pi)$; (d) $[-9, -6]$ **17.** Increasing: (a); decreasing: (c); neither: (b), (d)   **19.** Increasing $[0, 1]$; decreasing $[-1, 0]$; many possible answers   **21.** Increasing: (a), (e); decreasing (b); neither: (c), (d), (f)

Chapter 3 Test, or Review, p. 105

1. (b, a), $(b, 1)$, $(b, 3)$, $(1, a)$, $(1, 1)$, $(1, 3)$, $(3, a)$, $(3, 1)$, $(3, 3)$

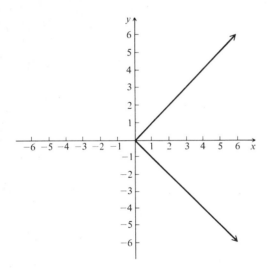

5. b, d, f   **7.** $x = 3y^2 + 2y - 1$ **9.** a, b, d   **11.** 4   **13.** $g^{-1}(x) = (2x - 4)^2$
15. (a)   **15.** (b)   **15.** (c)

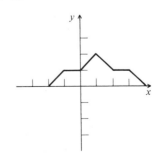

17. b, f   **19.** b, c   **21.** (a) yes; (b) no   **23.** $(0, 1]$ **25.** a   **27.** $f \circ g(x) = \dfrac{4}{(3 - 2x)^2}$; $g \circ f(x) = 3 - \dfrac{8}{x^2}$

Exercise Set 4.1, p. 112

1. $\frac{1}{8}$ **3.** $\frac{1}{2}$ **5.** $\frac{1}{\pi}$ **7.** $y = 4x - 10$ **9.** $y = 2x - 5$ **11.** $y = \dfrac{x}{2} + \dfrac{7}{2}$ **13.** $m = 2;\ b = 3$ **15.** $m = -3;\ b = 5$ **17.** $m = \frac{3}{4}$; $b = -3$ **19.** $m = 0;\ b = -\frac{10}{3}$ **21.** $y = 3.516x - 13.1602$ **23.** $y = 1.2222x + 1.0949$ **25.** Yes   **27.** $\overline{AB}, \overline{DC}$: same slope; $\overline{BC}, \overline{AD}$: same slope   **29.** $F = \frac{9}{5}C + 32$

Exercise Set 4.2, p. 115

1. No   **3.** No   **5.** 5   **7.** $3\sqrt{2}$ **9.** $\sqrt{a^2 + 64}$ **11.** $\sqrt{a^2 + b^2}$ **13.** $2\sqrt{a}$ **15.** Yes   **17.** $(-\frac{1}{2}, -1)$ **19.** $(a, 0)$ **21.** 18.80607   **23.** $(-0.4485, -0.27325)$ **25.** $(5, 0)$

Exercise Set 4.3, p. 120

1. (a) $(0, 0)$; (b) $x = 0$; (c) 0 is a minimum   **3.** (a) $(0, 0)$; (b) $x = 0$; (c) maximum   **5.** (a) $(\frac{1}{4}, 0)$; (b) $x = \frac{1}{4}$; (c) 0 is a minimum   **7.** (a) $(9, 0)$; (b) $x = 9$; (c) 0 is a maximum   **9.** (a) $(-7, 0)$; (b) $x = -7$; (c) 0 is a minimum   **11.** (a) $(-\frac{1}{2}, 0)$; (b) $x = -\frac{1}{2}$; (c) 0 is a maximum   **13.** (a) $(9, 5)$; (b) $x = 9$; (c) 5 is a minimum   **15.** (a) $(-4, 9)$; (b) $x = -4$; (c) 9 is a minimum   **17.** (a) $(2, -11)$; (b) $x = 2$; (c) -11 is a maximum   **19.** (a) $(-7, \frac{1}{2})$; (b) $x = -7$; (c) $\frac{1}{2}$ is a maximum   **21.** (a) $f(x) = -(x - 1)^2 + 4$; (b) $(1, 4)$; (c) $x = 1$; (d) 4 is maximum   **23.** (a) $f(x) = (x + \frac{3}{2})^2 - \frac{9}{4}$; (b) $(-\frac{3}{2}, -\frac{9}{4})$; (c) $x = -\frac{3}{2}$; (d) $-\frac{9}{4}$ is minimum   **25.** (a) $f(x) = -\frac{3}{4}(x - 4)^2 + 12$; (b) $(4, 12)$; (c) $x = 4$; (d) 12 is maximum   **27.** (a) $f(x) = 3(x + \frac{1}{6})^2 - \frac{49}{12}$, (b) $(-\frac{1}{6}, -\frac{49}{12})$; (c) $x = -\frac{1}{6}$; (d) $-\frac{49}{12}$ is minimum   **29.** $(3, 0), (-1, 0)$ **31.** $(4 \pm \sqrt{11}, 0)$ **33.** No x-intercepts

35.

37.

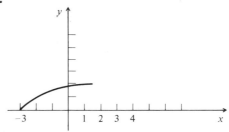

39. $f(x) = 3\left(x + \dfrac{m}{6}\right)^2 + \dfrac{11m^2}{12}$ **41.** Minimum, -6.95 **43.** Minimum, -6.081; ± 2.466 **45.** 6 cm by 4.5 cm; $27\ \text{cm}^2$

Exercise Set 4.4, p. 125

1. (a) $E = 0.15t + 72$; (b) 76.5, 77.25 **3.** (a) $P = 1.25t + 15$; (b) 65%, 90% **5.** (a) 1102.5 m after 15 sec; (b) after 30 sec **7.** 10×10 **9.** 30 **11.** 300 m^2

Exercise Set 4.5, p. 130

1. $\{3, 4, 5\}$ **3.** $\{0, 2, 4, 6, 8, 9\}$ **5.** $\{c\}$ **7.** Entire set of real numbers **9.** $-\frac{1}{2}$ and all numbers between $-\frac{1}{2}$ and $\frac{1}{2}$
11.   **13.**

15. $\{x \mid -3 < x\}$ **17.** $\{x \mid x > -2\}$ **19.** $\{x \mid x \geq -\frac{3}{2}\}$ **21.** $\{x \mid 4 < x\}$ **23.** $\{x \mid -3 \leq x < 3\}$ **25.** $\{x \mid 8 \leq x \leq 10\}$
27. $\{x \mid -\frac{3}{2} < x < 2\}$ **29.** $\{x \mid 1 < x \leq 5\}$ **31.** $\{x \mid -\frac{5}{8} \leq x \leq -\frac{3}{8}\}$ **33.** $\{x \mid 0 < x \leq \frac{4}{3}\}$ **35.** $\{x \mid x \leq -2 \text{ or } x > 1\}$
37. $\{x \mid x < -1 \text{ or } x > 3\}$ **39.** $\{x \mid x \leq -\frac{7}{2} \text{ or } x \geq \frac{1}{2}\}$ **41.** $\{x \mid x < 9.6 \text{ or } x > 10.4\}$ **43.** $\{x \mid x \leq -\frac{57}{4} \text{ or } x \geq -\frac{55}{4}\}$
45. $4.885 < w < 53.67$ cm **47.** $97\% \leq x \leq 100\%$; yes

Exercise Set 4.6, p. 133

1. $\{-7, 7\}$ **3.** $\{x \mid -7 < x < 7\}$ **5.** $\{x \mid x \leq -\pi \text{ or } x \geq \pi\}$ **7.** $\{-3, 5\}$ **9.** $\{x \mid -17 < x < 1\}$ **11.** $\{x \mid x \leq -17 \text{ or } x \geq 1\}$
13. $\{x \mid -\frac{1}{4} < x < \frac{3}{4}\}$ **15.** $\{-\frac{1}{3}, \frac{1}{3}\}$ **17.** $\{-1, -\frac{1}{3}\}$ **19.** $\{x \mid -\frac{1}{3} < x < \frac{1}{3}\}$ **21.** $\{x \mid -6 \leq x \leq 3\}$ **23.** $\{x \mid x < 4.9 \text{ or } x > 5.1\}$
25. $\{x \mid -\frac{7}{3} \leq x \leq 1\}$ **27.** $\{x \mid -\frac{1}{2} \leq x \leq \frac{7}{2}\}$ **29.** $\{x \mid x < -8 \text{ or } x > 7\}$ **31.** $\{x \mid x < -\frac{7}{4} \text{ or } x > -\frac{3}{2}\}$ **33.** $\{x \mid \frac{3}{8} \leq x \leq \frac{9}{8}\}$
35. $\{a + e, a - e\}$ **37.** $\{x \mid a - e < x < a + e\}$ **39.** $\{x \mid 1.9234 < x < 2.1256\}$ **41.** $\{x \mid 0.98414 \leq x \leq 4.9808\}$ **43–45.**
No solution. Absolute value is never negative. **47.** (a) $\left| x - \dfrac{a + b}{2} \right| < \dfrac{b - a}{2}$ is equivalent to $-\dfrac{b - a}{2} < x - \dfrac{a + b}{2} <$
$\dfrac{b - a}{2}$. Then $\dfrac{a + b}{2} - \dfrac{b - a}{2} < x < \dfrac{a + b}{2} + \dfrac{b - a}{2}$ and $a < x < b$; (b) $|x| < 5$; (c) $|x| < 6$; (d) $|x - 3| < 4$; (e) $|x + 2| < 3$

Exercise Set 4.7, p. 137

1. $\{x \mid -1 < x < 2\}$ **3.** $\{x \mid x < -2 \text{ or } x > 2\}$ **5.** $\{x \mid -1 \leq x \leq 1\}$ **7.** $\{x \mid x < 1 - \sqrt{6} \text{ or } x > 1 + \sqrt{6}\}$ **9.** All real
numbers **11.** $\{x \mid 3 - \sqrt{5} < x < 3 + \sqrt{5}\}$ **13.** $\{x \mid -2 \leq x \leq 10\}$ **15.** $\{x \mid -2 < x < 4\}$ **17.** $\{x \mid x < 2 \text{ or } x > 3\}$
19. $\left\{ x \mid \dfrac{-5 - \sqrt{37}}{2} \leq x \leq \dfrac{-5 + \sqrt{37}}{2} \right\}$ **21.** $\{x \mid -3 < x < \frac{5}{4}\}$ **23.** $\left\{ x \mid x > \dfrac{-1 + \sqrt{41}}{4} \text{ or } x < \dfrac{-1 - \sqrt{41}}{4} \right\}$
25. $\{x \mid \frac{3}{2} < x \leq 4\}$ **27.** $\{x \mid x \leq -\frac{5}{2} \text{ or } x > -2\}$ **29.** $\{x \mid x < -\frac{11}{7}\}$ **31.** $\{x \mid x > 1\}$ **33.** $\{x \mid x > 0 \text{ and } x \neq 2\}$
35. $\{x \mid x < 0 \text{ or } x \geq 1\}$ **37.** $h > -2 + 2\sqrt{6}$ cm **39.** (a) 10, 35; (b) $10 < x < 35$; (c) $x < 10 \text{ or } x > 35$ **41.** $\{x \mid x <$
$-1.6712 \text{ or } x > 1.1787\}$ **43.** (a) $k > 2 \text{ or } k < -2$; (b) $-2 < k < 2$

Chapter 4 Test, or Review, p. 138

1. -2 **3.** $y - 1 = \frac{1}{3}(x - 4)$ **5.** $(\frac{1}{2}, \frac{11}{2})$ **7.** (a) $f(x) = -2(x + \frac{3}{4})^2 + \frac{57}{8}$; (b) $(-\frac{3}{4}, \frac{57}{8})$; (c) $x = -\frac{3}{4}$; (d) $\frac{57}{8}$, maximum

9.

11. $\{8, 32\}$ **13.**

15. $10\,\text{m} < b < 18\,\text{m}$ **17.** $\{x \mid -\frac{9}{2} \leqslant x \leqslant \frac{15}{2}\}$ **19.** $\{3, -4\}$ **21.** $\{x \mid -2 < x < \frac{1}{8}\}$ **23.** $b = 20, h = 20$

Exercise Set 5.1, p. 145

1. No   **3.** $(-1, 3)$ **5.** $(\frac{39}{11}, -\frac{1}{11})$ **7.** $(-4, -2)$ **9.** $(-3, 0)$ **11.** $(10, 8)$ **13.** $(1, 1)$ **15.** $(-12, 0)$ **17.** $(0.924, -0.833)$
19. $(-\frac{1}{4}, -\frac{1}{2})$ **21.** $\{(5, 3), (-5, 3), (5, -3), (-5, -3)\}$

Exercise Set 5.2, p. 148

1. $(-4, 4)$ **3.** $(x, 3x - 5)$ or $\left(\dfrac{y + 5}{3}, y\right)$ **5.** $\varnothing$ **7.** Consistent: 1, 2, 3   **9.** $\left(x, \dfrac{5 - 3x}{2}\right)$ **11.** $\left(x, \dfrac{4x + 3}{6}\right)$

13. $-\frac{11}{2}, -\frac{9}{2}$ **15.** $20\,\text{km/hr}, 3\,\text{km/hr}$ **17.** $12.5\,l, 7.5\,l$ **19.** $\left(x, \dfrac{2013x - 9160}{724}\right)$ **21.** 2

Exercise Set 5.3, p. 153

1. Yes   **3.** $(3, -2, 1)$ **5.** $(-3, 2, 1)$ **7.** $(\frac{1}{2}, \frac{2}{3}, -\frac{5}{6})$ **9.** No solution   **11.** $\left(\dfrac{10 + 11z}{9}, \dfrac{-11 + 5z}{9}, z\right)$; $(\frac{10}{9}, -\frac{11}{9}, 0)$,   etc.
13. $(\frac{11}{9}z, \frac{5}{9}z, z)$; $(\frac{11}{9}, \frac{5}{9}, 1)$, etc.   **15.** $(4z - 5, -3z + 2, z)$; $(-1, -1, 1)$, etc.   **17.** $(0, 0, 0)$ **19.** $(-1, \frac{1}{5}, -\frac{1}{2})$ **21.** $y = 2x^2 + 3x - 1$ **23.** (a) $E = -4t^2 + 40t + 2$;   (b) \$98   **25.** A: 4 hr;   B: 6 hr;   C: 12 hr   **27.** $(1.49, 0.538, 2.03)$
29. $(-2, 4, -1, 1)$

Exercise Set 5.4, p. 156

1. $(\frac{3}{2}, \frac{5}{2})$ **3.** $(-1, 2, -2)$ **5.** $(\frac{1}{2}, \frac{3}{2})$ **7.** $(\frac{3}{2}, -4, 3)$ **9.** $(1, -3, 3)$ **11.** $(-3, -2, -1, 1)$ **13.** 4 dimes, 30 nickels   **15.** 10 nickels, 4
dimes, 8 quarters   **17.** 5 lb of \$4.05, 10 lb of \$2.70   **19.** \$30,000 at 5.5%; \$40,000 at 6%   **21.** $(1.012, -4.891)$
23. $(1.23, -2.11, 1.89)$ **25.** $\left(\dfrac{\pi + 3\sqrt{2}}{\pi^2 + 2}, \dfrac{3\pi - \sqrt{2}}{\pi^2 + 2}\right)$

Exercise Set 5.5, p. 160

1. -11 **3.** $x^3 - 4x$ **5.** -109 **7.** $-x^4 + x^2 - 5x$ **9.** $\left(-\frac{25}{2}, -\frac{11}{2}\right)$ **11.** $\left(\dfrac{4\pi - 5\sqrt{3}}{3 + \pi^2}, \dfrac{4\sqrt{3} + 5\pi}{-3 - \pi^2}\right)$ **13.** $\left(\frac{3}{2}, \frac{13}{14}, \frac{33}{14}\right)$ **15.** $\left(\frac{1}{2}, \frac{2}{3}, -\frac{5}{6}\right)$

17. Evaluate the two sides separately.   **19.** Evaluate the determinant and compare with two-point equation of a line. **21.** Details follow from hint.

Exercise Set 5.6, p. 165

1.

3.

5.

7.

9.

11.

13.

15.

17.

19.

21.

23.

25.

27.

29.

31.

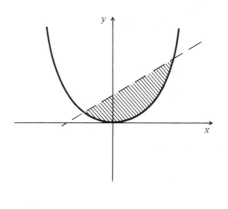

Exercise Set 5.7, p. 167

1. Max 168, when $x = 0$, $y = 6$; min 0, when $x = 0$, $y = 0$ **3.** Max 152, when $x = 7$, $y = 0$; min 32, when $x = 0$, $y = 4$ **5.** Max 102, 8 of A, 10 of B   **7.** $7000 bank X, $15,000 bank Y, maximum income $1395   **9.** Max $192, 2 knits, 4 worsteds

Exercise Set 5.8, p. 172

1. $\begin{bmatrix} -2 & 7 \\ 6 & 2 \end{bmatrix}$ **3.** $\begin{bmatrix} 1 & 3 \\ 2 & 6 \end{bmatrix}$ **5.** $\begin{bmatrix} 9 & 9 \\ -3 & -3 \end{bmatrix}$ **7.** $\begin{bmatrix} 11 & 13 \\ 5 & 3 \end{bmatrix}$ **9.** $\begin{bmatrix} -4 & 3 \\ -2 & -4 \end{bmatrix}$ **11.** $\begin{bmatrix} 17 & 9 \\ -2 & 1 \end{bmatrix}$ **13.** $\begin{bmatrix} 0 & 0 \\ 0 & 0 \end{bmatrix}$ **15.** $\begin{bmatrix} 1 & 2 \\ 4 & 3 \end{bmatrix}$ or A

17. $\begin{bmatrix} -5 & 4 & 3 \\ 5 & -9 & 4 \\ 7 & -18 & 17 \end{bmatrix}$ **19.** $\begin{bmatrix} -2 & 9 & 6 \\ -3 & 3 & 4 \\ 2 & -2 & 1 \end{bmatrix}$ or C **21.** $[-16]$ **23.** $[2 \quad -19]$ **25.** $\begin{bmatrix} 3 & -2 & 4 \\ 2 & 1 & -5 \end{bmatrix} \begin{bmatrix} x \\ y \\ z \end{bmatrix} = \begin{bmatrix} 17 \\ 13 \end{bmatrix}$

27. $\begin{bmatrix} 1 & -1 & 2 & -4 \\ 2 & -1 & -1 & 1 \\ 1 & 4 & -3 & -1 \\ 3 & 5 & -7 & 2 \end{bmatrix} \begin{bmatrix} x \\ y \\ z \\ w \end{bmatrix} = \begin{bmatrix} 12 \\ 0 \\ 1 \\ 9 \end{bmatrix}$ **29.** $\begin{bmatrix} -40.19 & 37.94 & 142.24 \\ -36.78 & 16.63 & 119.62 \\ -1.659 & 14.97 & 12.65 \end{bmatrix}$

31. $(A + B)(A - B) = \begin{bmatrix} -2 & 1 \\ 2 & -1 \end{bmatrix}$, $A^2 - B^2 = \begin{bmatrix} 0 & 3 \\ 0 & -3 \end{bmatrix}$

Chapter 5 Test, or Review, p. 173

1. $(-2, -2)$ **3.** 31 nickels, 44 dimes **5.** $(-3, 4, -2)$ **7.** Consistent **9.** Dependent **11.** $y = -x^2 - 2x + 3$ **13.** Min 20 at $(0, 2)$, max 56 at $(6, 2)$

15. $\begin{bmatrix} 0 & 1 & 5 \\ 1 & 0 & -1 \\ 2 & 0 & -3 \end{bmatrix}$ **17.** $\begin{bmatrix} -1 & -1 & -3 \\ 0 & -2 & 1 \\ -2 & 1 & 0 \end{bmatrix}$ **19.** $\begin{bmatrix} 3 & -2 & 4 \\ 1 & 5 & -3 \\ 2 & -3 & 7 \end{bmatrix} \begin{bmatrix} x \\ y \\ z \end{bmatrix} = \begin{bmatrix} 13 \\ 7 \\ -8 \end{bmatrix}$

Exercise Set 6.1, p. 179

1. (a) and (b)

(c) Horizontal translation 2 units to the right of (a); (d) horizontal translation 2 units to the right of (b)

3. $5^2 = 25$ **5.** $6^1 = 6$ **7.** $b^N = M$ **9.** $\log_{10} 1 = 0$ **11.** $\log_5 \frac{1}{25} = -2$ **13.** $\log_{10} 2 = 0.3010$ **15.** $\log_a c = -b$ **17.** 9
19. 4 **21.** $\frac{1}{2}$ **23.** 6 **25.** 2 **27.** 1 **29.** $\frac{1}{2}$ **31.** -3 **33.** $4x, (x > 0)$ **35.** 3.2 **37.** π **39.** 7.5 **41.** $x^2 + 3$ **43.** $\sqrt{x^2 + y^2}$

45.

47.

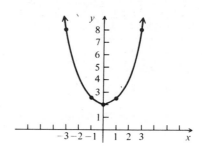

Exercise Set 6.2, p. 182

1. $2 \log_a x + 3 \log_a y + \log_a z$ **3.** $\log_b x + 2 \log_b y - 3 \log_b z$ **5.** $\log_b 4$ **7.** $\log_a \dfrac{2x^4}{y^3}$ **9.** $\log_a \dfrac{\sqrt{a}}{x}$ or $\frac{1}{2} - \log_a x$
11. $\frac{1}{2}[\log_a (1 - x) + \log_a (1 + x)]$ **13.** 0.602 **15.** 1.699 **17.** 1.778 **19.** -0.088 **21.** 1.954 **23.** -0.046 **25.** False
27. True   **29.** False   **31.** $\frac{1}{2}$ **33.** $\sqrt{7}$ **35.** -2

Exercise Set 6.3, p. 187

1. 0.3909 **3.** 0.7251 **5.** 2.5403 **7.** 1.7202 **9.** 5.7952 **11.** $8.8463 - 10$ **13.** $6.3345 - 10$ **15.** $7.5403 - 10$ **17.** 233
19. 1800 **21.** 25.2 **23.** 0.00346 **25.** 0.654 **27.** 190 **29.** 272 **31.** 8.77 **33.** 3.64 **35.** 25.7

Exercise Set 6.4, p. 190

1. 1.6194 **3.** 0.4689 **5.** 2.8130 **7.** $9.1538 - 10$ **9.** $7.6291 - 10$ **11.** $9.2494 - 10$ **13.** 2.7786 **15.** $9.8445 - 10$
17. 224.5 **19.** 14.53 **21.** $70,030$ **23.** 0.09245 **25.** 0.5343 **27.** 0.007295 **29.** 0.8268

Exercise Set 6.5, p. 193

1. 5 **3.** $\frac{12}{5}$ **5.** $\frac{1}{2}, -3$ **7.** 2.7093 **9.** 10 **11.** 1 **13.** 5 **15.** 1 or 100 **17.** 1 or 10^4 **19.** $\pm 2\sqrt{6}$ **21.** $x = \log_3(t \pm \sqrt{t^2 - 1})$ **23.** $x =$
$\frac{1}{2} \log_5 \dfrac{t + 1}{1 - t}$ **25.** $\log_x y - \log_x a = n$ **27.** $t = \dfrac{100(\log_e P - \log_e P_0)}{r}$ **29.** $t = -\dfrac{1}{k} \log \left[\dfrac{T - T_0}{T_1 - T_0} \right]$ **31.** 11.9 yr   **33.** 65 db

35. 140 db   **37.** 6.7 **39.** $10^5 \cdot I_0$ **41.** (a) 82; (b) 68 **43.** 9 mos   **45.** 4.2 **47.** $\left(\dfrac{\log 2}{\log 5}, 4 \right)$ **49.** No solution

51. $(2.392, 2.060)$

Exercise Set 6.6, p. 199

1. 1.4037 **3.** 2.1609 **5.** 0.9266 **7.** 2.9266 **9.** 0 **11.** −0.4055 **13.** −0.004833 **15.** 2.3026 **17.** −0.2614 **19.** 0
21. $k = 0.0201$, $P = 1{,}243{,}000$ **23.** 0.4 grams **25.** 1.2 days **27.** (a) 3000 yr; (b) 5100 yr **29.** 583 mb
31. $N = N_0 2^{-t/H}$

Chapter 6 Test, or Review, p. 200

1.

3.

5. $\log_7 2x = 2.3$ **7.** $\frac{1}{2}$ **9.** $3, -2$ **11.** 0.544 **13.** 0.2385 **15.** 1.4200 **17.** 73.9 **19.** 0.0276 **21.** $x^2 + 1$ **23.** $\frac{1}{5}$
25. 14.2 yr **27.** 30 db

Exercise Set 7.1, p. 206

1. 52° **3.** 17.5 **5.** $\sin \theta = \frac{3}{5}$, $\cos \theta = \frac{4}{5}$, $\tan \theta = \frac{3}{4}$, $\cot \theta = \frac{4}{3}$ **7.** $\sin \theta = \frac{7}{\sqrt{65}}$, $\cos \theta = \frac{4}{\sqrt{65}}$, $\tan \theta = \frac{7}{4}$, $\cot \theta = \frac{4}{7}$ **9.** (a) 53.5°; (b)
16.77; (c) 22.7 **11.** (a) 52.5; (b) 36.5; (c) 46.0

Exercise Set 7.2, p. 210

1. (a) $(-5, -2)$; (b) $(5, 2)$; (c) $(5, -2)$; (d) yes, by symmetry **3.** $M(0, 1)$; $N\left(-\frac{\sqrt{2}}{2}, \frac{\sqrt{2}}{2}\right)$; $P(0, -1)$; $Q\left(\frac{\sqrt{2}}{2}, -\frac{\sqrt{2}}{2}\right)$

5.

7.

9.

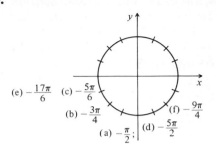

11. $M: \frac{2}{3}\pi, -\frac{4}{3}\pi; \ N: \frac{5}{6}\pi, -\frac{7}{6}\pi; \ P: \frac{5}{4}\pi, -\frac{3}{4}\pi; \ Q: \frac{11}{6}\pi, -\frac{\pi}{6}$ **13.** $\left(\frac{\sqrt{3}}{2}, -\frac{1}{2}\right)$

Exercise Set 7.3, p. 214

1.

3. (a) See Exercise 1;
(b)

(c) Same as (b)   (d) Same as (b)

5. (a) See Exercise 1;
(b)

(c) Same as (b)   (d) Same as (b)

7. (a) See Exercise 2;
(b)

(c) Same as (b)   (d) Same as (b)

9. $\cos x$ **11.** $-\sin x$ **13.** $-\cos x$ **15.** $\cos x$ **17.** $-\cos x$ **19.** (a) $\frac{\sqrt{2}}{2}$; (b) 0; (c) $-\frac{\sqrt{2}}{2}$; (d) -1; (e) $-\frac{\sqrt{2}}{2}$; (f) 0; (g) $\frac{\sqrt{2}}{2}$; (h) 1
21. (a) $\frac{\sqrt{2}}{2}$; (b) -1; (c) $-\frac{\sqrt{2}}{2}$; (d) 0; (e) $\frac{\sqrt{2}}{2}$; (f) -1; (g) $-\frac{\sqrt{2}}{2}$; (h) 0

Exercise Set 7.4, p. 220

1. $y = \tan x$

3. $y = \sec x$

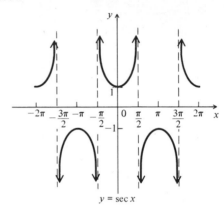

5. cos, sec **7.** sin, cos, sec, cosec **9.** Positive: I, III; negative: II, IV **11.** Positive: I, IV negative: II, III **13.** sec; $(-x) \equiv$
$$\frac{1}{\cos(-x)} \equiv \frac{1}{\cos x} \equiv \sec x$$ **15.** $\cot(x + \pi) \equiv \dfrac{\cos(x + \pi)}{\sin(x + \pi)} \equiv \dfrac{-\cos x}{-\sin x} \equiv \dfrac{\cos x}{\sin x} \equiv \cot x$ **17.** $\sec(x + \pi) \equiv \dfrac{1}{\cos(x + \pi)} \equiv$
$$-\frac{1}{\cos x} \equiv -\sec x$$ **19.** $\tan(\pi - x) \equiv \dfrac{\sin(\pi - x)}{\cos(\pi - x)} \equiv \dfrac{\sin x}{-\cos x} \equiv -\tan x$

Exercise Set 7.5, p. 224

1. $\cot^2 x \equiv \csc^2 x - 1$, $\csc^2 x - \cot^2 x \equiv 1$ **3.** (a) $\csc x \equiv \pm\sqrt{1 + \cot^2 x}$; (b) $\cot x \equiv \pm\sqrt{\csc^2 x - 1}$
5. $\cos\left(s + \dfrac{\pi}{2}\right) \equiv -\sin s$

$\sin\left(s - \dfrac{\pi}{2}\right) \equiv -\cos s$

$\cos\left(s - \dfrac{\pi}{2}\right) \equiv \sin s$

$\sin\left(s + \dfrac{\pi}{2}\right) \equiv \cos s$

7. $\tan\left(x - \dfrac{\pi}{2}\right) \equiv -\cot x$ **9.** $\sec\left(\dfrac{\pi}{2} - x\right) \equiv \csc x$

11. $\sin\left(\dfrac{\pi}{2} - x\right) \equiv \cos x,\ \cos\left(\dfrac{\pi}{2} - x\right) \equiv \sin x,\ \tan\left(\dfrac{\pi}{2} - x\right) \equiv \cot x,\ \cot\left(\dfrac{\pi}{2} - x\right) \equiv \tan x,\ \sec\left(\dfrac{\pi}{2} - x\right) \equiv \csc x,\ \csc\left(\dfrac{\pi}{2} - x\right) \equiv \sec x$

13. A circle of radius r is $x^2 + y^2 = r^2$. Compare with circle of radius 1. By similar triangles, $x = r \cos \theta$ and $y = r \sin \theta$, so the coordinates of P are $(r \cos \theta, r \sin \theta)$.

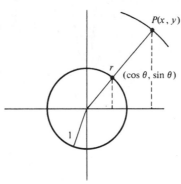

Exercise Set 7.6, p. 228

1.

3.

5.

7.

9.

11.

13.

15.

17.

19.

21.

23.

25.

27.

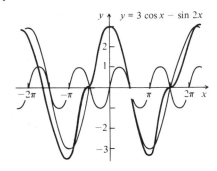

29. Amplitude, 3; period, $\frac{2\pi}{3}$; phase shift, $\frac{\pi}{6}$ **31.** Amplitude, 5; period, $\frac{\pi}{2}$; phase shift, $-\frac{\pi}{12}$ **33.** Amplitude, $\frac{1}{2}$; period, 1; phase shift, $-\frac{1}{2}$

Exercise Set 7.7A, p. 230

1. $\sin^2 x - \cos^2 x$ **3.** $\sin x - \sec x$ **5.** $\sin y + \cos y$ **7.** $\cot x - \tan x$ **9.** $1 - 2 \sin y \cos y$ **11.** $2 \tan x + \sec^2 x$
13. $\sin^2 y + \csc^2 y - 2$ **15.** $\cos^3 x - \sec^3 x$ **17.** $\cot^3 x - \tan^3 x$ **19.** $\sin^2 x$ **21.** $\cos x (\sin x + \cos x)$ **23.** $(\sin y - \cos y) \times$
$(\sin y + \cos y)$ **25.** $\sin x (\sec x + 1)$ **27.** $(\sin x + \cos x)(\sin x - \cos x)$ **29.** $3(\cot y + 1)^2$ **31.** $(\csc^2 x + 5)(\csc x + 1) \times$
$(\csc x - 1)$ **33.** $(\sin y + 3)(\sin^2 y - 3 \sin y + 9)$ **35.** $(\sin y - \csc y)(\sin^2 y + 1 + \csc^2 y)$ **37.** $\sin x (\cos y + \tan y)$
39. $-\cos x (1 + \cot x)$

Exercise Set 7.7B, p. 231

1. $\tan x$ **3.** $\frac{2 \cos^2 x}{9 \sin x}$ **5.** $\cos x - 1$ **7.** $\cos x + 1$ **9.** $\frac{2 \tan x + 1}{3 \sin x + 1}$ **11.** $\cos x + 1$ **13.** $\frac{\cos x - 1}{1 + \tan x}$ **15.** 1 **17.** $\cos x - 1$

19. $-\tan^2 y$ **21.** $\frac{1}{2 \cos x}$ **23.** $\frac{3 \tan x}{\cos x - \sin x}$ **25.** $\frac{1}{3} \cot y$ **27.** $\frac{1 - 2 \sin y + 2 \cos y}{\sin^2 y - \cos^2 y}$ **29.** -1 **31.** $\frac{5(\sin x - 3)}{3}$

Exercise Set 7.7C, p. 233

1. $|\sin x| \cos x$ **3.** $\sqrt{\sin y}\,(|\sin y| + |\cos y|)$ **5.** $|\sin x + \cos x|$ **7.** $1 - \sin y$ **9.** $\sin x\,(\sqrt{2} + \sqrt{\cos x})$ **11.** $\dfrac{\sqrt{\sin x \cos x}}{|\cos x|}$

13. $\dfrac{\sqrt{\cos x}}{|\cot x|}$ **15.** $\dfrac{\sqrt{2}\,|\cot x|}{2}$ **17.** $\dfrac{|\cos x|}{|1 - \sin x|}$ **19.** $3,\ -7$ **21.** $\dfrac{3}{4},\ -\dfrac{1}{2}$ **23.** $-10,\ 1$ **25.** $2,\ -3$ **27.** $3 \pm \sqrt{13}$ **29.** $\dfrac{5 \pm \sqrt{73}}{12}$

Chapter 7 Test, or Review, p. 234

1. $(-3, -2)$ **3.** $(3, 2)$ **5 and 7.**   **9.** Set of all real numbers **11.** 2π

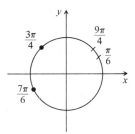

13.   **15.** 2π **17.** I, IV **19.** 1 **21.** $-\sin x$ **23.** $-\cos x$

	$\dfrac{\pi}{4}$	$\dfrac{\pi}{2}$	$\dfrac{3\pi}{4}$	$\dfrac{5\pi}{4}$
$\sin x$	$\dfrac{\sqrt{2}}{2}$	1	$\dfrac{\sqrt{2}}{2}$	$-\dfrac{\sqrt{2}}{2}$
$\cos x$	$\dfrac{\sqrt{2}}{2}$	0	$-\dfrac{\sqrt{2}}{2}$	$-\dfrac{\sqrt{2}}{2}$

25.   **27.** 2π **29.** $\dfrac{1}{\sin x}$ **31.** $\dfrac{\sqrt{\sec x \tan x}}{|\sec x|}$

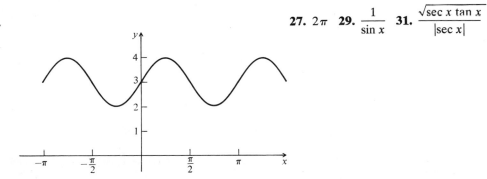

Exercise Set 8.1, p. 240

1. I **3.** III **5.** I **7.** II **9.** $\dfrac{\pi}{6}$ **11.** $\dfrac{\pi}{3}$ **13.** $\dfrac{5\pi}{12}$ **15.** 2.093 **17.** 5.582 **19.** 3.489 **21.** 57.32° **23.** 1440° **25.** 135°
27. 1.1 radians, 63° **29.** 5.233 radians **31.** 16 m **33.** 0.2095π **35.** 1.1922π **37.** 2.0560 **39.** 0.0236 **41.** 74.66°
43. 2171° **45.** 1477° **47.** 135.6° **49.** 105°

Exercise Set 8.2, p. 242

1. 3150 cm/min **3.** 52.3 cm/sec **5.** 1047 mph **7.** 75.4 ft **9.** 68.8 radians/sec **11.** 377 radians **13.** 10 mph
15. 2.093 radians/sec

Exercise Set 8.3, p. 247

1. $\sin\theta = \frac{5}{13}$, $\cos\theta = -\frac{12}{13}$, $\tan\theta = -\frac{5}{12}$, $\cot\theta = -\frac{12}{5}$, $\sec\theta = -\frac{13}{12}$, $\csc\theta = \frac{13}{5}$ **3.** $\sin\theta = -\frac{3}{4}$, $\cos\theta = -\dfrac{\sqrt{7}}{4}$, $\tan\theta = \dfrac{3}{\sqrt{7}}$,

$\cot\theta = \dfrac{\sqrt{7}}{3}$, $\sec\theta = -\dfrac{4}{\sqrt{7}}$, $\csc\theta = -\frac{4}{3}$ **5.** $\sin 30° = 0.5$, $\cos 30° = 0.866$, $\tan\theta = 0.577$, $\cot\theta = 1.732$, $\sec 30° = 1.155$,

$\csc 30° = 2$ **7.** -1 **9.** Does not exist. **11.** 1 **13.** 1 **15.** 0.5 **17.** 1.732 **19.** 1.414 **21.** 1 **23.** 0.5 **25.** 0.577
27. 0.707 **29.** -0.577

Exercise Set 8.4, p. 250

1.

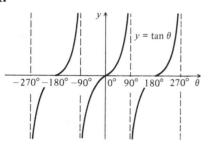

3. $\sin(x \pm 180°) \equiv -\sin x$ **5.** $\sin x \equiv \sin(x + k \cdot 360°)$

7. $\sin(x + 90°) \equiv \cos x$ **9.** $\sin(90° - x) \equiv \cos x$ **11.** $\tan(x + 180°) \equiv \tan x$ **13.** $\tan(x + 90°) \equiv -\cot x$ **15.** $\cos\theta =$
$-\dfrac{\sqrt{8}}{3}$, $\tan\theta = \dfrac{1}{\sqrt{8}}$, $\cot\theta = \sqrt{8}$, $\sec\theta = -\dfrac{3}{\sqrt{8}}$, $\csc\theta = -3$ **17.** $\sin\theta = \dfrac{\sqrt{5}}{3}$, $\tan\theta = -\dfrac{\sqrt{5}}{2}$, $\cot\theta = -\dfrac{2}{\sqrt{5}}$, $\sec\theta = -\dfrac{3}{2}$,

$\csc\theta = \dfrac{3}{\sqrt{5}}$ **19.** $\sin 25° = 0.4226$, $\cos 25° = 0.9063$, $\tan 25° = 0.4663$, $\cot 25° = 2.145$, $\sec 25° = 1.103$, $\csc 25° = 2.366$

Exercise Set 8.5, p. 253

1. 2°30′ **3.** 46°23′ **5.** 67°50′ **7.** 45.75° **9.** 76.88° **11.** 0.2306 **13.** 0.5519 **15.** 0.4176 **17.** 0.7720 **19.** −0.9228
21. −0.3854 **23.** −1.590 **25.** 1.053 **27.** 0.4728 **29.** 0.5894 **31.** −0.1859 **33.** 0.2995 **35.** 0.2563 **37.** 13°40′
39. 68°10′ **41.** 69°17′ **43.** 0.4392 **45.** 0.8145

Chapter 8 Test, or Review, p. 254

1. I, 0.483π, 1.52 **3.** I, 0.167π, 0.524 **5.** 270° **7.** 5.5 cm **9.** 1130 cm/min **11.** $\sin\theta = \dfrac{3}{\sqrt{13}}$, $\cos\theta = -\dfrac{2}{\sqrt{13}}$, $\tan\theta =$

$-\dfrac{3}{2}$, $\cot\theta = -\dfrac{2}{3}$, $\sec\theta = -\dfrac{\sqrt{13}}{2}$, $\csc\theta = \dfrac{\sqrt{13}}{3}$ **13.** $\dfrac{\sqrt{2}}{2}$ **15.** $\sqrt{3}$ **17.** $-\dfrac{2}{3}$ **19.** $\dfrac{\sqrt{5}}{2}$ **21.** $-\dfrac{3}{2}$ **23.** 0.6820 **25.** 0.9325
27. 1.3673 **29.** 47.55° **31.** 0.5147 **33.** 16°10′

Exercise Set 9.1, p. 261

1. $\sin P \cos Q + \cos P \sin Q$ **3.** $\cos A \cos B + \sin A \sin B$ **5.** $\dfrac{\tan P - \tan Q}{1 + \tan P \tan Q}$ **7.** $\sin 45° \cos 30° + \cos 45° \sin 30°$, or

$\dfrac{\sqrt{6} + \sqrt{2}}{4}$ **9.** $\cos(A + B)$ **11.** $\sin(P + Q)$ **13.** $\tan(A - B)$ **15.** $\sin(37° + 22°)$, or $\sin 59°$ **17.** $\tan(20° + 32°)$, or
$\tan 52°$ **19.** $2\sin\alpha\cos\beta$ **21.** $2\cos\alpha\cos\beta$ **23.** $\cos u$ **25.** $2\sin\theta\cos\theta$

27.

$$\cot(\alpha + \beta) = \frac{\cos(\alpha + \beta)}{\sin(\alpha + \beta)} = \frac{\cos\alpha\cos\beta - \sin\alpha\sin\beta}{\sin\alpha\cos\beta + \cos\alpha\sin\beta} \cdot \frac{\dfrac{1}{\sin\alpha\sin\beta}}{\dfrac{1}{\sin\alpha\sin\beta}} = \frac{\dfrac{\cos\alpha\cos\beta}{\sin\alpha\sin\beta} - 1}{\dfrac{\sin\alpha\cos\beta}{\sin\alpha\sin\beta} + \dfrac{\cos\alpha\sin\beta}{\sin\alpha\sin\beta}} = \frac{\cot\alpha\cot\beta - 1}{\cot\alpha + \cot\beta}$$

29. $\cos x$ **31.** $\sin 45° + \sin 30° = 0.7071 + 0.5 = 1.2071$; $\sin 75° = 0.9659$ **33.** 1 **35.** 0 **37.** Undefined **39.** 0.8448
41. $\sin(\sin x) \cdot \cos(\sin y) + \cos(\sin x) \cdot \sin(\sin y)$

Exercise Set 9.2, p. 265

1. $\sin 2\theta = \frac{24}{25}$, $\cos 2\theta = -\frac{7}{25}$, $\tan 2\theta = -\frac{24}{7}$; 2θ in quadrant II **3.** $\cos 2\theta = \frac{7}{25}$, $\sin 2\theta = \frac{24}{25}$, $\tan 2\theta = \frac{24}{7}$; 2θ in quadrant I
5. $\sin 2\theta = \frac{24}{25}$, $\cos 2\theta = -\frac{7}{25}$, $\tan 2\theta = -\frac{24}{7}$; 2θ in quadrant II **7.** $8\sin\theta\cos^3\theta - 4\sin\theta\cos\theta$, or
$4\sin\theta\cos^3\theta - 4\sin^3\theta\cos\theta$ **9.** $\dfrac{3 - 4\cos 2\theta + \cos 4\theta}{8}$ **11.** $\dfrac{\sqrt{2 + \sqrt{3}}}{2}$ **13.** $2 + \sqrt{3}$ **15.** $\dfrac{\sqrt{2 + \sqrt{2}}}{2}$ **17.** $\cos x$ **19.** $\cos x$
21. $\sin x$ **23.** $\cos x$ **25.** 1 **27.** 1 **29.** 8 **31.** $\sin 2x$ **33.** 0.6421 **35.** 0.9844 **37.** 0.1734

Exercise Set 9.3, p. 269

1.

$\dfrac{1}{\sin x} - \cos x \dfrac{\cos x}{\sin x}$	$\sin x$
$\dfrac{1 - \cos^2 x}{\sin x}$	
$\dfrac{\sin^2 x}{\sin x}$	
$\sin x$	

3.

$\dfrac{1 + \cos\theta}{\sin\theta} \cdot \dfrac{\cos\theta}{\cos\theta} + \dfrac{\sin\theta}{\cos\theta} \cdot \dfrac{\sin\theta}{\sin\theta}$	$\dfrac{1 + \cos\theta}{\sin\theta\cos\theta}$
$\dfrac{\cos^2\theta + \cos\theta + \sin^2\theta}{\sin\theta\cos\theta}$	
$\dfrac{1 + \cos\theta}{\sin\theta\cos\theta}$	

5.

$\dfrac{1 - \sin x}{\cos x}$	$\dfrac{\cos x}{1 + \sin x}$
$\dfrac{1 - \sin x}{\cos x} \cdot \dfrac{\cos x}{\cos x}$	$\dfrac{\cos x}{1 + \sin x} \cdot \dfrac{1 - \sin x}{1 - \sin x}$
$\dfrac{\cos x - \sin x \cos x}{\cos^2 x}$	$\dfrac{\cos x - \sin x \cos x}{1 - \sin^2 x}$
	$\dfrac{\cos x - \sin x \cos x}{\cos^2 x}$

7.

$\dfrac{1 + \tan\theta}{1 + \cot\theta}$	$\dfrac{\sec\theta}{\csc\theta}$
$\dfrac{1 + \dfrac{\sin\theta}{\cos\theta}}{1 + \dfrac{\cos\theta}{\sin\theta}}$	$\dfrac{\sin\theta}{\cos\theta}$
	$\tan\theta$
$\dfrac{\dfrac{\cos\theta + \sin\theta}{\cos\theta}}{\dfrac{\sin\theta + \cos\theta}{\sin\theta}}$	
$\dfrac{\cos\theta + \sin\theta}{\cos\theta} \cdot \dfrac{\sin\theta}{\sin\theta + \cos\theta}$	
$\dfrac{\sin\theta}{\cos\theta}$	
$\tan\theta$	

9.

$\dfrac{\sin x + \cos x}{\sec x + \csc x}$	$\dfrac{\sin x}{\sec x}$
$\dfrac{\sin x + \cos x}{\dfrac{1}{\cos x} + \dfrac{1}{\sin x}}$	$\dfrac{\sin x}{\sec x}$
$\dfrac{\sin x + \cos x}{\dfrac{\sin x + \cos x}{\sin x \cos x}}$	
$(\sin x + \cos x) \cdot \dfrac{\sin x \cos x}{\sin x + \cos x}$	
$\sin x \cos x$	
$\dfrac{\sin x}{\sec x}$	

11.

$$\frac{1 + \tan\theta}{1 - \tan\theta} + \frac{1 + \cot\theta}{1 - \cot\theta} \qquad\qquad 0$$

$$\frac{1 + \dfrac{\sin\theta}{\cos\theta}}{1 - \dfrac{\sin\theta}{\cos\theta}} + \frac{1 + \dfrac{\cos\theta}{\sin\theta}}{1 - \dfrac{\cos\theta}{\sin\theta}} \qquad\qquad 0$$

$$\frac{\dfrac{\cos\theta + \sin\theta}{\cos\theta}}{\dfrac{\cos\theta - \sin\theta}{\cos\theta}} + \frac{\dfrac{\sin\theta + \cos\theta}{\sin\theta}}{\dfrac{\sin\theta - \cos\theta}{\sin\theta}}$$

$$\frac{\cos\theta + \sin\theta}{\cos\theta} \cdot \frac{\cos\theta}{\cos\theta - \sin\theta} + \frac{\sin\theta + \cos\theta}{\sin\theta} \cdot \frac{\sin\theta}{\sin\theta - \cos\theta} \qquad\qquad 0$$

$$\frac{\cos\theta + \sin\theta}{\cos\theta - \sin\theta} + \frac{\sin\theta + \cos\theta}{\sin\theta - \cos\theta}$$

$$\frac{\cos\theta + \sin\theta}{\cos\theta - \sin\theta} - \frac{\cos\theta + \sin\theta}{\cos\theta - \sin\theta}$$

$$0$$

13.

$$\frac{1 + 2\cos^2\theta - 1}{2\sin\theta\cos\theta} \qquad \bigg| \qquad \frac{\cos\theta}{\sin\theta}$$

$$\frac{\cos\theta}{\sin\theta}$$

15.

$$\frac{1}{\cos 2\theta} \qquad\qquad \bigg| \qquad\qquad \frac{1 + \tan^2\theta}{2 - 1 - \tan^2\theta}$$

$$\frac{1}{\cos^2\theta - \sin^2\theta} \qquad\qquad \frac{1 + \tan^2\theta}{1 - \tan^2\theta}$$

$$\frac{1 + \dfrac{\sin^2\theta}{\cos^2\theta}}{1 - \dfrac{\sin^2\theta}{\cos^2\theta}}$$

$$\frac{\cos^2\theta + \sin^2\theta}{\cos^2\theta - \sin^2\theta}$$

$$\frac{1}{\cos^2\theta - \sin^2\theta}$$

17.

$\dfrac{\sin \alpha \cos \beta + \cos \alpha \sin \beta}{\cos \alpha \cos \beta}$	$\dfrac{\sin \alpha}{\cos \alpha} + \dfrac{\sin \beta}{\cos \beta}$
	$\dfrac{\sin \alpha \cos \beta + \cos \alpha \sin \beta}{\cos \alpha \cos \beta}$

19.

$1 - [\cos 5\theta \cos 3\theta + \sin 5\theta \sin 3\theta]$	$1 - \cos 2\theta$
$1 - \cos (5\theta - 3\theta)$	
$1 - \cos 2\theta$	

21.

$\dfrac{1}{2} \left[\dfrac{\dfrac{\sin \theta + \sin \theta \cos \theta}{\cos \theta}}{\dfrac{\sin \theta}{\cos \theta}} \right]$	$\dfrac{1 + \cos \theta}{2}$
$\dfrac{1}{2} \left[\dfrac{\sin \theta(1 + \cos \theta)}{\cos \theta} \cdot \dfrac{\cos \theta}{\sin \theta} \right]$	
$\dfrac{1 + \cos \theta}{2}$	

23.

$(\cos^2 x - \sin^2 x)(\cos^2 x + \sin^2 x)$	$\cos^2 x - \sin^2 x$
$\cos^2 x - \sin^2 x$	

25.

$\dfrac{\tan (3\theta - \theta)}{\tan 2\theta}$	$\tan 2\theta$

27.

$\dfrac{(\cos x - \sin x)(\cos^2 x + \cos x \sin x + \sin^2 x)}{\cos x - \sin x}$	$\dfrac{2 + 2 \sin x \cos x}{2}$
$1 + \cos x \sin x$	$1 + \sin x \cos x$

29.

$(\sin \alpha \cos \beta + \cos \alpha \sin \beta)(\sin \alpha \cos \beta - \cos \alpha \sin \beta)$	$1 - \cos^2 \alpha - (1 - \cos^2 \beta)$
$\sin^2 \alpha \cos^2 \beta - \cos^2 \alpha \sin^2 \beta$	$\cos^2 \beta - \cos^2 \alpha$
$\cos^2 \beta(1 - \cos^2 \alpha) - \cos^2 \alpha(1 - \cos^2 \beta)$	
$\cos^2 \beta - \cos^2 \beta \cos^2 \alpha - \cos^2 \alpha + \cos^2 \alpha \cos^2 \beta$	
$\cos^2 \beta - \cos^2 \alpha$	

31.

$\cos \alpha \cos \beta - \sin \alpha \sin \beta + \cos \alpha \cos \beta + \sin \alpha \sin \beta$	$2 \cos \alpha \cos \beta$
$2 \cos \alpha \cos \beta$	

33. $2 \sin\left(2x + \dfrac{\pi}{3}\right)$ **35.** $5 \sin(x + b)$, where $\cos b = \frac{4}{5}$, $\sin b = \frac{3}{5}$

37. $y = \sqrt{2} \sin\left(2x - \dfrac{\pi}{4}\right)$

39. $7.89 \sin(0.374x + 31.2°)$

Exercise Set 9.4, p. 274

1. $\dfrac{\pi}{4} + 2k\pi, \dfrac{3\pi}{4} + 2k\pi$ **3.** $\dfrac{\pi}{4} + 2k\pi, -\dfrac{\pi}{4} + 2k\pi$ **5.** $\dfrac{5\pi}{4} + 2k\pi, -\dfrac{\pi}{4} + 2k\pi$ **7.** $\dfrac{3\pi}{4} + 2k\pi, \dfrac{5\pi}{4} + 2k\pi$ **9.** $\dfrac{\pi}{3} + k\pi$ **11.** $\dfrac{\pi}{4} +$

$k\pi$ **13.** $\dfrac{5\pi}{6} + k\pi$ **15.** $\dfrac{3\pi}{4} + k\pi$ **17.** $0 + 2k\pi$ **19.** $\dfrac{\pi}{2} + 2k\pi$ **21.** $23° + k \cdot 360°, 157° + k \cdot 360°$ **23.** $39° + k \cdot 360°,$

$141° + k \cdot 360°$ **25.** $36°58' + k \cdot 360°, 323°02' + k \cdot 360°$ **27.** $21°25' + k \cdot 360°, 338°35' + k \cdot 360°$ **29.** $20°10' + k \cdot 180°$

31. $38°20' + k \cdot 180°$ **33.** $31° + k \cdot 360°, 329° + k \cdot 360°$ **35.** $9°10' + k \cdot 360°, 170°50' + k \cdot 360°$ **37.** $\dfrac{\pi}{4}$ **39.** $\dfrac{\pi}{3}$

41. $-\dfrac{\pi}{3}$ **43.** $\dfrac{3\pi}{4}$ **45.** $-\dfrac{\pi}{6}$ **47.** $\dfrac{2\pi}{3}$ **49.** $13°30'$ **51.** $-39°30'$ **53.** $152°50'$ **55.** $-22°10'$ **57.** $169°30'$

Exercise Set 9.5, p. 277

1. 0.3 **3.** -4.2 **5.** $\dfrac{\pi}{3}$ **7.** $-\dfrac{\pi}{4}$ **9.** $\dfrac{\pi}{5}$ **11.** $-\dfrac{\pi}{3}$ **13.** $\dfrac{\sqrt{3}}{2}$ **15.** $\dfrac{1}{2}$ **17.** 1 **19.** $\dfrac{\pi}{6}$ **21.** $\dfrac{\pi}{3}$ **23.** $\dfrac{\pi}{2}$ **25.** $\dfrac{x}{\sqrt{x^2 + 4}}$ **27.** $\dfrac{3}{\sqrt{11}}$

29. $\dfrac{1}{3\sqrt{11}}$ **31.** $-\dfrac{1}{2\sqrt{6}}$ **33.** $\dfrac{1}{\sqrt{1 + y^2}}$ **35.** $\dfrac{1}{2}$ **37.** $\dfrac{\sqrt{2 + \sqrt{3}}}{2}$ **39.** $\dfrac{24}{25}$ **41.** $\dfrac{119}{169}$ **43.** $\dfrac{3 + 4\sqrt{3}}{10}$ **45.** $\dfrac{-\sqrt{2}}{10}$ **47.** 0.9861

Exercise Set 9.6, p. 281

1. $\dfrac{2\pi}{3}$ **3.** $0°$ **5.** $86°40'$ **7.** $135°$ **9.** $90°$ **11.** Neither   **13.** Perpendicular   **15.** $y = 3x + 3$ **17.** $x = 3$ **19.** $y = -3$

21. $y + 5 = -\dfrac{2}{5}(x + 3)$ **23.** $y = 3$ **25.** $x = -3$ **27.** $y + 2 = -\dfrac{7}{3}(x - 4)$ **29.** $\dfrac{1}{7}$ **31.** $\dfrac{1}{6}$ **33.** $y = 0.6114x + 3.4094$

35. $173°$, approximately

Exercise Set 9.7, p. 285

1. $\dfrac{\pi}{3} + 2k\pi, \dfrac{2\pi}{3} + 2k\pi$ **3.** $\dfrac{\pi}{4} + 2k\pi, \dfrac{-\pi}{4} + 2k\pi$ **5.** $20°10' + k \cdot 360°, 159°50' + k \cdot 360°$ **7.** $236°40', 123°20'$ **9.** $\dfrac{4\pi}{3}, \dfrac{5\pi}{3}$

11. $123°40', 303°40'$ **13.** $\dfrac{\pi}{6}, \dfrac{5\pi}{6}, \dfrac{7\pi}{6}, \dfrac{11\pi}{6}$ **15.** $\dfrac{\pi}{6}, \dfrac{5\pi}{6}, \dfrac{7\pi}{6}, \dfrac{11\pi}{6}$ **17.** $\dfrac{\pi}{6}, \dfrac{5\pi}{6}, \dfrac{3\pi}{2}$ **19.** 0 **21.** $0, \dfrac{\pi}{6}, \dfrac{5\pi}{6}, \pi, \dfrac{7\pi}{6}, \dfrac{11\pi}{6}$ **23.** $\dfrac{\pi}{6},$

$\dfrac{5\pi}{6}$ **25.** $109°30', 250°30', 120°, 240°$ **27.** $\dfrac{\pi}{6}, \dfrac{5\pi}{6}, \pi$ **29.** $0, \pi, \dfrac{\pi}{2}, \dfrac{3\pi}{2}$

Exercise Set 9.8, p. 288

1. $0, \pi$ **3.** $\dfrac{3\pi}{4}, \dfrac{7\pi}{4}$ **5.** $\dfrac{\pi}{2}, \dfrac{3\pi}{2}, \dfrac{\pi}{6}, \dfrac{5\pi}{6}$ **7.** $\dfrac{\pi}{2}, \dfrac{3\pi}{2}, \dfrac{\pi}{4}, \dfrac{3\pi}{4}, \dfrac{5\pi}{4}, \dfrac{7\pi}{4}$ **9.** $0, \dfrac{\pi}{2}, \pi, \dfrac{3\pi}{2}$ **11.** 0 **13.** $0, \dfrac{\pi}{2}, \pi, \dfrac{3\pi}{2}$ **15.** $\dfrac{\pi}{6}, \dfrac{5\pi}{6}, \pi$

17. $\dfrac{\pi}{6}, \dfrac{5\pi}{6}, \dfrac{7\pi}{6}, \dfrac{11\pi}{6}$ **19.** 63°30′, 243°30′, 101°20′, 281°20′ **21.** $\dfrac{\pi}{6}, \dfrac{\pi}{2}, \dfrac{5\pi}{6}, \dfrac{7\pi}{6}, \dfrac{3\pi}{2}, \dfrac{11\pi}{6}$ **23.** $\dfrac{2\pi}{3}, \dfrac{4\pi}{3}$ **25.** $\dfrac{\pi}{4}, \dfrac{7\pi}{4}$

27. $\dfrac{\pi}{12}, \dfrac{5\pi}{12}$ **29.** $\dfrac{\pi}{6}, \dfrac{3\pi}{2}$

Chapter 9 Test, or Review, p. 288

1. $\cos X \cos Y - \sin X \sin Y$ **3.** $\cos 11°$ **5.** $\tfrac{1}{2}\sqrt{2 - \sqrt{2}}$

7.

$\tan 2\theta$	$\dfrac{2 \tan \theta}{1 - \tan^2 \theta}$
$\dfrac{\sin 2\theta}{\cos 2\theta}$	$\dfrac{2 \dfrac{\sin \theta}{\cos \theta}}{\dfrac{\cos^2 \theta}{\cos^2 \theta} - \dfrac{\sin^2 \theta}{\cos^2 \theta}}$
$\dfrac{2 \sin \theta \cos \theta}{\cos^2 \theta - \sin^2 \theta}$	$\dfrac{2 \sin \theta}{\cos \theta} \cdot \dfrac{\cos^2 \theta}{\cos^2 \theta - \sin^2 \theta}$
	$\dfrac{2 \sin \theta \cos \theta}{\cos^2 \theta - \sin^2 \theta}$

9. $81° + k \cdot 180°$ **11.** $\tfrac{7}{8}$ **13.** Parallel **15.** Perpendicular **17.** $0, \pi$

Exercise Set 10.1, p. 295

1. $B = 53°50'$, $b = 37.2$, $c = 46.1$ **3.** $A = 77°20'$, $a = 436$, $c = 447$ **5.** $B = 72°40'$, $a = 4.24$, $c = 14.3$ **7.** $A = 66°50'$, $b = 0.0148$, $c = 0.0375$ **9.** $B = 42°30'$, $a = 35.6$, $b = 32.6$ **11.** $A = 7°40'$, $a = 0.131$, $b = 0.973$ **13.** $c = 21.6$, $A = 33°40'$, $B = 56°20'$ **15.** $b = 12.0$, $A = 53°10'$, $B = 36°50'$ **17.** $a = 3.57$, $A = 63°20'$, $B = 26°40'$ **19.** 47.9 ft **21.** 1°40′ **23.** 30°10′ **25.** 3.52 mi **27.** 109 km **29.** 23.9 km **31.** 7.92 km **33.** 3.45 km **35.** $b = \sqrt{3}$, $s = \sqrt{19}$, $\theta = 23°30'$

Exercise Set 10.2, p. 300

1. $C = 17°$, $a = 26.3$, $c = 10.5$ **3.** $A = 121°$, $a = 33.4$, $c = 14.0$ **5.** $B = 68°50'$, $a = 32.3$, $b = 32.3$ **7.** $B = 56°20'$, $C = 87°40'$, $c = 40.8$, and $B = 123°40'$, $C = 20°20'$, $c = 14.2$ **9.** $B = 19°$, $C = 44°40'$, $b = 6.25$ **11.** $A = 74°30'$, $B = 44°20'$, $a = 33.3$ **13.** 76.3 m **15.** 50.8 ft **17.** 1470 km **19.** 10.6 km

Exercise Set 10.3, p. 302

1. $a = 14.9$, $B = 23°40'$, $C = 126°20'$ **3.** $a = 24.8$, $B = 20°40'$, $C = 26°20'$ **5.** $b = 74.8$, $A = 95°30'$, $C = 11°50'$
7. $A = 36°10'$, $B = 43°30'$, $C = 100°20'$ **9.** $A = 73°40'$, $B = 51°50'$, $C = 54°30'$ **11.** $A = 25°40'$, $B = 126°$, $C = 28°20'$ **13.** 28.2 nautical mi, S 55°20'E   **15.** 37 nautical mi   **17.** 59.4 ft   **19.** 68°, 68°, 44°

Exercise Set 10.4, p. 304

1. 57, 38°   **3.** 18.4, 37°   **5.** 20.9, 58°   **7.** 68.3, 18°   **9.** 13 kg, 67°   **11.** 655 kg, 21°   **13.** 21.6 ft/sec, 34°   **15.** 726 lb, 47°
17. 174 nautical mi, S 15°E   **19.** An angle of 12° upstream

Exercise Set 10.5, p. 307

1. $(5, 16)$ **3.** $(4.8, 13.7)$ **5.** $(-662, -426)$ **7.** $(5, 53°10')$ **9.** $(18, 303°40')$ **11.** $(5, 233°10')$ **13.** $(18, 123°40')$
15. $(3.46, 2)$ **17.** $(-5.74, -8.19)$ **19.** $(17.3, -10)$ **21.** $(70.7, -70.7)$ **23.** Vertical 118, horizontal 92.4   **25.** S. 192 km/h, W. 161 km/h   **27.** 43 kg, S 35°30'W   **29.** (a) N. 28, W. 7; (b) 28.8, N. 13°40'W

Exercise Set 10.6, p. 310

25. $(4\sqrt{2}, 45°)$ **27.** $(5, 90°)$ **29.** $(4, 0°)$ **31.** $(6, 60°)$ **33.** $(2, 30°)$ **35.** $(6, 30°)$ **37.** $\left(\dfrac{4}{\sqrt{2}}, \dfrac{4}{\sqrt{2}}\right)$ or $(2.83, 2.83)$ **39.** $(0, 0)$

41. $\left(\dfrac{-3}{\sqrt{2}}, \dfrac{-3}{\sqrt{2}}\right)$ **43.** $(3, -3\sqrt{3})$ **45.** $(5\sqrt{3}, 5)$ **47.** $(4.33, -2.5)$ **49.** $3r\cos\theta + 4r\sin\theta = 5$ **51.** $r\cos\theta = 5$ **53.** $r^2 = 36$

55. $r^2(\cos^2\theta - 4\sin^2\theta) = 4$ **57.** $x^2 + y^2 = 25$ **59.** $y = x$ **61.** $y = 2$ **63.** $x^2 + y^2 = 4x$ **65.** $x^2 - 4y = 4$

67. $x^2 - 2x + y^2 - 3y = 0$ **69.** $y^2 = -4x + 4$ **71.** Since $\alpha = \beta = \gamma$ and $r_1 = r_2 = r_3$, the triangle is equiangular, hence equilateral. By the distance formula, $AC = \sqrt{(\sqrt{3})^2 + 3^2} = \sqrt{12}$ or $2\sqrt{3}$.

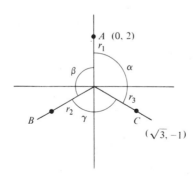

Exercise Set 10.7, p. 313

1. Cable 224-lb tension, boom 167-lb compression **3.** Horizontal rod 168-kg tension, other rod 261-kg compression **5.** Lift 2472 lb, drag 1315 lb **7.** 60 kg **9.** 9°40′ **11.** Horizontal rope 400 kg, other rope 566 kg **13.** 2000 kg in each **15.** 2242 kg on left, 1830 kg on right

Chapter 10 Test, or Review, p. 315

1. $A = 58°10′$, $B = 31°50′$, $c = 4.53$ **3.** 1748 cm **5.** 420 cm **7.** 75.8 mph, N 20°10′E **9.** $(\sqrt{13}, 123°40′)$ **11.** 577 kg

Exercise Set 11.1, p. 320

1. $i\sqrt{15}$ **3.** $4i$ **5.** $-2i\sqrt{3}$ **7.** $9i$ **9.** $i(\sqrt{7} - \sqrt{10})$ **11.** $-\sqrt{55}$ **13.** $2\sqrt{5}$ **15.** $\frac{\sqrt{5}}{\sqrt{2}}$ or $\frac{\sqrt{10}}{2}$ **17.** $\frac{3}{2}$ **19.** -2 **21.** $6 + 5i$
23. $11 + i$ **25.** 8 **27.** 0 **29.** $2 + 4i$ **31.** $5 - 7i$ **33.** $-4 - i$ **35.** $-5 + 5i$ **37.** $13 + i$ **39.** 13 **41.** $-6 + 12i$ **43.** $-5 + 12i$ **45.** $5 - 12i$ **47.** i **49.** i **51.** Yes **53.** No **55.** $x = -\frac{3}{2}$, $y = 7$ **57.** $x = 2$, $y = 3$ **59.** $-400.4595 + 1598.5665i$
61. $1834.9099 - 490.3471i$ **63.** -1

Exercise Set 11.2, p. 323

1. $\frac{4}{25} - \frac{3}{25}i$ **3.** $\frac{5}{29} + \frac{2}{29}i$ **5.** $-i$ **7.** $\frac{i}{4}$ **9.** $\frac{1}{2} + \frac{7}{2}i$ **11.** $\frac{22}{41} - \frac{7}{41}i$ **13.** $\frac{1}{3} + \frac{2}{3}\sqrt{2}i$ **15.** $2 - 3i$ **17.** $\frac{1}{5} + \frac{2}{5}i$ **19.** $\frac{12}{61} + \frac{10}{61}i$
21. $-\frac{1}{2} - \frac{i}{2}$ **23.** $\frac{28}{65} - \frac{29}{65}i$ **25.** $\frac{719}{3233} + \frac{955}{3233}i$ **27.** $\frac{2a^2 - 2b^2}{4a^2 + b^2} + \frac{5ab}{4a^2 + b^2}i$ **29.** $-\frac{1}{2} + \frac{3}{2}i$ **31.** $\frac{5}{2} + \frac{13}{2}i$ **33.** $\frac{3}{2} + \frac{3}{2}i$
35. $3\bar{z}^5 - 4\bar{z}^2 + 3\bar{z} - 5$ **37.** $7\bar{z}^4 + 5\bar{z}^3 - 12\bar{z}$ **39.** $5\bar{z}^{10} - 7\bar{z}^8 + 13\bar{z}^2 - 4$ **41.** $\frac{1}{z} = \frac{a}{a^2 + b^2} - \frac{b}{a^2 + b^2}i$

Exercise Set 11.3, p. 326

1. $x^2 + 4 = 0$ **3.** $x^2 - 2x + 2 = 0$ **5.** $x^2 - 4x + 13 = 0$ **7.** $x^2 - 3x - ix + 3i = 0$ **9.** $x^3 - x^2 + 9x - 9 = 0$
11. $x^3 - 2x^2i - 3x^2 + 5xi + x - 2i + 2 = 0$ **13.** $x^3 + x - 2x^2i - 2i = 0$ **15.** $\frac{2}{5} + \frac{6}{5}i$ **17.** $\frac{8}{5} - \frac{9}{5}i$ **19.** $2 - i$
21. $\frac{11}{25} + \frac{2}{25}i$ **23.** $1 \pm 2i$ **25.** $2 \pm 3i$ **27.** $-\frac{3}{2} \pm \frac{\sqrt{7}}{2}i$ **29.** $\frac{-1 + i \pm \sqrt{-6i}}{2}$ **31.** $-i, \frac{i}{2}$ **33.** $\frac{-1 - 2i \pm \sqrt{-15 + 16i}}{6}$
35. $\sqrt{2} + \sqrt{2}i; -\sqrt{2} - \sqrt{2}i$ **37.** $2 + i, -2 - i$ **39.** $-1 \pm \sqrt{3}i, 2$ **41.** $-5; \frac{5 \pm 5i\sqrt{3}}{2}$

Exercise Set 11.4, p. 330

1.

3.

5.

7.

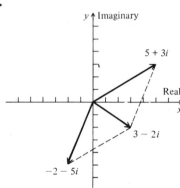

9. $\dfrac{3\sqrt{3}}{2} + \dfrac{3}{2}i$ **11.** $-2\sqrt{2} + 2\sqrt{2}i$ **13.** $-10i$ **15.** $\dfrac{5\sqrt{2}}{2} - \dfrac{5\sqrt{2}}{2}i$ **17.** $2 + 2i$

19. $2\sqrt{3} + 2i$ **21.** $-2 - 2i$ **23.** $\sqrt{2}$ cis $315°$ **25.** 2 cis $30°$ **27.** 20 cis $330°$ **29.** 2 cis $90°$ **31.** 5 cis $180°$

33. 4 cis $270°$ **35.** 4 cis $0°$, or 4 **37.** 40 cis $0°$, or 40 **39.** 8 cis $120°$ **41.** cis $90°$, or i **43.** $\dfrac{\sqrt{2}}{2}$ cis $105°$ **45.** 2 cis $270°$,

or $-2i$ **47.** $z = a + bi$, $|z| = \sqrt{a^2 + b^2}$; $-z = -a - bi$, $|-z| = \sqrt{(-a)^2 + (-b)^2} = \sqrt{a^2 + b^2}$. $\therefore |z| = |-z|$

49. $z \cdot w = (r_1 \text{ cis } \theta_1)(r_2 \text{ cis } \theta_2) = r_1 r_2 \text{ cis } (\theta_1 + \theta_2)$, $|z \cdot w| = \sqrt{[r_1 r_2 \cos (\theta_1 + \theta_2)]^2 + [r_1 r_2 \sin (\theta_1 + \theta_2)]^2} = \sqrt{(r_1 r_2)^2} = |r_1 r_2|, |z|$
$= \sqrt{(r_1 \cos \theta_1)^2 + (r_1 \sin \theta_1)^2} = \sqrt{r_1^2} = |r_1|, |w| = \sqrt{(r_2 \cos \theta_2)^2 + (r_2 \sin \theta_2)^2} = \sqrt{r_2^2} = |r_2|$. Then $|z| \cdot |w| = |r_1| \cdot |r_2| =$
$|r_1 r_2| = |z \cdot w|$

Exercise Set 11.5, p. 333

1. 8 cis π **3.** 64 cis π **5.** 8 cis $270°$ **7.** $-8 - 8\sqrt{3}i$ **9.** $-8 - 8\sqrt{3}i$ **11.** i **13.** 1 **15.** $\sqrt{2}$ cis $60°$, $\sqrt{2}$ cis $240°$; or $\dfrac{\sqrt{2}}{2} + \dfrac{\sqrt{6}}{2}i$,

$\dfrac{-\sqrt{2}}{2} - \dfrac{\sqrt{6}}{2}i$ **17.** cis 30°, cis 150°, cis 270°; or $\dfrac{\sqrt{3}}{2} + \dfrac{1}{2}i$, $\dfrac{-\sqrt{3}}{2} + \dfrac{1}{2}i$, $-i$ **19.** 2 cis 0°, 2 cis 90°, 2 cis 180°, 2 cis 270°; or 2, 2i,

-2, $-2i$ **21.** 4.09, $-2.045 + 3.542i$, $-2.045 - 3.542i$

Chapter 11 Test, or Review, p. 334

1. $14 + 2i$ **3.** $2 - i$ **5.** $x = 2$, $y = -4$ **7.** $x^2 - 2x + 5 = 0$ **9.** $\dfrac{(-3 \pm \sqrt{5})i}{2}$

11.

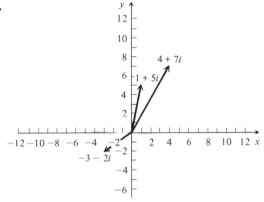

13. $\sqrt{2}$ cis 45° **15.** $\sqrt[6]{2}$ cis 15°, $\sqrt[6]{2}$ cis 135°, $\sqrt[6]{2}$ cis 255°

Exercise Set 12.1, p. 337

1. 4 **3.** 1 **5.** 2 **7.** 0 **9.** No degree **11.** No degree **13.** 2 yes, 3 no, -1 no **15.** (a) yes; (b) no; (c) no **17.** $Q(x) = x^2 + 8x + 15$, $R(x) = 0$, $P(x) = (x - 2)(x^2 + 8x + 15) + 0$ **19.** $Q(x) = x^2 + 9x + 26$, $R(x) = 48$, $P(x) - (x - 3) \times (x^2 + 9x + 26) + 48$ **21.** $Q(x) = x^2 - 2x + 4$, $R(x) = -16$, $P(x) = (x + 2)(x^2 - 2x + 4) - 16$ **23.** $Q(x) = x^2 + 5$, $R(x) = 0$, $P(x) = (x^2 + 4)(x^2 + 5) + 0$ **25.** (a) -32; (b) -32; (c) -65; (d) -65 **27.** (a) -2; (b) -2

Exercise Set 12.2, p. 339

1. 6 **3.** -1 **5.** -12 **7.** 0 **9.** $-5 - 24i$ **11.** 0 **13.** No **15.** Yes **17.** Yes **19.** Yes **21.** (a) yes; (b) $x^2 + 3x + 2$; (c) $P(x) = (x - 1)(x + 2)(x + 1)$ **23.** $(x - 3)$, $(x + 4)$, $(x + 1)$, $(x - 1)$ **25.** 3 **27.** $P(-a) = (-a)^{2n} - \overline{a}^{2n}$. Since $(-a)^{2n} = a^{2n}$, $P(-a) = 0$. ∴ $x + a$ is a factor of $x^{2n} - a^{2n}$. **29.** $P(a) = a^n - a^n = 0$. Since $P(a) = 0$, then $x - a$ is a factor of $x^n - a^n$.

Exercise Set 12.3, p. 341

1. $Q(x) = x^2 - 9x + 5$, $R(x) = -7$ **3.** $Q(x) = 2x^3 + x^2 - 3x + 10$, $R(x) = -42$ **5.** $Q(x) = x^2 - 4x + 8$, $R(x) = -24$ **7.** $Q(x) = x^2 - 3x + 9$, $R(x) = 0$ **9.** $Q(x) = x^3 + x^2 + x + 1$, $R(x) = 0$ **11.** $Q(x) = 2x^3 + x^2 + \frac{7}{2}x + \frac{7}{4}$, $R(x) = -\frac{1}{8}$ **13.** $Q(x) = x^3 + x^2y + xy^2 + y^3$, $R(x) = 0$ **15.** $Q(x) = x^2 - ix + (1 + i)$, $R(x) = 4 + i$ **17.** $P(1) = 0$, $P(-2) = -60$, $P(3) = 0$ **19.** $P(20) = 5{,}935{,}988$, $P(-3) = -772$ **21.** -3 yes, 2 no **23.** -3 no, $\frac{1}{2}$ no **25.** i yes, $-i$ yes, -2 yes **27.** (a) -485.15873; (b) -485.15882 **29.** (a) 1004

Exercise Set 12.4, p. 345

1. $-3(m2)$, 1 $(m1)$ **3.** $3(m2)$, $-4(m3)$, $0(m4)$ **5.** $3(m2)$, $2(m2)$ **7.** $x^3 - 6x^2 - x + 30$ **9.** $x^3 - 2x^2 + x - 2$ **11.** $x^3 - 7x^2 + 17x - 15$ **13.** $x^3 - \sqrt{3}x^2 - 2x + 2\sqrt{3}$, no   **15.** $x^4 - 10x^3 + 25x^2$ **17.** $x^4 - 3x^3 - 7x^2 + 15x + 18$ **19.** $-3 - 4i$, $4 + \sqrt{5}$ **21.** $1 + i$ **23.** $x^3 - 4x^2 + 6x - 4$ **25.** $x^3 + 2x^2 + 9x + 18$ **27.** $x^4 - 6x^3 + 11x^2 - 10x + 2$ **29.** $x^4 + 4x^2 - 45$ **31.** i, 2, 3 **33.** $-2i$, 2, -2 **35.** $2 - i$, $2 + i$ **37.** $-1 + \sqrt{3}i$, $-1 - \sqrt{3}i$ **39.** Use the *fundamental theorem of algebra* and the theorem concerning complex roots occurring in conjugate pairs.

Exercise Set 12.5, p. 348

1. -3, $\sqrt{2}$, $-\sqrt{2}$ **3.** $-\frac{1}{5}$, 1, $2i$, $-2i$ **5.** -1, -2, $3 + \sqrt{13}$, $3 - \sqrt{13}$ **7.** 1, -1, -3 **9.** -2, $1 \pm i\sqrt{3}$ **11.** $\frac{1}{2}$, $\frac{1 \pm \sqrt{5}}{2}$

13. None   **15.** None   **17.** None   **19.** -2, 1, 2 **21.** $4\,\mathrm{cm}$ **23.** $3\,\mathrm{cm}$, $\dfrac{7 - \sqrt{33}}{2}\,\mathrm{cm}$ **25.** If n is even, x^n is nonnegative for any x, so $x^n + b$ positive for any x. Thus $x^n + b$ is never 0, and thus has no roots.

Exercise Set 12.6, p. 352

1.

3.

5.

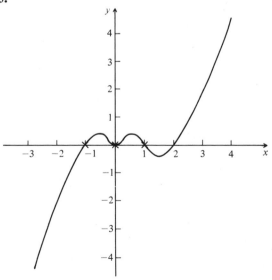

7. No irrational roots   **9.** 2.2   **11.** No irrational roots   **13.** ± 1.4 **15.** No irrational roots   **17.** $4.2\,\mathrm{cm}$ **19.** -1.27

Exercise Set 12.7, p. 358

1.

3.

5.

7.

9.

11.

13.

15.

17.

19.

21.

23.

25.

27.

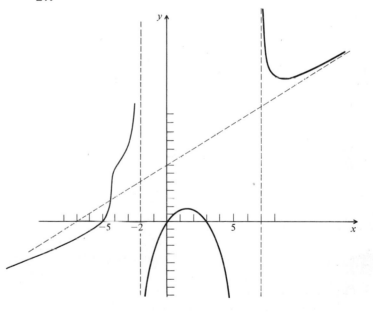

Chapter 12 Test, or Review, p. 359

1. 0   **3.** $x^3 - 3x^2 + 2x$ **5.** $(x - 1)\left(x + \dfrac{1}{2} + i\dfrac{\sqrt{3}}{2}\right)\left(x + \dfrac{1}{2} - i\dfrac{\sqrt{3}}{2}\right)$ **7.** 88   **9.** No   **11.** −0.9, 1.3, 2.5

Exercise Set 13.1, p. 363

1. The union of the graphs of $y = -x$ and $y = x$ **3.** The union of the graphs of $y = -\frac{1}{3}x$ and $y = \frac{1}{3}x$ **5.** The union of the graphs of $y = -x$ and $y = \frac{3}{2}x$ **7.** Just $(0, 0)$

Exercise Set 13.2, p. 365

1. $x^2 + y^2 = 49$ **3.** $(x + 2)^2 + (y - 7)^2 = 5$ **5.** $C(-1, -3)$; $r = 2$ **7.** $C(8, -3)$; $r = 2\sqrt{10}$ **9.** $C(0, 0)$; $r = \sqrt{2}$ **11.** $C(5, 0)$; $r = \frac{1}{2}$ **13.** $C(-4, 3)$; $r = 2\sqrt{10}$ **15.** $C(-\frac{25}{2}, -5)$; $r = \frac{\sqrt{677}}{2}$ **17.** $C(2, 0)$; $r = 2$ **19.** $C(0, 0)$; $r = \frac{1}{3}$ **21.** $x^2 + y^2 = 25$ **23.** $(x - 3)^2 + (y + 2)^2 = 64$ **25.** $(x - 2)^2 + (y - 4)^2 = 16$ **27.** $C(-4.123, 3.174)$; $r = 10.071$ **29.** $(x - 1)^2 + (y - 2)^2 = 41$ **31.** (a) no; (b) $y = \pm\sqrt{4 - x^2}$; (c) yes, domain $\{x \mid -2 \leqslant x \leqslant 2\}$, range $\{y \mid 0 \leqslant y \leqslant 2\}$; (d) yes, domain $\{x \mid -2 \leqslant x \leqslant 2\}$, range $\{y \mid -2 \leqslant y \leqslant 0\}$

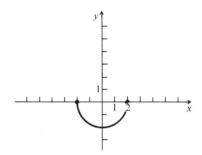

33. $(x - h)(x - h) - (y - k)[-(y - k)] = r^2$, so $(x - h)^2 + (y - k)^2 = r^2$ **35.** Yes **37.** Yes **39.** Yes **41.** No **43.** Yes **45.** No

Exercise Set 13.3, p. 370

1. $C(0, 0)$; V: $(2, 0)$, $(-2, 0)$, $(0, 1)$, $(0, -1)$; F: $(\sqrt{3}, 0)$, $(-\sqrt{3}, 0)$ **3.** $C(1, 2)$; V: $(3, 2)$, $(-1, 2)$, $(1, 3)$, $(1, 1)$; F: $(1 + \sqrt{3}, 2)$, $(1 - \sqrt{3}, 2)$ **5.** $C(-3, 2)$; V: $(2, 2)$, $(-8, 2)$, $(-3, 6)$, $(-3, -2)$; F: $(0, 2)$, $(-6, 2)$ **7.** $C(0, 0)$; V: $(-3, 0)$, $(3, 0)$, $(0, 4)$, $(0, -4)$; F: $(0, \sqrt{7})$, $(0, -\sqrt{7})$ **9.** $C(-2, 1)$; V: $(-10, 1)$, $(6, 1)$, $(-2, 1 + 4\sqrt{3})$, $(-2, 1 - 4\sqrt{3})$; F: $(-6, 1)$, $(2, 1)$ **11.** $C(0, 0)$; V: $(-\sqrt{3}, 0)$, $(\sqrt{3}, 0)$, $(0, \sqrt{2})$, $(0, -\sqrt{2})$; F: $(-1, 0)$, $(1, 0)$ **13.** $C(0, 0)$; V: $(-\frac{1}{2}, 0)$, $(\frac{1}{2}, 0)$, $(0, \frac{1}{3})$, $(0, -\frac{1}{3})$; F: $(-\frac{\sqrt{5}}{6}, 0)$, $(\frac{\sqrt{5}}{6}, 0)$ **15.** $C(2, -1)$; V: $(-1, -1)$, $(5, -1)$, $(2, 1)$, $(2, -3)$; F: $(2 - \sqrt{5}, -1)$, $(2 + \sqrt{5}, -1)$ **17.** $C(1, 1)$; V: $(0, 1)$, $(2, 1)$, $(1, 3)$, $(1, -1)$; F: $(1, 1 + \sqrt{3})$, $(1, 1 - \sqrt{3})$ **19.** $C(2.003125, -1.00515)$; V: $(5.0234302, -1.00515)$, $(-1.0171802, -1.00515)$, $(2.003125, -3.0186868)$, $(2.003125, 1.0083868)$, $(2.003125, -3.0186869)$ **21.** $\dfrac{x^2}{4} + \dfrac{y^2}{9} = 1$ **23.** $\dfrac{(x - 3)^2}{4} + \dfrac{(y - 1)^2}{25} = 1$ **25.** $\dfrac{(x + 2)^2}{\frac{1}{4}} + \dfrac{(y - 3)^2}{4} = 1$

27. $\dfrac{x^2}{9} + \dfrac{5y^2}{484} = 1$

29. (a) no; (b) $y = \pm 3\sqrt{1-x^2}$; (c) yes, domain $\{x \mid -1 \le x \le 1\}$, range $\{y \mid 0 \le y \le 3\}$; (d) yes, domain $\{x \mid -1 \le x \le 1\}$, range $\{y \mid -3 \le y \le 0\}$ **31.** Circle with $C(0, 0)$; $r = a$ **33.** (a) $A = \pi ab$; (b) 20π; (c) $2\pi\sqrt{3}$

Exercise Set 13.4, p. 377

1. $C(0, 0)$; V: $(-3, 0)$, $(3, 0)$; F: $(-\sqrt{10}, 0)$, $(\sqrt{10}, 0)$; A: $y = \frac{1}{3}x$, $y = -\frac{1}{3}x$ **3.** $C(2, -5)$; V: $(-1, -5)$, $(5, -5)$; F: $(2 - \sqrt{10}, -5)$, $(2 + \sqrt{10}, -5)$; A: $y = -\dfrac{x}{3} - \dfrac{13}{3}$, $y = \dfrac{x}{3} - \dfrac{17}{3}$ **5.** $C(-1, -3)$; V: $(-1, -1)$, $(-1, -5)$; F: $(-1, -3 + 2\sqrt{5})$, $(-1, -3 - 2\sqrt{5})$; A: $y = \frac{1}{2}x - \frac{5}{2}$, $y = -\frac{1}{2}x - \frac{7}{2}$ **7.** $C(0, 0)$; V: $(-2, 0)$, $(2, 0)$; F: $(-\sqrt{5}, 0)$, $(\sqrt{5}, 0)$; A: $y = -\frac{1}{2}x$, $y = \frac{1}{2}x$ **9.** $C(0, 0)$; V: $(0, 1)$, $(0, -1)$; F: $(0, \sqrt{5})$, $(0, -\sqrt{5})$; A: $y = -\frac{1}{2}x$, $y = \frac{1}{2}x$ **11.** $C(0, 0)$; V: $(-\sqrt{2}, 0)$, $(\sqrt{2}, 0)$; F: $(-2, 0)$, $(2, 0)$; A: $y = \pm x$ **13.** $C(0, 0)$; V: $(-\frac{1}{2}, 0)$, $(\frac{1}{2}, 0)$; F: $\left(-\dfrac{\sqrt{2}}{2}, 0\right)$, $\left(\dfrac{\sqrt{2}}{2}, 0\right)$; A: $y = \pm x$ **15.** $C(1, -2)$; V: $(0, -2)$, $(2, -2)$; F: $(1 - \sqrt{2}, -2)$, $(1 + \sqrt{2}, -2)$; A: $y = -x - 1$, $y = x - 3$ **17.** $C(\frac{1}{3}, 3)$; V: $(-\frac{2}{3}, 3)$, $(\frac{4}{3}, 3)$; F: $(\frac{1}{3} - \sqrt{37}, 3)$, $(\frac{1}{3} + \sqrt{37}, 3)$; A: $y = 6x + 1$, $y = -6x + 5$ **19.** See text **21.** See text **23** $C(1.023, -2.044)$; V: $(2.07, -2.044)$, $(-0.024, -2.044)$; A: $y = x - 3.067$, $y = -x - 1.021$ **25.** $x^2 - \dfrac{y^2}{3} = 1$ **27.** $\dfrac{x^2}{4} - \dfrac{y^2}{9} = 1$ **29.** (a) no; (b) $y = \pm\frac{1}{2}\sqrt{x^2 - 4}$; (c) yes, domain $\{x \mid x \le -2 \text{ or } x \ge 2\}$, range $\{y \mid y \ge 0\}$; (d) yes, domain $\{x \mid x \le -2 \text{ or } x \ge 2\}$, range $\{y \mid y \le 0\}$

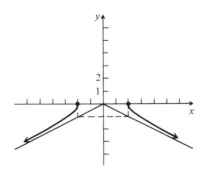

31. $\left(\dfrac{x-h}{a}\right)\left(\dfrac{x-h}{a}\right) - \left(\dfrac{y-k}{b}\right)\left(\dfrac{y-k}{b}\right) = 1 \quad \therefore \quad \dfrac{(x-h)^2}{a^2} - \dfrac{(y-k)^2}{b^2} = 1$

Exercise Set 13.5, p. 381

1. $V(0,0)$; $F(0,2)$; D: $y = -2$ **3.** $V(0,0)$; $F(-\frac{3}{2},0)$; D: $x = \frac{3}{2}$ **5.** $V(0,0)$; $F(0,1)$; D: $y = -1$ **7.** $V(0,0)$; $F(0,\frac{1}{8})$; D: $y = -\frac{1}{8}$ **9.** $V(-2,1)$; $F(-2,-\frac{1}{2})$; D: $y = \frac{5}{2}$ **11.** $V(-1,-3)$; $F(-1,-\frac{7}{2})$; D: $y = -\frac{5}{2}$ **13.** $V(0,-2)$; $F(0,-1\frac{3}{4})$; D: $y = -2\frac{1}{4}$ **15.** $V(-2,-1)$; $F(-2,-\frac{3}{4})$; D: $y = -1\frac{1}{4}$ **17.** $V(5\frac{3}{4},\frac{1}{2})$; $F(6,\frac{1}{2})$; D: $x = 5\frac{1}{2}$ **19.** $y^2 = 16x$ **21.** $y^2 = -4\sqrt{2}x$ **23.** $(y-2)^2 = 14(x+\frac{1}{2})$ **25.** The graph of $x^2 - y^2 = 0$ is the union of the lines $y = x$, $y = -x$; the others are respectively a hyperbola, a circle, and a parabola **27.** $V(0,0)$; $F(0,2014.0625)$; D: $y = -2014.0625$ **29.** $(x+1)^2 = -4(y-2)$ **31.** (a) no; (b) no, unless $p = 0$ **33.** $(y-k)(y-k) - (x-h)(4p) = 0$, $(y-k)^2 = 4p(x-h)$

Exercise Set 13.6, p. 384

1. $(-4,-3)$, $(3,4)$ **3.** $(0,-3)$, $(4,5)$ **5.** $(3,0)$, $(0,2)$ **7.** $(-2,1)$ **9.** $(3,2)$, $(4,\frac{3}{2})$ **11.** $\left(\dfrac{5+\sqrt{70}}{3}, \dfrac{-1+\sqrt{70}}{3}\right)$, $\left(\dfrac{5-\sqrt{70}}{3}, \dfrac{-1-\sqrt{70}}{3}\right)$ **13.** $\left(\dfrac{15+\sqrt{561}}{8}, \dfrac{11-3\sqrt{561}}{8}\right)$, $\left(\dfrac{15-\sqrt{561}}{8}, \dfrac{11+3\sqrt{561}}{8}\right)$ **15.** 9, 5 **17.** 6 cm, 8 cm **19.** 4 in., 5 in. **21.** $(0.965, 4402.33)$, $(-0.965, -4402.33)$ **23.** $2(L+W) = P$, $L+W = \dfrac{P}{2}$, $LW = A$, $L = \dfrac{P}{2} - W$, $W\left(\dfrac{P}{2} - W\right) = A$,

$W^2 - \dfrac{WP}{2} + A = 0$, $W = \dfrac{\dfrac{P}{2} \pm \sqrt{\left(\dfrac{P}{2}\right)^2 - 4A}}{2} = \dfrac{P}{4} \pm \dfrac{\sqrt{P^2 - 16A}}{4} = \dfrac{1}{4}(P \pm \sqrt{P^2 - 16A})$ **25.** $(x-2)^2 + (y-3)^2 = 1$

Exercise Set 13.7, p. 387

1. $(-5,0)$, $(4,3)$, $(4,-3)$ **3.** $(3,0)$, $(-3,0)$ **5.** $(4,3)$, $(-4,-3)$, $(3,4)$, $(-3,-4)$ **7.** No solution **9.** $(\sqrt{2},\sqrt{14})$, $(-\sqrt{2},\sqrt{14})$, $(\sqrt{2},-\sqrt{14})$, $(-\sqrt{2},-\sqrt{14})$ **11.** $(1,2)$, $(-1,-2)$, $(2,1)$, $(-2,-1)$ **13.** $(3,2)$, $(-3,-2)$, $(2,3)$, $(-2,-3)$ **15.** $\left(\dfrac{5-9\sqrt{15}}{20}, \dfrac{-45+3\sqrt{15}}{20}\right)$, $\left(\dfrac{5+9\sqrt{15}}{20}, \dfrac{-45-3\sqrt{15}}{20}\right)$ **17.** 13, 12 and -13, -12 **19.** 1 m, $\sqrt{3}$ m **21.** 16 ft, 24 ft **23.** $(8.53, 2.53)$, $(8.53, -2.53)$, $(-8.53, 2.53)$, $(-8.53, -2.53)$ **25.** $\left(x + \dfrac{5}{13}\right)^2 + \left(y - \dfrac{32}{13}\right)^2 = \dfrac{5365}{169}$

Chapter 13, Test, or Review, p. 388

1.

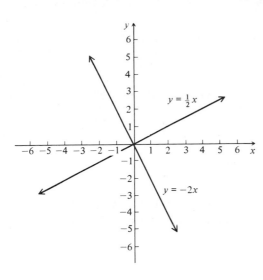

3. $C(\frac{3}{4}, \frac{5}{4})$; $r = \frac{1}{4}\sqrt{10}$

5. $F(-3, 0)$; $V(0, 0)$; $D:\ x = 3$

7. $C(-2, \frac{1}{4})$; $V:\ (0, \frac{1}{4}),\ (-4, \frac{1}{4})$; $F:\ (-2 + \sqrt{6}, \frac{1}{4}),\ (-2 - \sqrt{6}, \frac{1}{4})$; $A:\ y - \frac{1}{4} = \pm\frac{\sqrt{2}}{2}(x + 2)$ **9.** $\left(3, \frac{\sqrt{29}}{2}\right),\ \left(-3, \frac{\sqrt{29}}{2}\right),$
$\left(3, -\frac{\sqrt{29}}{2}\right),\ \left(-3, \frac{-\sqrt{29}}{2}\right)$ **11.** $\dfrac{16\sqrt{6}}{7} \approx 5.6$

Exercise Set 14.1, p. 392

1. 4, 7, 10, 13; 31; 46 **3.** $1, \frac{1}{2}, \frac{1}{3}, \frac{1}{4}; \frac{1}{10}; \frac{1}{15}$ **5.** $\frac{1}{2}, \frac{2}{3}, \frac{3}{4}, \frac{4}{5}; \frac{10}{11}; \frac{15}{16}$ **7.** 0, 1, 4, 9; 81; 196 **9.** 2, $2\frac{1}{2}$, $3\frac{1}{3}$, $4\frac{1}{4}$; $10\frac{1}{10}$; $15\frac{1}{15}$
11. 2, 4, 8, 16; 2^{10} or 1024; 2^{15} or 32,768 **13.** $2n - 1$ **15.** $\dfrac{n + 1}{n + 2}$ **17.** $(\sqrt{3})^n$ **19.** $-(3n - 2)$ **21.** Infinite **23.** Finite **25.** 4,
$1\frac{1}{4}$, $1\frac{4}{5}$, $1\frac{5}{9}$ **27.** 64, 8, $2\sqrt{2}$, $\sqrt{2\sqrt{2}}$ **29.** $1 + 2 + 3 + 4 + 5 + 6 + 7$ **31.** $2 + 4 + 6 + 8 + \cdots + 2n$ **33.** $\frac{1}{2} + \frac{1}{4} + \frac{1}{6} + \frac{1}{8} + \frac{1}{10}$
35. $2^0 + 2^1 + 2^2 + 2^3 + 2^4 + 2^5$ **37.** $\log 7 + \log 8 + \log 9 + \log 10$ **39.** $\displaystyle\sum_{k=1}^{6} \frac{k}{k+1}$ **41.** $\displaystyle\sum_{k-1}^{6} (-2)^k$ **43.** $\displaystyle\sum_{k=1}^{\infty} k^2$ **45.** $\displaystyle\sum_{k=1}^{\infty} -k$
47. $\displaystyle\sum_{k=1}^{\infty} \frac{k}{2^k}$ **49.** $1 + \frac{1}{2} + \frac{1}{3} + \frac{1}{4} + \cdots$ **51.** $-3 + 9 + (-27) + 81 + \cdots$ **53.** $\frac{2}{6} + \frac{5}{7} + \frac{10}{8} + \frac{17}{9} + \cdots$

Exercise Set 14.2, p. 397

1. $a_1 = 2$; $d = 5$ **3.** $a_1 = 7$; $d = -4$ **5.** $a_1 = \frac{3}{2}$; $d = \frac{3}{4}$ **7.** $a_{12} = 46$ **9.** $a_{17} = -41$ **11.** 27th **13.** 102nd **15.** $a_{17} = 101$
17. $a_1 = 5$ **19.** $n = 28$ **21.** $a_1 = 8$; $d = -3$; 8, 5, 2, −1, −4 **23.** 624 ft **25.** 670 **27.** 375 **29.** 2550 **31.** 1683

33. 990 **35.** 432 **37.** 16,195 **39.** 465 **41.** 524.011, 524.6609, 525.3108, 525.9607, 526.6106, 527.2605, 527.9104, 528.5603, 529.2102, 529.8601 **43.** $S_n = 1 + 3 + 5 + \cdots + (2n - 1)$, $S_n = \dfrac{n}{2}[1 + (2n - 1)]$, $S_n = \dfrac{n}{2}[2n]$, $S_n = n^2$

Exercise Set 14.3, p. 402

1. 2 **3.** $-\frac{1}{3}$ **5.** -1 **7.** $\dfrac{1}{x}$ **9.** $a_6 = 243$ **11.** $a_5 = 1250$ **13.** \$933.12 **15.** $\frac{1}{256}$ ft **17.** 161,051 **19.** 762 **21.** 1275 **23.** $\frac{547}{18}$
25. $-\frac{171}{32}$ **27.** $\frac{63}{32}$ **29.** 10,485.75 in. **31.** \$259,056.52

Exercise Set 14.4, p. 405

1. $r = 2$; no **3.** $r = \frac{1}{3}$; yes **5.** $r = \frac{1}{10}$; yes **7.** $r = -\frac{1}{5}$; yes **9.** 8 **11.** 125 **13.** 2 **15.** $\frac{160}{9}$ **17.** $\frac{7}{9}$ **19.** $\frac{7}{33}$ **21.** $\frac{170}{33}$ **23.** 2, 2.5, 2.666666667, 2.708333334, 2.716666667, 2.718055556; $S_\infty = e$ (≈ 2.718281828; See Chapter 6) **25.** 24 ft

Exercise Set 14.5, p. 410

1. S_n: $1 + 2 + 3 + \cdots + n = \dfrac{n(n + 1)}{2}$

S_1: $1 = \dfrac{1(1 + 1)}{2}$

S_k: $1 + 2 + 3 + \cdots + k = \dfrac{k(k + 1)}{2}$

S_{k+1}: $1 + 2 + 3 + \cdots + k + (k + 1) = \dfrac{(k + 1)(k + 2)}{2}$

1. *Basis step:* S_1 true by substitution.
2. *Induction step:* Assume S_k. Deduce S_{k+1}.
   Starting with the left side of S_{k+1}, we have

   $\underbrace{1 + 2 + 3 + \cdots + k} + (k + 1)$

   $= \quad \dfrac{k(k + 1)}{2} + (k + 1) \qquad$ (by S_k)

   $= \quad \dfrac{k(k + 1) + 2(k + 1)}{2} \qquad$ (adding)

   $= \quad \dfrac{(k + 1)(k + 2)}{2} \qquad$ (distributive law)

3. S_n: $1 + 5 + 9 + \cdots + (4n - 3) = n(2n - 1)$
   S_1: $1 = 1(2 \cdot 1 - 1)$
   S_k: $1 + 5 + 9 + \cdots + (4k - 3) = k(2k - 1)$
   S_{k+1}: $1 + 5 + 9 + \cdots + (4k - 3) + [4(k + 1) - 3]$
   $\qquad\qquad = (k + 1)[2(k + 1) - 1]$
   $\qquad\qquad = (k + 1)(2k + 1)$

1. *Basis step:* S_1 true by substitution.
2. *Induction step:* Assume S_k. Deduce S_{k+1}.
   Starting with the left side of S_{k+1}, we have

   $\underbrace{1 + 5 + 9 + \cdots + (4k - 3)} + [4(k + 1) - 3]$.

   $= \qquad k(2k - 1) + [4(k + 1) - 3] \qquad$ (by S_k)

   $= \qquad 2k^2 - k + 4k + 4 - 3$

   $= \qquad (k + 1)(2k + 1)$

5. S_n: $\dfrac{1}{1 \cdot 2} + \dfrac{1}{2 \cdot 3} + \cdots + \dfrac{1}{n(n+1)} = \dfrac{n}{n+1}$

S_1: $\dfrac{1}{1 \cdot 2} = \dfrac{1}{1+1}$

S_k: $\dfrac{1}{1 \cdot 2} + \dfrac{1}{2 \cdot 3} + \cdots + \dfrac{1}{k(k+1)} = \dfrac{k}{k+1}$

S_{k+1}: $\dfrac{1}{1 \cdot 2} + \dfrac{1}{2 \cdot 3} + \cdots + \dfrac{1}{k(k+1)} + \dfrac{1}{(k+1)(k+2)}$

$$= \dfrac{k+1}{k+2}$$

1. Basis step: S_1 true by substitution.

2. Induction step: Assume S_k. Deduce S_{k+1}.

Starting with the left side of S_{k+1}, we have

$$\underbrace{\dfrac{1}{1 \cdot 2} + \dfrac{1}{2 \cdot 3} + \cdots + \dfrac{1}{k(k+1)}} + \dfrac{1}{(k+1)(k+2)}$$

$$= \dfrac{k}{k+1} + \dfrac{1}{(k+1)(k+2)} \quad \text{(by } S_k\text{)}$$

$$= \dfrac{k(k+2) + 1}{(k+1)(k+2)}$$

$$= \dfrac{k^2 + 2k + 1}{(k+1)(k+2)}$$

$$= \dfrac{(k+1)^2}{(k+1)(k+2)} = \dfrac{k+1}{k+2}$$

15. The answer is left to the student.

19. *2. Induction step:* Assume S_k. Deduce S_{k+1}.

Starting with the left side of S_{k+1}, we have

$[r(\cos\theta + i\sin\theta)]^{k+1}$

$= [r(\cos\theta + i\sin\theta)]^k [r(\cos\theta + i\sin\theta)]$

$= r^k[\cos k\theta + i\sin k\theta][r(\cos\theta + i\sin\theta)]$

$= r^{k+1}(\cos k\theta + i\sin k\theta)(\cos\theta + i\sin\theta)$

$= r^{k+1}[\cos k\theta \cos\theta + i\sin k\theta \cos\theta + i\cos k\theta \sin\theta$
$\qquad\qquad\qquad\qquad - \sin k\theta \sin\theta]$

$= r^{k+1}[(\cos k\theta \cos\theta - \sin k\theta \sin\theta) + i(\sin k\theta \cos\theta$
$\qquad\qquad\qquad\qquad\qquad + \cos k\theta \sin\theta)$

$= r^{k+1}[\cos(k\theta + \theta) + i\sin(k\theta + \theta)]$

$= r^{k+1}[\cos(k+1)\theta + i\sin(k+1)\theta]$

7. *2. Induction step:* Assume S_k. Deduce S_{k+1}. Now

$\quad k < k + 1 \qquad$ (by S_k)

$k + 1 < k + 1 + 1 \qquad$ (adding 1)

$\therefore k + 1 < k + 2$

9. *2. Induction step:* Assume S_k. Deduce S_{k+1}.

$\quad 2 \leqslant 2^k \qquad$ (by S_k)

$2 \cdot 2 \leqslant 2^k \cdot 2 \qquad$ (multiplying by 2)

$2 < 2 \cdot 2 \leqslant 2^{k+1} \qquad$ since $2 < 2 \cdot 2$, $\therefore 2 \leqslant 2^{k+1}$.

11. *2. Induction step:* Assume S_k. Deduce S_{k+1}.

$\quad 2^k < 2^{k+1} \qquad$ (by S_k)

$2 \cdot 2^k < 2 \cdot 2^{k+1} \qquad$ (multiplying by 2)

$2^{k+1} < 2^{k+2}$

13. *2. Induction step:* Assume S_k. Deduce S_{k+1}.

$\quad 2k \leqslant 2^k \qquad$ (by S_k)

$2 \cdot 2k \leqslant 2 \cdot 2^k \qquad$ (multiplying by 2)

$4k \leqslant 2^{k+1}$

Since $1 \leqslant k$, $k + 1 \leqslant k + k$, or $k + 1 \leqslant 2k$. Then $2(k + 1) \leqslant 4k$. Thus

$$2(k + 1) \leqslant 4k \leqslant 2^{k+1}, \text{ so } 2(k + 1) \leqslant 2^{k+1}$$

17. The answer is left to the student.

21. *2. Induction step:* Assume S_k. Deduce S_{k+1}
We start with the left side of S_{k+1}.

$$\underbrace{\cos x \cdot \cos 2x \cdots \cos 2^{k-1}x} \cdot \cos 2^k x$$

$$= \dfrac{\sin 2^k x}{2^k \sin x} \cdot \cos 2^k x$$

$$= \dfrac{\sin 2^k x \cos 2^k x}{2^k \sin x}$$

$$= \dfrac{\frac{1}{2} \sin 2(2^k x)}{2^k \sin x} \quad \text{(since } \sin 2\theta = 2\sin\theta\cos\theta\text{)}$$

$$= \dfrac{\sin 2^{k+1} x}{2^{k+1} \sin x} \cdot$$

23. The answer is left to the student.

25. Cannot prove $S_1 \to S_2$ because there is no overlap of sets B and C

Chapter 14 Test, or Review, p. 412

1. $3\frac{3}{4}$

3. 11

5. 0.27, 0.0027, 0.000027

7. $7.38, $1365.10

9. Use mathematical induction. Prove: For all natural numbers n,

$$1 + 4 + 7 + \cdots + (3n - 2) = \frac{n(3n - 1)}{2}$$

$$S_n: \; 1 + 4 + 7 + \cdots + (3n - 2) = \frac{n(3n - 1)}{2}$$

$$S_1: \; 1 = \frac{1(3 - 1)}{2}$$

$$S_k: \; 1 + 4 + 7 + \cdots + (3k - 2) = \frac{k(3k - 1)}{2}$$

$$S_{k+1}: \; 1 + 4 + 7 + \cdots + [3(k + 1) - 2]$$
$$= 1 + 4 + 7 + \cdots + (3k - 2) + (3k + 1)$$
$$= \frac{(k + 1)(3k + 2)}{2}$$

1. *Basis step*: $1 = \dfrac{2}{2} = \dfrac{1(3 - 1)}{2}$ is true.

2. *Induction step*. Assume S_k. Prove S_{k+1}.

$$\underbrace{1 + 4 + 7 + \cdots + (3k - 2)} + (3k + 1)$$

$$= \frac{k(3k - 1)}{2} + (3k + 1)$$

$$= \frac{k(3k - 1)}{2} + \frac{2(3k + 1)}{2}$$

$$= \frac{3k^2 - k + 6k + 2}{2}$$

$$= \frac{3k^2 + 5k + 2}{2}$$

$$= \frac{(k + 1)(3k + 2)}{2}$$

Exercise Set 15.1, p. 417

1. $4 \cdot 3 \cdot 2$, or 24 **3.** $_{10}P_7 = 10 \cdot 9 \cdot 8 \cdot 7 \cdot 6 \cdot 5 \cdot 4$, or 604,800 **5.** 120; 3125 **7.** 120; 24 **9.** $\dfrac{5!}{2! \, 1! \, 1! \, 1!} = 5 \cdot 4 \cdot 3 = 60$

11. $9 \cdot 9 \cdot 8 \cdot 7 \cdot 6 \cdot 5 \cdot 4$, or 544,320 **13.** $\dfrac{9!}{2! \, 3! \, 4!} = 1260$ **15.** 12! or 479,001,600 **17.** (a) 120; (b) 3840

19. $52 \cdot 51 \cdot 50 \cdot 49 = 6,497,400$ **21.** $\dfrac{24!}{3! \, 5! \, 9! \, 4! \, 3!} = 16,491,024,950,400$ **23.** 11 **25.** 9

Exercise Set 15.2, p. 420

1. 126 **3.** 1225 **5.** $\dfrac{n(n - 1)(n - 2)}{3!}$ **7.** 8855 **9.** 210 **11.** $\binom{8}{2} = 28$, $\binom{8}{3} = 56$ **13.** $\binom{10}{7} \cdot \binom{5}{3} = 1200$

15. $\binom{58}{6} \cdot \binom{42}{4}$ **17.** $\binom{4}{3} \cdot \binom{48}{2} = 4512$ **19.** 2,598,960 **21.** 10; 5 **23.** $\dfrac{n(n - 1)}{2}, \dfrac{n(n - 3)}{2}$ **25.** 5 **27.** 7

Exercise Set 15.3, p. 424

1. $15a^4b^2$ **3.** $-745{,}472a^3$ **5.** $1120x^{12}y^2$ **7.** $-1{,}959{,}552u^5v^{10}$ **9.** $m^5 + 5m^4n + 10m^3n^2 + 10m^2n^3 + 5mn^4 + n^5$
11. $x^{10} - 15x^8y + 90x^6y^2 - 270x^4y^3 + 405x^2y^4 - 243y^5$ **13.** $x^8 + 4x^4 + 4x^{-4} + x^{-8} + 6$ **15.** $140\sqrt{2}$ **17.** $-7 - 4\sqrt{2}i$
19. 1.072 **21.** 0.951 **23.** $\binom{n}{0} - \binom{n}{1} + \binom{n}{2} - \binom{n}{3} + \cdots + \binom{n}{n}(-1)^n$ **25.** 1.015 **27.** Use the property $\binom{k}{r-1} + \binom{k}{r} = \binom{k+1}{r}$ in the induction step.

Exercise Set 15.4, p. 428

1. 52 **3.** $\frac{1}{4}$ **5.** $\frac{1}{13}$ **7.** $\frac{1}{2}$ **9.** $\frac{2}{13}$ **11.** $\frac{5}{7}$ **13.** 0 **15.** $\frac{11}{4165}$ **17.** $\frac{28}{65}$ **19.** $\frac{1}{18}$ **21.** $\frac{1}{36}$ **23.** $\frac{30}{323}$ **25.** $\frac{9}{19}$ **27.** $\frac{1}{38}$ **29.** $\frac{1}{19}$
31. $2{,}598{,}960$ **33.** (a) 36; (b) 1.23×10^{-5} **35.** (a) $13 \cdot \binom{4}{3}\binom{4}{2} \cdot 12 = 3744$; (b) 0.00144 **37.** (a)

$13\binom{4}{3}\binom{48}{2} - 3744 = 54{,}912$; (b) 0.0211 **39.** (a) $\binom{13}{2}\binom{4}{2}\binom{4}{2}\binom{44}{1} = 123{,}552$; (b) 0.0475

Exercise Set 15.5, p. 434

1. $\frac{2}{23}$ **3.** 0.988 **5.** 0 **7.** $\frac{37}{56}$ **9.** 0.999 **11.** 0.051 **13.** $\frac{55}{144}$ **15.** (a) $\frac{3}{13}$; (b) $\frac{10}{13}$; (c) $\frac{1}{4}$; (d) $\frac{3}{4}$ **17.** $\frac{3}{13}$ **19.** (a) $\frac{3}{10}$; (b) $\frac{3}{25}$; (c) $\frac{1}{5}$;
(d) $\frac{31}{50}$; (e) $\frac{19}{50}$ **21.** $\frac{5}{7}$ **23.** (a) $\frac{15}{32}$; (b) $\frac{14}{32}$ (c) $\frac{3}{32}$ **25.** $(1-p)q$ **27.** (a) $\frac{13}{52} \cdot \frac{12}{51} \cdot \frac{11}{50}$, or $\frac{11}{850}$; (b) $4 \cdot \frac{11}{850}$, or $\frac{22}{425}$; (c) $\frac{26}{52} \cdot \frac{25}{51} \cdot \frac{24}{50}$, or $\frac{2}{17}$;
(d) $\frac{4}{17}$; (e) $\frac{12}{52} \cdot \frac{11}{51} \cdot \frac{10}{50}$, or $\frac{11}{1105}$; (f) $\frac{4}{52} \cdot \frac{3}{51} \cdot \frac{2}{50}$, or $\frac{1}{5525}$

Chapter 15 Test, or Review, p. 435

1. 3024 **3.** $n = 36$ **5.** $\frac{3}{36}$ **7.** $m^7 + 7m^6n + 21m^5n^2 + 35m^4n^3 + 35m^3n^4 + 21m^2n^5 + 7mn^6 + n^7$ **9.** 3780 **11.** $\frac{5}{24}$

Index